POETRY
for Students

Advisors

Susan Allison: Head Librarian, Lewiston High School, Lewiston, Maine. Standards Committee Chairperson for Maine School Library (MASL) Programs. Board member, Julia Adams Morse Memorial Library, Greene, Maine. Advisor to Lewiston Public Library Planning Process.

Jennifer Hood: Young Adult/Reference Librarian, Cumberland Public Library, Cumberland, Rhode Island. Certified teacher, Rhode Island. Member of the New England Library Association, Rhode Island Library Association, and the Rhode Island Educational Media Association.

Ann Kearney: Head Librarian and Media Specialist, Christopher Columbus High School, Miami, Florida, 1982–2002. Thirty-two years as Librarian in various educational institutions ranging from grade schools through graduate programs. Library positions at Miami-Dade Community College, the University of Miami's Medical School Library, and Carrollton School in Coconut Grove,

Florida. B.A. from University of Detroit, 1967 (magna cum laude); M.L.S., University of Missouri-Columbia, 1974. Volunteer Project Leader for a school in rural Jamaica; volunteer with Adult Literacy programs.

Laurie St. Laurent: Head of Adult and Children's Services, East Lansing Public Library, East Lansing, Michigan, 1994. M.L.S. from Western Michigan University. Chair of Michigan Library Association's 1998 Michigan Summer Reading Program; Chair of the Children's Services Division in 2000–2001; and Vice-President of the Association in 2002–2003. Board member of several regional early childhood literacy organizations and member of the Library of Michigan Youth Services Advisory Committee.

Heidi Stohs: Instructor in Language Arts, grades 10–12, Solomon High School, Solomon, Kansas. Received B.S. from Kansas State University; M.A. from Fort Hays State University.

POETRY
for Students

Presenting Analysis, Context, and Criticism on
Commonly Studied Poetry

VOLUME 28

GALE
CENGAGE Learning™

Detroit • New York • San Francisco • New Haven, Conn • Waterville, Maine • London

GALE
CENGAGE Learning™

Poetry for Students Volume 28

Project Editor: Ira Mark Milne

Rights Acquisition and Management: Vernon English, Jocelyne Green, Aja Perales, Sue Rudolph, Robyn Young

Composition: Evi Abou-El-Seoud

Manufacturing: Drew Kalasky

Imaging: Lezlie Light

Product Design: Pamela A. E. Galbreath, Jennifer Wahi

Content Conversion: Civie Green, Katrina Coach

Product Manager: Meggin Condino

For product information and technology assistance, contact us at
Gale Customer Support, 1-800-877-4253.
For permission to use material from this text or product,
submit all requests online at **www.cengage.com/permissions.**
Further permissions questions can be emailed to
permissionrequest@cengage.com

Gale
27500 Drake Rd.
Farmington Hills, MI, 48331-3535

ISBN-13: 978-0-7876-9892-8
ISBN-10: 0-7876-9892-X

ISSN 1094-7019

This title is also available as an e-book.
ISBN-13: 978-1-4144-3833-7
ISBN-10: 1-4144-3833-8
Contact your Gale, a part of Cengage Learning sales representative for ordering information.

Printed in the United States of America
1 2 3 4 5 6 7 12 11 10 09 08

Table of Contents

Just a Few Lines on a Page

I have often thought that poets have the easiest job in the world. A poem, after all, is just a few lines on a page, usually not even extending margin to marginhow long would that take to write, about five minutes? Maybe ten at the most, if you wanted it to rhyme or have a repeating meter. Why, I could start in the morning and produce a book of poetry by dinnertime. But we all know that it isn't that easy. Anyone can come up with enough words, but the poet's job is about writing the *right* ones. The right words will change lives, making people see the world somewhat differently than they saw it just a few minutes earlier. The right words can make a reader who relies on the dictionary for meanings take a greater responsibility for his or her own personal understanding. A poem that is put on the page correctly can bear any amount of analysis, probing, defining, explaining, and interrogating, and something about it will still feel new the next time you read it.

It would be fine with me if I could talk about poetry without using the word "magical," because that word is overused these days to imply "a really good time," often with a certain sweetness about it, and a lot of poetry is neither of these. But if you stop and think about magicwhether it brings to mind sorcery, witchcraft, or bunnies pulled from top hatsit always seems to involve stretching reality to produce a result greater than the sum of its parts and pulling unexpected results out of thin air. This book provides ample cases where a few simple words conjure up whole worlds. We do not actually travel to different times and different cultures, but the poems get into our minds, they find what little we know about the places they are talking about, and then they make that little bit blossom into a bouquet of someone else's life. Poets make us think we are following simple, specific events, but then they leave ideas in our heads that cannot be found on the printed page. Abracadabra.

Sometimes when you finish a poem it doesn't feel as if it has left any supernatural effect on you, like it did not have any more to say beyond the actual words that it used. This happens to everybody, but most often to inexperienced readers: regardless of what is often said about young people's infinite capacity to be amazed, you have to understand what usually does happen, and what could have happened instead, if you are going to be moved by what someone has accomplished. In those cases in which you finish a poem with a "So what?" attitude, the information provided in *Poetry for Students* comes in handy. Readers can feel assured that the poems included here actually are potent magic, not just because a few (or a hundred or ten thousand) professors of literature say they are: they're significant because they can withstand close inspection and still amaze the very same people who have just finished taking them apart and seeing how they work. Turn them inside out, and they will still be able to come alive, again and again. *Poetry for Students* gives readers of any age good practice in feeling the ways poems relate to both the reality of the time and place the poet lived in and the reality of our emotions. Practice is just another word for being a student. The information given here helps you understand the way to read poetry; what to look for, what to expect.

With all of this in mind, I really don't think I would actually like to have a poet's job at all. There are too many skills involved, including precision, honesty, taste, courage, linguistics, passion, compassion, and the ability to keep all sorts of people entertained at once. And that is just what they do with one hand, while the other hand pulls some sort of trick that most of us will never fully understand. I can't even pack all that I need for a weekend into one suitcase, so what would be my chances of stuffing so much life into a few lines? With all that *Poetry for Students* tells us about each poem, I am impressed that any poet can finish three or four poems a year. Read the inside stories of these poems, and you won't be able to approach any poem in the same way you did before.

David J. Kelly
College of Lake County

Introduction

Purpose of the Book

The purpose of *Poetry for Students* (*PfS*) is to provide readers with a guide to understanding, enjoying, and studying poems by giving them easy access to information about the work. Part of Gale's "For Students" Literature line, *PfS* is specifically designed to meet the curricular needs of high school and undergraduate college students and their teachers, as well as the interests of general readers and researchers considering specific poems. While each volume contains entries on "classic" poems frequently studied in classrooms, there are also entries containing hard-to-find information on contemporary poems, including works by multicultural, international, and women poets.

The information covered in each entry includes an introduction to the poem and the poem's author; the actual poem text (if possible); a poem summary, to help readers unravel and understand the meaning of the poem; analysis of important themes in the poem; and an explanation of important literary techniques and movements as they are demonstrated in the poem.

In addition to this material, which helps the readers analyze the poem itself, students are also provided with important information on the literary and historical background informing each work. This includes a historical context essay, a box comparing the time or place the poem was written to modern Western culture, a critical overview essay, and excerpts from critical essays on the poem. A unique feature of *PfS* is a specially commissioned critical essay on each poem, targeted toward the student reader.

To further aid the student in studying and enjoying each poem, information on media adaptations is provided (if available), as well as reading suggestions for works of fiction and nonfiction on similar themes and topics. Classroom aids include ideas for research papers and lists of critical sources that provide additional material on the poem.

Selection Criteria

The titles for each volume of *PfS* were selected by surveying numerous sources on teaching literature and analyzing course curricula for various school districts. Some of the sources surveyed included: literature anthologies; *Reading Lists for College-Bound Students: The Books Most Recommended by America's Top Colleges;* textbooks on teaching the poem; a College Board survey of poems commonly studied in high schools; and a National Council of Teachers of English (NCTE) survey of poems commonly studied in high schools.

Input was also solicited from our advisory board, as well as educators from various areas. From these discussions, it was determined that each volume should have a mix of "classic" poems (those works commonly taught in literature classes) and contemporary poems for which information is often hard to find. Because of the interest in expanding the canon of literature, an emphasis was also placed on including works by international, multicultural, and women poets. Our advisory board members—educational professionals—helped pare down the list for each volume. If a work was not selected for the present volume, it was often noted as a possibility for a future volume. As always, the editor welcomes suggestions for titles to be included in future volumes.

How Each Entry Is Organized

Each entry, or chapter, in *PfS* focuses on one poem. Each entry heading lists the full name of the poem, the author's name, and the date of the poem's publication. The following elements are contained in each entry:

Introduction: a brief overview of the poem which provides information about its first appearance, its literary standing, any controversies surrounding the work, and major conflicts or themes within the work.

Author Biography: this section includes basic facts about the poet's life, and focuses on events and times in the author's life that inspired the poem in question.

Poem Text: when permission has been granted, the poem is reprinted, allowing for quick reference when reading the explication of the following section.

Poem Summary: a description of the major events in the poem. Summaries are broken down with subheads that indicate the lines being discussed.

Themes: a thorough overview of how the major topics, themes, and issues are addressed within the poem. Each theme discussed appears in a separate subhead and is easily accessed through the boldface entries in the Subject/Theme Index.

Style: this section addresses important style elements of the poem, such as form, meter, and rhyme scheme; important literary devices used, such as imagery, foreshadowing, and symbolism; and, if applicable, genres to which the work might have belonged, such as Gothicism or Romanticism. Literary terms are explained within the entry, but can also be found in the Glossary.

Historical Context: this section outlines the social, political, and cultural climate *in which the author lived and the poem was created.* This section may include descriptions of related historical events, pertinent aspects of daily life in the culture, and the artistic and literary sensibilities of the time in which the work was written. If the poem is a historical work, information regarding the time in which the poem is set is also included. Each section is broken down with helpful subheads.

Critical Overview: this section provides background on the critical reputation of the poem, including bannings or any other public controversies surrounding the work. For older works, this section includes a history of how the poem was first received and how perceptions of it may have changed over the years; for more recent poems, direct quotes from early reviews may also be included.

Criticism: an essay commissioned by *PfS* which specifically deals with the poem and is written specifically for the student audience, as well as excerpts from previously published criticism on the work (if available).

Sources: an alphabetical list of critical material quoted in the entry, with full bibliographical information.

Further Reading: an alphabetical list of other critical sources which may prove useful for the student. Includes full bibliographical information and a brief annotation.

In addition, each entry contains the following highlighted sections, set apart from the main text as sidebars:

Media Adaptations: if available, a list of audio recordings as well as any film or television adaptations of the poem, including source information.

Topics for Further Study: a list of potential study questions or research topics dealing with the poem. This section includes questions related to other disciplines the student may be studying, such as American history, world history, science, math, government, business, geography, economics, psychology, etc.

Compare & Contrast: an "at-a-glance" comparison of the cultural and historical differences between the author's time and culture and late twentieth century or early twenty-first century Western culture. This box includes pertinent parallels between the major scientific, political, and cultural movements of the time or place the poem was written, the time or place the poem was set (if a historical work), and modern Western culture. Works written after 1990 may not have this box.

What Do I Read Next?: a list of works that might complement the featured poem or serve as a contrast to it. This includes works by the same author and others, works of fiction and nonfiction, and works from various genres, cultures, and eras.

Other Features

PfS includes "Just a Few Lines on a Page," a foreword by David J. Kelly, an adjunct professor of English, College of Lake County, Illinois. This essay provides a straightforward, unpretentious explanation of why poetry should be marveled at and how *Poetry for Students* can help teachers show students how to enrich their own reading experiences.

A Cumulative Author/Title Index lists the authors and titles covered in each volume of the *PfS* series.

A Cumulative Nationality/Ethnicity Index breaks down the authors and titles covered in each volume of the *PfS* series by nationality and ethnicity.

A Subject/Theme Index, specific to each volume, provides easy reference for users who may be studying a particular subject or theme rather than a single work. Significant subjects from events to broad themes are included, and the entries pointing to the specific theme discussions in each entry are indicated in **boldface**.

A Cumulative Index of First Lines (beginning in Vol. 10) provides easy reference for users who may be familiar with the first line of a poem but may not remember the actual title.

A Cumulative Index of Last Lines (beginning in Vol. 10) provides easy reference for users who may be familiar with the last line of a poem but may not remember the actual title.

Each entry may include illustrations, including photo of the author and other graphics related to the poem.

Citing *Poetry for Students*

When writing papers, students who quote directly from any volume of *Poetry for Students* may use the following general forms. These examples are based on MLA style; teachers may request that students adhere to a different style, so the following examples may be adapted as needed.

When citing text from *PfS* that is not attributed to a particular author (i.e., the Themes, Style, Historical Context sections, etc.), the following format should be used in the bibliography section:

> "Angle of Geese." *Poetry for Students*. Eds. Marie Napierkowski and Mary Ruby. Vol. 2. Detroit: Gale, 1998. 8–9.

When quoting the specially commissioned essay from *PfS* (usually the first piece under the "Criticism" subhead), the following format should be used:

> Velie, Alan. Critical Essay on "Angle of Geese." *Poetry for Students. Eds.* Marie Napierkowski and Mary Ruby. Vol. 2. Detroit: Gale, 1998. 7–10.

When quoting a journal or newspaper essay that is reprinted in a volume of *PfS*, the following form may be used:

> Luscher, Robert M. "An Emersonian Context of Dickinson's 'The Soul Selects Her Own Society.'" *ESQ: A Journal of American Renaissance* Vol. 30, No. 2 (Second Quarter, 1984), 111–16; excerpted and reprinted in *Poetry for Students*, Vol. 1, eds. Marie Napierkowski and Mary Ruby (Detroit: Gale, 1998), pp. 266–69.

When quoting material reprinted from a book that appears in a volume of PfS, the following form may be used:

> Mootry, Maria K. "'Tell It Slant': Disguise and Discovery as Revisionist Poetic Discourse in 'The Bean Eaters,'" in *A Life Distilled: Gwendolyn Brooks, Her Poetry and Fiction*. Edited by Maria K. Mootry and Gary Smith. University of Illinois Press, 1987. 177–80, 191; excerpted and reprinted in *Poetry for Students*, Vol. 2, eds. Marie Napierkowski and Mary Ruby (Detroit: Gale, 1998), pp. 22–24.

We Welcome Your Suggestions

The editorial staff of *Poetry for Students* welcomes your comments and ideas. Readers who wish to suggest poems to appear in future volumes, or who have other suggestions, are cordially invited to contact the editor. You may contact the editor via E-mail at: **ForStudentsEditors@cengage.com**. Or write to the editor at:

Editor, *Poetry for Students*
Gale
27500 Drake Road
Farmington Hills, MI 48331-3535

Literary Chronology

1799: Alexander Pushkin is born on June 6 in Moscow, Russia.

1830: Emily Dickinson is born on December 10 in Amherst, Massachusetts.

1837: Alexander Pushkin dies on February 10 in St. Petersburg, Russia, from injuries sustained in a duel.

1841: Alexander Pushkin's "The Bronze Horseman" is posthumously published.

1854: Arthur Rimbaud is born on October 20 in Charleville, France.

1883: Arthur Rimbaud's poem "The Drunken Boat" is published.

1886: Emily Dickinson dies of nephritis (kidney disease) on May 15 in Amherst, Massachusetts.

1886: Siegfried Sassoon is born on September 8 in Kent, England.

1886: H.D. is born Hilda Doolittle on September 10 in Bethlehem, Pennsylvania.

1890: Emily Dickinson's "I Died for Beauty" is posthumously published.

1891: Arthur Rimbaud dies on November 10 in Marseilles, France.

1904: Pablo Neruda is born Ricardo Eliecer Neftalí Reyes Basoalto on July 12 in Parral, Chile.

1916: H.D.'s "Sea Rose" is published.

1917: Siegfried Sassoon's "'Blighters'" is published.

1919: Lawrence Ferlinghetti is born on March 24 in Yonkers, New York.

1920: Charles Bukowski is born on August 16 in Andernach, Germany.

1927: John Ashbery is born on July 28 in Rochester, New York.

1932: Sylvia Plath is born on October 27 in Jamaica Plains, Massachusetts.

1943: Nikki Giovanni is born Yolanda Cornelia Giovanni on June 7 in Knoxville, Tennessee.

1944: Fleda Brown is born in Columbia, Missouri.

1947: Pablo Neruda's "The Heights of Macchu Picchu" is published.

1953: Mark Doty is born on August 10 in Maryville, Tennessee.

1955: Marilyn Chin is born on January 14 in Hong Kong.

1958: Lawrence Ferlinghetti's poem "Christ Climbed Down" is published.

1961: H.D. dies of a heart attack on September 27 in Geneva, Switzerland.

1963: Charles Bukowski's "The Tragedy of the Leaves" is published.

1963: Sylvia Plath commits suicide in London on February 11.

1965: Sylvia Plath's poem "Daddy" is published posthumously.

1967: Siegfried Sassoon dies of cancer on September 1 in England.

1971: Pablo Neruda is awarded the Nobel Prize for Literature.

1972: Nikki Giovanni's "Ego-Tripping" is published.

1973: Pablo Neruda dies of leukemia on September 23 in Santiago, Chile.

1975: John Ashbery's "Self-Portrait in a Convex Mirror" is published.

1976: John Ashbery is awarded the Pulitzer Prize for Poetry for *Self-Portrait in a Convex Mirror: Poems.*

1982: Sylvia Plath is posthumously awarded the Pulitzer Prize for poetry.

1993: Mark Doty's "The Wings" is published.

1994: Marilyn Chin's "How I Got that Name" is published.

1994: Charles Bukowski dies of leukemia on March 9 in San Pedro, California.

2004: Fleda Brown's "The Women Who Loved Elvis All Their Lives" is published.

Acknowledgments

The editors wish to thank the copyright holders of the excerpted criticism included in this volume and the permissions managers of many book and magazine publishing companies for assisting us in securing reproduction rights. We are also grateful to the staffs of the Detroit Public Library, the Library of Congress, the University of Detroit Mercy Library, Wayne State University Purdy/Kresge Library Complex, and the University of Michigan Libraries for making their resources available to us. Following is a list of the copyright holders who have granted us permission to reproduce material in this volume of PFS. Every effort has been made to trace copyright, but if omissions have been made, please let us know.

COPYRIGHTED EXCERPTS IN *PFS*, VOLUME 28, WERE REPRODUCED FROM THE FOLLOWING PERIODICALS:

American Literature, v. 68, March, 1996. Copyright, 1996 Duke University Press. All rights reserved. Used by permission of the publisher.—*Chicago Review*, v. 27, autumn 1975. Copyright © 1975 by *Chicago Review*. Reproduced by permission.—*Contemporary Literature*, v. 10, autumn 1969; v. 27, winter 1986; v. 42, summer, 2001. Copyright © 1969, 1986, 2001 by the Board of Regents of the University of Wisconsin System. Both reproduced by permission.—*ESQ: A Journal of the American Renaissance*, v. 24, 1978 for "Dickinson and the Divine:

The Terror of Integration, the Terror of Detachment," by Evan Carton. Copyright 1978 by Evan Carton. Reproduced by permission of the author.—*Explicator*, v. 53, spring 1995; v. 55, summer 1997. Copyright © 1995, 1997 by Helen Dwight Reid Educational Foundation. All reproduced with permission of the Helen Dwight Reid Educational Foundation, published by Heldref Publications, 1319 18th Street, NW, Washington, DC 20036-1802.—*Journal of Modern Literature*, v. 5, September 1976. Copyright © Indiana University Press. Reproduced by permission.—*Kenyon Review*, v. 17, spring 1995 for "Try Bondage," by Terese Svoboda. Reproduced by permission of the author.—*Kliatt*, v. 38, September, 2004. Copyright © 2004 by KLIATT. Reproduced by permission.—*Melus*, v. 9, autumn 1982. Copyright *MELUS: The Society for the Study of Multi-Ethnic Literature of the United States,* 1982. Reproduced by permission.—*The Montserrat Review*, 2005-2006. Copyright © 1999-2007 Dragonfly Press. All rights reserved. Reproduced by permission.—*New Literary History*, v. 15, spring 1984. Copyright © 1984 by *New Literary History*. Reproduced by permission of The Johns Hopkins University Press.—*Parnassus*, v. 20, 1995 for "These AIDS Days," by Calvin Bedient. Copyright © 1995 Poetry in Review Foundation, NY. Reproduced by permission of the author.—*Progressive*, v. 58, May 1994. Copyright © 1994 by The Progressive, Inc.

Reproduced by permission of *The Progressive,* 409 East Main Street, Madison, WI 53703, www.progressive.org.—*Renascence,* v. 8, spring 1996. Copyright © 1996 Marquette University Press. Both reproduced by permission.—*Slavic Review,* v. 58, summer, 1999. Copyright © 1999 by the American Association for the Advancement of Slavic Studies, Inc. Reproduced by permission.—*SubStance,* v. 11, 1983. Copyright © 1983 by the Board of Regents of the University of Wisconsin System. Reproduced by permission.—*Symposium,* v. 28, summer 1974. Copyright © 1974 by Helen Dwight Reid Educational Foundation. Reproduced with permission of the Helen Dwight Reid Educational Foundation, published by Heldref Publications, 1319 18th Street, NW, Washington, DC 20036-1802.—*World Literature Today,* v. 79, May-August, 2005. Copyright © 2005 by *World Literature Today.* Reproduced by permission of the publisher.

COPYRIGHTED EXCERPTS IN *PFS,* VOLUME 28, WERE REPRODUCED FROM THE FOLLOWING BOOKS:

Broe, Mary Lynn. From *Protean Poetic: The Poetry of Sylvia Plath.* University of Missouri Press, 1980. Copyright © 1980 by The Curators of the University of Missouri. All rights reserved. Reprinted by permission of the University of Missouri Press.—Brown, Fleda. From *The Women Who Loved Elvis All Their Lives.* Carnegie Mellon University Press, 2004. Copyright © 2004 by Fleda Brown. All rights reserved. Reproduced by permission.—Dickinson, Emily. From "I Died for Beauty," in *The Complete Poems of Emily Dickinson.* Edited by Thomas H. Johnson. Cambridge, Mass.: The Belknap Press of Harvard University Press, Copyright © 1951, 1955, 1979, 1983 by the President and Fellows of Harvard College.—Doty, Mark. From *My Alexandria.* National Poetry Series, 1993. Copyright © 1995 by Mark Doty. Used with the permission of the poet and the University of Illinois Press.—Duval, Jean-Francois. From "Bukowski: The Counterculture's Dissident," in *Bukowski and the Beats.* Edited by Alison Ardron. Sun Dog Press, 2002. Copyright © 2002 by Jean-Francois Duval and © 1998 by Editions Michalon. All rights reserved. Reproduced by permission.—Fowlie, Wallace. From *Rimbaud and Jim Morrison: The Rebel as Poet.* Duke University Press, 1996. Copyright © 1994 Duke University Press. All rights

reserved. Used by permission of the publisher.—Giovanni, Nikki. From *Ego-Tripping and Other Poems for Young People.* Lawrence Hill Books, 1993. Reproduced by permission.—Hobson, Charles, Sheila Smith and Nikki Giovanni. From "The Poet and Black Realities," in *Conversations with Nikki Giovanni.* Edited by Virginia C. Fowler. University Press of Mississippi, 1992. Copyright © *Tuesday Magazine* [a supplement to Newark Sunday News], v. 4, June 1969 for "The Poet and Black Realities," by Charles Hobson and Shelia Smith. Copyright © Tuesday Magazine. All rights reserved. Reprinted by permission of the Newark Public Library.—Loercher, Diana and Nikki Giovanni. From "Nikki Giovanni's Poems Radiate Black Pride, Woman Pride," in *Conversations with Nikki Giovanni.* Edited by Virginia C. Fowler. University Press of Mississippi, 1992. Copyright © 1992 The Christian Science Publishing Society. All rights reserved. Reproduced by permission from *Christian Science Monitor, (www.csmonitor.com).*—Macklin, Gerald Martin. From "Arthur Rimbaud," in *Dictionary of Literary Biography, Vol. 217, Nineteenth-Century French Poets.* Edited by Robert Beum. The Gale Group, 1999. Reproduced by permission of Gale, a part of Cengage Learning.—McDowell, Margaret B. From "Siegfried Sassoon," in *Dictionary of Literary Biography, Vol. 20, British Poets, 1914-1945.* Edited by Donald E. Stanford. Gale Research, 1983. Reproduced by permission of Gale, a part of Cengage Learning.—Nance, Guinevara A., and Judith P. Jones. From "Doing Away with Daddy: Exorcism and Sympathetic Magic in Plath's Poetry," in *Critical Essays on Sylvia Plath.* Edited by Linda W. Wagner. G. K. Hall 1984 by Linda W. Wagner. All rights reserved. Reproduced by permission of Gale, a part of Cengage Learning.—Neruda, Pablo. From "The Heights of Macchu Picchu," in *Translating Neruda: The Way to Macchu Picchu.* Translated by Nathaniel Tarn. Translation copyright © 1966 renewed © 1994 by Nathaniel Tarn. Reprinted by permission of Random House Group Limited. In the U.S. reprinted by permission of Farrar, Straus and Giroux, LLC.—Pushkin, Alexander. From *The Bronze Horseman and Other Poems.* Translated by D.M. Thomas. Penguin Books, 1982. © copyright D. M. Thomas, 1982. Secker Rimbaud, Arthur. From *Rimbaud: Complete Works, Selected Letters: A Bilingual Edition.* Translated by Wallace Fowlie. University of Chicago Press,

2005. Copyright © 2005 by The University of Chicago. All rights reserved. Reproduced by permission.—Sassoon, Siegfried. From *The War Poems of Siegfried Sassoon*. W. Heinemann, 1919. Copyright 1936, 1946, 1947, 1948 by Siegfried Sassoon. Reproduced by kind permission of The Estate of George Sassoon. In the U.S. used by permission of Viking Penguin, a division of Penguin Group (USA) Inc.—Weinburg, Bernard. From *The Limits of Symbolism: Studies of Five Modern French Poets*. University of Chicago Press, 1966. Copyright © 1966 by The University of Chicago. All rights reserved. Reproduced by permission.

COPYRIGHTED EXCERPTS IN *PFS*, VOLUME 28, WERE REPRODUCED FROM THE FOLLOWING WEBSITES OR OTHER SOURCES:

From *Contemporary Authors Online*. "Mark Doty," www.gale.com, Gale, 2007. Reproduced by permission of Gale, a part of Cengage Learning.

Contributors

Jennifer A. Bussey: Bussey is an independent writer specializing in literature. Entries on *How I Got That Name* and *I Died for Beauty*. Original essays on *How I Got That Name* and *I Died for Beauty*.

Catherine Dominic: Dominic is an author and freelance editor. Entry on *Self-Portrait in a Convex Mirror*. Original essay on *Self-Portrait in a Convex Mirror*.

Klay Dyer: Dyer holds a Ph.D. in English literature and has published extensively on fiction, poetry, film, and television. He is also a freelance university teacher, writer, and educational consultant. Entry on *The Women Who Loved Elvis All Their Lives*. Original essay on *The Women Who Loved Elvis All Their Lives*.

Neil Heims: Heims is a writer and teacher living in Paris. Entries on *Christ Climbed Down*, *Daddy*, and *The Drunken Boat*. Original essays on *Christ Climbed Down*, *Daddy*, and *The Drunken Boat*.

Diane Andrews Henningfeld: Henningfeld is a professor and literary critic who writes widely for educational publications. Entry on *Blighters*. Original essay on *Blighters*.

Sheri Metzger Karmiol: Karmiol has a doctorate in English Renaissance literature. She teaches literature and drama at the University of New Mexico, where she is a lecturer in the University Honors Program. Karmiol is also a professional writer and the author of several reference texts on poetry and drama. Entries on *Ego-Tripping* and *Sea Rose*. Original essays on *Ego-Tripping* and *Sea Rose*.

Claire Robinson: Robinson has an M.A. in English. She is a former teacher of English literature and creative writing, and is currently a freelance writer and editor. Entries on *The Bronze Horseman*, *The Tragedy of the Leaves*, and *The Wings*. Original essays on *The Bronze Horseman*, *The Tragedy of the Leaves*, and *The Wings*.

Carol Ullmann: Ullmann is a freelance writer and editor. Entry on *The Heights of Macchu Picchu*. Original essay on *The Heights of Macchu Picchu*.

"Blighters"

SIEGFRIED SASSOON

1917

Until 1914, young Siegfried Sassoon, a wealthy English gentleman, spent his days fox hunting and playing sports. He was also a poet, albeit a minor one, of the Georgian school, a group of poets dedicated to infusing English poetry with the beauty of nature. All this changed when Europe exploded into war in August of 1914. The rest of Sassoon's long life would be spent coming to terms with his experiences fighting in the trenches of the Western Front as a Second Lieutenant in the Royal Welch Fusiliers from 1915 to 1918. A courageous war hero who rescued his men from certain death on the field, Sassoon also protested the war and risked court-martial.

"'Blighters,'" published in 1917 as a part of the collection *The Old Huntsman and Other Poems* is an excellent example of Sassoon's talent for satiric, confrontational poetry, and is still in print in many collections of Sassoon's poetry, including *The War Poems of Siegfried Sassoon*, reprinted by Echo Press in 2006. Written in response to a revue at the Liverpool Hippodrome, which Sassoon attended in January, 1917, "'Blighters'" attacks the civilians at home in England, the "blighters" of the title, for their ill-founded, excessive, and shallow patriotism. Their lack of understanding of the reality of war and of the conditions in the trenches elicits hatred in the narrator of the poem.

AUTHOR BIOGRAPHY

Siegfried Sassoon was born on September 8, 1886, to the wealthy family of Alfred Ezra Sassoon and Theresa Georgiana Thornycroft Sassoon near Warminster, Kent, England. Alfred Sassoon's family were Sephardic Jews who had historically established a large merchant business, extending from Baghdad to Bombay through Europe. Theresa Thornycroft was from a wealthy country family, many of whom were sculptors, including her uncle and mother. She was eight years older than Alfred Sassoon, and she was a Christian, making her doubly unsuitable in the eyes of Alfred's family. The couple married secretly in 1884 without the approval of the Sassoon family, and chose to live in the country near the Thornycrofts.

Siegfried was the second of three sons born to Alfred and Theresa. However, the marriage proved to be an unhappy one. Sassoon's father left the family in 1891 and went to London with his lover. In 1895, Alfred Sassoon died of tuberculosis. Siegfried Sassoon suffered extreme grief over his father's death and was not permitted to attend the funeral. The sense of loss apparently haunted him for much of his life.

Sassoon's education was largely carried out at home, and he was very close to his mother. In 1902, he matriculated at Marlborough College and ultimately attended Clare College, Cambridge. He was not a particularly talented scholar, and left Cambridge without a degree, spending the next years living in the country, fox hunting and writing poetry. He self-published a series of books between 1906 and 1914. He belonged to a school of poets referred to as the Georgians. The group produced beautiful sounding poetry that took nature as its subject.

By 1914, Sassoon had grown increasingly dissatisfied with his life. He enlisted in the military three days before England declared war on Germany. After breaking his arm in a fall from a horse, he left the cavalry and obtained a commission as a lieutenant in the Royal Welch Fusiliers, arriving in France in November, 1915. It was at his first assignment as a transport officer that he met fellow poet and writer Robert Graves, a man who was to have tremendous importance in Sassoon's life. During this period, Sassoon wrote a number of poems about the glory of war, somewhat in the manner of Rupert

Siegfried Sassoon (© *Pictorial Press Ltd / Alamy*)

Brooke, a popular English soldier who died early in the war while in transit to battle.

By 1916, much of the glamour of the war had faded for Sassoon. His brother Hamo had been killed fighting at the terrible defeat at Gallipoli in Turkey in 1915, and David Thomas, a young soldier Sassoon was in love with, also was killed in 1916. March of 1916 found Sassoon in the trenches, earning a reputation as a heroic and reckless officer. He rescued a number of his men from No-Man's-Land (the area between the English and the German trenches) while under fire, and earned for himself the nickname "Mad Jack." All in all, his behavior was both brave and suicidal.

Sassoon became ill with trench fever in July of 1916 and was sent home to England to recover. During this time, he began writing the war poetry for which he became famous, including "'Blighters.'" He returned to the trenches, only to be shot in the shoulder in 1917. Again, he was sent to England to recover. At this time, he became friendly with members of the British peace movement, including Lady Ottoline Morrell, and became increasingly disenchanted with the war. Significantly, Sassoon always supported his fellow soldiers, but grew angry and bitter about the politicians and people at the home front.

While on recovery leave, Sassoon attended a musical review at the Liverpool Hippodrome that filled him with anger and distaste. It was this review that was the inspiration for "'Blighters,'" a poem that he included in *The Old Huntsman, and Other Poems*, published in 1917.

In May 1917, Sassoon wrote an essay called "A Soldier's Declaration." This statement, sent to Sassoon's commanding officer, the *London Times*, and many influential people, stated his belief that the war was being mishandled by the politicians and that soldiers were paying the price for their corruption. His words bordered on treason.

Robert Graves, working behind the scenes, convinced Sassoon's superiors that he was suffering from shell shock, and that he should not be held responsible for his words. As a result, Sassoon was sent to Craiglockhart War Hospital near Edinburgh, Scotland, to be treated. There he met Captain William H. R. Rivers, a psychiatrist, who treated him for three months. The relationship proved to be an important one for Sassoon who found in Rivers the father he had missed since childhood. Sassoon also befriended and deeply influenced the young poet Wilfred Owen, also at Craiglockhart being treated for shell shock.

Eventually, Sassoon asked to be sent back to France to be with his soldiers. On July 18, 1918, he was shot in the head by one of his own men who mistook him for a German. He was sent back to England again to recover, and only the November 11 armistice prevented him returning yet again to the trenches. In 1918, Sassoon's second volume of war poems, *Counter-Attack, and Other Poems* was published.

Sassoon returned to the years of his youth, ending with his experiences during World War I, again and again in his later writing. He wrote three novels that were thinly veiled personal memoirs between 1929 and 1936. He followed this by writing three books of memoirs, revisiting the same territory, between 1938 and 1945. In all, Sassoon published over sixty books before his death from cancer in Wiltshire, England in 1967. His diaries were published during the 1980s.

MEDIA ADAPTATIONS

- *Poets of the Great War* is an audiobook featuring the poetry of Siegfried Sassoon, Wilfred Owen, and Isaac Rosenberg, among others. The audiobook was produced by NAXOS Audibooks in 2001.

Although Sassoon attempted to distance himself in later years from the war poetry, it is ironic that these are the very poems for which Sassoon is best remembered.

POEM TEXT

The house is crammed: tier beyond tier they
   grin
And cackle at the Show, while prancing ranks
Of harlots shrill the chorus, drunk with din;
"We're sure the Kaiser loves the dear old
   Tanks!"

I'd like to see a Tank come down the stalls,   5
Lurching to rag-time tunes, or "Home, sweet
   Home,"—
And there'd be no more jokes in Music-halls
To mock the riddled corpses round Bapaume.

POEM SUMMARY

"'Blighters'" is a poem comprised of eight lines, divided into two stanzas. As such, it is a very compact poem; Sassoon packs many meanings into just a few short lines.

The title of the poem itself, for example, is particularly interesting. In the first place, Sassoon places the title in quotation marks, suggesting that the title is a quotation from some common soldier, or that there is something ironic about the title. A blight is a disease or by extension, affliction. It can also be used as a verb: a war can blight the land. To complicate matters, soldiers during World War I called England (and, by extension, wherever their home was) "blighty." In addition, in common slang, a blighter is an unfortunate fellow. (North Americans might use the term "poor guy" in the same way.) Consequently, blighters means, simultaneously, someone or something that causes a blight; someone who lives in England or at home; and an unfortunate fellow. The title, then, becomes both pitying when directed at the soldiers at the front, and accusatory when directed at the people at home.

Stanza 1

In the first line, Sassoon writes: "The house is crammed: tier beyond tier they grin." The house he refers to is a music hall where "they" sit crowded together to watch a show. In one sense, they are the blighters of the title: people who have stayed at home and have the free time to go to the theater to watch chorus girls sing and dance.

In the second line, the people in the audience "cackle at the Show," and Sassoon capitalizes the word show. This small detail lets readers know that he is referring not only to the show that the audience is watching, but also to the war. The soldiers often referred to a battle or military engagement as a "show." The effect is emphasized by placing the chorus girls in "ranks," meaning a row or file, but also a term often used in connection with military maneuvers.

Sassoon calls the chorus girls singing on the stage "harlots" in line three. A harlot is a prostitute, and Sassoon's use of this word to describe the chorus girls suggests his deep anger at the women. In addition, as prostitutes, harlots debase themselves by acting lewdly. Thus, as they "shrill" the chorus, they are acting out what Sassoon sees as a depraved and debauched treatment of a serious issue. In addition, by using the word shrill as a verb rather than as an adjective, he makes the whole scene more graphic and more active.

The chorus that the girls sing in line four: "We're sure the Kaiser loves the dear old Tanks!" also disgusts the narrator of the poem. The Kaiser is the king of Germany. His image was used in many propaganda posters and images in England during the time. The line from the song is sarcastic and satiric in its own right: of course the Kaiser does *not* love the tanks. What the song implies is that the British tanks are so strong that they will destroy the Kaiser and all his soldiers. It is a way of taunting the enemy and asserting the superiority of British technology. However, Sassoon takes offense at people at home joking about things they know nothing about.

Stanza 2

Line five opens the second quatrain. In this line, the narrator speaks in his own voice for the first time, contrasting what he would "like to see" with what he is seeing on the stage. In disgust and anger, he says that he would "like to see a Tank come down the stalls." The stalls are simply the places where people sit; however, the word stall also refers to a place where animals are kept. The double meaning helps paint a picture of the crowd as bestial in its response to the show.

In line six, Sassoon creates an image of a tank, dancing to ragtime music, or the popular song "Home, sweet Home." Were this to somehow be real, the raucous scene in the music hall would quickly shift from one of laughter, noise, and disrespect to one of terror and fear. The juxtaposition of a tank with the song "Home sweet Home" is particularly troubling; supposedly, the army is fighting in France to protect the people at home. However, their lack of understanding of the situation in France and of the men who are dying horrible deaths there moves the narrator to wish for the death and destruction of "Home sweet Home." It is a deep paradox that Sassoon uncovers in this line: he hates the blighters at home, the very people he is sworn to protect.

In the final two lines, Sassoon delivers his message. He states that if the people at home were really to see a tank in their midst, they would not find themselves in a joking mood. He makes clear that he finds music hall shows about the war to be disrespectful to the men who die in large numbers in places like Bapaume, France. The image of "riddled corpses" in the final line of the poem is a stark contrast to the image of women dancing on the stage established in the early lines of the poems. It is clear that the narrator's sympathies (and by extension, Sassoon's) lie with the dead in France, rather than with the living in England.

THEMES

Soldiers' and Civilians' Vastly Different Experiences of World War I

Of course, Sassoon would not have identified his theme as World War I himself because he could not have known when writing "'Blighters'" that the terrible war raging in France and throughout

TOPICS FOR FURTHER STUDY

- Read Robert Graves's autobiography, *Good-bye To All That*, and Siegfried Sassoon's autobiography, *Siegfried's Journey*. In an essay, compare and contrast their memories of similar and identical events. What do the differences and similarities between these two book indicate about writing memoir, and by extension, writing history?

- Read Vera Brittain's memoir, *Testament of Youth*. How was her experience of the war in France similar to, and different from, that of the young men who served there? Write a paper exploring gender difference in the experience of war.

- Seek out posters and images of propaganda circulated among the public in England during the years 1914–1918. Create a collage of these materials, and write an essay about the uses of propaganda in a time of war. To what end does a government use such devices?

- From a variety of sources, gather descriptions of life in the trenches during World War I. What was life like for a common soldier during this time? Write a creative, first-person narrative in which you imagine yourself in a similar situation.

- Read a number of poems from writers such as Rupert Brooke, Edmund Blunden, Wilfred Owen, and Isaac Rosenberg. Note the dates on each poem that you read. Write an essay describing the changes you see in the poetry as time goes by. How does Brooke's work, for example, differ from Rosenberg's?

Europe would be the first of two global catastrophes. Nonetheless, Sassoon's war, still commonly referred to as the Great War by Europeans, is always part of his writing.

In the case of "'Blighters,'" Sassoon's theme is not his hatred of the German enemy, but rather his hatred of the people for whom the war is being fought. In this and other poems, he ironically illustrates how complacent, insensitive, and lacking in dignity are the British civilians. Their excessive show of patriotism has no connection to their brothers and sons dying in France, and is a mockery of the soldiers' ultimate sacrifice. In the situation of this poem, the home population uses the excuse of the war to go out and have a good time at the music hall. People who have never seen a tank roll over the bodies of dead friends co-opt the vehicle, turning it from a weapon of death and destruction into a prop in a music hall number. For Sassoon, home on medical leave, and having lost two of his closest relationships to the war, seeing the war ridiculed on stage is cause for anger and reproach.

In "'Blighters,'" Sassoon embellishes a theme that he will continue to pursue for years to come. For Sassoon, the gulf between those who have been in the trenches and those who have not is an unbridgeable chasm. The poet reserves his greatest venom for the politicians and merchants who are making a profit on the war, and for women, who are represented by the harlots dancing on the stage.

The Irony of War

Sassoon taps into the inherent irony of war in "'Blighters'" as well as in poems such as "The General" and "They." It is a commonplace that only people who have participated in war can understand what it means.

For Sassoon, watching a music hall show in which dancing girls promise that the Kaiser will love British tanks, the irony is overwhelming. He knows, as he sits in his comfortable chair in the Liverpool Hippodrome, that not more than two hundred miles away in France, men he knows are living in muck-filled, rat-infested trenches. He also knows that the Kaiser himself will never see a tank in action, and that this war, unlike others in the past, is not a war of battles won and lost, but is rather a war of attrition. Because the war has quickly devolved into a stalemate with the two armies facing each other from trenches across a devastated landscape known as No Man's Land, there are no great heroic battles, but rather the wholesale slaughter of thousands within hours of any new offensive.

This slaughter, as represented by The Battle of the Somme, is clearly one of the ironies that Sassoon is addressing in "'Blighters.'" Bapaume, mentioned in the last line of the poem, is a town in France, and the objective of the British forces for the first day of the Battle of Somme, an initiative that was supposed to bring the war quickly to a close. The British did not reach Bapaume on the first day, nor did they ever reach Bapaume in the entire four months that the battle raged. Sassoon, watching the music hall performance, knows that over 600,000 men have died, their bodies littering the ground round about Bapaume, as the performers and the audience joke about tanks.

Jingoism

Jingoism is extreme, unthinking, chauvinistic patriotism. It often refers to a popular sentiment held among the general population that force must be used to protect a country's national interests. Jingoism can also be thought of as shallow, militaristic patriotism, common among the uneducated masses, who take pride in military show of force, no matter the cost in human lives. Jingoism comes from the term "By Jingo!", an expression found in a song by G. H. Hunt called "MacDermott's War Song," written in 1878 and performed in London music halls. The first two lines of the chorus are as follows: "We don't want to fight but by jingo if we do / We've got the ships, we've got the men, and got the money too!" This song became very popular among patrons of British pubs who sang it as an expression of the swaggering military might of the British Empire.

For Sassoon, an upper class gentleman and a veteran of the trenches, jingoism of any sort is utterly distasteful. It reveals the ignorance and stupidity of the masses of civilians, safe in Britain, and willing to send their young men to die in a cause that has little value. Sassoon expresses this theme throughout many poems, but it is in "'Blighters'" that it finds its most vicious expression. The jingoistic bravado of the song sung by the chorus girls in "'Blighters,'" "We're sure the Kaiser loves the dear old Tanks!", represents for Sassoon a betrayal by the population, a population who cannot even imagine the horrors of the Western Front.

STYLE

Epigram

Critics have generally agreed that Sassoon's best verse, including "'Blighters,'" is generally epigrammatic. An epigram is a pithy saying. The Greeks wrote epigrams, as did the Romans. In the English language, there have been several masters of the form, although none has surpassed Ben Jonson, the seventeenth century contemporary of William Shakespeare. Increasingly, epigrams were used for satirical purposes; Jonson often set up his epigrams with an introduction, and then came sharply to the point in his conclusion.

This description fits the construction of Sassoon's best epigrammatic poetry. In *Siegfried Sassoon: A Study of the War Poetry*, Patrick Campbell notes that in *Siegfried's Journey*, Sassoon writes that his method includes "two or three harsh, peremptory, and colloquial stanzas with a knock-out blow in the last line." Indeed, Sassoon received praise for this style from none other than the famous English writer, Thomas Hardy, to whom *The Old Huntsman, and Other Poems* is dedicated.

"'Blighters'" begins with a quatrain (a four line stanza) that sets the scene. Readers clearly see that the poem is set in a music hall, complete with a raucous audience and dancing show girls. The poem turns at the end of the quatrain when the harlots sing "We're sure the Kaiser loves the dear old Tanks!" A first person narrator enters in the next line, shifting the focus from the action on the stage to a fantasy of the narrator's, that tanks will come and crush the people sitting in the stalls. It is in the last two lines that Sassoon drives home his point: the dead young men, lying in foreign fields, have made a sacred sacrifice. Their loss should be a cause for mourning, not an occasion for boasts, swaggering, or empty threats.

Satire

Satire is an ancient form of writing created to criticize and ridicule people, institutions, actions, and beliefs. The earliest expression of satire still in writing can be found in the comedies of Aristophanes. Roman writers Plautus and Terence continued the form, and much later, Shakespeare and Ben Jonson's dramatic satires reworked the form for English audiences.

Sometimes, satire takes a comedic form and even becomes parody. The audience watching the show in "'Blighters,'" for example, is enjoying a parody of military might in the prancing ranks of chorus girls singing about tanks. This, however, was not a vision that coincided with Sassoon's, whose satire often took the tragic route. In "'Blighters,'" there is an ironic gap opened between the audience's experience and Sassoon's point in the poem. The contrast between the two opposing notions of satire contributes to the overall power of the poem.

Sassoon's work has its roots in the formal verse satire of Roman writers Horace and Juvenal. These two writers took very different approaches to satire. Horace, on the one hand, wrote verse that poked urbane, genial fun at the follies and shortcomings of governments and institutions. Juvenal, on the other hand, is bitter and filled with rage. His work reveals a man sickened and horrified by corruption. Sassoon's poems such as "'Blighters'" may be identified as Juvenalian satires. In "'Blighters,'" Sassoon is clearly angry, so angry that he wishes death and destruction on the people in the music hall. Through poems like "'Blighters,'" Sassoon attempts to educate his readers about the betrayal of the British soldiers by corrupt politicians and a complacent citizenry. According to Patrick Campbell in *Siegfried Sassoon: A Study of the War Poetry*: "That politicians, parsons and parents, indeed most of 'Blighty' as far as Sassoon was concerned, seemed blissfully unaware of the war's actual character mean that the revelations needed to be more rather than less shockingly veracious."

HISTORICAL CONTEXT

The Oscar Wilde Case and Aftermath

Toward the end of the nineteenth century, there was a relaxation of the strict moral codes of Victorian England, and within the literary community, homosexuality was a relatively well-accepted way of life. However, during the final decade of the century, there was an event that was to have long-lasting consequences for the gay community in general, an event that in all probability influenced Sassoon's understanding of his own homosexuality.

The noted writer Oscar Wilde, flamboyant in the extreme, began a well-documented affair with Lord Alfred Douglas in about 1891. Douglas's father, the Marquess of Queensberry, was a very powerful man, and was violently angry over his son's affair. He accused Wilde of being a "sodomite," the legal term for those who perform homosexual intercourse. Although those accused of sodomy were rarely prosecuted, it was nonetheless illegal.

In response to the Marquess's accusations, Wilde sued him for criminal libel. The case did not go well for Wilde. Not only did he lose the case, he was also arrested and ordered to stand trial for sodomy, shocking members of the literary community, and particularly other gay writers. Wilde was found guilty, and forced to serve two years at hard labor. When he was released in 1897, he was broken and bankrupt. He left England for France, and died there in 1900.

That someone could be arrested, tried, and punished for having a homosexual affair was deeply troubling for artists and writers. Many chose, in response to the Wilde affair, to hide their sexuality and to distance themselves from known gay men. For Sassoon, reaching puberty near the time of Wilde's death, the pressures to conform must have been tremendous.

As a consequence of cultural pressure, Sassoon became very much a man's man. He excelled at sport, hunting, and riding. In addition, he enlisted in the military just as England entered the war. As a soldier, he distinguished himself with bravery and courage. At the same time, paradoxically, he also developed a close group of literary friends with whom he spoke guardedly about his sexual identity.

Sassoon's writings reveal that he was content in the world of men he found in the military. This is not to say that he necessarily consummated sexual affairs with men, but rather that he found joy and beauty in the company of men such as David Thomas, a young subaltern Sassoon memorialized in a poem at his death. In addition, it is tempting to credit Sassoon's deep love for the soldiers subordinate to him to his attraction to men younger than himself.

In any event, seeing the young men of his unit mown down by German guns, and losing both his brother and David Thomas within a year, pushed Sassoon away from the beautiful verses of his youth, and toward the gritty, angry protest of poems like "'Blighters.'"

World War I

On July 28, 1914, a young Serb terrorist named Gavril Princip assassinated the Austrian Archduke Franz Ferdinand and his bride in Sarajevo, Serbia. This action, like a bolt falling into place, started a series of responses from all over Europe. Treaties that had been signed privately or publicly were put into play; by the time the air cleared, nearly every country in Europe was on

COMPARE
&
CONTRAST

- **1917:** Soldier-poets such as Siegfried Sassoon, Wilfred Owen, and Isaac Rosenberg write poetry and memoirs recording the realities of their lives on the battlefields of France during World War I.

  Today: Soldier-writers such as Anthony Swofford and Brian Turner record their experiences in the Gulf War and the Iraq War.

- **1917:** The war is nearing its end, and by that time over 900,000 British soldiers will be dead, with a total battlefield death count of 8.5 million people.

Today: In the first four years of the War in Iraq, about 3,600 Americans have been killed, with an additional estimated 70,000 Iraqis dead.

- **1917:** Britain instituted a military draft in 1916 and the United States does likewise at this time, thus bolstering the ranks of what was at first a volunteer army.

  Today: Both the British and the American military are volunteer forces, despite ongoing participation in the war in Iraq.

---

one side or another, readying for war. The assassination, as tragic as it was, was not so large an event that it should have caused the response that it did. However, the growing militarism of Germany, and the subsequent military response of both France and England, made the events of 1914 seem somehow fated.

In August 1914, the Germans invaded Belgium, shooting some five thousand civilians and setting fire to buildings and homes along the way. These atrocities were played up in the British newspapers, and probably led to the British decision to enter the war, although the Germans had expected them to remain neutral. (After all, King George V of England and Kaiser Wilhelm of Germany were first cousins.) At the Battle of the Marne, the combined forces of Britain and France stopped the German invasion, in an important victory. However, they did not push the Germans back to their own country. Instead, both sides fortified lines of trenches that ended up extending from the North Sea to the Swiss border. The armies held the line that came to be known as the Western Front with very little movement for the next four years.

Each side fortified the areas outside their trenches with barbed wire and mines. The technology of the machine gun rendered obsolete all the previous history of warfare. No longer could

men march in a line toward an opposing side. Whereas in earlier wars, soldiers would march forward, shoot, then drop to their knees to reload guns while the next line moved forward to shoot, and so on and so forth; in the new modern warfare, machine gunners sitting in nests at the trench lines simply mowed down everything that moved in an area that quickly came to be called No Man's Land. In addition, both sides developed mustard gas, a deadly poison that could be dropped on an opposing side and cause terrible pain, suffering and death.

It is difficult to describe the conditions in the trenches; that the conditions were so terrible and beyond the power of conventional language is probably what spurred Sassoon and other trench poets to render their experiences metaphorically. Countless accounts report that the stench of the Front met soldiers miles before they actually reached the front line. Mutilated, rotting corpses of men and beasts littered No Man's Land. Further, the winter of 1914 was one of the coldest and wettest in modern European history, and many men drowned in mud. Rats were everywhere.

It was into to this hell that Sassoon arrived in 1915. He found at the front the chance to distinguish himself as a hero, which he did. Called "Mad Jack" by his men, he single-handedly captured a German trench and rescued members of his unit from certain death in No Man's Land. Yet by 1916, Sassoon, as well as many other soldier-writers, believed that the politicians and leaders of their countries had led them to death and destruction without a clear strategy for success. Sassoon came to believe that the loss of life in the war was simply unconscionable, and that the people responsible for sending young men to horror and death were both corrupt and culpable.

This anger is evident in poems such as "'Blighters,'" as well as in "The General" and "They," poems that suggest that the real enemy is not the German army bogged down on the Western Front, but rather the people in power on the Home Front.

CRITICAL OVERVIEW

The poems of the *Old Huntsman* were composed over a several year period, with "'Blighters'" and the other war poems largely composed shortly before the book's publication in 1917. Indeed, "'Blighters'" was written in January 1917, while Sassoon was in England recuperating from trench fever. In his biography of the poet, titled *Siegfried Sassoon*, John Stuart Roberts describes the volume: "Its contents ranged from a long autobiographical poem of an ageing and ailing huntsman to the savage realities of war. Sassoon also included many of his pastoral compositions and early lyrical evocations of his youthful experience." There are, then, striking differences between the early and later poetry of the volume. As Roberts continues: "The seventy-two poems ... constitute a progression from callow youth to 'happy warrior,' to the confused soldier and angry man of 1916." Certainly, "'Blighters'" was a very late poem in the volume, and foretells the direction that Sassoon's poetry would take during the rest of the war.

Indeed, the poems in *The Old Huntsman, and Other Poems* signal a shift in Sassoon's poetry, away from the romanticized notions of life, nature, and especially the war, toward a bitter and realistic appraisal of the situation in the trenches. Michael Thorpe, in his *Siegfried Sassoon: A Critical Study*, notes the discrepancy among the poems in *The Old Huntsman, and Other Poems*. He writes: "A few poems in *The Old Huntsman* show Sassoon striving, during his first months in France, to hold fast the innocent vision that had animated the early nature poems." Poems such as "'Blighters,'" "The Hero," and

"The General," on the other hand, shift into the bitter satire that marks the bulk of Sassoon's war poetry. Thorpe argues that these poems at least partially owe their power to the fact that they resemble "Georgian rhyming verse in everything but the diction, so that the satiric effect is accentuated by clothing a disreputable body in formal dress." That is, by using forms and structures he previously employed in his Georgian period, and substituting sometimes ugly words and phrases from the trenches for the beautiful, high-flown vocabulary of his earlier work, Sassoon creates poems that are deeply ironic and savagely satiric. Indeed, if the poems of *The Old Huntsman, and Other Poems*, notably poems such as "'Blighters,'" indicate a transition for Sassoon, then the shift is fully realized in his next collection, *Counter-Attack*.

When *The Old Huntsman* was published in 1917, it met with critical and popular success, although there were those who found the war poetry too brutal for their tastes. One of the earliest published reviews was by Sassoon's friend Edmund Gosse, appearing in the *Edinburgh Review* in October, 1917. Although Gosse was impressed by the volume, in his review he finds it necessary to temper Sassoon's more bitter responses for the reading public: "The bitterness of Lieut. Sassoon is not cynical, it is the rage of disenchantment, the violence of a young man eager to pursue other aims.... His temper is not altogether to be applauded, for such sentiments must tend to relax the effort of the struggle, yet they can hardly be reproved when conducted with so much honesty and courage."

With the passage of time, Sassoon's war poetry assumed a more and more important place in the body of his work, and various critics have taken very different approaches. Both John H. Johnston in 1966 and Fred D. Crawford in 1988 comment on Sassoon's disgust for the home front displays of patriotism. In *English Poetry of the First World War: A Study in the Evolution of Lyric and Narrative Form*, Johnston calls "'Blighters'" "the last poem of Sassoon's early satiric period" and "the bitterest of his early productions; it attacks the frivolous and vulgar jingoism of the music hall and the hectic approval of the audience." Likewise, Crawford writes in *British Poets of the Great War* that "In "'Blighters,'" Sassoon attacks the frenzied jingoism of the music hall."

The 1st Lancashire Fusiliers line up in a trench and fix bayonets prior to the assault on Beaumont Hamel, during the Battle of Albert (Hulton Archive / Getty Images)

Other critics explore Sassoon's emotional and psychological state as a means of approaching the wary poetry. Daniel Hipp in *The Poetry of Shell Shock: Wartime Trauma and Healing in Wilfred Owen, Ivor Gurney and Siegfried Sassoon*, argues that by writing the war poetry found in *The Old Huntsman* and *Counter-Attack*, Sassoon was able to "resolve his crisis of protest and rejoin his men in France." Further, Hipp asserts that writing the war poetry immediately before and at the same time as receiving care at Craiglockhart proved a complementary therapy to that provided by his psychiatrist.

Paul Moeyes in *Siegfried Sassoon: Scorched Glory* argues that Sassoon was not only interested in the literary quality of his work, but also in the emotional release writing such poetry gave him. Moeyes asserts that "Sassoon's characteristic attitude towards all his literary work throughout his career was never to judge it by literary standards only: at least as important was

the emotional value it had for him personally." The inclusion of pastoral pieces as well as the satires of *The Old Huntsman* speaks to Sassoon's mixed emotional state from 1915 through 1916.

More recent criticism of Sassoon's work, including "'Blighters,'" relegates Sassoon to a place somewhere behind Wilfred Owen in talent. It is of course possible that had Sassoon died like Owen, ironically just days before the November 11, 1918, Armistice, his work would have been considered the gift of a martyr. On the other hand, critics such as Brooke Allen have rediscovered Sassoon. In a *New Criterion* article she writes that "much of the power of Sassoon's poetry derives from a trick he had picked up from Thomas Hardy, that of ending his poems with what he called a 'knock-out blow.' . . . his real gifts were more epigrammatic than poetic . . . [and] his epigrammatic poems have mostly proved more memorable than his lyrical ones."

Certainly, for all of Sassoon's repeated attempts to tell the story of his war experience, and finally get it right, it is (again, ironically) his first attempts that have proved the most lasting. Although he lived a very long time after the World War I, Sassoon's legacy to British literature will likely remain this slim collection of poems, written between 1914 and 1918.

CRITICISM

Diane Andrews Henningfeld

Henningfeld is a professor and literary critic who writes widely for educational publications. In the following essay, she closely reads Sassoon's "'Blighters,'" using a type of literary theory known as New Criticism and focusing on the poet's tightly controlled vocabulary and irony.

During the years between the World War I and World War II, a type of literary criticism called New Criticism flourished. As a result, many school and university students through much of the twentieth century learned a technique called "close reading" as a means of literary analysis. The New Critics (such as Cleanth Brooks) believed that literary analysis ought to focus on the work itself, rather than on the subjective feelings of the reader or the intentions of the author. They did so by concentrating on the words of the poem, and the images, symbols, and irony that the words contain. They were eager to demonstrate that a poem functions as an organic unit, due to the interaction of its parts. At its most extreme, the New Critics believed that all one needed to read a poem successfully was the poem itself and a dictionary.

In the closing years of the twentieth century and the beginning of the twenty-first century, however, the New Criticism was relegated to the past. Students were taught to read poems and literature from a wide variety of critical perspectives, including reader response, psycho-analytical, new historical, Marxist, and queer theories, among others. From these theories arose many important and interesting new ways of looking at literature.

Nevertheless, there is something about a poem like "'Blighters'" that begs to be closely read, using New Critical theory. It is only eight lines long, yet those eight lines are so compacted with meaning that without a careful understanding of the nuances of the language and the

WHAT DO I READ NEXT?

- Vera Brittain's *The Testament of Youth*, published in 1933 and continuously in print since that time, offers a look at World War I in France from the perspective of a young volunteer nurse.

- Siegfried Sassoon's fictionalized memoirs, *Memoirs of a Fox Hunting Man*, published in 1928, and *Memoirs of an Infantry Officer*, published in 1930, provide significant context and background for the poems in *The Old Huntsman*.

- *All Quiet on the Western Front* (1929), by Erich Maria Remarque, provides another picture of the World War I stalemate along the trenches of the Western Front, from the perspective of a young German soldier. Many critics view this novel as the most representative piece of literature produced by a writer from either side of the conflict.

- Jon Stallworthy's *Great Poets of World War I* (2002) offers an examination of a number of war poets, including Sassoon, and provides striking illustrations and photographs as well.

- Poetry by Wilfred Owen, included in *The Collected Poems of Wilfred Owen*, published in 1965 and still in print, is often considered by critics to be among the best poetry written about World War I. Owen spent time at Craiglockhart Hospital with Sassoon and Owen was deeply influenced by his contact with Sassoon.

- *Good-bye to All That* (1929), written by Sassoon's friend Robert Graves, is a memoir of his time on the Western Front. Sassoon figures prominently in the memoir.

- British writer Pat Barker used the experiences of Siegfried Sassoon, Robert Graves, Wilfred Owen, and Dr. William Rivers as the basis for her trilogy of novels about World War I, *Regeneration* (1991), *The Eye in the Door* (1994), and the Booker Award-winning *The Ghost Road* (1995).

> THERE IS LITTLE DOUBT THAT SASSOON HAS
> CREATED A GENUINE POEM, ITS THEME THE IRONIC
> DISCONNECT BETWEEN THE HOME FRONT AND
> THE WESTERN FRONT, ITS REALITY THE 'RIDDLED
> CORPSES' WHO WILL NEVER FIND THEIR WAY BACK
> HOME AGAIN."

interplay of ironies in the text, the poem simply becomes a witty little epigram. Brooks' essay, "Irony as a Principle of Structure" (reprinted in *Contexts for Criticism*), becomes particularly instructive in a close reading of "'Blighters.'"

To begin, it is important to establish working definitions for both metaphor and for irony. A metaphor is a figure of language in which two unlike things are compared to each other, often in an unexpected way. For example, when Shakespeare writes "All the world's a stage, and we are but poor players in it," he is comparing life to theater. When a young man calls his girlfriend "Honey," he is also using a metaphor, comparing his girlfriend to something very sweet. Metaphor is at the heart of modern poetry; Brooks writes "One can sum up modern poetic technique by calling it the rediscovery of metaphor and the full commitment to metaphor."

Further, irony is a rhetorical device which reveals a gap or a contradiction or an incongruity between an expectation and reality. When an audience knows more than the characters in a play or novel, the characters' actions become ironic, because the audience recognizes the gap between what the characters expect to happen and what will really happen. Likewise, when a speaker in a poem makes a statement that is unexpected by the reader, or is the opposite of what the speaker means, the result is irony. The New Critics would argue that all metaphors are essentially ironic because of the gap that opens between the literal and figurative meanings of the items being compared.

Sassoon's language in "'Blighters'" is shot through with multiple meanings, and metaphors. Further, it is clear that the narrator of the poem is telling his audience (those who are reading his poem) something very different from the expectations of the audience *in* the poem, the people watching the music hall show. Thus, "'Blighters'" in its eight lines, becomes a vehicle for tragic irony, cloaked in the cackling laughter of the crowd.

Sassoon makes clear his ironic intent before the opening line. The title of the poem is in itself ironic because Sassoon places it within quotation marks. Typically, quotation marks are used to indicate spoken language. It is not clear, however, who might be saying the word "blighters" in the poem, or even to whom the word blighters refers. Further, sometimes a person will place a word in quotation marks to actually imply the opposite of the word, an obviously ironic usage.

What is a blighter? In the first place, it is a term, often ironically endearing, applying to a common fellow, sometimes in unfortunate circumstances. For example, one might say: "The poor blighter got a 'Dear John' letter from his wife." A blighter can also refer to anyone living in Blighty, another term for England, or home. A blighter is also someone who damages or destroys something through blight. When the last of these two definitions coalesce, they take on a sinister cast. The people who live in Britain not only live in Britain, they are blighting Britain.

For Sassoon, the most obvious disconnect is that between "home, sweet home" and "Blighty." On the one hand, Sassoon clearly uses the song title "Home, sweet Home" ironically. England is anything but sweet to him. He is angry at the nation and angry with the citizens of the nation. Blighty, the term used by common soldiers to denote England, and by extension home, is also ironic. A blighted country can scarcely also be "home, sweet home." The contradiction here is between what the soldiers expect from their nation and what they receive. Sassoon, as narrator, sees the gap. As he recovers in England from his illness, he knows that there are men in the trenches of the Western Front who want nothing more than to return to old Blighty. These men believe that when they return home, all will be well. Sassoon, however, understands that not only is home not sweet, it is blighted. As the narrator, he is in a position to observe the difference between the sentimental and conventional meaning of "home" that the soldiers hold as a fantasy, and the reality of the home front, a place where the citizens exhibit ignorant patriotism without regard to the death of soldiers, a place where an audience laughs when they should be weeping. Brooks writes that "the 'meaning' of any particular item is modified by the context. . . . The context endows the particular word or image or statement with significance." In "'Blighters,'" the context of soldiers fighting and dying for their home in a foreign country lends particular, ironic significance to the entire concept of home.

Brooks further argues: "The poet can legitimately step out into the universal only by first going though the narrow door of the particular. The poet does not select an abstract theme and then embellish it with concrete details. On the contrary, he must establish the details, must abide by the details, and through his realization of the details attain whatever general meaning he can attain." Sassoon structures his poem precisely as described by Brooks. He fills the first six lines with concrete details about the music hall. The house is "crammed," the audience members "grin" and "cackle." Chorus girls prance and sing shrilly. The careful details of the first stanza are the "narrow door" through which Sassoon goes to reach the universal truth of the last lines of the poem.

Indeed, it is not until readers reach the second stanza that the metaphoric nature of the first stanza becomes clear. The "house" of the first line, for example, can mean not only the theater, it can also mean a house of Parliament, the governing body of Britain. This conjecture is supported by the fact that in the Houses of Parliament, members sit in tiers that rise from ground level upward, just as in the music hall. Patrick Campbell agrees with this interpretation. He writes that "The 'House' could also signify that chamber where politicians spout just as obscenely about the glamorous heroics of the conflict." Sassoon, in many of his writings, expresses his belief that politicians are despicable because they are the ones sending boys to die unnecessarily. It is a small leap, therefore, to identify the audience of the music hall show with the politicians watching the show, particularly since the word show not only refers to a stage performance, it also is a term used by soldiers to refer to a battle or fight. One of the biggest "shows" of World War I was the Battle of the Somme, an exquisitely violent, and monumentally unsuccessful attempt to break the German lines that cost 21,000 British lives on the first day alone. That Sassoon has this particular battle in mind as he writes "'Blighters'" is clear from the final two lines of the poem: "And there'd be no more jokes in Music-halls / To mock the riddled corpses round Bapaume."

These lines are Sassoon at his ironic best. Bapaume, the name of a French town that conveniently rhymes with "home," and thus provides an ironic contrast to the notion of home, was to have been the first day's objective for the British soldiers in the Battle of the Somme. What the generals and politicians expected of the soldiers in the field was a far cry from what the soldiers were able to accomplish, and it was those expectations that contributed to the heavy death toll. The soldiers were not properly equipped for the fight, nor were the tactics of the battle connected to the reality of the field. Consequently, the Battle of the Somme itself became a horrific irony: so many men lost, so little ground gained. The corpses in "'Blighters'" are "round Bapaume," not in it. The English soldiers never reached their objective, nor will they ever have any home again but for the French soil on which they fell.

In addition, the corpses of whom Sassoon writes are "riddled." The word riddle has its roots in Anglo-Saxon English, and is deeply engrained in the language, particularly in its second sense. The obvious meaning of this word is that the bodies of the men who fought in the Battle of the Somme were shot full of holes. The second sense of the word "riddle" is a statement that is ambiguous, paradoxical, or puzzling. The great ancient Anglo-Saxon warriors, predecessors of the British soldiers who died near Bapaume, were famous for their riddles. In Sassoon's text, the corpses themselves pose a riddle in their death: why have so many young men been slaughtered in a senseless war?

Cleanth Brooks writes near the end of his essay that "the theme in a genuine poem does not confront us as abstraction—that is as one man's generalization from the relevant particulars. Finding its proper symbol, defined and refined by the participating metaphors, the theme becomes a part of the reality in which we live." There is little doubt that Sassoon has created a genuine poem, its theme the ironic disconnect between the home front and the Western front, its reality the "riddled corpses" who will never find their way back home again.

Source: Diane Andrews Henningfeld, Critical Essay on "'Blighters,'" in *Poetry for Students*, Gale, Cengage Learning, 2008.

Patrick Campbell

In the following essay, Campbell closely examines the language in "'Blighters,'" noting that the description of the music hall is ironic.

Home on leave before returning to "unmitigated hell," Siegfried Sassoon went to a revue at the Hippodrome, Liverpool. The date was 4 February 1917. Although the company, that of "a pleasant and intelligent" "fellow officer" apparently made for "an amusing evening," the show, Sassoon recalled, "provided me with a bit of material for satire... I wrote the afterwards well-known lines called 'Blighters' in which I asserted that I'd like to see a tank come down the stalls at a music hall performance where—in my opinion the jingoism of the jokes and songs appeared to 'mock the riddled corpses round Bapaume.'"

No poem in *The Old Huntsman* is briefer, the poet's recipe of "two or three harsh, peremptory and colloquial stanzas" here reduced to a minimum of two terse quatrains. As Sassoon's "farewell to England," he wanted to keep it short—and satiric. For the targets of the title are "blighters" and the writer was consciously using the colloquialism both as a general indictment of anything that blights, of contemptible people, and, more specifically, in reference to those who had stayed in "Blighty" (England) and profited from the misfortunes of others. In the poem both general and specific meanings coalesce.

The structure appears to mirror that of another epigram, "They"—the "nation at home" pictured in the first quatrain and the "nation overseas" in the second. But the tour de force, literally, resides in Sassoon's imaginative vision of war, in the form of a "Lurching" tank that comes crashing down the stalls of the Hippodrome. Only the shock of real terror can stir audience and reader alike out of their complacency and jingoism.

The piece is shot through with heavy irony. The "tier beyond tier" of the house superficially reminds the sardonic observer of serried and disciplined soldiers anticipating a "Show" (the soldiers' jargon for a big offensive) in which many will inevitably die. But here the verbs emphasize the vulgarity of an audience that is deliberately demeaned and disparaged by the epithets "grin" and "cackle." Worse, the chorus line of "prancing" women are no better than harlots showing off their bodies in an atmosphere of dissipation and false bonhomie generated not by the heat of battle but by inebriation ("drunk with din"). So impervious is the audience to the reality of war that it responds by indulging in the sentimental claptrap of some vapid music-hall number ("We're sure the Kaiser loves our dear old Tanks").

The poet's reaction, that of one who has "been there," is predictably fierce. These "blighters" need a nightmarish vision to awaken them to the real horror of war, something that will dispel forever the misplaced notion of "dear old Tanks."

The absurd sentimental humanizing of these lumbering leviathans gives the poet an opportunity to expand the stock personification in a grimly comic way and to wish on this "House" a nightmarish vision of the hell that is trench warfare. For Sassoon's tanks do lurch in a manner reminiscent of drunken blighters or chorus girls swaying to syncopated ragtime tunes. But now, if the poet has his way, they will lurch towards the wealthy cacklers in the stalls, the jerky rhythms of their progress as metronomic as those of ragtime but mechanical, remorseless, inhuman. Now it will be the turn of these blighters to experience that sense of abject terror that is daily currency for the ordinary soldier.

The trooper may dream of "Home, Sweet Home" but the words of this song also embody a falsehood. For this world of the Hippodrome mirrors, if more nakedly, the values of a blighted nation; a place where, in Sassoon's words, "the jingoism of the songs and jokes" appears to "mock" the victims of war. It is left to the soldier-poet (here identified by the personal pronoun) and not the music-hall chorus to remind his readers of the carnage of "riddled corpses." Bapaume, the site of a bloody offensive, may rhyme with "home," but the name, remote and echoic, sounds a death knell at the poem's conclusion.

Source: Patrick Campbell, "Sassoon's 'Blighters,'" in *Explicator*, Vol. 53, Spring 1995, pp. 170–71.

Margaret B. McDowell

In the following essay, McDowell gives a critical analysis of Sassoon's work.

Siegfried Sassoon's poetry was published over a period of more than sixty years, almost to the moment of his death in 1967, a few days before his eighty-first birthday. In the history of British poetry, he will be remembered primarily for some one hundred poems—many satirical and almost all short—in which he protested the

OTHER POEMS WRITTEN BEFORE HIS DEPAR-
TURE FOR FRANCE (OR SHORTLY AFTER HIS ARRIVAL)
PRESENT WAR AS A POSITIVE AGENT THAT DEVELOPS
STRENGTH AND CHARACTER."

continuation of World War I through 1917 and 1918. Many of his war poems reflect with absolute authenticity the sufferings of the soldiers in the French trenches, in hospitals, or in their homeland after many of them returned disabled or traumatized. The poetry Sassoon wrote in the last half of his life drew less attention than his war poems and is, on the whole, far less arresting and original. For the most part, these later poems are meditative, reflecting his search for identity, and are important for their psychological revelations. His lyrics became increasingly religious in nature, a trend that reached its culmination in his last ten years, when he celebrated in his poems the spiritual peace and security that he had eventually found in Roman Catholicism in 1957.

Sassoon also wrote six memorable autobiographical books. In three of these—*Memoirs of a Fox-Hunting Man* (1928), *Memoirs of an Infantry Officer* (1930), and *Sherston's Progress* (1936)—he presented his life in a partially fictionalized form through the "journeys" of a character named George Sherston. (The trilogy appeared in one volume in 1937 as *The Complete Memoirs of George Sherston.)Memoirs of a Fox-Hunting Man* sold extremely well in both England and the United States and secured an audience for the two later volumes. It introduced Sassoon as an excellent writer in prose and won for him two distinguished awards: The Hawthornden Prize and the James Tait Black Memorial Prize. In a second autobiographical trilogy—*The Old Century and Seven More Years* (1938), *The Weald of Youth* (1942), and *Siegfried's Journey, 1916-1920* (1945)—Sassoon presented his life to 1920 without a fictional facade.

Siegfried Lorraine Sassoon grew up in Kent, loving the weald and the outdoor sports of the country gentry—fox hunting, golf, and cricket. His parents separated in 1901, and his father,

Alfred Ezra Sassoon, died of tuberculosis when Siegfried was not quite nine. Because he had had little contact with his father, Siegfried Sassoon wrote in *The Weald of Youth* that he had not understood how long he should feel grief, after his father's funeral in London, which he was too upset to attend with his younger brother, Hamo, and older brother, Michael. Brought up by his mother, Theresa Georgina Thornycroft Sassoon, in the Church of England, Sassoon expressed surprise later in life at how deeply his Spanish-Jewish heritage affected him and at how greatly the psychological inheritance from his father's people had conditioned his responses, his values, and his attitudes: "I sometimes surmise that my eastern ancestry is stronger in me than the Thornycrofts'. The daemon in me is Jewish. Do you believe in racial memories? Some of my hypnogogic visions have seemed like it, and many of them were oriental architecture."

Alfred Ezra Sassoon, Siegfried's father, was the first Sassoon to marry a Gentile. Alfred's mother opposed the marriage, said all the Jewish funeral prayers for him, and uttered a curse upon his unborn children. Never relenting, she cut off his allowance and never permitted her grandchildren to visit her at Ashley Park, near Walton-on-the-Thames, an estate which included a large fifteenth-century hall, a cricket field, and a golf course. Sometimes called "the Rothschilds of the East," the millionaire Sassoon families had typically resided in India and in the Near East since the time of the Spanish Inquisition. In the mid-nineteenth century Siegfried's paternal grandfather and several of his uncles moved to Europe and were important in the arts as well as commerce and banking. In England some of the Sassoons exercised power in Parliament, and one entertained the Shah of Persia during his much-publicized visit to London in the 1890s. Alfred Sassoon's sister, Rachel Beer, owned and edited two London newspapers, the *Observer* and the *Sunday Times*, from the early 1890s to 1904, and she wrote extensively for them. Against her mother's protests, she remained in close contact with Alfred's family and left an inheritance for Siegfried and his surviving brother, Michael, at her death in 1927.

Sassoon in *The Old Century and Seven More Years* suggested he had been endowed, in the Old Testament sense, with the gift of prophecy through his Jewish blood, and that this gift had found its most powerful expression in his crying out for social justice and compassion in his war poetry. Nevertheless, he identified more strongly with his mother than with his father. If he inherited from his father a contemplative spirit, an urge to speak as a minor prophet through his poetry, he, nevertheless, gained from the Thornycrofts the "common-sense" and the creative perspective that had allowed him to develop as an artist: "how I bless the Thornycroft sanity.... Introspective though I have been, I could stand aside and look at myself—and laugh." His mother chose his name because of her love of Wagner's *Der Ring des Nibelungen*, and he himself always liked the name for its heroic associations. In a letter to Dame Felicitas Corrigan in 1965, he remarked upon his mother's having given him for his third birthday a copy of Coleridge's *Lectures on Shakespeare*. Theresa's family, like the Sassoons, was wealthy, but its wealth derived from land. Her immediate family included notable sculptors: her grandfather John Francis; her father, Thomas; her mother, and her brother Hamo. Another brother, John, was an architect for the British navy. Theresa's mother painted many portraits of the royal family, and Theresa and her two sisters were minor painters and sculptors. Siegfried's education included private tutoring until he was fourteen, the study of law at Marlborough College from ages sixteen to nineteen, and the study of history—while he was also writing poetry—at Clare College, Cambridge. When he decided to return to Kent without taking a degree, he continued his writing and began to publish his poems privately. His mother introduced him to her friend Sir Edmund Gosse, who in turn introduced him to such literary figures as Edward Marsh and Rupert Brooke. Gosse encouraged Sassoon to spend much time in London. Marsh used some of Sassoon's early poems in his anthology, *Georgian Poetry, 1916-1917*. Sassoon later developed some doubts about Georgian poetry, which he described as "crocus-crowded lyrics."

In Sassoon's early poetry his ideas and his technique are conventional and sometimes reveal the influence of the Pre-Raphaelites or the Rhymers' Club poets, whom he had read as an adolescent and as a university student. Such poets as Algernon Charles Swinburne, Dante Gabriel Rossetti, Lionel Johnson, Ernest Dowson, Thomas Hardy, and George Meredith served as his models. Not all of his early poems have survived, but many appeared in pamphlets that he published privately between 1906 and 1916. Of those early efforts selected for inclusion in his collected poems, several bear titles that are pagan in orientation: "Goblin Revel," "Dryads," and "Arcady Unheeding." The poems are replete with romantic references to "hooded witches," "dulcimers," "mournful pennons," "the gloom of the glade," and gentle shepherds. . . . As an older man, Sassoon attributed his frequent references to dawn in his early lyrics to the influence of George Meredith, and he thought his choice of archaic diction (words such as *noisome, darkling, marish, weir, jollity*) had derived from a desire to imitate Dante Gabriel Rossetti and other poets who had used medieval associations for romantic effects.

But these early poems also differ from the fin de siècle works that he read as a student. For example, his poems of fantasy have a more positive tone, a more direct style, and a more energetic pace than Dowson's fantasies, with their longing for death or for a return to lost innocence. In contrast to the older poets that Sassoon admired, he rarely wrote about love and sex. While in more than half of the early lyrics nature is a principal source of his imagery, his preoccupation with nature derives not only from attempts to follow pastoral conventions but also from a deeply felt love of outdoor life and an intimate knowledge of Kentish wildlife. Sassoon's depiction of nature even in the early poems reveals a freshness and a firsthand authenticity often absent in the poetry of the fin de siècle poets and the Georgian movement. This emphasis on nature continued throughout his lifetime. Even in his seventies a deep feeling for nature gave vitality to his poems of religion and the supernatural.

Much of his privately printed early verse was pallid and stilted, making his achievement as a war poet a few years later startling and unexpected. His revisions of early works, however, imply an ability to criticize his poetry and revise it in the direction of the simple and the specific. [. . .] Yet, in moving away from conventional artifice in diction to a more direct language and syntax, he was still far from the forceful colloquial utterances in his best war poems.

Sassoon was the earliest of the World War I poets to enlist in the British service, although not the first to see action in France. On 1 August 1914 at the age of twenty-seven, he passed his examination for enlistment; England declared war on 4 August; and Sassoon found himself in uniform on 5 August. He left for France in November 1915 with the First Battalion of the Royal Welch Fusiliers.

Some of the eight poems included by Marsh in *Georgian Poetry: 1916-1917* and some printed in *The Old Huntsman and Other Poems* (1917) adumbrate the growth that was to occur between Sassoon's earliest poetry and the poetry that he produced during and after the Somme offensive in 1916. "Haunted," a two-page, blank-verse poem, is conventionally romantic in its descriptions and in the image of a pale and solitary forest wanderer, who is doomed by an evil spell. But a few lines also hint at Sassoon's developing realism. For example, [...] and he depicts the pale victim's unequal encounter with Fate in terms as specific as those in the war poems: [...].

"The Kiss," written in 1916 (another poem in Marsh's anthology and in *The Old Huntsman*), depicts the violence of the war dramatically, but, unlike the war poems, written after he had seen action in the trenches, "The Kiss" seems to celebrate militarism. In this poem the soldier hopes that, as his heel holds his enemy, he will feel him "quail" as the bayonet penetrates. According to Sassoon, he wrote this poem after hearing a Colonel Campbell address his class in military training on "The Spirit of the Bayonet." It was written in the weeks when, according to Robert Graves, Sassoon was vacillating between being a "happy warrior" and a pacifist. Later Sassoon maintained that he had designed this poem as a satirical parody, but this assertion is of doubtful validity because he had similarly celebrated war as a cathartic experience in several other early poems.

Other poems written before his departure for France (or shortly after his arrival) present war as a positive agent that develops strength and character. [In the chauvinistic "Absolution," composed in summer 1915], [...] [r]eferring to the army as "the happy legion," he implies that soldiers may be glad to give up their lives in a great cause. The poet adopts the view that war occupies only a moment in history: [...]. This sense of war's brevity minimizes its agony, as does the comparison of that agony with the glory that comes from self-sacrifice. In "Absolution" Sassoon questions neither the necessity of the war nor the motives that led to it. This poem, influenced by poetry of Rupert Brooke, was written shortly after Brooke died.

In "The Redeemer," written in his first weeks in the trenches, Sassoon uses vivid details characteristic of his later war poems [...], and the soldier is depicted realistically as a "simple duffer" [...]. The sardonic tone of Sassoon's later war poems is not yet fully developed. The speaker, seeing the duffer loaded down with planks across his shoulders in a midwinter rain, too readily envisions him as Christ. Unearned religious sentiment dominates the poem until it ends suddenly in a blunt declaration of nationalism [...].

Several conventional lyrics which emphasize nature (such as "Morning Glory," "Daybreak in a Garden," "Tree and Sky," "Storm and Sunlight," and "Wind in the Beechwood") appear in *The Old Huntsman and Other Poems*, and a number of the early war poems in the volume similarly treat nature in an artificial manner. "France" praises the "vivid green [...]." [...] In another mood he complains in "To Victory," a poem written just after his arrival in France, of the colorlessness of the gray November landscape. In "The Dragon and the Undying" he identifies the bursting flares as dragons. The soldiers lying in the trenches relate to the landscape and the night sky as if meeting a significant destiny, in harmony with the cosmos. [...] "Before the Battle" is replete with similar language and conventional imagery. Such poetry—much like the popular war verse of Robert Nichols—contrasts strikingly with even the better war poems that appear in this early book.

"To My Brother" (Autumn 1915) holds special personal significance because in it Sassoon—still in training in England—addresses his younger brother, Hamo, who was killed in action on the Gallipoli Peninsula in August 1915 and buried at sea. This graceful work is not an elegy or lament but an expression of the author's anxiety that fear may overwhelm him and of his longing for his brother's companionship in the ordeal he faces on the battlefield: [...]. Unfortunately, Sassoon allows the speaker's uncertainty to be too easily resolved in the last two lines, in which the heroism of the dead is hailed impersonally as an omen of victory: [...].

A second loss was to come a few months later with the death of Sassoon's "dream friend," Lt. David Thomas, whom Sassoon calls Dick Tiltwood in the Sherston trilogy. Thomas is lamented in "The Last Meeting," written in May 1916 at Flixecourt, during Sassoon's brief respite from front-line action. In these calm surroundings after months of devastating warfare, Sassoon also wrote the excellent poem "Stand-To: Good Friday Morning," which he later identified as the single poem which pointed toward the satirical style that was to prove so successful in many of his poems in the next three years.

Besides the war poems and the pastoral poems in *The Old Huntsman*, the long title poem is of particular interest. Marked by colloquial diction and conversational rhythms, this poem is a blank-verse monologue in which an old huntsman recalls scenes and people from his past. He wonders about the religious convictions of "the old Duke" and of the clergy he has known, but he himself feels remote from heaven and hell—and finally also remote from a world "that's full of wars." The huntsman's series of descriptive pictures reveal a grasp of realistic detail, and the huntsman's speech is an improvement over Sassoon's only other long poem in colloquial blank verse, *The Daffodil Murderer* (1913), a parody on John Masefield.

Of even greater interest, however, are the new war poems, written after Sassoon was sent to the front. These poems present trench warfare graphically, stress the ordinariness and the humanity of the soldiers, and usually employ colloquial diction and conversational rhythms. While "The Old Huntsman" is relaxed and humorous, the majority of the war poems in this volume lament human suffering and express rage at the futile deaths of the young men.

Sassoon's combat career from 1916 to 1918 was marked by several long leaves and hospitalizations for injuries and illnesses. For example, he was hospitalized for a gastric illness, so that he missed the worst fighting of the Somme offensive, in which British casualties were heaviest, from July to October 1916. He also found himself in 1916 and again in 1917 in close contact in England with influential pacifists: art critic Robert Ross; Lady Ottoline Morrell and her husband, an influential pacifist member of Parliament; Bertrand Russell, who had already lost his professorship because of his antiwar statements at Cambridge; and John Middleton Murry, literary critic and friend of antiwar authors such as D.H. Lawrence. Sassoon, in part through the urging of these friends, made a formal declaration of protest against the war in July 1917. He had already received the Military Cross for bringing in under heavy fire a wounded lance-

corporal who had fallen near the German lines; and he had been recommended for the Victoria Cross after he captured alone some German trenches in the Hindenburg Line. When he sent his letter of protest to the war department, he threw the ribbon of his Military Cross into the River Mersey. In the protest, Sassoon said: "I believe that the War is being deliberately prolonged by those who have the power to end it.... I believe that this War, on which I entered as a war of defence and liberation, has now become a war of aggression and conquest. I believe that the purpose for which I and my fellow soldiers entered upon this war should have been so clearly stated as to have made it impossible to change them, and that, had this been done, the objects which actuated us would now be attainable by negotiation.... I can no longer be a party to prolong these sufferings for ends which I believe to be evil and unjust. I am not protesting against the conduct of the war, but against the political errors and insincerities for which the fighting men are being sacrificed." Sassoon's declaration was read in the House of Commons at the instigation of Bertrand Russell, and he was in danger of court-martial. Robert Graves, a fellow poet, interceded at his hearing, pleading his view that Sassoon was suffering shell shock. As a result, in July 1917 Sassoon entered Craiglockhart War Hospital in Edinburgh, where Wilfred Owen was already receiving treatment. Sassoon and Owen became friends. (After Owen was killed during the week of the Armistice, Sassoon collected and edited Owen's poems—almost all previously unpublished—for publication in 1920.) By summer 1917 *The Old Huntsman* had been widely read, and Sassoon was writing and compiling the poems that were to appear in *Counter-Attack*.

While *The Old Huntsman and Other Poems* includes a variety of poems, the next volume, *Counter-Attack and Other Poems* (1918), does not. All thirty-nine poems are harshly realistic laments or satires. The typical satirical poem is short and marked by rhythms of conversation, strong and regular rhyme, considerable slang, and often a singsong, lilting verse at variance with the tragic subject. Sassoon's satires are marked by bitter irony, and they specifically attack patriotic and complacent civilians, politicians unconcerned with peacemaking, military strategists in high positions, clergymen who preach an apparently merciless God and who identify warlikeness with godliness, and all the popular media, especially the kind of journalism which emphasized military goals of absolute conquest and minimized the extent of British casualties. The horror of the battlefield and the trenches emerges as Sassoon relentlessly builds detail upon detail (rats, fragments of dead bodies, stench of rotting flesh, winter rain, mud that slows each step, sounds of guns, and sounds of ominous silence before shelling).

At the close of the war when Sassoon selected sixty-four poems for *The War Poems of Siegfried Sassoon* (1919), he included eighteen from *The Old Huntsman* (1917), nearly all of the poems in *Counter-Attack* (1918), and nine from the privately published volume *Picture Show* (1919). The war poems he excluded were primarily those in *The Old Huntsman* that were written prior to his combat experience—poems such as "Absolution," "The Redeemer," and "Victory"—that romanticized warfare. Most of the poems included in *The War Poems* were written in 1917 and 1918. Some reflect his own hospital experience; many were undoubtedly written in the hospital or rest home during the long leaves that Sassoon had in England and Scotland during the last year and a half of his army service. Although these periods of relief from combat service permitted him to see his experiences in perspective, he was still far from tranquil when he wrote about them. He admitted to Robert Graves that when he was back in England, he had at times visions of horror in which he saw the bodies of the dead on the city pavements. During his long leave at Craiglockhart in the summer and fall of 1917, Sassoon was torn between his wish to return to the front in order to share the sufferings of his comrades and his wish to stay in England in order to continue his protest against continuing the war to absolute victory. Poems reflecting his hospital experience include "Sick Leave," "Banishment," "Repression of War Experience," "Autumn," and "Survivors."

Public response to *Counter-Attack* was more vocal and violent than the response to *The Old Huntsman* had been in the previous year. The satirical poems in the earlier volume followed the genial, long title poem, and harsh poems were interspersed among more conventional lyrics primarily in praise of nature. Even the gray and black book cover of *The Old Huntsman* contrasted with the cover of *Counter-Attack*, an orange cover overlaid with red, as if to call attention to the violent experiences described inside. *Counter-Attack* featured an introduction by Robert Nichols, whose war poetry, though inferior in its sentimentality and its lack of artistry, enjoyed great popularity in 1915-1917. (Sassoon's *The Old Huntsman* sold even more copies in 1917 than did Nichols's *Ardours and Endurances*.) In the introduction to *Counter-Attack*, Nichols acknowledged that war destroys more often than it develops nobility in men. He suggests, however, that Sassoon's anger may weaken his poems aesthetically. Both the British and American editions of *Counter-Attack* began with an excerpt from Fitzwater Wray's translation of Henri Barbusse's *Le Feu*, a book that Sassoon had read at Craiglockhart. The passage from *Le Feu* maintains that war destroys its participants morally as well as physically: war, in short, "outrages common sense, debases noble ideas, and dictates all kind of crime." It enlarges "every evil instinct."

The satirical poems here are all short. In most of them Sassoon employs epigrammatic statements, often climactically in the last line or two. There is also a tautness in the diction and structure evident in many of the poems. The typical figure is a simple, honorable, and patient soldier who is incapable of sophisticated argument against war. The soldiers are "poor duffers" who accept their unheroic lot. The poetry is not marked by an unusual degree of richness, and there is not much subtlety or ambiguity present. If the soldier protagonist is capable of intense feeling, the poetry is seldom complicated enough to require reflection and analysis on the reader's part.

Some readers became angry with Sassoon's blatant lack of patriotism in poems such as "Lamentations" and "How to Die." Some others became angry with Sassoon's apparent blasphemy and disrespect for the Christian religion in poems such as "The Investiture," "To Any Dead Officer," "Stand To: Good Friday Morning," "The Choral Union," and "They." In "Stand To: Good Friday Morning," for example, a soldier mocks the benevolence and compassion universally attributed to Christ, and in his hope for a sick leave shouts, "[...] send me a wound [...] And I'll believe [...]." Similarly glad for a wound that has allowed him to go home, the veteran in "The One-Legged Man" breathes a [thankful] prayer in the last line [...].

Even the responses of Wilfred Owen, John Middleton Murry, and Virginia Woolf to *Counter-Attack* were not wholeheartedly enthusiastic, although their points of view on the war were similar to Sassoon's. Like Nichols, they questioned whether Sassoon's technique of shocking the reader is aesthetically valid and whether he might not be writing propaganda rather than poetry. Not long before he was killed in action, Wilfred Owen wrote Sassoon in October 1918 that he had been made more fearful by reading the *Counter-Attack* poems than he had been when he had held a young soldier wounded in the head for half an hour and felt the soldier's blood soak through to his own shoulder. He wrote, "My senses are charred." For Owen, Sassoon's poetry failed to place the intense and horrible moment into a more general context of human association. Rather, Sassoon's poetry tended to hypnotize the reader so that he saw the horrible moment only in isolation. The reader is confronted with a violent "spot in time" which, intense in itself, leads to no discernible resolution or reasoned conclusion. In his preoccupation with the irrationality of war, Sassoon deliberately angered the reader and left him with a cryptic epigram that could give him little comfort. Owen at least must have appreciated Sassoon's revulsion against war, even though Sassoon was apparently unable to attain Owen's measured response to it.

John Middleton Murry wrote in his review of *Counter-Attack* that he found a city of pain in each poem, but he did not find a finished artistry. After reading Sassoon's poems, Murry could only conclude that there was no meaning at all left to human experience. Sassoon, said Murry, tends to numb his readers, to terrify them, and to deaden their sensibilities, all responses fatal to full aesthetic experience. For Murry, Sassoon failed to universalize his experience, because he concentrated so fanatically on one part of it. A truly great poet, Murry contended, must be able to get beyond even an annihilating experience to see it in its unusual implications; Sassoon gave us only the shocking intensity of the annihilating moment in many of his poems. Murry cited two lines from "Prelude: The Troops" to illustrate the element of balance he could not find in most of the poems: [...]. These lines, because of the reference to the blossoming sky, present "a full octave of emotional experience ... from serenity to desolation," a range of emotion lacking in most of Sassoon's grim new poems. Murry

thought, moreover, that Sassoon had become too greatly dependent upon a single mode of expression in these poems, "the irony epigram."

Virginia Woolf's views on *Counter-Attack* are similar to Murry's. She suggested in the *Times Literary Supplement* that Sassoon had deserted art in his compulsion to express the intolerable. "Beauty and art have something too universal about them to meet our particular case," she commented as she criticized the narrow range of the individual poems. Like Murry, Woolf felt that rage by itself could never lead to the aesthetic effect that requires its presentation against a background of harmony—or some hope, however dim, of an orderly universe with which the horrible moment contrasts. Some sense of harmonious resolution must be present for a genuine artistic expression of emotional experience. Yet, in spite of Sassoon's inability to reach a largeness of vision in his war poetry, Woolf sees in his "contempt for palliative or subterfuge ... the raw stuff of poetry." She says, in effect, that without his unusual and violent experience Sassoon would not have written at all.

Actually, at times in his war poems Sassoon shows the range of imaginative power that Murry and Woolf deny him. In these instances he can relate the violence about which he writes to a larger humanistic context, and his irony depends upon his suggestion that what would be the normally expected in peacetime cannot be relied upon to happen in wartime when human values must at times yield to struggle for survival. In two poems, "The Rear-Guard, Hindenburg Line, April, 1917" (sometimes published under the title "The Deceiver") and "The Dug-Out, St. Venant, July, 1918," Sassoon relates incidents in which a soldier mistakes a comrade's death for sleep in one case and mistakes a comrade's sleep for death in the other. The protagonist's terror in "The Rear-Guard" when he discovers the man is dead strikes suddenly. In "The Dug-Out," the narrator's recognition that the boy is only asleep calms his fears—but only for the moment. Any sleeping man can remind him of the many dead men he has seen. The incident punctuates his chronic fear, a fear which is appropriate in the trenches and the only possible emotion, perhaps, that can be experienced in the uncertainty of existence there. (Sassoon also describes this incident in *Sherston's Progress.*) In "The Rear-Guard" the soldier's actions and speech are presented by a detached narrator. In "The Dug-Out" the point of view is first person as the protagonist muses but never speaks aloud to the sleeping boy. In "The Rear-Guard" the poet implies that sleep constitutes the normal state and death is a shocking aberration. Conversely, in "The Dug-Out" the poet's awareness that death is the norm in the trenches has made sleep an abnormal state. Sassoon masterfully communicates that in wartime the normal expectations of one's previous experience are unlikely to be realized and that the unexpected converse of these expectations becomes the usual pattern for men who live under abnormal and distorted circumstances.

In spite of Murry's implication that a balanced view is unusual for Sassoon, Sassoon frequently uses natural backgrounds of beauty—sky, sunset, or dawn—to intensify his sense of desolation in the trenches. Always he describes the desolation of no-man's-land for what it is. Sassoon's poems avoid the artifice in some sentimental and popular war poems. No nightingale or lark is needed to heighten the effect of Sassoon's battlefields with their blighted trees and twisted wire, as in this description from "Counter-Attack": [....]

The depth and intensity of Sassoon's rendition of experience in itself provide a degree of universality in his poems which his critics often felt was not there.

Though Sassoon's satirical war poems possess strengths that his early critics tended to ignore, these works also reveal some weaknesses. In "Base Details" and "The General" Sassoon satirizes too easily the high-ranking military officers. His complacent generals and his irresponsible majors are so stereotypical that they become scapegoats without much human substance. More effective, but equally biased, are poems which regard women as insensitive civilians. In "The Hero" a soldier visits his comrade's mother and tries to keep secret his knowledge that her son was not courageous under fire. She continues to idealize the boy and refuses to recognize that he might have been a fearful and suffering individual before he died. In "Their Frailty" Sassoon presents women as complacent about the deaths of thousands of men mowed down by German machine guns, as long as the men in their own families are safe. In "Glory of Women" Sassoon inveighs against women who demand that soldiers be heroes and who do not

realize that even British soldiers may flee from combat when fear grips them: [...]. In the last three lines of the poem Sassoon shifts abruptly to German grandmothers who knit socks for their men—men whose faces have already been ground into the mud by the retreating British. These complacent women, like the British women, cannot view their soldiers as suffering human beings. Sassoon's characteristic distrust of women, revealed in all his verse, finds its strongest expression in these poems.

In Sassoon's best war poems he achieved new dimensions in literary art through his use of techniques already established in fiction but not common in poetry—short, trenchant statements; colloquial language punctuated with oaths; the accumulation of graphic detail; the use of cryptic language; and the presentation of shocking incidents accompanied by little authorial comment. If his prewar poems had been overly conventional and dulled by artifice, his war poems either succeeded or failed because of their unconventionality and unpredictability. In his poems written after the war he seldom sought to shock, he used satire far less frequently, and he seldom employed the colloquial and epigrammatic technique that had marked his wartime verse. He did not lapse into the conventionality of his prewar romantic poems, but his work was more traditional and the emotional appeal was muted. His diction, though consistently simple, was not colloquial. His maturity as poet appeared in the order and grace of the verse rather than in its originality of thought or image. He aptly described his own style in the decades after the war as his "cello voice."

In July 1918 Sassoon was accidentally shot in the head by a member of his own company, and he was discharged prior to the Armistice. He seems to have lost his subject for a time. He briefly but vigorously supported the campaign of Philip Snowden in the general election following Armistice because Snowden had attempted to shorten the war and had supported postwar assistance for widows and for unemployed former soldiers. Since Snowden was involved in the Labour movement, Sassoon's "Tory-minded," fox-hunting companions taunted him for becoming a "budding Bolshevik."

If his occasional poems, often requested in the 1920s and 1930s, addressed social problems, the prophetic fervor and the intensity that had characterized the poems from 1915 to 1919 had largely vanished. In his war poems he had attained considerable universality, attacking war itself rather than the German forces or even World War I itself. Nevertheless, after the Armistice was signed, his rage against war and its madness, which had given the war poems their intensity, was inadequate to the resolution of the complex social and political problems emanating from the war and to the treatment of contemporary issues generally.

Sassoon spent nearly all of 1920 in the United States, speaking and reading his poetry to large audiences. In collecting new war poems in *Picture Show* (1919) and collecting previously published war poems for republication in *The War Poems of Siegfried Sassoon* (1919), he saw the need to exhort readers not to forget the horror of one war, lest another war might someday occur. Such purpose also prompted his writing of the poems in *The Road to Ruin* (1933). In the satiric "An Unveiling" he has an orator call for the building of a "bomb-proof roofed Metropolis" in London, dedicated to "for What-they-died-for's sake," and the orator praises the courage of victims of poison gas. Sassoon did not protest England's entry into World War II and regarded that war as necessary to exorcize the evil of Hitler's regime. In his old age, he still regarded his protest declaration and his poems of World War I as a significant dramatization of the horror of war, although he had begun to doubt their permanent impact.

Sassoon returned to his practice of having single poems or small pamphlet editions of a few poems privately printed, particularly in the 1920s and again following World War II. The poems in these small publications were periodically collected in larger, commercially published volumes. In his old age, he said that *The Heart's Journey* (1927) was the last of his books of poetry to receive any favorable or full acknowledgment. Actually, in the twenty-five years following World War I, Sassoon wrote relatively little poetry and concentrated upon his seven major prose works: *Meredith* (1948) and the two autobiographical trilogies. Perhaps the best of his war poems is a lyric which heralds the Armistice, "Everyone Sang" (*Picture Show*, 1919). [...] In 1965, two years before his death, Sassoon was startled to see this poem printed on the back page of the *Times* as a memorial to Winston Churchill, who as a member of Parliament had fifty years before heard his protest against war.

The lyric, with its childlike simplicity and joyous spirit, typifies much in Sassoon's maturity and old age.

In each decade Sassoon produced a few fine poems, which are not widely known. In "Alone" (1924) he shows his ability to enliven an abstract lament with the sharp specificity of the ordinary. As he speaks of the strange person that one becomes when alone, he contrasts that desolate state with the everyday, ritualistic, common acts of community. In "Revisitation" (*Vigils*, 1934) he speaks to his psychiatrist, Dr. W. H. R. Rivers, who returns as a ghost to his "heart room"; they continue to talk as they had done in summer 1917 at Craiglockhart. Sassoon portrays Rivers as a man who is both a good scientist and a "fathering friend." In him Sassoon sees "human sainthood," and he recognizes that the spiritual healing which Rivers had begun in him has been truly augmented by memory in the passing years. The poem's dignity precludes sentimentality.

During the late 1930s Sassoon wrote several brief poems on his son's birth and early years. In the best of these, "Meeting and Parting," Sassoon looks with love at his newborn son and then thinks of the grown-up man looking down at him at the time of his death. (Sassoon in his last years commented on the pleasure he had in talking with his son, who had recognized in his father his "second self." George Sassoon was present at his father's death.)

In the 1950s and 1960s Sassoon wrote meditative and philosophical poetry, focusing often on religious issues. He was preoccupied with such issues as the essential mystery of God as other and God as immanent in the spirit of the individual. The poems lack concentration and intensity and seldom achieve profundity. Very short—often only four lines long—they articulate momentary insights into what constitutes for Sassoon an ultimate reality, or they represent momentary affirmations of belief, or they are prayerlike and spontaneous celebrations of a unity recognized between God and himself. Often the poems of this period focus on a single image, like the opening of one flower. Biblical juxtapositions recur with the oxymoronic overtones that sometimes occur in the scriptures: losing oneself in order to find the self, becoming blind in order to see, dying in order to live. Familiar truths and paradoxes are presented with a sense of rediscovery or surprise.

In 1953 Sassoon remarked that he had remained under the spell of Swinburne, not only in his prewar poems but in all of his poetry after the war—that he had the rhythms of Swinburne in his mind and that their effect continued to hypnotize him. He related Swinburne's overpowering "auditory" influence to his own "cello voice" in a poetry characterized by the use of melancholy, nostalgic, and somewhat monotonous rhythms. Actually, in his best poems Sassoon may still have found Thomas Hardy to be a more dominant influence than Swinburne. During the war Sassoon had dedicated his first commercially produced collection, *The Old Huntsman and Other Poems*, to Hardy, and he had referred to his having read Hardy's novels in a dugout and not wanting to be killed before finishing the Hardy novel that he was then reading. In one of the later poems that reflects Hardy's ability to create graceful, if rugged, poems and to limn a sharp portrait, Sassoon created a memorable picture of the aged Hardy. The sonnet "At Max Gate" (1950) recalls a visit to Hardy in 1924. Hardy sits beside the fire, petting his dog, and appears as a man of hope and contentment. In the ironic and surprising last line—typical of Hardy but in its subtlety less typical of Sassoon's final lines—the poet expresses his recognition in 1950 that someone else "had taken Mr. Hardy's place."

In 1953 Sassoon sought to describe in his diary his various types of poetry: (1) his declamatory poems with their "loud-speaker" style; (2) his "strongly-drawn cartoons," which had given him wartime success as a satirist but had not satisfied him; (3) his poems characterized by an "indirect" style, which he felt that he had not yet perfected but which he longed to perfect; and (4) his "soliloquies," which dominate his late work. He observed that his poems were not visually evocative, and that he had much difficulty in trying to make them so, although while writing them he had always thought in terms of visual images. He also expressed distaste for the "loud ones" with their closing "fortissimo line," which had brought him fame thirty-five years earlier. He now saw himself as a poet whose work could not be appropriately evaluated aesthetically because of stereotypical opinions about it. He had been typed as a war poet who had written dramatic and strident poems. Sassoon felt that the poet should communicate directly with the common reader, and he believed that his audience had diminished as critics turned readers

toward the predominant mode of the period, an intense, concentrated, elliptical, and intellectualized kind of poetry. To Sassoon, T. S. Eliot seemed "too professorial," and he commented that he could make neither head nor tail of *The Waste Land.* But he amiably conceded a few years before his death that Eliot had become an important touchstone by which his contemporaries were to be measured: [...]. Sassoon thought that even his friend Dame Edith Sitwell had been encouraged to turn away from his work as "old-fashioned," and he also felt that it was difficult for devotional religious poetry to be evaluated on its aesthetic merits.

Sassoon chose to live a relatively solitary existence in the last two decades of his life, but he was never a recluse. In 1933, at the age of forty-seven, he had married Hester Gatty and became a father three years later. The couple apparently lived together about ten years and then separated, but they remained good friends. During the years of World War II, Heytesbury House was largely taken over for refugees—some of whom Sassoon complained were unclean and ill-behaved. He complained also of the cold in the large house during those years, but the years of his son's childhood were happy ones for him. In the 1950s and 1960s his letters and diary entries comment on the extended visits of his son and his wife. Though he was practicing a disciplined preparation for death and eternity through meditation and prayer and writing, he had considerable contact with neighbors, particularly the nuns from Stanbrook Abbey. He greatly missed old friends such as Thomas Hardy, Max Beerbohm, Robert Ross, T. E. Lawrence, Edith Sitwell, E. M. Forster, and Walter de la Mare. (One of his last public speeches was the dedication of the memorial for de la Mare at St. Paul's Cathedral in December 1961.) But some old friends remained. He wrote that the high point of his eightieth birthday, 8 September 1966, was his having received a letter from John Masefield, the poet he had parodied in *The Daffodil Murderer* (1913), and he also rejoiced that year that his old friend of fifty years, Edmund Blunden, had received double the votes "of his American adversary, Robert Lowell" for the Oxford Professorship of Poetry: [...].

For his eightieth birthday, the Arts Council of Britain honored him with the publication of eight short poems, *An Octave.* In honor of this birthday the Stanbrook Abbey Press presented him with a calligraphic edition of *Something*

About Myself a story about cats that Sassoon had written at age eleven and illustrated for his mother. The dedication described Sassoon as "poet, warrior, and fox-hunting man, who even to serene old age has kept the heart of a child." As the dedication indicates, Sassoon had lived the active life of one concerned about and enjoying society, and he had lived the passive, contemplative life. The paradox is that as a poet he had actualized his career as a soldier so much more memorably than his life as a religious seeker. On 3 September 1967, he died in the company of his son quietly at home, an occasion toward which he had looked with joyful anticipation.

Source: Margaret B. McDowell, "Siegfried Sassoon," in *Dictionary of Literary Biography*, Vol. 20, *British Poets, 1914–1945*, edited by Donald E. Stanford, Gale Research, 1983, pp. 321–35.

SOURCES

Allen, Brooke, "Rediscovering Sassoon," in the *New Criterion*, Vol. 24, No. 3, November 2005, pp. 15–20.

Brooks, Cleanth, "Irony as a Principle of Structure," reprinted in *Contexts for Criticism*, 2nd edition, edited by Donald Keesey, Mayfield Publishing, 1994, pp. 74–81.

Campbell, Patrick, *Siegfried Sassoon: A Study of the War Poetry*, McFarland, 1999, pp. 15, 42, 58, 134–35.

Crawford, Fred D., *British Poets of the Great War*, Susquehanna University Press, 1988, pp. 119–38.

Fussell, Paul, *The Great War and Modern Memory*, Oxford University Press, 2000, pp. 7–8, 75–105.

Gosse, Edmund, "Some Soldier Poets," in the *Edinburgh Review*, Vol. 226, No. 4, October 1917, pp. 296–316.

Hipp, Daniel, *The Poetry of Shell Shock: Wartime Trauma and Healing in Wilfred Owen, Ivor Gurney and Siegfried Sassoon*, McFarland, 2005, pp. 152–53.

Johnston, John H., *English Poetry of the First World War: A Study in the Evolution of Lyric and Narrative Form*, Princeton University Press, 1964, pp. 71–112.

Moeyes, Paul, *Siegfriend Sassoon: Scorched Glory*, St. Martin's Press, 1997, pp. 16–18, 58–59.

Roberts, John Stuart, *Siegfried Sassoon*, Metro, 2005, pp. 88–89.

Sassoon, Siegfried, "'Blighters,'" in *The War Poems of Siegfried Sassoon*, Echo Library, reprinted edition, 2006, p. 30, originally published 1919.

Thorpe, Michael, *Siegfried Sassoon: A Critical Study*, Oxford University Press, 1966, pp. 15–38.

FURTHER READING

Featherstone, Simon, *War Poetry: An Introductory Reader*, Routledge, 1995.

This book contains both an anthology of poetry and prose commentary from World War I and World War II, as well as a comprehensive discussion of critical and cultural concerns related to the poems.

Giddings, Robert, ed., *The War Poets*, Bloomsbury, 1988.

This book includes biographies, paintings, illustrations, and commentary on World War I poets.

Howard, Michael, *The First World War: A Very Short Introduction*, Oxford University Press, 2002.

This volume offers a short, readable history of World War I by a noted historian.

Hynes, Samuel, *A War Imagined: The First World War and English Culture*, Pimlico, 1998.

This study, along with Paul Fussell's *The Great War and Modern Memory*, is one of the most important cultural studies of World War I.

The Bronze Horseman

ALEXANDER PUSHKIN

1841

"The Bronze Horseman" is a narrative poem by the Russian poet Alexander Pushkin. Originally written in 1833 and titled "Mednyi Vsadnik," it was not published until 1841, after Pushkin's death, and it was printed as a stand-alone piece. The delay was due to the disapproval of Tsar Nicholas I, who objected to its themes and portrayal of his royal ancestor, Tsar Peter I. One frequently used English translation (which is also used throughout this entry), is by the British novelist and poet D. M. Thomas (Alexander Pushkin, *The Bronze Horseman and Other Poems*, 1982), which, as of 2007, is out of print, but second-hand copies are available. The poem is also available in an English translation by Robert Powell-Jones (Alexander Pushkin, *Bronze Horseman*, Stone Trough Books, 1999).

The poem's background theme is the building of the Russian city of St. Petersburg on the orders of Tsar Peter I (Peter the Great, 1672–1725) on marshland on the banks of the river Neva. The city was built by forced labor, and thousands of peasant builders are said to have died in the harsh conditions. This bloody history of the city informs the themes of the poem, which include the conflict between the interests of the state or historical destiny and those of the common man, a conflict that prefigures the struggle that was to rage in Russia for the next century. The main event of the poem is the flood that occurred in St. Petersburg in November of 1824.

The poem has three main characters: Tsar Peter I, who appears first as a historical person and then as the bronze equestrian statue of Tsar Peter I, that stands in the city (which has been known since the poem became popular as the Bronze Horseman), and the humble clerk Yevgeni. It is widely considered a masterpiece, and has helped to cement Pushkin's reputation as Russia's greatest and most influential writer of the early nineteenth century.

AUTHOR BIOGRAPHY

The Russian poet, dramatist, novelist, and short story writer Alexander Pushkin was born on June 6, 1799 in Moscow, Russia, the son of Sergei Lvovich, an army officer, and Nadezhda Osipovna Pushkin. (Some sources predate the dates given here by several days, giving Pushkin's birth date, for instance, as May 26. This is because until 1918, Russia followed the Julian calendar, which was several days behind the Gregorian calendar used in Europe. The Julian calendar dates are often referred to as Old Style and the Gregorian calendar dates as New Style. Dates given here are New Style.)

Pushkin's family was descended from aristocracy, though it no longer held the prestige it once enjoyed. Pushkin was proud of his maternal great-grandfather, Abram Petrovich Hannibal (sometimes spelled Gannibal), a black Abyssinian prince who became a favorite of Tsar Peter I and a renowned general and engineer.

From 1811 to 1817, Pushkin attended the Lyceum school at Tsarskoe Selo near St. Petersburg. After graduating, he was given a sinecure as a civil servant in the Ministry of Foreign Affairs in St. Petersburg.

Pushkin finished his first major poem, "Ruslan and Lyudmila," in 1820. He was remarkable for writing in Russian at a time when most Russian literary figures wrote in French and English. In Tsarist Russia, royalty and aristocracy (including Pushkin himself) usually spoke French, and Russian was considered the language of the peasants. Thus, Pushkin has acquired the status of a founder of Russian literature. He was also instrumental in moving Russian literature away from the sentimentality of eighteenth-century works and towards a realistic and psychological approach that would be taken

Alexander Pushkin (The Library of Congress)

up by later writers such as Leo Tolstoy and Fyodor Dostoevsky.

In 1820, Pushkin's liberal political views and his biting satires about Tsar Alexander I and his officials led to his being interrogated and exiled to South Russia. He also traveled to the Caucasus and Crimea. This proved a productive time for Pushkin. During three years in Kishinev (in contemporary Moldova), he wrote verse narratives in the style of the English poet George Gordon, Lord Byron. These included "The Prisoner of the Caucasus" (1822). He also started his verse novel *Eugene Onegin*, which was written in the period 1823–1831, published serially beginning in 1825, and published in full in 1833.

In 1824, officials intercepted a letter in which Pushkin supported atheism. He was sent into deeper exile, to his mother's estate of Mikhaylovskoe in north Russia, where he spent two years under surveillance. In this period he wrote a narrative poem, "The Gypsies" (1827) and the drama *Boris Godunov* (completed in 1825, though censors prevented it from being published until 1831).

In 1826, Pushkin petitioned Tsar Nicholas to release him from exile. The Tsar agreed, and told Pushkin that he personally would be the censor of his works. Pushkin at first believed that he would be free to publish and to travel freely. However, he soon found that without advance permission he could do neither, and he was repeatedly questioned by the police about his poems.

In 1830, Pushkin was betrothed to Natalia Goncharova, a society beauty. He traveled to his father's estate at Boldino to make arrangements for his father's wedding gift to him of half the estate, and found himself trapped there for three months in quarantine due to a cholera epidemic. During this period, Pushkin wrote dramas, including *Mozart and Salieri* (first produced in 1832) and *The Stone Guest* (first produced in 1847). He completed "The Bronze Horseman" in the fall of 1833 during another stay at Boldino. The poem was first published individually in 1841 as *Mednyi Vsadnik*.

Pushkin married Natalia in Moscow in 1831. The couple briefly settled in Tsarskoe Selo and then in St. Petersburg, where they lived until Pushkin's death. Pushkin intended to live simply, but the proximity of the royal family and Natalia's expensive tastes meant that he became dependent on favors from Tsar Nicholas. The marriage, while it produced four children, was unhappy. Natalia's interests lay in leading an active social life in court circles, and her flirtations provoked frustration in Pushkin. In 1834, Natalia miscarried after dancing at a ball. An indignant letter from Pushkin to his wife, who was convalescing in the country, was intercepted by the Tsar's police. A furious Pushkin handed in his resignation from the civil service, though he soon retracted it due to fear of the Tsar's displeasure.

Pushkin was burdened by managing his father's estate, which he took over in 1834, and by the debts of his brother, which he had undertaken to settle. He asked the Tsar either to let him retire to the country or to grant him a large loan; the first request was refused, but the second granted. In 1836, the Tsar agreed to let Pushkin publish a journal, *The Contemporary*, which involved Pushkin in more debt and trouble with the censors.

In 1834, Natalia met Baron Georges d'Anthès-Heeckeren, a French émigré who worked in the Russian service. Rumors of an affair circulated. In the fall of 1836, Pushkin received an anonymous letter accusing him of being a cuckold. He challenged d'Anthès-Heeckeren to a duel, which took place on February 8, 1837. Pushkin died of his bullet wounds two days later at his home in St. Petersburg. D'Anthès-Heeckeren was slightly wounded, and court society sympathized with him, though ordinary people felt differently. They flocked by the thousands to the dying Pushkin's bedside. The authorities, fearing a public revolt, shifted his funeral from St. Isaac's Cathedral to a small and secluded church, and secretly sent his body for burial at night. He was buried near his mother at Svyatye Gory Monastery near Mikhaylovskoe.

POEM TEXT

A Tale of St Petersburg
Introduction

On a shore washed by desolate waves, *he* stood,
Full of high thoughts, and gazed into the
  distance.
The broad river rushed before him; a wretched
  skiff
Sped on it in solitude. Here and there,
Like black specks on the mossy, marshy banks,   5
Were huts, the shelter of the hapless Finn;
And forest, never visited by rays
Of the mist-shrouded sun, rustled all round.

And he thought: From here we will outface the
  Swede;
To spite our haughty neighbour I shall found   10
A city here. By nature we are fated
To cut a window through to Europe,
To stand with a firm foothold on the sea.
Ships of every flag, on waves unknown
To them, will come to visit us, and we   15
Shall revel in the open sea.

A hundred years have passed, and the young city,
The grace and wonder of the northern lands,
Out of the gloom of forests and the mud
Of marshes splendidly has risen; where once   20
The Finnish fisherman, the sad stepson
Of nature, standing alone on the low banks,
Cast into unknown waters his worn net,
Now huge harmonious palaces and towers
Crowd on the bustling banks; ships in their
  throngs   25
Speed from all ends of the earth to the rich
  quays;
The Neva is clad in granite; bridges hang
Poised over her waters; her islands are covered
With dark-green gardens, and before the
  younger
Capital, ancient Moscow has grown pale,   30
Like a widow in purple before a new empress.

I love you, Peter's creation, I love your stern

Harmonious look, the Neva's majestic flow,
Her granite banks, the iron tracery
Of your railings, the transparent twilight and   35
The moonless glitter of your pensive nights,
When in my room I write or read without
A lamp, and slumbering masses of deserted
Streets shine clearly, and the Admiralty spire
Is luminous, and, without letting in   40
The dark of night to golden skies, one dawn
Hastens to relieve another, granting
A mere half-hour to night. I love
The motionless air and frost of your harsh
     winter,
The sledges coursing along the solid Neva,   45
Girls' faces brighter than roses, and the sparkle
And noise and sound of voices at the balls,
And, at the hour of the bachelor's feast, the hiss
Of foaming goblets and the pale-blue flame
Of punch. I love the warlike energy   50
Of Mars' Field, the uniform beauty of the
     troops
Of infantry and of the horses, tattered
Remnants of those victorious banners in array
Harmoniously swaying, the gleam of those
Bronze helmets, shot through in battle. O
     martial   55
Capital, I love the smoke and thunder
Of your fortress, when the empress of the north
Presents a son to the royal house, or when
Russia celebrates another victory
Over the foe, or when the Neva, breaking   60
Her blue ice, bears it to the seas, exulting,
Scenting spring days.

          Flaunt your beauty, Peter's
City, and stand unshakeable like Russia,
So that even the conquered elements may make   65
Their peace with you; let the Finnish waves
Forget their enmity and ancient bondage,
And let them not disturb with empty spite
Peter's eternal sleep!

There was a dreadful time—the memory of it   70
Is still fresh ... I will begin my narrative
Of it for you, my friends. My tale will be sad.

1

November over darkened Petrograd.
With a roar of waves splashing against the
     edges
Of her shapely bounds, the Neva tossed   75
Like a sick man in his restless bed.
It was already late and dark; against
The window angrily the rain was beating,
And the wind blew, howling sadly. At that time
Came young Yevgeni home, from friends ...
     We'll call   80
Our hero by this name. It's pleasant, and
Has long been congenial to my pen.
We do not need his surname, though perhaps
In times gone by it shone, under the pen
Of Karamzin, rang forth in our native legends;   85
But now it is forgotten by the world

And fame. Our hero lives in Kolomna, works
Somewhere, avoids the paths of the famous,
     mourns
Neither dead relatives nor the forgotten past.

And so, having come home, Yevgeni tossed   90
His cloak aside, undressed, lay down. But for
A long time could not fall asleep, disturbed
By divers thoughts. What did he think about?
About the fact that he was poor, by toil
Would have to earn honour and independence;   95
That God might have granted him more brains
     and money;
That there are lazy devils, after all,
For whom life is so easy! That he had been
A clerk for two years; he also thought the
     weather
Was not becoming any calmer; that   100
The river was still rising; as like as not,
The bridges on the Neva had been raised,
And for two or three days he would be cut off
From Parasha. At that point Yevgeni sighed
From his heart, and fell to dreaming like a poet.   105

'Get married? Me? Why not! It would be hard,
Of course; but then, I'm young and healthy,
     ready
To toil day and night; somehow or other
I'll fix myself a humble, simple shelter
Where Parasha and I can live in quiet.   110
After a year or two I'll get a job,
And Parasha will bring up our children ...
     Then
We shall begin to live, and thus we'll go
Hand in hand to the grave, and our
     grandchildren
Will bury us ...'   115

Thus he dreamed. And he felt sad that night,
And wished the wind would not howl gloomily,
The rain not beat so angrily at the window ...

At last he closed his sleepy eyes. And now
The foul night thins, and the pale day draws on
     ...   120
The dreadful day!

          All night the Neva rushed
Towards the sea against the storm, unable
To overcome the madness of the winds ...
She could no longer carry on the struggle ...   125
By morning, throngs of people on her banks
Admired the spray, the mountains and the
     foam
Of maddened waters. But harried by the gale
Out of the gulf, the Neva turned back, angry,
Turbulent, and swamped the islands. The
     weather   130
Raged more fiercely, Neva swelled up and
     roared,
Bubbling like a cauldron; suddenly
Hurled herself on the city like a beast.
Everything ran before her, everything
Suddenly became deserted—suddenly   135

The waters flowed into the cellars underground,
The canals surged up to the railings,
And Petropolis floated up, like Triton,
Plunged to the waist in water.

   Siege! Assault! The sly waves climb like thieves 140
Through the windows. Scudding boats smash
   the panes
With their sterns. Hawkers' trays, fragments of
   huts,
Beams, roofs, the wares of thrifty trading,
The chattels of pale poverty, bridges swept
Away by the storm, coffins from the buried 145
Cemetery—all float along the streets!

   The people gaze upon the wrath of God
And await their doom. Alas! All's swept away:
Shelter and food—where shall they find them?

   In that dread year the late Tsar in his glory 150
Still ruled Russia. He came out on to the
   balcony,
Sad, troubled, and said: 'Tsars cannot master
The divine elements.' He sat down and with
   thoughtful
Sorrowful eyes gazed on the dire disaster:
The squares like lakes; broad rivers of streets 155
Pouring into them. The palace a sad island.
The Tsar spoke—from end to end of the city,
Along streets near and far, a dangerous journey
Through the storm waters, generals set off
To save the people, drowning in their homes. 160

   There, in Peter's square, where in the corner
A new house towers, where over the lofty porch
Two guardian lions stand like living creatures
With upraised paw—there sat, astride the marble
Beast, hatless, his arms crossed tightly, 165
Motionless and fearfully pale, Yevgeni.
He was afraid, poor fellow, not for himself.
He did not hear the greedy billow rise,
Lapping his soles; he did not feel the rain
Lashing his face, nor the wind, wildly howling, 170
Tear his hat from his head. His desperate gaze
Was fixed on one distant point. Like
   mountains,
There the waves rose up from the seething
   depths,
And raged, there the storm howled, there
   wreckage
Rushed to and fro ... God, God! There— 175
Alas!—so close to the waves, almost by the gulf
Itself, is an unpainted fence and a willow
And a small ramshackle house: there they live,
A widow and her daughter, Parasha, his dream
   ...
Or is all this a dream? Is all our life 180
Nothing but an empty dream, heaven's jest?

   And he, as though bewitched, as if riveted
To the marble, cannot get down! Around him
Is water and nothing else! And, his back turned
To him, in unshakeable eminence, over 185
The angry river, the turbulent Neva, stands

The Image, with outstretched arm, on his
   bronze horse.

2

   But now, satiated with destruction, wearied
By her insolent violence, the Neva drew back,
Revelling in the chaos she had caused, 190
And carelessly abandoning her booty.
Thus a marauder, bursting into a village with
His savage band, smashes, slashes, shatters,
And robs; shrieks, gnashing of teeth, violence,
Oaths, panic, howls! And weighed down by
   their plunder, 195
Fearing pursuit, exhausted, the robbers
   leave
For home, dropping their plunder on the way.

   The water fell, the roadway was visible,
And my Yevgeni, in hope and fear and grief,
Hastened with sinking heart to the scarcely
   abated 200
River. But full of their victory the waves
Still seethed angrily, as though beneath them
Fires were smouldering; foam still covered
   them,
And heavily the Neva breathed, like a horse
Galloping home from battle. Yevgeni looks; 205
He sees a boat; he runs towards his find;
Shouts to the ferryman—and for ten kopecks
The carefree ferryman rows him across the
   billows.

   And long the experienced oarsman struggled with
The stormy waves, and all the time the skiff 210
Was on the point of plunging with its rash crew
To the depths, between the ranges of the waves
—And at last he reached the bank.

         The wretched man
Runs down a familiar street to familiar places. 215
He gazes, and can recognize nothing.
A dreadful vision! All is piled up before him:
This has been hurled down, that has been torn
   away;
The little houses have become twisted, others
Have completely collapsed, others have been
   shifted 220
By the waves; all around, as on a battlefield,
Corpses are strewn. Yevgeni rushes headlong,
Remembering nothing, exhausted by torments,
To the place where fate awaits him with
   unknown tidings,
As with a sealed letter. And now he is 225
Already rushing through the suburb, and here
Is the bay, and close by is the house ...
What is this? ...

         He stopped. Went back and turned.
Looked ... walked forward ... looked again. 230
Here is the place where their house stood;
Here is the willow. There were gates here—
   swept
Away, evidently. But where is the house?
And, full of gloomy anxiety, he walks, he walks

Around, talks loudly to himself—and then,   235
Striking his forehead with his hand, he
    laughed.

Darkness fell upon the city, shaking
With terror; long its people did not sleep,
But talked among themselves of the past day.

Dawn's light shone over the pale capital   240
And found no trace of the disaster; loss
Was covered by a purple cloak. And life
Resumed its customary order. People
Walked coldly, impassively, along cleared
    streets.
Government officials, leaving their night's
    shelter,   245
Went to their jobs. The indomitable tradesman
Opened his cellar looted by the Neva,
Hoping to make good his loss at his neigh-
    bour's expense.
Boats were being hauled away from
    courtyards.

Already Count Khvostov, beloved of heaven,   250
Was singing the disaster of Neva's banks
In his immortal verses.

But my poor, poor
Yevgeni! ... Alas! his confused mind could not
    endure
The shocks he had suffered. His ears still heard   255
The boom of Neva and the winds. Silently
He wandered round, filled with dreadful
    thoughts.
Some sort of dream tormented him. A week,
A month, went by—still he did not go home.
When the time ran out, his landlord leased   260
His abandoned nook to a poor poet. Yevgeni
Did not come to collect his belongings. He grew
A stranger to the world. All day he wandered
On foot, and slept at night on the embankment;
He fed on scraps handed to him through
    windows.   265
Tattered and mouldy grew his shabby clothes.
Children threw stones at him. Often the whips
Of coachmen lashed him, for he could not find
    his way;
It seemed he noticed nothing, deafened by
An inner turmoil. And so he dragged out his
    life,   270
Neither beast nor man, neither this nor that,
Not of the living world nor of the dead ...

Once he was sleeping on the Neva banks.
The days of summer were declining towards
    autumn.
A sickly wind was breathing. The sullen wave   275
Splashed against the embankment,
    reproachfully
Grumbling and beating against the smooth
    steps,
Like a petitioner at the door of judges
Who keep turning him away. The poor wretch
    woke.

It was dark: rain dripped, the wind howled
    gloomily;   280
A distant watchman traded cries with it.
Yevgeni started up; recalled his nightmare;
Hastily he set off wandering, until
He suddenly stopped—and slowly began to cast
His eyes around, with wild fear on his face.   285
He found himself at the foot of the pillars of
The great house. Over the porch the lions stood
On guard, like living creatures, with their paws
Upraised; and eminently dark and high
Above the railed-in rock, with arm
    outstretched,   290
The Image, mounted on his horse of bronze.

Yevgeni shuddered. Terribly his thoughts
Grew clear in him. He recognized the place
Where the flood played, where greedy waves
    had pressed,
Rioting round him angrily, and the lions,   295
And the square, and him who motionlessly
Held aloft his bronze head in the darkness,
Him by whose fateful will the city had
Been founded on the sea ... How terrible
He was in the surrounding murk! What
    thought   300
Was on his brow, what strength was hidden in
    him!
And in that steed what fire! Where do you
    gallop,
Proud steed, and where will you plant your
    hoofs?
O mighty master of fate! was it not thus,
Towering on the precipice's brink,   305
You reared up Russia with your iron curb?

The poor madman walked around the pedestal
Of the Image, and brought wild looks to bear
On the countenance of the lord of half the
    world.
His breast contracted, his brow was pressed
    against   310
The cold railings, his eyes were sealed by mist,
Flames ran through his heart, his blood
    boiled.
Sombrely he stood before the statue;
His teeth clenched, his hands tightened,
    trembling
With wrath, possessed by a dark power, he
    whispered: 315
'All right then, wonder-worker, just you wait!'
And suddenly set off running at breakneck
    speed.
It seemed to him that the face of the dead Tsar,
Momentarily flaring up with rage,
Was slowly turning ... Across the empty
    square   320
He runs, and hears behind him—like the
    rumble
Of thunder—the clash and clangor of hoofs
Heavily galloping over the shaking square.
And lit by the pale moonlight, stretching out
His hand aloft, the Bronze Horseman rushes   325

After him on his ponderously galloping mount;
And all night long, wherever the madman ran,
The Bronze Horseman followed with a ringing
  clatter.

  And from that time, whenever his wanderings took
    him
Into that square, confusion appeared on his
    face.   330
Hastily he would press his hand to his heart,
As though to ease its torment, he would doff
His tattered cap, he would not raise his
    troubled
Eyes, and would go on by some roundabout
    way.

  A small island can be seen off-shore. Sometimes 335
A fisherman out late will moor there with
His net and cook his meagre supper. Or
Some civil servant, boating on a Sunday,
Will pay a visit to the barren island.
No grass grows, not a blade. The flood, in
    sport,   340
Had driven a ramshackle little house there.
Above the water it had taken root
Like a black bush. Last spring a wooden barge
Carried away the wreckage. By the threshold
They found my madman, and on that very spot   345
For the love of God they buried his cold corpse.

POEM SUMMARY

Introduction

This lengthy narrative poem is divided into three sections, the Introduction and parts 1 and 2. The opening stanza of the Introduction to "The Bronze Horseman" (lines 1–8) portrays an unnamed man (the historical Tsar Peter I) standing on the banks of the river Neva. He is gazing into the distance and is "Full of high thoughts." As becomes clear in the second stanza, he is planning to build a great city on this site. That city is St. Petersburg, which Tsar Peter I founded in 1703, so the Introduction is set at an unspecified date before this. For now, the place consists of dark forest and inhospitable marshland dotted with small huts inhabited by Finnish people (St. Petersburg is located on the eastern shore of the Gulf of Finland, with Finland's coastline on the northern shore).

The second stanza (lines 9–16) describes the man's vision. He aims to found a city that will thwart Swedish expansionist aims in the Baltic Sea (the Gulf of Finland connects the Baltic Sea with St. Petersburg). The city will be Tsar Peter's "window through to Europe" and will attract

ships from every country. The vision concludes with Tsar Peter's vision of joyful Russian seafarers celebrating the success of the scheme at some point in the future when the city is built.

In the third stanza (lines 17–31), the poem jumps forward in time one hundred years. The man's vision has been fulfilled: the city of St. Petersburg has been built. Where once Finnish fishermen plied their trade, now huge palaces and towers have sprung up. Ships from all over the world come to the harbors, and the banks of the river Neva are encased in granite. The poet likens the city to "a new empress" who makes the previous capital, Moscow, seem like a pale old widow in comparison. The widow wears purple because this was the royal color of the Byzantine Empire. The poet is connecting Russia with Constantinople, the centre of the Byzantine Empire, which shared its Orthodox Christian faith. The city is likened to a widow bowing before a new empress because Tsar Peter I has abandoned her: Tsar Peter I made St. Petersburg the capital of Russia in 1712, taking that title from Moscow.

The fourth stanza (lines 32–62) changes to an odic tone (an ode is a lyric poem that expresses exalted or enthusiastic emotion to praise a person, place, quality, or object). The poet addresses St. Petersburg directly as if he were speaking to a beloved woman, and for the first time, the unnamed man is identified as Tsar Peter I: "I love you, Peter's creation." The poet describes aspects of the city's beauty. He notes the phenomenon of the White Nights. St. Petersburg is so far north that in summer, the nights remain light enough that he can read and write without a lamp. He sees the spire of the Admiralty (constructed between 1806 and 1823) shining. He lists other sensory impressions of the city, including the sight of girls in sledges coursing along the frozen river, their faces bright with cold; the hiss of foaming goblets at the balls; and the sight of military drills on the city's parade ground, the Field of Mars. The poet addresses the city as "martial / Capital," referring to the cannons at the Peter and Paul Fortress being fired to mark the birth of a son to the Tsarina, a Russian victory over an enemy, or the melting of the river Neva in spring.

The fifth stanza (lines 62–68) has the flavor of a prayer. The poet invites the city to flaunt its beauty and stand "unshakeable like Russia," so that even the "conquered elements," the sea and river that have been captured within the granite banks of the city, can make peace with it. Here, the poet calls into question the sense of invincibility of Tsar Peter's creation that has been built up in the previous sections.

In the sixth stanza (lines 69–71), the poet announces that he will recount a sad tale of a dreadful time.

Part 1

Part 1 consists of the poet's dramatized account of a historical event on November 19 (New Style), 1824, when a catastrophic flood occurred in St. Petersburg. Here, the city is called by the alternative name, Petrograd, which translates as Peter's town. In the first stanza (lines 1–17), the scene opens on the river Neva, tossing in the darkness "Like a sick man in his restless bed." The focus shifts to inside a house, on the window of which the rain is beating. The house is that of a young man, Yevgeni, who has just returned home after visiting friends. He lives in Kolomna, a working-class area of St. Petersburg, and has an undistinguished job. The poet suggests that Yevgeni's family may have been important in ancient times but has declined in influence: his family name may have featured in traditional legends or in the Russian author Nikolai Karamzin's *History of the Russian State* (1818), which ended its chronicle in 1613.

The second stanza (lines 18–33) recounts how Yevgeni goes to bed, but lies awake worrying about his poverty. He thinks that he will have to earn his independence by hard work, though for some, life is easy. He has been a clerk for two years. He is concerned about the worsening weather. The river is rising, and he fears he will be cut off from Parasha, the woman he loves and hopes to marry.

The third stanza (lines 34–43) focuses on Yevgeni's thoughts as he plans out his future with Parasha. His desires are humble: a simple house in which he and Parasha will enjoy a quiet life. He will have a job, children, and in time, grandchildren. The fourth and fifth stanzas (lines 44–49) describe Yevgeni going to sleep as the wind howls and the rain beats around him.

The sixth stanza (lines 50–67) describe how the wind, coming in from the Gulf of Finland, fights against the river Neva, which is flowing towards the Gulf. By morning, the gale has turned the river back, and it has swamped the islands on which the city stands. The river sweeps along everything in its path, and the city's canals reach the height of the railings. The city is referred to by its Greek name of Petropolis (Peter's city). Because it is half submerged in water, it is likened to Triton, who in Greek mythology is the messenger of the ocean and son of the sea god, Poseidon.

The seventh stanza (lines 68–74) likens the flood to a siege, and the waves to sly thieves that climb into buildings through windows. Street hawkers' equipment, pieces of huts, and even coffins unearthed from the cemetery float along the streets.

In the eighth stanza (lines 75–77), the poet shifts his attention to the people of the city. They gaze at the flood, which is portrayed as God's judgment, and await their end. They have no food or shelter.

In the ninth stanza (lines 78–88), the poet turns his attention to Tsar Alexander I. The Tsar's palace (known as the Hermitage) has been spared flooding, but has become an isolated island. The Tsar reflects sadly that "Tsars cannot master / the divine elements," and then sends his generals on a dangerous mission through the streets to save the people drowning in their homes. It is the generals who are the heroic men of action, while the Tsar passively philosophizes. The fact that the Tsar is shown standing on his balcony, as well as the island status of his palace, denotes his removal from the common people.

The tenth stanza (lines 89–109) tells how Yevgeni escapes the flood. He sits on top of a huge sculpture of a stone lion, one of a pair of guardian lions that flank the staircase of the mansion of the Lobanov-Rostovsky family in Senate Square, where the statue of Peter the Great is located. The poet here calls Senate Square "Peter's square," after its creator and the statue of Tsar Peter I. Senate Square was renamed Decembrist Square in 1925, after the Decembrist Revolt that took place there in December 1825.

Yevgeni is afraid not for himself, but for Parasha. He strains to see the ramshackle house where she lives with her widowed mother, and notes that it is close to the waves. He recalls his "dream" of marrying Parasha, but then asks a bitter question as to whether life itself is "Nothing but an empty dream, heaven's jest?"

The eleventh stanza (lines 110–15) describes Yevgeni's terror at his realization that he cannot get down from the lion, as there is water all around him. Across the flooded river, its back turned to him, is the equestrian statue of Peter the Great, with arm outstretched: the Bronze Horseman.

Part 2

Part 2 marks a transition forward in time to when the flood has retreated and the waters have begun to fall. The first stanza (lines 1–10) likens the river to violent robbers who plunder a village and flee, dropping their plunder as they go.

The second stanza (lines 11–21) describes how, as the waters slowly fall, the road becomes visible. Yevgeni rushes to the river bank and hires a boatman to row him across the river.

The third stanza (lines 22–47) tells how, fighting against the current, the boatman at last delivers Yevgeni to the opposite bank. Yevgeni runs down the street where Parasha lived, but sees only devastation. Houses have collapsed, and corpses are strewn around, as on a battlefield. Reaching the spot where Parasha's house stood, Yevgeni sees that it has been swept away. He walks around, talking to himself, then strikes his forehead with his hand (a gesture that perhaps denotes a bitter realization) and laughs. This is the first sign that Yevgeni may be losing his reason.

The fourth and fifth stanzas (lines 48–60) portray night falling on a terrified people, and the next day dawning on a return to normal life for the survivors. The purple color describes the dawn sky, but also recalls the purple-wearing widow of the Introduction. In both instances, the color purple denotes imperial power: in this instance, the reference denotes a return to imperially imposed order after the devastation wrought by nature. The streets have been cleared of debris. The people are in a state of cold indifference; government officials go to work; and a merchant whose cellar has been robbed of goods by the flood cynically hopes to make good his loss at his neighbor's expense.

The sixth stanza (lines 61–63) notes that Count Khvostov, a poet and contemporary of Pushkin, has already begun composing verses on the disaster. The poet begins the seventh stanza (lines 63–82) with an expression of pity for the traumatized Yevgeni and goes on to describe his state of mind as "tormented" by "Some sort of

dream." In Yevgeni's head, he can still hear the sounds of the wind and the flooding waves from the night of the flood. He wanders the streets as a tramp, living on scraps that people hand to him through windows. The landlord of the house where he lived lets his room to a poor poet. He seems to live a half-life, neither in the world of the living nor of the dead.

The seventh stanza (lines 83–101) jumps forward in time to a year after the flood, which would place the action just before the Decembrist Revolt of 1825. The poet recounts how one night, Yevgeni is sleeping on the banks of the Neva when he wakes with a start. Filled with fear, he wanders to Senate Square, where the lions and the Bronze Horseman, the statue of Tsar Peter I, still stand.

In the eighth stanza (lines 102–116), Yevgeni recalls his ordeal in the flood. He gazes at the statue of Tsar Peter I, and muses on him, by whose "fateful will" the city was "founded on the sea." He wonders where the horse will gallop, and plant his hooves, next. He addresses Tsar Peter I as "mighty master of fate," and notes that as he is making his horse rear up by pulling on the iron curb bit, he also "reared up Russia" out of the sea by means of his indomitable will.

The ninth stanza (lines 117–38) tells how the furious Yevgeni presses his face against the railings that surround the statue of Tsar Peter I and issues an unspecified threat to the dead Tsar before running away. As he runs across the square, he feels that the statue's face is flaring up with rage and that the statue is galloping after him. Yevgeni runs all night, but wherever he goes, he feels that he is followed by the Bronze Horseman.

The tenth stanza (lines 139–44) jumps forward in time. The poet tells how, ever since that episode, whenever Yevgeni wandered into that square, he would hastily press his hand to his heart to ease the torment, and doff his cap in deference to the statue, without looking at it.

The eleventh and last stanza (lines 145–56) jumps forward in time once more. The poet describes a small island that can be seen from the banks of the Neva, where occasionally a fisherman stops to cook supper. The island is so barren that not a blade of grass grows there. The flood drove "a ramshackle little house there": Parasha's. The poet notes that last spring, a barge carried away the wreckage. By

TOPICS FOR FURTHER STUDY

- Consider Pushkin's portrayals of Tsar Peter I and Yevgeni in "The Bronze Horseman." Write an essay showing how the poet elicits or alienates the reader's sympathy for each character. Where do your own sympathies lie? Why?

- Research the literary movements of neoclassicism, romanticism, and realism, and list the primary characteristics displayed by works belonging to each movement. Analyze the characteristics from each movement as they appear in "The Bronze Horseman." Does the work fit into any one movement, or does it contain elements from two, or all three movements? Give a class presentation on your findings.

- Research the lives and history of three of Russia's autocratic rulers from any time in the country's history (Tsarist or Soviet periods). An autocracy is a government in which one person (in the case of Russia, the Tsar or Soviet leader of the country) has unlimited authority over others. Write an essay comparing and contrasting their methods of government and the lives of different social classes under their rule. Use your findings to draw contrasts or comparisons with contemporary government in your own country.

- Research the history of St. Petersburg, Russia, from the events leading up to its foundation in 1703 to the present day. Write an essay (using illustrations if you wish) detailing some of the events and influences that shaped the city.

- Research the 1824 flood in St. Petersburg, Russia, and the 2005 flood in New Orleans caused by Hurricane Katrina. Write a report comparing and contrasting the causes and effects of the two events. Possible areas of examination might include social, political, economic, environmental, and public health aspects. Include in your report any measures that are currently being taken in both cities to try to prevent future floods, as well as any measures that you believe should be, but are not being, implemented.

the threshold of the house, Yevgeni's body was found. He was buried in that spot.

THEMES

Conflict between the Needs of the State and the Desires of the Individual

The main theme of "The Bronze Horseman" is the conflict between the needs and desires of the imperial state, as embodied by Tsar Peter I and symbolized by his statue, and the desires of the individual, as embodied by Yevgeni.

Yevgeni's fate symbolizes the sacrifice of the thousands of peasants who, drafted in as forced labor by Peter, perished in the building of the city. This story of the peasant builders is not directly recounted in "The Bronze Horseman." Instead, the poet shows Peter planning the construction of the future capital of the Russian Empire, and then jumps forward in time a hundred years, when the city is already built. This deliberate omission of important events is a narrative device called ellipsis. However, the story of the peasants is vividly present in the poem in symbolic form, portrayed by the fate of Yevgeni. In deliberate contrast with Peter's grand vision, Yevgeni has simple desires: marriage to his beloved Parasha, a house, children, and grandchildren. Yet he is denied fulfillment of these desires by Peter I's act of will in constructing a city on flood-prone, low-lying land. Peter wanted the city in this place because it was strategically important, both for stopping Swedish expansion in the Baltic region and for trade and cultural exchange with Europe. In Peter's view, Europe was commercially, technologically, and artistically more advanced than Russia.

The Vulnerability of the Poor and Powerless Compared with the Strength of the Wealthy and Powerful

Pushkin makes clear that it is the poorer residents of the city, such as Yevgeni, who suffer most in the flood. In Part 1 of "The Bronze Horseman" he identifies the detritus that is being washed away as street hawkers' trays, fragments of huts, and "The chattels of pale poverty." The poor people's houses were made of wood, which made them especially vulnerable to natural disasters. Parasha's house is completely swept away, ending up washed up on an island outside the city. Yevgeni makes a pathetic attempt at defiance of Peter's hubristic vision, issuing a vague threat to the dead Tsar's statue. When the statue seems to come alive and chase Yevgeni through the streets, Yevgeni is cowed with fear at this royal rebuke of his insolence. He loses his mind and ends his life at the threshold of his sweetheart's broken-up house. Thus, symbolically, the poor and insignificant, along with their desires and aspirations, are terrified by the powerful into submission, before being swept away and forgotten as utterly as the peasants who died in the building of the city.

Moving up the socioeconomic scale, the middle-class merchants' houses, more solidly constructed of stone, are left intact by the flood. The merchant loses his goods, but there is a chance that he may make good his loss at a neighbor's expense. At the top of the social scale, the houses and monuments of the rich and influential, such as the sculptural lions, the grand mansions, and the Bronze Horseman itself, emerge from the flood untouched. The poem contrasts the resilience of absolute power with the vulnerability of the ordinary people, and shows that this is as true at the time of writing as it was in 1703, when Peter founded the city.

Conflict between Nature and Civilization

A subsidiary theme in the poem is the conflict between nature and civilization, as represented by the elemental water of the river and rain, and the stone of the city. This theme is first presented in the Introduction, when Tsar Peter I invokes nature as a partner in his grand scheme: "By nature we are fated / To cut a window through to Europe." This image is of the river's banks being encased in granite on the orders of Tsar Peter I. Tsar Peter I has imposed his will on nature, but nature fights back. The river breaks out of its manmade boundaries and overwhelms the city. Even absolute temporal power, as embodied in the Tsars of Russia, is ineffectual against the uprisings of nature's elements. Tsar Alexander I is shown reflecting that "Tsars cannot master / The divine elements."

Even when the flood subsides, Yevgeni is awoken from his sleep on the embankment to the sound of the "sullen wave … reproachfully / Grumbling and beating against the smooth steps." The image suggests that the river's power is only temporarily latent, but is not defeated, even by Tsar Peter I's mighty will. While civilization has in the short term won a battle against nature, the war continues. Thus, while the poem shows the relative vulnerability of the poor and powerless, it also emphasizes the fragility of all human endeavor, whether it be that of a powerful Tsar such as Peter I or an ordinary person such as Yevgeni.

STYLE

The Heroic or Epic Poem

The heroic (otherwise known as epic) mode of poetry was popular in eighteenth-century Russian literature. It is characterized by an elevated style of language, and involves a warrior or statesman protagonist whose actions determine the fate of an empire. In Russia, it was commonly used to praise Tsars and their generals or officials. Pushkin uses the heroic mode in the Introduction of "The Bronze Horseman" to describe Tsar Peter I and his grand vision of building the city of St. Petersburg on the marshes. However, he departs from the heroic tradition by juxtaposing the heroic or epic mode with the realistic mode, which is used to describe the humble Yevgeni's activities.

Russian Romanticism

Russian romanticism began to emerge from eighteenth-century sentimentalism around 1815. Its early proponents included the poet, writer of fairy tales, and translator Vasilii Andreevich Zhukovsky, whom Pushkin acknowledged as a major influence, and the poet Konstantin Batiushkov. Romanticism reached its heights in the 1820s and 1830s with writers such as Mikhail

Monument to Peter the Great in St. Petersburg, Russia. This is the statue that the poem refers to
(© Tibor Bognar / Alamy)

Lermontov and by the early 1840s was being displaced by realism, in the works of writers such as Nikolai Gogol (who is, however, primarily classed as a romantic).

Pushkin is usually classed as a Romantic writer. It is true that he influenced Russian romantic writers such as Lermontov, and that his writings include the major themes of European romantic writers. These include the special role of the poet, the importance of freedom from social and political restrictions, the value of emotion and the subjective experience as a means to truth, and an interest in folk literature. A special emphasis of Russian romanticism was a nationalistic pride. Examples of romantic themes in "The Bronze Horseman" include Pushkin's acknowledgement of the role of the poet Count Khvostov in immortalizing the flood in verse; the sympathy he shows for Yevgeni's suffering under the tyrannical will of Peter I; the emphasis on the emotions experienced by Yevgeni, Tsar Alexander, and Peter I; and the poet's pride in the city of St. Petersburg and in the history and achievements of Russia. Aspects of the romantic stance apparent in "The Bronze

Horseman" include irony and a sympathy with Yevgeni's opposition to the existing order.

Nevertheless, Pushkin's poem also exemplifies classical virtues such as clarity, rationality (both Peter I's and Yevgeni's viewpoints are presented and honored), and moderation, in that the poet does not identify himself with extremes of emotion, but stands apart from it and observes it. The poem, in common with the rest of Pushkin's works, also lacks the passion borne of moral commitment that has come to be associated with Russian romanticism and which passed into Russian realism.

Rather than classifying Pushkin as a romantic writer, it may be more accurate to call him primarily a romantic writer with strong elements of classicism and realism.

Personification

Throughout the poem, the river Neva is personified (personification is a literary device in which an inanimate object is given the attributes of a person). In the Introduction, the poet states that in the construction of the city, the river has been encased in granite. This is presented as nature's elements being "conquered." The water appears to resent its "enmity and ancient bondage," as the poet pleads with it to forget this history of conflict with Peter and avoid disturbing his "eternal sleep" with its "empty spite." "Bondage" refers explicitly to the tamed river, but Pushkin's Russian readers would also have made the connection to the enslaved peasant builders of the city. In this poem, the original peasant inhabitants of the area are presented almost as part of the landscape, as part of nature: their huts are "Like black specks on the mossy, marshy banks," merging with the natural surroundings. Thus the enmity and memory of bondage that threatens Peter's rest (and his city) is held by the river and possibly by the thousands of dead peasant builders.

Initially, at the start of the storm that will create the flood, the river Neva seems to be on the side of the city, struggling to flow out to sea against the gale-force winds blowing in from the Gulf of Finland. But when its struggle proves futile, the river becomes "maddened" and "Hurled herself on the city like a beast." Here, the river is personified as a hostile and violent attacker. This is reinforced by the description of the flood as "Siege! Assault!" Then the poet shifts to describing the flood waves as cunning thieves that climb into houses through windows and steal people's goods. While this image seems to condemn the river, it is subsequently portrayed as the deliverer of God's wrath: "The people gaze upon the wrath of God / And await their doom." It is not explicitly said why God is angry with the city, but one possible answer is suggested by the other religious imagery of the poem, the description of Peter I as "The Image." The Russian word for "Image" is *kumir*, a word that normally designates a pagan idol. While Pushkin was not religious in the orthodox sense, he may have been suggesting that Peter blasphemously (and in defiance of the laws of nature) elevated himself to godlike status in his hubristic act of founding his city so close to the water.

It would, however, be wrong to conclude that Pushkin was condemning the creation of the city. His paean to the city beginning "I love you, Peter's creation," detailing the beautiful sights and sounds of St. Petersburg, is heartfelt and sincere. It is more accurate to suggest that Pushkin, like many Russians, had an ambivalent attitude to the city. He was able simultaneously to maintain gratitude to Peter for his creation of St. Petersburg, and his sense of outrage committed against nature and thousands of peasant laborers in the process of creation.

Personification is also used in the poem to animate the Bronze Horseman, the statue of Peter I, into a character embodying his spirit. The scene in which the statue seems to come to life and pursues Yevgeni through the streets in retribution for his defiance emphasizes the all-powerful nature of Peter's regal authority, undaunted even by death.

HISTORICAL CONTEXT

The Founding of St. Petersburg

Tsar Peter I founded the Russian city of St. Petersburg on May 27, 1703 (New Style) on land, in an area known as Ingria, won back from Sweden in the beginning of the Great Northern War (1700–1721). Historically, Ingria was populated by the Finnic peoples, which is why the Introduction to "The Bronze Horseman," mentions Finns living at the site of the future St. Petersburg.

The story of how Peter I founded St. Petersburg is well known in Russia. Using his prerogative

as Tsar, he drafted in forced labor, specifying a quota of 40,000 peasants per year. The peasants left their homes and walked to the site under armed guard, often for hundreds of miles. They had to supply their own tools and food, and many were shackled to prevent desertion. They raised Peter's city out of inhospitable marshland under brutal climatic conditions. Thousands died from exposure, starvation, and disease, meaning that in any one year, losses through mortality would amount to fifty percent and the total workforce would number 20,000. Thus it is said in Russia that St. Petersburg is founded on the bones of the peasants who built it. In "The Bronze Horseman," the fate of Yevgeni is symbolic of that of the laborer peasants, in that they are all seen as victims of Peter I's autocratic will.

Peter's aims in building St. Petersburg were fulfilled, in history as in the poem. By the latter half of the nineteenth century, St. Petersburg was a leading trading port and industrial center which was instrumental in lifting Russia out of the medieval state. Because Peter employed the greatest European architects and planned the city as a unified whole, the city is a model of town planning and is famed for its beautiful and impressive baroque architecture.

The Flood of 1824

The flood in St. Petersburg that is recounted in "The Bronze Horseman" took place on November 19 (New Style), 1824. It remains the most serious flood in the recorded history of the city. Pushkin was in exile in South Russia at the time. His source for the facts of the flood was V. N. Berch's *A Detailed Historical Account of All the Floods That Occurred in St. Petersburg* (1826), which Pushkin had in his library. Assessments of the fatalities that occurred in the 1824 flood vary widely, but the "St. Petersburg Flood Protection Barrier Environmental Impact Assessment Study: Executive Summary" cites a figure of over 300 people.

Autocracy in Russia

Peter I was largely responsible for making Russia an autocratic state. He abolished the old Boyar Duma, or advisory Council of Nobles, and replaced it with a senate, to which he assigned the job of collecting taxes on his behalf. He also abolished all vestiges of local government and forced all nobles into state service. This

COMPARE
&
CONTRAST

- **1830s:** Tsar Nicholas I (reigned 1825–1855) is known as one of the most autocratic of Russian monarchs. After the Decembrist Revolt, Nicholas tightens control over education and publishing, and runs an efficient network of spies and informers against his own people.

  Today: In 2004, Russia's President Vladimir Putin alarms some international observers when he tightens the presidency's control over parliament, civil society, and regional government.

- **1830s:** Tsar Nicholas I censors works of literature, including Pushkin's "The Bronze Horseman," and has its author watched closely.

  Today: International concern rises over the unsolved murders of Russian journalists, many of whom are known to be critical of President Vladimir Putin and his regime.

- **1830s:** St. Petersburg suffers annual floods sufficiently serious to inundate streets and basements in low-lying areas of the city.

  Today: St. Petersburg continues to flood with what appears to be increasing frequency. The St. Petersburg Flood Prevention Facility Complex (also known as the St. Petersburg Dam) is under construction to try to prevent serious floods in the future. President Vladimir Putin has set a target of 2008 to finish the dam.

autocratic model of monarchy was followed by subsequent Tsars of Russia and prevailed in Pushkin's time. Two great revolutions against autocracy occurred in 1825 (the Decembrist Revolt) and the Russian Revolution of 1917. The latter revolution abolished the monarchy and marked the beginning of communist rule in Soviet Russia. Autocratic rule flourished under communism, with dictators such as Joseph Stalin (1878–1953) establishing near total control over society and centralizing the power base. Since the breakup of the Soviet Union in 1991, the rise of a multiparty system led to a decentralization of power, though President Vladimir Putin, who came to office in 1999, has been criticized for reversing this liberalization process.

The Decembrist Revolt

The Decembrist Revolt or Uprising took place on December 26, 1825 (New Style). The trigger for the revolt was the conservative Nicholas I's assuming the throne after his older brother Constantine relinquished his claim to the succession. A group of liberal Russian army officers led three thousand soldiers in a protest in Senate Square, St. Petersburg. They refused to pledge allegiance to the new Tsar, instead demanding a constitution. The Tsar's troops easily suppressed the revolt. Afterwards two hundred and eighty-nine Decembrists were tried. Five were executed, thirty-one imprisoned, and the rest exiled to Siberia. They were viewed as martyrs by later generations of Russian dissidents. Because the revolt occurred in December, the rebels were called the Decembrists. In 1925, to mark the centenary of the revolt, Senate Square was renamed Decembrist Square.

Pushkin was not directly involved in the revolt as he was in exile in South Russia, though he realized that he was implicated when Decembrists were found to have copies of his early political poems. Pushkin destroyed all of his papers that he felt were dangerous and escaped retribution, later concluding that fate had singled him out as the sole survivor of his generation's best hopes. For the rest of his life, however, Nicholas I had Pushkin closely watched and had his works censored.

The Decembrist Revolt had a profound influence on Russian romantic literature. Russian writers such as the playwright Alexander Gri-boyedov and the poet and novelist Mikhail Ler-montov came to view themselves as adversaries of the existing order. Pushkin makes a heavily veiled reference to the Decembrist Revolt in part 2 of in "The Bronze Horseman," when he takes up Yevgeni's story a year after the November 1824 flood, in the fall of 1825. All of his readers would have known that Yevgeni's final angry yet futile confrontation with Peter I's statue ("All right then, wonder-worker, just you wait!") took place just before the Decembrist Revolt. This adds a special pathos to Yevgeni's body being found soon afterwards at the threshold of Parasha's ruined house: he becomes symbolic of the fallen Decembrists. The fact that his body is found and buried on an island outside St. Petersburg is a symbolic reference to exile, which became the fate of many writers (including Pushkin) and intellectuals in both Tsarist and Soviet Russia.

Falconet's Statue

The equestrian statue of Peter I that stands in Decembrist Square (formerly Senate Square) in St. Petersburg is by the French sculptor Étienne Maurice Falconet (1716–1791) and was commissioned by Tsarina Catherine II (Catherine the Great, reigned 1762–1796) to commemorate her royal predecessor. The statue faces west, in the direction of Europe, symbolizing Peter's determination to westernize Russian culture and technology. The statue has come to be known as the Bronze Horseman, after Pushkin's poem, and is a symbol of the city in the same way in which the Statue of Liberty is a symbol of New York City.

Adam Mickiewicz

According to Andrew Kahn in *Pushkin's "The Bronze Horseman,"* Pushkin indicated in a footnote to the poem that his description of the statue of Peter I forms a response to a work by the Polish romantic poet Adam Mickiewicz (1798–1855). The work is Mickiewicz's verse drama *Forefather's Eve*, which recounts the narrator's travels to St. Petersburg and his philosophical musings on the capital. "He ponders what will happen to the statue, which he calls a 'cascade of tyranny,' when the warm sun of freedom begins to shine on Russian society." The narrator sees the city as the whim of an aristocrat rather than an organic product of Russian culture, and as a symbol of the inhuman quality of life in Russia.

CRITICAL OVERVIEW

Although Pushkin is widely considered to be the most influential Russian writer of the early nineteenth century, his work is rarely read outside Russia, largely because it is difficult to convey the power and music of his verse in English translation. Nevertheless, in Russia and internationally, "The Bronze Horseman" is generally viewed as one of Pushkin's greatest works, second only to *Eugene Onegin*, his novel in verse.

One of the first readers of "The Bronze Horseman" was Pushkin's censor, Tsar Nicholas I. Nicholas objected to Pushkin's portrayal of his royal predecessor, Peter I. He insisted that references to the statue as "The Image," a pagan idol, be removed. He objected to the passage about Moscow's decline, and wanted to cut the crucial final confrontation between Yevgeni and the statue. Pushkin refused to make the cuts and withheld publication. The poem was published in bowdlerized (censored) form, with changes largely in line with the Tsar's requests, in 1841, four years after Pushkin's death. The cuts severely distorted the poem's meaning. This version formed the basis of its critical reception throughout the nineteenth century. Many editions published after 1841 also feature versions that were censored to some degree, and it was not until Pavel Shchegolev's 1924 edition that the text was reconstructed as Pushkin had intended it. The discovery of new material and variants of the poem among Pushkin's manuscripts led to the publication of as precise a version as possible in N. Izmailov's edition of 1978.

The stature of the poem has grown with these attempts to restore its integrity. It was barely noticed until the 1870s, though as early as 1832, Pushkin himself was lauded as the "Russian national poet" by another famous Russian writer, Nikolai Gogol, in his essay "A Few Words About Pushkin." In his essay (reprinted in the *Russian Literature Triquarterly*) Gogol writes: "All the richness, power, and versatility of our language is contained in him." The influential critic Vissarion G. Belinsky (1811–1848), using the censored version of the poem, emphasizes the positive portrayal of Tsar Peter I in the Introduction. Indeed, according to Andrew Kahn in *Pushkin's "The Bronze Horseman,"* Belinsky sees "in its celebration of the Petrine creation an argument that the practical ends

(Westernisation) justify the political means (tyranny)." Further, Belinksy writes of the poem: "meek in our heart we admit the triumph of the general over the individual without forfeiting our empathy for the suffering of that individual."

Leonid Grossman (cited by Kahn), in his biography of 1939 titled *Pushkin*, continued the tradition of interpreting the poem in a pro-Petrine manner. In language reminiscent of contemporary eulogies of the then Russian leader Joseph Stalin, Grossman draws attention to "the mighty creative energy of Peter's character."

In a 1992 article for *Partisan Review*, John Bayley notes that Pushkin "saw through" authority "and yet was fascinated by it, and in a sense admiring." He adds that the poem is as much a celebration of Peter I "as it is a cry of pity and protest from underneath, for the little man who only wants to marry his sweetheart and live a quiet life." Bayley notes how this ambivalence became a characteristic feature of Russian realism as exemplified by writers such as Gogol, Dostoevsky, and Tolstoy.

Peter I. Barta, in his 1995 *Reference Guide to World Literature* essay, draws attention to the poem's role in contributing to the myth of St. Petersburg. Barta emphasizes the ambiguity in the poet's treatment of the city, which Barta sees as defined by dichotomies: "European splendour and Russian poverty; urban civilization and unsuitable climatic conditions"; and "the fantastic city in which human aspirations come to nought." Alexandra Smith notes in *Two Hundred Years of Pushkin, Volume II: Alexander Pushkin: Myth and Monument* that Pushkin himself was ambivalent about the city. Though he chose to settle there after his marriage, when he received news of the flood in 1824, he wrote to his brother that this was "the very thing for cursed Petersburg."

The poem continues to attract critical praise and attention, with many critics focusing on the poem's elements of psychological interest and irony.

CRITICISM

Claire Robinson

Robinson has an M.A. in English. She is a former teacher of English literature and creative writing, *and is currently a freelance writer and editor. In the following essay, Robinson explores how Pushkin uses the heroic and realistic modes to comment on the action and characters in "The Bronze Horseman."*

In "The Bronze Horseman," Pushkin uses two distinct modes: the heroic and the realistic. The heroic (otherwise known as epic) mode prevailed in eighteenth-century Russian literature. It is characterized by an elevated style of language, and involves a warrior or statesman protagonist whose actions determine the fate of an empire. In Russia, it was commonly used to praise Tsars and their generals or officials. Pushkin uses the heroic mode in the Introduction of "The Bronze Horseman" to describe Peter I, and his grand plan. Peter I is described as "Full of high thoughts" aimed at strengthening Russia's strategic position. Then the poet moves to the odic style (often used in heroic verse) to praise the city: "I love you, Peter's creation." At the end of the Introduction, the poet addresses the city as if in a prayer: "Flaunt your beauty, Peter's / City, and stand unshakeable like Russia."

Unlike his predecessors, Pushkin was not content to rest with the heroic mode. He juxtaposes the heroic with the realistic mode. The realistic mode, introduced in part 1, is used to describe the humble clerk Yevgeni, and his actions. The style is very different from the one Pushkin uses to describe Peter I and his actions: it is everyday, conversational, and ordinary. He writes as if chatting to the reader: "We'll call / Our hero by this name. It's pleasant, and / Has long been congenial to my pen." With wry humor, he describes the mundane, unsung, and day-to-day nature of Yevgeni's existence: he "works / Somewhere, avoids the paths of the famous, mourns / Neither dead relatives nor the forgotten past." These facts are all in contrast to the lives of great people like Tsar Peter and Tsar Alexander, whose actions are far from anonymous and affect numerous people, and who derive their power from ancient bloodlines (dead relatives and the past).

Pushkin then brings together the heroic and the realistic, with revealing results. Having described the flood in realistic mode, he introduces Tsar Alexander with a reminder of the heroic mode: "the late Tsar in his glory." All the glorious Tsar can do, however, is to stand on his balcony at a remove from the people and reflect sadly on the disaster. He concludes, rightly, that

WHAT DO I READ NEXT?

- *The Collected Stories* (Everyman's Library edition, 1999), by Alexander Pushkin, presents Pushkin's most highly regarded and accessible prose works, including "The Tales of the Late Ivan Petrovich Belkin," "The Captain's Daughter," and "The Queen of Spades." Written in his clear, spare style, these stories encompass romantic, melancholy, humorous, and psychological themes.

- *The Collected Tales of Nikolai Gogol* (2003), by N. V. Gogol and translated by Richard Pevear and Larissa Volokhonsky, offers Gogol's most notable short stories, set in the Ukraine and St. Petersburg. Gogol was a famous Russian writer who was influenced by Pushkin. Elements that these works have in common with Pushkin's "The Bronze Horseman" are supernatural mystery and a sympathy for the ordinary man, although the experiences of Gogol's average men are infused with the extraordinary.

- *Lord Byron: The Major Works* (2000), by George Gordon Byron and edited by Jerome J. McGann, contains the major poetry and prose of the English romantic writer. Byron had a significant influence on Pushkin in terms of ironic style and rebellious, alienated attitude. Readers new to Byron may consider beginning with the narrative poems "Childe Harold's Pilgrimage" or "Don Juan."

- *St. Petersburg: A Cultural History* (1997), by Solomon Volkov, offers a fascinating overview of the writers, artists, and composers who contributed to the cultural evolution of St. Petersburg from its founding in 1703 into the modern age. Individuals featured include writers Dostoevsky, Gogol, and Anna Akhmatova; and composers Pyotr Ilyich Tchaikovsky, Modest Petrovich Mussorgsky, Nikolai Andreyevich Rimsky-Korsakov, Dmitri Shostakovich, and Alexander Porfiryevich Borodin.

- In *Sunlight at Midnight: St. Petersburg and the Rise of Modern Russia* (2002), W. Bruce Lincoln traces the story of the city's beginnings, then depicts the glorious buildings of eighteenth-century Tsars, followed by the rise of industrial slums, disaffection, violence, intellectual ferment, and revolution. Lincoln also recounts the heroism of the city's 900 days under siege in World War II.

"Tsars cannot master / The divine elements." All the imperial power in the world is ineffectual against the workings of nature. As for Peter, who at this point in the poem is symbolized by his statue, he only turns his back on the suffering of Yevgeni and his fellow townspeople: "his back turned / To him, in unshakeable eminence." He maintains his imperious gesture, his hand outstretched in command, but he has no power to command the elements. Thus Pushkin undermines the traditional heroic mode with the realistic mode.

One way in which Pushkin undermines the heroic is by the use of ironic parallels: he mirrors a heroic event or gesture with a decidedly unheroic counterpart in a way whereby the latter comments on the former. Such parallels include themes and images.

An example of a parallel theme is that of the dream. Both Peter I and Yevgeni have a dream. Peter dreams of founding a great city that will check the Swedes and serve as Russia's window onto Europe; Yevgeni dreams of a quiet life in a humble house with Parasha and their children. The contrast between the two dreams is stark. Though on the surface, it would seem that Peter's dream would be the most difficult to fulfill, as it turns out, it is Yevgeni's most basic and unambitious dream that proves impossible. Yevgeni's unfulfilled dream is swept away by

PETER'S BUILDING OF THE CITY REFLECTS THE CREATION OF THE UNIVERSE AS DESCRIBED IN THE BIBLE'S BOOK OF GENESIS, IN WHICH GOD FIRST CREATES LIGHT OUT OF DARKNESS."

Peter's fulfilled dream. Peter builds his city on a flood plain, and the flood destroys Yevgeni's beloved and, indirectly, his entire life. After the flood, Yevgeni's dream of life with Parasha turns into a despairing thought that the whole of life is "Nothing but an empty dream, heaven's jest."

An example of a parallel image is that of the equestrian statue, two versions of which are present in the poem. The first is the bronze horseman, the statue of Peter I that stands in Senate Square. This statue is referred to in the poem as "The Image," reminiscent of a revered idol. The statue portrays Peter with arm outstretched in a gesture of command, as if decreeing, godlike, the creation of St. Petersburg. His horse rears up under the force of Peter's "iron curb," the harsh bit that can cause a horse pain if insensitively handled and can make it rear in an effort to escape the pressure on its mouth. Pushkin draws the analogy explicitly: this action is likened to the way in which Peter "reared up Russia" with his indomitable will. It is an act of violence and tyrannical power. What is more, the horse rears "on the precipice's brink," as the statue stands on a huge rock that resembles a cliff face. This connotes the enormous risk that Peter took in building his city on marshland prone to flooding, an exercise that in modern parlance might be termed *brinkmanship*. The statue shows the supreme confidence that attends absolute power such as Peter enjoyed. It is a godlike power, extending over the life and death of the citizens of St. Petersburg, as is shown in the fate of Yevgeni.

The ironic counterpart to the equestrian statue is the statue of the lion on which Yevgeni perches to escape the flood. Yevgeni's state of mind and the physical attitude he adopts are in direct contrast to Peter's: where Peter is confident, Yevgeni is terrified; where Peter gazes into the distance "Full of high thoughts," Yevgeni gazes into the distance trying to see Parasha's house; where Peter's arm is outstretched in command, Yevgeni's arms are crossed tightly in a defensive pose. Even the lion takes on an ironic tone: it is a guardian lion, but its guardianship is selective: while the mansion outside which it stands outlasts the flood, Parasha's house and the goods of the city's poor are swept away. The contrast between the two equestrian images is between imperial power and Yevgeni's helplessness, though much irony lies in the fact that imperial power is as helpless as the humble clerk in the face of nature's forces. Imperial power, when faced with something it cannot control, simply assumes an attitude of indifference, as symbolized by the image of Peter's statue with its back towards Yevgeni. While imperial power is ineffectual in assisting the ordinary people, it is also "unshakeable."

Reinforcing this idea of the intransigence of power, in the Introduction, an implied analogy is drawn between Peter I and God as creator. Peter is not referred to by name, but only, reverentially, as "*he*," recalling the Old Testament proscription against mentioning the name of God. Peter's building of the city reflects the creation of the universe as described in the Bible's Book of Genesis, in which God first creates light out of darkness. The site on which Peter builds St. Petersburg is described in images of primordial darkness: even the forest, a place of "gloom," is "never visited by rays / Of the mist-shrouded sun." The poet characterizes the built city, on the other hand, as a place of light. He describes the White Nights, during which he can read and write without a lamp; the streets "shine clearly," "the Admiralty spire / Is luminous," girls with bright faces travel in sledges along the frozen river, the balls are full of "sparkle" and the light blue flames of burning punch.

The effect of this likening of Peter I to God is to suggest that his will is no less than Russia's historical destiny, and to bear out his claim that "we are fated / To cut a window through to Europe." Once more, a bringing in of the light (Europe was considered to be a higher civilization than Russia at the time) to a Russia sunk in medieval darkness is suggested in the image of the window.

Although Peter gains his window onto Europe, he cannot banish the forces of nature, symbolized by darkness. Peter's heroic aspirations are set against the realistic forces of nature.

As Tsar Alexander is shown stating in the poem, Tsars have no power over the elements, which are equally as "divine" as Peter's omnipotent will. The flood threatens Peter's creation: it is described as occurring at night, in "darkened Petrograd." When Yevgeni realizes that Parasha's house has been swept away in the flood, this moment is followed by a description of the darkness of night falling on the city, and of the people discussing the terrors of the disaster. With the dawn light comes an apparent restoration of Peter's order, with no trace of the disaster remaining. In reality, however, the losses of the night have not disappeared, but have merely been "covered by a purple cloak," the cloak of Imperial power and will.

Nature's elements have been temporarily suppressed, but not conquered, any more than day conquers night. Nature and civilization, like darkness and light, the common people and their rulers, and the realistic and the heroic, are destined to coexist in Pushkin's Russia, sometimes in an uneasy truce, and at other times in open conflict.

Source: Claire Robinson, Critical Essay on "The Bronze Horseman," in *Poetry for Students*, Gale, Cengage Learning, 2008.

Catharine Theimer Nepomnyashchy

In the following excerpt, Nepomnyashchy claims that Pushkin's "The Bronze Horseman" was heavily influenced by Washington Irving's short story "The Legend of Sleepy Hollow."

... Both Evgenii and Ichabod, in the parallel passages in which they elaborate their visions of future marital bliss, reveal their powers of imagination. While Evgenii's musings ("Zhenit'sia? Nu ... za chem zhe net? ..." [Get married? Well ... why shouldn't I? ...]), in which he envisions the course of his life to the grave, are pointedly prosaic, this passage is prefaced by the remark, "i razmechtalsia kak poet" (and, like a poet, set to musing), cautioning us not to dismiss his ability to dream too lightly. In the corresponding passage from "The Legend of Sleepy Hollow," Ichabod reveals himself as a restless Yankee, his heart set more on the bounty Katrina represents than on the young woman herself. He confuses Katrina with the property owned by her father and dreams of the liquidation of these holdings, the transformation of the place into movable assets, disclosing an imagination as fertile as the land he covets:

> IN THIS REGARD WE MUST FIRST RECOGNIZE THAT THE CONFRONTATION BETWEEN EVGENII AND THE TSAR, AUTOCRAT AND SUBJECT, CONSTITUTES AT LEAST AS MUCH A *WRITER'S* PROBLEM—THAT IS, SPECIFICALLY A DEFINING CONDITION OF THE LITERARY CULTURE OF PUSHKIN'S DAY—AS IT DOES A PURELY POLITICAL ISSUE."

Both Evgenii's and Ichabod's dreams of course come to naught, defeated by the competing visions of their more powerful rivals.

In this context I would finally point to what to my mind is the most significant convergence between the Pushkin and Irving works: the nature and function of the "supernatural" horsemen. In both cases, the figure represents an incursion of the past into the present. Moreover, the Headless Hessian, like the Falconet statue of Peter the Great, embodies a historical moment of revolutionary social upheaval, the effects of which shape contemporary life just as the Petrine "revolution" has created not only the physical setting but the social context that determines the sad course of Evgenii's life and demise. The confrontations between Ichabod and the Headless Horseman, on the one hand, and between Evgenii and Peter, on the other, thus represent a clash of historical forces that, despite appearances, leaves the "victor" and his "victory" in an ethically and even ontologically and aesthetically ambiguous position.

... We might do well to emulate Irving's critics in suggesting that the prevailing sociopolitical, historical, and even religious readings of *The Bronze Horseman* may yet not exhaust the interpretive possibilities of the poem. I have argued elsewhere that there is sufficient evidence in Pushkin's poem that Evgenii may be read as a poet figure. I will not repeat that argument here, but will merely adduce briefly the evidence I believe supports a reading that views Evgenii as a "writer" caught in the same net of constraints that conditioned Pushkin's own literary endeavors. Pace any number of scholars on *The Bronze Horseman*, I am not suggesting that Evgenii be read "autobiographically" (although autobiographical parallels between Pushkin and his protagonist support my argument). Evgenii "is" no more Pushkin than the comically preposterous Ichabod Crane "is" Washington Irving. Rather, I am suggesting that Pushkin placed Evgenii in a situation with unquestionable resonances with his own literary context.

In this regard we must first recognize that the confrontation between Evgenii and the tsar, autocrat and subject, constitutes at least as much a *writer's* problem—that is, specifically a defining condition of the literary culture of Pushkin's day—as it does a purely political issue. Pushkin's own tormented relationship with the tsar is too well documented to demand revisitation here, except to recall the extent to which it dominated Pushkin's literary fortunes. In this respect, *The Bronze Horseman* offers a characteristic case in point. Pushkin was counting on the profits from the sale of the works he hoped to produce at Boldino in the autumn of 1833 to ease his ever precarious financial position, as evidenced by the letter he wrote to the tsar on 30 July of that year requesting leave to absent himself from the capital:

> In the course of the past two years I have been occupied with historical research alone, not writing a single line of the purely literary. I must spend a month or two in complete isolation, in order to rest up from my very important occupations and to finish a book I began a long time ago, and which will bring me money I need. I am myself sorry to waste time on vain pursuits, but what can I do? They alone bring me independence and a means of living with my family in Petersburg, where my labors, thanks to the sovereign, have a more important and useful goal.

Nicholas I's fundamental objections to the publication of *The Bronze Horseman* dashed Pushkin's hopes. Thus, while Irving lamented the absence of aristocratic patronage of the arts left at the mercy of the growing commercialism of American literature, Pushkin in essence found himself between these two worlds: his dependence on the tsar (a vestige of the old patronage system) and his need to live primarily off his own works in a cultural economy that favored potboiler prose over "gentleman poets." Moreover, Pushkin's distaste for the "rabble" of the reading public, given voice most famously in such works as his "Razgovor knigoprodavtsa s poetom" (Conversation between the bookseller and the poet), are echoed in *The Bronze Horseman* as well. If Evgenii is to be viewed as a representative of the "people," then the callous indifference of the Petersburg *narod* to his fate appears all the more jarring, particularly Pushkin's insistence on its mercantile nature:

> ...(And order was again restored. / With cold insensitivity / The masses walked upon the streets / So recently freed by the waters. / Emerging from their past night's shelters, / Officials hurried to their jobs. / The fearless merchant, not despairing, / Opened up his plundered cellar / And counted up his heavy losses / For which he planned to wreak revenge.)

In the final analysis, Evgenii *is* a "writer," a clerk who "serves" (*sluzhit*) the state for money, a sad comedown for the scion of a noble family that once "shone beneath Karamzin's pen" (*pod perom Karamzina ... prozvuchalo*) and a sad commentary on the writer's abasement, not only before the public, but also before the state for his livelihood.

Let us then turn to the crucial confrontation between Evgenii and the statue. First of all, we should note that Evgenii's challenge to the statue—"Dobro, stroitel' chudotvornyi! ... Uzho tebe!" (Just wait, proud miracle creator!)—constitutes the sole instance of direct speech in the poem, and his words are specifically addressed to Peter the Great as the miraculous builder of the city, the poser, dare I say, of a creative challenge. The Bronze Horseman's response to Evgenii's challenge lends itself to two possible interpretations: either the statue really comes alive or the event transpires only in Evgenii's imagination. I would argue, however, that the latter, "naturalistic" explanation yields a richer reading of the poem. If the statue comes alive only in Evgenii's mind, then the poor clerk becomes a poet surrogate who not only forces a reaction from the hitherto impassive statue but in essence "rewrites" Peter in the Gothic mode, "displacing" the statue out of material reality into the realm of the poet's fantasy. It would seem, then, that the poema presents us with two symmetrical creative acts—Peter's at the beginning and Evgenii's at the end—the juxtaposition of which suggests a mode of being for the writer in the autocratic state. Thus, Pushkin seems to suggest, the creative imagination may yield to political reality on the historical plane—Peter's city will remain standing long after Evgenii's fleeting moment of poetic inspiration has passed. Yet, at the same time, the artistic act—intangible though its fruits may be—has the power to transform, to "displace" the matter of the historical world. In the confrontation between poet and tsar, the poet emerges victorious in the invisible space of the mind.

Let me conclude by reiterating that, hardly surprisingly, both Pushkin and Irving address in what are among their most enduring works the forces that shaped and circumscribed their own careers as writers, standing at the beginning of the emergence of their national literatures on the world stage, haunted by the specter of the overtowering legacy of the western European cultural past. Clearly the threats posed to literature by their respective cultures were different, as history has generously demonstrated. Equally clearly, Pushkin's knowledge of America was limited and his attitude toward the new democracy, as he would express it several years after completing *The Bronze Horseman* and only shortly before his death, mixed grudging admiration with distinct hostility. Yet in Irving, it would seem, he found a kindred spirit, or, perhaps more to the point, a fellow writer caught, like himself, in the growing pains of a young literary culture to which he, like Pushkin after him, gave enduring shape through his works.

Source: Catharine Theimer Nepomnyashchy, "Pushkin's 'The Bronze Horseman' and Irving's 'The Legend of Sleepy Hollow': A Curious Case of Cultural Cross-Fertilization," in *Slavic Review*, Vol. 58, No. 2, Summer 1999, pp. 337–51.

SOURCES

Barta, Peter I., "The Bronze Horseman: Overview," in *Reference Guide to World Literature*, 2nd edition, edited by Lesley Henderson, St. James Press, 1995.

Bayley, John, "Pushkin's Tales," in *Partisan Review*, Vol. 59, No. 2, Spring 1992, pp. 197–215.

Gogol, Nikolai, "A Few Words about Pushkin," in *Russian Literature Triquarterly*, Vol. 10, 1974, pp. 180–83.

Gutsche, George J., "Aleksandr Sergeyevich Pushkin," in *Dictionary of Literary Biography, Volume 205: Russian Literature in the Age of Pushkin and Gogol: Poetry and Drama*, edited by Christine A. Rydel, The Gale Group, 1999, pp. 243–80.

Kahn, Andrew, *Pushkin's "The Bronze Horseman,"* Bristol Classical Press, 2006, pp. 9–11, 99–100.

NEDECO, *St. Petersburg Flood Protection Barrier Environmental Impact Assessment Study Executive Summary*, August 16, 2002, pp. 1–2.

Pushkin, Alexander, "The Bronze Horseman," in *The Bronze Horseman and Other Poems*, translated with an introduction by D. M. Thomas, Penguin Books, 1982, pp. 247–57.

Smith, Alexandra, "Pushkin's Imperial Image of St Petersburg Revisited," in *Two Hundred Years of Pushkin, Volume II: Alexander Pushkin: Myth and Monument*, edited by Robert Reid and Joe Andrew, Rodopi, 2003, pp. 117–38.

FURTHER READING

Feinstein, Elaine, *Pushkin: A Biography*, Ecco, 2000.
    This book by a British poet and novelist is one of the more readable biographies of Pushkin, detailing his turbulent personal life, love affairs, and the events that led up to the duel in which he died.

Gore, Al, *An Inconvenient Truth: The Planetary Emergency of Global Warming and What We Can Do About It*, Rodale Books, 2006.
    Many climate scientists believe that natural disasters such as hurricanes, floods, and droughts are increasing because of an excess of carbon dioxide in the atmosphere caused by man's burning of fossil fuels, a phenomenon known as global warming. Gore's book (and his film of the same name) brings together the scientific evidence for manmade climate change in an easily understandable form, and puts forward practical solutions to the problem.

Kahn, Andrew, ed., *The Cambridge Companion to Pushkin*, Cambridge University Press, 2007.
    This book provides a collection of essays by leading scholars discussing Pushkin's work in its political, literary, social, and intellectual contexts.

Massie, Suzanne, *Land of the Firebird: The Beauty of Old Russia*, Simon and Schuster, 1980.
    This popular and meticulously researched book provides an accessible and engaging overview of Russian history and culture from 987 to 1917. It has become a seminal text for anyone who wants to understand the Russian nation and people.

McQuaid, John, and Mark Schleifstein, *Path of Destruction: The Devastation of New Orleans and the Coming Age of Superstorms*, Little, Brown, 2006.
    In 2005, the United States suffered its own catastrophic flood on a par with the St. Petersburg flood of 1824. This book examines the events leading up to Hurricane Katrina and the subsequent flooding of New Orleans, and shows how a series of mistakes over 300 years culminated in this preventable disaster.

Shvidkovsky, Dmitri O., *St. Petersburg: Architecture of the Tsars*, with photographs by Alexander Orloff, translated by John Goodman, Abbeville Press, 1996.

No study of St. Petersburg is complete without an exploration of its architecture, and the best way of achieving this in the absence of a personal visit may be to study this book on the buildings constructed by the Tsars since the time of Peter I. The text is informative and the sumptuous photographs do justice to the beauty and harmony of this planned city.

Christ Climbed Down

LAWRENCE FERLINGHETTI

1958

"Christ Climbed Down," like much of Lawrence Ferlinghetti's work, is a poetry of social criticism forged in direct response to the culture it springs from. It is a poetry written in opposition to what the Beats, a group of artists (of which Ferlinghetti was a highly prominent member) called the "square" world (the mainstream), to which they counterpoised the "gone" world. Ferlinghetti's first book of poetry, published in 1955, in fact, was called *Pictures of the Gone World*.

The 1950s were a time of great social injustice in the United States. Racism, especially against African Americans, not only existed as a matter of fact, it was institutionalized and accepted, sometimes even celebrated, as a way of life. In addition to the institutionalized racism of the time, there was the continuous threat of nuclear war between the United States and the Soviet Union. In America, money, brain power, and labor were dedicated to, or, some would have argued, sacrificed to the arms race—the attempt to build more deadly weapons than the Russians.

In reaction to this climate, the Beats flaunted a freedom from conformity. They lived communally on little money, disdained employment, and worked for money only when absolutely necessary. They broke with sexual conventions and racial prejudices, and sought to liberate an inner creative and spiritual force through art, often aided by mind altering substances like alcohol,

marijuana, and other drugs. They were also, as a rule, pacifistic with regard to the Cold War and against militarism and regimentation in general.

Thus, very much rooted in this tradition, "Christ Climbed Down" employs the images of the conventional Christmas icons it satirizes and hopes to erase. Ferlinghetti does not disdain Christ or Christmas. He is instead pointing to their subversion by consumerism and materialism, a subversion that blocks the spirit from being expressed. One of Ferlinghetti's best-known and most controversial poems, "Christ Climbed Down" appears in *A Coney Island of the Mind*, a collection of Ferlinghetti's poetry, which was published in 1958 by New Directions and has not been out of print since then.

AUTHOR BIOGRAPHY

Lawrence Ferlinghetti was born in Yonkers, New York, on March 24, 1919, the youngest of five boys. His father, an Italian immigrant and auctioneer, made his fortune in real estate in New York and was providing handsomely for his family. Several months before Lawrence's birth, Charles Ferlinghetti died. Ferlinghetti's mother, Clemence, was ill equipped to support her family; she moved them to ever cheaper quarters until she was hospitalized and the family split apart. Ferlinghetti was taken in by his maternal grand uncle, Ludovico, and his wife, Emily. Theirs was a troubled marriage. When Emily left Ludovico, she took the baby with her and settled in Strasbourg in Alsace, France. Thus, French was Ferlinghetti's first language. Four years after leaving her husband, Emily returned to him and to New York. Ludovico, a language instructor at City College, taught Ferlinghetti English. When Ludovico lost his job and the family became impoverished, Emily placed Ferlinghetti, age six, in an orphanage.

Once Emily managed to obtain the position of governess for the wealthy Lawrence-Bisland family, whose forebears had founded Sarah Lawrence College, she brought Ferlinghetti to live with her at their mansion. When Emily left one day and did not return, the Lawrence-Bisland's adopted Ferlinghetti. After a while, however, he was moved again to live with another family, the Wilsons. He thrived in that environment, going to good schools and becoming an Eagle Scout. He also was a member of a

Lawrence Ferlinghetti (AP Images)

boys' gang and was once arrested for shoplifting. His scoutmaster bailed him out.

Ferlinghetti was then sent to a private boys's school, strong on discipline, in Connecticut. There he began reading literature seriously and engaging in intellectual and philosophical discussions with his schoolmates. He attended the University of North Carolina, where he worked on the student newspaper and began trying to write fiction. After his sophomore year, Ferlinghetti and a few friends bummed their way to Mexico. From there Ferlinghetti sent off stories on the social and political scene to American magazines like *Time*, but nothing was ever accepted. After college and a summer spent idyllically on an island off Maine, Ferlinghetti joined the Navy. It was 1941.

After the war, Ferlinghetti lived in New York's Greenwich Village, wrote derivative poetry and discovered the new American vernacular poets like Kenneth Patchen, e.e. cummings, William Carlos Williams, and Marianne Moore. He also worked in the mail room at *Time* magazine, and, although he continued to submit news stories, none were accepted. After tiring of his job, Ferlinghetti enrolled at Columbia University by using the G.I. Bill of Rights. There he became interested in painting as well as writing. After obtaining his M.A., Ferlinghetti left for Paris, still supported by the G.I. Bill, where he earned a doctoral degree at the Sorbonne. On one of his voyages back to Paris after a visit to New York, Ferlinghetti met Selden Kirby-Smith (Kirby), who became his wife and sometimes breadwinner as she brought in money while he wrote. In Paris, Ferlinghetti met the American poet, Kenneth Rexroth, who persuaded him to come to San Francisco, which was beginning to enjoy a literary and social renaissance, even while the United States as a whole was benighted and hobbled by the repressive conditions of loyalty oaths and Congressional anti-communist investigations.

In this climate, in 1953, with friend Peter D. Martin, Ferlinghetti began a magazine called *City Lights*, after Charlie Chaplin's film of that name. He opened the City Lights Bookstore in San Francisco and began a publishing company. City Lights Books became famous for its square shaped editions of poems by Williams, Ferlinghetti himself, and Allen Ginsberg, particularly his 1955, culturally revolutionary poem, "Howl," which Ferlinghetti successfully defended in a court trial against the United States Government's attempt to impound and ban it. Since then, Ferlinghetti has been a cultural institution, running a bookstore and a publishing house, writing poetry and drama, and actively participating in protest activities against U.S. militarism and imperialism.

Ferlinghetti's first book of poetry, *Pictures of the Gone World*, was published in 1955. This was three years before *A Coney Island of the Mind* introduced him as a poet as well as a Beat bookstore owner and publisher. Nevertheless, it was *A Coney Island of the Mind* (1958), which includes "Christ Climbed Down," that brought Ferlinghetti lasting recognition as one of the principal figures among the Beat poets. It has sold over a million copies since first being published.

Ferlinghetti has also written several plays, among them *Unfair Arguments with Existence* (1963), and *Routines* (1964). In 1970, he published *The Mexican Night*, a travel journal. In 1998, he looked back to *A Coney Island of the Mind* in a book he called *A Far Rockaway of the Heart*.

On December 8, 2006, Ferlinghetti was made *Commandeur dans L'Ordre des Arts et Lettres* by the Minister of Culture of the French

MEDIA ADAPTATIONS

- *A Coney Island of the Mind* is available as a recording on vinyl or CD from Rykodisc (1999). Ferlinghetti reads the poems from the collection, including "Christ Climbed Down," while saxophonist Dana Colley plays jazz in the background.

Republic. Later, in 2007, at the age of eighty-eight, Ferlinghetti released a book of prose called *Poetry as Insurgent Art*.

POEM SUMMARY

Stanza 1

The poem is a catalogue of variations on the theme that Christ stepped down from the cross as a protest against American culture. The first image of that culture is of "rootless Christmas trees / hung with candy canes and breakable stars." It is an image of contempt for nature—growing pines for Christmas cutting depletes the earth and suggests the rootlessness of alienation—of shallow values and a lack of enduring things. Despite the seriousness of Ferlinghetti's criticism of middle-class American culture and the shallowness of American religion, the first stanza immediately reveals that Ferlinghetti will use satire to make his points. Saying something shocking is more palatable if it is said comically or made to seem a little grotesque. The image of Christ climbing down from the cross might at first seem blasphemous, but Ferlinghetti undercuts that negative possibility by showing immediately that his poem is not about Christ as much as about America. He offers criticism of American culture in the name of Christ.

Stanza 2

The second stanza begins matter-of-factly with the lines "Christ climbed down / from His bare Tree / this year," as if reported by a newscaster.

The tone gives a ridiculous verisimilitude to the image. The action is funny and ought to be startling, but the report of it is deadpan. The cross and the Christmas tree are both related to each other and separated from each other by Ferlinghetti's identification of the cross as a "bare tree" The cross is an emblem of spiritual redemption through suffering. It is an impoverished tree, a bare tree, a tree that has been killed. Its beams of wood have been hewn from nature to become instruments of torture. It is an abused tree. Yet the paradox of the cross is that the dead tree is a tree of eternal life. The tree, as represented by the Christmas tree, is not bare, but it is rootless and dead—it is temporary. The Christmas tree, which ought to suggest life's abundance and eternal hope, is shown here as representing impoverishment and emptiness of the spirit. As Ferlinghetti established in the first section, it is gaudy and far from eternal. In the second stanza Christ runs "away to where / there were no gilded Christmas trees" or in each succeeding line, where there are no "tinsel ... tinfoil ... pink plastic ... gold ... black" and "powderblue Christmas trees." Ferlinghetti follows the catalogue of vulgar trees with the mention of clichéd accoutrements which add to the cheapening of the Christian sacrifice: "electric candles ... electric trains ... and clever cornball relatives."

Stanza 3

The third stanza is essentially more of the same, a catalogue of references to stereotypical images, now not of Christmas trees but of a soulless country composed of pushy bible salesmen driving fancy cars, of plastic, that is, ersatz, representations of the nativity scene, of mail-order catalogues, of Christmas imagery prostituted by advertising—a whiskey commercial on television with the three Wise Men endorsing the brand, for example. In each instance, Ferlinghetti is showing how sacred things are commercialized and robbed of their sanctity.

Stanza 4

The litany continues with Santa Claus and consumerism being the objects of the poet's contempt and ridicule. Santa Claus is described as a "fat handshaking stranger / in a red flannel suit / and a fake white beard." The image is boilerplate; the contempt for it arises out of several things. Familiarity in its negative sense is suggested by the "handshaking." It is familiarity, not contact or intimacy. Buried in the image of the "red flannel suit" is an allusion to a popular stereotype of the 1950s, the man in the gray flannel suit, who represented the junior executive in a corporation, an organization man whose life was regulated by his job. One of Ferlinghetti's criticisms of Santa Claus is that he is simply a version of the men who are owned by their corporations. Santa Claus, as the stanza ends, becomes a delivery man for the great department stores, his magical sleigh turned into a Volkswagen Beetle. The children are treated to such opulent gifts because of the religion of consumerism, of which they, not Christ himself, seem to be the divine incarnation. Ferlinghetti is not demeaning the story or spirit of Santa Claus but its debasement by a culture out of touch with the reality of the spirit and convinced only of the reality of material things.

Stanza 5

The next vignette shows how the spirit and the sense of wonder and longing associated with it are exploited in the garish and sentimental Christmas entertainments of show business. Ferlinghetti mocks the clichéd image of Christmas carolers by using the image of drunken carolers singing sentimental pop songs like those sung by one of the famous crooners of the time, Bing Crosby, who is mentioned in the poem. From that village image Ferlinghetti segues to the urban vulgarity of Christmas stage shows at movie palaces and actual church services that have become entertainment spectacles instead of spiritual ceremonies.

Stanza 6

In the final stanza, Christ climbs down from the cross but does not run away from things as in the previous stanzas but "stole away into / some anonymous Mary's womb again / where in the darkest night / of everybody's anonymous soul / He waits again / an unimaginable and impossibly / Immaculate Reconception." Something is missing, Ferlinghetti is arguing, from the spiritual understanding and the religious celebration that surrounds him. He calls for reconceptualizing the way spirit is understood and celebrated, punning on the possible meaning of the word "conception" which signifies both the beginning of life and the process of thinking and imagining. What will make the Reconception of Christ immaculate is not that it will be the result of a virgin birth but that it will be celebrated cleanly, cleansed of the materialism and consumerism that debase the spirit and contradict what is eternal. When Ferlinghetti says "the very craziest of Second Comings," he is using crazy not to mean insane but the way it is used to mean something out of the ordinary, at odds with how things are but better. Something crazy is something able to dislocate fustian attitudes.

THEMES

An Alternative World Vision
Although "Christ Climbed Down" presents a picture of a spiritually corrupt world governed by vulgarity, materialism, and conspicuous consumption; a world of many-colored Christmas trees, high-powered salesmen, mail-order religion, and intoxication rather than exaltation; its theme implies that there is an alternative vision possible. It imagines an "Immaculate Reconception" that will supersede the original birth of Christ, called the Immaculate Conception because it was a virgin birth. The reconception is not only a new birth or another birth, but a new idea of Christ, a new conception of the godhead. It will be immaculate, without a taint, because it will be without a taint of the influences Ferlinghetti has unrolled in the poem. Consequently, the implicit theme of the poem is a call for a human revolution in values which will transcend the base materialism and vulgarity Ferlinghetti describes. This change will alter the human attitude towards Christ as it is manifest in the celebration of Christ's birth. That will be the immaculate reconception. It will also signal Christ's second coming. The second coming is the awaited return of the Messiah. When Ferlinghetti describes it as "the very craziest / of Second Comings," the word "craziest" suggests an event unlike the events he described in the poem, an event that both subverts what is and replaces it with something that is sacred.

Consumerism
Nearly all the things that Christ runs away from are consumer products. They are examples of vulgar conspicuous consumption, whether they are the variously designed Christmas trees, the Bible salesman's two tone cadillac, the glad handing department store Santas, or the pageant at the Radio City Music Hall. The culture being celebrated is the culture of consumption, not the religion of sacrificing oneself for the good of

TOPICS FOR FURTHER STUDY

- Write a dialogue in which a rebellious person and a person who believes in strictly conforming to the values of society discuss the virtues of their positions and the problems with their opponent's position. Give them specific social issues to talk about to illustrate why they believe what they do. With a partner, perform this dialogue for the class.

- Research the Beat Generation and present a report to your class describing who they were, what they did, how they lived, and what the times were like in which they flourished.

- Research the growth and development of Christmas as a holiday in the United States. In your report, focus on how it was celebrated throughout the nation's history. Discuss the customs and traditions that have been associated with it. Has the tree always been a part of the celebration? What about Santa Claus? When did the intense commercialization of Christmas begin? How has Christmas been used in literature?

- Perhaps the most famous Christmas story is Charles Dickens's *A Christmas Carol*, and the most popular Christmas movie is Frank Capra's *It's A Wonderful Life*. Comparing and contrasting these two works and Ferlinghetti's "Christ Climbed Down," write an essay discussing how the novelist, the filmmaker, and the poet understand the meaning of Christmas and use Christmas in their analysis or criticism of social customs and institutions.

others. Christ, then, the quintessential sacrificial figure, the Lamb of God, is, by definition, excluded from the Christmas celebration of His birth in the form Ferlinghetti is describing it, and reasonably gets down from the cross to try again.

Debasement and Corruption
The vulgarity of the way Christmas is celebrated is emblematic in the poem of the debasement of human and spiritual values. Ritual and

solemnity are corrupted and become vulgar displays as the various Christmas trees, the caroling and the stage show are drawn to be. The purity of a "White" is transformed into the sleaze of a "tight" Christmas.

Hypocrisy

Implicitly, the theme of hypocrisy threads through "Christ Climbed Down." While the pretense is that the birth of Christ is being celebrated, the reality Ferlinghetti is trying to show is otherwise. Consumption and wealth are being celebrated in honor of a spiritual force—who decreed that it is easier for a camel to fit through the eye of a needle than for a rich person to gain entrance to paradise, and one of whose disciples argued that cupidity or covetousness lies at the root of evil.

Withdrawal

In Ferlinghetti's understanding of him, Christ disapproves of American culture in exactly the same way Ferlinghetti does. Christ's response to the culture he is conceived as condemning is to withdraw from it, to remove himself from the cross and seek a new life different from the one represented by gaudy Christmas trees, materialism, and vulgar celebrations. It is a nonviolent response. In the poem, Christ is not only used as the vehicle for Feringhetti's criticism of America but as an actual surrogate for the poet who symbolically acts as the poet in fact has acted in real life. Ferlinghetti withdrew from the mainstream American society, renounced militarism, renounced employment in corporate America. He withdrew, that is, from the world as it was and sought a reconception. He designed another world: opening an exclusively paperback bookstore before paperbacks became popular; writing poetry that was unlike the academic, hermetic poetry of his time; founding a small press that was not in business to make money but to make books; and associating with people who were artists and bohemians, anarchists and pacifists, who lived on the margins of society and were attempting to invent a new culture and to reconceive themselves.

STYLE

Repetition

Each of the six stanzas of "Christ Climbed Down," except the last one, begin with the same four lines. The sixth stanza repeats the three first lines and varies the fourth. That minimal variation gives the poem a sense of movement. This sense of movement is particularly important because the primary structural feature of the poem is repetition rather than development.

Polysyndeton

Polysyndeton signifies a repetition of the word "and." In "Christ Climbed Down" roughly one fourth of the lines begin with "and." The most concentrated example is in the second stanza's litany of kinds of Christmas trees. The effect is to give the piece a rhythmic sense of forward thrust through a build up of examples, where each example must top the previous one in absurdity or vulgarity.

Satire

"Christ Climbed Down" is a satire of how Christmas is celebrated and of the values that govern society at the time of its composition, the mid-1950s. It is intent on making a mockery of what is acceptable practice with the purpose of eliminating that practice through the implicit criticism that resides in satire, of making it unacceptable by showing it to be ridiculous.

Colloquial Speech

At a time when poetry was defined by its difficulty, when obscurity could be seen as a mark of profundity, and when formal and metrical skills marked the quality of a poet as a poet, "Christ Climbed Down" flaunts all these criteria. The language of the poem is colloquial and sometimes even uses slang. Expressions like "ran away," "covered the territory," complete with "parcel post," "televised," "went around passing himself off as," "some sort of," and "craziest" govern the diction of "Christ Climbed Down."

Cultural References

Rather than being stuffed with learned allusions and literary references, "Christ Climbed Down" uses common and familiar cultural references available to all of Ferlinghetti's readers, regardless of their level of education. In order to understand the poem, all a reader need know is the popular culture of the time, which, even if it requires some footnotes for twenty-first century readers, was entirely accessible to readers in its own time.

COMPARE
&
CONTRAST

- **1950s:** Beat poets meet in cellar clubs and read their poetry (commonly known as spoken word and believed to be a predecessor to rap) with jazz accompaniment. Their audiences and venues are usually small.

  Today: Rappers and hip-hop artists perform their rhymes to mass audiences in concerts and through mass distribution of their soundtracks.

- **1950s:** Critics of American consumer society complain of the commercialization of Christmas.

  Today: Christmas has become even more commercialized, and some advocates of "tradi-

tional values" fear that Christmas has become secularized and is treated like a multicultural, seasonal celebration rather than a Christian holiday.

- **1950s:** Televisions, carrying at most seven channels, are introduced into the home and change the way people live. Televisions are large, clunky machines usually housed in a table-topped wooden console.

  Today: There are hundreds of television channels and televisions are either portable or boast immense flat screens. Computers and cell phones can also display television shows.

HISTORICAL CONTEXT

The Advent of Television

The force of television in the 1950s as a determiner of social values and, as an instrument of cultural homogenization, is difficult to exaggerate. Although prototypes of television were on display in New York City at the 1939 World's Fair, it was not until a few years after World War II that television was introduced into the American home where it soon became a dominant feature of family life, a primary fashioner of individual consciousness, and a powerful influence on social values and habits. Besides programming, television brought entertaining advertising in the form of commercials into the home. Poets like Ferlinghetti and the Beats lived and wrote impelled by a desire to offer an alternative to mainstream culture and to weaken the burgeoning mass conformist and consumerist culture of television.

Advertising

Although advertising and public relations preceded and outlasted the 1950s as a powerful force in the American economy, culture, and politics, advertising achieved a social prestige in

the 1950s that it had not had previously. Often referred to as "Madison Avenue" because of the New York City street where a number of advertising agencies were located, advertising became the fundamental mode of social communication. Glamorized in the mainstream of society, advertising and careers in advertising were vilified by social critics like the Beats. Much of "Christ Climbed Down" is dedicated to mocking advertising.

The Beats

The original Beats were a group of friends, primarily writers, including Allen Ginsburg, Jack Kerouack, William Burroughs, Lucien Carr, and Neal Cassady, who either attended or hung around Columbia University in New York City in the 1940s, both during and after World War II. They were inspired by their reading of literature and especially by the poetry of the French Symbolist Arthur Rimbaud (1854–1891), by the radical politics of the 1930s, by the experiments of painters like Jackson Pollack, and by their own sense of disaffection from their contemporary culture, which they found repressive, constraining, and hostile to experience. They cherished spontaneity and the sanctity of individual vision and desire in both life and art. They sought to transcend the racial and sexual prejudices that governed how people lived, and they sought to live as much as possible outside the money economy of conspicuous consumption and corporate employment.

Another similarly alienated and influential group of writers and intellectuals was forming around the same time in San Francisco, centered around the poet Kenneth Rexroth and the newly formed Pacifica radio station KPFA, begun by Lou Hill and a group of people whose politics were defined by their anarchism and pacifism. Ferlinghetti was among them. The opening of City Lights Bookstore by Ferlinghetti gave writers and readers a place to congregate. Ferlinghetti forming his press gave writers from San Francisco and New York a place to publish their work. The existence of the store and the press, as well as the tireless public relations work Allen Ginsberg carried on, turned the small literary movement into a national phenomenon called the Beat Generation. The popularity of Ginsberg's 1956 poem, "Howl," and of Kerouack's novel *On the Road*, written in 1952 and published in 1957, also played a large part in bringing the group to prominence.

The term "Beat" is thought to have been introduced by the small-time hood and junky, Herbert Huncke, whom Burroughs met in Times Square in the 1940s. Kerouack picked up the term, and used it to suggest the sense of beatific or blessed, as well as beaten. On November 16, 1952, the writer John Clellon Holmes used the phrase in an article, "This Is the Beat Generation" published in the *New York Times Magazine*. The Beat style, wearing black, being scruffy, playing bongo drums, smoking marijuana, disdaining mainstream society and its values, caught on among high school and college students across the country by the late 1950s.

HUAC and McCarthyism

During the first half of the 1950s, the United States Government carried out investigations into people's political beliefs and political associations. In the House of Representatives such an investigation was carried on by the House Committee on Un-American Activities, or HUAC. The committee had subpoena power and the power to order witnesses to jail if their answers to the committee members' questions did not satisfy the committee. From the floor

of the Senate, the junior senator from Wisconsin, Joe McCarthy, accused a number of people in the government itself and in the Army's chain of command of being communists or sympathizers with communism. McCarthy's influence was so great that he gave his name to an era. The early 1950s are called the McCarthy era. Entertainers were banned from performing, schoolteachers lost their jobs, and the general cultural tone was homogenous and conformist. In opposition to this social context, Beat writers like Ferlinghetti emerged.

Packaging

With the proliferation of supermarkets replacing small grocery stores, and the merchandising of prepackaged goods rather than fresh goods, as well as the increased importance of brand names that came about because of the spread of advertising on television, the package itself became the commodity. People were taught to purchase the package as much as the product that was being packaged. As in "Christ Climbed Down," image became more important than actuality.

The Trial of "Howl" for Obscenity

As a publisher, too, Ferlinghetti played an important role in insuring freedom of the press. He was at the center of the trial in which the United States Government attempted to prevent the distribution of Allen Ginsberg's poem "Howl," which Ferlinghetti had published in 1956 as Number Four in his Pocket Poets Series. For reasons of economy, Ferlinghetti had Howl printed in England. The first printing of *Howl* passed through customs in October 1956. In March 1957, the second printing was confiscated. On April 3, the American Civil Liberties Union challenged the legality of the seizure. On May 19, the *San Francisco Chronicle* gave Ferlinghetti a column in the paper to write in defense of the poem. On May 29, the U.S. Attorney in San Francisco released the confiscated copies of "Howl" after he was advised by a Washington, DC, customs official not to take action against *the book*. But that was not the end. On May 21, a week before the second printing was released by customs, two plainclothes policemen bought a copy of *Howl* at the City Lights Bookstore. Afterwards, Ferlinghetti and the clerk at City Lights, who sold the book to the undercover policemen, were arrested. They faced six months in jail and five hundred dollar fines. Their trial began on August 22, 1957. It drew a great deal of media attention. In October,

Judge Clayton W. Horn, a Sunday school Bible teacher, ruled in favor of the poem. Ferlinghetti had effectively defeated the attempt by the United States Government at censoring not just a poem but at inhibiting what was to become a culture-changing event.

CRITICAL OVERVIEW

According to critic James A. Butler, in his article in *Renascence* magazine, Ferlinghetti was quoted in *Poetry* magazine in November 1958 as saying, "I have been working toward a kind of *street poetry* ... to get poetry out of the inner esthetic sanctum and out of the classroom into the street." Ferlinghetti adds: "The printing press has made poetry so silent that we've forgotten the power of poetry as oral messages. The sound of the street-singer and the Salvation Army speaker is not to be scorned." It is probably for just this reason that, as Larry Smith wrote in a 1995 review of *Pictures of the Gone World* in the *Small Press Review*: "Ferlinghetti has never received his due as a poet." Nevertheless, Ferlinghetti's poetry is appreciated by a vast audience of readers who have kept *A Coney Island of the Mind* in print since it was first published in 1958.

Ferlinghetti's poetry is also highly regarded by many of the poets who were his contemporaries. Barry Silesky, Ferlinghetti's biographer and author of *Ferlinghetti: The Artist in His Time*, quotes the poet Robert Creeley: "His poetry is ... what [Robert] Frost always claims to have written. ... It's a very subtle commonness of address, that makes everyone feel that they're not threatened by what he has to say. ... He's also capable of an extraordinarily warm and terrific humor." Silesky himself notes that "the often overt political attitudes in Ferlinghetti's poems ... while contributing to the poems' popularity, are at the same time ... partly responsible for the generally poor treatment he's received at the hands of critics." The poet Allen Ginsberg, whose work Ferlinghetti's City Lights Press published over the span of Ginsberg's career, was good friends with Ferlinghetti, and he told Silesky that much of Ferlinghetti's poetry "depended on ... witty references, the paraphrases and puns, and a sort of melodic cello feeling ... but not enough pictorial" detail. Silesky also cites the San Francisco poet Michael McClure's statement that

Painting of Jesus on the cross (© *Visual Arts Library* (*London*) | *Alamy*)

Ferlinghetti's "influence has been primarily in initiating an enormous audience into poetry" on account of the accessibility and surface clarity of his poetry. The poet Anne Waldman confirms this, Silesky reports, by citing her own experience of reading "Christ Climbed Down": "I distinctly remember reading aloud 'Christ Climbed Down' ... Ferlinghetti's poem struck home. It had the litany-like cadence of formal church litany, it had a hypnotic quality, it was also outrageous and somewhat brave." What Ferlinghetti is most celebrated for, Silesky quotes the critic Ralph Mills as saying, is the "exhilarating ... sense of *openness* that came from his poems on the page—a visual freedom that went along with the directness of speech."

No account of Ferlinghetti's significance to the renaissance in American poetry in the 1950s is complete without recognizing his importance not only as a poet but as a publisher. While many of Ferlinghetti's own books, like *A Coney Island of the Mind*, were published by the avant-garde New York City-based press, New Directions, a host of poets ranging from William Carlos Williams to Gregory Corso, and including Allen Ginsberg, were published by Ferlinghetti's own San Francisco-based press, City Lights Books. Ferlinghetti's idea was to make handsome, inexpensive pamphlet-like books of poetry that could be easily carried around. In addition, Ferlinghetti published poets who would have otherwise gone unpublished because Ferlinghetti saw his press as functioning outside the mainstream, and while he did not have the resources that bigger presses had in order to advertise his writers, his press gained a cachet among those in the know.

CRITICISM

Neil Heims

Heims is a writer and teacher living in Paris. In the following essay on "Christ Climbed Down," he discusses Ferlinghetti's use of common speech in his poetry.

What Ferlinghetti wrote in *A Coney Island of the Mind* in 1958, including the poem "Christ Climbed Down," was something new. It was not what poetry had been in the twentieth century until then. Poetry that was respected as poetry was difficult and elusive. It was poetry of hidden meanings, learned allusions, and distance from the object of its discourse. It was poetry that might just as easily exist in a void as in a social context. Modern poetry, Ferlinghetti wrote in 2001:

> has suffered from a kind of exhausted or "defeated" romanticism. We heard it in the 1920s in T. S. Eliot's *Waste Land* (especially in "The Love Song of J. Alfred Prufrock"), in Ezra Pound's *Cantos* that couldn't possibly be sung [a *canto* in Italian is a song] and in the increasing stoicism, if not cynicism, of many who came of age during the war or returned from it with radically changed perspectives. . . . Politically, it all started with the disillusionment of intellectuals with the Communist dream in the 1930s . . . In the postwar years, this led to increasing resistance to commitment of any kind, in literature as well as in politics. And it was a part of a growing alienation of artists and writers from mainstream society.

Ferlinghetti and those who thought like him about poetry, Allen Ginsberg and Gregory Corso, for example, wrote with a conscious opposition to the intellectual, academic, disembodied, and

WHAT DO I READ NEXT?

- Edgar Z. Friedenberg's *The Vanishing Adolescent* (1959) is a study of adolescent culture and rebellion in the context of the American social and economic institutions of the 1950s.

- Allen Ginsberg's poem "A Supermarket in California," first published in 1956 by Ferlinghetti along with Ginsberg's revolutionary poem, "Howl," in *The Pocket Poets Series, Number Four* combines a meditation on what it is to be a poet within the context of American consumer culture as exemplified by a supermarket.

- Jack Kerouac's novel *On the Road*, written in 1951 and published in 1957, aside from Allen Ginsberg's "Howl" and Ferlinghetti's *A Coney Island of the Mind*, is one of the defining works of Beat literature.

- "Every One of the Cleaning Women" is the last poem in the 2001 collection *Love and Politics*. Written by Judith Malina, a cofounder, with Julian Beck, of The Living Theater, it juxtaposes the youthful dreams of women workers and the life that economic necessity forced upon them with the poet's own life as a bohemian radical. Malina brings to the poem the common diction and the common concerns that recur in the kind of poetry Ferlinghetti wrote, as well as the radical social consciousness that he presents in terms of everyday experience.

- J. D. Salinger's classic coming-of-age novel, *The Catcher in the Rye* (1951), depicts the breakdown of a boy caught in a conflict between his idealism and the materialism of post-war American culture.

remote poetry of the time. They strove for immediacy and sensation and for a quality that might be called down-to-earth in their poetry. They wanted their poetry to swing, to be lyrical and committed, engaged in a cultural overthrow of what they saw

"'CHRIST CLIMBED DOWN' CONTAINS WITHIN IT THE ESSENTIAL MOTIFS OF THE BEAT SENSIBILITY. IT IS WRITTEN IN THE COMMON LANGUAGE, NOT IN WHAT THE BEATS WOULD CONSIDER THE ELITE JARGON THAT HAD CHARACTERIZED THE POETRY AROUND THEM."

as a spirit-killing culture run in the interest of vulgar materialism and which spawned and supported injustice, nationalism and war. They wanted to make a poetry that did not ignore the body and that unshackled the mind, as they saw it, from dull conformity to receive ideas and to see ideas and beliefs spread throughout and by the newly burgeoning mass media of television and news magazines.

Rather than a poetry defined by delicate indirection and elevated speech, the poets who came to be called the Beat poets wrote a poetry defined by shouting or repetition and colloquial speech, the speech of the everyday world, including obscene speech. They also incorporated, as Ferlinghetti does in "Christ Climbed Down," the kind of speech being broadcast on television and often devised by public relations and advertising firms on Madison Avenue. They took that kind of language, which could be used for satiric or sarcastic effect, and put it beside the language of the street, speech of anguish and violence, funny speech, or speech of spirit-crushing vacuity. Because polite society was seen as the source of misery and hypocrisy, poets like Ferlinghetti and the Beats used impolite speech and were unafraid of vulgarity or obscenity.

The words that came from television and the street and from daily, down-to-earth experience constituted not only a different language for poetry from the one poets were writing but also asserted a different content from the usual content of poetry after World War II. It was a poetry that was concerned with immediate situations, with wars, with continuously generated fear of a Soviet and a Chinese menace, with militarism, with the daily experiences imposed and denied by the culture. It was a poetry immersed in sociology and mystical enlightenment. It attempted to give voice and expression to the alienated

internal experience of the self, whether conforming or rebelling.

Decorum, keeping up appearances, reflecting an uncomplaining cheerfulness in demeanor and behavior were the ideals that shaped the rather homogenous American culture of the 1950s. Against this the Beat poets wrote their poetry. "Christ Climbed Down" contains within it the essential motifs of the Beat sensibility. It is written in the common language, not in what the Beats would consider the elite jargon that had characterized the poetry around them. Ferlinghetti introduced into the verbal landscape of the poem words like "candycanes," "pink plastic," "tinfoil," "powderblue," "cornball," "two-tone Cadillacs," "Sears Roebuck," "parcel post," "special delivery" (with its knowing pun on delivery, as in birth), "televised," "went around passing himself off," "Volkswagon," "jinglebell heaven," and "craziest." These are all words that could be heard on radio and television or in popular songs or read in the newspapers and mass-circulation magazines. They had not been the words with which poets had been making poetry. The use of such words for Ferlinghetti, as well as conveying the actual subject of a poem, constituted the dramatic matter of the poem. Such defilement of poetry in "Christ Climbed Down" is occurring in a poem that has taken as its subject the defilement of Christmas by commercial interests. But to the poet, his use of language is not a defilement but a gesture towards restoring poetry to the broad mass of people and restoring social existence and relevance to poetry.

The subject of "Christ Climbed Down" is its social project: exposing the subversion of the spirit accomplished through the practice of consumption. The images used to represent that subject and express its conflict are common cultural images, images of various kinds of Christmas trees as garish negations of the cross, which is described as a bare tree. A bare tree is a fitting image for the dolorous death that the cross represents. But Christmas is not the story of Christ's death. It is the story of the God's birth. The trees and other cultural artifacts that Ferlinghetti assembles in the poem are not signs of birth but of death-in-life, of death—since they are rootless—masquerading as life—since they are so gaudily adorned. Consequently, Christ climbs down from the cross, the true tree, bare and dead, in protest against the false celebration of a misbegotten birth in search of a new birth story and the elements with which to construct that new birth story. He hopes to dismantle the corrupt imagery of consumerism and commercialism.

The main rhetorical strategy of "Christ Climbed Down" is repetition. It is a simple structural form that was popular among poets of the Beat generation. It links elements together in a long chain. Formally such a poem is closer to hypnotic incantation than carefully constructed metrical verse. The poem, rather than constructing speech, reproduces and pours forth common speech. Ferlinghetti's lines are held together by the linking repetition of "Christ climbed down / from His bare tree / this year / and ran away to where." And then it is like a game to fill in the blanks. It allows an exercise in unfettered imagination, free to express itself as it will as long as it stays within the broadly drawn boundaries of the poem's subject. The lines themselves that follow in "Christ Climbed Down" are actually emphatic prose broken up to look like the verse of poetry. There is something naïvely democratic about this. The form of the poem proclaims that making poetry is a possibility open to everyone. It is not the musical skill of metrics or a Homeric capacity for metaphor and simile that makes a poet. It is only swinging with the beat, drawing on the common language, laying down image clusters, and having a connection with how we actually live that the poet wants to say something about. In a sense, a poem like "Christ Climbed Down" is a precursor to rap, except that some rap shows a verbal dexterity, felicity, and obscenity, as well as a rhyming ingenuity and metric complexity more challenging and complex than Ferlinghetti's rather gentle screed. But in the late 1950s, what seems tame now was, inside the culture of the time, unsettling.

Readers who are familiar only with "Christ Climbed Down," as representative of Ferlinghetti's stance and diction as it is, are missing one of the essential qualities of Ferlinghetti's poetic voice. "Christ Climbed Down" is a hip and funny poem, a routine full of one-liners, gags drawn from the mass culture of its time. But what is just as characteristic of Ferlinghetti as his punning and social satire is his lyricism. This quality is evident in the poem in *A Coney Island of the Mind* that directly follows "Christ Climbed Down." Although "The Long Street" also is full of social satire and cultural criticism, to "deserts of advertising men" and "brittle housewives / sheathed in nylon snobberies," it also reveals the long breath of common speech broken up into small line segments in graceful, dancing turns decorated with rhyme and repetition: "The long street / which is the street of the world / passes around the world / filled with all the people of the world / not to mention all the voices / of all the people / that ever existed / Lovers and weepers / virgins and sleepers."

The lyricism that is an essential quality of Ferlinghetti's rhythm is one of the characteristics that tempers, but does not diminish, his satiric social criticism. "Christ climbed down / from his bare Tree / this year / and ran away to where," although repeated, is far from strident. The subtle slant rhyme (a slight rhyme that is not exact) of "bare," "year," and "where" along with the near baby talk creates a gentle and friendly environment for the put-down that the poem essentially is. Ferlinghetti's lyrical power also deepens the experience of his poetry because lyricism imitates a rhythm that transcends the rhythm of momentary experience and suggests something eternally ongoing.

Indeed, he has moved away from the passing delights of appetite to a timeless lament for its transience. Inside the context of that realization, the burden of spiritual responsibility revealed in "Christ Climbed Down" becomes more deeply meaningful than social critique and suggests the hidden dimension of what it entails to be alive, to be connected to the earth, not alienated from it by cultural constructs that deny both the transience and the immortality that shape veritable human consciousness.

Source: Neil Heims, Critical Essay on "Christ Climbed Down," in *Poetry for Students*, Gale, Cengage Learning, 2008.

James A. Butler

In the following article, Butler presents a critical overview of A Coney Island of the Mind *and argues that Ferlinghetti's poetry transcends the Beat movement.*

The public first began to suspect Lawrence Ferlinghetti was a dirty old man in 1955, when he published through his own City Lights Press his poetic *Pictures of the Gone World.* This first volume identified Ferlinghetti with the "Beat Generation Poets"—Allen Ginsberg, Jack Kerouac, Gregory Corso, and others—none of whom a girl could comfortably bring home to

IT IS TEMPTING TO MERELY CATEGORIZE FER-
LINGHETTI AS A BUSH-LEAGUE SICK POET OF A SICK
POETIC MOVEMENT, BUT SEVERAL FACTORS MAKE THIS
POET WORTHY OF CONSIDERATION."

meet the family. The public's dirty-old-man sus-
picions were heightened when Ferlinghetti was
tried in a 1957 obscenity case for publishing
Ginsberg's "Howl." Finally, Ferlinghetti's fame
for filthiness was assured by a 1965 *Time* article
describing a "happening" at the American Students and Artists Center in Montparnasse: "Beat
Poet Lawrence Ferlinghetti intoned his latest
work while a naked couple made love vertically
in a burlap bag, black light playing on their
shoulders."

It is tempting to merely categorize Ferlinghetti as a bush-league sick poet of a sick poetic
movement, but several factors make this poet
worthy of consideration. His major work, *A
Coney Island of the Mind* (1958), is now in its
twelfth printing and has sold 130,000 copies to
rank near the top of contemporary poetic best-
sellers. In addition, *Coney Island* was received as
"highly readable and often very funny" by *The
New York Times* and as having "something of
the importance 'The Waste Land' had in 1922,"
(*Library Journal*). Finally, if a man may be
known by the company he keeps, it is significant
that the 1965 Spoleto Festival of Two Worlds
presented poetry readings by Russia's Yevgeny
Yevtushenko, Stephen Spender, Ezra Pound,
and Lawrence Ferlinghetti.

In the light of Ferlinghetti's popularity, it is
necessary for the critic to determine whether the
poet is a best-selling one because of his somewhat scandalous vocabulary and somewhat
more scandalous activities, or whether there is
intrinsic value in the poetry. The method of
this paper is to first develop an evolving understanding of the poetic devices of Ferlinghetti by
examining selected instances. The poet's philosophy of a "street poetry" will next be discussed to
determine whether Ferlinghetti accomplishes his
end. After the above considerations, an attempt

will be made to reconcile the dirty old man and
the poet.

The first Ferlinghetti poem to be analyzed is
from *Coney Island* (No. 25):

Cast up
   the heart flops over
      gasping 'Love'
a foolish fish which tries to draw
   its breath from flesh of air
And no one there to hear its death
      among the sad bushes
   where the world rushes by
      in a blather of asphalt and delay

Perhaps the first thing that strikes the reader
in the above poem by Ferlinghetti is the absence
of traditional poetic devices: rhyme, meter, uniform left-hand margin. Ferlinghetti's free verse
is, of course, indebted to such prosodic pioneers
as Walt Whitman and especially William Carlos
Williams:

IT IS MYSELF,
   not the poor beast lying there
      yelping with pain
   that brings me to myself with a start—
      as at the explosion
   of a bomb, a bomb that has laid
   all the world waste,

"To a Dog Injured in the Street" (W. C.
Williams)

In addition to being influenced by Williams'
free verse, Ferlinghetti also shows in other
poems that he has absorbed some of the visual
effects of Williams; e.g., the line visually accen-
tuating the meaning:

And the way the bell-hop runs downstairs:
   ta tuck a
      ta tuck a
         ta tuck a
            ta tuck a
               ta tuck a

(*Paterson*—W. C. Williams)

like
   a
      ball
         bounced
down steps

(*Coney Island*, No. 22)

But these influences on Ferlinghetti's prosody, although important, are not dominant; it is
rather the "Projective Verse" of Charles Olson

that has not only influenced Ferlinghetti, but has become the new poetics of the new poetry.

Charles Olson's "Projective Verse" first appeared in *Poetry New York* of November 3, 1950. Summary of this complex essay is difficult, but basically Olson says that "form is never more than an extension of content." The syllable, not the foot or meter, is the building block of poetry. The syllables thus do not combine into a foot, but into a line. The length of this line comes only from "the *breathing* of the man who writes at the moment he writes." Meter and rhyme are therefore unimportant in the line length; the line is determined by those places in which the poet takes, and wants the reader to take, a breath. Ferlinghetti has much the same philosophy of sound:

> The printing press has made poetry so silent
> that we've
> forgotten the power of poetry as oral mes-
> sages. The
> sound of the streetsinger and the Salvation
> Army speaker
> is not to be scorned . . .

The application of the "projective verse" theory is evident in the first poem selected for analysis. The breathing stops arc so placed as to emphasize various lines. The first line, for example, "Cast up," receives very strong stress from the breath taken both before and after. Other short lines also receive stress through breathing: "gasping 'Love'," and "among the sad bushes." On the other hand, the longer lines pound quickly, partly because of the strong, regular, iambic rhythm and partly because of the harsh, spitting *t*'s, *b*'s, *d*'s and *f*s:

> a *f*oolish *f*ish which *t*ries *t*o *d*raw
> i*ts* brea*th* *fr*om *f*lesh *o*f air

Throughout the poem, the line length and breathing are not used randomly as may first appear, but to accentuate the meaning.

Ferlinghetti does not, in spite of unconventional metrics, operate independently of poetic tradition. His entire poem is, of course, a metaphor comparing a fish out of water with a heart in love. The lines quoted immediately above represent a highly sophisticated use of metaphor: a heart in love that tries to exist from flesh is as helpless as a fish gasping for air. On the audio level, Ferlinghetti in this poem shows his competence at matching sound and meaning. One example of this skill is the explosive sounds (*t*'s, *b*'s, *d*'s, and *f*s) used in the line above which through the explosion of sound, then unstressed syllable, then another explosion suggest breathlessness and gasping for air. "Gasping" in 1.3 is in itself onomatopoetic. The only true rhyme in the poem, the feminine rhyme of bushes and rushes, draws our attention to the pun on the meaning of rushes as plants. Finally, the last line plays with the *a* sound in a manner reminiscent of the slant rhymes of Yeats, Auden, Thomas, and Owen. The *a*'s are all short vowels and move quickly to suggest the speed of which the poet speaks until the last, long *a* of "delay" slows the tempo:

> in *a* bl*a*ther of *a*sphalt and del*a*y.

We have seen in this poem how Ferlinghetti works with a modern prosody based on Whitman, Williams, and Olson. The poet is, in addition, a master of audio effects and in matching sound and meaning. Ferlinghetti also seems to delight in the pun by deliberately drawing attention to it. The following poem (*Coney Island*— No. 14) should reinforce those conclusions and add others:

> Don't let that horse
>   eat that violin
>   cried Chagall's mother
>   But he
>   kept right on
>   painting
> And became famous
> And kept on painting
>   The Horse With Violin In Mouth
> And when he finally finished it
> he jumped up upon the horse
>   and rode away
>   waving the violin
> And then with a low bow gave it
> to the first naked nude he ran across
> And there were no strings
>   attached

Here Ferlinghetti is seen in a more playful vein than in the previous selection. The projective verse is again used for startling emphasis; e.g. "painting" in 1.6 and "attached" in 1.17. But the onomatopoetic use of syllable is not as prominent in this more humorous offering. The lines are kept quick-moving—in accordance with the light tone of the poem—by a majority of short vowels and short lines.

The reference by Ferlinghetti to something such as Chagall's "The Horse With Violin in Mouth" is typical of the poet. Much of

Ferlinghetti's work is predicated on the reader's familiarity with culture, both past and present. In the twenty-nine short poems of *Coney Island of the Mind*, the poet refers, directly or indirectly, to Goya, Cervantes, Thoreau, Keats, T. S. Eliot, Hieronymous Bosch, Dante, Kafka, Longfellow, Stockton ("The Lady or the Tiger?"), Cellini, Picasso, Hemingway, Shakespeare, Proust, Lorca, Nichols (*Abie's Irish Rose*), Tolstoy, Freud, and Joyce. Sometimes the entire meaning of a Ferlinghetti poem is based on the reader's ability to recognize a famous line out of context, e.g., Keats' "silent upon a peak in Darien." Obviously, this heavy reliance on cultural allusions somewhat limits Ferlinghetti's audience and will have major implications in regard to his "street poetry."

Ferlinghetti has a strong sense of humor as is evident both in this poem and in several others, notably one which describes the secular excitement of the erecting of a Saint Francis statue, with all the reporters and workers and Italians, "while no birds sang." In the Chagall poem, Ferlinghetti relies on the pun for humorous effect: "bow" meaning both a violin's bow and a bending of the body; "ran across" meaning both run under the horse's hooves and met in passing; and, "no strings attached" referring to the violin and to a gift. The linking of two synonymous words to create an enhanced meaning is also a favorite Ferlinghetti trick. In this poem, he uses "naked nude" for double emphasis; elsewhere he employs such figures as "sperm seed." By such puns and double emphases, Ferlinghetti is clearly trying to combat American semiliteracy, where all read but few stop to understand. Another method this poet uses to stop the reader in his tracks and make him go back to think is the twisting of a familiar saying so that it sounds much the same but means far more. Of several dozen examples, representative effects of this kind include the following: drugged store cowboys; cinemad matrons; unroman senators; conscientious non-objectors; [Christ hanging on the cross] looking real Petered out; My country tears of thee; I hear America singing / in the yellow pages; televised Wise Men / praised the Lord Calvert Whiskey; [Santa Claus] bearing sacks of Humble Gifts from Saks Fifth Avenue.

This second poem thus clearly reveals two more characteristics of Ferlinghetti's work: 1) The poet is heavily dependent on cultural allusions; and, 2) the poet attempts his humorous effects through puns, double emphasis, and changed clichés.

The following poem will be the last considered before turning to an analysis of Ferlinghetti's "street poetry" and an overall evaluation of the poet.

> Constantly risking absurdity
>   and death
>   whenever he performs
>   above the heads
>   of his audience
> the poet like an acrobat
>   climbs on rime
>   to a high wire of his own making
> and balancing on eyebeams
>   above a sea of faces
>   paces his way
>   to the other side of day
> performing entrechats
>   and sleight-of-foot tricks
> and other high theatrics
>   and all without mistaking
>   any thing
>   for what it may not be
>   For he's the super realist
>   who must perforce perceive
>   taut truth
> before the taking of each stance or step
> in his supposed advance
>   toward that still higher perch
> where Beauty stands and waits
>   with gravity
>   to start her death-defying leap
>   And he
>   and a little charleychaplin man
>   who may or may not catch
>   her fair eternal form
>   spreadeagled in the
> empty air
> of existence

(Coney Island—No. 15)

Like many of Ferlinghetti's poems, this one shows an eye for the commonplace. Elsewhere he speaks of "The penny candy store beyond the El / . . . jelly beans . . . / and tootsie rolls / and Oh Boy Gum," but here he compares a poet and a trapeze artist. Much of the skill of the poem is in this comparison as a detailed prose retelling should demonstrate. The poem begins with the statement that the poet, like the acrobat, risks absurdity and death "whenever he performs / *above the heads* / of his audience" (italics mine). The acrobat risks actual death because he is performing at a great height from the ground, while the poet risks literary death when he writes at a higher intellectual level than that to which his audience is accustomed. Like the acrobat, the poet climbs to the high wire to perform, but the poet climbs on rhyme. In his performance, the acrobat balances on steel I-beams, but also figuratively on the "eyebeams" of the spectators below. The poet also performs before eyebeams, the eyebeams of those reading his poems. Both the acrobat and poet do "sleight-of-foot tricks": the acrobat walking the high wire and the poet dealing with another kind of foot—iambic, trochaic, etc. The "high theatrics" of the acrobat are literally high above the ground, but the poet's actions are figuratively "high theatrics." Both the acrobat and the poet must, of necessity, perceive "taut truth" for if the acrobat's wire is not truly taut, he will fall; and if the poet does not see tightly-drawn truth, he will not succeed. This "taut truth" is necessary before the acrobat takes his "stance" (mode of standing) and before the poet takes his "stance" (intellectual or emotional attitude). The comparison continues with the acrobat waiting to catch his leaping female partner in that traditional trick of the high wire, while the poet tries to catch not a beautiful girl, but Beauty itself. Both the girl and Beauty jump and may or may not be caught by the acrobat and poet.

The mechanics of this poem again admirably enhance the meaning. The projective verse is used for heavy emphasis at crucial points (taut truth) and to visually and vocally correspond to the sense of the words:

> where Beauty stands and waits
> with gravity
> to start her death-defying leap

In these lines, the spacing suggests a sudden drop and, in addition, the excitement of the last line is metrically shown by increased speed since it is a long line coming after a shorter one. Although the metaphors of the poem are all well made, perhaps the best is the picture of the poet trying to catch Beauty as "a little charley-chaplin man". This metaphor conveys the perfect picture of a man—hands at his sides and a deadpan expression on his face—running helplessly in circles. In this poem, Ferlinghetti caught Beauty.

With some idea of Ferlinghetti's characteristics in mind, the philosophy of the poet will now be considered in order to determine whether he reaches his personally-set goals. This philosophy was quoted in *Poetry* of November, 1958:

> I have been working toward a kind of *street poetry* ... to get poetry out of the inner esthetic sanctum and out of the classroom into the street. The poet has been contemplating his navel too long, while the world walks by. The printing press has made poetry so silent that we've forgotten the power of poetry as oral messages. The sound of the street-singer and the Salvation Army speaker is not to be scorned ...

In evaluating Ferlinghetti's success, or lack of it, with poetry for all, three characteristics of "street poetry" should be considered. First, poetry for all the people should be *lively, rhythmic,* and *iterative.* The advertising jingle would be an example of those traits, as would Vachel Lindsay's successful "popular poetry":

> Booth led boldly with his big bass drum—
> (Are you washed in the blood of the Lamb?)
> The Saints smiled gravely and they said:
> "He's come."
> (Are you washed in the blood of the Lamb?)

Second, popular poetry should be *narrative* as in the ballad or in Lindsay's poem narrating General Booth entering heaven. Third, poetry for all should contain allusions *familiar* to nearly all.

Consideration of Ferlinghetti's poetry in regard to those three points shows definitely that his lines are not "street poetry." In the first place, Ferlinghetti's poetry is mostly tuneless, arhythmic, and hard to remember. Without the printing press, the heavy beat, repetitiveness, and alliteration of Lindsay's lines would make them easy to remember. In contrast, the following lines by Ferlinghetti offer little aid to memorization and are hardly likely to be on the tip of everyone's tongue:

> We squat upon the beach of love
> among Picasso mandolins struck full of
> sand
> and buried catspaws that know no sphinx
> and picnic papers
> dead crabs' claws
> and starfish prints

(*Coney Island*—No. 24)

Secondly, few of Ferlinghetti's poems have a narrative content, as the representative poems selected for analysis show. In regard to the third requirement—familiar allusions—the twenty literary and artistic references mentioned above of this paper are allusions generally specialized to the more widely-read of the populace. Indeed, if an entire poem hangs on a line from Keats or a reference to Kafka, it is not a "street poem."

There is one other trait sometimes found in popular poetry—the erotic—that leads to the consideration of Ferlinghetti as a dirty old man. As might be expected of a dirty old man, Ferlinghetti places prominently last in *Coney Island* a poem that maintains, in a style and vocabulary similar to the conclusion of *Ulysses* that all is sex and sex is all. Nevertheless, the reputation of Ferlinghetti as an erotic poet is exaggerated—only five of the twenty-nine poems of *Coney Island* have sexual themes. In spite of such description of himself as "the poet obscenely seeing," Ferlinghetti's poems do not show as a dominant trait the ribaldness that to many seems to characterize his personal life.

Turning from the dirty old man to the poet, the poems selected for analysis show that there is great intrinsic value in Mr. Ferlinghetti's lines. The poem containing the dying fish—love metaphor, for example, demonstrates the poet's capabilities with a free verse inherited from Whitman, Williams, and Olson, in addition to a stunning use of metaphor and a skillful matching of sound and meaning. On the other hand, the Chagall poem shows Ferlinghetti's humor and punning both to be delightful, without becoming strained. In the acrobat-poet poem, Ferlinghetti creates a *tour de force* in metaphor.

Thus Ferlinghetti is both dirty old man *and* poet. But the poet is far too gifted to let himself be dominated or destroyed by the dirty old man. The time has come for Ferlinghetti to abandon his "beat" themes and his "beat" vocabulary: "square-type, cool, king-cat," etc. *A Coney Island of the Mind* should be remembered as the early work of an excellent and universal poet and not as the best work of a "beat poet." The poet once wrote:

I am a social climber
climbing downward
and the descent is difficult

The *ascent* into excellence is too near for Ferlinghetti to climb downward into that morass populated by dirty old men and "beat poets."

Source: James A. Butler, "Ferlinghetti: Dirty Old Man?" in *Renascence*, Vol. 8, Spring 1996, pp. 115–23.

SOURCES

Butler, James A., "Ferlinghetti: Dirty Old Man?," in *Renascence*, Vol. 8, Spring 1966, pp. 115–23.

Carruth, Hayden, "Four New Books," in *Poetry*, November 1958, pp. 111–16.

Ferlinghetti, Lawrence, "Christ Climbed Down," in *A Coney Island of the Mind*, New Directions, 1958, pp. 69–70.

———, "The Long Street," in *A Coney Island of the Mind*, New Directions, 1958, p. 71.

———, "Toward a New Lyricism," in *Exquisite Corpse*, No. 8, 2001, http://www.corpse.org/issue_8/critiques/ferling.htm (accessed August 31, 2007).

Silesky, Barry, *Ferlinghetti: The Artist in His Time*, Warner Books, 1990, pp. 256–65.

Smith, Larry, Review of *Pictures of the Gone World*, in *Small Press Review*, Vol. 27, No. 9, September 1995, p. 12.

FURTHER READING

Allen, Donald M., *The New American Poetry: 1945–1960*, Grove Press, 1960.
   This anthology was groundbreaking when first published, not just for introducing a new generation of poets but for showing the great change those poets had brought about in poetry with regard to form, subject, and language.

Goodman, Paul, *Growing Up Absurd: Problems of Youth in the Organized System*, Vintage Books, 1960.
   A classic in its time, *Growing Up Absurd* is an analysis of the culture that Goodman argues is an unworthy environment for children. He believes that the shallowness of American culture has lead to several generational responses, which characterized juvenile delinquents, junior executives, and beatniks, each in a particular way.

Heims, Neil, *Allen Ginsberg*, Chelsea House Publishers, 2005.
   In this biography of Ginsberg, Heims presents a picture of the social, cultural, literary, and intellectual milieu in which Ginsberg and his contemporaries (like Ferlinghetti) lived and worked.

Packard, Vance, *The Hidden Persuaders*, Ig Publishing, 2007, originally published 1957.
   Packard's examination of the power of the advertising and public relations industries was a million-copy bestseller in the late 1950s.

Daddy

SYLVIA PLATH

1965

Sylvia Plath's poem "Daddy" appeared in her collection *Ariel*, which was published in 1965. Yet, the poems in the collection were written mere months before Plath's death in February 1963. These poems are some of the best examples of confessional poetry, or poetry that is extremely personal and autobiographical in nature. Indeed, in the 1970s, the publication of Plath's autobiographical novel *The Bell Jar* under her own name—it was published in England in 1963 under the pseudonym Victoria Lucas— amplified the context for "Daddy" and set the poem firmly inside Plath's life story. That poem and the book taken together made Plath an emblem of the conflicted intellectual woman simultaneously starved for and revolted by male affection. In the 1970s "Daddy" was celebrated perhaps more as a confessional anthem of female oppression, subversion, and resistance in a world dominated by male power and the power of male definition than it was celebrated as a poem.

General critical opinion indicates that the poems in *Ariel*, not just "Daddy," reveal a mastery of the craft that was often suggested but not fully realized in Plath's earlier poems. *Ariel* set Plath among the first-ranking American poets of the second half of the twentieth century. After her death, her novel, her journals, and some children's stories she wrote were published. In 2004, the version of *Ariel* as Plath had intended it, edited by her daughter, Frieda Hughes, was released by HarperCollins. In the first version,

her husband, the poet Ted Hughes, had dropped several poems, and rearranged the order in which they appeared.

AUTHOR BIOGRAPHY

Sylvia Plath was born on October 27, 1932, in Jamaica Plain, Massachusetts. Her German-born father, Otto Plath, was professor of zoology and German at Boston University and was also an expert on bees. Her Austrian-born mother, Aurelia Schober Plath, was twenty years her husband's junior. In 1934, she gave birth to Plath's brother, Warren. Six years later, just after Plath's eighth birthday, her father died of complications from a case of diabetes he had neglected to treat. Later that same year, Plath published her first poem at the age of eight in the children's section of the *Boston Herald*. Plath, who began keeping a diary when she was eleven, continued to do so until her death.

Plath was an excellent student in high school, and she was accepted by Smith College with a full scholarship funded by the American novelist Olive Higgins Prouty, in 1950. In 1953, Plath spent the summer in New York City after being chosen to be one of the college student editors of *Mademoiselle* magazine. Back at Smith for her junior year, she attempted suicide with pills but did not succeed, was hospitalized, with the financial help of Olive Prouty again, and later returned to school. She graduated from Smith *magna cum laude* in 1955. After Smith, she went to England on a Fulbright scholarship and studied at Cambridge, where she met the English poet Ted Hughes. They were married a year later, in June 1956, and Plath moved back to Massachusetts with Hughes. She taught at Smith, attended Robert Lowell's poetry seminars in Boston, and wrote. In 1959, Plath and Huges returned to England, living first in London and then in Devon. Plath suffered a miscarriage and then gave birth to two children. Her marriage to Huges went badly, as her husband took mistresses. At the time Plath wrote "Daddy," either during the last months of 1962 or the first of 1963, they were in the process of divorcing. The poem was first published in *Ariel*, posthumously, in 1965.

Indeed, "Daddy" well may be Plath's best known work, just as *Ariel* is her best known collection of poetry. Her 1960 collection, *The*

Sylvia Plath (The Library of Congress)

Colossus and Other Poems, is not considered to have the power and individuality that *Ariel* has. But her novel, *The Bell Jar* (1963), is still immensely popular.

By 1963, Plath was living in London, in a house where the great Irish poet William Butler Yeats had once lived. It was here that Plath killed herself by putting her head in the oven after having turned on the gas the morning of February 11. After her death, her reputation as a poet and a feminist icon quickly became formidable. In 1982, after the publication of her collected poems, Plath was posthumously awarded a Pulitzer Prize.

POEM SUMMARY

Stanza 1

"Daddy" begins on a note of rejection by means of the repetition of the phrase "You do not do." Uttered once, it is a statement of a fact or of an opinion. Repeated, it denotes a realization that, the poem shows, is simultaneously painful and liberating. Although the second line reveals that it is a "black shoe" that does "not do," the fact that the first line appears directly under the

MEDIA ADAPTATIONS

- There is an audio recording of Plath reading "Daddy" available on tape called *In Their Own Voices: A Century of Recorded Poetry*, edited by Rebekah Presson, and distributed by Rhino Entertainment, 1997.

poem's title pulls the reference backward to the title as well, leaving the intended, pervasive suggestion that it is the speaker's father who does "not do." With a focus on the shoe, "in which" the speaker has "lived like a foot / For thirty years, poor and white," Plath is expressing a claustrophobic condition that has haunted the narrator lifelong. Additionally, she is coloring that personal suffering with the hint of social oppression suggested by the allusion to the squalid conditions in which the poor must live and the power the color black has to overwhelm the color white.

The world she has lived in, like a black shoe, is severe, formal, confining, and constricting. She experiences herself to be more like a foot, a limb or appendage, than a person, integral unto herself. In contrast to the shoe, she is blanched, poor, devitalized. Because of the constraint of the shoe-like environment she has "Barely dar[ed] to breathe or" sneeze. Instead of saying "sneeze" Plath use the onomatopoeic "Achoo." Using the sound of the sneeze rather than the word "sneeze," Plath is able to rhyme with the "oo" sound that runs throughout the poem. It is a sound of fear and dread and of surprise and release. It reflects the conflicting emotions that have determined the speaker's life and that are addressed in the poem. The speaker needs her father and needs to be rid of that need. The need for him that haunts her is a little girl's need that has never been satisfied. Consequently, neediness has not let go of the girl, even after she has become a woman. The child inside the adult is conjured by the word "Achoo." Using the sound instead of the word suggests the child's limited

capacity for abstraction and untempered connection to immediacy. "Achoo" also suggests the German word "Achtung," Attention! Thus, it foreshadows the imagery of Nazi atrocities the speaker will introduce as metaphor for her situation. In addition, using "Achoo" for its sound quality suggests the same thing may be done to its companion rhyme "shoe." "Shoe" may suggest the onomatopoeic homonym "shoo," a word spoken along with a dismissive gesture of the wrist, meaning, go away, leave me alone, one of the characteristic themes of "Daddy"

Stanza 2

The contemplative address to the shoe in the first stanza gives way in the second to words addressed to the speaker's dead father: "Daddy, I have had to kill you." The force of the confession is tempered by the irony that, although he is dead, although she has had to break so determinedly with him that it has the force of murder, her father is alive enough in her, for her, that she still can, must, speak to him. The poem, then, is the actual and finalizing act of murder. It is the complaint against him that will sever her from him just by having been spoken. The poem, consequently, is also a defense of murder and an explanation of the necessity for murder. "You died before I had time,—" she says, without repeating the phrase, to kill you, suggesting that there might be something else beside murder which was prevented, but which, now, has been lost.

The underlying matter of the poem is autobiographical. Otto Plath died when Sylvia was eight—in the poem she says ten. It is an age when a child still needs her father, before she reaches the age when she needs to rid herself of her childish attachments in order to become available for mature ones.

The last three lines of the stanza offer contrasting images of the dead father. Two aspects or two perceptions of him are thus revealed. He is "a bag full of God," and is consequently "marble heavy" for her. He is also a one-legged cadaver. One of Otto Plath's legs was in fact amputated as a result of the diabetes that actually killed him. His intact leg is shown with a gangrenous big toe sticking out under the sheet covering his corpse. The sight of that toe to his daughter deflates—although it does not destroy—his divinity. The existence of the poem attests to that.

Stanza 3

In her description of the big toe, which is introduced as "Big as a Frisco seal," at the end of the second stanza but developed in the third, Plath introduces into the poem the method by which she can accomplish the murder. The ghastly toe becomes the opportunity for a verbal cadenza, for the exercise of poetry. The poem in this stanza is very deliberately announcing itself as a poem by the display of virtuosity in lines like "Big as a Frisco seal / And a head in the freakish Atlantic / Where it pours bean green over blue / In the waters off beautiful Nauset." The poet is asserting herself as a poet, as if saying "Look what I can do." To write like that is to grab hold of one's independence.

Nauset is a beach in Cape Cod, Massachusetts, near Plath's home. The introduction of Nauset not only enhances the scenery of the poem. It is allusive, suggesting Nausicaa, the girl in Homer's *Odyssey*. Nausicca is playing on a beach in Greece with her companions when she spots Odysseus, who has been washed up half-dead upon the beach. She rescues him and brings him to her father, in whose court he tells his story. The hint of Nausicaa's presence in "Daddy" provides a counter-image to the murderous girl, the poet who must kill her father, in the image of the savior girl who brings life back to Odysseus, a man old enough to be her father.

Following the display of poetic virtuosity, the poet returns to a straight declarative sentence: "I used to pray to recover you." "Pray" is particularly apt in the context of having to bear "a bagful of God." The last line of the stanza abandons sentence structure entirely for a kind of disgusted exclamation, dismissing her father in his mother tongue: "Ach, du," You. It is not an address but a reflection on how impossible he was.

Stanza 4

After the exclamation that ended the third stanza, the fourth begins with a halting return to syntax, but the first three lines are unable to form themselves into a sentence. "In the German tongue, in the Polish town / Scraped flat by the roller / Of wars, wars, wars." is missing a verb. "Scraped" is only a predicate adjective modifying the Polish town. What about the German tongue or war ravaged Polish town? The next line does not say. It only reveals that "the name of the town is common." That fact is then supported by two more lines of testimony from the speaker's "Polack friend." Does the demeaning term suggest her father's snobbery. Why is this important to the poem? Perhaps it indicates how difficult it is for the speaker to focus on the complexity of her relationship with her father.

Stanza 5

The fourth stanza spills over into the fifth. The speaker does not even know the specific town in Poland from which her father came, since many have the same name, and the name was German rather than in Polish. This want of knowledge is symptomatic of the entire relationship the poet had with her father. Not knowing where he came from, "I never could talk to you. / The tongue stuck in my jaw."

Stanza 6

Not talking about her father who is so unknowable to her, the poet speaks of his effect on her, of her inability to speak. The fifth stanza ended with a near cliché: her tongue stuck in her jaw when she tried to speak with him. Now she describes that blockage using imagery that has been prepared earlier through references to war and, through references to the German language and black shoes, to Nazism. Her inability to speak is expressed in the image of "a barb wire snare." That snare is represented linguistically in the repetition four times over of "ich," the German word for "I." But the line of "ichs" represents not only the metal thorns of barb wire. It gives voice to a guttural blockage and anger that constitute a prime component of the speaker's character and that lie at the bottom of this poem.

Her tongue somewhat loosened by grinding out angry "ichs," the poet begins to express that anger in images of Nazi barbarity. She "could hardly speak" to anyone she tells her father. He so invaded her consciousness that she saw him in others: "I thought every German was you." He has, in addition tainted the German language for her. She calls it "obscene"

Stanza 7

Having identified his oppressiveness, she begins to express her anger at her father in a convoluted manner, identifying herself as a victim, his victim, and calling up images of Nazi brutality, identifying herself with the recipients of violence, the Jews taken by cattle cars to extermination terminals, rather than as an agent of anger.

Stanza 8

Freely associating around German themes, the speaker segues into what momentarily seems a lyrical invocation of Germanic Austrian pastoral landscapes, the Tyrol and Vienna. But she subverts that lyricism in the next line. "The snows of the Tyrol ... /Are not very pure," and "the clear beer of Vienna / [is] not very ... true." By extension, there is something deceptive about her father's charm. The poet challenges the lie of his authority as well as asserting the power of her vulnerability. Being wounded seems to be a source of insight as she speaks of her "gypsy ancestress and my weird luck" and her pack of Tarot cards, cards that are used in divination and seeing the future.

Stanza 9

Returning from the reverie of the preceding stanzas to addressing her father directly, the speaker says she has "always been scared of" him. Rather than addressing that fear directly, Plath returns to metaphor as a means of expressing what was frightening about him without really saying anything specific. She turns her father into a stereotype or caricature, drawing him in the costume of a Nazi and defining him by means of that costume. She really says nothing specific about him when she describes him "With your Luftwaffe, your gobbledygoo. / And your neat mustache / And your Aryan eye, bright blue. / Panzer-man, panzer-man, O you." She is saying something, however, about herself in relation to him: she feels his awful power the way Jews felt the awful power of their Nazi tormentors.

Stanza 10

The Nazi imagery of the last stanzas challenges the sense of divinity that the speaker had indicated, in the second stanza, hovered around her father, but not her sense of his power. "Not God but a swastika," is the emblem she uses now to define him. The swastika becomes a huge, looming blackness that entirely blots out the sky. "Every woman adores a Fascist," the poet proceeds to assert without either connection to the preceding lines or substantiation. The line can, consequently, be conceived as a kind of self-defense, an excuse for the affection she has felt for him and apparently still does, despite her response to him as if he were a Nazi. But she does not say "I." She says "Every woman." Such generalization absolves her from being responsible for the unwanted affection to which she still

is prone. At the same time, by her continuing description of his fascist allure ("The boot in the face, the brute / Brute heart of a brute like you"), she is expressing contempt for her own womanish admiration for and her own inclination to surrender to brutality.

Stanza 11

Leaving the allusive for the actual, the speaker recalls her actual father not wearing the Nazi uniform with which she had invested him. She refers not to her own memory of him but to a picture of him. He is standing at a blackboard. He was a college teacher. Her evidence of his evil now is the fact that he had a cleft in his chin. This ordinary physical characteristic takes her, by association, to represent him as the devil because the devil is popularly pictured as having a cleft foot. Although the cleft was in his chin and not his foot, she says he is no less the devil.

Stanza 12

Her substantiation of his diabolical nature returns her to metaphor. He "Bit my pretty red heart in two," she says, apparently because, the following line suggests, he died while she was still a child. By dying he broke her heart. Her bitterness is not just the fruit of anger, it seems, but also of an unassimilated grief: "At twenty I tried to die / And get back, back, back to you. / I thought even the bones would do." The father she began to describe with loathing is actually a man she sought with longing so strong that she tried to realize the great romantic trope of attempting to join him, to meet him, in death.

Stanza 13

"But they pulled me out of the sack, / And they stuck me together with glue" she writes. Plath's suicide attempt was unsuccessful and she was treated with electroconvulsive therapy. She was stuck back together, but still stuck with her ambivalent desire for her father. She trumped those who her defeated effort to merge with her father in death with a clever piece of spite work: "I made a model of you / A man with a Meinkampf look." The stanza ends before the sentence is completed, structurally representing the thread of her life pulling through its various moments.

Stanza 14

"And a love of the rack and the screw" finishes the sentence and begins a new stanza but continues old business, although she claims to be "through." Not being able to join her father in death, she constructed a death–bearing man in life, whom she married, to whom she "said I do, I do." Because her father did not "do" she said "I do."

Stanza 15
But it was to a man whom she characterizes as a "vampire" who "drank my blood for a year," she says first but then changes the number to "seven years." Seven years is actually the amount of time Plath was married to the poet Ted Hughes at the time she wrote "Daddy." That marriage, at the time she wrote the poem, was disintegrating and, she includes her husband along with her father as one of her victims: "If I've killed one man, I've killed two." The irony is that she seems rather the victim of both of those men's denial of love. Only in the angry, love-hungry fantasy of her poem are they her victims. Marriage, although unsuccessful, perhaps just because it was unsuccessful and required a second "killing," unbound her from her father, whom she has, figuratively, roused from death. He is the one to whom she is confessing in this confessional poem. The confession made, he "can lie back now."

Stanza 16
The image of the vampire she attached to her husband reverts to her father. She addresses him as if he has been killed in the only way a vampire can be killed, with a stake through his heart. Unlike hers, which she described in stanza twelve as "pretty red" his is a "fat black heart."

The poem concludes as the speaker transposes her feelings onto a whole group of people. As before, through all the Nazi imagery, the speaker transforms the offense against her into a larger offense against an entire community of people, so weak is her ego in a reality the poem cannot change: "And the villagers never liked you / They are dancing and stamping on you. They always knew it was you." The final line "Daddy, daddy, you bastard, I'm through," is ambiguous. At first glance, it seems to be saying, I am through with you; I have exorcised you successfully, killed your hold on me. But the word "you" does not appear. It seems what she is actually doing in the last line is saying that she has finished speaking to him, finished her confession, finished the poem, succeeded in the assertion of herself accomplished by her

invocation of him. But he is still a "bastard" and his ability to keep a hold on her despite all her poetic bravado is confirmed by that angry word.

THEMES

Ambivalence
There is a fundamental contradiction at the heart of "Daddy." The poet needs to kill her father in order to liberate herself from her love for him, yet she needs to tell her father that she has killed him in order for her to satisfy that need to kill him. Thus she needs to have him alive for her in order to experience for herself his death. Killing him is, in actuality, her way of showing her anger at a need for him that she does not experience as being gratified.

Death
The theme of death, pervasive in Plath's work and in her life—*The Bell Jar* is an account of her first suicide attempt in 1953—hovers over "Daddy." It appears as the inconclusive death of the poet's father, the slaughter of the European Jews by the Nazis, the poet's own attempt at suicide, the recurring wars that have marred the landscape of history, and the poet's own need to kill her already dead father in order to obliterate his presence within her once and for all.

Purgation
Implicitly, "Daddy" is a poem of purgation, written to liberate the poet from the ghost of her relationship with her father. Purgation through an act of murdering the pollutant is the overt method of cleansing Plath speaks of in the poem, but it appears that writing the poem is in itself the real purgative action. The poet, by writing her situation and separating her psychic tangles, is attempting to achieve and enact the power to govern and define her psychic reality herself, taking the power back from her father.

Resentment
Resentment, broken down into its components, means to feel again. The person who reveals herself as the speaker of "Daddy" is haunted and driven by resentment. Feelings that might have expired still breathe within her and determine her overall emotional condition, which is resentment against her father. The poem itself is

TOPICS FOR FURTHER STUDY

- Using "Daddy" as a basis, write an "answer poem," written by Plath's father from his point of view.

- Write an essay describing your relationship to one of your parents or to a strong parental figure in your life.

- Research the subject of feminism and present a report to your class describing what the expectations were that shaped the roles males and females were expected to play in society. How does "Daddy" reflect, or not reflect, feminism and traditional gender roles?

- Construct a collage of images from the 1960s that reflects the concerns and sensibilities in "Daddy."

an expression of that resentment, not an attempt to extirpate it but to satisfy it. Plath's real-life suicide a few months after composing the poem shows that resentment, when it festers, cannot be satisfied. It can only be momentarily allayed, but it recharges and demands repeated release.

Sadomasochism

"Every woman adores a Fascist, / The boot in the face, the brute / Brute heart of a brute like you" has become one of the best known lines not just from this poem but from the entirety of the Plath canon. It gives expression to a fundamental masochism Plath asserts is an inherent component of an abstract, female psyche. Whether the assertion is actually true or not, it is a governing defense for the attitude of the poet and a fundamental explanation of her malaise. She loves a father who not only did not reciprocate that love, but whose manner towards her was such that the only thing she could attach her love for him to was his cruelty. She is in the paradoxical situation of seeing herself as an archetypal victim, symbolized by the image of the Jews who were carried to extermination in cattle cars.

At the same time as she is being destroyed, she is erotically overwhelmed by the power that is destroying her, wishing, against her will, to submit to it for the strange frisson such surrender can offer. Love for her father has become the dominant mechanism of her libidinal interest. Her identification with his power to obliterate her leads her to attempt suicide. When that fails, she finds a more subtle method of self obliteration, spite: "And then I knew what to do. / I made a model of you, / A man in black with a Meinkampf look / And a love of the rack and the screw. / And I said I do, I do." She deliberately recapitulated her father, particularly in his brutal aspects, in a husband. But her choice is not a pure exercise of masochism. She was setting up for herself the opportunity to accomplish her father's death by killing her husband, whom she describes, with masochistic relish at her power to withstand assault as she experiences it—"The vampire who said he was you / And drank my blood for a year, / Seven years if you want to know." The masochism she perversely celebrates is a cover under which she hides her own sadistic wishes.

STYLE

Assertion

"Daddy" is a poem whose grammatical mode is the declarative sentence used in the service of the assertions that give the poem both its strength and its ambiguity, for the assertions, from the first "You do not do" to "They always *knew* it was you," as strongly and elaborately delivered as they are, are presented without substantiation.

Assonance and Consonance

Rhyme is usually a phenomenon that occurs at the end of a line when the sound of one word at a line's end echoes the sound of another word ending a previous line. Assonance and consonance are varieties of rhyme that appear inside the lines of a poem. They occur when vowel sounds (assonance) and consonant sounds (consonance) repeat, reflect, or suggest each other throughout the body of a poem. In "Daddy," Plath relies heavily on both these sorts of internal rhymes. Most prominent is the "oo" sound, introduced emphatically in the first line, that dominates the aural texture of the poem. But even a cursory perusal of the poem reveals such combinations as "In which I have lived like a foot." where the sound of the short "i" is prominent, "v" and "l" are repeated, as are the related "t" and "d." Just about every line will yield to such aural analysis.

Onomatopoeia

Onomatopoeia refers to the use of a sound to signify the thing that makes that sound. "Daddy" is replete with it, starting with the last word of the first stanza, and occurring in words like "chuffing" and "scraped," and "gobbledygoo."

Repetition

Plath uses repetition throughout "Daddy," beginning in the first line of the poem, where the first four words are repeated exactly and continuing the technique with variations, as in "In the German tongue, in the Polish town," or "I could hardly speak / I thought every German," or the number of lines beginning with "I." Repetition gives the poem a rhythm of insistence that reflects the intensity of the narrator's obsession with her subject, her father.

HISTORICAL CONTEXT

Confessional Poetry

In part the rise of confessional poetry in the 1950s was a response to the difficulties of hermetic academic poetry, to the learned and allusive work of poets like the highly influential Ezra Pound and T. S. Eliot, and to the puzzling complexities of stripped down modernism with its forests of symbols and obscure imagery. The confessional poetry of American poets like Robert Lowell, who practiced making poetry out of his family history and his own personal and often agonizing experience, or of W. D. Snodgrass, who wrote addressing his daughter about his separation from her because of divorce, brought a new range of subjects and opened a new realm of discourse for poets, their life experiences, anxieties, losses, shameful moments. Although confessional poetry as a genre was new, a poetry of confession was not. Shakespeare, Milton, Wordsworth, Coleridge, and Keats, for example, all wrote poems that are essentially confessional. What distinguished the confessional poetry of the second half of the twentieth century was its closeness to the bone of its practitioners' experience and the climate in

which it was produced, its depth of revelation in a culture of conformity where "dirty laundry" was not, properly, aired in public.

Feminism

In 1963, the same year that the poems in *Ariel* were written and that Plath killed herself, an American journalist and union activist, Betty Friedan, who had graduated from Smith college thirteen years before Plath, published *The Feminine Mystique* and ushered in what is called the second wave of feminism in the United States. (The first wave ended when (white) women in the United States won the right to vote in 1919.) The second wave brought to the surface problems of female inequality, diminished opportunity, biological determinism—because women can bear children, women must bear children—and social and sexual freedom. Plath herself, who became a powerful presence for late twentieth-century feminism, was not a feminist but a woman whose turmoil and experience served to explain and justify the eruption of feminism. Caught between her own genius as a poet, her savage intellect, and sharp, indignant insights on the one hand and the gender expectations and roles women (and men) were trained to believe were inherent aspects of human nature, Plath, particularly because of her grim and tragic response to the contradictions that bedeviled her, became a model for many well-educated young women who resisted the roles that awaited them independent of their individual characteristics or desires.

The Holocaust

Plath's comparison of herself to a Jew and her allusions to "your Aryan eye, bright blue," "Dachau, Auschwitz, Belsen," " an engine / Chuffing," "a swastika," and the "Luftwaffe," as well as a "neat mustache" and "a Meinkampf look" all allude to what has come to be called the Holocaust or the Shoa. The Holocaust was the deliberate and carefully executed extermination of the majority of the population of European Jewry. This was carried out in Nazi Germany during the period beginning with Adolph Hitler's rise to power in Germany in 1933 and ending in 1945, when the Allied Forces of the Soviet Union, the United States, and Great Britain defeated Germany at the end of World War II. Hitler, a man with a trademark black moustache, mobilized the German people particularly with the tool of anti-Semitism and by promulgating the racist idea

COMPARE
&
CONTRAST

- **1962:** The great changes that feminism will bring about at the end of the 1960s have not yet occurred. Women, even if they are college graduates, are still expected to pursue the role of homemaker and mother, perhaps devoting some time to charity work or the Parent Teachers Association, but essentially dedicating themselves to domesticity.

  Today: Many women enter the corporate world and can attain high positions within their companies. Many women also balance, or at least attempt to balance, the demands of work with the demands of motherhood.

- **1962:** Psychological and emotional distress is still commonly treated by electroconvulsive therapy, as it has been since the 1940s and throughout the 1950s (when Plath was subjected to it). Sometimes called "electroshock therapy," it resets the brain in a process that can be said to be similar to rebooting a computer.

  Today: Electroconvulsive therapy is still used but less regularly and in a more carefully regulated fashion than it was in the 1950s and early 1960s. Medication is the favored means of dealing with psychological and emotional disturbances.

- **1962:** The Cold War, a power struggle between the United States and the Soviet Union (now Russia) and some of its neighboring states, is at its height as United States President John Kennedy and Russian Premier Nikita Khrushchev confront each other with the threat of nuclear war.

  Today: The Soviet threat has been replaced in the United States by the threat of a worldwide terrorism that is not located in one particular country but is often represented by the terms "*Al Qaeda*" or "*Jihad*."

- **1962:** Germany, as a result of its defeat in World War II, is a country divided into two countries, West Germany and East Germany. That division is symbolized by the Berlin Wall, built in 1961 in order to prevent the people of East Berlin from fleeing to West Berlin.

  Today: Germany was reunited after the fall of the Berlin wall in 1989 and its citizens can now freely travel inside and outside Germany.

---

that there was a "master race" of Aryans, notable for their blue eyes, and inferior races, like the Jews, who were compared to vermin in Nazi propaganda. Auschwitz, Bergen-Belsen, and Dachau are the names of death camps where Jews were taken to be gassed and then cremated. *Mein Kampf* is the name of the book Hitler wrote around 1925 during a relatively brief imprisonment for leading his followers in subversive and violent demonstrations. *Mein Kampf* sets forth the Nazi ideology and expresses Hitler's anti-Jewish stance. The Luftwaffe was Hitler's air force. The incomprehensible, open, and proud barbarity of the Nazis hovered throughout the 1950s and beyond as the indelible emblem of brutality and cruelty.

CRITICAL OVERVIEW

Linda W. Wagner reports in *Critical Essays on Sylvia Plath* that the critic George Steiner has called "Daddy" "the *Guernica* of modern poetry," comparing Plath's poem to Pablo Picasso's monumental 1937 painting depicting the sufferings of Spaniards under the violence of the Nazi bombardment during the Spanish Civil war. "Daddy," like *Guernica*, Steiner asserts, "achieves the classic art of generalization, translating a private, obviously intolerable hurt into a code of plain statement, of instantaneously public images which concern us all." Wagner also cites Katha Pollit, writing in the *Nation* in 1982. Pollit declares that "by the time she [Plath] came

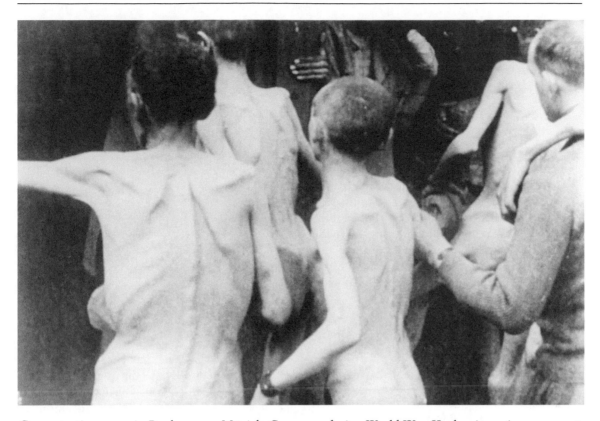

Concentration camp in Dachau near Münich, Germany, during World War II, showing prisoners gaunt from malnutrition (© Pat Behnke / Alamy)

to write her last seventy or eighty poems, there was no voice like hers on earth."

Indeed, during the second wave of feminism in the late 1960s and in the 1970s, "Daddy" became a feminist anthem, a sort of "We Shall Overcome" of the Women's Liberation Movement. It was a poem immediately accessible to readers outside academia. It had the force of a social provocation. Gary Lane declares in *Sylvia Plath: New Views on the Poetry* that "Plath has grown into a cult figure. ... For some she became the symbol of woman oppressed." Toni Saldívar argues in *Sylvia Plath: Confessing the Fictive Self* that in "Daddy" "the speaker negates a paternal bond by emptying out an image of father and of husband as a repeat of father until that image is itself unfathered and thus finished." "The effectiveness of 'Daddy,'" A. R. Jones writes in *The Art of Sylvia Plath: A Symposium*, "can largely be accounted for by Sylvia Plath's success in associating the world of the poem with [the] structure of the nursery rhyme world, a world of carefully contained terror in which

rhythm and tone are precariously weighed against content to produce a hardly achieved balance of tensions." Roger Platizky, writing in the *Explicator* in 1997, notes: "Images of victimization ... of Nazis, swastikas, barbed wire, fascists, brutes, devils, and vampires—are so frantic, imposing, and vituperative that the poem seems more out of control than it actually is." He then goes on to compare "Daddy" to "a runaway train," but he argues that Plath's formal mastery of poetic technique asserts her power over her tormentors in the poem and over the poem itself.

CRITICISM

Neil Heims

Heims is a writer and teacher living in Paris. In the following essay, he considers the importance of a very interesting omission in "Daddy": while the poet condemns her father, she does not actually say what he has done to make him worthy of her intense scorn.

WHAT DO I READ NEXT?

- Robert Lowell's *Life Studies* (1959) is a collection of Lowell's confessional poetry. In poems like "Skunk Hour," "Man and Wife," "Memories of West Street and Lephe," "Waking in the Blue," and "Grandparents," Lowell reveals parts of his life and describes the intersection between autobiographical events and his deepest responses to them.

- Kate Millet's *Sexual Politics* (1969) exerted a tremendous cultural influence on American gender consciousness and was one of the principle texts of the Women's Movement in the 1970s.

- Shulamith Firestone's *The Dialectic of Sex: The Case for Feminist Revolution* (1970) is a classic radical feminist text in which Firestone examines and criticizes the patterns of culture that have formed the social and cultural constructs of female and male.

- William Wordsworth's *The Prelude* (1850) is a book-length epic poem, but Wordsworth took for the subject of the poem the events of his own life and the development of his mind and ideas.

- Grace Paley's collection of stories *The Little Disturbances of Man* (1959) presents the lives of various women at various ages and stages of life as they cope with gender definition, expectations, growth, men, and love.

"Daddy" can be read as a very angry poem, even a mad poem. It lends itself to such a reading just by its rhythm and by the fact that most of its words are monosyllabic (one syllable) and many of its syllables echo each other, repeating similar sounds and rhythms. It is a poem of "telling off," of finally saying just what is on your mind. Its imagery of Nazi criminals and death camps crowd their way into its center along with references to a boot stomping on the face and a heart-

> THE QUESTION REMAINS, WHY IS SHE SO ANGRY? FOR ALL ITS SHOWY ELOQUENCE, THE POEM LEAVES THE REASON UNSTATED. THE EFFECTS OF HER ANGER, HOW ANGER AT HER FATHER MAKES HER FEEL, HER PICTURE OF HIM, THESE ARE EXPRESSED. BUT WHAT HE ACTUALLY DID TO HER, BESIDES DYING, IS NOT."

---

destroying vampire. Most significantly, it is a poem written only months before the poet killed herself. But, when one listens to Plath's reading of the poem on *In Their Own Voices: A Century of Recorded Poetry*, one can hear something else. Her reading does not have the quality of a fierce poet ranting, out of control, blisteringly spitting out a catalogue of condemnations. It is a rather dry reading of a very carefully constructed text. She is petulant, flirtatious, spiteful, taunting, and there is a sense of anger in her voice. But it is all very controlled, almost theatrical. The anger is cold, resigned anger. She would prefer, it seems, that she had not needed to be angry, the tone of the lines suggests. This realization is almost funny to her, for the poem is witty and pleased with itself, almost smug in its proficiency. All the distancing, posing, and awareness that Plath builds into the text—the layering—make the anger something different from a simple flash of personal rage. It is a studied anger that looks forward to cruelty whether received or given. Rather than expressing her own personal anger, the poet is conveying an attitude of anger. It is more like an intellectual anger than a vulnerable, emotional one. It is a cultivated rather than an explosive anger.

But whether "Daddy" is read with fierceness or detachment, there is still the question: What is the poet angry at, exactly? We know at whom, her father. But why? Because he died of diabetes? Perhaps. Abandonment is abandonment, no matter what the reason, especially to a ten year old. But his death is not the full reason for her anger at him, if it is even a part. The fact of his death is introduced to show that he died before she could kill him, so she has got to kill him instead in the poem. Thus, according to the speaker of the poem, her wanting to kill him is not the result of his dying when she was ten. The poem is a kind of declaration or catalogue not of his faults, but of the way his faults felt to her. She must make him disappear by her willing it, freeing herself from being the victim of the circumstance of his death. In order to be able to kill him with impunity, she must construct and represent him as the very model of evil. The poet's father's actual death and the death he will suffer at her hand are very different things. In actuality he is dead. To his daughter, he is immortal. The poet does not kill him; she constructs and controls his image. That is her power as a poet, and it is the power of poetry. In the actual world, his death is a natural fact. Killing him in poetry is a psychic fact, accomplished by turning him into a vampire. But who, then, is really the vampire? She feeds her anger and her poem with his blood.

Indeed, the poet's father, dead in the world, remains alive in her as a perceived cause of her rage and an object of it. The question remains, why is she so angry? For all its showy eloquence, the poem leaves the reason unstated. The effects of her anger, how anger at her father makes her feel, her picture of him, these are expressed. But what he actually did to her, besides dying, is not. "Daddy" says nothing about what happened to the speaker, what he did to her, only what it felt like.

Yet, the poem remains powerful. It is talking about some wrong, some injustice, some brutality, but not the brutality that forms the metaphorical content regarding Nazis and vampires. Instead the poem represents a way of feeling that readers can identify with, a sense of ill-treatment recognizable as one's own. Plath's "luck," the "weird luck" that seems to arise from "gypsy ancestr[y]" and that gives her the visionary power of a reader of Tarot cards, is the luck of history. It is the luck that gives her not the fate of the tormented Jew but the vision of that persecution. It is a luck derived from her own psychic experience, and her response to it and to the social malaise that finds its expression in feminism (for feminism is a response to a perception of widespread and systemic persecution by a system privileging males and demeaning females). It is a vision of patriarchy as a fundamentally evil system that defines a certain category of persons as less than persons, as a lower order. This is where the Nazi and the patriarchal systems converge.

What tends to weaken the narrator's confession, the lack of specific charges against her father, strengthens her poem as a vehicle for drawing reader response. The passion of her reaction to the unstated injuries and the way she demonizes them is an easily transferable emotion accessible to anyone. What may be of no great proportion objectively and under the aspect of eternity may take up, as it is experienced, all the psychic space there is. Plath's image of the "swastika [the twisted cross composed by four sevens whose stems touch at right angles to each other and that was the primary emblem of the Nazi Party] / So black no sky could squeak through" is an image of the overwhelming psychic perception of the experience of being stifled. Her father is transformed from the man he was, whatever he was actually like, into a symbol of stifling itself, of patriarchy, and the abstract designation for the system of female negation. The poet's response to him is a model for the response to the psychic tremors created by a sense of having been, in one's deepest core, obliterated.

There is strength in numbers, especially for anyone who feels marginalized and for the solitary sufferer of an injustice. In "Daddy," Plath relies heavily for vindication of her anger on the broader community, first of women, and then of women and men, as characterized by the image of "the villagers." "Every woman adores a Fascist," she writes. Whether this is a valid and true assertion is of little importance in the poem or for the poem. After all, it is a poem, a personal, confessional poem. What is revealing about the formulation is that the poet moves, with it, away from the "I" that she has used until then. In just the previous stanza, she wrote "I have always been scared of *you*." But now she does not say "I adore a Fascist," which would be a valuable personal insight, but "Every woman" The narrator now has set the stage for an entire disavowal of the personal. The venom she felt and the condemnation she expressed throughout, in the final stanza becomes generalized rather than hers: "the villagers never liked you. / They are dancing and stamping on you. / They always *knew* it was you." The problem is not hers but everybody's. The angry dismissal and the happy revenge are not hers. They are everybody's. The emotion the poem generates is greater than the untold sins of her father. The effect is to universalize the object of her wrath. It is not her father who becomes the object of her scorn and her readers's scorn but the system of elevating fathers; the object of her scorn is patriarchy itself.

Source: Neil Heims, Critical Essay on "Daddy," in *Poetry for Students*, Gale, Cengage Learning, 2008.

Guinevara A. Nance and Judith P. Jones

In the following excerpt, Nance and Jones consider the psychological aspects of the infantile regression that is suggested by some of the language in "Daddy." They also discuss the corresponding transformation of childish love into adult venom.

Sylvia Plath's ironic reference to two of her most venomous poems, "Lady Lazarus" and "Daddy," as "some light verse" shows an aesthetic distance that not many of her readers have been able to achieve. Alvarez recalls that when Plath first read these two poems to him, he responded to them more as "assault and battery" than as poetry. Subsequent critical responses to "Daddy" in particular have reacted to the most grizzly stanzas in categorizing the poem as symbolic enactment of patricide and have accentuated its macabre quality by focusing on the parallels between the daddy of the poem and Plath's own father. Readings of the poem as a ritualistic murder have overlooked evidence that the father—whether purely an artistic construct or a derivative of the poet's father—is the fabrication of a persona who attempts to exorcise her childish view of her daddy. Plath has said that "the poem is spoken by a girl with an Electra complex" whose "father died while she thought he was God." Significantly, she refers to the thirty-year old person as a "girl," for the psychological restrictions of an infantile love and fear of the father have retarded the possibility of autonomy. In the declaration that "You do not do, you do not do / Any more, black shoe," the speaker recognizes as untenable her puerile perspective of daddy; and the poem depicts her attempts to free herself from an image which she created of the father as deity and demon. Anthony Libby comes closest to recognizing the speaker's participation in the creation of her father when he says that she is as much operator as victim: "She creates the man in black ... and she finally destroys him" in a destruction that is "internal and theoretical." The process of doing

> THE PERSONA'S SYSTEMATIC RECOLLECTION OF ALL THE MENTAL PROJECTIONS OF HER FATHER AMOUNTS TO AN ATTEMPT AT DISPOSSESSION THROUGH DIRECT CONFRONTATION WITH A DEMON PRODUCED IN HER IMAGINATION."

away with daddy in the poem represents the persona's attempts at psychic purgation of the image, "the model," of a father she has constructed. Her methods, however, are more akin to magic than murder, since it is through a combination of exorcism and sympathetic magic that she works to dispossess herself of her own fantasies.

The first twelve stanzas of the poem reveal the extent of the speaker's possession by what, in psychoanalytic terms, is the *imago* of the father—a childhood version of the father which persists into adulthood. This *imago* is an amalgamation of real experience and archetypal memories wherein the speaker's own psychic oppression is represented in the more general symbol of the Nazi oppression of the Jews. For example, the man at the blackboard in the picture of the actual father is transformed symbolically into the "man in black with a Meinkampf look." The connecting link, of course, between each of these associations is the word "black," which also relates to the shoe in which the speaker has lived and the swastika "So black no sky could squeak through." Thus the specific and personal recollections ignite powerful associations with culturally significant symbols. The fact that the girl is herself "a bit of a Jew" and a bit of a German intensifies her emotional paralysis before the *imago* of an Aryan father with whom she is both connected and at enmity. Commenting on the persona in a BBC interview, Plath herself suggests that the two strains of Nazi and Jew unite in the daughter "and paralyze each other"; so the girl is doubly incapacitated to deal with her sense of her father, both by virtue of her mixed ethnicity and her childish perspective. As the persona recalls the father of her early years, she emphasizes and blends the two perspectives of impotence: that of the child before its father and of the Jew before the Nazi. The child's intimidation is clear, for example, in "I never could talk to you. / The tongue stuck in my Jaw"; but the sense of the childhood terror melds into a suggestion of the Jewish persecution and terror with the next line: "It stuck in a barb wire snare."

What Plath accomplishes by the more or less chronological sequencing of these recollections of childhood, and on through the twenty year old's attempted suicide to the point at thirty when the woman tries to extricate hersel from her image of daddy, is a dramatization of the process of psychic purgation in the speaker. The persona's systematic recollection of all the mental projections of her father amounts to an attempt at dispossession through direct confrontation with a demon produced in her imagination. Both psychoanalysis and the religious rite of exorcism have regarded this process of confrontation with the "trauma" or the "demon" as potentially curative; and from whichever perspective Plath viewed the process, she has her persona confront—in a way almost relive—her childhood terror of a father whose actual existence is as indistinct as the towns with which the girl tries to associate him. Plath also accentuates linguistically the speaker's re-living of her childhood. Using the heavy cadences of nursery rhyme and baby words such as "Chuffing," "Achoo," and "gobbledygoo," she employs a technical device similar to Joyce's in *A Portrait of the Artist as a Young Man*, where the child's simple perspective reflected through language. Like Joyce, Plath wants to recreate with immediacy the child's view. But whereas Joyce evolves his Stephen Dedalus from the "baby tuckoo" and the "moocow" stage into maturity, she has her speaker psychically regress to her childhood fantasies, where every German is potentially her father and the German language seems to be an engine "chuffing" her off to Dachau. Because the persona's past is pathologically connected to her present, this regression requires minimal distance for the adult woman who has been unable to relinquish the childish perspective.

The tough, even brutal, language to which Alvarez reacted provides an ironic contrast to the language associated with a child's vision of "daddy." This juxtaposition is most evident in the early lines:

Barely daring to breathe or Achoo.
Daddy, I have had to kill you.

It is inaccurate to see this last statement entirely as a suggestion of patricide, for the persona's threat is against the infantile version of the father which the word "daddy" connotes. These lines accentuate the irony of the impotent little girl's directing her rage at a monumental fantasy father.

As the language of the poem begins to exclude baby talk and to develop more exclusively the vocabulary of venom, it signals a change in the persona's method of dealing with this image of the father. She moves from confrontation with her childhood projections to an abjuration of the total psychic picture of the father in an attempt at exorcism. Sounding more like Clytemnestra than a little girl playing Electra, she renounces the deity turned demon with a vengeance in the declaration, "Daddy, daddy, you bastard, I'm through." The virulence of this and the statements immediately preceding it indicates a ritualistic attempt to transform the little girl's love into the adult's hatred and thereby kill the image which has preyed upon her.

The turning point in the poem and in the speaker's efforts to purge herself of the psychological significance of the father image occurs in the following stanza:

But they pulled me out of the sack.
And they stuck me together with glue.
And then I knew what to do.
I made a model of you.

The statement, "I made a model of you," suggests several levels of meaning. On the most obvious level, the speaker implies that she made of her father a prototype of all men; and this is borne out in the merging of the father with the man to whom she says "I do, I do." Her image of the "man in black with a Meinkampf look" is superimposed upon the husband so that instead of having one unreality to destroy, she has two— the prototypic father and the husband who is fashioned in his likeness. The poem "Stings" establishes a similar relationship between the dead-imaginary father and the living but spectral husband:

A third person is watching.
He has nothing to do with the bee-seller or
    me.
Now he is gone

In eight great bounds, a great scapegoat.

A more complicated implication of the speaker's action in making a model of the father, but one which is also consonant with the allusions to folklore in the later references to vampirism, concerns the persona's use of magic to rid herself of the mental impressions associated with her father. The making of a model, image, or effigy suggests symbolically a reaction not so much to the real father but to the *imago*, or projection of his image in the mind of the persona. She employs what Frazer in *The Golden Bough* refers to as "sympathetic magic"—a generic term for various forms of magic which are based on the premise that a correspondence exists between animate and inanimate objects. One form, homeopathic magic, is predicated on the belief that any representation may affect what it depicts. For example, a picture of a person, a voodoo doll, or any other sort of portrayal can, when acted upon, influence its prototype. In "Daddy," it is the model of the father that the persona destroys; and the solution suggested in the making of the model seems to occur as a consequence of its association with the speaker's own reconstruction after her attempted suicide, when she is "stuck ... together with glue." Her remodeling, described in a way that recalls the assembling of a collage, seems to be the associative stimulus for the idea of constructing the model through which to effect her dispossession. It is this model, a fabricated representation of a distorted vision of the father—a patchwork mental impression of him—that she seeks to destroy.

Ironically, of course, she is also destroying a portion of her own psychological constitution with which she has lived, however detrimentally, all of her life. With the special significance which Carl Jung gives to the the idea of "image" as a "concentrated expression of the *total psychic situation*," it is obvious that in attempting to destroy her image of the father, the persona risks total psychic destruction for herself. The final words of the poem, "I'm through," which have been so variously interpreted, imply both that the magic has worked its power of dispossession and also that the speaker is left with nothing. Dispossessed of the *imago* which has defined her own identity and with which she has been obsessed, she is psychically finished, depleted. The villagers, in a kind of ritual death dance, demolish the model of the father, both as it is representative of daddy and of the shadowy vampire-husband behind whose mask that

image lurks; and in a final excoriation reminiscent of exorcism rites in which the pride of Satan is attacked by calling him vile names, the daughter declares, "Daddy, daddy, you bastard, I'm through." The ambiguity which Plath creates here in the multiple meanings of "through" indicates the irony of the persona's finishment. Her freedom from the father image which she has created leaves her psychologically void, done in ...

Source: Guinevara A. Nance and Judith P. Jones, "Doing Away with Daddy: Exorcism and Sympathetic Magic in Plath's Poetry," in *Critical Essays on Sylvia Plath*, edited by Linda W. Wagner, G. K. Hall, 1984, pp. 124–29.

Mary Lynn Broe

In the following excerpt, Broe regards "Daddy" as a failed attempt at the ritual exorcism of the speaker's father and her image of him.

... The speaker in "Daddy" performs a mock poetic exorcism of an event that has already happened—the death of her father who she feels withdrew his love from her by dying prematurely: "Daddy, I have had to kill you. / You died before I had time—."

The speaker attempts to exorcise not just the memory of her father but her own *Mein Kampf* model of him as well as her inherited behavioral traits that lead her graveward under the Freudian banner of death instinct or Thanatos's libido. But her ritual reenactment simply does not take. The event comically backfires as pure self-parody: the metaphorical murder of the father dwindles into Hollywood spectacle, while the poet is lost in the clutter of the collective unconscious.

Early in the poem, the ritual gets off on the wrong foot both literally and figuratively. A sudden rhythmic break midway through the first stanza interrupts the insistent and mesmeric chant of the poet's own freedom:

> You do not do, you do not do
> Any more, black shoe
> In which I have lived like a foot
> For thirty years, poor and white,
> Barely daring to breathe or Achoo.

The break suggests, on the one hand, that the nursery-rhyme world of contained terror is here abandoned; on the other, that the poet-exorcist's mesmeric control is superficial, founded in a shaky faith and an unsure heart—the worst possible state for the strong, disciplined exorcist.

At first she kills her father succinctly with her own words, demythologizing him to a ludicrous piece of statuary that is hardly a Poseidon or the Colossus of Rhodes:

> Marble-heavy, a bag full of God,
> Ghastly statue with one grey toe
> Big as a Frisco seal
>
> And a head in the freakish Atlantic
> Where it pours bean green over blue
> In the waters off beautiful Nauset.
> I used to pray to recover you.
> Ach, du.

Then as she tries to patch together the narrative of him, his tribal myth (the "common" town, the "German tongue," the war-scraped culture), she begins to lose her own powers of description to a senseless Germanic prattle ("The tongue stuck in my jaw. / It stuck in a barb wire snare. / Ich, ich, ich, ich"). The individual man is absorbed by his inhuman archetype, the "panzer man," "an engine / Chuffing me off like a Jew." Losing the exorcist's power that binds the spirit and then casts out the demon, she is the classic helpless victim of the swastika man. As she culls up her own picture of him as a devil, he refuses to adopt this stereotype. Instead he jumbles his trademark:

> A cleft in your chin instead of your foot
> But no less a devil for that, no not
> Any less the black man who
>
> Bit my pretty red heart in two.

The overt Nazi-Jew allegory throughout the poem suggests that, by a simple inversion of power, father and daughter grow more alike. But when she tries to imitate his action of dying, making all the appropriate grand gestures, she once again fails: "but they pulled me out of the sack, / And they stuck me together with glue." She retreats to a safe world of icons and replicas, but even the doll image she constructs turns out to be "the vampire who said he was you." At last, she abandons her father to the collective unconscious where it is *he* who is finally recognized ("they always *knew* it was you"). *She* is lost, impersonally absorbed by his irate persecutors, bereft of both her power and her conjuror's discipline, and possessed by the incensed villagers. The exorcist's ritual, one of purifying, cleansing, commanding silence and then ordering the evil spirit's departure, has dwindled to a comic picture from the heart of darkness. Mad villagers stamp on the devil-vampire creation.

In the course of performing the imaginative "killing," the speaker moves through a variety of emotions, from viciousness ("a stake in your fat black heart"), to vengefulness ("You bastard, I'm through"), finally to silence ("the black telephone's off at the root"). It would seem that the real victim is the poet-performer who, despite her straining toward identification with the public events of holocaust and destruction of World War II, becomes more murderously persecuting than the "panzer-man" who smothered her, and who abandoned her with a paradoxical love, guilt, and fear. Unlike him, she kills three times: the original subject, the model to whom she said "I do, I do," and herself, the imitating victim. But each of these killings is comically inverted. Each backfires. Instead of successfully binding the spirits, commanding them to remain silent and cease doing harm, and then ordering them to an appointed place, the speaker herself is stricken dumb.

The failure of the exorcism and the emotional ambivalence are echoed in the curious rhythm. The incantatory safety of the nursery-rhyme thump (seemingly one of controlled, familiar terrors) also suggests some sinister brooding by its repetition. The poem opens with a suspiciously emphatic protest, a kind of psychological whistling-in-the-dark. As it proceeds, "Daddy's" continuous life-rhythms—the assonance, consonance, and especially the sustained *oo* sounds—triumph over either the personal or the cultural-historical imagery. The sheer sense of organic life in the interwoven sounds carries the verse forward in boisterous spirit and communicates an underlying feeling of comedy that is also echoed in the repeated failure of the speaker to perform her exorcism.

Ultimately, "Daddy" is like an emotional, psychological, and historical autopsy, a final report. There is no real progress. The poet is in the same place in the beginning as in the end. She begins the poem as a hesitant but familiar fairy-tale daughter who parodies her attempt to recon-struct the myth of her father. Suffocating in her shoe house, she is unable to do much with that "bag full of God." She ends as a murderous member of a mythical community enacting the-ritual or vampire killing, but only for a surro-gate vampire, not the real thing ("the vampire who said he was you"). Although it seems that the speaker has moved from identification with the persecuted to identity as persecutor, Jew to vampire-killer, powerless to powerful, she has simply enacted a performance that allows her to live with what is unchangeable. She has used her art to stave off suffocation, and performs her self-contempt with a degree of bravado ...

Source: Mary Lynn Broe, "A Performing Self: 'the theat-rical / comeback in broad day,'" in *Protean Poetic: The Poetry of Sylvia Plath*, University of Missouri Press, 1980, pp. 165–79.

SOURCES

Jones, A. R., "On 'Daddy,'" in *The Art of Sylvia Plath: A Symposium*, edited by Charles Newman, University of Indiana Press, 1970, pp. 230–36.

Lane, Gary, Introduction, in *Sylvia Plath: New Views on the Poetry*, edited by Gary Lane, Johns Hopkins Univer-sity Press, 1979, p. ix.

Plath, Sylvia, "Daddy," in *Ariel*, Faber and Faber, 1972, pp. 54–56.

Platizky, Roger, "Plath's 'Daddy,'" in the *Explicator*, Winter 1997, Vol. 55, No. 2, p. 105.

Presson, Rebekah, ed., *In Their Own Voices: A Century of Recorded Poetry* (audiotape), Rhino Entertainment, 1997.

Saldívar, Toni, *Sylvia Plath: Confessing the Fictive Self*, Peter Lang, 1992, p. 180–81.

Wagner, Linda W., *Critical Essays on Sylvia Plath*, G. K Hall, 1984, pp. 1–2.

FURTHER READING

Bassnet, Susan, *Sylvia Plath*, Rowman & Littlefield, 1987.
Bassnet argues that Plath's poetry ought not be read as strictly autobiographical, but as works that set contradictions of experience and response against each other.

Friedan, Betty, *The Feminine Mystique*, W. W. Norton, 1963.
Published the same year Plath died, Friedan's classic study of how women's social roles and psychic make-up were constructed reflects the tensions Plath herself faced as a young woman coming of age in the years following World War II.

Plath, Sylvia, *The Bell Jar*, Harper & Row, 1971.
Plath's only novel draws strongly on her per-sonal experience, chronicling the summer of 1953 when Plath was working in New York City for a fashion magazine, her growing dis-tress, her suicide attempt, her electroshock treatments, and her return to 'normal' life.

Rose, Jacqueline, *The Haunting of Sylvia Plath*, Virago Press, 1991.
Among other things, Rose addresses and defends the presence of Holocaust references and imagery in "Daddy."

Wood, David John, *A Critical Study of the Birth Imagery of Sylvia Plath, American Poet 1932–1963*, Edwin Mellen Press, 1992.
Wood reads the body of Plath's poetry as one essential poem divided into a number of parts, and argues that there is a unifying theme and set of images throughout suggesting birth and coming into being.

The Drunken Boat

ARTHUR RIMBAUD

1884

Arthur Rimbaud's "The Drunken Boat" was written in 1871 but was not published until 1884, when it appeared in an anthology of poetry called *Les Poètes maudits*. What makes this poem difficult is its lack of a narrated plot. It is instead a narrative of a state of being. As such, it requires symbols to express internal psychic events and experiences. Rimbaud writes as if he were dreaming.

Symbolic poetry representing a symbolic voyage, the kind of poetry represented by "The Drunken Boat," was not invented by Rimbaud. His older contemporary, Charles Baudelaire, in many ways served as a precursor for Rimbaud. Particularly noteworthy are Baudelaire's two later voyage poems, "A Voyage to Cythera" and "The Voyage," published in 1857, in *Les Fleurs du Mal* (translated as *The Flowers of Evil*). Baudelaire's influence is also felt in the very Symbolist technique that informs the type of imagery in "The Drunken Boat." Given these strong influences, Rimbaud's poem is also considered one of the finest examples of symbolist poetry.

One of the best English translations of the poem, Wallace Fowlie's version of "The Drunken Boat" appears in *Rimbaud: Complete Works, Selected Letters, A Bilingual Edition*, published by the University of Chicago Press in 2005.

AUTHOR BIOGRAPHY

Arthur Rimbaud was born Jean Nicolas Arthur Rimbaud in the French village of Charleville on October 20, 1854. He was one of the four surviving children born to Frédéric Rimbaud, soldier, adventurer, and man of letters, who deserted his family when Rimbaud was six, and to a strict, religious, unaffectionate mother, Marie-Cathérine-Vitalie Cuif. In October of 1861, Rimbaud and his elder brother were sent to school at the Institut Rossat. Rimbaud excelled, winning prizes in subjects ranging from Latin and French to History, Geography, and Arithmetic. Because the Institut Rossat was too liberal for her strict beliefs, Madame Rimbaud transferred the boys to the municipal school, the Collège de Charleville in April of 1865. Rimbaud distinguished himself there, too, especially for his essays. At fifteen years of age, Rimbaud was writing accomplished verse in Latin as well as French and was allowed to read whatever books he wished. Many of his school assignments in Latin verse were published in a journal devoted to the work of school children. His first published poem in French appeared in *La Revue pour Tous*, a journal for mature poets, in 1870, while he was still in school.

That year, too, Rimbaud met Georges Izambard, a teacher at the College who devoted himself to mentoring the fifteen-year-old poet. Although he was writing in the elevated Parnassian style of the time, Rimbaud had begun to subvert that style, creating the poetry of sensory derangement that became his hallmark. Rimbaud was vocal in his opposition to Napoleon III's invasion of Germany in 1870. He sold some of his books, and without the knowledge of his mother, ran away to Paris at the end of August. There he was arrested as a vagabond when he disembarked at the Gare du Nord and held in the Paris municipal jail, where he was probably raped, and was then transferred to prison. A letter to Izambard asking for his help secured money for Rimbaud's release and a trip to Izambard's home in Douai. While staying with Izambard, Rimbaud read and wrote until, as his mother demanded, Izambard returned Rimbaud to Charleville and his mother's strict discipline.

Early in 1871, after the Prussian defeat of the French toppled Napoleon III's government, and the Third Republic was formed, Rimbaud returned to Paris. He introduced himself to a

Arthur Rimbaud (The Library of Congress)

host of literary men who remained cold to him, wandered around Paris, composed poetry, and after two weeks, returned to Charleville. He returned to Paris later that year during the days of the Paris Commune and, bearing an invitation from Paul Verlaine—a well-known poet more than twenty tears his senior, to whom he had sent some of his work—introduced himself and began living with Verlaine and his wife. Verlaine and Rimbaud became lovers, and Verlaine left his wife and young son in pursuit of the affair. Rimbaud and Verlaine traveled, drank absinthe and smoked hashish, while living in England in the fall of 1872. In the summer of 1873, the two quarreled with such fury that Verlaine, in a jealous rage, shot Rimbaud, who, in fright, turned Verlaine in to the police. Even though Rimbaud dropped the charges, Verlaine was incarcerated for two years.

Rimbaud stopped writing poetry in 1873; from then on, he traveled in Europe, joined the Dutch army, deserted in Java, lived in his mother's house in Charleville, worked on her farm, read, and studied languages. In 1879, after recovering at his mother's from the typhoid fever he caught in Cypress, he returned to

Cypress and then, from 1880 until his death, he lived and traveled through Africa, working for several French colonial enterprises and seeking his fortune as a gun runner and slave trader in Abyssinia (now Ethiopia). Rimbaud had no contact with anyone in Europe, but he did write letters to his mother, which are extant; he also wrote an account of some of his travels in Africa, which was published by a geographical society. Rimbaud died of syphilis in a hospital in Marseilles, on November 10, 1891. "The Drunken Boat" was first published, along with other poems, in an 1884 collection, *Les Poètes maudits*, edited by Paul Verlaine. Its appearance solidified Rimbaud's reputation as a poet.

Rimbaud's reputation as a decadent and revolutionary artist has survived through to the present, influencing poets like Allen Ginsberg and musicians like Bob Dylan and Patti Smith. In *Total Eclipse*, the 1995 film about Rimbaud's life, Leonardo Di Caprio played Rimbaud. The same sort of sensory distortion and imagistic intensity displayed in "The Drunken Boat" can be found in Rimbaud's two other major works, *Une Saison en Enfer* (1873; translated as *A Season in Hell*) and *Illuminations* (1874).

MEDIA ADAPTATIONS

- The Allen Browne Quintet, an Australian Jazz Band, issued a recording of poetry and jazz featuring Rimbaud's poem in 2007. They have divided "The Drunken Boat" into five suites, each comprising five of the poem's twenty-five stanzas. The album is available through Jazzhead Records.

POEM TEXT

As I was going down impassive Rivers,
I no longer felt myself guided by haulers:
Yelping redskins had taken them as targets
And had nailed them naked to colored stakes.

I was indifferent to all crews,   5
The bearer of Flemish wheat or English cottons
When with my haulers this uproar stopped
The Rivers let me go where I wanted.

Into the furious lashing of the tides
More heedless than children's brains the other
    winter   10
I ran! And loosened Peninsulas
Have not undergone a more triumphant hubbub

The storm blessed my sea vigils
Lighter than a cork I danced on the waves
That are called eternal rollers of victims,   15
Ten nights, without missing the stupid eye of
    the lighthouses!

Sweeter than the flesh of hard apples is to children
The green water penetrated my hull of fir
And washed me of spots of blue wine
And vomit, scattering rudder and grappling-hook   20

And from then on I bathed in the Poem
Of the Sea, infused with stars and lactescent,

Devouring the green azure verses; where, like a
    pale elated
Piece of flotsam, a pensive drowned figure
    sometimes sinks;

Where, suddenly dyeing the blueness, delirium   25
And slow rhythms under the streaking of
    daylight,
Stronger than alcohol, vaster than our lyres
The bitter redness of love ferments!

I know the skies bursting with lighting, and the
    waterspouts
And the surf and the currents; I know the
    evening,   30
And dawn as exalted as a flock of doves
And at times I have seen what man thought he
    saw!

I have seen the low sun spotted with mystic horrors,
Lighting up, with long violet clots,
Resembling actors of very ancient dramas,   35
The waves rolling far off their quivering of
    shutters!

I have dreamed of the green night with dazzled
    snows
A kiss slowly rising to the eyes of the sea,
The circulation of unknown saps,
And the yellow and blue awakening of singing
    phosphorous!   40

I followed during pregnant months the swell,
Like hysterical cows, in its assault on the reefs,
Without dreaming that the luminous feet of the
    Marys
Could constrain the snout of the wheezing
    Oceans!

I struck against, you know, unbelievable Floridas 45
Mingling with flowers panthers' eyes and
    human
Skin! Rainbows stretched like bridle reins

Under the horizon of the seas to greenish herds!

I have seen enormous swamps ferment, fish-traps
Where a whole Leviathan rots in the rushes!　　50
Avalanches of water in the midst of a calm,
And the distances cataracting toward the
　　abyss!

Glaciers, suns of silver, nacreous waves, skies of
　　embers!
Hideous strands at the end of brown gulfs
Where giant serpents devoured by bedbugs　　55
Fall down from gnarled tress with black scent!

I should have liked to show children those sunfish
Of the blue wave, the fish of gold, the singing
　　fish.
—Foam of flowers rocked my drifting
And ineffable winds winged me at times.　　60

At times a martyr weary of poles and zones,
The sea, whose sob created my gentle roll,
Brought up to me her dark flowers with yellow
　　suckers
And I remained, like a woman on her knees . . .

Resembling an island tossing on my sides the
　　quarrels　　65
And droppings of noisy birds with yellow eyes
And I sailed on, when through my fragile ropes
Drowned men sank backward to sleep!

Now I, a boat lost in the foliage of caves,
Thrown by the storm into the birdless air　　70
I whose water-drunk carcass would not have
　　been rescued
By the Monitors and the Hanseatic sailboats;

Free, smoking, topped with violet fog,
I who pierced the reddening sky like a wall,
Bearing, delicious jam for good poets　　75
Lichens of sunlight and mucus of azure,

Who ran, spotted with small electric moons,
A wild plank, escorted by black seahorses,
When Julys beat down with blows of cudgels
The ultramarine skies with burning funnels;　　80

I, who trembled, hearing at fifty leagues off
The moaning of the Behemoths in heat and the
　　thick Maelstroms,
Eternal spinner of the blue immobility
I Miss Europe with its ancient parapets!

I have seen sidereal archipelagos! and islands　　85
Whose delirious skies are open to the sea-
　　wanderer:
—Is it in these bottomless nights that you sleep
　　and exile yourself,
Million golden birds, o future Vigor?—

But, in truth, I have wept too much! Dawns are
　　heartbreaking
Every moon is atrocious and every sun bitter.　　90
Acrid love has swollen me with intoxicating
　　torpor
O let my keel burst! O let me go into the sea!

If I want a water of Europe, it is the black

Cold puddle where in the sweet-smelling
　　twilight
A squatting child full of sadness releases　　95
A boat as fragile as a May butterfly.

No longer can I, bathed in your languor, o
　　waves,
Follow in the wake of the cotton boats,
Nor cross through the pride of flags and
　　flames,
Nor swim under the terrible eyes of prison
　　ships.　　100

POEM SUMMARY

Stanza 1

"The Drunken Boat" begins in the middle of an action on a note of savage and liberating violence. The forces that guide his boat have vanished, as the mariner/poet is rushing "down impassive Rivers." These rivers are metaphorical rivers. The poet's boat is a metaphorical boat, a symbol used to represent the poet himself. The poet has relocated the wild rivers of the world within himself. They are used to express symbolically his sensation of being alive and to represent the conflicts that are generated within him by his experience of the surging of that force of life. As he is rushing down impassive rivers, rivers which assert themselves no matter what resistance is attempted against them, the narrator feels the boat is being drawn by the river. It is unguided by haulers, the navigators who guide its course. "Yelping redskins had taken them as targets / And had nailed them to colored stakes." Savage and gaudy force has overcome strictness, direction, decorum, and control. The poet has been freed from the constraints imposed by social order. In terms that had yet to be introduced, the superego, symbolized by the haulers, has been conquered by the id, symbolized by the "redskins."

Stanza 2

Like the Ancient Mariner in Coleridge's poem, the narrator is telling of a strange water journey, and like that other mariner's, it is a symbolic one. He imagines himself as a merchant of wheat from Flanders or of cotton from England, a businessman who abandons the discipline of business. As the rivers are impassive, the narrator is indifferent to the loss of the haulers. In fact, once they are defeated by the upsurge of savagery, of lawlessness, once resistance yields and stops struggling against the primal forces which are frightening in their tempestuousness, the "uproar stopped / The rivers let me go where I wanted." The deliberate guidance overcome, there is a guidance of spontaneity that takes its place. The tempest is allayed because individual and wish are in accord.

Stanza 3

With passion unleashed and restraint abandoned the narrator, the person represented by the boat, runs with an intoxicated joy "Into the furious lashings of the tide." To show the magnitude of the sensation this liberty gives him, the poet conceives himself as a geographical entity whose feelings are commensurate with the feelings of "loosened Peninsulas"

Stanza 4

The narrator continues to celebrate the triumph of his liberation from constraint. "The storm blessed my sea vigils," he says. He was euphoric: "Lighter than a cork, I danced on the waves." Later in 1933, William Butler Yeats will give this phenomenon definition with his question "How can we know the dancer from the dance?" in his poem "Among School Children." In Rimbaud's poem, dancer and dance have become identical. The poet/sailor, the boat, and the ocean have become one substance. Alive inside the tempest because of his submission to it, the sailor/poet dances on the dancing waves whose rolling and raging tidal dance has been a deluging death to other mariners. He has moved with the waves for "ten nights," and has never wanted a lighthouse.

Stanza 5

"Sweeter than the flesh of hard apples is to children" shifts readers visually away from the savage freedom of the tossing sea to a scene of children in an orchard relishing the sweet skins of sour apples. It is a momentary flash of an image from childhood, when all the world is a mixture of the self within experiencing the world without. That is happening again in the river. The poet's growth is accomplished by a kind of reversion. The world and inner experience have grown more complex than they had been when they involved only chewing an apple. But the liberating principle of yielding to experience is the same.

The image of the child chewing the sweet skin of a sour apple does not exist only by itself.

It does double work. It suggests a scene from the sailor/poet's past and it serves as the first term of an epic simile. He is comparing the present experience to that past one: "Sweeter than the flesh of hard apples is to children," was "The green water" that "penetrated my hull of fir / And washed me of spots of blue wine / And vomit, scattering rudder and grappling-hook." Rather than drowning the sailor/poet, the water that destroyed his boat cleansed him. It "washed me of spots of blue wine / And vomit."

Stanza 6

That water initiated him, too. "From then on I bathed in the Poem / Of the Sea," he says. The turbulence, which destroys the moorings that social convention constructs around us, is itself the actual Poem that the poet must enter in order to make poetry. The Sea is "infused with stars and lactescent." The waves are lactescent. They are milk in its condition of becoming milk. Thus, they are incipient nourishment for the Poet. But the image is firmly grounded in the nature of the sea. The foam that crests breaking waves is milky in color. It is the sea's milk. In the sea, too, he finds the food for his verses, which he describes as blue. As such, they are "Silences crossed by Angels and Worlds." The line is Rimbaud's description of blue in his poem, "Vowels." Rimbaud attributed visual characteristics to each vowel and gave blue to "O." He then begins to experience a symbolistic scenario: a corpse pale and ravished by drowning, pensive and sinking into the depths. What follows is the descent under the sea with the drowned body.

Stanza 7

Its presence dyes the blue water red—Rimbaud's color for "I" and signifying "blood coughed up, laughter of lovely lips / In anger or ecstatic penitence," as Rimbaud wrote in his poem "Vowels." It is a fermenting, bubbling, bitter redness, the visual representation of the ghastly effects of love upon the spirit.

Stanza 8

Just as the intensity of the poet's vision violates the boundaries of the natural world, so stanzas 8 through 12, although divided into the quatrains that define the poem's structure, violate the formal structure of the poem by their intense, interwoven, and unrelenting focus on the interconnected aspects of the poet/mariner's experience. They form one integrated unit in which apparent boundaries are not boundaries. Stanza 8 introduces the "I" that introduces each of theses stanzas and weaves through them. Having been granted a poet's drink, drawing from the red fermentation of the last image, Rimbaud here becomes an "I" and asserts the "I" of the poet in a frenzy of perception and experience. "I know the skies bursting with lightening," he writes, and continues to represent a violent upsurge of external nature that corresponds to his inner liberation. But he knows not only the rage of "waterspouts" but also the calmness of evening or the "dawn as exalted as a flock of doves." The range and intensity of his experience allows him to say "I have seen what man thought he saw!"

Stanza 9

I have seen the low sun spotted with mystic horrors," the explorer/poet continues, "Lighting up, with long violet clots, / Resembling actors of very ancient dramas, / The waves rolling far off their quivering shutters!" Inside the phenomena of nature, transformed now into a poetic vision, he sees the form of an ancient drama as the violet light of the sun illuminates the rolling waves in a mystic conjunction of fire and water. In his psyche, the poet unites opposites.

Stanza 10

"I have dreamed of the green night with dazzled snows," he writes. With this image the poet/explorer is symbolizing the vibrancy and peace that can exist in nature as nature goes through its cycles. For Rimbaud, green is the color for the vowel "U" and, as he wrote in his poem "Vowels," green signifies "divine vibrations and virescent seas, / Peace of the pastures sown with animals." (Virescent means becoming green.) He has dreamed of "dazzled snows / A kiss slowly rising to the eyes of the sea, / The circulation of unknown saps / And the yellow and blue awakening of singing phosphorous!" He has experienced the sea eroticized as a kiss and glowing with an energy that can energize him. He has felt the colors contained in the sea and expressed by it. He has known the movement of the sea as life's energy and as a source of poetry.

Stanza 11

"I followed during pregnant months the swell, / . . . in its assault on the reefs." The poet is symbolically representing the gestation of a poem. The poem as it comes into being is like an assault, a natural force in a struggle against the restraints religion places on nature as symbolized by the "luminous feet" of the biblical "Marys" that are suggested by the "reefs."

Stanza 12

The poet continues his catalogue of conquests. "I struck against, you know, unbelievable Floridas." He has become a poet/hero, a poet who goes through the unknown realms for his education and brings back what has not yet been known. His experience, he proclaims, has been authentic. He has known exaltation in his experience of stormy skies, of evenings and of bright mornings. He has observed the violent and gorgeous surfaces of nature and he has seen the terrors beneath the surfaces. He has undergone a process of breaking boundaries and intermingling aspects of nature that nature keeps separate, of striking "against . . . unbelievable Floridas / Mingling with flowers panthers' eyes and human / skin!" The image is of Bacchic, or drunken, abandon. The only constraint is imposed by the shaping power of the imagination upon nature's intensity: "Rainbows stretched like bridle reins / Under the horizon of the seas to greenish herds!" The rainbows of poetry harness the horsepower of the sea.

Stanza 13

As the narrator continues his account, the nature of what he has seen and experienced changes from the billowing and blooming force of creation to the rotting and decaying energy of decomposition and destruction. Fermenting swamps, a whale rotting in the rushes, avalanches, cataracts, and "the abyss" now are revealed to him. The surge has become the fall.

Stanza 14

The fourteenth stanza details the fall, shifting away from a collage of silver suns, mother of pearl waves, and embers glowing in the skies. Against this blanched ground, "Hideous strands at the end of brown gulfs" appear "Where giant serpents devoured by bedbugs / Fall down from gnarled trees with black scent!" The symbolism has moved from the pregnant to the putrid.

Stanza 15

The "I" that has been speaking of itself and its experience becomes reflective now. The past tense is replaced by a past conditional: "I should have liked to show children those sunfish / Of the blue wave, the fish of gold, the singing fish."

Although upheaval has been his own interior experience, he wishes he could have shown to children, whose contact with experience is still immediate, the world it revealed. The hero/poet ventures through forbidden, unknown regions and in his verse returns with verbal maps of his explorations—his poetry. And he offers two lines of such poetry: "—Foam of flowers rocked my drifting / And ineffable winds winged me at times."

Stanza 16

In the next stanza the poet moves away from reverie back to the experience of his oceanic turmoil. He is "a martyr weary of poles and zones," of traveling, of being uprooted. As if in consolation or because he has earned it by those wearying travels, he is preserved by the poetry he can draw from his voyage. "The sea ... / Brought up to me her dark flowers," and he was grateful: "And I remained, like a woman on her knees."

Stanza 17

The poet/boat "sailed on," "resembling an island" and going through the squawking of birds and their droppings, and the image intensifies to "Drowned men" who "sank backward to sleep" because he could not prevent them from slipping through his "fragile ropes."

Stanza 18

The drowned are lost and so is he. The "I" of the poet and the boat are deliberately merged now, as they had implicitly been all along. But before, at the outbreak of his liberation, the poet was still being conveyed in a vessel. Now the boat, which has been identified as a symbolic representation of the poet himself is "lost in the foliage of caves, / Thrown by the storm into the birdless air." The carcass of the poet/boat is "water-drunk" and the boat is beyond rescue.

Stanza 19

There follows, in three interconnected stanzas, a brief lament, a memorial testimony of its conquests that the lost boat delivers for itself. It "pierced the reddening sky like a wall," breaking through the violence of the real world and penetrating into the visionary realm of poetry, and he brought back "delicious jam for good poets," the nurturing sweetness of real poetry.

Stanza 20

He continues recounting his accomplishments and the madness of his poetic experience, figured as a symbolic journey. He "ran, spotted with small electric moons, / A wild plank, escorted by black seahorses, / When Julys beat down with blows of cudgels / The ultramarine skies with burning funnels." The symbolic imagery has become delirious, as if the product of sick intoxication resulting from a beating by the cudgels of hot July.

Stanza 21

The poet/boat concludes the memorial lament with a confession: "I, who trembled, hearing at fifty leagues off / the moaning of Behemoths [sea monsters] in heat and the thick Maelstroms, / Eternal spinner of the blue immobility [the silence of death] / I miss Europe with its ancient parapets!" The poet who has seen what others have only imagined, and crossed into the turbulence of nature and psyche when guiding limits have been demolished, after everything, confesses he misses the order that antiquity has given to Europe.

Stanza 22

There is one last boasting lament. The poet proclaims his power as a seer. He has "seen sidereal archipelagos," islands of stars in the sea of the sky, in an image that symbolically merges the terrestrial and the celestial as one dazzling world. And then comes a question, not about himself or the value of his experience to himself but about its power beyond him: "—Is it in these bottomless nights that you sleep and exile yourself, / Million golden birds, o future Vigor?—" Does the strength of the future, symbolized by the "million golden birds" derive from the kind of psychic experience, the "bottomless nights" in which sleep is a form of visionary exile from the present world?

Stanza 23

But he does not really consider the question and refocuses on the anguish that has launched his defiant voyage: "But, in truth I have wept too much! Dawns are heartbreaking / Every moon is atrocious and every sun bitter." Waking consciousness brings cruelty and bitterness to him. The reason? "Acrid love has swollen me with intoxicating torpor." A disturbance in loving has become a disease in him and poisoned him into his visions. His torment is such that entering all the way into it seems to be the only way out of it. "O let my keel burst! O let me go into the sea!" It seems he is courting oblivion, death by drowning, but it is just as likely that he is wishing not death but metamorphosis into a poet and his poem. As such, he is dependent upon the internal power of his poet's imagination and he is free of the world, whether constrained or turbulent.

Stanza 24

"O let me go into the sea!" the culminating desire of the last stanza, gives way to "If I want a water of Europe, it is the black / Cold puddle where in the sweet-smelling twilight / A squatting child full of sadness releases / A boat as fragile as a May butterfly" The awful voyage of the drunken boat takes him round to its starting point, the sad child daydreaming inside his sadness as he pushes his toy boat, delicate in itself, and in its journey through the puddle made more delicate by the fragility of the child's psyche. The Poet's journey has dispelled a hunger for liberating grandeur and returned him to the child's world of all encompassing and calmly satisfying imagination.

Stanza 25

This tender reprise precedes the poet's return to his present and his sense of wanting to be away from everything he has been writing about. Bathing in the waves, he has still been following in the wake of the cotton boats, and he does not want to. He is still in the realm of controlled commerce, where he does not wish to be. He refuses to participate in the business of the civilized world, to "cross through the pride of flags and flames," to navigate his way through nationalism and war. And, he concludes with a refusal to "swim under the terrible eyes of prison ships." He makes a concluding declaration of defiance, seeing the Europe that he missed, nevertheless, as a center of constraints and, symbolically, even a drunken boat is monitored by prison ships. Any act of liberty is endangered because of the constraint inherent in the European culture.

THEMES

Savagery

"The Drunken Boat" begins with the triumph of savagery over the technology of civilization. "Redskins" slaughter the navigators guiding

TOPICS FOR FURTHER STUDY

- Write a ballad describing some strange and unnerving experience that you have had.

- In an essay, compare and contrast "The Drunken Boat" and Samuel Taylor Coleridge's "The Rhime of the Ancient Mariner" (1798). The latter is a confessional poem charting a life-changing sea voyage.

- Choose one of the scenes described in "The Drunken Boat" and select five images depicting that scene. In an accompanying paper, discuss the artists who created the images you've selected, and note why these particular works apply to the poem.

- Rimbaud, especially in his relationship with Verlaine, lived a life of debauchery, not only because of their promiscuous and volatile sexual relationship, but because of their intoxication, especially through the use of absinthe. In his poetics, Rimbaud asserted the need to break through the ordered and the rational to a deranged realm that fostered creativity. Choose a particular painter, composer, poet, or performer known to have regularly used drugs or alcohol. How does the artist's use of drugs and alcohol enhance or weaken your understanding of the artist's work overall? Present your findings to the class.

- Rimbaud in his poetry and in his life sought to subvert established patterns of behavior and modes of thought. In your opinion, what contemporary patterns of culture, morality, or thought ought to be reconsidered and replaced? Write an essay defending your position.

the boat, and the boat enters the state of savagery, drunk on its own liberation from constraint. The poet and boat then, throughout the poem, traverse the savage realms of unrestraint, of explosive and destructive nature, experiencing the force of savagery that the rules of European middle-class order exist to subdue.

The Tension Created by the Struggle between Constraint and Liberation

Implicit throughout "The Drunken Boat" is a tension between the constraints of authority, of the forces guiding behavior, thought, and perception and the experience of freedom, which is represented by the poet's escapes from those constraints. Freedom is felt as a kind of intoxication as the poem begins and the poet experiences his first moments of liberation. He compares himself to a cork dancing on the waves. He senses himself inundated and cleansed by the sea water he feels rushing over him. He experiences delirium and an immediate contact with the source of poetry and inspiration. Phenomena burst upon him, like lightening in its flashes and waterspouts in their jetting. But shortly after enjoying the headiness of liberation and the consciousness of psychic expansion, he begins to experience contraction. The boat becomes "lost in the foliage of caves." He perceives himself as a "water-drunk carcass." He confesses, after the elation of his riot has subsided, that he "miss[es] Europe," which symbolizes the restraint and the order civilization imposes on the individual. The once drunken poet is now like a man with a hangover who feels the dawn as "heartbreaking." Yet the poem ends not with his recantation of freedom but a rededication to escape from constraint: "No longer can I ... swim under the terrible eyes of prison ships."

Disintegration of the Self

Constructed of symbols used to represent internal psychic experience, "The Drunken Boat" takes the imagery of a sailor besieged by a tempest, who enters into the tempestuous experience rather than resisting the disintegration of ego. The poet/sailor abandons his socially constructed self and willingly allows himself to be drawn into the dark mysteries of a world full of wild, unbridled energetic experience that decomposes him, that sets him into a psychic freefall. The self is replaced by the fantastic visions the poet reports he has undergone on his voyage after he emerges from his orgy of intoxicated disintegration.

The Poet as a Visionary Hero/Adventurer

Poets are sometimes called seers. More than simply a writer, a poet is potentially an artist with visionary power. He may see into the depths that are hidden to most people. He is even sometimes believed to be endowed with the power to perceive and to shape the future. The persona Rimbaud assumes in "The Drunken Boat" is such hero poet/seer. Through his power as a poet, he is able to discover and to reveal in his poetry what until then had been unseen. "I have seen what man thought he saw," Rimbaud writes. The poet can enter unknown worlds, or worlds that were perceived, perhaps, only by madmen. But madmen are not poets. They can enter into the realms of chaos, but lack the resources and the power to return and to bring something back from the terrible realms beyond the boundaries of the civilized world and the well-ordered mind. The poet, because of his initiation into the art of poetry, can encounter and travel through the hidden realms and return, bringing back with him, in his poetry, what he has known there. That ability to return with a coherent vision of what he saw distinguishes him from a madman and confers on him the name of hero. A hero, in myth after myth, is the person who can go down to Hell and return with news from the forbidden realms. Dante, the poet of *The Divine Comedy* is such a poet hero. He travels through the realms of Hell, Purgatory, and Paradise and returns to tell the tale of what he has seen.

The narrator of "The Drunken Boat" is hurled into an abyss, propelled into an adventure in strange forbidden realms comparable to Paradise and Hell, on a symbolic sea of overwhelming experiences. His grip on ordered reality is loosened. His past attachments to the formal order and the regulating conventions of bourgeois European culture are lost. His vision takes him through the realm of Paradise before Hell. Paradise is the experience of his power as a poet. He "bathe[s] in the Poem / Of the Sea," and is nourished by the Sea, which is a zone of energy and a repository of images and symbols which the poet mines for his poetry. But the elation of his unfettered power is like drunkenness. Paradise transforms into Hell midway through the poem, reversing Dante's path from Hell to Paradise. Dante's vision is organized by the guidance of the doctrines of the Catholic Church. Rimbaud's is not. It is completely unhinged from anything but the poet's power of poetry, the power to return with the fragments of his experience and reveal them in symbolic, metric, rhyming language. Rimbaud returns with a vision of the true turmoil that underlies human life and with a vision of the insufferability of the systems which attempt to control chaos, the "prison ships." He also brings back a wish that there are "in these bottomless nights ... / [a] Million golden birds ... future Vigor."

STYLE

Symbolism

Symbolism is a poetic technique that allows a poet to write about intangible experience in concrete terms, replacing psychic events with symbols representing them. The first stanza of "The Drunken Boat" offers a good example. The poet was not really traveling in a boat. He symbolically describes his experience of being as "going down impassive rivers." The experience of the social control a person exercises to regulate his behavior is symbolized by "haulers" and the liberation from that constraint when repressed material breaks out in the psyche and affects the nature of one's ideas is symbolized by the slaughter of the haulers by "yelping redskins."

Repetition

In a poem of one hundred lines, Rimbaud uses the word *je*, I, twenty-four times in the original French. In Wallace Fowlie's English translation, it occurs twenty-six times. The repetition establishes not just the subjectivity of the poet's vision, but his own presence as the navigator that he said had been overwhelmed. Perhaps in the experience of the action of the poem he has been overwhelmed, but as a craftsman he has not. He is asserting his presence as the master poet/creator of the poem as well as the hero of the experience recounted by the poem.

Formal Control over Chaotic Material

Less apparent in the English translation, and, consequently, robbing the poem of its full strength, is the great control Rimbaud exercised over his material. While the content of the poem concerns the chaotic eruption of repression into an abandoned liberty, the construction of the poem shows the carefully crafting hand of a very skillful, metrically expert, practitioner of poetry. An example is the tight rhyming pattern Rimbaud creates. Although the English translation keeps the four-line stanza of the original, it sacrifices the discipline of the *abab* alternating rhyme scheme that runs through the poem. The contrast between the chaotic material and the formally shaped structure is one of the major factors turning what might be near-mad ranting into visionary and subversive poetry.

Synesthesia

Synesthesia is a poetic device of sensory derangement that Rimbaud practiced. The senses no longer have their proper object. Colors can have taste; texture can have smell; what is seen can be felt. Sight becomes texture. "Evening / And dawn" are described as being "as exalted as a flock of doves." A visual phenomenon is described in terms of the phenomenon of motion. The color red is compared to fermenting alcohol. Rainbows stretch under water and become the "bridle reins" for the "greenish herds" of the sea. This kind of derangement, while it makes for difficult poetry, is a kind of discipline, like meditation, designed to undo the boundaries of the self and liberate the poet's and the reader's experiential capability.

HISTORICAL CONTEXT

The Second Republic, the Second Empire, the Third Republic, and the Paris Commune

Nephew of Napoleon, Louis Napoleon, after years of exile and imprisonment under the restored French monarchy, was elected president of the Second French Republic, which was established in 1848 with the overthrow of the monarchy. In 1852, having consolidated power, Louis Napoleon dissolved the Republic and restored the Empire, designating himself Napoleon III. He began a course of imperial conquests and restored France to the military power it had lost in 1815 with the French defeat at the Battle of Waterloo. By the late 1860s, French military domination in Europe was threatened by Prussia and its leader, Otto von Bismarck. When Bismarck invaded Austria, Napoleon failed to enter the battle on the side of Austria. The defeat of Austria gave Prussia added might and Napoleon began The Franco-Prussian War with a preemptive invasion of Prussia in 1870. The French attack was a disaster. Napoleon was captured. A few days later, in July 1870, the Third French Republic was formed. Social and economic conditions were such in Paris, however, that discontent among workers was both strong and

COMPARE & CONTRAST

- **1870s:** The French suffer defeat after the invasion of Prussia by Napoleon III's army, the government abandons Paris, and Parisian workers establish a Commune and introduce revolutionary democratic reforms.

  Today: France has elected the rightist Nicolas Sarkozy as president on a platform of rolling back social reforms like the thirty-five hour work week. Paris is governed by a socialist mayor who institutes ecologically friendly programs like *velib*, which discourages the use of automobiles by making tens of thousands of bicycles available throughout the city. In the suburbs, which are populated largely by Islamic immigrants, there is little of the prosperity that is apparent in Paris.

- **1870s:** Paris is a center of radical movements in the arts, particularly in painting and

  poetry, and is a gathering spot for artists and poets.

  Today: Paris has lost its avant-garde status regarding painting and poetry to cities like Berlin and New York. Nonetheless, it thrives on its cultural past, often being regarded as a great museum rather than as a center of new creativity.

- **1870s:** Poets like Rimbaud and Verlaine induce intoxicated states of mind using absinthe and hashish. Their works reflect this in that they attempt to present the world in new and different ways.

  Today: The tradition of using mind-altering substances to enhance performance and creativity continues. Many popular musicians are known to regularly use drugs and alcohol.

---

unifying. There was a workers' uprising in July 1870 after the French defeat, and conditions of impoverishment and inequality continued, especially because of the Prussian siege of Paris. In 1871, the government of the new Third Republic attempted to negotiate an armistice with Prussia. One of Prussia's terms was for the French to permit a German ceremonial entrance into, but not an occupation of, Paris. The French workers had already formed an armed militia, the National Guard, and they were prepared to fight the Germans if their triumphal march through Paris turned violent. The government of France, in order to be more secure against a possible Prussian attack by German soldiers marching through Paris, retreated to Versaillles. The Prussians entered Paris and left the city without a violent confrontation. But the retreat of the Republican government to Versailles left a power vacuum in Paris that was filled by the steadily increasing strength and authority of the armed workers. Alarmed that the workers

had even commandeered cannons, the government in Versailles dispatched troops to Paris to seize the weaponry. Instead, the soldiers made common cause with the workers. In March 1871, after the workers' National Guard defeated those soldiers who did attack, the Paris Commune was declared by the Central Committee of the National Guard and remained in existence for two months until the end of May, when French army troops, which had been sent from Versailles and had been fighting the communards since the establishment of the Paris Commune, triumphed and the Third Republic was returned to power in Paris. Government reprisals against all who supported the Commune were numerous and severe.

The importance of the Paris Commune far outlasted its short existence because of its revolutionary nature. Among the social policies the communards inaugurated were the equality of women, including the right to vote, the separation of church and state, the right of the workers

Men in Tavern Drinking Absinthe (© *Bettmann | Corbis*)

to control factories and businesses that had been abandoned, the introduction of humane working conditions, the restoration to the workers of the tools of their trade that need had forced them to pawn, and the abolition of interest on debts.

Rimbaud was in Paris during the days of the Commune experiencing a society where men and women were being liberated, in a radically revised world, from repressive social, economic, and political conditions. It was a world he experienced that formed the context for his radically disruptive theory and practice of poetry.

Parnassians and Decadents

Nineteenth-century French poetry is divided into several classifications. During the early part of the century, the dominant poetry was called romantic. Romantics like Victor Hugo and Alphonse de Lamartine wrote poetry concerned with individual emotional expression and social rectification. Parnassianism developed around mid-century and its practitioners sought to focus poetry on the art of poetry itself for the sake of the art, wishing to free poetry from social or even psychological concerns. They sought formal perfection and the reconstitution of

traditional poetic forms. Parnassianism spawned a reaction that was at once a rebellion against it and a development of it. Charles Baudelaire practiced formal perfection in his poetry but nevertheless introduced an element of what he called spleen, meaning malice toward his fellow man, and distemper in general. He was branded as a decadent. Rimbaud's poetry reflects the influence of both of these trends. His formal poetic skill was prodigious, and his dedication to art was strong, but he brought to his poetry a subversive decadent sensibility.

CRITICAL OVERVIEW

The playwright, poet, and novelist, Samuel Beckett observes (according to Damian Love writing in the *Modern Language Quarterly*), that Rimbaud "stands on the threshold of modern literature" and "points the way into the promised land of modernism." Eric Ormsby asserts in the *New Criterion* that Rimbaud changed the course of French poetry by virtue of the fact that with "only a few savage but well-aimed swings of his rhetorical wrecking ball he seemed to fracture and upend all the flimsy subterfuges of the Parnassians." Rimbaud, Love argues, "embraced the divide" that he experienced between his observing "I" and the evolving and experiencing self that I observed. "He flung his life," Love suggests, "more passionately than most into the trajectory of his art—passionately enough, in the end, to turn his back on poetry when it failed him—and this inevitably led to extremes." It also made Rimbaud "a seer discovering new spiritual realms for mankind" Rimbaud was, according to Harold Bloom in *Genius: A Mosaic of One Hundred Exemplary Creative Minds*, "the genius of adolescence [who] achieved an astonishing originality." Bloom calls Rimbaud "a great innovator within French poetry."

One of the sources for Rimbaud's innovation, Daryl Lee argues in *Nineteenth-Century French Studies*, is his experience of the Paris Commune and particularly the ruins of buildings destroyed by the communards, which punctuated Paris and are known as "open ruins." "The open ruin," Lee argues, "links up with the azure sky, the desert, the abyss—so many anti-sites—because it tends toward the indistinct, undifferentiated." Lee argues that Rimbaud's verse stands, like the open ruin, admitting the "anti-sites" of his seemingly mad illuminations into his verse. In this vein, Enid Starkie, writing in *Arthur Rimbaud*, calls "The Drunken Boat" "one of the greatest poems in the French language."

CRITICISM

Neil Heims

Heims is a writer and teacher living in Paris. In the following essay, he discusses the psychic division that is expressed and charted in "The Drunken Boat."

"As I was going down impassive Rivers," the first line of "The Drunken Boat," establishes the cooperation of opposites that Pablo Picasso brought into his 1960 sketch of Rimbaud, a sober portrait surrounded by chaotic black scribbles. The "I" of the poet is set against the "impassive Rivers." But those rivers are another, symbolic aspect of the poet—the repressed energy of the poet, chaotic and turbulent. The second line also tells a story of opposition: "I no longer felt myself guided by haulers." In fact, a

third element is introduced, the term "myself." The river, which was the counterforce to the "I" in the first line, has been replaced by the haulers who guide the boat. But they are no longer available to control and protect the "I." Lodged between the "I" and the haulers is "myself" The poet is split into three parts now, the two recognized as "I" and "myself" on one side, and the haulers, the repressing and guiding forces, on the other. As I and myself, he is equally subject and object, the narrator and the thing narrated. In the third line, the haulers have been killed by "Yelping redskins." Now the opposition is between the haulers and the redskins; once again, both are opposing terms and both are opposing aspects of the poet. Control and savage liberation compete with one another. The primordial bursts through the "I," that aspect of the narrator/poet/sailor formed by the repression that society demands. The onrushing psychic and bodily energy that follows the breakdown of repression, the internal flood, is symbolized by the flood upon which the boat tosses. Both floods, the psychic and the symbolic, represent a void—Picasso's blackened scribble—the void of himself that Rimbaud penetrated in order to illuminate that blackness, in order to find what is within it and, in consequence, what is in him and what he is. That exploration and what is found become the double matter of his art. Once he penetrates that blackness in his drunken boat, he begins to see the phantoms of energy that have been pent-up and are now exploding.

Rimbaud is a divided person. There are two of him, just as Picasso's drawing suggests. There is the straight-laced, constrained man, the man, strict in his bearing, and there is the chaos within him, which he also is; when he delves into it he becomes, in consequence, like a madman. The poet's consciousness is a mystery for him to explore, and there he finds another man, a man without boundaries, awash on the oceanic tide of sensation that merges with everything it senses. He sets out to explore his consciousness and to free it from its formative bonds. The independent yet interdependent parts, his several selves, contradict each other; they also require each other.

In a letter dated May 13, 1871, which Rimbaud sent to Georges Izambard, his old teacher from the College de Charleville, Rimbaud wrote a sentence that has come to be understood as an

WHAT DO I READ NEXT?

- "Howl" (1956), by Allen Ginsberg, presents a journey through the nightmare experiences of poets and hipsters in revolt against conventional society. Its pile-up of violent imagery and its assault on the senses are partially rooted in Rimbaud's work and sensibility.

- "Sad-Eyed Lady of the Lowlands," a long song of tribute to an inscrutable woman with often inscrutable lyrics and images that are reminiscent of the kind Rimbaud employed, appeared on Bob Dylan's album *Blonde on Blonde*, released in 1966 by Columbia Records, now a division of Sony.

- *The Divided Self*, R. D. Laing's 1960 study of schizophrenia, argues that schizophrenic speech is not necessarily mad speech but appears that way because the schizophrenic speaker and his non-schizophrenic interlocutor do not share the same set of references. As a visionary poet, Rimbaud used language that was not placed against a shared social background but against the private background of his own inner meanings, divorced

from common understanding. It can therefore appear mad and deranged until a reader finds or creates its proper context, entering into Rimbaud's linguistic reality as Laing argues the psychiatrist must enter into the schizophrenic's.

- In *The Ego and the Id*, published in 1923, Dr. Sigmund Freud discusses the fundamental structure of the psyche as involving a dynamic interrelation of conscious and unconscious elements. Rimbaud is a great poet of the unconscious, bringing it into consciousness through symbolism, much as dreams in their bizarre imagery do, and he is also a poet of the struggle between the conscious and the unconscious for control of the person. His poetic journey anticipates Freud's analytic quest.

- Spanish poet Federico García Lorca's collection *A Poet in New York*, written in 1930 and published in 1940, has a rebellious awareness similar to what can be found in Rimbaud, as well as energetic imagery that is reminiscent of Rimbaud's imagery.

---

essential statement of his poetic stance and perhaps, beyond that, the secret motto of the century that came after him, *Je est un autre*, literally translated, "I is another." By this statement, Rimbaud likely meant that if the self is alien, then what we call "I" is not the person. It is a thing, something that has been made, constructed by a set of external forces. "I" signifies the *concept of I*. Thus, "I" means something other than what I identify myself as being. Such swirling thought indeed has the dizzying, unhinged wildness of a drunken boat.

Je est un autre is the creed of the Rimbaud that Picasso presents in his sketch. It expresses the fundamentally divided nature of integrity, the fragmented process of consciousness. There is the conscious being and the being he is

conscious of. But it is the same person who bears both perspectives. It is the fact that unity is composed of duality, and even of multiplicity, that is essential for a radical understanding of "The Drunken Boat," and this concept is at the heart of its composition. In addition, if there is a conscious "I" and if there is an "I" that the "I" is conscious of, that second "I" is potentially an unconscious "I." Thus, there is a third term, the unconscious being, the being the "I" is not conscious of when it is conscious of itself. The third term becomes manifest by the shifting manifestation of the "autre," the other. It is another part of the self that the constructed "I" obscures. The poem is a confrontation with this other that is "I" and consequently not "I." It is the turbulent sea the sailor/poet bathes in. In order to realize

> RIMBAUD IS NOT SAYING 'I AM LIKE A DRUNKEN
> BOAT.' HE IS SAYING 'I AM A DRUNKEN BOAT.' HIS MES-
> SAGE IS THAT PART OF ME THAT I AM DISCOVERING IS A
> HIDDEN PART OF ME THAT I CAN ONLY REVEAL
> THROUGH THE LANGUAGE OF SYMBOLS."

it, according to Rimbaud, the poet must break through the order and discipline of consciousness, must go beyond the frame of consciousness, into blackness. Rimbaud devised a technique to accomplish this. In that letter of May 13 to Izambard, and in a letter he wrote two days later, on the fifteenth of May, 1871, to his friend Paul Demeny, Rimbaud outlined that technique.

On the thirteenth, Rimbaud wrote to Izambard:

> I'm working at turning myself into a *Seer*. You won't understand any of this, and I'm almost incapable of explaining it to you. The idea is to reach the unknown by the derangement of *all the senses*. It involves enormous suffering, but one must be strong and a born poet. And I've realized that I am a poet.

In his letter on the fifteenth, Rimbaud wrote: "The first study of the man who wishes to be a poet is complete knowledge of himself." Unlike the Socratic injunction "Know thyself," Rimbaud's commission is not to know who he is but to know who he is not, to know the parts of him that are the "other." The need for a "derangement of *all the senses*" suggests that before such an attempt, the senses form a sort of boundary that not only receives and perceives sensation and information but also prevents the transmission of sensation and information. The senses are like sentinels guarding a position. In order to breach their line and discover what they are guarding, it is necessary to disrupt the order of their formation, to throw them off guard, to make them neglect their duty, to get them drunk.

Drunkeness, then, is not a metaphor or a simile for the poet's condition. Rimbaud is not saying "I am like a drunken boat." He is saying "I am a drunken boat." His message is that part of me that I am discovering is a hidden part of me that I can only reveal through the language of symbols. The language of metaphor is used for clarification. Something is compared to something else in order to amplify our understanding of it. The language of symbols is revelatory. Something is represented symbolically because it is so obscure in its existence that symbols are the only way it can be detected. The poet's hidden consciousness is not "like" a drunken boat. It is the same thing.

The "I" that is known, the socially constructed "I," the "I" that obscures and limits the experience of the psyche is provisional and deceptive. It is not the eternal psyche or the true "I" (which is unknowable). The true "I," the eternal "I" can only be discovered when the "I" that is known and the "I" that is not known is discovered as distinct. Rimbaud expresses this simply, even if symbolically, in a poem he sent to Verlaine, probably around 1873: "It's been found again. / What?—Eternity. / It's the sea gone off / With the sun."

Source: Neil Heims, Critical Essay on "The Drunken Boat," in *Poetry for Students*, Gale, Cengage Learning, 2008.

Gerald Martin Macklin

In the following essay, Macklin gives a critical analysis of Rimbaud's work.

It would be difficult to overestimate the influence of Arthur Rimbaud's poetry on subsequent practitioners of the genre. His impact on the Surrealist movement has been widely acknowledged, and a host of poets, from André Breton to André Freynaud, have recognized their indebtedness to Rimbaud's vision and technique. He was the enfant terrible of French poetry in the second half of the nineteenth century and a major figure in symbolism.

Jean-Nicolas-Arthur Rimbaud was born in Charleville in northeastern France on 20 October 1854, the second son of an army captain, Frédéric Rimbaud, and Marie-Cathérine-Vitalie Rimbaud, née Cuif. He had an older brother, Frédéric, born in 1853, and two younger sisters: Vitalie, born in 1858, and Isabelle, born in 1860. The father was absent during most of Rimbaud's childhood. Rimbaud's difficult relationship with his authoritarian mother is reflected in many of his early poems, such as "Les Poètes de sept ans" (The Seven-Year-Old Poets, 1871). Rimbaud's mother was a devout Christian, and Rimbaud associated her with many of the values that he rejected: conventional religious belief and

> IN THE LAST WORDS OF THE POEM, 'PRESSENT-ANT VIOLEMMENT LA VOILE' (HAVING A VIOLENT PREMONITION OF THE SAIL), THE IMAGE OF ANTICI-PATED SEA VOYAGES IS RELATED TO THE VISIONARY AND LINGUISTIC ADVENTURE THAT EMERGES IN 'LE BATEAU IVRE' (TRANSLATED AS 'THE DRUNKEN BOAT,' 1931) AND THAT REPRESENTS THE QUINTESSENTIAL RIMBAUD OF THE LATER PROSE POETRY."

practice, the principles of hard work and scholarly endeavor, patriotism, and social snobbery.

In 1870-1871 Rimbaud ran away from home three times. The outbreak of the Franco-Prussian War in July 1870 led to the closing of his school, the Collège de Charleville, ending Rimbaud's formal education. In August he went to Paris but was arrested at the train station for traveling without a ticket and was briefly imprisoned. He spent several months wandering in France and Belgium before his mother had him brought home by the police. In February 1871 he ran away again to join the insurgents in the Paris Commune; he returned home three weeks later, just before the Commune was brutally suppressed by the army. During this time he was developing his own poetic style and elaborating his theory of *voyance*, a visionary program in which the poetic process becomes the vehicle for exploration of other realities. This theory is expressed in his much-quoted letters of 13 May 1871 to his friend and tutor, Georges Izambard, and of 15 May 1871 to Paul Demeny. Rimbaud still felt drawn to Paris, where he might encounter the leading poets of the day—Théodore de Banville, Charles Cros, and Paul Verlaine. His letter to Verlaine in September 1871, which included samples of his poetry, elicited the reply, "Venez, chère grande âme, on vous appelle, on vous attend" (Come, great and dear soul, we are calling out to you, we are awaiting you). Rimbaud arrived in Paris in September and moved in with Verlaine and Verlaine's wife, Mathilde Mauté. A homosexual relationship developed between Rimbaud and Verlaine, causing Verlaine's marriage to become increasingly unstable.

Rimbaud's early poems, the *Poésies*, were written between 1869 and 1872 and published by Verlaine in 1895. They are, superficially, his most orthodox works in technical terms. Closer inspection, however, reveals in them many indicators of a precocious poet setting out "trouver une langue" (to find a language), as he said in the letter of 15 May 1871, and, ultimately, to revolutionize the genre. In thematic terms, the *Poésies* exhibit virtually all of the subjects and preoccupations usually associated with Rimbaud. "Le Mal" (Evil) and "Le Dormeur de val" (The Sleeper in the Valley) illustrate the absurdity of war; "Le Châtiment de Tartufe" (The Punishment of Tartuffe) represents Molière's eponymous impostor in sonnet form as the epitome of hypocrisy; "Au Cabaret-vert" (At the Green Tavern), "La Maline" (The Cunning One), and "Ma Bohème" (My Bohemian Existence) celebrate the physical joys of the bohemian lifestyle as an alternative to the moral rectitude of bourgeois existence. In "A la musique" (To Music) Rimbaud revels in his cherished role of observer as he satirizes the bourgeoisie through the technique of grotesque caricature. "Les Effarés" (The Frightened Ones) reveals both his humorous, cartoonlike presentation of figures on the margins of conventional society—in this case, five Christlike children peering into a bakery—and his social conscience as a commentator on exclusion, poverty, and hunger. "Oraison du soir" (Evening Prayer) shows his anti-Christian venom and his desire to shock and outrage accepted ideas of good taste by depicting himself as a rebellious angel who urinates skyward in a blasphemous gesture of defiance against his Creator.

The *Poésies*, however, also display Rimbaud's urge to extend the poetic idiom, to transcend the strictures and constraints of orthodox verse and to take poetry on an audacious journey into previously unsuspected technical and visionary realms. In this respect the *Poésies* anticipate Rimbaud's more fascinating later work and his profound impact both on the poetry of his own time and on that of the twentieth century. In the 15 May 1871 letter he says that "Viendront d'autres horribles travailleurs" (Other horrible workers will come along)—a prophetic assertion of his role as initiator of a process that would continue long after he himself had ceased writing.

The lengthy "Les Poètes de sept ans" combines many of Rimbaud's thematic preoccupations but also intimates the technical, linguistic, and visionary release that became a concomitant of his celebrated revolt. In the opening lines he establishes an opposition between the repressive mother and the disaffected seven-year-old boy who outwardly complies with her dictates but is inwardly seething with disdain: [...]. The child leads a double life that involves a superficial deference to material strictures and a secret other existence in which he gravitates to locations, confederates, and activities that would be anathema to the society embodied in the mother:[...].

Rimbaud is quite self-conscious in his choice of "distasteful" vocabulary, such as "latrines"; integral to his poetic credo was the principle that the sacred cows of traditional verse, such as the concept of "poetic" and "nonpoetic" terminology, needed to be challenged. The child-poet seeks out the mud as both a symbol of his rejection of the bourgeois totem of cleanliness and an indicator of his preference for the basic stuff of the natural environment. He consorts with the filthy ragamuffins of the district in an instinctive rejection of his mother's social stuffiness and a desire to find companionship among the outcasts of society; thus, the use of the plural *Les Poètes* in the poem's title is vindicated. The child most dreads the Christian Sabbath and Bible-reading; this negative reaction is balanced by his positive response to the working men of the district.

The most important elements of "Les Poètes de sept ans" are in the middle and later sections, where Rimbaud explores the visionary activities of the child-poet—activities conducted far from the watchful gaze of the parent that constitute a different, other life. One is reminded of the emphasis in the two May 1871 letters on the self as other—"Je est un autre" (I is an other)—and how these letters map out the function of the poet as medium between everyday reality and a hitherto unexplored *"ailleurs"* (elsewhere). The seven-year-old poet uses exotic journals to assist him in conjuring up new worlds: [...].

In the finale of the poem the child has retreated to the privacy of his room, blinds drawn to create an intense and intimate atmosphere. Here the scene is set for an imaginative flight triggered by "son roman sans cesse médité" (his endlessly considered novel), and the concluding six lines evoke a surreal landscape. The life of the neighborhood goes on below, acting as a counterpoint to the novelty of the inner world being explored by the child, a world with "lourd ciels ocreux" (heavy ochre skies) and "forêts noyées" (drowned forests). In the last words of the poem, "pressentant violemment la voile" (having a violent premonition of the sail), the image of anticipated sea voyages is related to the visionary and linguistic adventure that emerges in "Le Bateau ivre" (translated as "The Drunken Boat," 1931) and that represents the quintessential Rimbaud of the later prose poetry.

Many of the later poems of the *Poésies* prefigure Rimbaud's subsequent experimentation with language. The 15 May 1871 letter to Demeny combines Rimbaud's visionary program with a linguistic agenda and indicts a whole tradition of French verse, from Jean Racine to the Romantics, with only Charles-Pierre Baudelaire and, to a lesser extent, Victor Hugo escaping criticism. Rimbaud's search for a universal language is a defining feature of his work and is particularly manifest in "Voyelles" (1884; translated as "Vowel Sonnet," 1931), "Ce qu'on dit au poète à propos de fleurs" (What the poet is told about flowers), and "Le Bateau ivre" (1871-1872). The very idea of coloring the vowels, of composing a poem from their subjective associations, speaks volumes for Rimbaud's involvement with the minutiae of language and for his desire to challenge and reconstruct accepted idioms. The title "Ce qu'on dit au poète à propos de fleurs" is an audacious challenge to established poets; the piece mocks the inanities of Romantic commonplaces, deriding current practitioners as *faroeur* (jokesters) and outlining a new agenda for them as *jongleurs* (tricksters) conjuring up unsuspected visions. And "Le Bateau ivre," which is well known for its concatenation of dazzling imagery, is just as memorable for its linguistic inventiveness.

In March 1872 Rimbaud returned to Charleville to allow the Verlaines a chance to reconcile. During this period he wrote the *Derniers Vers* (Last Verses), which were published in *La Vogue* in 1886, highly experimental verse poems that are heavily influenced by Verlaine's style. Verlaine's poetry is characterized by a wistful tenderness, the muted evocation of landscape and character, the half-light of in-between states, a refusal of all that is aggressively stated or depicted, and above all by musicality. In the *Derniers Vers* Rimbaud adopts many of these technical features but allies them to unusual images and a dense conceptual content. The outcome is a strange blend of ostensible levity and musical airiness with weighty thematic elements, elements that are all the more intriguing for being conveyed in such apparently incongruous forms. All of this represents a major stride away from the poetry of the *Poésies*, where one finds many conventional features, and a retrospective view from the vantage point of the later prose poetry enables one to identify the *Derniers Vers* as a key phase in Rimbaud's rejection of orthodox verse, his abandonment of rhyme, and his evolution toward a more supple, less constricted form. That such is the case is confirmed in "Délires II" (Delirium II), a section of *Une Saison en enfer* (1873; translated as "A Season in Hell," 1931) where Rimbaud looks back on the *Derniers Vers*, ironically and affectionately repeats some of the poems, and ambivalently sees them as "L'histoire d'une de mes folies" (the account of one of my follies) and as a stage in the process of the "alchimie du verbe" (alchemy of the word), the creation of a new poetic language.

One is immediately struck by the almost surreal quality of "Larme" (Tear), the opening piece in *Derniers Vers*. The first words, "Loin des . . . " (Far from . . .), suggest a pressing need for the poet to separate himself from the trite and the commonplace. This escape is facilitated by an obscure potion, a golden liqueur that opens up a fantastic landscape presided over by an "orage" (storm), where the elements are liberated to generate a chaos that will slake the poet's metaphysical thirst. The poem "Comédie de la soif " (Comedy of Thirst) suggests in its five-part structure the influence of the five acts of classical tragedy, as well as having a distinctly operatic flavor. In parts one through three the *"Moi"* (Me) curtly rejects the overtures and solicitous attentions of family, friends, and "L'Esprit" (The Spirit), preferring to indulge in a death wish and the kind of landscape seen in "Larme" rather than accept their offer of a conventional life in familiar surroundings with banal occupations. Parts four and five afford the *Moi* some moments of recuperative calm in which to plot an alternative future course and anticipate dissolution in nature. "Comédie de la soif " is particularly musical; the slenderness of its lines in parts one through four gives an

impression of levity that is belied by its thematic content, and there is a marked sense of understatedness throughout. But the superficial lightness and musical simplicity of the poem are wedded to a linguistic concentration and intensity that repays endless revisiting.

Just as this poem advertises itself as a "comédie," so "Chanson de la plus haute tour" (Song of the Highest Tower) draws attention to itself as musically inspired. The narrowness of the lines on the page calls to mind the architecture of the tower where the poet has imaginatively secluded himself. The six lines of the opening stanza are repeated verbatim in the closing stanza, creating the effect of a chorus with the poem closing on itself. The poet presents himself as having gone to seed, laments the loss of his youth, and tries to transcend his own anguish in a call for a universal love: [...].

The immediately following poems, "L'Eternité" (Eternity) and "Age d'or" (Golden Age), have a structure and line length similar to those of "Chanson de la plus haute tour." "L'Eternité" encapsulates the essence of the *Derniers Vers* in its engaging musicality, its deceptively slim appearance, and its dense and obscure intellectual foundation. One is especially struck by the original manner in which Rimbaud has brought a musical form usually associated with a simple celebration or a joyous expression of love together with an abstract content replete with terms such as "suffrages" (approbation), "élans" (urges), "Devoir" (Duty), "espérance" (hope), and "supplice" (torture). The effect of this combination is to disorient the reader, for the musicality leads one to expect a text that will be readily intelligible; one is, however, left with a work that compels one to return again and again in search of an elucidation of its central meaning. The simplicity of the opening and closing quatrain— [...] —is at odds with the imprecise and abstract nature of the ensuing vocabulary.

While other poems, such as "Fêtes de la faim" (Feasts of Hunger) and "O Saisons, ô châteaux" (Oh Seasons, Oh Castles), share these features, the collection also includes the substantial poem "Qu'est-ce pour nous, mon coeur . . ." (What is it to us, my heart . . . ?) which deals with both sociopolitical upheaval and a private apocalypse; the celebrated complexity of "Mémoire" (Memory), with its rich allusiveness and intricate tapestry of evocations of the past, the self, and the family; and the charming and humorous idiosyncrasies of "Bruxelles" (Brussels), where Rimbaud admires an unusual cityscape and uses it as a bridge to something beyond itself.

In May 1872 Verlaine called Rimbaud back to Paris; in July he deserted his wife and child and went to London with Rimbaud. In April 1873 Rimbaud returned to his family's farm at Roche, near Charleville, where he began writing *Une Saison en enfer*. In May 1873 he again accompanied Verlaine to London. After many quarrels and another separation the two men met in July 1873 in Brussels, where Rimbaud tried to break off their relationship. Distraught, Verlaine shot the younger poet in the wrist; at the hospital where Rimbaud was treated, the two claimed that the wound had been inflicted accidentally. The next day the two men were walking down the street when Verlaine reached into his pocket; Rimbaud thought he was about to be shot again and ran to a nearby policeman. The truth about the shooting came out, and Verlaine was sentenced to two years at hard labor in a Belgian prison. While there, he wrote "Crimen amoris" (Crime of Love, 1884), in which Rimbaud is depicted as a radiant but evil angel outlining a new spiritual credo. Meanwhile, Rimbaud returned to the farm in Roche, where he completed *Une Saison en enfer*.

Even more dramatically than the *Derniers Vers*, *Une Saison en enfer* illustrates Rimbaud's proclivity for reinventing himself and redefining the direction and form of his poetry. No poet is more apt than Rimbaud to slough off one skin and put on another, more easily disillusioned with his most recent artistic endeavors, or readier to experiment with untried forms. The year 1873 thus marks his engagement with prose poetry, although there is still some disagreement concerning the dates of composition of many of the individual prose poems in *Les Illuminations* (1886; translated as "Illuminations," 1953). Much of this controversy was generated by the fact that the last of the nine sections of *Une Saison en enfer* seems to be a definitive farewell to literature, and this, allied to the fact that Rimbaud did abandon his poetic career at an early age, led many commentators to seek a simple and convenient solution by postulating that *Une Saison en enfer* is his swan song. There is now a consensus, however, that at least some of the poems in *Les Illuminations* postdate those of *Une Saison en enfer* and were written in 1874

and possibly 1875. The critical endeavor that has been wasted in the pursuit of a final adjudication on this chronological dispute would have been more constructively spent in examining the texts themselves. Since the mid 1970s, however, this situation has been rectified with excellent studies by critics such as Steve Murphy, Paule Lapeyre, André Guyaux, Nathaniel Wing, Nick Osmond, James Lawler, and Roger Little.

Rimbaud persuaded his mother to pay to have *Une Saison en enfer* published in Brussels in 1873. It is a diary of the damned that affords insights into his preoccupations and casts light on the artistic inspiration for the *Derniers Vers*. At the same time, the nine parts of the diary display an utterly new technical direction, and "Délires II" is all the more remarkable for the way it interweaves this new prose style with extracts from the *Derniers Vers* so that both modes are thrown into dramatically stark relief. *Une Saison en enfer* is an intensely personal account of private torture and the search for a spiritual and an artistic resolution; a prose style studded with laconic formulae that are also seen in the one-liners of *Les Illuminations*; a sustained investigation of self, Christianity, and alternative spiritual and poetic options that is frequently lit up by the flare of Rimbaud's memorable imagery; and a conscious pushing of language to the point of disintegration, so that verbal crisis and personal trauma are perfectly matched.

From the outset Rimbaud engages with abstractions, often personified in a Baudelairean manner: "[...] I sat Beauty on [...]," he begins the opening section, showing the irreverence that is a hallmark of his entire output. The death wish already seen in the *Derniers Vers* and to be repeated in many of the finales of *Les Illuminations* is also present here. The terse statements "Le malheur a été mon dieu. [...]" (Misfortune was my god. [...]) anticipates the enigmatic, clipped comments and sibylline quality of many of the prose poems in *Les Illuminations*. One of the most important sections of *Une Saison en enfer* follows this brief introductory sequence: "Maivais sang" (Bad Blood) is a sustained investigation into the narrator's genealogical origins [...]. One is reminded of the importance of revolt in the early *Poésies* as the narrative voice seems bent on contravening all received ideas about morality and decency; this unorthodoxy escalates into a full-scale assault on Christian values.

"Mauvais sang" registers the wrestling of a tormented soul that initially rebels against Christian teaching and then apparently finds grace and redemption, only to withdraw into a pursuit of fulfillment in the religions of the East or a personal spiritual agenda that is part of the poetic experience. Known above all for his delight in revolting against norms and conventions, Rimbaud impresses on the reader from the start of "Mauvais sang" that he is conscious of his "otherness," his inability to follow the accepted orthodoxies of Western Christian civilization. He extols "vices" such as idolatry, sloth, and anger; he refuses to comply with the received wisdom that one must work to live[...]; and he mocks traditional family and civic values. He traces these characteristics to his earliest ancestry, associating his "bad blood" or "bad stock" with previous lives as a leper or pariah, and he insists on his essential loneliness. He derides the scientific "progress" of the late nineteenth century, rejecting rationalism in favor of an internal spiritual debate. [...] he establishes his own form of mysticism and faith as an alternative to the Christian orthodoxies he had rejected in the *Poésies*.

The remainder of "Mauvais sang" and the subsequent section, "Nuit de l'enfer" (Night in Hell), pursue the diarist's spiritual crisis in all its intensity and complexity. Oscillating between salvation and damnation, the poet struggles with his dilemma in an increasingly fractured and tormented style that dramatically reflects his inner trauma. Guyaux has written of Rimbaud's *La Poetique du fragment* (fragmentary poetics), a formula that is admirably suited to the tortured style of these pages of unanswered questions, emotionally charged outpourings, lucidly trenchant affirmations of intent that seem unshakable but are almost immediately undermined by another change in direction, and a prose that seems informed by delirium. Seeing himself as a martyr in the line of Joan of Arc, Rimbaud [denies being a Christian] but soon afterward enters a sequence of contemplative calm in which salvation is enjoyed in dreamlike serenity. At the end of "Mauvais sang" the poet evokes his own extinction as language disintegrates in a proliferation of punctuation marks and linguistic fragments.

The next two sections of *Une Saison en enfer* share a title—"Délires I" and "Délires II," the latter of which carries the secondary heading "Alchimie du verbe." It is generally agreed that "Délires I" is a commentary on Rimbaud's relationship with Verlaine; it takes the form of a religious confession in which the speaker is the "Vierge folle" (Foolish Virgin), a thinly disguised image of Verlaine, who reflects on "her" stormy affair with the "Epoux infernal" (Infernal Bridegroom), Rimbaud. As well as being another irreverent parody of a religious source, this confession is a highly original form of self-presentation on Rimbaud's part as he sees himself through the refracted and selective memory of a confederate. The *Vierge folle* registers her failure to understand the complexities of her Infernal Companion, a blend of compassion and cruelty, innocence and malice, and ideological power and near insanity. This is a love affair in which the older partner is in thrall to the paradoxes and enigmas of the younger one; the relationship is characterized as a messiah leading a disciple, offering new ideas and experiences and then abandoning the weaker partner just when the *Vierge* is least emotionally prepared for the separation. All of these elements can be linked to the stages in the unfolding relationship between Rimbaud and Verlaine in 1872-1873, but the text is more significant for what it reveals about Rimbaud's defiance of the norm [...]; his compassion for underdogs such as drunks, children, and outcasts; his ideological fervor [...]; and his need to escape from reality.

"Délires II" has a quite different complexion. It reflects on the genesis of the *Derniers Vers*, affectionately and ironically recalling the poet's ambitions and artistic preferences during the earlier period. No fewer than fifteen sources of inspiration are listed at the outset, including obsolete literature, church Latin, fairy tales, and old operas, all of which assist in a quest—now seen as "one of my follies"—to create a new poetic idiom. Linking his predilection for hallucinatory experiences to "l'hallucination des mots" (the hallucination of words), Rimbaud weaves reprises from the *Derniers Vers* into his new prose style. The reader soon notices his preference for lapidary formulae, which stud not only *Une Saison en enfer* but *Les Illuminations*, as well: [...].

While sections six and seven of *Une Saison en enfer*, "L'Impossible" (The Impossible) and "L'Eclair" (Flash), continue the spiritual and philosophical probing of earlier parts of the work, it is the penultimate and final chapters,

"Matin" (Morning) and "Adieu" (Farewell), that have attracted the most detailed comment. At the end of "Matin" comes a sense of uplift as the poet anticipates a glorious day of renewal and transformation, a time when an outmoded religious belief will be superseded by a fresh spiritual awakening and the first authentic Noel: [...].

"Adieu" comes at the end of *Une Saison en enfer*, leading many to see this section as the conclusion not only of the collection but also of Rimbaud's poetic career. An initial reading of the text lends support to this interpretation, as the poet describes himself as a fallen angel and a writer who must give up the pen and embrace a more prosaic existence [...]. It is also noticeable that the concluding paragraphs of "Adieu" are couched in the future tense, which appears to prefigure yet another redefinition of the poet and his mission.

For many critics, *Les Illuminations* is Rimbaud's most important and technically sophisticated work. While the collection maintains a clear thematic continuity in many ways with the earlier verse—the idea of revolt, the preeminence accorded to the world of the child, the fascination exerted by the elements, the motif of travel in pursuit of the ideal, and so on—here one is manifestly in the presence of a poet intent on experimentation with new poetic structures, the deployment of unusual and often bizarre terminology, and even an exploration of the creative power of punctuation dynamically reinvented and released from its conventionally subservient role as a prop for language. These and many other ingredients have created a sense of bewilderment in some readers of the poems; the critic Atle Kittang has even referred to the "illisibilité" (unreadability) of the collection. One often associates the poetry of Stéphane Mallarmé with such hermeticism, but it is a significant feature of the critical reception of *Les Illuminations* that readers have produced such widely divergent interpretations of the poems and that some have declared themselves incapable of arriving at any sustainable reading of given texts. "Parade," "Matinée d'ivress" (Morning of Drunkenness), "Barbare" (Barbaric), "Fairy," "H," and "Dévotion" (Devotion) are some of the poems that have provoked perplexity and a polarization of critical opinion.

Critics such as Osmond and Albert Py have attempted to classify the poems in *Les Illuminations*; while no definitive labeling is possible—or, perhaps, even desirable—some distinctive groupings can be observed among the forty-two texts. A prominent source of inspiration in all of Rimbaud's poetry is the fairy tale, which is clearly linked with his preoccupation with the child and the child's imagination. In *Les Illuminations* "Conte" (Tale), "Aube" (Dawn), and "Royauté" (Royalty) are obviously based on the structure of the fairy tale. Each poem has a distinctly narrative development, and "Conte" and "Royauté" include regal characters (prince, king, and queen) involved in the pursuit of happiness on a personal or public level. Rimbaud, however, tends to subvert the traditional fairy-tale happy ending by setting up an apparently happy outcome and then destabilizing it. Other poems that might be loosely grouped under a common heading are those that seem to constitute riddles, puzzles, and enigmas. In these poems Rimbaud poses problems for his readers and often uses the finale of the text to tantalize, disconcert, or confuse them. A master of beginnings and endings, he frequently deploys an isolated final line to set a problem or issue a challenge; these final lines are a most original feature of *Les Illuminations*: [...]. Other sequences in the collection enhance a sense of mystery and the unknown. For example, in "Enfance III" (Childhood III), "Enfance IV," "Veillées I" (Vigils I), "Solde" (Sale), and "Fairy" a concatenation of linguistic units bound together by the same linguistic formula perplexes the reader as to just what is being described.

Equally prominent as a motif in *Les Illuminations* is Rimbaud's quest for the ideal cityscape in poems such as "Ville" (City), "Villes" (Cities), "Villes II," and "Métropolitain" (Metropolitan). Whereas "Ville" is a mournful evocation of the soulless existence endured by many in contemporary urban conglomerations, the other texts are characterized by a vitality and exuberance that reflect the poet's desire to transcend the everyday banality of late-nineteenth-century life and reveal an alternative world of daring new architecture populated by unexpected characters. Thus, the grayness, repetitiveness, and tastelessness of "Ville" is superseded by the enormous proportions of "Villes," in which a "Nabuchodonsor norwégien" (Norwegian Nebuchadnezzar) is one of the architects of a complex metropolis that goes far beyond anything that London or Paris might offer. Even more dazzling is the vertiginous drama acted out in

"Villes II," where a miscellany of extraordinary figures is set before the mind's eye to the accompaniment of a stereophonic operatic "score." This poem gravitates toward the apprehension of some hitherto unattained understanding designated by the expressions "les idées des peuples" (the ideas of the peoples) and "la musique inconnue" (the unknown music). Finally, the opening paragraph of "Métropolitain" evokes a richly colored realm where another complex architectural system—crisscrossing "boulevards de cristal" (crystal boulevards)—is the venue for the emergence of "jeunes familles pauvres" (young poor families), a mysterious constituency of inhabitants whose lifestyle is enthusiastically endorsed by the poet in the words "la ville!"

The pursuit of a new religion is a constant in Rimbaud's work, but *Les Illuminations* takes this quest to a new plane. The collection is heavily populated by gods and goddesses of the poet's invention, including the mysterious Reine (Queen) or Sorcière (Witch) in "Après le déluge" (After the Flood), an enigmatic figure who withholds privileged knowledge from mere mortals; the object of worship in "Being Beauteous," a poem with many Baudelairean connections; the Génie in the poem of that title, who also appears in "Conte" as a key player in the Prince's creative rampage; the "idole" (idol) in " Enfance I"; the goddess pursued by the poet in "Aube" ; the spirit referred to in "A une raison" (To a Reason); and Elle (She), who appears in both "Angoisse" (Anguish) and "Métropolitain." "Après le déluge," the first poem in the collection, harks back to the deluge in the Old Testament to evoke new floods that might cleanse the earth again; [...] in the first part of "Vies" (Lives) he refers to a "brahmane" (Brahman) who explained the Book of Proverbs to him; and "Matinée d'ivresse" is predicated on the imperative to supersede the tired Christian opposition of good and evil and to develop a new religious faith.

The persona of traveler is one of Rimbaud's preferred identities, and the motif of the journey is a central element in such works as "Le Bateau ivre." In *Les Illuminations* this motif is reconstituted and reinvented in a variety of ways. The "piéton de la grand'route par les bois nains" (traveler on the highway amid dwarfish forests) in "Enfance IV" anticipates the nomadic tendency that leads the prince on his pilgrimage in "Conte," stimulates the boy to pursue the goddess in "Aube," and prompts the brief text

"Départ" (Departure) as a celebration of the dynamic and the shifting over the static and the familiar. Other examples include the wandering poet and his bizarre confederate Henrika drifting on the fringes of an industrial city but desirous of an "autre monde" (other world) in "Ouvriers" (Workers); the circus troupe on the move in "Ornières" (Ruts); and the wretched couple in "Vagabonds," wandering in search of "le lieu et la formule" (the place and the formula). In poems such as "Nocturne vulgaire" (Ordinary Nocturne) and "Barbare" Rimbaud depicts imaginative voyages or drug-induced "trips" that take him and the reader to the further limits of the psyche. In "Nocturne vulgaire" the reader is taken on a highly unusual journey that involves a destabilizing of the contours of the known world as a prelude to a departure in a "carrosse" (carriage) that transports the poet to an "ailleurs" that proves to be trite and unsatisfactory. Then a flood of green and blue abruptly curtails the journey in the carriage and permits a much more satisfying adventure in the elemental ferment of the storm, one of Rimbaud's most favored contexts, in which a mixture of creation and destruction occurs: [...].

This pattern of creative immersion in the elements—including earth, air, and fire, as well as water—is seen in many finales in *Les Illuminations*, such as those of "Angoisse," "Soir historique" (Historic Evening), and "Métropolitain." "Barbare" includes a particularly engrossing example of the function of elemental imagery in Rimbaud's prose poetry. As its title suggests, "Barbare" sets out to challenge and transcend all that is conventional and familiar. It achieves this objective in two ways: in its mysterious and absorbing imagery, which evokes another bizarre journey of the imagination; and in its unprecedented linguistic experimentation, which takes one to the verge of verbal disintegration. From the opening line [...], it is apparent that Rimbaud is determined to sever links with normal time and space as a prelude to his departure into an uncharted realm of the imagination. Much ink has been spilled in attempts to "decode" the "pavillon en viande saignante" (ensign of bleeding meat) that binds the poem together in a cyclical pattern by virtue of its triple deployment in the text; yet, just as striking is the concatenation of elemental imagery that runs through the piece—arctic seas, infernos, frosty squalls, flames, foams, blocks of ice, volcanoes. One passage is remarkable for its dense compression of ingredients derived from each of the four elements: [...].

Here water *(pluie)*, fire *(feux, carbonisé)*, air *(vent)*, and earth *(le coeur terrestre)* are fused to register an experience of the eternal. "L'Eternité" in the *Derniers Vers* and "Matinée d'ivresse" in *Les Illuminations* similarly relate a sense of the eternal to a fusion of elemental opposites; yet, in "Barbare" this amalgamation is effected by virtue of Rimbaud's audacious approach to language, punctuation, and poetic form.

Rimbaud's pursuit of a new poetic language is the defining and enduring aspect of his artistic career. His essential thematic preoccupations—the journey of discovery, the world of the child, the phenomenon of revolt—are developed in conjunction with his ambition to redefine the poetic word, to liberate it from the shackles of debilitating forms and rules, and to arrive at a much more supple and flexible medium of expression, untrammeled by inhibitions and fusty convention and characterized by a vitality and an exciting "otherness" that permit endless innovation and surprise. The injunction to the poet in "Ce qu'on dit au poèt à propos de fleurs" to become a "Jongleur" dispensing shocks and revelations to the reader is an apposite characterization of Rimbaud's entire enterprise. *Les Illuminations* represents the culmination of this process: the collection is studded with all sorts of verbal discoveries—from the foreign terms such as the German *wasserfall* (waterfall) in "Aube" and the English title "Being Beauteous" to the highly unusual *Baou* in "Dévotion." The collection is also remarkable for its proliferation of dashes, intriguing capitalizations, and baffling italicizations. The odd punctuation fragments texts in fascinating ways, creating unsuspected rhythms and internal arrangements and highlighting individual words and clauses, and, in conjunction with the foreign and unusual terms, it turns *Les Illuminations* into a venue for all sorts of linguistic surprises. Among these surprises are the vast number of puzzling proper nouns in the collection—*Reine, Sorcière, Barbe-Bleue, Prince, Génie, Elle, Hottentots, Molochs, Proverbes, Mabs, Solymes, Damas, Hélène*, and so on. The poem-puzzle "H" invites the reader to consider the properties of the capital letter *H*, some of which are tantalizingly offered within the poem itself with the proper name Hortense and the word *hydrogène*, which reminds the

reader that H is the atomic symbol for hydrogen. This text sets author and reader in opposition, Rimbaud withholding his secrets and the reader being teased to attempt to discover them. This situation is seen frequently in *Les Illuminations* in poems such as "Parade," "Solde," and "Dévotion." In "Vies" the poet sets himself up as an oracular figure with revelations to make: [...].

The key term here is *chaos*, a traditionally pejorative word characteristically given a positive meaning by Rimbaud. *Les Illuminations* is a realization of that positive state of "chaos" so ardently desired by its creator: a flux in which language disintegrates and reconstitutes itself into an entity that transcends what has preceded it.

Rimbaud abandoned poetry at the age of twenty-one, having written it for only five years. In 1875-1876 he traveled to England, Germany, Italy, and Holland; he enlisted in the Dutch army but deserted from it in Sumatra. In 1876 he settled briefly in Vienna, then traveled to Egypt, Java, and Cyprus, where he worked as a foreman in a quarry. In 1880 he went to Ethiopia as the representative of a French coffee trader, Alfred Bardey, based in Aden (today part of Yemen); Rimbaud was one of the first Europeans to visit the country. He remained there as a trader and explorer. Scholars have long been intrigued by the fact that Rimbaud's extensive correspondence from Africa to France includes no references to poetry but is taken up with utilitarian and commercial considerations relating to his trading activities; the phrase "le silence de Rimbaud" is used to designate his abrupt abandonment of poetry. Nevertheless, his fame as a poet occurred during this period when Verlaine included some of his poems in *Les Poètes maudits: Tristan Corbière; Arthur Rimbaud; Stéphane Mallarmé* (The Accursed Poets: Tristan Corbière; Arthur Rimbaud; Stéphane Mallarmé) in 1884 and published *Les Illuminations* two years later. In February 1891 Rimbaud developed a tumor on his right knee; he returned to France for treatment, and his leg was amputated in a Marseille hospital. He went back to the farm in Roche to recuperate, but his health continued to deteriorate. He went back to Marseille, where he was diagnosed with cancer. He died in the hospital there on 10 November 1891; his sister Isabelle, who was with him at the time, claimed that he accepted the Catholic faith before his death. He was buried in Charleville.

"

Source: Gerald Martin Macklin, "Arthur Rimbaud," in *Dictionary of Literary Biography*, Vol. 217, *Nineteenth-Century French Poets*, edited by Robert Beum, The Gale Group, 1999, pp. 243–57.

Wallace Fowlie

In the following essay, Fowlie examines Rimbaud's childhood experiences, which are reflected in "The Drunken Boat." Fowlie also provides a brief interpretation of the poem's several sections.

In August 1871, when Rimbaud wrote this poem, he was sixteen years old and living with his mother, his brother, and his two sisters at 7, quai de Moulinet in Charleville. The poem marks the beginning of his period of most mature and significant writing, and represents an achievement in the history of French lyric poetry.

A little over a year's poetic activity preceded the composition of "Le Bateau ivre." Rimbaud had written poems in Latin and had received prizes for his skill in executing classical hexameters. In French he had written long and short poems on themes of mythology, love, and violence, some of which reveal parnassian ancestry. May 1871 seems to have been one of the most fertile months in Rimbaud's life. This was probably the month in which he wrote "Le coeur volé" and his first major poem, "Les Poètes de sept ans." May was also the month in which he wrote his two letters to Izambard and Demeny on the function of the poet. In these *lettres du voyant* he formulated a poetic creed of which "Le Bateau ivre" was to be the first successful illustration.

In Rimbaud's childhood experience there was no great river and no great ocean. But there was a small boat on the Meuse River. Where it flowed near the college there was a small island, and midway between the island and the shore floated a raft used by the workmen

from the tanneries. A small boat for the use of the tanners was attached to the shore by means of a long padlocked chain and an iron stake. After school, Arthur and his brother often threw themselves into the boat, pushed it out into the river as far as the chain would permit, and then, leaning first to the right and then to the left, would cause the boat to rock as in a storm. Arthur would lie down flat and look down into the depths of the river water. This often repeated scene on the Meuse plays its own part in the storms and contemplations of "Le Bateau ivre."

Another kind of experience, important in the genesis of the one-hundred-line poem, is that of Rimbaud as reader. No precise allusions are in the poem, but it contains many reminiscences. Several of the images have literary sources, but they have been subjected to Rimbaud's own personal experience.

Two authors above all seem to have stimulated the boy-poet: Chateaubriand and Hugo. *Les Natchez* and *Atala* of Chateaubriand, with their scenes of Indian torture and North American forests, and the pictures of the sea in Hugo's *Travailleurs de la mer* are two rich sources, both in language and vision. James Fenimore Cooper's *La Prairie*, in its French translation, and Jules Verne's *Vingt mille lieues sous la mer* were popular novels of adventure widely read by boys at the time. They provided Rimbaud with further images of prairies and solitary figures sinking into the sea. The work of two poets should be added to these titles. "Les Odes funambulesques" of Banville, because of their technical brilliance, and "Le Voyage" of Baudelaire, because of its symbol of the sea, left their mark on Rimbaud. Phrases from the Latin poets exist: Horace's *levior cortice* (*plus léger qu'un bouchon*, "lighter than cork"). More important are biblical verses from Job, chapters 32 and 38, which abound in questions the ancient Hebrew visionary might have asked the youthful poet of the Ardennes who had defined his vocation as that of visionary: "Hast thou entered into the springs of the sea? or hast thou walked in the search of the depth?" The vision of "Le Bateau ivre" may well be the answer to questionings which had sunk into the boy's subconscious after his reading of Job: "Hast thou entered into the treasures of the snow? or hast thou seen the treasures of the hail?"

The real introduction, however, to "Le Bateau ivre" is the earlier poem, "Les Poètes de sept ans." There we learn something of the mental and psychical activity of the boy Arthur which finally becomes projected and crystallized in his art. There we learn about his Bible readings, his dreary Sundays, his revolt against maternal domination, his efforts to love children and workmen. But especially we learn about the successful adventures of his childhood, those of his imagination: the novels he invented about life (*les romans sur la vie*), the litany of exotic lands (*forêts, soleils, rives, savanes*), the power of pictures (*journaux illustrés*), and of fictional sailings which converted prairies into sea billows.

"Le Bateau ivre" is a complete intellectual autobiography. All of Rimbaud's past is in it, and, prophetically, the general lines of his future.

The Poem

Not only for convenience' sake, but because they seem to follow a design, the twenty-five stanzas of the poem may be divided into four parts.

1. The first five stanzas serve as an introduction and announcement of the major theme: liberation. The boat speaks; it is clearly the symbol of the poet who in his intoxication has discovered a release from the world of conventions. The first step in the boat's liberation is the disappearance of the haulers, who had been seized by Indians and nailed naked to colored stakes. This places the scene in North America, possibly by the Mississippi, where the savages crucify in a ritual of blood, sadism, and uproar the foreign invaders seeking to impose an unholy order and commercial exploitation on a pagan civilization. After losing its haulers, the boat loses its crew and cargo. It is now able to follow its own will and feel the freedom of the river waters. It has a child's lust for the disorderly and the noisy, a lust which is a natural self-affirmation. There are not even any shore lights to direct its course through the domains of excitement and haste and fracas. The pure element of the sea, limitless and powerful, enters into the very being of the boat, and its taste is like that of hard apples to a child, the taste of danger and stolen fruit. With the crashing of the water on the deck, the last elements of direction and control disappear. Anchor and rudder are swept into the sea. The liberation is complete. The poem of the sea can begin.

2. The second section (stanzas six through fifteen) begins with the temporal statement "Et dès lors" and is a long litany of what the boat saw in its disordered and uncharted voyage. The sound of litany is in the simple verbs at the beginning of each stanza: "je sais," "j'ai vu," "j'ai rêvé," "j'ai suivi," "j'ai heurté," "j'ai vu" (I know, I saw, I dreamed, I followed, I struck against, I saw). The first verb affirms the new knowledge of violence and peace, of the lightning-drenched evening sky and the dove-swarming sky of dawn. The second verb affirms the new vision of the setting sun when its rays stretch out across the water like long ceremonial figures of ancient actors. The third affirms a dream of polar nights when light seems to mount from the snow as yellow phosphor mounts up from the ocean depths. The fourth affirms the boat's quest for the unseizable power and the unseizable form of the ocean swells. The fifth and sixth verbs affirm the boat's collision with the mainland and the subsequent vision of sea monsters caught in the gulfs along the coast. This, the longest section of the poem, is the boat's discovery of the universe: of its splendor, its gigantism, its violence. Each sensation leads to another in a wild chase for sensation.

3. The third section (stanzas sixteen through twenty-two) interrupts the tone of violence and vision and serves as a transition from the mad ornateness of the second section to the pathos of the final movement. The boat suddenly becomes conscious of itself in the midst of its voyages. The freedom of the boat has brought itself against an impasse. It feels itself to be a woman on her knees, humbled and quieted. Then begins a period of self-examination. Around this woman, now a "bateau perdu," drowned men sink silently into the sea, and the skies collapse over the boat. "Je regrette l'Europe" (I miss Europe) is the honest confession. The boat misses its origins. Throughout the nights and days of this drunken voyage, the boat's real Vigor has been asleep. The visions were mental and unreal. They were experiences of dispersal and indulgence. Behind them, the reality of a boat's function waited soberly for the last excesses to spend themselves.

4. The last section (stanzas twenty-three through twenty-five) narrates the rising up of his real desire, divested of imagination. Rimbaud's return to the small street puddle, known to him as a child, on which he could sail a paper boat and which he could encompass with his thin arms is the return to his origin and his personal experience. The simplicity and pathos in the final

image of the mud puddle in a European street are the return of sobriety

Interpretation

1. *literal*: The distance between the voyage of the drunken boat through its grandiose décors and the small boat at the end of a chain on the Meuse River is cosmic. The composing of "Le Bateau ivre" was the literal experience; it hardly relates one. The will to be a poet and a visionary is the real experience of the poem. In the letter to Izambard (May 12, 1871), Rimbaud stated his creed emphatically: "One must be strong and be born a poet, and I have recognized myself as a poet."

2. *moral*: The world is both our fortune and our peril. To realize fully the voyages which a boy's imagination invents would equate the realization of a failure, and this is the moral meaning of the poet, whose final scene is not a triumphant vision but a humble and pathetic scene of reality: the sea becomes a puddle, the boat becomes a paper boat as frail as a butterfly, intoxication becomes sadness.

3. *spiritual*: Twice in the poem the word "love" is used. In both instances it is associated with the sea. The ocean is first that place "where the bitter rednesses of love ferment." Secondly, love is the bitter element which has swollen the boat with intoxicating torpor. The anagoge or spiritual meaning of modern works of art is their prophetic quality. Rimbaud's destiny is announced in this poem he wrote at the age of sixteen. The boy Arthur is already the legendary character who, after traveling throughout the world, will return to the land of his origin in order to die there. The experience of love is immobilization, far different from the restless motion of the drunken boat of Rimbaud's subsequent voyages.

Source: Wallace Fowlie, "'Le Bateau Ivre': (The Drunken Boat: The Poet's Imagination)," in *Rimbaud and Jim Morrison: The Rebel as Poet*, Duke University Press, 1996, pp. 47–53.

Bernard Weinberg

In the following excerpt, Weinberg presents a lengthy explication of the original French text of "The Drunken Boat." The critic also considers the symbolic and the non-symbolic elements that constitute the poem.

… "Le Bateau ivre" is unclear and highly complex. It is unclear not because we have

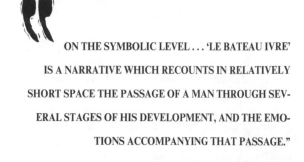

ON THE SYMBOLIC LEVEL … 'LE BATEAU IVRE' IS A NARRATIVE WHICH RECOUNTS IN RELATIVELY SHORT SPACE THE PASSAGE OF A MAN THROUGH SEVERAL STAGES OF HIS DEVELOPMENT, AND THE EMOTIONS ACCOMPANYING THAT PASSAGE."

doubts about the fact that the boat is a symbol for something else, but because that something else is not readily identifiable. The thing symbolized, the "other half" of the metaphor, is vague and dubious, partly because there seem to be various conflicting suggestions within the poem, partly because certain partial and occasional indicators have led to a traditional reading that is not corroborated by the rest of the poem. "Le Bateau ivre" is complex through its length and the number of narrative episodes involved; through the many aspects of the symbol presented for consideration; through the multitude of descriptive details; and—resulting from all these—through the variety of emotions that succeed one another both in what the boat says about itself and in what the reader is made to feel with respect to the boat.

Complexity of this kind carries with it a great danger for the interpretation of the poem: the danger of an allegorical reading, the danger of seeing the poem as a vast enigma each part of which must be "solved" in terms of a central meaning. That danger raises a theoretical question with respect to the analysis of symbolist poetry in general: How much of a symbolist poem is actually involved in the central symbol about which the poem is built, and what purpose is served by such parts of the poem as are not involved in that symbol? Unless the poem is an allegory or an enigma, there will be parts of it that are not immediately translatable into terms of the central symbol and the thing symbolized. The artistic reasons for the presence of those parts, either in terms of internal structure or of external effect, need to be sought and discovered. Once found, they may be related both to the symbol and to the thing symbolized, to the literal meaning and the symbolic meaning, and the poem as a whole may be more fully understood.

On the literal level, "Le Bateau ivre" is a narrative which recounts in relatively short space the adventures of a boat and the emotions accompanying those adventures. The boat passes, at the beginning, from a state of servitude to one of liberty, and the joy of liberation is indicated. Next come the multiple voyages and adventures as the boat drifts or is blown over the surface of all the world's oceans, adventures accompanied by great exultation in the sense of boundless freedom, but also by a premonition of lassitude and regret. Finally, it is these latter emotions which dominate as the boat, its drunken career having ended in debilitation, disintegration, and a tragic sense of impotence, yearns to end its voyagings in a final sinking to the bottom of the sea—or else to return to its original state of servitude. The progression of the narrative is thus from liberation, to unrestrained adventure, to a disillusionment with adventure; the progression of the emotions is from joy, to exultation mixed with regret, to despair and a wish for an end of suffering.

On the symbolic level (and I suggest here a hypothetical interpretation which I hope to substantiate in the course of the following analysis), "Le Bateau ivre" is a narrative which recounts in relatively short space the passage of a man through several stages of his development, and the emotions accompanying that passage. The man passes, at the beginning, from the restrictions and servitude of childhood to a state of adult manhood, and the joy of liberation is indicated. Next come the multiple adventures as the man, free of all restraint, participates fully in all the activities of a certain kind of adult life, adventures accompanied by great exultation in the sense of boundless freedom, but also by a premonition of lassitude and regret. Finally, it is these latter emotions which dominate as the man, his adult life having brought a sense of discouragement, impotence, and corruption, yearns to end his life in final death—or, as an alternative, to return to the peace and the orderly security of his childhood years. The progression of the narrative is thus from a state of childhood, with all its restrictions, to a state of manhood involving disappearance of these restrictions and complete liberty of action, to a disillusionment with this liberty; the progression of the emotions

is from joy, to exultation mixed with regret, to despair and a wish for an end of suffering.

I have purposely insisted upon these two aspects of the poem, the parallelism of the literal and the symbolic action, the identity of the emotion, because this is the poetic device by which the ultimate effect of the poem is achieved. The emotions attributed to the boat are from the outset those which belong not to a boat—which as an inanimate object would have none—but to a man in like circumstances and progressing through a similar series of episodes. The boat speaks throughout, saying what a boat might say about the actual adventures which it relates, but expressing an emotional accompaniment proper only to a man. The identity of the emotions is the basis of the symbolical relationship. The problem of the poet is so to express the literal action that the symbolic action becomes apparent through it, thereby rendering the expression of the emotions more vigorous and more poignant to the reader. The problem of the reader is to discover the symbolic meaning through the literal one; as he does so, he understands more clearly, the emotions become more intelligible and more personally alive for him, and his pleasure in the reading is enhanced.

... I do not think that I need to insist further on the symbolical relationship between boat and man and on the successive stages of development through which the symbol moves, each accompanied by a meaning for the man symbolized and by an emotional effect proper both to boat and to man, but especially to man. In so far as emotions are involved for the boat, they are those of a man in like circumstances, and they are recognized by a reader who identifies them as such and who feels them as a man having similar capacities for feeling. But several problems of interpretation of the symbol still remain. One may ask whether the "man" represented is all mankind or a particular man, whether the "adventure" symbolizes the passage of everyman from childhood to adult life or the passage of one particular man from childhood to a particular kind of adult life. The text, I believe, corroborates the latter hypothesis. For rather than attempting to generalize, it speaks constantly of a specifically "drunken" boat in a peculiarly "drunken" adventure: of complete liberation from restraint and restriction, of wild passage through every variety of episode and circumstance, of passivity, of confusion and disorder.

In this way it perhaps answers another question, that relative to the causes of the boat's and the man's failure. The causes lie in part in the choice of this life rather than another, in part in the character which led the man to make this choice rather than another. I do not mean that there is any moral lesson present or implied; merely that action in the poem comes from a particular choice and that this choice springs from character. The indications of character are however of the most summary, and are for the most part derived by working backwards from action.

As for the problem of the nonsymbolic elements of the poem, the solution should now appear fairly simple. I have from the start insisted that the poem, both on the literal and on the symbolic level, possessed an essentially narrative form. The emphasis, however, is not on the series of events which constitute the narrative, but rather on the series of emotions which accompany those events (hence its essential lyricism). The structure is one which effects the passage from an initial emotional state to a final emotional state. The function of the symbolic elements is to state the events and the essential emotions which they produce. The function of the nonsymbolic elements—those which seem not to lend themselves to direct identification with any specific aspects of the thing symbolized—is to contribute to the nature and the intensity of the emotions aroused. This they do by rendering action and circumstance more concrete, more sensible, by surrounding them with affective accompaniments. In a sense, they prolong and complete the symbol.

One must therefore apply to them a canon of appropriateness which involves not only the poem as a whole as point of reference, but the particular place in the order of the poem at which the passage appears. This is abundantly clear in such a poem as "Le Bateau ivre," where the emotional effects change so subtly and so clearly as one passes from one part of the poem to another. Any judgment of the usefulness or the "goodness" of any such nonsymbolic passages must thus depend (as must, indeed, any judgment of a detail) upon a prior analysis of the total structure of the poem. Since in "Le Bateau ivre" the total emotional range is considerable, the variety of effect possible in the individual images will be commensurately large. This does not mean that "all" emotions are treated or suggested either in the poem or in the individual passages; for the boat and the man (and the contemplator) move in the essentially restricted area between "joy" and "despair." As a matter of fact, the unity of the poem and of its effect is a function of the fact that the adventure and its accompanying emotions (either on the literal or on the symbolic level) are restricted to and productive of a single emotion contained in the passage from one state of feeling to another. It is indeed very difficult to describe or define the exact accretion to emotion made by an individual passage or image; for the language of the passions is extremely inexact and imperfect, and this inexactness and imperfection must reflect itself in the language of criticism. The best that one can do is to "classify" the particular effect of a passage under the general effects of the poem, then to indicate what nuances are produced by it, how they are produced, and what they contribute to the formation and the development of the general effect.

Perhaps this last statement may be used as a basis for asking a final question about these nonsymbolic passages. Suppose that they had not been included in the poem; what then would be lacking from it? Clearly, the whole of the central structure, both literal and symbolic, would still be present. Moreover certain passages, especially at the beginning and at the end of the poem, would be unchanged. But from the two long central sections of the poem something would indeed be lacking. The statements of the boat would be skeletal. They would say what was essential, but would not add to it those "supplementary" or "auxiliary" elements which either provide the shades of feeling desired or reinforce the statement of the central emotions. The poem might produce the same overall effect; but it would do so less fully, less richly, less successfully. The function of these "additional" passages would seem to be to provide the nuance and the shading, the color and the differentiation; and in this sense they are not additional at all, since the poem produces not its general effect but its specific effect, and this specific effect results from the combination of all its particular elements.

To suggest that the nonsymbolic elements of the poem are "additional" or "excessive" would be to posit a lack of unity which, in the case of "Le Bateau ivre," is corroborated neither by sensitivity nor by analysis. Rather, one feels and one discovers that both symbolic and nonsymbolic elements are integral to the creation of the total resultant effect. Perhaps we might say that the broad general character of the emotions is determined by the development which the symbol undergoes, both in its literal and in its symbolic phases, and that the other "unilateral" components add to these general emotions nuance and color and specification. I do not wish to intimate that, from a theoretical standpoint, the symbol itself can do no more than establish the general emotion; although since it depends upon likeness or comparison it might tend to establish such likeness on the basis of common characteristics which cannot become too specific. I merely wish to say that in the present poem the two types of development work in the kind of relationship indicated. Again from the theoretical standpoint, one might presumably say that the totally symbolic poem would be extremely difficult if not impossible of achievement; but the poet who achieved it would display the folly of any such generalization. In this particular poem, the poet has preferred not to do so. He has effected, instead, a combination of symbolic and nonsymbolic elements, in a proportion and in a relationship demanded by the peculiar conditions of his poem. The limits which he placed upon his symbolism were such as to assure on the one hand the intelligibility and the emotional accessibility of his poem, on the other hand the maximum creation of the desired poetic effect.

Source: Bernard Weinberg, "Rimbaud: 'Le Bateau ivre,'" in *The Limits of Symbolism: Studies of Five Modern French Poets*, University of Chicago Press, 1966, pp. 89–127.

SOURCES

Bloom, Harold, "Rimbaud," in *Genius: A Mosaic of One Hundred Exemplary Creative Minds*, Warner Books, 2002, p.483–85.

Lee, Daryl, "Rimbaud's Ruin of French Verse: Verse Spatiality and the Paris Commune Ruins," in *Nineteenth-Century French Studies*, Fall–Winter 2003, Vol. 32, No. 1–2, p. 69.

Love, Damian, "Doing Him into the Eye: Samuel Beckett's Rimbaud," in *Modern Language Quarterly*, December 2005, Vol. 66, No. 4, pp. 477–504.

Ormsby, Eric, "Rimbaud: Sophist of Insanity," in the *New Criterion*, June 2001, Vol. 19, No. 10, p. 16.

Peyre, Henri, "Rimbaud, or the Symbolism of Revolt," in *What Is Symbolism?*, translated by Emmett Parker, University of Alabama Press , 1980, pp. 33–47.

Rimbaud, Arthur, "The Drunken Boat," in *Rimbaud: Complete Works, Selected Letters: A Bilingual Edition*, updated, revised, and with a foreword by Seth Whidden, University of Chicago Press, 2005, pp. 115–20.

——, "It's Been Found Again," in *Rimbaud*, by Graham Robb, W. W. Norton, 2000, p. 84.

——, "Vowels," translated by Louise Varèse, in *An Anthology of French Poetry from Nerval to Valéry in English Translation*, edited by Angel Flores, Doubleday/Anchor, 1958, p. 113.

Starkie, Enid, *Arthur Rimbaud*, W. W. Norton, 1968, p. 143.

FURTHER READING

Baudelaire, Charles, *The Flowers of Evil*, selected and edited by Marthiel and Jackson Mathews, New Directions, 1962.
> *The Flowers of Evil* includes such poems as "To the Reader," a condemnation of what Baudelaire saw as the nastiness of the human disposition; "Correspondences," a poem about poetic symbolism; and his voyage poems, which were the precursors to "The Drunken Boat."

Edwards, Stewart, *The Paris Commune, 1871*, Quadrangle Books, 1971.
> Edwards provides a thorough and sympathetic account of the Paris Commune, referring to documents of the time.

Fowlie, Wallace, *Rimbaud and Jim Morrison: The Rebel as Poet*, Duke University Press, 1994.
> Fowlie was an academic scholar and a translator of Rimbaud's work. This is a serious comparative study of Rimbaud and Jim Morrison, the lead singer and lyricist of the 1960s rock group The Doors.

Robb, Graham, *Rimbaud*, W. W. Norton, 2000.
> Intertwining an account of Rimbaud's life with a discussion of its relation to his work and his work's relation to his life, Robb's biography is thorough and never tedious.

Ego-Tripping

NIKKI GIOVANNI

1972

The poem "Ego-Tripping," written by Nikki Giovanni, was first published in 1972 in a collection of poetry titled *My House*. Best known under this shortened title, the poem's full title is actually "Ego-Tripping (there may be a reason why)." The poem is also included in a children's book of poetry, titled *Ego-Tripping and Other Poems for Young People*, which was published the following year. This latter book includes illustrations by George Ford that offer positive images for children that reflect a feeling of black pride. The illustrations and words advocate strength and power; whatever can be imagined is possible. Giovanni eschews periods, commas, and other forms of punctuation. There are no pauses or places for the reader to stop and catch a breath. The title, "Ego-Tripping," suggests an ego so large that the author is tripping over it, but that is not the poem's purpose. Giovanni's first trip to Africa was in 1972, the year of the publication of this poem. Many of the great ancient African civilizations, the Egyptians, the Carthagians, and the Ethiopians, contributed to the greatness of Greek, Roman, and Norman life, and in these civilizations, much of modern life finds its origins. Giovanni aligns herself with these beginnings and the possibilities they offer in "Ego-Tripping," as she celebrates being black and female. Her style is both original and individualistic and is accessible to all levels of readers. Giovanni's love for "Ego-Tripping," is evident, since she has recorded it on at least

Nikki Giovanni *(Hulton Archive / Getty Images)*

two compact disks, placed an audio file of her reading it on her website, and included it in at least three of her poetry collections, the two collections noted above and *The Selected Poems of Nikki Giovanni*, published in 1996.

AUTHOR BIOGRAPHY

Born Yolanda Cornelia Giovanni on June 7, 1943, Nikki Giovanni grew up in Lincoln Heights, a predominately black suburb of Cincinnati, Ohio. Growing up, she frequently visited Knoxville, Tennessee, the city of her birth and the home of her grandparents. When she was fourteen, she moved back to Knoxville to live with her maternal grandparents. Giovanni enrolled at Fisk University after her junior year at Austin High School, under an early admission policy, but was expelled at the end of her first semester when she left campus to visit her

grandparents at Thanksgiving. After a new Dean of Women replaced the one who had expelled her, Giovanni returned to Fisk. She graduated with honors in 1967, with a degree in history. After graduation, Giovanni moved back to Cincinnati. After her grandmother's death only a month after she received her degree, Giovanni began to write poetry as a way to deal with her grief. Most of the poems that she wrote during this period of grief were later published in her first collection of poetry, *Black Feeling Black Talk*, in 1968. At the same time, Giovanni enrolled at the University of Pennsylvania School of Social Work but soon left the program.

She received a grant from the National Endowment for the Arts and was able to move to New York City, where she continued writing poetry while enrolled at Columbia University's School of Fine Arts; she dropped out of their M.F.A. program during the first year. A second collection of poetry, *Black Judgement*, was also published in 1968. Giovanni began teaching, first at Queens College and later at Rutgers University, and then gave birth to her only child, Thomas Watson Giovanni, in 1969. *Re: Creation*, published in 1970, was the third and the last of Giovanni's books to have a revolutionary tone that advocated militant change for the black community.

Single motherhood softened Giovanni's poetry, and she also began writing poetry for children. The following year, she published her first collection of poems for children, *Spin a Soft Black Song* and also published a lengthy autobiographical essay, *Gemini*. Also in 1971, Giovanni recorded a spoken-word album, *Truth is on its Way*, with the New York Community Choir. This bestselling album received the National Association of Television and Radio Announcers Award for Best Spoken Word Album. *My House* (the first collection to include "Ego-Tripping,") was published in 1972, while a second children's book, *Ego-Tripping and Other Poems for Young People*, was published in 1973. Both of these books included the poem, "Ego-Tripping."

Giovanni has received a number of awards, including being honored as Woman of the Year by *Ebony Magazine* (1970), *Mademoiselle Magazine* (1971), and *Ladies Home Journal* (1973). She was also named to the Ohio Women's Hall of Fame (1985) and received the Governor's Awards from both Tennessee (1996) and Virginia (1998). Giovanni was also awarded the Langston Hughes Medal for poetry (1996) and the Rosa L. Parks Woman of Courage Award (2002). Giovanni's children's book about Rosa Parks, *Rosa* (2005) was selected as a Caldecott Honors Book. Between 1968 and 2005, Giovanni published thirty-two books and many essays and individual poems. She is a prolific writer and also a teacher. Giovanni has been a professor at Virginia Polytechnic Institute and State University (Virginia Tech) since 1987. In 1999, she was given the title of University Distinguished Professor, the highest award given to university faculty. She resides in Virginia.

POEM TEXT

I was born in the congo
I walked to the fertile crescent and built
    the sphinx

MEDIA ADAPTATIONS

- A recording of Nikki Giovanni reading her poem "Ego-Tripping" is posted on her website: http://nikki-giovanni.com/egotrip pingqt. shtml.

- Although she did not publish the poem until the following year, Giovanni reads "Ego-Tripping" on a 1971 recording titled *Truth Is on Its Way*. This is her first recording, and it was re-released on CD in 1993 by Collectables.

- Giovanni reads "Ego-Tripping" on *In Philadelphia*, a recording released in 1997 by Collectables that is still available on compact disk.

- Giovanni also reads "Ego-Tripping" on a short video titled *Spirit to Spirit: Nikki Giovanni*, released in 1987. This film was directed and produced by Mirra Bank and is distributed by Direct Cinema Limited. It is twenty-eight minutes long and was released as a DVD in 2007.

I designed a pyramid so tough that a star
    that only glows every one hundred years falls   5
    into the center giving divine perfect light
I am bad

I sat on the throne
    drinking nectar with allah
I got hot and sent an ice age to europe   10
    to cool my thirst
My oldest daughter is nefertiti
    the tears from my birth pains
    created the nile
I am a beautiful woman   15

I gazed on the forest and burned
    out the sahara desert
    with a packet of goat's meat
    and a change of clothes
I crossed it in two hours   20
I am a gazelle so swift
    so swift you can't catch me

For a birthday present when he was three
I gave my son hannibal an elephant
He gave me rome for mother's day   25

My strength flows ever on

My son noah built new/ark and
I stood proudly at the helm
  as we sailed on a soft summer day
I turned myself into myself and was   30
  jesus
  men intone my loving name

  All praises All praises
I am the one who would save

I sowed diamonds in my back yard   35
My bowels deliver uranium
  the filings from my fingernails are
  semi-precious jewels
  On a trip north
I caught a cold and blew   40
My nose giving oil to the arab world
I am so hip even my errors are correct
I sailed west to reach east and had to round off
  the earth as I went
  The hair from my head thinned and gold was   45
  laid across three continents

I am so perfect so divine so ethereal so surreal
I cannot be comprehended
  except by my permission

I mean ... I ... can fly   50
  like a bird in the sky ...

POEM SUMMARY

Stanza 1

"Ego-Tripping." begins with a simple declarative statement. The speaker declares her origins as having been "born in the Congo." Each line of the poem asserts the speaker's strength and power, as she imagines herself a female god. In the first section, the speaker claims that the sphinx and the pyramids are her creations. She professes to have walked to the Fertile Crescent, the area that encompasses the lands of ancient Mesopotamia and ancient Egypt. The Fertile Crescent is watered by the Nile, Jordan, Tigris, and Euphrates rivers and so is an important ecological, agricultural, and economic feature of that area. In the rest of this stanza, the poet incorporates both science and religion into her poem. In our galaxy, the Milky Way, supernova stars burn out every 100 years. The death of a supernova creates an explosion that appears as a very bright star. Some scientists think that the star over Bethlehem might have been a supernova, and so the bright star can have religious significance. Giovanni's poem notes that the star "that only glows every one hundred years" gives

"divine perfect light." The final line of this stanza, the simple "I am bad" should not be understood as a literal statement. Instead, the phrase adopts 1970s slang, and "I am bad" should be understood as "I am awesome." This final line of the stanza tells the reader that the poet is proud of her identity and her accomplishments.

Stanza 2

The second stanza of this poem clearly establishes the narrator as a goddess. She is the mother of Nefertiti, whose name means the beautiful or perfect woman. Nefertiti was a much loved wife, but there is no real knowledge about her origins. The poem's speaker can safely claim her as a daughter without contradicting history. Making Nefertiti's mother a goddess would not be unusual, either, since many of the Pharaohs claimed to be descended from their gods and goddesses. The narrator is also equal to Allah, since she "sat on the throne / drinking nectar with allah." She sat next to him and not below him as a subject would have done. The speaker claims that her childbirth tears created the Nile River, which is the longest river in the world at 4000 miles in length. The Nile was so important in early Egyptian life that its flood and drought cycle became the basis for the Egyptian seasons. In the final line, the speaker asserts that "I am a beautiful woman." This line establishes the speaker as female and also reinforces the image of her as supremely confident and proud of her identity as a woman. The last line refers back to the earlier reference to Nefertiti, the most perfect and beautiful of women.

Stanza 3

This third stanza continues the poet's claim to superlative powers. Her gaze is so powerful that she is able to look at the forest and burn "out the sahara desert." The Sahara desert is the largest in the world, and so in keeping with the speaker's creation of the largest river in the world in the previous stanza, this stanza continues the speaker's claim to great fame and ability. The desert is 3000 miles wide from east to west and between 800 and 1200 miles long from north to south. Thus the poet's claim to be able to cross it in "two hours" requires a goddess of superior strength and power. To put this claim into perspective, flying this distance in an airplane would require more than two hours. The speaker, though, is "a gazelle so swift" she cannot be caught. The gazelle is part of the antelope family and is known as one of the fastest animals in the world. Gazelles are also herbivores, and so while the speaker carries goat's meat for her journey, the analogy of the speaker as a gazelle refers only to her swiftness in escaping those who see her as prey.

Stanza 4

In this stanza the goddess speaker again claims a child. In this case the child is a son, Hannibal. Hannibal was a great Carthaginian general. In the First Punic War (264–241 B.C.E.), Carthage lost important territories to the Roman Empire. In the Second Punic War (218–201 B.C.E.), Hannibal crossed the Pyrenees with thirty-five elephants. He did not, however, succeed in taking Rome, although he did control large parts of the Roman Empire before being finally defeated. Hannibal is best known as a general who, despite winning almost all of the battles, finally lost the war. After losing several battles, Rome chose to just sit and wait until Hannibal was short on men and supplies. He was defeated at that point. Giovanni's lines in this stanza are correct in their reference to Hannibal's use of the elephant, but he was never able to give anyone "rome for mother's day," or for any day. As has been the case with the previous stanzas, this fourth stanza ends with the speaker's affirmations that her "strength flows ever on." Although Hannibal was ultimately defeated and killed, the goddess-speaker is not diminished. Hannibal was renowned for his strength, and the goddess mother's strength is matchless.

Stanza 5

In the next lines, the speaker refers to two men who are renowned for saving mankind. The first reference is to Noah, who saved his family and the animals on earth, thus allowing the world to be repopulated after a period of sin and destruction. The goddess speaker accompanied her son, Noah, on his journey to preserve mankind, standing "proudly at the helm / as we sailed on a soft summer day." Biblical text does not mention "a soft summer day." Instead Genesis 7:12–13 states: "And rain fell upon the earth forty days and forty nights. On the very same day Noah and his sons" entered the ark. The speaker, however, suggests another meaning within these lines. The first line of this stanza refers to "new/ark." Newark has significance in several ways. It is the birthplace of American dramatist, poet, novelist, and political activist, Amiri Baraka,

whom Giovanni greatly admired. Baraka brought new life to black poetry and drama through the Black Arts Repertory Theatre, which he founded in Harlem in 1958 to provide a forum for poetry readings, concerts, and plays created by black writers. Then in 1966, Baraka established a black community theater in Newark, New Jersey, called Spirit House. His activism on behalf of all blacks, but especially black poets and playwrights can be read into Giovanni's words: "My son Noah built new/ark." Newark is notable for another reason, as well. In July 1967, the city of Newark was the site of six days of racially based rioting that ultimately changed the city. After the riots, many white residents moved to the suburbs, and for the first time, black residents were given a voice in city politics. African Americans refer to the riots as the Newark Rebellion and consider it a rebellion against oppression. Only three years later, Newark became the first major northeastern city to elect a black mayor. In a sense, then, the "new/ark" provided not only a new start for mankind but a new beginning for Newark's black population.

The poet next undergoes a metamorphosis from goddess to Jesus. The speaker "turned myself into myself" and was transformed into the savior of mankind. The female deity has already claimed the Old Testament in a previous stanza; now she is not excluded from the New Testament, when she can merge into Jesus. Traditional biblical teachings embrace patriarchy and religion as a way to exclude women from roles that assert their independence. As a result, biblical texts make women reliant upon and subordinated to men. The goddess speaker turns those ideas upside down by claiming that Jesus is both god and goddess. She has even more power and adoration, given that "men intone my loving name." Rather than a more generic use of mankind or people, the speaker makes clear that it is "men" who praise her.

Stanza 6

Just to make sure that the point is not lost on the reader, the speaker repeats twice: "All praises All praises." The final line then refers back to the topic of this section, with a reminder that the goddess is the "one who would save."

Stanza 7

In this long stanza, the focus changes to the many riches that the goddess has provided to mankind. She is responsible for diamonds, uranium, semiprecious jewels, oil, and gold. Again, the goddess speaker returns to the theme of ultimate self-confidence. She is "so hip" that even her "errors are correct." Thus she can make no mistakes. To be hip is to be better than anyone and to be above whatever is common and usual. Modern slang also defines hip as someone who knows all the answers and who is beyond simple trends or fashion. To be hip makes the speaker the ultimate authority on all topics. This reinforces the goddess image, who in this stanza, also claims to have made the earth round.

Stanza 8

Having spoken in specific details through the poem, the goddess speaker ends the poem with a broader comment about her own perfection. She is "so perfect so divine so ethereal so surreal." In the first section of this line ("so perfect"), she claims herself to be flawless, lacking anything that would detract from her perfection. In the second section ("so divine"), she reminds readers that she is a god. In the third section ("so ethereal"), she expands upon her divinity, to reinforce the idea that she is celestial, heavenly, and not confined to earthly land. In the final words of this line ("so surreal"), the goddess speaker defines her existence as so fantastic that she cannot be understood, unless, of course, she gives permission. The surreal provides an incongruent juxtaposition of imagery, such as blowing her nose and "giving oil to the arab world."

Stanza 9

These last few lines invite the reader to simply enjoy the poem and not question too closely. To reinforce this point, the poem ends with a line from a song by the singing group, The Temptations, called "I can't get next to you." The phrase "I ... can fly / like a bird in the sky" connects Giovanni's speaker to one of the important cultural experiences of the 1960s and 1970s— Motown and black music. The lyrics in this song say that a lovesick man can achieve anything, even "make the seasons change just by waving my hand." Even with all those god-like powers, he is unhappy because it is the girl who is "the key to my happiness." This old song by The Temptations acknowledges that women have the power and control over men. These lines assert that the male singer can have everything in the world but without a woman, his powers mean nothing. Giovanni's goddess speaker ends the

poem with an affirmation of her complete power. The complete title of "Ego-Tripping" is "Ego-Tripping (there may be a reason why)." The content of the poem proves that there is a reason for the goddess to have so great an ego that she might trip over it. She is the pinnacle of female strength, power, wisdom, and achievement, and this poem celebrates all that women can and have achieved.

THEMES

Ethnic and Cultural Roots

Much of the setting of "Ego-Tripping" is in Africa. By making the speaker a strong and powerful goddess, Giovanni counters the oppression that so many blacks have had to endure in the United States. The first line, "I was born in the Congo," establishes that the speaker is proud of her origins. The Democratic Republic of Congo is the center of vast mineral wealth, with exports of diamonds and oil, two of the riches that are named in Giovanni's poem as having been created by the goddess. Other areas of Africa export gold and uranium, also mentioned in Giovanni's poem. Egypt, with one of the oldest, most advanced civilizations in the ancient world, is also in Africa. The speaker claims this heritage as her own, even claiming one of Egypt's most beautiful queens, Nefertiti, as her own descendent. The great Carthaginian general, Hannibal, is claimed as another descendent. Africa is filled with meaning for black Americans, who look to the continent of their origin for a history that can make them proud and counter more than two hundred years of prejudice and subjugation. Giovanni's poem embraces her African heritage by creating a black goddess who is strong and proud of all that she has achieved.

Egoism/Pride

The full title of this poem, "Ego-Tripping (there may be a reason why)," suggests that one theme is egotism and pride. But as the subheading suggests, there may be a reason why the poet feels so compelled to boast. The poet uses this poem to celebrate a black heritage that is meant to counter some of the negative connotations about black life that are more prevalent in the media. Television and print media often reports on crime, drugs, poverty, and any number of other

TOPICS FOR FURTHER STUDY

- Take the first line of Giovanni's poem and use it as the first line of your own poem, changing the last word to reflect your own birthplace. Write a poem of at least twenty lines by continuing this new first line to whatever conclusion fits your own subject or ideas. Write a brief paragraph to attach to your poem, in which you evaluate what your poem says about your life's story.

- Giovanni's speaker identifies herself as a female of infinite power. She is a goddess in the Greek tradition. Research the role of Greek gods and goddesses in early Greek life and write an essay in which you discuss what you have discovered. Consider in what ways the Greek worship of these gods was similar to, and or different from, the Judeo-Christian-Islamic worship of just one god.

- Giovanni's poem was composed early in the 1970s. Research the economic and social status of African Americans in the 1960s and 1970s. Prepare an oral report in which you discuss the experiences of black Americans during this period and the role of the Black Power Movement.

- Select a poem by any nineteenth-century female author and compare it to Giovanni's poem. In a well-written essay, compare such elements as content, theme, tone, and word choice. In your evaluation of these two works, consider the different approaches of these two poets. Do you think that Giovanni's poem is different in tone and content from the poem by the nineteenth-century writer that you chose? In your evaluation, consider the differences and whether those differences can be attributed to the historical context of Giovanni's poetry or to some other influence.

---

issues and identifies these as obstacles that prevent blacks from succeeding; but these are social problems that affect many people, regardless of race or ethnicity. The poem's speaker is a proud black woman, who is strong enough to be a goddess. She is the creator of civilizations, from the biblical Noah to the Egyptian Pharaohs. She is the creator of vast wealth and is not afraid to acclaim her strength. The speaker declares that she is "so hip even my errors are correct." This poem makes an important point about pride—that it is important to be proud of both heritage and accomplishments. The speaker uses hyperbole to make the point that pride is not misplaced no matter how great or even how insignificant the accomplishment. The speaker's pride can serve as a model for women and young readers that they can accomplish much, if they have faith in their own strength and power. Giovanni uses this poem as a way to embrace the black pride movement that was part of the Black Power alliance of the mid–1960s.

Mother Earth

The speaker identifies herself in the Mother Earth role of creator. The first Greek god was the goddess, Gaia, the Mother Earth from whose womb all life on earth was created. Mother Earth is also commonly known as Mother Nature, who is responsible for all living things and all natural occurrences, from weather to earthquakes. Whether called Mother Earth, Gaia, or Mother Nature, this entity is also known as the healer, who maintains the natural balance of all things and makes our world fruitful. The earliest religions felt a natural connection to Mother Earth, who has always been a female representation. Giovanni's speaker, as a feminine entity, assumes the role of Gaia, the mythological earth mother. In her poem, the speaker claims she gave birth to great deserts and rivers. She also connects her mythological identify to the religions of the Judeo-Christian tradition by claiming to be the mother of Noah and that she "turned myself into myself and was / Jesus." In addition to the mythological Earth Mother, in the western tradition Eve and the Virgin Mary are also associated with the concept of the Earth Mother, and so Giovanni's reference to Jesus links nature with the mythological and with the Judeo-Christian tradition. Whether a Mother Earth, Gaia, or just Mother Nature, women are creators and mothers, and are representative of strength, wisdom, and authority.

Great Sphinx and Pyramid of Khafre at Giza in Egypt *(© Wolfgang Kaehler | Alamy)*

STYLE

Figurative Language

Giovanni employs figurative language to create images that are not necessarily intended to be taken literally. Figurative language allows the poet and the reader to use their imaginations to see the world differently, often through the use of simile or metaphor. In figurative language, the poet departs from customary meanings of words to help the reader understand a concept. For instance, when the speaker claims to have blown her "nose giving oil to the arab world," her claim is obviously not a literal one. The speaker asserts her power by claiming to have created the world. The image created by these words is more imaginative than the more literal descriptions of how oil originates from the decay of organic plant and animal life, which is then compressed by heat and pressure and sedentary rocks into fossil fuels. Figurative language brings new life and imagination to this action. In that same stanza, the speaker claims that her "bowels deliver uranium." This very figurative phrase creates an image that might be easier for

many readers to grasp than the one that scientists struggle with—that uranium is caused by supernovas exploding. The creation of uranium, though, provides a connection to the explosion of a supernova, which created the image of the star in the first stanza "that only glows every hundred years." Giovanni's poem can be enjoyed just for its imaginative use of language, but on a deeper level, there are some complex links between ideas that, if understood, create more enjoyment of the poem.

Free Verse

Free verse is verse with no discernable structure, rhyme scheme, or meter, and it allows the poet to fit the poetic line to the content of the poem. The poet is not restricted by the need to shape the poem to a particular meter but can instead create complex rhythm and syntax. Free verse is not the same as blank verse, which also does not use a rhyme scheme. Blank verse almost always adheres to iambic pentameter, while free verse relies on line breaks to create a rhythm. Free verse is most often associated with modern poetry, as it is with Giovanni's poem. There is no pattern of rhyme or meter to "Ego-Tripping," and instead, the irregular line breaks give the poem more of a sing-song rhythm that is best appreciated by reading it aloud. Giovanni rarely employs conventional forms of either stanza or line structure. She does not adhere to any standardized meter; nor is there any use of stanza division. Giovanni also eschews punctuation and most capital letters, which are used not for formal names but only for the first word of a line that begins all the way to the left of the page. Shorter lines that are indented do not begin with a capital letter. Giovanni rejects all formal rules for poetry format and punctuation, and instead creates her own meaning using only language.

Modern Poetry

The label, modern poetry, like modern novels and other forms of modern literature, refers to the poet's strong and conscious effort to break away from traditional literary forms and themes. Modern poetry attempts to create a new world by changing perceptions of the old world. Modern literary works identify the individual as more important than either society or social conventions and emphasizes the mind and the poet's inward thoughts. The imagination of the poet often prefers the unconscious actions of the individual. Giovanni's poem suggests that poets are free of conventional ideas and free of the stagnant responses that are expected of most individuals. Her poem moves beyond the practical world and into a world that privileges imagination and creativity, just as modern poetry values these freedoms.

Parallelism

Parallelism refers to a repetition in style or words within the poem. This stylistic device is one way to express several ideas of similar importance in a similar manner or to establish the importance of a particular idea. Giovanni uses parallelism to establish tone and to create tension. For instance, the opening words of line 2 "I walked" create a structure that is repeated a dozen times in phrases such as "I designed," "I gazed," "I crossed," etc. This repetition of style emphasizes the poet's strength. Another type of parallelism is in the poem's format. For example, the final line in each stanza also wraps back to the central idea expressed within the stanza. In the second stanza, Nefertiti is renowned for her great beauty. Her very name means beautiful or perfect woman. Then the final line of the stanza

links back to her beauty when the poet says: "I am a beautiful woman." This formula is repeated in other stanzas, such as the gazelle, who is linked to the goddess speaker who is "so swift you can't catch me." Another example is in the stanzas on Noah and Jesus, which end with the speaker claiming that "I am the one who would save." The final line reminds readers that Noah and Jesus saved others and their actions are now linked to the goddess speaker. This use of parallelism of words and ideas focuses the reader's attention on these lines and signifies that they are important elements of the poem.

HISTORICAL CONTEXT

The Civil Rights Movement

After the Civil War ended, Reconstruction was suppose to guarantee African Americans equal rights. In some cases, this appeared to be happening, but the reality of Reconstruction was quite different. In many communities, legislation was passed that was designed to circumvent the intent of Reconstruction. There were new laws that outlawed discrimination, but in several of the southern states, legislation was created that required that blacks pass educational and literacy tests before they could vote. Other laws, called Jim Crow Laws, required the separation of whites from anyone of black ancestry, who were commonly referred to as "persons of color." This segregation was applied to schools, restaurants, theaters, public transportation, hotels, and even cemeteries. An 1896 ruling by the Supreme Court legalized this segregation in *Plessy v. Ferguson*, which upheld separate but equal facilities for blacks and whites. This kind of segregation continued for the next sixty years. Many blacks felt that if they fought to defend the United States in World War II that segregation would end, but there was little change in the lives of black Americans in the United States after the war ended. Finally, there was some movement to end segregation in the mid 1950s. In a 1954 ruling, *Brown v. Board of Education*, the Supreme Court declared that separate educational facilities for black and white children was unequal and unconstitutional. The following year, a black woman, Rosa Parks, was arrested for refusing to give up her seat to a white man and move to the segregated rear of a bus, where there were no empty seats. Her arrest led to a lengthy

COMPARE
&
CONTRAST

- **1970s:** Social activist and Baptist minister, Dr. Martin Luther King Jr., was an influential leader in the civil rights movement in the United States. He was assassinated in April 1968, but his legacy of peaceful resistance against social injustice continued to influence his followers long after his death.

  Today: The third Monday of every January is set aside as a Federal holiday in the United States to honor the work of Dr. King, whose legacy serves as a reminder that nonviolent resistance can bring about social change.

- **1970s:** Shirley Chisholm is the first African-American woman to be elected to the U.S. Congress. She is a candidate for the U.S. Presidency as a Democrat in 1972 and wins 151 (some sources say 152) delegates before withdrawing from the race. She is a supporter of the Equal Rights Amendment. Chisholm serves in Congress from 1968–1983.

  Today: A total of twenty-five black women have served in the U.S. Congress, twenty-four in the House and one in the Senate. A total of fourteen black women serve in the 110th Congress in 2007. Women of all races hold only 16 percent of Congressional seats in 2007.

- **1970s:** The Black Aesthetic Movement is in full swing, bringing about a period of great literary and artistic development for African Americans. The movement is an effort to create a populist art that can be identified with African-American culture, through African-American publishers, theater groups, and literature. This movement asserts that black experiences, through art and literature, are different from those of other groups.

  Today: Although the Black Aesthetic Movement officially ended towards the end of the 1970s, its legacy is twofold. Academic studies of this movement flourish at college campuses around the United States. Another legacy has been a tradition of literature from writers like Alice Walker and Toni Morrison, whose work portrays the African-American experience and appeals to readers of all ethnic and racial groups.

- **1970s:** Huey Newton and Bobby Seale, along with Leroy Eldridge Cleaver, are among some of the founding members of the militant Black Panther Party in the late 1960s. After a shootout between Black Panthers and police in Oakland, CA, Cleaver fled charges in the United States and sought protection from imprisonment, first in Cuba and later in Algeria. By the early 1970s, the Black Panther Party had changed its focus from militant resistance to social programs to improve the lives of black children.

  Today: The original Black Panther Party dissolved in the mid–1970s, but many of the original members are still active in less militant community groups. The Black Panther Collective began working with old members of the original party in 1994 to protest police brutality against blacks and to educate youth about African-American history.

---

bus boycott, which was led by Martin Luther King, Jr. This boycott resulted in the Montgomery, Alabama, bus company desegregating their buses. Parks was one of Giovanni's personal heroes and the subject of a children's book that she wrote, called *Rosa*. A succession of boycotts, sit-ins, and other nonviolent actions led to desegregation of many theaters, stores, and other similar venues. In spite of the *Brown v. Board of Education* ruling, the federal government remained reluctant to force school desegregation where they met opposition in the south. In 1964, President

Lyndon Johnson succeeded in getting Congress to pass a Civil Rights Act that forbid discrimination in all public accommodations. This new law also had the authority to withhold government funds to communities that maintained segregated schools. The following year the Voting Rights Act did away with many of the rules that southern communities had used to prevent blacks from voting. None of these changes occurred without turmoil and in many cases, violence and murder. These changes in the laws also motivated many young blacks to become more militant in their demands for equality.

Black Power

Black frustration over poverty, poor housing, and unemployment led to race riots in Los Angeles in 1965. In the following three years, there were many more urban riots in Cleveland, Chicago, Atlanta, and in more than 125 other U.S. cities, including Newark, the site of one of the nation's worst riots, which Giovanni references briefly in line 27 of "Ego-Tripping," with "new/ark." The rage that was present during these race riots evolved into a demand for Black Power, which sometimes meant different things to many blacks. Some African Americans saw Black Power as a necessary violent response to injustice, but other people envisioned the movement as a way to embrace racial self-reliance and racial dignity and pride. While some members of the black community wanted a more violent defense against white racism and aggression toward blacks, other members of the black community saw Black Power as a way to achieve more political and economic power. Black Power also called upon blacks to take pride in their heritage. The movement divided into two primary groups, one that demanded black separation and economic and political self-reliance, and a second group that focused on integration and a true colorblind society, in which no individual's color or ethnicity was a defining feature of life. Giovanni's early poetry reflected the more militant side of Black Power, but in her poem "Ego-Tripping," she moves more solidly into the nonviolent approach of Black Power by embracing black pride as a primary theme. Eventually the Black Power movement led to white women adopting some of the nonviolent protest strategies of Black Power to fuel the Women's Rights Movement.

CRITICAL OVERVIEW

As has been the case with most poetry, Giovanni's collections were rarely reviewed by book critics, especially her earlier books. There are other ways, however, to evaluate the impact that her work has on her readers. In 1968, Giovanni self published her first two books of poetry, *Black Feeling, Black Talk* and *Black Judgement*. The second book sold 6,000 copies within the first six months, with Giovanni distributing the book in a limited area. In a 1973 *Ingenue* essay that focuses on Giovanni's poetry, Lorraine Dusky notes that "Publishing houses consider a poetry book to be doing well if it sells 2,500 copies in a year." By self-publishing her books, Giovanni had only limited distribution contacts, and so her feat of selling so many books, over twice as many as were typically sold, was a remarkable achievement that suggests she had already found a supportive audience. In *Racism 101*, Giovanni herself writes that she self-published her first books because she feared rejection, but as it turned out, that would not prove to be a problem. By the time that she published *My House* in 1972, she was already a popular and bestselling author. In a 2002 *Black Issues Book Review* article about Giovanni's work, Samiya Bashir comments that Giovanni's live readings of her poetry "rivaled the popularity of Amiri Baraka," the iconic poet and dramatist of the 1950s and 1960s. "Ego-Tripping." was included in the *My House* collection, which according to Bashir was "a watershed with an unheard of 50,000 copies, an unprecedented printing for a black poet at the time" (1972). In 1973, Giovanni staged a celebration at New York's Philharmonic Hall to celebrate her thirtieth birthday. In a combination of poetry readings and music, Giovanni entertained a sold out audience with readings that included selections from *My House*. In a review of the concert for the *New York Times*, columnist Laurie Johnston refers to "Ego-Tripping." as "an audience favorite" and that the audience "clapped along in rousing rhythm" as it was read. Indeed, "Ego-Tripping" seems to be one of Giovanni's favorite poems, given her frequent readings of the poem. The audience's response to it at this 1973 concert suggests that it is a favorite with her readers as well.

WHAT DO I READ NEXT?

- Nikki Giovanni's *Black Judgement* and *Black Feeling, Black Talk* (both 1968) are her first collections of poetry. They are representative of her early revolutionary writing.

- Nikki Giovanni's *Racism 101* (1994) is a collection of essays in which Giovanni writes about what it means to be a black American and how she feels about her experiences with race and racism.

- *African-American Music: An Introduction* (2005), edited by Mellonee V. Burnim and Portia K. Maultsby, is a collection of thirty essays that explore the various genres of African-American music, including the music of slaves and religious hymns, both of which are interests of Giovanni.

- A *History of Ancient Egypt: An Introduction* (1999), edited by Eric Hornung and translated by David Lorton, offers a good opportunity for readers to learn more about the country and events that Giovanni references in her poem. This book is filled with wonderful information about the history of ancient Egypt, including information about the society, politics, and artistic world of the ancient Egyptians.

- Sharon F. Patton's *African-American Art* (1998) includes information about the artistic achievements of black Americans, including art from the 1800s and 1900s created by both slaves and freemen.

- John Reader's *Africa: A Biography of the Continent* (1999) is a concise but thorough history of Africa. The book takes a multidisciplinary approach that includes history, anthropology, geology, and geography, as well as several other fields.

- At Giovanni's personal website, the author has provided audio files of some of her poetry readings, as well as links to other websites with additional biographical information: http://nikki-giovanni.com/index.shtml.

CRITICISM

Sheri Metzger Karmiol

Karmiol has a doctorate in English Renaissance literature. She teaches literature and drama at the University of New Mexico, where she is a lecturer in the University Honors Program. Karmiol is also a professional writer and the author of several reference texts on poetry and drama. In this essay on "Ego-Tripping," Karmiol examines Giovanni's poem as an anthem for women, a call to power and strength.

It is tough to undo a history of misogyny (hatred towards women) and patriarchy (male power structures) that promote women as weak vessels, whose words and actions put men at risk. Although it means combating a tradition of subordinating women that extends back thousands of years, the feminist movement has, since the early 1970s, tried to provide a voice for women that offers hope, provides strength, and suggests ways to fight for greater equality. Feminism does not, however, speak for all women, as writers and activists such as bell hooks (born Gloria Jean Watkins) and Nikki Giovanni have both stated in interviews and essays. These two women use their voices to argue for change for black women, but they do it in dramatically different ways. Where hooks insists that society change and that all women work together to demand an end to patriarchy, sexism, racism, and inequality, Giovanni calls for change from within. Giovanni's poem, "Ego-Tripping," is a call to power and equality through pride. It is an anthem for black women, with its effort to inspire pride in women's lives. These are women whose lives are filled with accomplishments that need to be acknowledged. "Ego-Tripping," celebrates all that women can, have, and should achieve.

In bell hooks' book, *Feminism is for Everybody: Passionate Politics*, hooks makes clear that her view about feminism, with its inability and lack of any desire to help black women, is especially negative. Hooks states that black women knew "that they were never going to have equality within the existing white supremacist capitalistic patriarchy." This is because the feminist movement had differing visions of what equal rights could be for women. Those whom hooks calls "reformist thinkers" wanted gender equality, while those women whom she labels "revolutionary thinkers" wanted to also end patriarchy and sexism. The reformist group, according to hooks, demanded rights for women "within the existing class structure." In other words, the feminist movement, who were largely composed of reformists, abandoned black women because many white women were willing to settle for some equality in the workforce, and less male domination, and were not willing to risk losing what few gains they had won by pushing for more equality for all women. These early feminists were willing to settle for less, according to hooks, because it was in their best interests to maintain a "white supremacist capitalist patriarchy," since doing so allowed white women to "maximize their freedom within the existing system."

This approach to equality does not benefit women who are poor or lower class or who are the objects of discrimination. Feminism, suggests hooks, has had no interest in helping lower class women, poor women, or women of color, since it did not benefit middle and upper class white women to do so. Hooks's bitterness is especially evident in her claim that these few privileged women "could count on there being a lower class of exploited subordinated women to do the dirty work they were refusing to do." In her condemnation of those women who use feminism only to advance their own lives, hooks maintains that women with more social standing chose to abandon their less fortunate sisters, who have not yet achieved parity. According to hooks, white women cannot continue to abandon black women and must work with women of color for equality. She states that feminism is not about equality for *some* women but about equality for *all* women, and to achieve that equality requires rejecting sexism.

The issue of class is an important one to consider in discussing feminism. For women of higher socioeconomic class, only the right to careers and promotions equal to those given to men matter, but for many women, who are forced to work to survive, equality of salary is the issue. Many women don't have the option to just stay home; they must work and they need to

> AND IN FACT, 'EGO-TRIPPING' DOES NOT PROVIDE AN OVERT CALL TO ACTION OR SUGGEST IN ANY WAY THAT THE SPEAKER/POET CAN SOLVE ANYONE'S PROBLEMS. INSTEAD, THE POEM IS ABOUT EGO AND ABOUT BEING PROUD."

earn what men earn. A study in 2007 by two Vanderbilt University professors reported that men continue to earn more than women for doing the same work. This was true in many fields, including accountanting, insurance sales, editing, and reporting, where women earned from 63 percent to 81 percent of their male colleagues' salaries. Women physicians, lawyers, and teachers also earn less than men, between 73 percent and 86 percent of their male colleagues' salaries, with teachers actually having the closest parity at 86 percent of male salaries.

Hooks is angry at white women whom she feels have forgotten their minority sisters; her perception is that the feminist movement has become more about maintaining patriarchy for men who felt threatened by feminists' demands than for equality for all women. This view of feminism as a white women's movement is one that Giovanni shares with hooks. In an interview with Diana Loercher, originally printed in the *Christian Science Monitor* and reprinted in *Conversations with Nikki Giovanni*, Giovanni tells Loercher that she "sees the women's liberation movement as 'very white.'" This is because black women do not yet possess all of those things that white women say are not enough. The majority of women who want equal rights are not poor; they are not needy; they are not the women who still lack housing, food, and basic necessities, which is still the condition of many black women. In a *Black American Literature Forum* interview with Carrington Bonner, Giovanni once again addresses feminism and the divisions between white and black women in the movement for equal rights. In responding to Bonner's query about why there are so few black women involved in the feminist movement, Giovanni responds that black women are interested in equality, and in fact, she argues that there "can't be a women's movement without Black women." Giovanni further suggests that "the feminist movement didn't recruit or have Black women in leadership roles," which accounts for some of the disparity of involvement for black women. However, Giovanni also claims that black women are still struggling for basic rights that are not on the feminist agenda. For instance, according to Giovanni, feminists "were arguing to be bank executives while we wanted to be in a position to have a bank account." Like hooks, Giovanni argues that the feminist movement was too narrowly focused on equality between men and women, without solving the problems of poorer women and those who need basic assistance.

One way that Giovanni has worked to deal with the class struggle and inequities of black life has been in her efforts to shape black identity into a more positive force through her poetry. Changing people's perception of themselves is sometimes the first step in changing their lives. One benefit of the black power movement of the late 1960s was the way that it transformed into a black pride movement. Those people who did not see violent and militant actions as the solution to prejudice and hate, saw racial pride as a viable way to fight the system. Giovanni sees a natural link between being a woman, being black, and having pride in all aspects of life. Her poem, "Ego-Tripping," presents a strong feminine speaker who is not afraid to say "I am a beautiful woman" or "I am the one who would save," because that is how she sees herself. That is what makes her strong, and indeed, her "strength flows ever on," especially as a mother. In her essay in *Her Words: Diverse Voices in Contemporary Appalachian Women's Poetry*, Virginia C. Fowler suggests that "Ego-Tripping" "exuberantly illustrates" that Giovanni's pride is "in her racial identity," which "is due to her perception and experience of it as a female." She does not separate being female from being black; nor does she see limitations that define her life based either on race or gender. She published her own first books of poetry, borrowing money to do so, when she thought that no one else would publish her work. She refused to fail. She had a child when she wanted one, defying a society that in 1970 condemned unwed mothers, and she rejected marriage because she did not want to be married. Fowler claims that "In her own personal life, Giovanni has consistently challenged traditional gender expectations, both those based on white norms and

those based on black ones." Fowler points to the women in Giovanni's life, especially her grandmother, who taught her "that women are the leaders for social change, the activists," as an important source of her strength. In her earlier poetry, according to Fowler, "Giovanni's celebrations of blackness have tended to be highly inflected by gender, so that 'black' seems to become almost synonymous with 'female.'" Her inability to separate race and gender is a primary way in which Giovanni's view of self merges to form a positive sense of identity that confronts inequality.

Giovanni feels very strongly that every person needs to deal with racism, inequality, and injustice. In a conversation with Frederick D. Murphy, originally published in the *Encore American & Worldwide News* and reprinted in *Conversations with Nikki Giovanni*, Giovanni states that "I don't want to be the one Black who did not carry her end." Her activism, which is evident in her prose works like *Racism 101* and in her poetry are ways that she can "carry her end" in the fight for equality. In Peter Bailey's article for *Ebony* magazine, Giovanni says that black artists have a responsibility to "tell it like it *can* and *should* be." This does mean, according to Giovanni, that black artists do not need to provide solutions to black problems. And in fact, "Ego-Tripping" does not provide an overt call to action or suggest in any way that the speaker/poet can solve anyone's problems. Instead, the poem is about ego and about being proud. Bailey notes that Giovanni has "an ego, a super one," which of course is also evident in her poem, since the title is all about her "ego." Bailey also points out that Giovanni "considers herself a good poetess," who once has been quoted as saying "I'm an arrogant bitch, culturally speaking." She is proud of her talent, but the phrase "culturally speaking," also suggests that she is proud of her heritage and her life, and most importantly, proud of herself as a black woman.

For Giovanni, poetry is one way to assert that she is in control of her life. It is also how she claims pride in who she is. In "Ego-Tripping," Giovanni uses her goddess speaker to claim that she can control the production of riches and the creation of magnificent rivers and deserts. Using language as art, then, is one way that black women can showcase strength and power. Giovanni does it with poetry; other women do it with music. In a *South Atlantic Quarterly* discussion of how black women use music to assert their authority and power, Marcyliena Morgan points out the "power of women to discursively claim a space and challenge both patriarchy and feminism was born during the discursive struggles of the black power movement." Black pride, then, was born out of the black power movement, when blacks decided that they no longer needed, in Morgan's words, "to speak in a deferential manner" to whites. This led to music that confronted prejudice and promoted strength and achievement. Morgan suggests that this new black discourse confronted white supremacy and "asserted a black presence ... that reflected a different consciousness and a sense of entitlement." Language no longer subordinates women; now, through poetry and music, language provides power and freedom. Black women, according to Morgan, "have worked to reframe family, womanhood, relationship, and sexuality to guarantee their right to represent women within the American life." Giovanni is one of those women whose actions have redefined definitions of womanhood, especially what it means to be a black woman. Giovanni has not only helped women to imagine achievement and reignite black pride; she has also paved the way for another generation of women, who can now redefine themselves through her words and each can claim that she, too is "a beautiful woman."

Source: Sheri Metzger Karmiol, Critical Essay on "Ego-Tripping," in *Poetry for Students*, Gale, Cengage Learning, 2008.

Diana Loercher and Nikki Giovanni

In the following 1973 essay, Loercher explains that Giovanni's poetry has evolved from the poetry of a black militant writer to the poetry of a woman who is proud of her black heritage. Indeed, Giovanni tells Loercher that her poetry has become more focused on people than on ideology.

In her poem "Ego-tripping," Nikki Giovanni writes, "I am a gazelle so swift / So swift you can't catch me."

The image lingers, for Miss Giovanni resembles a gazelle, with her topaz skin, lustrous eyes, and nervous grace.

It is rare to become a successful poet before the age of 30, and the fact that Miss Giovanni is black and a woman makes her achievement all the more unusual.

> MISS GIOVANNI FEELS THAT LOVE FOR THE INDIVIDUAL AND LOVE FOR HUMANITY 'GO HAND IN HAND ... BUT I DON'T THINK THAT YOU SHOULD EVER CONFUSE THE TWO. I DON'T THINK YOU CAN EVER APPROACH A GROUP PASSIONATELY. THERE HAS TO BE SOME *BODY*....'"

Raised in a middle-class family in Cincinnati, and a graduate of Fisk University, Miss Giovanni is the author of five books of poetry and a biographical essay about her grandmother called *Gemini*, nominated for a national book award this year. She also has received an honorary doctorate from Wilberforce University, and an award for outstanding achievement from *Mademoiselle* magazine. She now is an editorial consultant for *Encore* magazine.

One of her many speaking engagements recently brought her to Town Hall in New York City for a poetry reading. She easily charmed the audience with her earthy wit, incisive perceptions, and disarming candor, all delivered, like her poems, in a melodic, honey-tone voice.

Miss Giovanni's early poems, written in the turbulent '60s and collected under the title *Black Feeling, Black Talk/Black Judgement* are the poems of a black militant: angry, bitter, violent protests against racial injustice.

But gradually, as in her most recent book, *My House*, she has turned toward more personal and universal themes, and now deals with social ideas from a broadened perspective. Her poems now radiate black pride and woman pride—and also, most importantly, self-pride, that both depends on these categories and transcends them.

Miss Giovanni is a dedicated individualist who seems to value most highly (next to love perhaps) ideals of respect, responsibility, and flexibility.

In an interview held after the reading, the slender poet, who in certain lights looks like a

16-year-old, attributed the change in her poetry to "old age."

"I think that I've had a logical growth, a logical progression. I don't know how long I could have kept writing the poems that I wrote, and I think that certainly my son's had an effect on my world outlook. Children have a way of softening you, I should think."

Miss Giovanni continues, "I'm not trying to say that I'm 80—don't misunderstand—but a 21–29-year-old is very different from a person 30–39, and I don't like people who are 30 years old acting like they're 20. I don't believe in it.

"I think I'm now in what Victoria, [her press agent] and I call my 'love period,'" says Miss Giovanni. "Black poets traditionally don't write love poems... But black people do fall romantically in love. I think I'm more interested now in exploring people than I am in exploring ideologies—mostly because I've explored the ideologies, and there's a limit. It's always going to come back to *you*—no matter who you are, no matter what you believe in—it's going to come back to you."

Miss Giovanni feels that love for the individual and love for humanity "go hand in hand... But I don't think that you should ever confuse the two. I don't think you can ever approach a group passionately. There has to be some *body*.

But there is a residual that comes back and forth. In terms of black people, they've given a lot to me so that I do have a lot to give back. They call forth what I would consider the best in me, and I try to give back what I consider the best. In our case love is what we have and what we must built on." These sentiments echo a line from one of her most famous poems, "Nikki-Rosa": "Black love is Black wealth."

When Miss Giovanni speaks of her three-year-old son Thomas, her face softens and the extent of his influence on her life is obvious. Some of her poems she has written for and about him.

Miss Giovanni does not consider herself a feminist, in the current sense of the term. She sees the women's liberation movement as 'very white, and I think that's probably as it should be. What black women have called drudgery white women are now viewing in terms of liberation. And certainly the issues of child-care centers ... and equal pay are not new ones, and they're not something we have forgotten. These have been constant problems in our community because our community is a female-based community.

She continues, "I'm sympathetic of course... I think it has relevance to white women, and I wish them the best of luck. But I think it's going to be a long time before they have any black women involved in it or before black women and white women come together, because there's a lot of emotion.

"In my community if I would take the average woman and say, 'Okay, what do you want,' she wants a fur coat. And she wants a house. And she wants dresses. And she wants all the things that you all don't want. And you all sit there and say to her, 'What do you need with it? It doesn't make you happy.' It makes *her* happy. And if I'm going to talk to her I'm going to say exactly what I tried to say today, 'Hey, you can have it, if that's what makes you happy.'

"My grandmother all of her life wanted a set of sterling silver for six so that she could set her table with sterling silver. I said she was going to have sterling silver for six before she died, and she was going to set her table with it. And you can laugh and say it's ridiculous—all of that. She wanted it and it was my responsibility, if I was going to be responsible, to get it, which I did.

"Feminism says, 'Hey, you don't need it.' I know when I'm talking to those ladies that they need it. And I say, 'Hey, feminism says you can have it.' That's the ideological breakdown."

As for black people in general in the United States, Miss Giovanni does not feel that conditions have improved and is "very pessimistic about the President. I'm not happy. I'm not happy about any civil liberties. I'm not happy about the commitment that the administration refuses to make to anybody..."

She also points out that blacks, like white liberals, traditionally fear success, which they equate with corruption, and that they are "geared for failure." But her attitude toward the future of black people is not one of resignation or despair.

"I think that in terms of black people as a group it's out there. It's just that nobody's going to hand it to you. It's a lot of work. But if you want it, do it. The worst that can happen is that you fail. It is better to fail, I think, trying to do something than to fail because you say 'I'm gonna be cool. I ain't gonna try it.' You're still a failure."

Miss Giovanni speaks of her son as, in a sense, a microcosm of black manhood and black destiny. "I think that in terms of my baby he has the same chance that I had because he's probably receiving a very similar upbringing to mine. His chances are as good as my chances as long as he can understand, and it's certainly something that I would try to teach him, that there are responsibilities. Most people, I think, are not willing to shoulder responsibilities.

"Where I sympathize most with men is that there's nothing in the system that says that they can be wrong. There's nothing that says a man can say, 'I made a terrific mistake, and I'm sorry,' or, 'That hurt,' and sit down and cry. And I would hope, speaking of the feminist movement, that one of the things they'd do is give men the same space that they need. And I would hope that my son is enough of a man to be able to cry, to be able to be wrong, because once you can be wrong then you can be terrifically right. If you always have to be right, then you have to be safe which means you'll never do anything."

Source: Diana Loercher and Nikki Giovanni, "Nikki Giovanni's Poems Radiate Black Pride, Woman Pride," in *Conversations with Nikki Giovanni*, edited by Virginia C. Fowler, University Press of Mississippi, 1992, pp. 61–64.

Charles Hobson, Sheila Smith, and Nikki Giovanni

In the following interview, which took place very early in Giovanni's career, the poet talks about being a writer and teacher, as well as her reluctance to define herself or others according to how black they are.

Nikki Giovanni is a poet. To be more descriptive, she is (according to other publications) a revolutionary poet. When we asked what does the word "revolutionary" mean in relation to poetry (in relation to anything for that matter), Nikki replied this way:

"We (I) can't really be revolutionary anything without a revolution. I prefer to call myself a *black writer*, but I have no objections to the term "revolutionary" at all… All black poets, writers, etc., are revolutionary in the sense that they are read in print, seen in film, work in television. We're in places and doing things we've never done before. That's revolutionary. Besides, it doesn't hurt for people to get used to the word."

Nikki has published her own work, two paperbound books of poetry entitled *Black Feeling, Black Talk* and *Black Judgement*. She did so not because she couldn't find a publisher (actually, she admits that she didn't even look for one), but because she prefers to control her own product. Nikki feels also that by publishing her own work it is made more available to the people who want to read it.

"All black artists must be responsive to their community … politically. An artist has to come out of his community."

Nikki Giovanni was born in Knoxville, Tenn. She's been writing for most of her 25 years … not only poems but short stories, novellas and essays. She studied at Fisk University. Did she study writing and poetry?

"No, I never studied poetry. Writing classes kill your writing."

Nikki refuses to deal in negativism (as far as black people are concerned). She is one "revolutionary" writer who doesn't care to get into the who's-blacker-than-who game often played (with uneasy glee) by some "self-styled" revolutionaries.

"Why should I get into if Sidney Poitier is a black actor or if *Julia* is a black show. They're no less black than *Black Fire* (recently released book of black poetry) or *Uptight*. At least they reach millions of people while I only reach a few.

"We can't afford to be negative. You have to take care of business where you are."

Many poets deal with the religious experience, in one form or the other. Does Nikki Giovanni?

"I'm spiritual. I can't negate religion (established). I believe in God. I believe that God is everywhere. God is love. I believe that God has to be black. He made people in His image and likeness. Most of the people of the world are black. I believe that the Church is a great archive of black music. I wouldn't go to a church that didn't have black music. I dig Gospel, especially James Cleveland, he's saying a whole lot.

"Dr. King was a religious man. That's why he was so great because he was a Christian (he proved that you can really be a Christian). He was the *last* Christian."

There's a lot of talk about women's rights. What says Miss Giovanni about that?

"I don't deal with that. Black people are oppressed. Slaves are slaves. My role as a black woman is to be free ... by any means."

Nikki teaches at Queens College in New York City. She teaches English Literature and her class is reading books by black artists. Since she is very close to the current demands of black students for black studies (she teaches in the SEEK program which is geared towards black and Puerto Rican students), we asked her views on this.

"It's just a black way of looking at things. There *is* a black way of looking at things. We have the right to learn—like the white student—within our own cultural environment. It makes it easier to learn."

Another typical interview question: "Why do you write?" This caught the articulate Nikki Giovanni off guard. Long pause. A big grin.

"Writing is what I do best. We're writers because we don't have any skills."

A lot of writers can truly say this, but not Nikki Giovanni. She has a skill ... the skill of the written word ... the skill of the beauty and the power of words and the ugliness of words and the weakness of words. Words are usually so much scribbling on the naked paper. People like Nikki Giovanni make them more. They make them convictions, commitments, truths... sometimes not so pretty; they make them black realities.

Source: Charles Hobson, Sheila Smith, and Nikki Giovanni, "The Poet and Black Realities," in *Conversations with Nikki Giovanni*, edited by Virginia C. Fowler, University Press of Mississippi, 1992, pp. 3–5.

Arlene Elder and Nikki Giovanni

In the following excerpt from a 1982 interview, Giovanni discusses her relationship with Africa, how poetry evolves over time, what it's like to have her own poetry taught in classes, and the responsibility of the writer.

Throughout her career, Nikki Giovanni's poetry has been valued, at least in part, as a touchstone to the latest political and artistic ideas in Black American writing. She, however, never considered herself a spokesperson for any group. She says she is a "we" poet whose work might reflect the thoughts of others but judges it the height of "arrogance" to assume one is the "voice" of a people; people, she is confident, can speak perfectly well for themselves. She feels that her poetry

> I REALLY DON'T THINK I HAVE A RELATIONSHIP WITH AFRICA. I THINK I HAVE A RELATIONSHIP WITH MY MOTHER, MY SON, A NUMBER OF OTHER THINGS; I DON'T THINK I HAVE A RELATIONSHIP WITH THE CONTINENT."

is richer now because she understands more than she did when she was younger; as if to accommodate that fuller understanding, she is experimenting with longer pieces, some of 1200 to 1500 lines. Her forthcoming book is Those Who Ride The Night Winds, *to be published later this year by William Morrow.*

Interviewer: I was interested in your trip to Africa. Have you been there several times?

Giovanni: I've been there three times.

Interviewer: ... interested particularly in terms of your poetry and if you found that it affected your poetry in ways other than as subject matter. I am thinking of perhaps more of an emphasis on orality than you were conscious of previously.

Giovanni: No. No more than Mexico or Europe, or, probably, the moon. No. Of course, you are always conscious, just because of the nature of the African continent, that you are on the oldest continent and the richest, and that you're with the first people on earth who were, in fact, civilized, but you don't all of a sudden say, "Oh, now I'm a part of that; there's a tradition here." No, I don't think so.

First of all, it would be very difficult for me to be anything other than western, you know, because I am. I'm not wedded to tradition. I think that when we consider poetry, period, the nature of poetry, if we go pre-biblical, of course, we are going to get right into the African experience. And, of course, the oral arts in Africa are at an extremely high level. So you do have this involvement with the spoken word. I think that that is important, but I also think it's important to be able to write something down, so I don't have any conflict. It doesn't make my day, and it doesn't break it.

Interviewer: Has your attitude toward your relationship to Africa changed over the years, after your firsthand experience there?

Giovanni: I really don't think I have a relationship with Africa. I think I have a relationship with my mother, my son, a number of other things; I don't think I have a relationship with the continent. I enjoy traveling in Africa. I'm so happy: from the first time I went in 1972, until now, it's much cheaper to go, and one is more capable of going. And you don't really have to go through Europe; you can actually go from New York to Dakar without having to stop over, make what amounts to a courtesy stop in Europe. And I think that probably anybody who likes to travel would choose to travel to Africa at some point. I think to not go is a great loss. You are, as I said, on the richest continent, and you are among the first of civilized man. And I think that's an important part of your experience. I also feel, though, it's equally important to do other parts of the earth. I'm really looking forward to going to Antarctica. It's environmentally sound. I don't want you, or anyone, to think that I am denigrating Africa. Some people say, "well, why doesn't she have a relationship with Africa?" or "why doesn't she have her day made by going?" What I'm just trying to say is that you have to recognize, first of all, in 1982, Earth is a very small planet, and what we do is involve ourselves so that we are properly educated. I would still be remiss in my intellectual growth if I only did Africa. I would certainly be remiss if I did *not* do it. But it is not sufficient unto itself. We have to move around and utilize the best of all cultures.

I happen to be in an art that is almost overwhelmingly African because the poets started there. The first codification, of course, that western man recognizes is the Bible, and of course, we're still on the African continent—never understood how that became the Middle East, when the map says to me that it is Africa. You can see that, and we're very proud of it, but we also recognize that there are changes that have been made in the profession, and that those changes also are necessary to the life of the profession, in order for art to be serious, if I can use that—there must be a better word—to be viable. It has to remain alive; it has to remain adaptive to whatever forms. I have, of course, recorded some of my poetry: to gospel music in one case, and contemporary music, and some other albums just as a straight reading. It would be ridiculous, the only word I can think of, that I would live in an electronic age and not choose to electronically transmit my voice. That doesn't mean that I'm going to have the number-one-best-selling record. It's not likely at all; if I did, it would certainly be a fluke. But you do seek to use the tools that are available to you at that time. Always. You can't be so, I think the term is, purist. You get those people that say, "I would never print a book," and I'm sure that when the printing press came, "that's not the way you do it." And people continue to think that. I think that our obligation is to use whatever technology is available, because whether or not art is able to be translated tells us something about whether or not it's, in fact, living, whether or not it's part of us.

Interviewer: Whether it can be translated from one form to another, you mean?

Giovanni: To some degree. That's not the test of it, but to some degree. We were talking about a Shakespeare or a *Don Quixote*, particularly *Don Quixote*, but it has lasted so long. Not to denigrate *Don Quixote*, but essentially it's your basic soap opera. Every evening, the Spanish Court would gather, and somebody would read it. Well, it had to be interesting; it had to be true; it had to be something that people could connect to. And that's what you try to do. Now, I don't know that *Don Quixote* would make a great movie. Of course we did make it into a play, and I think we've done variations on the theme. I'm saying that you don't write for one medium to turn it into another. What I'm trying to say is that, as we are evolving, as the species evolves, we try to make use of all media. So if I were a poet when Gutenberg invented his press, I would say, "let me recite this, and you write it down, and we'll get it printed. And we'll see what this becomes," because you don't want to ignore the possibilities.

Interviewer: And if I understand you correctly, what you see remaining is that human quality that you said is essential for vital art to continue.

Giovanni: Well, people have made changes. You take a poem like the *Iliad* which was composed over some 400 years by a variety of people. We give Homer credit because Homer started it, and I'm sure Homer is delighted to take credit for it. But it kept evolving, because it was a poem being recited. And just a mere translation, just coming from Greek into anything else, just coming from Athens into Sparta would change it as much as coming from New York into Atlanta. So that what you have is something that, in fact, is alive. And it is alive because it has met the test of people.

Interviewer: It's curious, isn't it, that something like the Aeneid or the Odyssey, maybe even something like Don Quixote, meets the definition of what we now call "folk art," in the very real sense. And yet, "folk art" is not considered serious. Folk art is not important; it's not high art. What do you think happened in the course of our, as a people, listening to poetry, participating in poetry, that changed somebody's mind, anyway, about what was serious and what was not?

Giovanni: The rise of the merchant class. I really do. They did a lot for art. I don't take that away, because they were essentially an unlettered group, and what they did was to go out and purchase it, and at some points they were purchasing that which they understood. And as we got into "keeping up with the Joneses," it would almost be: "Well, *my* poet read this *poem* last night"; "Well, *my* poet read this *poem!*" Neither one of them gave a damn... But what we got into was more and more exotic, and the poets began, of course, to read for each other: "Anybody can do what *you* did. Let me show you what *I've* done."

Interviewer: ... I don't know if you know this or not, but you're being taught in a course at the University of Tennessee in Knoxville as an Appalachian writer.

Giovanni: Oh, that's fine. I was born in Knoxville. I think that's marvelous.

Interviewer: Do you ever think of yourself that way? You're being taught by a novelist named Wilma Dykeman, who is herself an Appalachian writer.

Giovanni: No, I didn't know that. I think that's great. You know, Agee is from Knoxville also, James Agee. Knoxville, for a little city, has produced a number of people that have done—I think—extremely well. I don't have any problem with being an Appalachian. I don't think of myself——I'm not particularly outdoorsy. We were talking about my nephew earlier. That would make his day, because he is off backpacking to Montana or something. I basically consider myself pretty urban, but because of birth I'm a Southerner, or in this particular case, I'm

an Appalachian, actually, because the Tennesseeans are very different from the rest of the South. Well, Tennessee is the Volunteer State, because Tennessee went with the Union. So you go up into the mountains, and you've got a whole other situation altogether. So you had West Virginia seceding from Virginia, you know; you get into that kind of thing. I think it's interesting.

I think that birth largely has to be considered an accident; I don't know another way around it. It's just a way of identifying. If it's not going to be positive, then it's pointless, because nobody chose the circumstances under which they were born, nor the place, nor the parents to whom they were born, nor their gender, nor any of that. So if it's not going to be a positive identification, then you really should let it go.

Interviewer: And yet it's so hard to let go for many people, isn't it?

Giovanni: Well, there is *something* you can do about it; you can change your behavior, if not your attitude. But I think, yes, we as a species need to let go, because it's enough that we do in life what we are responsible for. Somebody said, "we were calling you into account. Certainly we should not call you into account for your race, or your age, or your gender. You had nothing at all to do with that. You just happened to have survived. And the only reason we can complain about that is that you are alive. Because, if you weren't we wouldn't." On the other hand, I certainly see no reason that we should reward you, particularly for any of those three things. It's unacceptable that we continue to reward men for having been male. They didn't sit up in babyland and say, "well I think I'll be a boy, or I think I'll be a girl." It doesn't work out that way, so that we cannot continue to punish and reward people based upon something that they have absolutely no control over. It's illogical, just one of the things that human beings need to learn, and I should imagine at some point we will let go.

Interviewer: I hope so, but we were speaking earlier about the illogicality of human beings.

Giovanni: The rather interesting thing to me—I am a "Trekkie"—is that either we're going to come to a basic new understanding of what it is to be a human being, or we're going to destroy ourselves. So, I'm not blasé, but we would have to move away from a lot of things and pretty much all at once. We're talking race, gender, and age. It's not my fault I was born in the United States, and I shouldn't be disproportionately rewarded as to the world's minerals because of that. If that's the case, then everybody, all the little babies sitting up in baby heaven, will say, "well, I'm not gonna do Southeast Asia; I'm not gonna do Latin America. I want to go to the United States where I can disproportionately use up resources." It just doesn't happen. And I think it's time that we shut down the industrial age. We are really quite capable right now. We're moving into robotics and cybernetics, and it's time that we let go. I'm not picking on the industrial age, but that's when you've got your little machine, and then you run out, and you get your colonies so that you can take their raw materials, and then you can send the manufactured goods back. And all of that is just tiresome. It's moved us along, and I don't have a quarrel with history, otherwise you'd spend all of your time debating whether or not your mother should have had you. But if it did move us along, it cannot now. What it does, it leads to irreconcilable conflicts which frequently erupt into some level of war, which increases the possibility of a great error.

Interviewer: Of total destruction?

Giovanni: Oh sure. Which would not surprise me. I'm much too cynical and much too aware of the nature of human beings to be surprised, but it would be a disappointment, because it is not necessary. For what we are trying to hold on to and what that offers us, as opposed to what we can possibly become, it's just not necessary to hold on to the 15th century the way that we're doing it.

Interviewer: Do you think it's possible for writers to express their convictions strongly enough or imaginatively enough to change the mind of anybody?

Giovanni: I don't think that writers ever changed the mind of anybody. I think we always preach to the saved. Someone from the *Post* asked me, how would I describe myself, and I said, "I'm a preacher to the saved." And I don't think that anybody's mind has ever been changed. It has been enhanced by an already-meeting-of-the-minds. When the reader picks up the book and proceeds to begin a relationship, it will proceed based upon how that book and that reader are already in agreement. Because almost nobody really reads anything that they are

totally … I mean, I couldn't read a position paper about the *Ku Klux Klan*

Interviewer: You mean, you, literally, could not get through it?

Giovanni: I wouldn't even try. Why? Because I already know. To me it's like reading—which I guess I shouldn't say to you like this—, but it's like reading anti-abortion literature. I'm totally in opposition to their position. Unless I can read a headline that says they bring something new to the table, then no, I'm not going to do that, because I already know where they are, and what I'm going to do is look for a strengthening of my position, where I am. And everybody does that.

And again, I'm out of the tradition of the sixties that sort of crazily believed that there would be the poem that would free everybody. You would say to those people, "listen, fellows, that's not going to happen." The big term, of course, was "sell out," and everybody that didn't do what certain groups wanted—you know, Leroi Jones and all of them—everybody that didn't sort of hew the Black aesthetic line had "soldout." No. There will never be the poem that will free mankind. We would be fools … anybody that thinks that is a fool. And I don't really know another term for that.

Anybody that thinks any one thing or one person can make a difference in your life … If we could crucify Jesus, you know, whom we recognize in the western world as being the Son of God, then you know we would shoot down everybody. Now there are people who charismatically do make a difference. We were talking about holding two [opposing] thoughts, but I do that a lot. There are people who charismatically embody an age. But they didn't create the age. They personified it, and people often overlook that. They really think somebody … they really think Disraeli made [his age]. He didn't. He was the one who could personify it. Or Jack Kennedy. Now, I happen to like the Kennedys. I find them interesting people to read about. But Jack didn't make the sixties. Nor did Martin Luther King. We honor them, and we recognize them, because they personify the best within us. But they didn't create it. It was the little old ladies that said. "I'll walk," that made Martin Luther King. It was the kind that said, "even after his death we're antiwar. We're going to move even this image that we will maintain, but we're going to move it and make it much more." People overlook that, because they think that *you* could do something. They'll tell you, "Fidel Castro liberated Cuba." I'll be damned if he did, whatever you feel about Cuba. Fidel personifies that liberation. Therefore, to the Cuban people, it would probably be a loss had he been killed, say twenty years ago. I'm sure that they're ready to accept it now, not because Fidel was a loss, though of course it would be a loss to whomever loved him, but because he was the embodiment.

The same thing with our community. It was so unnecessary to shoot down Martin Luther King. And what happened there was that a man lost his life, but it was a message. And what it said was, "since we can't shoot a million people, we'll shoot this one, so that the million people will know that this is where we are." And of course what you got from that was a perfectly logical response: "Mother Fucker, since you did that, we will get you." So that you got, of course, the riots coming. There was no question that the Black community was going to respond to the white community. You sent the message, and we sent the answer. So that everybody said, "okay, well, tell you what, since I can't bring back my cities, and you can't bring back King, why don't we try peace." And you just wish that people would function on that a little bit, and earlier. We recognize that at some point if the message is sent, and an answer is sent, that we still have to come back to peace.

Interviewer: Sounds to me, and correct me if I misunderstood you, that in all that, the role of the writer is very much like that of the historian rather than the prophet. Or possibly, the prophecy comes in—and I used the word, "role," again, I realize, the function of the writer—is that the writer recognizes what you just expressed and communicates the meaning of some chaotic event or historical circumstance in whatever way he does it, and people read that because they recognize the writer as someone in whom they trust and believe, and possibly as a result of reading the meaning of what has happened, they are going to understand a little bit more of what's going to take place next, or, they will understand a little bit more of the consequences of behavior the next time something comes up. Not that they necessarily agree with what the writer said, but they understand a little bit more. And that's about all the writer can expect?

Giovanni: About all the writer can expect is to be read. That would probably be what most of us get. I think the word I was looking for is "vitality." You were using "role" and changed it to "function." But I think that the *vitality* of the writer, for those of us who are contemporary writers, who are writing contemporaneously—because some of us are literary writers who are not,—is that we are just a little bit of both. We're a little bit of a prophet, and we are a little bit of the historian. And we're saying, "this is the meaning that we find. You have to take what you can." We are not Marx; we're not sitting there saying, "A is A." We're not Ayn Rand either. We're sitting there saying, "I saw this through my eyes."

The word that you used that I do like is, "trust." There are certain writers that no matter what they have to say, no matter how much in agreement you would be with them, you simply don't trust the writer. I hate a damned liar. I really don't care what you have to say, or how awful you might think it is, or how awful I might think it is, but I hate a damned liar. Once you have given up that, once you have given up your basic integrity, then you have given up that, once you have given up your basic integrity, then you really have nothing else to offer. And maybe that's harsh, and I don't intend to be harsh. But when Norman Mailer, for example, had to pay off *Marilyn*, the book *Marilyn*, because it was plagiarized, I don't know what Mailer could write that I would read. It was hard enough to be bothered with his chauvinism and his crap before that, but to recognize that the man would be in a profession, but would take the work of somebody else ... There's just no way. It couldn't happen. I mean, Norman's spirit could descend in this room, and he could start to read from something, and I'd say, "well I have to leave."

Because the only thing you bring, the only thing any of us, any professional brings, is your honesty. You don't mind that the patient died on the table, as long as the surgeon wasn't drunk. It's sad if he did. It's sad to you; it's sad to the patient. It's probably sad to the surgeon. But you feel like, "well he tried." And in my profession, if you're not going to be honest ... It's not that you ask the reader to spend, which I think is ridiculous, 15 dollars upwards for a book, but that you're asking them for their time. Because they can go get another 15 dollars. That's not hard to do. You really cannot give back time; you think about the time you spend with a book. I mean, I'm a reader. You'd feel raped to think that you involved your heart and your mind and your time, that there were things you could have been doing, and you were sitting there reading a book to find out that it's essentially dishonest. You honestly came to that book. You chose it, and that it's a lie? I mean, it's not acceptable. Absolutely unacceptable. The profession is not really strong enough to me on your basic plagiarism. I know lawyers who worry about lawyers who are essentially dishonest. Because you can't always win. Those of us who are writers can't always be prescient, but we can always be honest. So that if we make a mistake, if we misunderstand something, if we're journalists and don't see something, that's all right, because we know that what was brought to bear there is the best that we have. That's all any of us are going to do, because you're going to miss a few calls there. One reason you don't shoot the umpire is that you know the guy is watching the ball. Now if you have to feel that other team gave him 10 bucks, then there's no game. There's absolutely no way that we can play the game. And life I think is like that.

Interviewer: It's tremendously fragile, isn't it, because it is back to "trust." We talked before about the formula, learning how to write the formula and just repeating it, repeating it. It takes a while for the reader to catch on that that's happening especially if that reader has read that writer before and has developed his trust and liking and is willing to invest not only 15 dollars, as you say, but the time and the emotional energy. And so it's really a very fragile kind of delicate thing between writer and reader.

Giovanni: I honestly think,—we were talking formula,—I think that formula is essentially dishonest. I'm not fighting with my fellow writers who are formula writers. I think it's essentially dishonest, but so is the circus, so is the Hall of Mirrors. And one of the things that I think happens to you when you are involved in that level of lazy writing is that you know what you're giving, and they know what they're getting. And I don't think that is a lack of trust. If I pick up a Frank Yerby, it's my fault. I'm not picking on Yerby, but it is, because I know exactly what he's going to do; What does the song say, "you knew I was a snake when you brought me in,"? I knew that. I happened to like

Jacqueline Susann when I'm doing junk-like reading. I can pick up a Jackie Susann and know exactly what I'm going to get. I don't feel misused.

I think that is true of all of us. You kind of know what you're getting when you pick up a certain level of book. What I do have a serious problem with, though, is your basic plagiarism, because that is actually taking someone else's work and putting it off as yours. What we are saying here is that, if I'm Steven King, ninety percent of my writing is going to be macabre. Take it or leave it. I'm sure that he considers that he writes as honestly and as well as any of the rest of us. As a matter of fact, he has a lot more money to show for it. What I'm saying is, I don't think that's your basic rape, because it's Steven King. You might say that someone was unaware that all his books are just alike. But that is very, very hard to do. That is like saying I didn't learn anything from "LaVerne & Shirley" this week; I'm disappointed. You know damn well you are not going to learn anything from "LaVerne & Shirley" or whatever it is that you're doing on TV. That is not to say that all of television is a waste. It's just that you know if you turn on TV, seven to ten, you're going to get mostly crap, unless it's Thursday night and there is a show called "Fame," which somehow or another is surviving; which makes my Thursdays. It's a great little show. I'm just saying, you've got to know that, and I don't think that that's the same level as your basic lie.

Interviewer: There is a distinction.

Giovanni: Sure. It's like your professor who reads the same notes every year. He's not lying. He says, "this is, for the level of energy that I'm willing to invest in this class, what you need to know. And if my notes have not changed in 5 years, that is not my problem. My subject hasn't changed, or at least it hasn't involved me." But that is not a lie. That's not the guy who stands in the lab and manufactures results that he knows never came up. Sure. You get into that, and I think that has to be dealt with much more stringently. A professor of medieval poetry might be dull, but he's not lying.

Interviewer: It seems as if a very mysterious relationship exists between the reader and the writer, which is one, frequently, and I think, charmingly, of awe; that this person has the ability to use language that makes me put down my $15 or makes me take that book out of the library. And

there is a love that develops there, because that person has that power over you, and trust, because any time you love, you want to trust.

Giovanni: I think that what essentially makes art so potentially dangerous is that it is totally egalitarian.

Interviewer: Explain that a little more.

Giovanni: Well, the term you use is "power," that the person has power over you. I don't think so. As a matter of fact, the writer is totally vulnerable to people that we shall never see. We sit someplace and create something, or explain something, research, and develop certain ideas. We convince a publisher to publish it, or a museum to hang it, or a producer to put it on Broadway, and we are subject to the judgment of people who never even knew us. We could have been dead 800 years before somebody discovered us.

Last year, here in Cincinnati, last September, October, and I think a little bit in November, I did a program. I don't know really how to express it, but I was invited, and I went to a number of elementary schools here in Cincinnati. And the thing that surprised the kids was that I was alive. It may sound strange, but that was the biggest thing, and when you think about how many dead authors we read, it was really not unusual. Just last night, I was at Morehead State. Even going there, people are really looking at you like, "she's really alive," and it's kind of strange. And, again, I think that the dangerous position is that we recognize not our power but people's power for themselves. The same way that I can sit here and decide whether or not Sy Hirsch, for Christ's sake, has written a creditable piece on Kissinger. That is a level of egalitarianism that most people don't have. Most people don't have to be bothered with that. Sy Hirsch should not have to worry about what some poet in Cincinnati thinks about his work. And I'm not saying that he does. I am just saying that I can make that judgment.

Interviewer: That certainly is a factor, but don't you feel power over your own interpretation of the world which really is not dependent upon how well someone else is going to agree with that?

Giovanni: Well, it really is, because if you are Ezra Pound and your interpretation of the world is markedly different from the country in which you happened to be born, you will find yourself adjudged insane, which is quite unfair. Do you

understand? And that does happen, I think, frequently enough to make us take pause. You get into the whole thing with the Soviets and their writers and, of course, we with ours. We don't do ours the same way as the Soviets do, because what we do with ours is just buy them out. The end result is the same thing, and if we can't buy them out, we simply refuse to publish them; we kind of hound them out of the country, essentially. But it all amounts to the same thing. I think that I have a view of the world, that I have an obligation, if not just your basic right, to share. But I don't consider that, in any respect, that that connotes any power. I still have to go upstairs [even though] they're locking CETA out. I still have to go to IGA.

You know, the artist is not a god, and I mention Mailer because he's such a prototypical, awful artist. Of all the real dumb things that he's said recently, the most stupid had to be on the Jack Abbott case. As a writer, you just simply cringe that somebody is justifying murder because the guy can put three words together. It's totally unacceptable. The writer is not god. It's what we do for a living. It's not who we are. And I have a great resentment—you haven't ruffled my feathers on that one at all, but you will see the hairs on the back of my neck rise— because writing is not who I am. It is what I do. And I think that anybody who fails to separate what they do from who they are, and that is from Ronald Reagan to Lyndon Johnson to Pope John Paul to whomever, is in serious, mental trouble. You've got to separate yourself; unfortunately, a lot of people don't.

Interviewer: And a lot of the people who don't are Reagan, and Pope John, the people who are in power.

Giovanni: But, hey, lot of people don't.—— The only reason we talk about the people in power is because that is who we know. You want to chart mental illness? We can go right up I-75 to Detroit and see a guy who has been laid off for six months who was a mechanic: who is nothing more. Now, we just don't talk about him, unless we are Studs Terkel. That appears to be a very human trait, but it also appears to be one that we have learned, because if we go back—again we are talking Africa or we go back to Chinese history, for two quickies and two good ones—you will see people and artisans, and what you did was not who you were.

Source: Arlene Elder and Nikki Giovanni, "A *Melus Interview: Nikki Giovanni*," in *Melus*, Vol. 9, No. 3, Autumn 1982, pp. 61–75.

SOURCES

Bailey, Peter, "I am Black, Female, Polite . . . ," in *Ebony*, February 1972, pp. 49–56.

Bashir, Samiya, "Giovanni's World," in *Black Issues Book Review*, Vol. 4, No. 6, November–December 2002, pp. 32–36.

Bonner, Carrington, "An Interview with Nikki Giovanni," in *Black American Literature Forum*, Vol. 18, No. 1, Spring 1984, pp. 29–30.

Dusky, Lorraine, "Fascinating Woman," in *Ingenue*, February 1973, pp. 20–24, 81, 83.

Fowler, Virginia C., "And This Poem Recognizes That: Embracing Contrarities in the Poetry of Nikki Giovanni," in *Her Words: Diverse Voices in Contemporary Appalachian Women's Poetry*, University of Tennessee Press, 2002, pp.112–35.

Giovanni, Nikki, "Ego-Tripping," in *Ego-Tripping and Other Poems for Young People*, Lawrence Hill, 1973, pp. 3–5.

———, *Racism 101*, in *The Prosaic Soul of Nikki Giovanni*, Perennial, 2003, p. 508, originally published by Morrow, 1994.

hooks, bell, *Feminism Is for Everybody: Passionate Politics*, South End Press, 2000, pp. 37–43.

Johnston, Laurie, "For Nikki Giovanni, Her Poetry Is Her Way of Life," in the *New York Times*, June 22, 1973, p. 19.

Loercher, Diana, "Nikki Giovanni's Poems Radiate Black Pride, Woman Pride," in *Conversations with Nikki Giovanni*, edited by Virginia C. Fowler, University Press of Mississippi, 1992, pp. 61–64, originally published in the *Christian Science Monitor*, April 23 1973.

May, Herbert G., and Bruce M. Metzger, eds., *The New Oxford Annotated Bible with the Apocrypha*, Oxford University Press, 1977, p. 9.

Morgan, Marcyliena, "Hip-Hop Women Shedding the Veil: Race and Class in Popular Feminist Identity," in the *South Atlantic Quarterly*, Vol. 104, No. 3, Summer 2005, pp. 425–44.

Murphy, Frederick D., "Nikki," in *Conversations with Nikki Giovanni*, edited by Virginia C. Fowler, University Press of Mississippi, 1992, pp. 104–12, originally published in the *Encore American & Worldwide News*, Vol. 4, May 5, 1975.

The Temptations, "I Can't Get Next to You," lyrics by Norman J. Whitfield and Barrett Strong, produced by Norman J. Whitfield for Motown, EMI Music, 1969.

Wolf, Amy, "Why Do Women Earn Less than Men?; Two Vanderbilt Economists Explain This Persistent Issue and Show Which Professions Are Worst at Pay Parity," http://www.sitemason.vanderbilt.edu/news/releases/2007/4/9/why-do-women-earn-less-than-men-two-vanderbilt-economists-explain-this-persistent-issue-and-show-which-professions-are-worst-at-pay-parity (accessed August 8, 2007).

FURTHER READING

Franklin, John Hope, and Alfred A. Moss, Jr., *From Slavery to Freedom: A History of African Americans*, Knopf, 2000.

> This book presents a history of African-American life in the United States. The authors recount black history beginning with slavery's origins and exploring the kidnapping of men and women in Africa and leading up to the Civil Rights movement of the last half of the twentieth century. The authors have included maps, charts, and many illustrations.

Higginbotham, A. Leon, Jr., et al, *Race-ing Justice, En-Gendering Power: Essays on Anita Hill, Clarence Thomas, and the Construction of Social Reality*, Pantheon, 1992.

> Toni Morrison wrote the introduction to this text, which is a collection of nineteen essays that deal with several aspects of black identity, civil rights, equality, and the public perception of race and gender equality. These essays explore important ideas about equality for black women, as well as illustrate that race and equality in the United States remains a complex issue for discussion.

Jago, Carol, *Nikki Giovanni in the Classroom: "The Same Ol Danger but a Brand New Pleasure,"* National Council of Teachers of English, 1999.

> This book provides a number of suggestions for how to use Giovanni's poetry in the classroom. The author includes a number of Giovanni's poems and excerpts from several of her essays, along with suggestions about how to get students immersed and involved in Giovanni's poetry.

Sniderman, Paul M., and Thomas Piazza, *Black Pride and Black Prejudice*, Princeton University Press, 2004.

> This book provides an often provocative look at race relations in the United States. The focus is on how black Americans view themselves and how they perceive that they are viewed by other groups. Some of the topics covered include black pride, black intolerance, and racism.

The Heights of Macchu Picchu

"The Heights of Macchu Picchu" was written by Chilean poet Pablo Neruda in 1945, following an inspirational trip to the ancient Incan mountaintop fortress of Macchu Picchu in October 1943. This period in time was one of great upheaval for Neruda and for the world. Neruda's first marriage had fallen apart; his daughter, father, and stepmother died within a few years of each other, after Neruda lost a number of friends in the Spanish Civil War. Concerned about Chile, Neruda became involved in politics. He was elected to the Chilean Senate and joined the Communist Party in 1945. That same year, the United States dropped two atomic bombs on Japan, devastating many people around the world with this brutal, controversial attack, Neruda included. Neruda first published his long twelve-part poem in Spanish in *Revista Nacional de Cultura* in 1946. "The Heights of Macchu Picchu" later became a key section in his book-length work, *Canto General* (1950). Additionally, a bilingual edition of "The Heights of Macchu Picchu," translated by Nathaniel Tarn, and first published in 1967, is available from publisher Farrar, Straus, and Giroux.

In "The Heights of Macchu Picchu," Neruda addresses mythology, memory, hardship, and community. His communist beliefs color a world of majestic indigenous architecture and the anguish of an enslaved people. Through "The Heights of Macchu Picchu," Neruda seeks to give voice to the voiceless and deliver

PABLO NERUDA

1946

Pablo Neruda *(Sam Falk / New York Times Co. / Getty Images)*

the glory of their work back into their own hands. He reaches back in time for truths about today, making this more than just a poem about ancient history.

AUTHOR BIOGRAPHY

Pablo Neruda was born Ricardo Eliecer Neftalí Reyes Basoalto on July 12, 1904, in Parral, Chile, to José del Carmen Reyes Morales, a railway worker, and Rosa Basoalto, a schoolteacher. Neruda's mother died when he was two months old. He instead grew up with his stepmother, Trinidad Candia Marverde, a half-brother, Rodolfo, and a half-sister, Laura. Neruda was interested in literature and writing from a young age and pursued it despite his father's discouragement. His first published piece was an essay for a local paper in 1917 when Neruda was only 13 years old. In 1920, he adopted the pseudonym of Pablo Neruda, in homage to Czech writer Jan Neruda; this later became his legal name.

In 1921, Neruda moved to Santiago, Chile, to study French at the University of Chile but instead he immersed himself in poetry and abandoned his studies. *Crepusculario* (*Twilights*), published in 1923, was Neruda's first volume of poetry. His famous volume *Twenty Love Poems and a Song of Despair* (1924) was his second volume of poetry; it continues to be popular today. Neruda's work made an immediate sensation although it was considered controversial for its eroticism, especially coming from a young writer. In 1927, in need of income, Neruda began working overseas as a diplomat for the government of Chile. He was stationed in a variety of locales, including Ceylon (modern Sri Lanka), Java, Singapore, Spain, Mexico, and France. While in Madrid, Spain, Neruda became friends with other writers such as Spanish poet Federico García Lorca and Peruvian poet César Vallejo. García Lorca's execution by Spanish dictator Francisco Franco motivated Neruda to become active in politics.

During these years abroad, Neruda was married twice and had a sickly daughter, who died at the age of eight. Neruda returned to Chile in 1943, much changed from the young, poor poet who left sixteen years earlier. His visit to the Incan fortress of Macchu Picchu on October 31, 1943 inspired him to write "Alturas de Macchu Picchu" ("The Heights of Macchu Picchu") two years later. Neruda first published the twelve-part poem in a Spanish-language magazine in 1946 but it was destined to become part of his famous 340-poem cycle, *Canto General* four years later.

Neruda was elected senator in Chile in 1945 and also joined the Communist Party. In 1948, Neruda and his second wife fled Chile for Argentina and then for Europe after Neruda publicly decried the president in the Senate. He was able to return in 1952 and largely remained in Chile for the rest of his life. After several near misses, Neruda won the Nobel Prize for Literature in 1971 "for a poetry that with the action of an elemental force brings alive a continent's destiny and dreams." Neruda's hard-won socialist government in Chile was overthrown in a military coup on September 11, 1973. Neruda, already quite ill, died of heart failure less than two weeks later, on September 23, 1973 at the Santa María Clinic in Santiago, Chile.

POEM TEXT

I

From the air to the air, like an empty net,
I went on through streets and thin air, arriving
    and
    leaving behind,
at autumn's advent, the coin handed out
in the leaves, and between spring and ripe grain,   5
the fullness that love, as in a glove's
fall, gives over to us like a long-drawn moon.

(Days of live brilliance in the storm
of bodies: steels transmuted
into silent acid: 10
nights raveled out to the final flour:
battered stamens of the nuptial land.)

Someone expecting me among violins
met with a world like a buried tower
sinking its spiral deeper than all   15
the leaves the color of rough sulfur:
and deeper yet, in geologic gold,
like a sword sheathed in meteors
I plunged my turbulent and gentle hand
into the genital quick of the earth.   20

I bent my head into the deepest waves,
dropped down through sulfurous calm
and went back, as if blind, to the jasmine
of the exhausted human spring.

MEDIA ADAPTATIONS

- Greek composer Mikis Theodorakis, exiled from his homeland for a time, was inspired by the Chilean poet and set Neruda's *Canto General* (of which "The Heights of Macchu Picchu" is a part) to music. Theodorakis's oratorio, *Canto General*, premiered in 1975 and is well known in Greece and Chile. It is available as a two-disc set from the Theodorakis label, sold on Amazon.com, or for purchase from iTunes.

- Neruda recited a selection of his poetry, including canto 6 from "The Heights of Macchu Picchu" for the Inter-American Development Bank on June 18, 1966, at the Mayflower Hotel in Washington, DC. The recital was wildly popular despite (or because of) Neruda's controversial communist politics, which nearly prevented his visit to the United States. The hour-long recording includes fifteen poems, eleven of which are freely available on the District of Columbia Commission on Arts and Humanities website, http://dcarts.dc.gov/dcarts/cwp/view,a,3,q,637717.asp.

- On June 20, 1966, two days after the recital for the Inter-American Development Bank, Neruda recorded part of "The Heights of Macchu Picchu" at the U.S. Library of Congress for their Archive of Hispanic Literature. The recording is available at the Library of Congress in Washington, DC, on reel-to-reel tape, and is thirty-six minutes long.

II

While flower to flower gives up the high seed   25
and rock keeps its flower sown
in a beaten coat of diamond and sand,
man crumples the petal of light he picks
in the deep-set springs of the sea
and drills the pulsing metal in his hands.   30
And soon, among clothes and smoke, on the
    broken table,
like a shuffled pack, there sits the soul:
quartz and sleeplessness, tears in the ocean

like pools of cold: yet still
man kills and tortures it with paper and with
 hate,   35
stuffs it each day under rugs, rends it
on the hostile trappings of the wire.

No: in corridors, air, sea, or roads,
who (like the crimson poppy) keeps
no dagger to guard his blood? Anger has
 drained   40
the tradesman's dreary trafficking in lives,
while in the height of the plum tree the dew
leaves its clear mark a thousand years
on the same waiting branch, oh heart, oh face
 ground down
among deep pits in autumn.   45

How many times in the city's winter streets or in
a bus or a boat at dusk, or in the densest
solitude, that of night festivity, under the sound
of shadows and bells, in the very cave of human
 pleasure,
have I wanted to stop and seek the timeless
 fathomless vein   50
I touched in a stone once or in the lightning a
 kiss released.

(Whatever in grain like a yellow history
of small swelling breasts keeps repeating its
 number
ceaselessly tender in the germinal shells,
and identical always, what strips to ivory,   55
and what is clear native land welling up, a bell
from remotest snows to the blood-sown
 waves.)

I could grasp only a clump of faces or masks
thrown down like rings of hollow gold,
like scattered clothes, daughters of a rabid
 autumn   60
that shook the fearful races' cheerless tree.

I had no place to rest my hand,
none running like linked springwater
or firm as a chunk of anthracite or crystal
to give back the warmth or cold of my outstretched hand.   65
What was man? Where in his simple talk
amid shops and whistles, in which of his metallic motions
lived the indestructible, the imperishable—life?

III

Lives like maize were threshed in the
 bottomless
granary of wasted deeds, of shabby   70
incidents, from one to sevenfold, even to eight,
and not one death but many deaths came each
 man's way:
each day a petty death, dust, worm, a lamp
snuffed out in suburban mud, a petty fat-
 winged
 death   75
entered each one like a short spear
and men were beset by bread or by the knife:

the drover, the son of seaports, the dark captain of the plow,
or those who gnaw at the cluttered streets:
all of them weakened, waiting their death, their
 brief death   80
 daily,
and their dismal weariness each day was like
a black cup they drank down trembling.

IV

The mightiest death invited me many times:
like invisible salt in the waves it was,   85
and what its invisible savor disseminated
was half like sinking and half like height
or huge structures of wind and glacier.

I came to the iron edge, the narrows
of the air, the shroud of fields and stone,   90
to the stellar emptiness of the final steps
and the dizzying spiral highway:
yet broad sea, oh death! not wave by wave you
 come
but like a gallop of nighttime clarity
or the absolute numbers of night.   95

You never came poking in pockets, nor could
you visit except in red robes,
in an auroral carpet enclosing silence,
in lofty and buried legacies of tears.

I could not in each creature love a tree   100
with its own small autumn on its back (the
 death of a
 thousand leaves),
all the false deaths and resurrections
with no earth, no depths:
I wanted to swim in the broadest lives,   105
in the openest river mouths,
and as men kept denying me little by little,
blocking path and door so I would not touch
with my streaming hands their wound of
 emptiness,
then I went street after street and river after
 river,   110
city after city and bed after bed,
and my brackish mask crossed through waste
 places,
and in the last low hovels, no light, no fire,
no bread, no stone, no silence, alone,
I roamed round dying of my own death.   115

V

Solemn death it was not you, iron-plumed bird,
that the poor successor to those dwellings
carried among gulps of food, under his empty
 skin:
something it was, a spent petal of worn-out rope,
a shred of heart that fell short of struggle   120
or the harsh dew that never reached his face.
It was what could not be reborn, a bit
of petty death with no peace or place:
a bone, a bell, that were dying within him.
I lifted the iodine bandages, plunged my hands   125

into meager griefs that were killing off death,
and all I found in the wound was a cold gust
that passed through loose gaps in the soul.

VI

Then on the ladder of the earth I climbed
through the lost jungle's tortured thicket   130
up to you, Macchu Picchu.
High city of laddered stones,
at last the dwelling of what earth
never covered in vestments of sleep.
In you like two lines parallel,   135
the cradles of lightning and man
rocked in a wind of thorns.

Mother of stone, spume of condors.

High reef of the human dawn.

Spade lost in the primal sand.   140

This was the dwelling, this is the place:
here the broad grains of maize rose up
and fell again like red hail.

Here gold thread came off the vicuña
to clothe lovers, tombs, and mothers,   145
king and prayers and warriors.

Here men's feet rested at night
next to the eagles' feet, in the ravenous
high nests, and at dawn
they stepped with the thunder's feet onto
    thinning mists   150
and touched the soil and the stones
till they knew them come night or death.

I look a clothes and hands,
the trace of water in an echoing tub,
the wall brushed smooth by the touch of a face   155
that looked with my eyes at the lights of earth,
that oiled with my hands the vanished
beams: because everything, clothing, skin, jars,
words, wine, bread,
is gone, fallen to earth.   160

And the air came in with the touch
of lemon blossom over everyone sleeping:
a thousand years of air, months, weeks of air,
of blue wind and iron cordillera,
that were like gentle hurricane footsteps   165
polishing the lonely boundary of stone.

VII

You dead of a single abyss, shadows of one
    ravine,
the deepest, thus on a scale
with your greatness there came
the true, the most consuming   170
death and from the drilled-out rocks,
from the red-topped columns,
from the laddered aqueducts
you plummeted as in autumn
to one sole death.   175
Today the empty air does not weep,
is not familiar with your clayey feet,
forgets your pitchers that filtered the sky

when knives of lightning spilled it out,
and eaten by mist the mighty   180
tree was cut down by gusts.

It held up a hand that fell suddenly
down from the height to the end of time.
You're no more now, spidery hands, frail
fibers, entangled web—   185
whatever you were fell away: customs, frayed
syllables, masks of dazzling light.

Yet a permanence of stone and word,
the city like a bowl, rose up in the hands
of all, living, dead, silenced, sustained,   190
a wall out of so much death, out of so much life
    a shock
of stone petals: the permanent rose, the
    dwelling place:
the glacial outposts on this Andean reef.

When the clay-colored hand
turned to clay and the eyes' small lids fell shut,   195
filled with rugged walls, crowded with castles,
and when man lay all tangled in his hole,
there remained an upraised exactitude:
the high site of the human dawn:
the highest vessel that held silence in: 200
a life of stone after so many lives.

VIII

Climb up with me, American love.

Kiss the secret stones with me.
The torrential silver of the Urubamba
sends pollen flying to its yellow cup.   205
The empty vine goes flying,
the stony plant, the stiff garland
over the silent mountain gorge.
Come, minuscule life, between the wings
of the earth, while—crystal and cold, a buffeted
    air   210
dividing the clash of emeralds—
oh wild water you come down from the snow.

Love, love, until the sudden night,
from the Andes' ringing flintstone,
to the red knees of dawn,   215
study the blind child of the snow.

Oh Wilkamayu of resonant threads,
when you shatter your bands of thunder
into white spume, like wounded snow,
when your steep gale   220
sings and slashes arousing the sky,
what language do you bring to the ear
barely uprooted from your Andean foam?

Who seized the lightning of the cold
and left it chained on the heights,   225
split into its chilling tears,
shaken in its rapid swords,
beating its war-worn stamens,
borne on its warrior bed,
stormed in its rock-bound end?   230

What do your tormented flashings say?
Your secret insurgent lightning—did it
once travel thronging with words?

Who goes on crushing frozen syllables,
black languages, banners of gold,   235
bottomless mouths, throttled shouts,
in your slender arterial waters?

Who goes clipping floral eyelids
that come to gaze from the earth?
Who hurls the dead stalks down   240
that drop in your cascading hands
to thresh their threshed-out night
in geologic coal?

Who flings down the linking branch?
Who yet again buries farewells?   245

Love, love, do not touch the brink
or worship the sunken head:
let time extend full span
in its hall of broken wellsprings,
and between ramparts and rapid water   250
gather the air in the pass,
the wind's parallel plating,
the blind channel of the cordillera,
the bitter greeting of the dew,
and climb through the denseness flower by
    flower,   255
trampling the serpent flung to earth.

In this cliff-hung region, stone and forest,
dust of green stars, jungle clarity,
Mantur breaks out like a living lake
or a new ledge of silence.   260
Come to my very being, to my own dawn,
up to the crowning solitude.

The dead realm lives on still.

And across the Sundial like a black ship
the ravening shadow of the condor cruises.   265

IX

Sidereal eagle, vineyard of mist.
Bulwark lost, blind scimitar.
Starred belt, sacred bread.
Torrential ladder, giant eyelid.
Triangled tunic, pollen of stone.   270
Granite lamp, bread of stone.
Mineral serpent, rose of stone.
Buried ship, wellspring of stone.
Lunar horse, light of stone.
Equinox square, vapor of stone.   275
Final geometry, book of stone.
Iceberg carved by the squalls.
Coral of sunken time.
Rampart smoothed by fingers.
Roof struck by feathers.   280
Branching of mirrors, ground of
    tempests.
Thrones overturned by twining weeds.
Rule of the ravenous claw.
Gale sustained on the slope.
Immobile turquoise cataract.   285
Sleepers' patriarchal bell.
Collar of subjected snows.
Iron lying on its statues.

Inaccessible storm sealed off.
Puma hands, bloodthirsty rock.   290
Shading tower, dispute of snow.
Night raised in fingers and roots.
Window on the mist, hardened dove.
Nocturnal plant, statue of thunder.
Root of the cordillera, roof of the sea.   295
Architecture of lost eagles.
Cord of the sky, bee of the heights.
Bloodstained level, constructed star.
Mineral bubble, moon of quartz.
Andean serpent, brow of amaranth.   300
Dome of silence, purebred homeland.
Bride of the sea, cathedral tree.
Salt branch, blackwinged cherry tree.
Snowswept teeth, cold thunder.
Scraped moon, menacing stone.   305
Crest of the cold, pull of the air.
Volcano of hands, dark cataract.
Silver wave, direction of time.

X

Stone upon stone, and man, where was he?
Air upon air, and man, where was he?   310
Time upon time, and man, where was he?
Were you too then the broken bit
of half-spent humankind, an empty eagle, that
through the streets today, through footsteps,
through the dead autumn's leaves,   315
keeps crushing its soul until the grave?
The meager hand, the foot, the meager life . . .
Did the days of unraveled light
in you, like rain
on pennants at a festival,   320
give off their dark food petal by petal
into your empty mouth?
Hunger, coral of humankind,
hunger, hidden plant, root of the woodcutter,
hunger, did your reef-edge climb   325
to these high and ruinous towers?
I question you, salt of the roads,
show me the trowel; architecture, let me
grind stone stamens with a stick,
climb every step of air up to the void,   330
scrape in the womb till I touch man.

Macchu Picchu, did you set
stone upon stone on a base of rags?
Coal over coal and at bottom, tears?
Fire on the gold and within it, trembling, the red   335
splash of blood?
Give me back the slave you buried!
Shake from the earth the hard bread
of the poor, show me the servant's
clothes and his window.   340
Tell me how he slept while he lived.
Tell me if his sleep
was snoring, gaping like a black hole
that weariness dug in the wall.
The wall, the wall! If every course of stone   345
weighed down his sleep, and if he fell
    underneath
as under a moon, with his sleep!

Ancient America, sunken bride,

your fingers too,

leaving the jungle for the empty height of the
    gods,   350

under bridal banners of light and reverence,

blending with thunder from the drums and
    lances,

yours, your fingers too,

those that the abstract rose and the rim of cold,
    the

bloodstained body of the new grain bore up   355

to a web of radiant matter, to the hardened
    hollows,

you too, buried America, did you keep in the
    deepest part

of your bitter gut, like an eagle, hunger?

XI

Through the dazing splendor,

through the night of stone, let me plunge my
    hand   360

and let there beat in me, like a bird a thousand
    years
  imprisoned,

the old forgotten human heart!

Let me forget today this joy that is broader
    than the sea,

because man is broader than sea and islands   365

and we must fall in him as in a well to rise from
    the bottom

with a branch of secret water and sunken
    truths.

Let me forget, broad stone, the sovereign
    symmetry,

transcendent measure, honeycombed stones,

and from the square edge let me this day slide   370

my hand down the hypotenuse of haircloth and
    bitter blood.

When, like a horseshoe of red-cased wings, the
    furious condor

hammers my temples in the order of flight

and the hurricane's blood-dipped feathers
    sweep the dark dust

on diagonal stairways, I see not the swift beast,   375

not the blind cycling of its claws,

I see the ancient human, a human slave,
    sleeping

in the fields, I see one body, a thousand bodies,
  a man, a
    thousand women

under black gusts, blackened by rain and night,   380

with the stonework's massive carving:

Jack Stonebreaker, son of Wiracocha,

Jack Coldbiter, son of the green star,

Jack Barefoot, grandson of the turquoise,

rise to be born with me, brother.   385

XII

Rise to be born with me, brother.

Give me your hand out of the deep

region seeded by all your grief.

You won't come back from bottom rock.

You won't come back from time under ground.   390

No coming back with your hardened voice.

No coming back with your drilled-out eyes.

Look at me from the bottom of earth,

plowman, weaver, voiceless shepherd:

trainer of guardian llamas: 395

mason on a dangerous scaffold:

water-bearer of Andean tears:

goldsmith with fingers bruised:

farmer trembling over the seed:

potter spilled on your clay: 400

bring all your age-old buried

griefs to the cup of this new life.

Show me your blood and your furrow,

say to me: here I was punished

when a gem didn't shine or the earth   405

give forth its stone or grain on time:

mark me the stone you stumbled on

and the wood they crucified you on,

strike light for me from your old flints,

the ancient lamps, the whiplash stuck   410

within your wounds through centuries,

and the axes' brightness stained with blood.

I come to speak through your dead mouth.

All through the earth join all

the silent wasted lips   415

and speak from the depths to me all this long
    night

as if I were anchored here with you,

tell me everything, chain by chain,

link by link, and step by step,

file the knives you kept by you,   420

drive them into my chest and my hand

like a river of riving yellow light,

like a river where buried jaguars lie,

and let me weep, hours, days, years,

blind ages, stellar centuries.   425

Give me silence, water, hope.

Give me struggle, iron, volcanoes.

Fasten your bodies to me like magnets.

Hasten to my veins to my mouth.

Speak through my words and my blood.   430

POEM SUMMARY

Canto 1

"The Heights of Macchu Picchu" opens in the first canto (a canto is a division used in long poetry) with the poet-narrator describing his work and life before ascending the mountain to Macchu Picchu. His concern with income is apparent in lines 3 and 4: "at autumn's advent, the coin handed out / in the leaves." Neruda then describes his approach to writing poetry in a characteristically erotic way: "like a sword sheathed in meteors / I plunged my turbulent and gentle hand / into the genital quick of the earth." His use of words such as "nuptial" and "spring" prepare the reader for the transportation back in time that will come later, as well as the personification of his homeland, Chile in specific, and Latin America in general.

Canto 2

In the second canto, Neruda expresses the exhaustion of modern life, both his own and that of his fellow humans. He evokes the seasons, giving a sense of time passing and renewing, from summer when the "flower gives up the high seed," to the "face ground down / among deep pits in autumn," to "the city's winter streets." The personification of the landscape continues to build as the poet confesses: "How many times ... // have I wanted to stop and seek the timeless fathomless vein / I touched in a stone once or in the lightning a kiss released." There is promise for renewal in the eternal promise of "germinal shells" of grain whereas, for humankind, "in which of his metallic motions / lived the indestructible, the imperishable—life?" This expresses the poet-narrator's existential disillusionment with the pattern of modern life.

Canto 3

Neruda now answers his questions posed at the end of canto 2. He underlines the struggle of everyday people, comparing them to the grain that nourishes the masses: "Lives like maize were threshed in the bottomless / granary of wasted deeds," as if their subjugation is justified by the needs of others. He dwells on the deaths that daily fill people's lives: "each day a petty death, dust, worm, a lamp / snuffed out in suburban mud." These "petty" deaths are a strain on humanity, "all of them weakened, waiting their death." The closing image, of "dismal weariness" likened to "a black cup" brings to mind the coffee and tea which many people around the world consume daily, just as the "maize" from the first line of Canto 3 is a staple food. They have accepted their miserable lives, Neruda is saying.

Canto 4

The fourth canto shifts focus to Neruda himself wherein he recounts his struggles with "the mightiest death." This is a death of more finite proportions than the petty deaths of the previous canto. "I wanted to swim in the broadest lives, /

in the openest river mouths" expresses Neruda's desire to move beyond the mundane. Yet, as this canto goes on to express, he has been held back from this by other people, people who do not want to hear his words or the truth within. The last line, "I roamed round dying of my own death," encapsulates Neruda's despair before ascending to Macchu Picchu: the frustration and seeming aimlessness of life.

Canto 5

The poet-narrator seeks renewal, even resurrection in canto 5. "I lifted the iodine bandages, plunged my hands / into meager griefs that were killing off death, / and all I found in the wound was a cold gust / that passed through loose gaps in the soul." He is struggling to cure these miseries of mediocrity with his poetic gift but is stymied by the lifelessness of that which he faces.

Canto 6

The poet-narrator arrives at Macchu Picchu and the despairing tone of the first five cantos is blasted away with a triumphal outcry at the magnificence of this place, even ruined as it now is. The poet uses epithets to celebrate Macchu Picchu, such as "Mother of stone, spume of condors. / High reef of the human dawn." These epithets frame Macchu Picchu as a mythical source, a mother, a place already standing at the beginning of humanity. The poet-narrator daydreams about what Macchu Picchu was like before falling to beautiful ruin: "Here men's feet rested at night / next to the eagles' feet." He sees these people who once were, in "the trace of water in an echoing tub, / the wall brushed smooth by the touch of a face," noting that now all else, "words, wine, bread / is gone, fallen to earth."

Canto 7

The poet-narrator imagines "one sole death" for this grand place, a place which has no living memory of what once was. And yet memory of stone is retained: "a permanence of stone and word, / the city like a bowl, rose up in the hands / of all, living, dead, silenced, sustained." Unoccupied by human beings, Macchu Picchu has now "a life of stone after so many lives."

Canto 8

Now at the summit of Macchu Picchu, the poet-narrator contemplates the source for the river Urubamba, known to the ancient Incas as Wilkamayu, and considered to be a sacred river because it was an earthly reflection of the celestial entity known today as the Milky Way. The "miniscule life" of "pollen"—the way nature continually renews—is transported, planted by the "wild water." He asks of the river: "Who seized the lightning of the cold / and left it chained on the heights" and "Who yet again buries farewells?" In other words, who were these ancient people who built their citadel on Macchu Picchu and what has become of them? He is also drawn to the loss of words by these Incans, who had only an oral tradition, and imagines their language breaking down and being washed away by the river, "who goes on crushing frozen syllables, / black languages, banners of gold, / bottomless mouths, throttled shouts, / in your slender arterial waters?" Neruda concludes: "The dead realm lives on still" and "the ravening shadow of the condor cruises." This again underlines his themes of renewal and death.

Canto 9

Canto 9 is almost completely composed of epithets, which the poet-narrator uses to describe the magnificence of Macchu Picchu. She is the "mineral serpent, rose of stone," "rule of the ravenous claw," "architecture of lost eagles," and "silver wave, direction of time." The litany of this list is chant-like and ritualistic. The long list of descriptive phrases adds dimension and layers of meaning to Macchu Picchu with an economy of words, drawing out this ancient site as much older, more mythological.

Canto 10

Addressing Macchu Picchu herself, the poet-narrator asks what humankind's involvement has been in her history: "Stone upon stone, and man, where was he?" "Hunger, did your reef-edge climb / to these high and ruinous towers?" he asks, wondering who ruined who, the mountain or the man. Hunger is a central theme of these last three cantos, which now draws a more direct correlation between the voiceless slaves of antiquity and the miserable masses of contemporary times. Neruda sees the "rags," tears," and "blood" the fortress was built upon and cries out: "Give me back the slave you buried!" "Ancient America, sunken bride," he addresses Macchu Picchu, "did you keep in the deepest part / of your bitter gut, like an eagle, hunger?" This hunger, the poet argues, has been central to the creations of humankind (i.e., Macchu Picchu) as well as the undoing of human beings, suffering for the brief glory of others.

Canto 11

Recalling the primary action of canto 1, the poet-narrator declares "let me plunge my hand / and let there beat in me . . . / the old forgotten human heart!" This heart is not found in Macchu Picchu's splendor but rather in "the ancient human, a human slave, sleeping / in the fields, I see one body, a thousand bodies, a man, a thousand women." Neruda's socialist beliefs, his compassion for others, draw him to the raw hands and bent backs of the people who were conscripted by others to build this now-ruined grand estate. He calls out to those laborers in the last line, "rise to be born with me, brother."

Canto 12

In canto 12, the closing canto of "The Heights of Macchu Picchu," the poet-narrator repeats the last line of the previous canto, as if in incantation, "Rise to be born with me, brother." Neruda calls forth the ancient laborers, using a brief list of epithets to describe their variety, their work, and their lives, much as he used epithets in canto 9 to describe Macchu Picchu's splendor—that splendor which is explicitly owed to the skills of these people. "I come to speak through your dead mouth." "Tell me everything" the poet asks, "let me weep, hours, days, years." He promises them: "Fasten your bodies to me like magnets. // Hasten to my veins to my mouth. // Speak through my words and my blood." "The Heights of Macchu Picchu" then is about the hundreds of slaves yoked to Macchu Picchu, whose blood was spilled to raise her up, here within the seat of the gods, so close to the sky. Neruda feels their ancient miseries and invokes them, to give them voice so they are not forgotten. Translator John Felstiner writes: "When the poet says 'rise to be born with me, brother,' he is not only summoning the past to the present but urging the present into the future." "The Heights of Macchu Picchu" as mythology is as much about what has already happened as it is about what is yet to come.

THEMES

Slavery

Slavery is a condition wherein one person, the slave, is owned by another person and can be forced to do work by the owner. Slavery has existed throughout human history wherever disproportionate power gives certain people the advantage over others and law does not forbid

TOPICS FOR FURTHER STUDY

- "The Heights of Macchu Picchu" was heavily influenced by Neruda's communist beliefs. Research communism and write an essay about how the poet's political beliefs shaped this poem. Give examples from the poem. Do you agree with Neruda's arguments? Why or why not?

- Neruda was, for many years, an outspoken supporter of Russian leader Joseph Stalin. Late in the 1950s, he had a change of heart. Why did Neruda change his views? What did Stalin do and how were his actions eventually revealed to the rest of the world? Research this period in history (1930s–1950s) and then write a research paper that answers these questions.

- Neruda began writing his masterpiece *Canto General* after his father died in 1938. It was originally titled "Canto de Chile" but Neruda later decided to broaden its scope to encompass all of Latin America. Write your own poem or short story that tells the story of a place you know well. Personify the place, like Neruda did: give it emotions, thoughts, and other human qualities. Share your work with another student or with the entire class in a group reading.

- Macchu Picchu is believed to have been a summer retreat for Pachacuti, the Inca ruler who famously turned the Kingdom of Cuzco into the Inca Empire, which spanned six modern nations. Inca culture fascinates people to this day for its grand architecture, masterful stonework, record-keeping methods, complex social organization, and other beliefs and technologies. Choose an area of Inca culture to investigate and prepare a class presentation on what you learned. Use visual aids and prepare a short speech.

slave ownership. As an ardent and outspoken socialist, Neruda opposed slavery. Socialists believe that a community should be supported by a shared effort of everyone living within the community. In "The Heights of Macchu Picchu," Neruda's poet-narrator comes to the heart of his quest at this mountain top fortress when, in canto 10, he asks: "Macchu Picchu, did you set / stone upon stone on a base of rags? / Coal over coal and at bottom, tears? / Fire on the gold and within it, trembling, the red / splash of blood?" From here he delves into the life of poverty and deprivation he has imagined for the slaves who built Macchu Picchu, and calls out to the slaves who constructed her in canto 11: "Jack Stonebiter, son of Wiracocha, / Jack Coldbiter, son of the green star, / Jack Barefoot, grandson of the turquoise, / rise to be born with me, brother." Wiracocha is a temple in the ancient Incan capital of Cuzco; here, Neruda is implying that the parents of Jack Stonebiter were also slaves, conscripted to build this temple. "Green star" and "turquoise" are probably references to mining and gem production for ornamenting royalty and magnificent architecture. "Man is broader than sea and islands / and we must fall in him as in a well to rise from the bottom." The poet emphasizes solidarity between human beings as the way for humans to rise above mortal miseries. In canto 12, calling these laborers to him, the speaker says "bring all your age-old buried / griefs to the cup of this new life," which echoes back to the last two lines in canto 3 ("their dismal weariness each day was like / a black cup they drank down trembling"). Neruda is commenting on the slavery of contemporary times, much of which is self-imposed or hidden within the structures of culture and government. He sees modern people suffering as much as slaves ever did and calls all to come together for collective improvement of life.

Death and Resurrection

Neruda, as a poet, was known for his love poetry, his sensuality, and, in his early verses, for loneliness. Death is a popular theme for writers all over the world but it was new to Neruda in "The Heights of Macchu Picchu." His life was also changing dramatically at this time as he lost several friends in the Spanish Civil War and quite soon thereafter his father, his stepmother, and his daughter all died. "The Heights of Macchu Picchu" marks a turning point in Neruda's literary career. He does not give up on his sensuous nature imagery but adds to it the darker elements of renewal, marked by the failure, sometimes, to renew at all. The first 5 cantos concern Neruda's life before he visits Macchu Picchu and these verses are grim, almost to the point of hopelessness. Moving through the daily lives of contemporary laborers who appear numb to their fate, "a black cup they drank down trembling," Neruda also describes himself as impotent to the world that has been circumscribed for him by other people as "I roamed round dying of my own death." He also distinguishes between "petty" deaths that make up a miserable life and the "mightiest death" which irrevocably transforms a life. Despite his own wretchedness and frustration, which the poet-narrator demonstrates in canto 4, he is not ready for the "mightiest death" and instead pushes past the obvious darkness to the mountaintop where clarity comes to him. He sees the suffering and death of laborers from 500 years ago; nothing has changed. Little tangible evidence of these common people are left; only a suggestion of memory in the timeless stone they laid. From these cold roots, a poet such as Neruda can resurrect their essence, give voice to their Marxist plight, a pattern he saw as stretching throughout the history of Latin America, backwards and forwards.

STYLE

Canto

A canto is a division used in long-form poetry. It is an Italian word derived from the Latin word for song and may be related to the oral tradition of storytelling, before writing was used to capture tales. Use of cantos is evocative of epic poetry, which was a popular narrative form up to and including the medieval period. "The Heights of Macchu Picchu" is divided into twelve cantos and, through the use of other literary devices, is heavily influenced by the styling found in epic poetry. This gives the poem a sense of antiquity and grandeur, emphasizing the timelessness of Neruda's themes of death, resurrection, and enslavement. The cantos, being a structural element, pace the poem and give the poet an opportunity to focus on different images and use different tones with each canto. For example the focus of canto 9 is the mountain-top fortress of Macchu Picchu and this canto celebrates her grand beauty. The focus shifts dramatically in canto 10 when the poet turns attention to those who constructed Macchu Picchu and his tone becomes accusatory and outraged.

Epithet

An epithet is a fixed descriptive phrase which adds layers of meaning to the object it is applied to. For example, these two epithets from canto 9: "Root of the cordillera, roof of the sea" (cordillera is the Spanish word for mountain range). Epithets were used to great effect in epic poetry, drawing bold portraits of heroes and villains, describing scenery, and generally adding dimension to a story overall. Epithets are believed to be a holdover from the oral tradition because these fixed descriptive phrases made for easier memorization or even improvisation. In "The Heights of Macchu Picchu," Neruda uses epithets when trying to describe Macchu Picchu's majestic and historic quality. Rather than liberally use them throughout the poem as one would find in epic poetry, he reserves this technique to use in particular places so that it will have a bolder impact on the reader. The epithets celebrating the beauty of Macchu Picchu, for example, begin building in canto 8, then crescendo in canto 10, which is almost all epithets. Following this, Neruda criticizes Macchu Picchu for the cost of human life which was demanded in her construction.

HISTORICAL CONTEXT

Inca Empire

The Inca Empire emerged during the thirteenth century in the highlands of Peru and quickly established dominance over western South America through both assimilation and warfare. The Empire spread up and down the Pacific Coast and included parts of modern Columbia, Ecuador, Bolivia, Peru, Chile, and Argentina. The capital city of the Inca Empire was Cuzco, located in what is today southern Peru. The major expansion of the Inca Empire occurred during the reign of Pachacuti ("earth-shaker") who developed the four-part provincial system, which divided the Empire into manageable portions. Pachacuti aggressively assimilated neighboring royalty by offering them a choice of payment to join the empire, or warfare; many chose payment and joined the Incas. The children of foreign royalty were sent to Cuzco for education, then returned to their homelands to spread the Incan way of life.

Incan government was highly bureaucratic and systematic, which gave it stability despite the uneven loyalties of its oppressed citizens. Taxes were extremely high with the benefit being that

COMPARE
&
CONTRAST

- **1400s:** The Inca Empire is established in 1438 by ruler Pachacuti and is the dominant power in western South America.

  1900s: Socialist Senator Salvador Allende is elected president of Chile in 1970. He is overthrown by a military coup three years later.

  Today: Socialist candidate Michelle Bachelet is elected president of Chile in January 2006. She is the first woman to serve in this office for the nation of Chile.

- **1400s:** Yanas are the lowest social class in Inca society. They are not slaves, but because they have been permanently separated from their families and no reciprocal service or payment is owed to them, they are similar to slaves.

  1900s: Peru is ruled by a wealthy oligarchy and, although slavery is illegal (as of 1854), many poor people, especially the indigenous minority, have no choice but servitude to the interests of the wealthy.

  Today: In Peru, unemployment is high and a significant portion of the population is under the age of eighteen. Poor women and children, especially girls, are the primary victims of human trafficking in Peru and are coerced or sold into hard labor in mines, domestic labor, or the sex trade.

- **1400s:** Christopher Columbus sails for the West Indies but, in 1492, "discovers" America instead. Spanish explorers and conquistadors soon follow, bringing ruin to the indigenous populations of North and South America.

  1900s: Indigenous populations are a fraction of what they once were and many tribes are extinct. Those cultural groups trying to live alongside modern society find themselves discriminated against and they often live in extreme poverty. Young people abandon the old traditions in hopes of improving their situation.

  Today: Rights for indigenous people are being asserted and restitution of tribal lands is being made, as in the case of the Mapuche people of southern Chile. The process is slow and difficult while old prejudices prevail, but forward progress is definitely being made.

areas that were poorer (possibly because the land was not farmable) were distributed extra goods, perhaps giving those people a better quality of life than they knew before Inca rule. This government model shares some similarities with that of the Romans.

Pachacuti commissioned the construction of Macchu Picchu around 1450 B.C.E., probably as a royal estate for his family; it was located only fifty miles from Cuzco. By the mid-1500s, Macchu Picchu was abandoned as the Inca Empire collapsed following the Spanish conquest of the region. The Inca Empire lasted a hundred years, abruptly interrupted by foes they could not fight: diseases, such as smallpox, and technologically advanced weapons that easily overcame their Bronze Age armaments.

Communism

Communism is a political theory advocating a classless society. Ownership is communal and everyone works to the best of their abilities for the improvement of the community. Communism became very controversial in the early twentieth century, especially following World War II, because it was associated with totalitarian regimes, such as Stalin's Russia and Mao's China, where people were poor and ideas were oppressed so as to not threaten the stability of the communist society. The controversy surrounding communism largely arose from the strong anticommunist sentiment in the free-market economy of the United States. Highly individualistic Americans were discomforted with the impression that

Ruins of the old Inca city of Machu Picchu in the Andes in Peru (© nagelestock.com | Alamy)

communism would turn people into anonymous drones.

Outside the United States, communism—and its parent ideology, socialism—had a strong draw for many other nations including Chile, Mexico, Cuba, Poland, Hungary, East Germany, North Korea, and Vietnam. Some countries eventually abandoned communism when it proved merely a vehicle for a single political party to absolutely control the government and use communist ideals to tyrannize the foment of new ideas. This abuse of communist ideals does not negate the potential for good and, indeed, some nations, like North Korea and Cuba, continue to structure their government and society under communism.

Neruda was an outspoken communist throughout his life, a position that many people considered to be controversial in an otherwise highly admirably poet. Beginning with his career as

a Communist Senator in 1945, Neruda actively sought to establish a communist government within his homeland of Chile. He ardently believed in communist ideology, going so far as to verbally attack President Gabriel González Videla in the Chilean Senate when Neruda learned that the President broke up a labor strike by interring the striking miners in prisons and concentration camps. Neruda then had to flee the country for fear of his life; he remained in exile for four years until González Videla's government destabilized and new elections were held.

CRITICAL OVERVIEW

Neruda began publishing his work when he was only thirteen years old, although his family discouraged him from pursuing writing as a career. He published his first two books of poetry while still a young man in college and quickly gained notoriety both within Chile and abroad. His second book, *20 Poems and a Song of Despair*, was an instant success and continues to be one of his most well-known, beloved works both in South America and around the world. Jonathan Cohen, writing in a *Romance Notes* article covering early critical reception of Neruda's work in English, notes that early reviewers were paying attention to this young poet, although not all were captivated by his work. "English translations of Neruda's poems were slow in coming, despite his growing international reputation as a major poet. A book-length collection [*Residence on Earth and Other Poems*] would not appear in the United States until 1946." Neruda was an established poet and diplomat by the time he published "The Heights of Macchu Picchu"—first on its own in a Spanish-language magazine in 1946, then a few years later, in 1950, as part of *Canto General*. Many scholars and critics have noted that "The Heights of Macchu Picchu" marks a turning point in Neruda's poetry, as he had grown out of the loneliness of his youth and was becoming increasingly concerned with the plight of the everyday people he represented as a Senator in Chile.

Writing for the *Wilson Quarterly*, Edward Hirsch describes *Canto General* thusly: "What started out as a poem about Chile eventually grew into a poem that delineated the full geological, biological, and political history of South America. It became a comprehensive song, a general chant, a Whitmanian epic of the New World, a mythification of America." Michael Wood, in his overview of Neruda's early works for the *New York Review of Books*, asserts that this poem cycle is "the best of all introductions to Neruda, since his gifts receive their full expression there." James Wright, a critic for *Poetry*, reviews Nathaniel Tarn's 1968 translation of "The Heights of Macchu Picchu." Wright is mild in his praise of Tarn, but calls Neruda "one of the precious few great masters of our time and of any time" and even compares the endurance of his work to that of Shakespeare. Indeed, the popularity of Neruda's work continues unabated.

CRITICISM

Carol Ullmann

Ullmann is a freelance writer and editor. In the following essay, she examines the mythological

WHAT DO I READ NEXT?

- *Stalin: A Biography* (2006), by Robert Service, is a modern and comprehensive look into the life of this controversial communist leader known both for his defeat of Nazi Germany and the torture of his own people.

- *On the Blue Shore of Silence*, written by Pablo Neruda, was produced as a special bilingual edition in 2003 to celebrate the 100th anniversary of the poet's birth. It is translated by Alastair Reid and illustrated by the painter Mary Heebner. The volume focuses on Neruda's poetry about the sea.

- *Leaves of Grass* (1855), by American poet Walt Whitman, heralded a new poetic tradition that was organic, sensual, and lyrical. Although fame eluded Whitman during his lifetime, scholars now acknowledge the tremendous influence of this poet; he was also one of Neruda's favorites.

- *Gypsy Ballads*, by Spanish poet and playwright Federico García Lorca, was written in Spanish in 1928 and published in English in 1953. This volume established Lorca's fame; Lorca, like Neruda, was a popular writer at a young age.

- *Trilce* (1922), by César Vallejo, was a significant avant-garde book of poetry. Vallejo was forced to flee his native Peru in 1923, remaining in Europe for the rest of his life; he met Neruda while visiting Spain.

- *Tales of the Little Quarter* (1878), by Czech writer Jan Neruda, is a collection of short stories that takes place in the Little Quarter neighborhood of Prague. This book was translated by Ellis Peters in 1957.

- *T. S. Eliot: An Imperfect Life* (2000), by Lyndall Gordon, provides insight into the life of the famed poet whom Neruda has been compared to stylistically and thematically. Eliot, like Neruda, also held strong social views that were highly controversial.

> ALTHOUGH MYTHS CAN BE SPIRITUAL AND EVEN ESOTERIC, THEY ARE ALWAYS BOUND TO THE HUMAN CONDITION."

nature of Neruda's long poem "The Heights of Macchu Picchu."

Neruda sought to establish a unified Latin American mythology with "The Heights of Macchu Picchu" and later, *Canto General*. Mythology is a set of stories or beliefs shared by a cultural group. Neruda was not ignoring the existence of already established indigenous beliefs and in fact drew on many of those symbols for this verse. But these indigenous cultural groups—such as the Bora, the Matsés, and the Yagua—have known no cultural unity, if ever, since the Inca Empire. Although called Indians by the Spanish after Christopher Columbus's mistake (he thought he had sailed to India), these people did not view themselves as a unified group.

Neruda was moved by the poverty he saw when he returned to Chile in 1943. This, coupled with his horrific and sad experiences while in Spain during the Spanish Civil War, drove the poet, who was always an optimist and a populist, to seek answers and solutions. He found these on top of a mountain in 1943. Neruda's journey, from his early manhood to the day he saw Macchu Picchu, was an expedition of mythic quality and he indeed includes this as the first half of the poem. Joseph Campbell, the renowned mythographer, writes about the hero's journey in his book *The Hero with a Thousand Faces*. The hero's journey begins with a summons; throughout his quest he is offered help and he meets with tribulation. He encounters gods, who are simultaneously aid and tribulation to him; he looses friends; and eventually acquires the boon that he seeks. This journey, is, of course, not about the material object the hero returns home with; it is about the hero's spiritual growth, often symbolic in specific tales as a boy becoming a man, or a prince becoming king.

Neruda's growth, then, in this journey leading up to Macchu Picchu, was one of politi-

cization. He did not exchange his naturalistic, erotic style for something new. He did not *change*, he grew, adding to his stylistic repertoire themes of death, populism, and history. Neruda was no longer just a poet, no longer solitary—now he was a poet of the people, giving voice to those who have forgotten how to talk: "I come to speak through your dead mouth."

The mythology Neruda brings from this mountaintop citadel is an old and oft-repeated tale of servitude—the slaves of the Inca who built their cities, followed by the Incas who were killed or enslaved by the Spanish, who are in turn politically enslaved by weighty influence of their northern neighbor, the United States. To Neruda, this enslavement of humans by humans is the source of misery and ultimately self-destruction. He writes in canto 10: "Macchu Picchu, did you set / stone upon stone on a base of rags?" And in canto 7: "on a scale / with your greatness there came / the true, the most consuming / death … // you plummeted as in autumn / to one sole death."

Subjugation, death, and innocent renewal form a pattern that repeats endlessly throughout the history of Latin America, spiraling into the despair that grips people today, as they go through their daily grind, lost in their cities, lost to each other. Neruda begins "The Heights of Macchu Picchu" with a contemporary view, taking in both his own loneliness, and the "dismal weariness" he sees in people around him. His expedition to Macchu Picchu takes him back in time and it is there that Neruda finds a promise for the future. His mythology is a racial awareness—a memory—and like all of humanity's oldest stories, Neruda's mythology of Latin America has been *resurrected* as a tool for memory, to combat today's wretchedness. His myth of Macchu Picchu teaches that it is only by working together and sharing life that a community can mitigate its miseries and overcome this ancestral need to possess and be possessed.

Why has Neruda chosen Macchu Picchu as the site of this myth, this awakened memory, and not some other site, like Cuzco, which was the heart of the Inca Empire and only fifty miles away? In part, it can be inferred that it is because Neruda was moved by the experience of visiting Macchu Picchu (he also visited Cuzco on the same trip). More significantly, Macchu Picchu was never discovered by the Spanish conquistadors, who frequently burned and tore down indigenous architecture as part of their campaign of subjugation. Until the early twentieth century, it was untouched and perhaps unseen by human eyes for almost four hundred years. Macchu Picchu is a citadel of the dead, quiet, unliving, frozen in time, but Neruda does not merely see a monument to what once was: "The dead realm lives on still."

In canto 7, Neruda directly expresses concern with memory: "Today the empty air does not weep, / is not familiar with your clayey feet, / forgets your pitchers that filtered the sky" and "whatever you were fell away: customs, frayed / syllables, masks of dazzling light." This begins the poet's mourning for those who constructed Macchu Picchu out of their blood and sweat; from these intense feelings, Neruda constructs memories he cannot literally posses. He must create the words for these memories from blind stone and senseless river, but it is as if these people have waited for him, for a voice, and as he moves among the ruins, he is possessed by their anger and grief. He sees their presence in that which has been left behind; he also sees that which is missing and, like the bodies of these people, has returned to the earth. By canto 10, Neruda's anger is mounting to outrage and his questions directed at Macchu Picchu are accusatory. "Give me back the slave you buried!" he cries out.

A lover and bride at the dawn of this history, America is also positioned as a mother figure. Neruda characterizes her as "buried" and "sunken," making her powerless to act on behalf of herself and her children—that is, the mountains, rivers, birds, plants, and people. Neruda writes of those people in canto 11: "I see the ancient human, a human slave, sleeping / in the fields, I see one body, a thousand bodies, a man, a thousand women." With "The Heights of Macchu Picchu" he seeks to wake them up, revive America, and dispel the shadows of oppression.

It is an idealistic mission but it works because it is presented in a mythological context. As stated earlier, myths are instruments of instruction. The conveyance of a lesson is not had only from a story's content—delivery is just as important. In this poem, Neruda has not chosen a traditional epic model of the kind usually associated with mythology and legend but has instead borrowed pieces of time-honored composition: epithets to summarily describe

(and although it is a device of economy, he makes long lists of epithets), cantos to divide the story and pace it, and, in the original Spanish, as described by John Felstiner in his translation of "The Heights of Macchu Picchu," use of classic eleven-syllable meter.

Although myths can be spiritual and even esoteric, they are always bound to the human condition. Neruda's new myth of Latin American is deeply concerned with the human condition. Stone will keep, rivers will flow—but what about the "old forgotten human heart"? It must be renewed, like spring-flowering trees, resurrected from a buried, miserable past. Joining these hands, these faces, their voices, Neruda pulls the old to the new. The laborers of antiquity are the farmers, the miners, and the factory workers of today. They were, are, and will be exploited until given a powerful voice, such as that of a senator and a world-renowned poet.

A secular savior, Neruda resurrects the dead laborers by might of memory. That is the gift of his unifying mythology: those who time would forget will be remembered. Sites like Macchu Picchu, built upon the exhausted bodies of slaves, will now stand as testament to their skill rather than the glory of gods and kings. He does not remember them out of a sense of duty but rather out of kinship. They worked as he works, with their hands, for their community. This message of communism is what Neruda seeks to convey in "The Heights of Macchu Picchu," but it is not political disingenuousness. He sincerely believes that communism—a classless, egalitarian society—is the answer to peace between human beings: "Give me your hand out of the deep / region seeded by all your grief."

Source: Carol Ullmann, Critical Essay on "The Heights of Macchu Picchu," in *Poetry for Students*, Gale, Cengage Learning, 2008.

Agnes Gullón

In the following review, Gullón explores the themes in "The Heights of Macchu Picchu" and remarks on the variations in narrative voice throughout the poem.

The painter of outdoor art allows the pedestrian who passes by the moving figures of a mural to merge momentarily with them, or at least to walk with them side by side. Bustling along a city street, brushing against others who form the real mass mirrored in such a mural, one comes eerily close to mistaking one's footsteps for those of the painted feet, the sidewalk for the wall. Yet this shifting identity barely shocks, because the mural after all is meant to depict us, the nameless many; all of us in private and perhaps secret worlds, but each able to stop to ask or give the time, or name the street.

The poet who would unite us attempts quite a bit more. Neruda achieves this fusion in *Alturas de Macchu Picchu*, the dozen poems set like an island in the vast sea of his *Canto general*. And I would like to stop there, where this synthesis of souls finds its most dramatic expression, to consider the genius of his poetry.

Just to read this sequence of poems is to reach great heights. Its surge of life—the poet's, the earth's, mankind's—makes a formal analysis seem somehow inappropriate to me. Their spirit balks at that sort of treatment.

So I propose instead to trace that spirit, or follow in its path, with stops along the way.

From the air to the air, like a net
empty,
I moved through the streets and the atmos-
     phere,
  arriving and leaving
at the coming of fall, the scattered money
of the leaves, and between spring and tassels,
what the greatest love, as if into a glove
falling, gives us like a long moon.

The opening lines happen in the air and suggest movement everywhere: from place to place, from the motion of the net to the heart, from season to season, from one expanse (of leaves) to another (of love). Comparisons are irresistible from the outset, because the poet carries ever-forming correspondences with him on his journey. This first stanza introduces Neruda's sense of himself as a creature susceptible to sensations embracing the subjective in the cosmic; a creature whose humanity derives so

intimately from the earth he inhabits that a certain confusion of essences occurs. A transmigration of sorts, and one that the poet records in a language of materials, as the second stanza shows:

Days of brilliancy I live in the unshelteredness
of bodies: steel converted
to the silence of acid:
nights unravelled to the final flour:
assaulted stamens of the nuptial land.

Bodies, steel, acid, nights, stamens: how life palpitates in each is what the poet catches in a stream of language heading for incoherence, collecting in its currents whatever drops in. And Neruda's perception is incredibly fine, picking up significance in matter usually appreciated only by geologists. The quantity of such geological detail can be a bit excessive in some of the *Canto general*, recalling a too thickly vegetated area where the tangles and knots of branches strike one more than the trees and plants themselves. In *Macchu Picchu* there is more restraint, less fixation on this aspect of nature, and I think the book benefits from it. The broad theme, that of attaining union with all men, undoubtedly lent more structure to the compositions.

There is a cosmic intensity throughout, an intermittent awareness of totality that gives the miniscule a special importance, one I would call Blakean were it not for the inevitable associations with mysticism. Neruda is no mystic, certainly. But his vision of the earth, of its evolution and engendering of man with his own peculiar, tragic history, makes the terrestrial sacred. Neruda loves the earth as Lorca did: not its rose gardens and seascapes alone, but first its minute creatures and basic elements—ants, seeds, sand, quartz, water, air, and of course stone, which in *Macchu Picchu* later dominates. Poetry, as Neruda often said, is like the dew, the disappearing essence that profiles the earth at dawn. And on his climb—soon an ascent—the most earthly matter accompanies him. In poem 2 he says:

And soon, between clothes and smoke, on
     the table
  sunken
like a shuffled quantity, lies the soul:
quartz and sleeplessness, tears in the ocean
like pools of cold

Isolation, complexity, and disorder are the facets of man's soul that Neruda feels have always existed. He starts his journey with this awareness and seeks assurance that there is at least some continuity, some kind of unity:

> I wanted to pause and look for the eternal abysmal vein
> I had already touched in stones or in the flash of
> lightning that gave off a kiss.

Touching, more than seeing, hearing, smelling or tasting, is the sense which discovers most in this book, and it is understandable that tactile qualities should attract Neruda as he explores part of the earth. What gives this book its peculiar radiance is that the poet never abandons his faith in touching, even when he is trying to 'touch' what is completely intangible: a thread of continuity from primitive to present man. The link, he suggests, is the earth; knowing and loving the only live presence which our forebears also experienced. The rest is dead: beliefs, artifacts, entire races of people, countries... Architecture, whether mental or physical, is destructible, leaving only ruins to be studied, whereas the earth in obeying a cosmic order lives on. The substance of man, throughout its changes, is what the poet hopes to find. At the end of poem 2 he asks:

> What was man? In what part of his open conversation
> near shops and whistling, in which of his metallic movements
> lived the indestructible, the unperishing— life?

The question is an ancient one, probably predating its first written formulation, and inevitably leads not to an answer but to a consciousness of death, the refinement of which prepares us for venturing an answer. Consciousness of mortality marks the next three poems (3,4,5), where Neruda faces the power of death in its many guises, especially the "short daily death," and he faces the issue dramatically rather than philosophically, thus making it personal. In poem 4 the poetic voice no longer narrates; it addresses death directly, and the dialogue is a prelude to other dialogues with successive interlocuters. Whether consciously adopted or not, the technique is adroit, for it eliminates a rhetorical atmosphere. If Neruda had begun *Alturas de Macchu Picchu* by addressing other men (to whom the poems are eventually dedicated), our entrance into the text could not but have seemed facile and unprivate. Dealing with the most intimate area of each man, the soul, the poet must

tread questioningly. This for me is one of the book's supreme achievements: Neruda reveals a prodigious amount about his soul, respects the mystery of others and gradually fuses us all in a vision of mankind. Neruda the lyricist has triumphed over Neruda the politician, the latter of whom in lesser poems makes immediate assumptions about what we are or should be, but who supplies only stereotypes. The issue is pertinent, I believe, for too often the political and the poetical have been mistaken in Pablo Neruda. Political implications may be detected in these poems, true; but politics is not necessary, nor even relevant really.

To return to the technical question of the introduction of dialogue, it is curious that Neruda speaks first to death, then to a place (the location, Macchu Picchu), then to the multifarious life of the South American continent (down to its minerals), and finally, decisively, to fellow man ("*hermano*"). Progressing from the abstract to an increasingly human life dramatizes the final unity between individuals. Musically, the movement is from an orchestration to a duo, a duo that symbolizes the linking of any man with any man. As the participants in the poetic dialogue change, so do the grammatical moods used; the indicative is preferred until the poet asks for company in poem 8, where the imperative (not at all mandatory) takes over: "Come, miniscule life," is how he urges living organisms from below to rise with him, revealing his very human desire to reach the heights in warm company, not solitary triumph. The message runs throughout Neruda's poetry and perhaps helps to explain its author's popularity today, when swarming technological inventions threaten our senses and, by extension, our sentiments. The ascent is an escape from all in contemporary life which separates us.

The poet states at the beginning of poem 6 that he has climbed to the "high city of scaled stones" out of "the atrocious tangle of lost jungles," and it is there—with arriving, "here"— that he feels the full impact of the cosmos he has experienced intermittently until now:

> Here man's feet rested at night
> next to the eagle's feet in high bloodthirsty
> lairs, and at dawn
> they tread with the feet of the thunder
> on rarified snow
> and they touched the earth and stones

until they could recognize them at night or in death.

An almost erotic magic. Neruda envisions primitive man secure even amidst danger and extremes, conquering the peaks of the earth as surely as the eagle and the thunder. The images of their feet contacting the earth transmit the power and closeness of the three—man, eagle, thunder. Like a pre-Columbian sculptor, Neruda insistently exaggerates hands, feet, eyes. Through the torrential metaphors that characterize his poetry, these three features recur again and again, as if obeying an instinct, or a wish to keep alive in verse the first South American man.

At the summits death reappears, this time historically, as the end of a civilization which Neruda presents as a falling: "all that you were fell: customs, worn out / syllables, masks of dazzling light." But although he is made conscious of death again, he is also on the verge of discovering the "eternal vein" he has been seeking; it is the stone, the material that has outlived catastrophes and recorded, past for future:

> But a permanence of stone and word:
> the city like a glass was raised in the hands
> of all, live, dead, silent, sustained
> by so much death, a wall, by so much life a
>   blow
> of petals of stone: the permanent rose, the
>   dwelling:
> this Andean reef of glacial colonies.

With this view of Macchu Picchu, we are ready for the synthesis given five lines further:

> the high site of man's dawn:
> the highest vessel that ever contained silence:
> a life of stone after so many lives.

These three lines depict the counterpart for all the life of the present below. Whereas no shape can contain the numerous, diverse lives and "short daily deaths," the wandering and anguish of the cities,—in sum, the palpitating presences Neruda describes—the lost Andean colony is like a vessel of stone whose petrification suggests at once former life, and lives, and their death.

The sight of the "glacial colonies" coincides with a sudden shift in Neruda's style. It is here in poem 8 that the imperative is introduced and his language becomes much tighter, more direct. Is the change inspired by the change in nature's panorama? (With the meandering, there is a more discursive style; with the arrival, conden-sation.) Whatever the cause, the effect is an artistic contraction which is accentuated in poem 9, where conventional syntactical orders vanish and are replaced by an exhaustive inventory of images ordered in a distinct way. The images are issued either one per line or are neatly grouped, two per line. Such form comes as a mild shock: Neruda's language usually flows, yet here it is abruptly locked into rhythms whose regularity suggests a litany. These lines are a sample of the symmetrical accentuation (two stresses per clause), more striking in the original Spanish:

> Triangular tunic, pollen of stone.
> Lamp of granite, bread of stone.
> Mineral serpent, rose of stone.

This type of verse contrasts with another, which is built on a single image rather than a pair and does not follow a strict pattern of accentuation; there are usually three stresses per line, but the distribution is not as symmetrical:

> Regime of the claw provoked.
> Gale withstood by the slope.
> Immobile turquoise waterfall.

Forty-three such lines are packed together, and conventional transitions are absent. At first reading, the poem is like a stone wall: so full of content (literally speaking) that meaning cannot be penetrated. It is a poem of pure impact, perhaps the effect of Macchu Picchu on the poet's imagination. Instead of exploring and wondering as he first did, or addressing some entity in his mind, the poet now stops and names; he regresses to the most primitive type of discourse: the utterance, which in this context hardly seems like utterance because of the profusion of metaphors. At this peak in his imagery, the poet captures the spatial, temporal, material, and spiritual complexity suggested by the ruins of Macchu Picchu.

And just as the poetic language has become concentrated, so has the matter described. Stone becomes in poem 9 the beginning, middle and end of human life. Present as primary rock, it is also the statues, walls and hand-carved objects preserving man's past. Seeing the stone remains of human labors in a rocky panorama where no one has survived calls to mind the power and durability of this first solid form of the creative rhythm (air→ fire→water→stone). The harmony achieved by the poet is impressive: his wandering and climbing stopped, he fixates at the summits on the only solid element—stone—

and the modifications in his verbal expression register his adjustment to the surroundings.

Confrontation with this world of stone intensifies the poet's awareness of man's precarious essence in a cosmic scheme where the elements seem so firmly established. Poem 10 opens with:

> Stone in stone, man, where was he?
> Air in air, man, where was he?
> Time in time, man, where was he?
> Were you also the little broken piece
> of the unfinished man, of an empty eagle
> that through the streets of today, in the tracks,
> through the leaves of a dead fall
> is hammering his soul into his grave?
> The poor hand, and foot, the poor life . . .

The spell has been broken. The cryptic assemblage in stone has provoked a single plaintive question: "Where was he?", which is perhaps the same as asking "Where am I?" No answer is offered, nor could it be, considering the beliefs of the questioner. Because Neruda, an incessant traveller in his own lifetime, never quenched his thirst for "the place." (An earlier book of poems hinted in its own title at this preoccupation: *Residence on Earth*.)

In the magnificent poem 10, Neruda's perceptions of matter are transfused by his awareness of orders of which matter is merely a vestigial reminder. He is at once dazzled by the real spectacle of Macchu Picchu and intent on getting beyond, to the men lost in it:

> I interrogate you, salt of the roads,
> show me the spoon, let me, architecture,
> gnaw with a stick at the stamens of stone,
> climb all the steps of air up to the void,
> scratch the entrails until I touch man.

Into the realm of the untouchable and indeed, the intangible, Neruda persists in his quest: to touch, even in disappearing matter, man. His insistently physical probing reveals a poet convinced of the power of every atom of life on the earth and determined to stay close to the organic matter that nourishes him.

The impact of the summits on Neruda is reproduced in the poetry, which transports us to that "confused splendor." And for the poet, there must have been a considerable struggle to both record his diverse impressions and manage his verbal material so as to create in us the illusion of finding that supreme reality at the summits: a sense of feeling for other men. There is evidence of this tension in the middle of poem 11:

> Let me forget, wide stone, and powerful proportion,
> the transcendent measurement, the stone of the
> honeycomb,
> and from the staff let me today slide
> my hand long the hypotenuse of stiff blood and hairshirt.

Faced with the "powerful proportion"— massive stone, the past disintegrating the present—Neruda's wish for unity is momentarily endangered: the scale is too enormous to be captured or shared. His perspective, unlike the sophisticated perspective of an elaborate camera designed to control visual fields, is that of the poor human eye, overcome by the summits and all they suggest to his spirit. So he pleads, almost humbly, for a chance to know, at these real and figurative altitudes, with his senses: "let me slide my hand . . .". Touching continues to be as important as speaking.

And his speech, which has been a confessing, telling, wondering, asking, inviting and uttering, becomes in the last line of poem 11 simply talking: "come up to be born with me, brother." The sentence is repeated as the opening line of the final poem, where it becomes a gentle urging, showing a simplicity and compassion that echo through poem 12. It is here that Neruda explicitly states his poetic purpose: "I come to speak for your dead mouths." He, the living, hopes to perpetuate those gone; and as poet, hopes to unite us with them. He offers his words and his body to join men. The closing line of *Alturas de Macchu Picchu* is:

> Speak through my words and blood.

A testimony to Pablo Neruda's concept of art and life.

Source: Agnes Gullón, "Pablo Neruda at Macchu Picchu," in *Chicago Review*, Vol. 27, No. 2, Autumn 1975, pp. 138–45.

Kay Engler

In the following excerpt, Engler examines the use of metaphor in Neruda's "The Heights of Macchu Picchu."

It is generally conceded that after *Residencia en la tierra* (1933–35), Pablo Neruda's finest work is *Las alturas de Macchu Picchu*, written in 1943 following the poet's first visit to the fabulous lost city of the Incas, first published in 1946 and later included in his *Canto general* (1950). *Las alturas de Macchu Picchu* is important not only because of its intrinsic literary merit, but also because, as critics have pointed out, it represents a key to Pablo Neruda's evolution as a poet. For example, Hernán Loyola has pointed out in *Ser y morir en Pablo Neruda* that *Las alturas de Macchu Picchu* is "[un] poema-sintesis ... [cuya] significación radica en el hecho de reflejar el punto culminante de una encrucijada dialéctica, la resolución final de una etapa del proceso interior que venía viviendo Neruda, y, al mismo tiempo, la apertura de una nueva etapa."

Amado Alonso's now classic *Poesía y estilo de Pablo Neruda* stands alone as an invaluable guide to the study of the first stage of Neruda's poetic development, the surrealist period of *Residencia en la tierra* (1933–35). Criticism of Neruda's later works has tended to be thematic rather than stylistic, a tendency which perhaps reflects the change in Neruda's poetry itself toward a more prosaic, less hermetic style. The criticism which exists on *Las alturas de Macchu Picchu* is either vague and impressionistic (Loyola, de Lellis, Larrea) or thematic (Rodriguez-Fernandez, Montes). Robert Pring-Mill's brief introduction to Nathaniel Tarn's English translation of the poem stands as an exception. Pring-Mill outlines the basic structure of the work and comments briefly on the poem's imagery. What follows is an attempt to expand on Pring-Mill's introduction, to study carefully and in depth the nature of the imagery and the metaphorical structure of the work.

The poet Pablo Neruda enters the world of Macchu Picchu with a two-fold inheritance from the past: the shattering experience of a world of chaos and disorder recorded in his *Residencia en la tierra* and *Tercera residencia*, and the kinship in human suffering experienced in the Spanish Civil War and recorded in *España en el corazón*. The poems of *Residencia*, in themselves, exhibit a spiritual duality: between a material world in chaos and disintegration and the plenum of nature and matter, of the vegetal universe which presages life and well-being; between the poet's horror at the insignificance and vulnerability of the individual human being confronted with the totality of Being and his longing to be a part of that Being; between the poet's awareness of his own discordant, disintegrating self and his

> **EACH METAPHOR SERVES AS THE CENTER OF A COMPLEX WEB OF ASSOCIATIONS AND IN TURN IS WOVEN INTO THE COMPLEX WEB OF ASSOCIATIONS WHICH IS MACCHU PICCHU ITSELF."**

search for meaning; between his profound tenderness and concern for human sorrow, fragility and weakness and his simultaneous repugnance before a distorted humanity, before what human weakness has wrought: a world which suffocates man and nature's full potentiality.

In reality, *España en el corazón* adds a third dimension. Neruda abandons, for the moment, the problem of his relationship with the material world and turns instead to the problem of his relationship with his fellow men. Probing behind the world of objects, of material things, he touches on the material basis of human fraternity: a common bond of suffering willfully toward a certain end. As Luis Monguió states: "Neruda suddenly saw himself no longer estranged, but 'reunited'—not with accidents of matter, in blind processes of cosmic fatality, as before, but with men in processes of will."

In the twelve poems of *Las alturas de Macchu Picchu* Neruda reflects and actually re-lives the earlier stages of his poetry. Macchu Picchu thus becomes the center of a complex web of associations which are only fully resolved in the context of his other works. The basic structure of the poem follows the dual vision established in the *Residencias*. The final resolution of the conflict, however, is profoundly influenced by the humanitarian vision of *España en el corazón*. Within the framework of the *Residencias*, the poem is a continuation of the poet's search for the individual's place in the universe and of the aesthetic used to convey that search. At the same time, the poem is an attempt to fit the mataphysics and aesthetics of the *Residencias* into the somewhat narrower social and historical framework of *España en el corazón*. Within the context of the *Canto general*, an epic-like work which explores the nature of Latin American history and culture, *Las alturas de Macchu Picchu* stands at the thematic center of the search for historical reality

Las alturas de Macchu Picchu and the *Canto general* of which it is a part stand as a monumental and grandiose effort to encompass the universal, to integrate the whole of reality. Macchu Picchu, symbolically and in a very real sense, offers the poet a kind of Archimedean point, beyond time and space, from which to survey the whole of being and to perceive the dimensions of its meaning. At the same time, Macchu Picchu stands at the center of reality past and present, temporal and eternal, particular and universal. It is, in Neruda's words, the destination of time, "dirección del tiempo," the destination of all things, the center of meaning, the point from which all makes sense. The central paradox of Macchu Picchu, above and beyond the world, yet standing at its existential center, is the principle around which the poem is structured. On the heights of Macchu Picchu, existence is made eternal, the particular becomes universal, many are made one, being is completed.

... Neruda's metaphors of Macchu Picchu function as the concrete universals of which Frye spoke. Each image represents a particular world—human, divine, animal, vegetable, mineral—which together form the oneness of Being. Macchu Picchu joins together the vegetable world (viña, polen, rosa, planta, árbol), the animal world (águila, serpiente, caballo, paloma, abeja), the mineral world (hierro, piedra, granito, cuarzo, amaranto), the human (párpado, cabellera, cinturón, manos, dentadura), and the heavenly (cielo, alturas, estrellas). In Macchu Picchu is joined the undisciplined life force (manantial, vendaval, catarata, temporal, volcán, ola, ráfaga) and man's attempts to control it (bastión, escala, muralla, techumbre, torre, ventana, techo, cúpula, catedral); the formless vastness (luz, vapor, noche, nieblas, bruma) and man's attempt to understand it (geometría, libro, arquitectura).

Each metaphor serves as the center of a complex web of associations and in turn is woven into the complex web of associations which is Macchu Picchu itself. A close examination of several of these epithets will suffice to show how the individual metaphor functions in creating the total Metaphor: (1) "aguila sideral": The eagle (representative of the animal world) flying high, reaches the stars (world of the heavenly bodies). Macchu Picchu itself reaches the height of the stars. The poet's ideal stands above the real world, reaching the level of the heavens. (2) "viña de bruma": The vine represents the fullness of the vegetal universe; it appears in the mist where water, the current of life, is in a state of suspicion in the air, enveloping the vine. The vine is a common communion symbol (the source of wine, spilt blood), yet it appears wrapped in the mists, the mysterious nature of the Eucharist. On a purely representational level, the dark stones of Macchu Picchu appear as vine leaves enveloped in mist on a dark night. (3) "escala torrencial": The stairway, a creation of man, made of stone, appears as a torrent of water. Water the life force, appears frozen in time, eternal. (4) "polen de piedra": The pollen of the vegetal world (agent of germination) has turned to stone. The process of creation is made eternal. (5) "témpano entre las ráfagas labrado": Interaction of water and wind on the cold heights have made Macchu Picchu an iceberg. Like the buried tower, its roots extend unseen far below the surface to the center of creation. (6) "muralla por los dedos suavizada": The stone walls of Macchu Picchu are softened by human fingers. The eternity of stone and the finitude of man are one.

The eternal refrain of permanence—stone, granite, rock—runs throughout the poem: "polen de piedra [...], pan de piedra [...], rosa de piedra [...], manantial de piedra [...], luz de piedra [...], vapor de piedra [...], libro de piedra [...], lámapara de granito [...]" as the poet evokes the apocalyptic world of oneness. Yet a disturbing note in a minor key jarrs the ear in a series of ambiguous images: "paloma endurecida," "manos de puma, roca sangrienta," "nivel sangriento," "luna arañada," "volcán de manos," "catarata oscura"; and other less ambiguous metaphors: "piedra amenazante," "dirección del tiempo."

The menacing stones overwhelm the poet at last, and in the next poem the subdued questioning breaks into full view: "Piedra en la piedra, el hombre, dónde estuvo? / Aire en el aire, el hombre, dónde estuvo?" Turning against Macchu Picchu, he demands:

> Macchu Picchu, pusiste
> piedras en la piedra, y en la base, harapo?
> Carbón sobre carbón, y en el fondo la
> lágrima?
> Fuego en el oro y en él, temblando el rojo
> goterón de la sangre?

Neruda abandons the "rosa abstracta" of Macchu Picchu because he cannot bear the thought of the human suffering required:

Antigua America, novia sumergida,

...

también, también tus dedos,
los que la rosa abstracta y la línea del frío, los
que el pecho sangriento del nuevo cereal
trasladaron
hasta la tela de materia radiante, hasta las
duras cavidades,
también también, America enterrada, guar-
daste en lo más bajo,
en el amargo intestino, como un aguila, el
hambre?

His vision of paradise was too abstract, too European (remember "alguien que me esperó entre violines encontró un mundo como una torre enterrada" and cannot be reconciled with his all too real love for his fellow men, past and present, and his concern for their suffering: "Déjame olvidar, ancha piedra, las piedras del panal, / y de la escuadra déjame hoy resbalar / la mano sobre la hipotenusa de áspera sangre y silicio."

His vision now must be consistent with that he brought with him from *España en el corazón*. He seeks not the collective permanence of the past, but "Juan Cortapiedras, hijo de Wiraco-cha, / Juan Comefrio, hijo de estrella verde, / Juan Piesdescalzos, nieto de la turquesa [. . .]." The abstract "Sube conmigo, amor americano" of the eighth poem has become, in the last poem, "Sube a nacer conmigo, hermano." His hand now grasps the hand of his brother. Neruda, who once spurned the trembling cup of human sorrows in favor of the stone chalice of Macchu Picchu, now asks the men of Macchu Picchu: "traed a la copa de esta nueva vida / vuestros viejos dolores enterrados." Not the abstract stone rose, but the real blood of his brothers, spilt in sacrifice, and now coursing through his veins, is the source of communion.

The style of the work changes considerably in the last three poems. Neruda now uses the prosaic style of *España en el corazón*, almost totally devoid of metaphor or complicated syntax. Like the style, the final vision of *Las alturas de Macchu Picchu* is that of *Tercera residencia*, where the poet has said: "Yo de los hombres tengo la misma mano herida, / yo sostengo la misma copa roja, / igual asombro enfurecido."

Neruda at last abandons the apocalyptic vision which had haunted him since the early years of *Residencia en la tierra*. He no longer projects his desires on a world of paradise, a near-divine world, but upon the human world

about him. The religious imagery of the last poem suggests his acceptance, instead, of the vision of the humanitarianism of a very human Christ. The poet asks his fellow men to reveal their sorrows, expressed in terms of the sorrows of Christ, and offers himself as a kind of substitute Christ figure who will express their sorrows for them and through whom communion is possible: "Yo vengo a hablar por vuestras bocas muertas [. . .] / Apegadme los cuerpos como imanes. / Acudid a mis venas y a mi boca. / Hablad por mis palabras y mi sangre."

Source: Kay Engler, "Image and Structure in Neruda's *Las alturas de Macchu Picchu*," in *Symposium*, Vol. 28, No. 2, Summer 1974, pp. 130–45.

SOURCES

Campbell, Joseph, *The Hero with a Thousand Faces*, Princeton University Press, 1973.

Cohen, Jonathan, "The Early History of Neruda in English (1925–1937)," in *Romance Notes*, Vol. 22, No. 3, Spring 1982, pp. 272–76.

Felstiner, John, *Translating Neruda: The Way to Macchu Picchu*, Stanford University Press, 1980, p. 190.

Hirsch, Edward, "Poetry: Pablo Neruda," in *Wilson Quarterly*, Vol. 22, No. 2, Spring 1998, pp. 113–14.

Neruda, Pablo, "The Heights of Macchu Picchu," translated by John Felstiner, in *Translating Neruda: The Way to Macchu Picchu*, by John Felstiner, Stanford University Press, 1980, pp. 202–39.

Nobel Foundation, Nobel Diploma for Pablo Neruda, translated by the Nobel Foundation, Nobel Prize in Literature, Stockholm, Sweden, 1971, http://nobelprize.org/nobel_prizes/literature/laureates/1971/index.html (accessed October 18, 2007).

Rivero, Eliana, "Pablo Neruda," in *Dictionary of Literary Biography, Volume 331: Nobel Prize Laureates in Literature, Part 3: Lagerkvist—Pontoppidan*, Gale, 2007, pp. 329–56.

Wood, Michael, "The Poetry of Neruda," in the *New York Review of Books*, Vol. 21, No. 15, October 3, 1974, p. 8.

Wright, James, "'I Come to Speak for Your Dead Mouths,'" in *Poetry* Vol. 112, No. 3, June 1968, p. 194.

FURTHER READING

D'Altroy, Terence N., *The Incas*, Blackwell Publishing, 2003.

    D'Altroy, a specialist in Incan archaeology, describes the rise of the Inca Empire, its technological innovations, its unique government, and the cultural landscape comprising this immense empire.

Dipiazza, Francesca Davis, *Chile in Pictures*, Twenty-First Century Books, revised edition, 2007.

Dipiazza has interspersed lavish photographs of the diverse Chilean landscapes with maps and text, creating a book that both informs and entertains. Neruda was born in the verdant South but dedicated his political career to the peoples of the arid North.

Poirot, Luis, *Pablo Neruda: Absence and Presence*, translated by Alastair Reid, W. W. Norton, 2004.

Poroit has created a unique collection in this book, assembling photographs of Neruda, his homes, and his possessions, and mingling these images with reminiscences by the poet's friends, such as Diego Muñus, Roberto Matta, and wife Matilde Urrutia. Poroit's book provides a refreshing new look inside the life of this famous poet.

Urrutia, Matilde, *My Life with Pablo Neruda*, translated by Alexandria Giardino, Stanford General Books, 2004.

Chilean singer Urrutia was Neruda's third wife and in this intimate memoir, she recalls her life alongside the famous poet as they overcame health problems, regime changes, exile, and persecution. Amongst the hardships they also shared an enduring friendship and passionate love.

How I Got That Name

MARILYN CHIN
1994

Published in 1994 in *The Phoenix Gone, The Terrace Empty*, Marilyn Chin's poem "How I Got That Name" is a self-described consideration of the issue of assimilation. Much of Chin's poetry explores this theme, and her personal struggle between two cultures is apparent. Not wanting to let go of her heritage, she honors it while taking aim at Chinese stereotypes that serve only to minimize the humanity of individual Chinese Americans. The poem explains how she got the name "Marilyn," but in the process, she covers themes of family, Americanization, and prevailing social attitudes. This poem appears in Chin's second volume of poetry, and it reflects the poet's comfort with her own voice. The book does not have a dedication, although Chin includes a brief prelude to her mother at the beginning of the book. Her mother is mentioned with honor in "How I Got That Name," and her disinterest in blind patriarchal honor for its own sake is abundantly clear.

"How I Got That Name" is a long, four-stanza poem in free verse. Its complexity is subtle, as the poem flows in a natural, conversational way. Yet, Chin changes tone and thematic focus with each stanza, all the while incorporating literary devices such as irony, alliteration, and assonance with a natural flow. This makes the poem very accessible to a wide range of readers, and this explains its continued popularity.

Marilyn Chin (Photo by Niki Berg. Reproduced by permission)

AUTHOR BIOGRAPHY

Award-winning poet Marilyn (Mei Ling) Chin was born on January 14, 1955, in Hong Kong. Her father, Gwock Gon, was a restaurant owner, and her mother's name was Yuet Kuen. As an infant, Chin was exposed to music, both informally and formally. In 1962, Chin and the women in her family joined the men in her family in Portland, Oregon. Chin's parents had a son and another daughter (in addition to Chin and her younger sister) in Portland. Her father worked as a chef in Chinese restaurants, but despite his efforts to invest in some partnerships, he struggled financially. He finally left his family, leaving them to depend on his parents. He remained estranged, although he never officially divorced his wife. Chin once described her painful confusion over his choosing a white woman over his own family. Her feelings of anger, rejection, and betrayal have colored her perspective on the traditional patriarchy of Chinese culture. Much of Chin's poetry praises womanhood and female strength and influence. As for her own relationships, she met, fell in love, and lived with a French Algerian man named Charles Moore, whom she met in 1992 in a coffee shop in California. In 2000, they enjoyed time together in Bali before returning to Taiwan, where Chin had been awarded a Senior Fulbright Fellowship. Tragically, Moore's plane exploded on take-off, and he was killed.

Chin attended the University of Massachusetts in Amherst, where she earned a B.A. in ancient Chinese literature in 1977. She then went on to the prestigious M.F.A. program at the University of Iowa, where she completed her degree in 1981. Following that, she taught comparative literature courses there and had previously worked as a translator for the university's International Writing Program. Chin currently resides in La Mesa, California, and is on staff with the Department of English and Comparative Literature at San Diego State University. She is a professor of English and the director of the M.F.A. program. Additionally, she has served as a visiting professor and lecturer all over the world, including at National Donghwa University in Taiwan and at the University of Technology in Sydney, Australia.

Chin writes poetry reflecting her unique experience and sensibility as a Chinese-American woman. Before seeing her poetry published, Chin worked as a translator and editor for other writers. Her first book of poems, *Dwarf Bamboo*, was published in 1987. This was followed by *The Phoenix Gone, The Terrace Empty* (which includes "How I Got That Name") in 1994, and *Rhapsody in Plain Yellow* in 2002. This last volume includes moving tributes to mother-daughter relationships, and includes a dedication to her own mother, who died in 1994. Chin's grandmother died in 1996, driving the poet to consider deeply the ties that bind generations of women together. Chin's poems are known for their direct style and their representation of a woman torn between two cultures. She also writes to express her political views and to destroy stereotypes. Reading her work as a whole, the reader begins to understand how different the American experience is for immigrant families and for those trying to find their social and ethnic place in the fabric of the United States. It is both complex and emotional. Identity issues figure prominently as Chin seeks to find the proper balance between the individual identity and the collective one. An undercurrent of Chin's work is the impulse for artistic expression and its role in Chinese and American cultures.

Chin has successfully tried her hand at short stories and drama, and saw her first play published in 2002. As a literary scholar, Chin has a strong reputation for her expertise and insight in the field of Asian American literature.

POEM SUMMARY

Stanza 1

The overall theme of the first stanza is family and surface assimilation. The speaker discusses the names her parents called her, while taking care not to equate what she was called with who she really is. The stanza opens with the speaker (in this case the poet) introducing herself. She makes a straightforward, declarative statement and takes pride in the ownership of her name as well as her identity apart from her name. She says she loves the "be" that lacks the uncertainty of "becoming." She then explains to the reader how her father changed her name from Mei Ling to Marilyn because he was fascinated by Marilyn Monroe. The two names sounded similar, so he thought it was a good idea. This was a decision he made while literally crossing to America on a boat with his family. The reader gets a strong sense of the father's willingness to uproot his family in every sense of the word, from lifestyle and culture to names, for the sake of better opportunities and a brighter future. He shares the same dream as countless immigrants to America, but here Chin only hints at it. Regarding the decision to name her after Marilyn Monroe, Chin says "nobody dared question / his initial impulse" despite the irony of a little Chinese baby being named after a blonde Hollywood bombshell. Chin disparages blind patriarchy, noting that men are driven by lust and turn their backs on decency.

Chin tells that her mother could not pronounce the "r" in her name, so she named her "Numba one female offshoot." This is because Chin was the firstborn, and it shows how the name her mother calls her is more personal and fitting than the one her father chose. Chin then casts her mother in a loving light, although she acknowledges her mother's naïve ignorance, and she describes her father as something of a lowlife. Again she says: "Nobody dared question his integrity." In this case, nobody dares challenge Chin's father because of his wonderful, hardworking children. Chin finds it ridiculous that a man would be measured by his children's

goodness rather than his own. Chin's distaste for patriarchal bias is clear in this stanza.

Stanza 2

The second stanza is cynical and sarcastic, with an overall theme of stereotypes. She reiterates how trustworthy the daughters are and how hard-working the sons are, ideas that continue from the first stanza. By linking this stanza with the first one, Chin is following part of her family's history, showing how they came to America with certain ideas of what it meant to be American, and then learned about ugliness such as stereotypes, prejudices, and the struggle of being from two cultures. As she opens the stanza, she seems to equate "daughters" and "sons" with Chinese women and men. She says how they have collectively fooled the experts into thinking that they are good at learning from books, but not at being creative. Given that this idea is presented in a poem by a highly talented and creative Chinese woman, the irony is sharp. In a line dripping with angry sarcasm, she writes: "Indeed, they can *use* us."

Chin next describes the turmoil of being caught between two cultures, longing for the East while working to make life work in the West. In very subtle terms, she explains the pain that often accompanies assimilation. While it is important to become part of the Western culture in which she lives, she longs to reconnect with her Eastern self. This stanza is not presented as a personal struggle, however, but as a collective one. She ends with the desperate statement: "We have no inner resources!"

Stanza 3

Moving from the intensity of the last stanza, the third stanza carries an air of resignation. Here, the overall theme is of indifference. Chin describes her family's Great Patriarch looking down on his family from heaven and seeing them as ugly. Their heads, noses, and profiles are all wrong. But Chin's patriarch probably sees them as ugly because of the ways they have assimilated. Perhaps if they were truer to their Chinese heritage and did not reconcile parts of it with life in America, he would be more approving. The patriarch describes Chin herself in the in-between terms of "not quite boiled, not quite cooked." She is neither one nor the other—the uncertainty of assimilation. She feels "listless" and unable to fight for her people's future, so she quietly awaits "imminent death." In the last lines, she admits the death is metaphorical and is thus a "testament to my lethargy."

Stanza 4

In the fourth and final stanza, Chin writes about herself as if she had died at the end of the previous stanza. The theme is Chin's life itself, and she offers a summary in a matter-of-fact tone. It is written as a lengthy gravestone text, complete with "here lies" in the beginning. In this stanza, she seeks to sum up her life. She has been a family member to some who were good and others who were not; "she was neither black nor white, / neither cherished nor vanquished," indicating she never really found her place in the world; she was a poet; and she was almost swallowed whole by forces much greater than she ("a mighty white whale" and "the jaws of a metaphysical Godzilla"), but she found herself strong and capable of overcoming the attempt at swallowing. This reference to her own death links this stanza with the one before it, providing a sense of continuity that is fitting in a poem about the poet's life. She is "a little gnawed, tattered, mesmerized," but she stays. In the last lines of the poem, Chin says she was mindful of all she was given and all that was taken away. In a vague way, she seems finally to have reconciled her identity and family crises of the rest of the poem.

THEMES

The Challenges of Assimilation

The subtitle of "How I Got That Name" is "an essay on assimilation." This alerts the reader right away to be sensitive to what Chin has to say on the topic of assimilating as a Chinese American. Throughout the poem, she shares her experience in direct and indirect ways. Explaining her name, she is very direct. Her father gave his daughter an Americanized name, and chose to name her after Marilyn Monroe. This shows that not only was her father beginning to characterize his family as Americans, but that his interests were in American pop culture. As her father began his process of assimilation, he led his family to do the same. Still, Chinese culture and traditions remained strong in the family, and with the example of Marilyn's name, she adds that "nobody dared question" her father, which is in keeping with traditional respect for the patriarchy in the Chinese family.

Chin describes assimilation in more subtle ways that give insight into the internal struggle of the process. In the second stanza, she writes: "The further west we go, we'll hit east; / the deeper down we dig, we'll find China." This is a poignant description of her intense need to hold onto her Chinese roots while living as an American. She is intentional and serious about finding the proper balance of the two cultures, and it is difficult. This dual identity not only affects her from within, but also from without. In the third stanza, she writes that the family patriarch in heaven is displeased with his descendants, and sees Chin as especially unfavorable. To him, she is "not quite boiled, not quite cooked." Then in the final stanza, Chin relates an imagined eulogy of sorts, and she describes herself in the third person as "neither black nor white, / neither cherished nor vanquished." These examples demonstrate how Chin feels that the outside world sees her as an assimilated woman who is forever stuck between two cultures. And although the poem begins with confidence in identity, the rest of the poem shows how precarious that confidence can be.

The Complications of Family Relationships

Because Chin comes from a Chinese background, family figures prominently in her experience and identity. Her father changes her name from her given Chinese name to a carelessly chosen American one. On the surface, it is a sensible choice because it sounds like her Chinese name (Marilyn sounds a bit like Mei Ling), and it is a mainstream American name, but the poet cannot let go of the source of the name, Marilyn Monroe. Whatever her personal feelings are, she and the others must accept it because it was decided by her father. Chin also explains that for all her father's shady dealings (gambling, bootlegging, being a thug), he is seen as respectable because of his trustworthy daughters and hard-working sons. The children are his validation because of the importance of family in their culture, even though it conceals the truth about her father. The other illustration of patriarchal importance in Chin's experience is her description of "the Great Patriarch Chin" who judges his descendants "from his kiosk in heaven" and declares them ugly. The family divinity is a heavenly patriarch whose words, however hurtful, are not questioned.

TOPICS FOR FURTHER STUDY

- Choose two other poems from *The Phoenix Gone, The Terrace Empty* that relate somehow to "How I Got That Name." Write a profile about Chin based only on these three poems. Include only what you learn about her in the text, but be sure to include your own analysis and conclusions about what the poet is revealing about herself in her work.

- Select another author or poet who grapples with the issue of assimilation and choose a work that exemplifies the writer's voice. How is this writer's experience and perspective different from or similar to Chin's? Deliver a twenty-minute lecture to your class about how Chin and your other chosen writer are representative of the immigrant experience in America, and take care to note how their experiences are also unique. Conclude with a few comments about individual and collective identities.

- Read the story of Frances Slocum, a Quaker girl who was abducted and raised in a Miami Indian tribe. What was her process of dealing with forced assimilation like, and how did she finally come to terms with her individual and collective identities? Pretend you are a social worker making a determination about whether or not she could return to her birth family. Write up a report explaining her story and your perceptions of the cultural and psychological issues surrounding her case.

- Read about the history of immigration in the United States and take notes on the points you think are most significant. Then keep a notepad with you for a day or two so you can make notes of anything you see that can be attributed to having diverse cultures in America. Using your notes about history and your notes about your observations, write a children's book about cultural diversity. Illustrate your text with drawings, photographs, or paintings.

In contrast to her descriptions of her father are her loving descriptions of her mother. Chin tells the reader that her mother could not pronounce the "r" in her name (a thoughtless oversight of her father), and so she called her daughter "Numba one female offshoot." Unlike Marilyn, this new name says something about Chin as an individual. Chin says that her mother will "live and die. . . . flanked by loving children." In the last stanza, she calls her mother "virtuous" and her father "infamous." Her love and preference for her mother is hard to miss, but her ties to her father are hard to sever.

STYLE

Free Verse

"How I Got That Name" is written in free verse. This means that it is not structured within even stanzas with consistent rhyme or meter. Instead, Chin adopts a very conversational approach to her poem, and the reader must follow the natural rhythms of the text and surrender to the line placement and stanza breaks chosen by Chin. Her lines range from only five syllables to over twice as many, depending on how she needs to break the lines for each particular observation or expression. The length of the stanzas also varies, allowing her to say what she needs to say in each without the constraints of structural concerns. The overall effect is very natural and comfortable for the reader, although it is deceptively simple on the part of the poet. It also lends itself well to the poem's subtitle as "an essay" because the flow of the language is more akin to prose.

Figurative Language

Chin's education and expertise in literature is apparent in her use of figurative language in

Immigration Station on Angel Island State Park in San Francisco Bay in California. Angel Island is mentioned in the poem (© Lee Foster / Alamy)

"How I Got That Name." Various literary devices are sprinkled throughout the poem, but they are all introduced in natural ways so that their use does not make the poem seem at all formal or contrived. For example: "bombshell blonde," "devout daughters," "plump pomfret," and "white whale" are all examples of alliteration, but they blend into the flow of the poem. Chin's use of irony, antithesis, and oxymoron are all used particularly well. Because they are all devices that rely on contrast to make a statement, they provide strong support to the theme of assimilation and dual identity. For example, Chin describes her infant self as "a wayward pink baby, / named after some tragic white woman," which presents a strong visual antithesis. Chin's sense of humor shows itself in the guise of oxymoron when she writes that her mother called her "'Numba one female offshoot' / for brevity," although her Chinese name was much shorter—Mei Ling. Chin cleverly uses irony in a self-referential way where she writes about negative stereotypes: "We're not very creative but not adverse to rote-learning." This is ironic because she is a poet parroting the stereotypical view that she is not creative.

Other literary devices include allusion ("red, red wheelbarrow" recalls the poem by William Carlos Williams, and "white whale" recalls Herman Melville's *Moby Dick*), metaphor ("plump pomfret simmering in my own juices"), and simile ("Solid as wood"). In each case, however, Chin is careful not to let the literary device itself overshadow the idea it is meant to portray. The result is that the poem sounds like an exercise in self-disclosure and not a forum for showing off technique.

Tone

Chin's "How I Got That Name" is interesting because each stanza addresses a different aspect of her experience and her struggle with assimilation, but each one also carries its own tone. Tone is an implied attitude, so Chin's changing tone throughout the poem underscores her changing attitudes about assimilation, identity, and external forces. The first stanza is about her name being changed to a Westernized version and her father's questionable ways. The tone of this stanza is very confident, and the speaker is not only proud of who she is today but she is sure of herself in her assessments of her parents. The second stanza is about stereotypes of Chinese Americans, and the tone is harsh and cynical. Here Chin uses sarcasm and ends with a cry to her people. The third stanza is about "the Great Patriarch Chin" and his disappointment in his descendants. The tone of this stanza is resigned, as Chin seems content to wait quietly for her metaphorical death. The fourth stanza is a summary of Chin's life, presented as if she has died, although the reader finds out at the end that she withstood the metaphorical attempt on her life. Although she came out a little battered, she survived. The tone is objective and matter-of-fact. Chin speaks of herself in the third person, giving the stanza an emotionless but kind tone.

HISTORICAL CONTEXT

Foreign-Born Americans in the 1990s
According to the United States Census Bureau, there were an average of 32.5 million foreign-born Americans in 2002. This was a significant increase since the 1990 estimate of 19.8 million. This means that in the 1990s, when "How I Got That Name" was written, the number of first-generation immigrants in the United States was on the rise. In 1994, 8.7 percent of the American population was foreign-born, with fully one-third of those living in California. The vast majority of the foreign-born population was from Mexico (6.2 million), and 556,000 of the foreign-born population was from China. In 1994, 3,953 babies were born to Chinese-American families, ensuring the growth of the next generation in this population.

Chinese-American Writers
American literature features the voices of diverse experiences and backgrounds, perhaps to a greater extent than any other nation. Chinese-American writers have long included their voices in this tradition, and in the late twentieth century, a number of prominent writers brought their culture and experience to the table. David Henry Hwang is a successful playwright, whose best known work to date is the Tony-award winning *M Butterfly*. Amy Tan is the author of

numerous books about her experiences as a Chinese-American woman striving to honor her family and her heritage, while folding America into her identity at the same time. Among her most famous titles are *The Joy Luck Club*, *The Kitchen God's Wife*, *The Bonesetter's Daughter*, and *The Hundred Secret Senses*. Laurence Yep writes children's books about various aspects of being Chinese American. He writes individual stories and series, and has had a prolific output.

Confessional Poetry
"How I Got That Name" is an example of confessional poetry, a type of modern poetry that reveals personal, often painful, insights by the speaker. Although the poetry is personal in nature, it is written with a public readership in mind, and sometimes even addresses the reader directly. In Chin's poem, for example, Chin is her own speaker talking autobiographically about her personal history and experiences. As is typical of the style, Chin's poem is unapologetic and unashamed. Confessional poetry rarely speaks through a fictitious voice, as that puts an artifice between the poet and his or her reader. It rose to popularity in the 1950s and 1960s and made a way for poets to explore themes and topics generally avoided in poetry because the personal nature of the expression calls for complete honesty. Among the best known confessional poets are Allen Ginsberg, Sylvia Plath, and Robert Lowell.

Angel Island
In "How I Got That Name," Chin relates that her American name was given to her while she was coming to America on a boat with her family. She specifically mentions Angel Island, which is in California and is home to Immigration Station. The station was a complex of buildings that included an administration building, a hospital, employee quarters, and barracks where immigrants stayed while awaiting entrance into the United States. It opened in 1910 and was planned as a sort of Ellis Island on the West Coast.

The first Chinese immigrants arrived in California in 1848 and the numbers grew rapidly with the gold rush and its attendant mining towns. When legislation prevented them from securing high-potential jobs, they were relegated to taking menial jobs or labor-intensive jobs. They worked on railroads, ran laundries, and worked in fisheries. Unemployment problems

COMPARE
&
CONTRAST

- **1990s:** Many Asian immigrants came to Angel Island before entering the United States, yet Cubans have no formal way to enter the country, even though they are given refugee status when they arrive. Thus, many Cubans desperate to leave Cuba board small rafts in the hopes of making it to the shores of the United States. Meanwhile, U.S. President Bill Clinton decides to order the Coast Guard to intercept Cuban rafters and take them back to the American naval base in Guantanamo Bay, Cuba—the antithesis of Angel Island.

  Today: Immigration policy is hotly debated as the number of illegal aliens, especially from Mexico, balloons. When President George W. Bush promotes legislation that would give amnesty to illegal aliens already working and residing in the United States, arguments erupt between and within political parties.

- **1990s:** American readers have a particular interest in fiction by Chinese-American authors. Many of them, such as Amy Tan, write about living in two cultures and incorporating both into their identities. Other popular Chinese-American authors include Ha Jin, Diana Chang, and C. Y. Lee.

  Today: American readers have taken an interest in the fiction of Indian and Indian-American writers and the unique perspective and storytelling they offer. Salman Rushdie continues to be popular among literary readers, and his work is included in coursework in universities all across the United States. Other authors include Jhumpa Lahiri, who writes about the difficult and sometimes humorous experiences of being both Indian and American; and Rohinton Mistry, who is regarded as having a gift for characterization. V. S. Naipaul, Anita Desai, Arundhati Roy, and Kamala Markandaya are other well-received Indian authors.

- **1990s:** Foreign-born Americans or Americans whose families are from abroad frequently change their names to something similar to their given names but that are more easily pronounced by Americans. In this way, they hold onto the letters or sounds of the names that honor their heritage while adopting more Americanized names. This helps them blend in to their new culture.

  Today: While the trend to Americanize ethnic names continues, more immigrants and their children are retaining their given names. In part, this is because American society is more aware and respectful of ethnic and cultural divides.

led to legislation that outright banned Asians, and Chinese in particular, from entering the United States. This was the Chinese Exclusion Act of 1882. Angel Island's Immigration Station was seen by many as a way to systematically block Chinese immigrants from entering the country. The Act was not repealed until 1943, but with many restrictions still in place. It was another twenty years before the Chinese were given equal standing among immigrant groups.

Angel Island Immigration Station was closed after World War II and was scheduled to be razed in the 1970s. When it was discovered that detainees had written poems and other statements in calligraphy on the walls of the barracks, funding was secured to restore and preserve it. Today, the station serves as a museum.

CRITICAL OVERVIEW

Critics are generous in their praise of Chin's work in general, and of *The Phoenix Gone, The Terrace Empty* (in which "How I Got That Name"

*Scene from the 1959 version of Some Like It Hot
(1959), with Tony Curtis and Marilyn Monroe*
(United Artists / The Kobal Collection / The Picture Desk, Inc.)

appears) specifically. Matthew Rothschild, writing
in *Progressive*, states that Chin "has a voice all
her own—witty, epigraphic, idiomatic, elegiac,
earthy." He adds that in *The Phoenix Gone, The
Terrace Empty*, "she covers the canvas of cultural
assimilation with an intensely personal brush."
Mary Slowik, writing in *MELUS*, echoes this
assessment when she describes Chin's immigration
poems as having "a boldness, even a brashness."
Also a fan of Chin's poetic voice, Slowik remarks:
"Marilyn Chin's language is terse, accusatory,
bristling with irony." A reviewer for *Publishers
Weekly* simply describes Chin's writing as "tough-
ened lyricism" with a "stalwart declaration [that]
gives the poetry a grounded force."

Assimilation is an overarching theme of
Chin's work, and it is explored fully in *The
Phoenix Gone, The Terrace Empty*, especially in
"How I Got That Name." Critics embrace
Chin's willingness to be honest about her strug-
gle and her experience. Whitney Scott, writing in
Booklist, observes that in her poetry, Chin
"reflects her dual-cultural perception in some
memorably wry observations." The *Publishers
Weekly* reviewer applauds Chin for achieving

"balance that is literary and also cultural."
Doris Lynch, writing in *Library Journal*, notes
that of all the poems in *The Phoenix Gone, The
Terrace Empty*, "the strongest poems ... present
an immigrant's view, combining old stories and
sensibilities with an American idiom." In *LIT:
Literature Interpretation Theory*, scholar John
Gery feels that Chin is not merely balancing
two cultures, but a whole range of competing
elements. He declares that her poetry is resilient
despite being "ensnared in a complex nexus of
gender, race, ancient traditions, and literary conventions." Gery points to "How I Got That
Name" as one of Chin's best poems. He notes
her willingness to indulge in "self-mockery and
satire" and to present a "bitterly satiric depiction
of Chinese American stereotypes."

In an interview with Bill Moyers, a tran-
script of which is included in *The Language of
Life: A Festival of Poets*, Chin speaks openly
about assimilation. She says: "I am afraid of
losing my Chinese, losing my language, which
would be like losing a part of myself, losing part
of my soul. Poetry seems a way to recapture that,
but of course the truth is we can't recapture the
past." She also adds: "There's a doubleness to
nearly all my work, to how I feel about things,
and perhaps especially about assimilation."
When asked about the lines in "How I Got
That Name" that describe her as "neither black
nor white, / neither cherished nor vanquished,"
she explains: "I feel rather invisible at times—
neither cherished nor vanquished. If I were black
I would be vanquished; if I were white I would be
cherished. So, I believe that much of my life has
been lived in a kind of mysterious opaqueness."

CRITICISM

Jennifer A. Bussey

*Bussey is an independent writer specializing in
literature. In the following essay, she demonstrates the intensely personal nature of Marilyn
Chin's "How I Got That Name."*

Published in her 1994 poetry collection, *The
Phoenix Gone, The Terrace Empty*, Marilyn
Chin's "How I Got That Name" ostensibly sets
out to explain to her readers how she, a wo
man born in China, ended up with a name like
Marilyn. Her name at birth was Mei Ling,
but her name was changed to something more
American-sounding. Her father, fascinated by

WHAT DO I READ NEXT?

- *Dwarf Bamboo* (1987) is Chin's debut volume of poetry. Already, readers will see her characteristic voice emerging in her handling of themes and language.

- Chin's 2002 poetry collection, *Rhapsody in Plain Yellow*, also expresses the poet's concerns about identity and heritage. Her poems touch on traditional themes, but discuss them in modern contexts and with modern subjects with which readers can readily identify.

- Lawrence A. Fuchs's 1990 book, *The American Kaleidoscope: Race, Ethnicity, and the Civic Culture*, addresses the topic of immigration and cultural diversity in the eighteenth and nineteenth centuries. He includes discussion of major immigrant groups and their assimilation into American culture.

- Written in 1980 by Him Mark Lai, Genny Lim, and Judy Yung, *Island: Poetry and History of Chinese Immigrants on Angel Island, 1910–1940* is a collection of poems taken from the detainee barracks on Angel Island, where Chinese immigrants were held before entering the United States. Accompanying the poems are historical passages and quotations.

Marilyn Monroe, decides that "Marilyn" is a good name for his Chinese daughter, so before she moves to America, she is given a new name and she has already moved toward her new dual identity as Chinese and American. This seemingly simple autobiographical anecdote is more than it seems at first, and so is the entire poem. A series of images and comments, the poem seems at first glance to be upholding its subtitle's promise to be "an essay on assimilation," but a closer look reveals that the speaker is revealing herself both directly and indirectly in the poem. It is intensely personal and revealing, and allows the reader a surprising level of emotional intimacy with the poet.

> CHIN DOES SOMETHING VERY SUBTLE, YET VERY REVEALING, AS SHE MOVES FROM STANZA TO STANZA. EACH STANZA ADDRESSES A DIFFERENT THEME AND SUBJECT MATTER, BUT CHIN ALSO ADOPTS A DIFFERENT TONE IN EACH STANZA THAT INDICATES A GREAT DEAL ABOUT HER FEELINGS...."

"How I Got That Name" has several layers. The first layer is the most accessible and direct. Her first line is a simple introduction. She then reveals that she embraces the "am" as a "be" instead of a "becoming." As she explains why she has the name Marilyn, she relates how her father gave it to her as they were preparing to begin new lives in America. He was already interested in American popular culture, and was introducing it into his family. But Chin begins to let the reader in on her personal feelings about her father. She notes that "nobody dared question" his decision about her name, and the line has a ring of bitterness to it. She writes that he was fixated on Marilyn Monroe because, like all men, he was subject to lust. Unfortunately, she adds, lust drives men away from decency. For those who have read Chin's biography, it is easy to read between the lines into another layer of the poem. Chin's father, after years of attempting to achieve financial success and working in restaurants, ultimately abandoned his family. Chin has strongly implied in interviews that he left his Chinese family for a white woman. Whatever the reason for his departure and permanent estrangement, he left his older daughter, Marilyn, angry, resentful, and disrespectful of patriarchies for their own sake. All of this history and emotion can be read into the lines in the first stanza of "How I Got That Name." Later in the stanza, she describes him as "a tomcat in Hong Kong trash— / a gambler, a petty thug, / who bought a chain of chopsuey joints / in Piss River, Oregon, / with bootlegged Gucci cash." Her ill will toward her father is unmistakable, and her willingness to disparage him publicly proves her rejection of the system of patriarchal respect that is part of Chinese tradition. Her mother, on the other hand, is described as simple, but genuinely loving and loved.

In the second stanza, Chin takes on Chinese stereotypes. She is forthright about her feelings and about the people she represents. In no time, Chin has replaced oversimplified, unfair stereotypes with the image of herself as a strong, outspoken individual who fights back against being dismissed as a stereotype. She begins: "Oh, how trustworthy our daughters, / how thrifty our sons!" Her sarcasm has the same effect as when the curtain is pulled back in Emerald City in Frank L. Baum's *The Wizard of Oz*. The lie is revealed. Chin says through her sarcasm that while many Chinese women are trustworthy and many Chinese men are thrifty, these are personal characteristics to be judged individually, not applied blindly across an entire people. She joins forces with her fellow Chinese Americans when she writes: "How we've managed to fool the experts," as if the stereotypes have been nothing but a big conspiracy. Throughout the stanza, she writes "we," meaning a collection of individuals, not a faceless group with one personality, identity, and group of skills.

Within the stanza about stereotypes is a subtle but deep insight into Chin's personal struggle. She writes: "The further west we go, we'll hit east; / the deeper down we dig, we'll find China." She expresses her fear of losing China in her assimilation into the west, and she hopes that if she keeps going and does not stand still, she will find China again. She will reconnect with the East that is as much a part of her identity as the West has become. For readers who are not torn between two cultures, this internal struggle is impossible to understand, but Chin allows the reader to see how it has dominated her thoughts.

The last stanza, written as a sort of eulogy to Chin's old self, contains more specific autobiographical information. Again she incorporates her parents into her identity, this time by name. She mentions Yuet Kuen Wong, which was her mother's real name, and she mentions her father only with his initials, G. G. Chin. Her father's real name was Gwock Gon. Her parental biases are again made clear as she preserves her mother's full name in her poetry, but only hints at her father's. Yet her parents are an inextricable part of her past, and she does not cut her father out of her autobiographical poem completely.

Chin does something very subtle, yet very revealing, as she moves from stanza to stanza.

Each stanza addresses a different theme and subject matter, but Chin also adopts a different tone in each stanza that indicates a great deal about her feelings regarding the various forces at play in her identity. In the first stanza, she exudes confidence sometimes to the point of condescension (to her father, not to the reader); in the second, the reader meets with a harsh, cynical tone; in the third stanza, the strength and assertiveness of the first two stanzas is replaced by vulnerability and resignation; and in the fourth stanza, Chin arrives at a matter-of-fact look at her life. She sees her life thus far with clarity, and she ends on an optimistic note befitting a woman who has been metaphorically killed, yet survived as a new, wiser person.

Source: Jennifer A. Bussey, Critical Essay on "How I Got That Name," in *Poetry for Students*, Gale, Cengage Learning, 2008.

Terese Svoboda

In the following excerpt, Svoboda reviews The Phoenix Gone, The Terrace Empty, *which includes "How I Got That Name." According to Svoboda, the collection represents a search for freedom, one in which "the oppressed and the oppressor live together."*

. . . "Isn't *bondage*, therefore, a *kind* of freedom?" ("Composed Near the Bay Bridge") asks China of Amerigo, her mohawked, dog-collared boyfriend in Marilyn Chin's second book, *The Phoenix Gone, the Terrace Empty*. That a woman of Chinese descent should make this observation resounds with irony—and truth—of the only kind of freedom she might traditionally expect. But, judging from the role of dominatress Chin takes on elsewhere in the book, the kind of freedom she looks for is more complex. Consider a freedom held in a duality, one in which both the oppressed and the oppressor exist together, at least symbolically. Think of Tienanmen Square, threaded as a place both psychic and physical throughout the book, where once revolutionaries came to rally, now the symbol of tragic violation of that freedom. Chin writes:

> The snake bites her own tail,
> meaning harmony at the year's end.
> Or does it mean
> she is eating herself
> into extinction?

> ("The Phoenix Gone, the Terrace Empty")

All people in the world dub themselves "the people," the xenophobic response to who's in and who's out. The Chinese built a wall to make the point. "*The barbarians are coming*: they are your fathers, brothers, teachers, lovers; and they are clearly an other" ("The Barbarians Are Coming"). They breach that wall and she is soon "only one woman, holding one broken brick in the wall." Chin acknowledges the inevitability of conquest. "The Ming will be over to make way for the Ch'ing / The Ch'ing will be over to make way for eternity" ("Barbarian Suite"). But knowing that there will always be conquerors does not make assimilation any less painful. "If my left hand is dying, will my right hand cut it off?" she continues. This division is most palpable in "Tienanmen, the Aftermath," in which a doppelgänger in China dislocates the speaker in America:

> I saw her in dream . . . a young girl in a
> *chipao*,
> bespeckled, forever lingering, thriving
> on the other side of the world, walking in my
> soles

In "How I Got that Name," Chin's "essay on assimilation," she is "mesmerized by all that was given her / all that was taken away!" In "A Break in the Rain," Chin instructs the recent immigrant on how to make the best of it:

> Better dance
> with the one named Rochester
> who likes your kind.
> Let us dub him
> "the point of entry."

Rochester, Jack Benny's straight man? Or Rochester, the seventeenth-century author of obscene verses? There is always an undertone of double entendre possible in these academically correct flush-left poems. Puns stud the final, brilliant poem of the book, "A Portrait of the Self as Nation, 1990–1991" as a way to conflate the personal with the political:

> my recent vagabond love
> driving a reckless chariot, lost
> in my feral country. *Country,* Oh I am
> so punny, so very very punny.

Chin admits there was "no Colonialist coercion; / sadly, we blended together well," and in embracing the lover/country, she remembers him/it with fondness: "We were fierce, yet tender, fierce and tender."

The critic Daryl Chin asserts that what is popular now is "victim subjectivity," a stage of liberalism that is happy to showcase artists—lesbian or gay, women, or those of color—just as long as they're victims. "If this doesn't please you, too bad," Marilyn Chin says to her lover in "Summer Love." This is the artists' only sane strategy.

Source: Terese Svoboda, "Try Bondage," in *Kenyon Review*, Vol. 17, No. 2, Spring 1995, pp. 154–60.

Matthew Rothschild

In the following excerpt, Rothschild reviews The Phoenix Gone, The Terrace Empty, *which includes "How I Got That Name." Rothschild finds that the poems in this collection are compelling in both their depiction of assimilation and in their portrayal of the sometimes conflicting emotional connections to American and Chinese cultural identities.*

Marilyn Chin has a voice all her own—witty, epigraphic, idiomatic, elegiac, earthy. In *The Phoenix Gone, The Terrace Empty,* she covers the canvas of cultural assimilation with an intensely personal brush. Born in Hong Kong and raised in Oregon, she pours herself into her poetry.

"How I Got That Name: An Essay on Assimilation" begins with the declaration, "I am Marilyn Mei Ling Chin," and recounts how her father "obsessed with a bombshell blonde / transliterated 'Mei Ling' to 'Marilyn,'" honoring her with the name of "some tragic white woman / swollen with gin and Nembutal." She goes on to warn that the stereotypes of Asian Americans are wrong: "We've managed to fool the experts," she writes, " . . . they can use us. / But the 'Model Minority' is a tease."

Worse than that, it can be fatal. Her "Elegy for Chloe Nguyen" tells of her precocious childhood friend, "Bipedal in five months, trilingual in a year; / at eleven she had her first lover." At thirty-three, she was dead. The last line reads: "Chloe, we are finally Americans now. Chloe, we are here!".

Similarly affecting are the ten little poems that make up "Homage to Diana Toy," a patient Chin tutored in a psychiatric hospital. When Toy, denied citizenship in the United States and sexually taken advantage of by an administrator, commits suicide, Chin blames herself, an "unworthy tutor," who "failed to tell her about the fifty paltry stars."

Chin concerns herself not only with the United States, but also, poignantly, with China. She dedicates a section of her book to the Chinese Democratic Movement. In "Beijing Spring," she embraces the protesters. "Lover, on Tienanmen Square, near the Avenue of Eternal Peace / I believe in the passions of youth, / I believe in eternal spring." She offers to "breathe life into your life" so rebellion can "begin again."

The immense charm that Chin brings to this book comes out in some of her "Love Poesies," as in, "Where Is the Moralizer, Your Mother?".

Here and in other poems, Chin parks the reader at the busy intersection of love, sex, family, and politics. This convergence makes for an astonishing conclusion in "A Portrait of the Nation, 1990–1991." This six-page poem includes sexual puns, remembrances of past lovers, praise for masturbation, remarks the judge made to her when she became a naturalized citizen, reminders of those denied citizenship, plus reflections on being in bed with a lover when the Persian Gulf war began: "Last night, in our large, rotund bed, / we witnessed the fall. Ours / was an 'aerial war.' Bombs / glittering in the twilight sky / against the Star Spangled Banner."

I've read this book three times now, and each time I go through it, I find it more compelling. For me, the most moving poem is "Tienanmen, the Aftermath," where Chin again juxtaposes being in bed while atrocities are committed: "These was blood and guts all over the road, / I said I'm sorry, darling, and rolled over." The poem closes with this haunting admonition: "leave the innocent ones alone, / those alive, yet stillborn, undead, yet waiting / in a fitful sleep undeserved of an awakening."

Source: Matthew Rothschild, "A Feast of Poetry," in *Progressive*, Vol. 58, May 1994, pp. 48–50.

SOURCES

Chin, Marilyn, "How I Got That Name," in *The Phoenix Gone, The Terrace Empty*, Milkweed, 1994, pp. 16–18.

Gery, John, "Mocking My Own Ripeness: Authenticity, Heritage, and Self-Erasure in the Poetry of Marilyn Chin," in *LIT: Literature Interpretation Theory*, Vol. 12, No. 1, April 2001, pp. 25–45.

Harmon, William, and Hugh Holman, eds., "Realistic Period in American Literature, 1865–1900," in *A Handbook to Literature*, Prentice Hall, 2003, pp. 422–23.

Lynch, Doris, Review of *The Phoenix Gone, the Terrace Empty*, in *Library Journal*, Vol. 119, No. 3, February 15, 1994, p. 164.

Moyers, Bill, "Marilyn Chin," in *The Language of Life: A Festival of Poets*, Doubleday, 1995, pp. 67–79.

Review of *The Phoenix Gone, the Terrace Empty*, in *Publishers Weekly*, Vol. 241, No. 9, February 28, 1994, p. 79.

Rothschild, Matthew, "A Feast of Poetry," in *Progressive*, Vol. 58, May 1994, pp. 48–50.

Scott, Whitney, Review of *The Phoenix Gone, the Terrace Empty*, in *Booklist*, Vol. 90, No. 14, March 15, 1994, p. 1322.

Slowik, Mary, "Beyond Lot's Wife: The Immigration Poems of Marilyn Chin, Garrett Hongo, Li-Young Lee, and David Mura," in *MELUS*, Vol. 25, No. 3–4, Fall–Winter 2000, pp. 221–42.

FURTHER READING

Cheung, King-Kok, ed., *An Interethnic Companion to Asian American Literature*, Cambridge University Press, 1996.

> Frequently referenced by scholars of Asian-American literature, this volume contains essays on topics pertinent to studying literature in this area. In addition to considering literature by ethnicity, the editor includes essays that compare works across ethnicity to uncover similarities in theme and style.

Ingersoll, Earl, *Breaking the Alabaster Jar: Conversations with Li-Young Lee*, BOA Editions, 2006.

> In this book, the prominent Chinese-American poet Lee answers questions about his background and experiences between cultures and between classes, and he discusses the differences in Western and Eastern thinking on a variety of issues.

McCormick, Adrienne, "Being Without: Marilyn Chin's "I" Poems as Feminist Acts of Theorizing," in *Critical Mass: A Journal of Asian American Cultural Criticism*, Vol. 6, Spring 2000, pp. 37–58.

> By looking at Chin's career as a whole and then examining a number of specific poems (including "How I Got That Name"), McCormick demonstrates how Chin expresses a feminist ideology in her poetry.

Weinberger, Eliot, ed., *The New Directions Anthology of Classical Chinese Poetry*, New Directions Publishing, 2004.

> This acclaimed anthology of classical Chinese poems has been carefully translated and edited for students of world literature. The book provides a helpful contrast to modern Chinese poetry, and helps readers understand the heritage of poetry in Chinese culture.

I Died for Beauty

EMILY DICKINSON

1890

Emily Dickinson's poem "I Died for Beauty" is an allegorical work that depicts someone who died for beauty interacting briefly with someone who died for truth. An allegory is a metaphorical work in which the characters and actions represent larger ideas or themes. Often in an allegory, abstract ideas are given physical form, as they are in Dickinson's poem. The poem equates the two as equally noble martyrs whose names are eventually covered with moss, as if to indicate that in the end, what one dies for is unimportant. Although is it uncertain when this poem was written, it is typical of Dickinson's work in its style, length, and content. It is a seemingly simple and straightforward poem that reveals deeper meaning with analysis. The length is only three quatrains (four-line stanzas), and the themes of death, beauty, and truth are frequent in her work.

Unlike most poets, Dickinson did not write with the intent of making a career as a poet. She kept most of her work private, which is why her poems often have a circa date indicating approximately when they were written. After her death, however, her sister enlisted a trusted editor to help get the poetry in publishable form. Because of these circumstances, the dates when Dickinson's work was published vastly differ from the dates when they were written. "I Died for Beauty" was written around 1862 and was first published in 1890. Editor Thomas Wentworth Higginson published the poem in a September issue of the *Christian Union*. Since then it has

Emily Dickinson (The Library of Congress)

been published repeatedly. Today, it is a popular and widely anthologized poem that is collected in virtually every volume of Dickinson's poems, as well as in other anthologies of American literature or poetry. Specifically, the poem appears in the only comprehensive edition of the works of Dickinson, *The Complete Poems of Emily Dickinson*, published by Back Bay Books in 1976.

AUTHOR BIOGRAPHY

Emily Dickinson was born on December 10, 1830, in Amherst, Massachusetts, to a young lawyer named Edward and his wife, Emily (Norcross). Dickinson had an older brother named William Austin and a younger sister named Lavinia, or "Vinnie." Edward became a successful politician who was known for being active in his community. His father had been a major force in the founding of Amherst College, and Edward often hosted and entertained visiting guests and lecturers, including Ralph Waldo Emerson. Less is known about Mrs. Dickinson, but many agree that she retained a love of learning, particularly in the sciences, for most of her life.

The Dickinson children attended Amherst Academy after completing their studies in a local one-room school. Dickinson was an enthusiastic student, and she seized the chance to attend college-level lectures while still at the Academy. Young women of the time enjoyed this educational season in their lives, where they grew their intellects and imaginations before settling into domestic lives. Dickinson certainly thrived. In addition to Milton, Emerson, and Thoreau, she embraced the writings of Emily and Charlotte Brontë, Robert and Elizabeth Barrett Browning, George Eliot, Charles Darwin, Nathaniel Hawthorne, Henry Wadsworth Longfellow, and Matthew Arnold. As Dickinson's friends began to marry and start their own lives, she delved deeper into her books.

When Dickinson completed studies at Amherst Academy, she continued her education at Mount Holyoke Female Seminary in nearby South Hadley. Although Dickinson had a strong sense of herself as a spiritual young woman, seminary authorities regarded her as hopeless. This was probably because some of her independent religious views flew in the face of the prevailing Calvinistic Puritanism. Dickinson left the seminary after only a year of study, raising eyebrows and questions. Whatever the reason, she returned to her parents' home and began her slow retreat from society. She generally stayed close to home, but entertained guests and maintained a few close relationships. At home, Dickinson had little interest in domestic work. She was content to pursue her own interests, such as writing and gardening.

Austin married Susan Gilbert, to Dickinson's delight. Susan had been a family friend since childhood, and she and Dickinson were good friends. Dickinson also corresponded with editors Samuel Bowles and Josiah Holland, literary figure Thomas Wentworth Higginson, and pastor Charles Wadsworth.

Between the late 1850s and 1865, Dickinson wrote as many as 1,100 poems. Then she began to have serious problems with her eyesight followed by devastating losses in the 1870s and 1880s. Edward died in 1874; Mrs. Dickinson suffered a stroke in 1875; Wadsworth and Mrs. Dickinson both died in 1882; and an eight-year-old nephew Dickinson held especially close to her heart died from typhoid fever in 1883.

A schism that seemed already to be forming was made worse with the arrival of Mabel Loomis Todd in 1881. A friend of Susan's, Todd was married to a professor at Amherst College. Dickinson is said never to have met her in person; she hid and eavesdropped when Todd came to visit Vinnie. But the next year, Todd began a love affair with Austin that lasted the rest of his life. Its openness created a great deal of tension among family members.

Dickinson suffered from an inflammation of the kidneys known as nephritis and died in Amherst on May 15, 1886. Despite having published seven poems in her lifetime, she asked Vinnie to burn her writings. Vinnie destroyed personal letters but preserved the poetry. It was Vinnie who pursued posthumous publication for Dickinson's poetry.

In 1890, Dickinson's first collection of poetry was published to great acclaim. Among the many now-popular poems was "I Died for Beauty," which was likely written around 1862. The first edition (500 copies) sold out in only a few weeks. Remarkably, it was printed in eleven editions in only two years. In editing early volumes, Todd and Higginson aggressively edited Dickinson's unusual style to make it more accessible. Later publications, however, presented the poems in their original style and with the original punctuation.

POEM TEXT

I died for Beauty—but was scarce
Adjusted in the Tomb
When One who died for Truth, was lain
In an adjoining Room—

He questioned softly "Why I failed"?   5
"For Beauty", I replied—
"And I—for Truth—Themself are One—
We Brethren, are", He said—

And so, as Kinsmen, met a Night—
We talked between the Rooms—   10
Until the Moss had reached our lips—
And covered up—our names—

POEM SUMMARY

Stanza 1

"I Died for Beauty" is told in the first person by someone who recently died "for Beauty." Each stanza is only four lines long, and in the first, the speaker introduces herself and goes right into the narrative. Readers may note that the poem begins with an image of Beauty being attended to by loved ones. She is not alone, as she is adjusted in the tomb. She seems to have been someone who was loved and has been respected with a proper burial. But just as she is left alone, she receives company. The speaker says she was just put in her tomb when another recently deceased person is brought into "an adjoining room," having died for truth.

Stanza 2

Sensing her presence, he addresses her softly. This suggests that he is apprehensive, afraid, or sensitive to what might be a painful topic for her. Given that he died for truth, he is not afraid of her answer, but might fear upsetting her. He was also brought in by others and has now been left, so he likely takes some comfort in the realization that he is not alone. He asks the speaker how she died, and she answers simply: "For Beauty." He responds by telling her that he died for truth, making them brethren. The two share an immediate kinship and mutual understanding. They have both given their lives on the altar of principle, and so they respect and identify with one another. As she did at the end of the first stanza, Dickinson ends this stanza with a hyphen. This essentially trails off the action and emotion of one stanza and leads the reader right into the next without the need for setting up anything new.

Stanza 3

The speaker refers to the two of them now as "kinsmen" although they just met. Their deaths for noble causes make them spiritually akin. Dickinson relates the friendship with something the reader may have experienced—striking up a kinship with someone one evening. The one who died for Beauty and the one who died for truth talk across their rooms as long as they could. The image is familiar; new relationships have enthusiasm and energy, and two new friends do not run out of things to discuss or learn about one another. This is what the two buried people experience, and the juxtaposition of the setting with the friendly interaction of the two (who are in reality corpses) is typical of Dickinson's work. The scene is macabre, but the reader almost forgets until Dickinson describes why the two stop talking. She says that they talk "between the rooms" for as long as they can. But when their physical selves are no longer able to speak ("Until the moss had reached our lips"), they go silent. The reader is abruptly reminded that the two characters in this allegory of Beauty and Truth are dead bodies. The grim reality of decay (and probably rigor mortis, which stiffens dead bodies) beings the cheerful kinship to a halt. The moss reaches their lips so they can no longer talk to one another. More broadly, the decay ends their ability to speak out on behalf of Beauty or Truth. The lips, which represent communication, expression, and relationship, go mute. They are silenced by the natural cycle of life and death. The speaker concludes with the image of the moss covering their names, apparently rendering them forgotten and anonymous. Not only does the moss cover the bodies' mouths, but it in effect erases the memories of those who are buried there. Their to-the-death stands for Beauty and Truth are forgotten (except for the poem), and the reader is left wondering for what did they really die? Were their deaths in vain? Without knowing the specifics of their individual deaths, it is impossible to say. It is, however, possible to conclude that even such great principles as beauty and truth are subject to the ravages of time.

THEMES

Beauty and Truth

"I Died for Beauty" deals very directly with the themes of beauty and truth. Dickinson portrays them as parallel in various ways. Both are represented by someone who died for them; both are buried in the same tomb near each other; both die and decay at around the same time; and both names are covered by the same moss. Further, the figures themselves feel an immediate bond when they each learn why the other died. The poem makes a strong and overt statement that beauty and truth are "brethren" and "kinsmen." Further, the two recognize one another as being kindred spirits.

An interesting point of interpretation is whether Dickinson means that the two figures died as martyrs for beauty and truth, or that the two figures died in order to attain beauty and truth. The phrasing "I died for beauty" and "And I for truth" leaves the door open to either interpretation. Regardless, the two figures felt strongly enough about them that their human lives were less valuable than beauty and truth.

Death and Mortality

"I Died for Beauty" takes place entirely inside a tomb. The speaker describes being placed in the

TOPICS FOR FURTHER STUDY

- Read John Keats's "Ode on a Grecian Urn." Do you find any relevant comments or parallels to "I Died for Beauty"? Write an essay comparing and contrasting these two poems. Add concluding remarks about the universal themes addressed by these two poets.

- Which is more worth dying for: beauty or truth? Stage a debate with a fellow student in which one of you takes the position that dying for beauty is nobler, while the other takes the position that dying for truth is nobler. Look for historical examples to strengthen your arguments. Have a three-person panel act as judges to determine who wins the debate.

- Read more about Dickinson's life and work. Although relatively little is known about her, try to get a sense of what kind of person she probably was. Write an introduction to a book of her poetry as if it was written by her and recently discovered among her letters. What do you think she would have wanted readers to know about her work? Be sure to include a few comments about "I Died for Beauty."

- Many students find that works of literature are more relatable when there is a visual component. Pretend you are a guest speaker to a group of college freshman art students. You want them to connect with literature in a way that is meaningful to them, so you collect five works of art that help bring "I Died for Beauty" to life. Using any format you like (slide show, packet handout, framed copies of the works), prepare a twenty-minute presentation that shows them how art and literature can complement each other.

tomb when another is placed in a nearby room within the tomb. There is hardly a stronger sense of death than such a setting. So everything about the poem must be considered within the context of death. The two figures have died and are now dealing with that reality, although they seem very content about it. They were aware of their own mortality when they gave their lives for the greater goods of beauty and truth. The poem takes an interesting twist, however, when the notion that beauty and truth are immortal comes into question. Initially, it seems that the figures have sacrificed their mortal lives for something that transcends death, namely beauty and truth. But in the end when the figures are rendered silent, and their names covered with moss, the reader must wonder if those things for which they died are also mortal.

Friendship

In typical Dickinson fashion, this poem about noble deaths and the process of dying also comments about something as ordinary and cheerful as friendship. In this case, the speaker (who died for Beauty) befriends a newcomer to her tomb who died for Truth. Both are placed in the tomb and then left, but they are not lonely for long when they realize that not only do they have each other, but that they have quite a lot in common. Dickinson demonstrates how easily some friendships form and the enthusiasm with which new friends engage each other. In this case, the two are bonded by their willingness to die for what they agree is the same thing (Beauty and Truth), but they are also bonded by their astonishing circumstances. Dickinson illustrates how a friendly relationship has the power to make even the most unusual and potentially frightening situation (such as being laid to rest in a tomb) seem pleasant. However, like most friendships, this one is eventually broken up by the passing of time. Although the poem ends on a melancholy note, the reader can not help but feel that the transition from life to death was made much easier by having formed one last meaningful friendship before passing on to eternity.

STYLE

Allegory

An allegory is a type of extended metaphor in which elements of the narrative (such as characters or events) represent something beyond what is immediately apparent. Just as any metaphor is a way of comparing two or more things for the sake of commenting on one of them, an allegory applies the same concept to a narrative. In "I Died for Beauty," Dickinson uses this form of metaphor to comment on beauty and truth. The narrative describes the bodies of those who died for beauty and truth being laid to rest in the same tomb, in adjoining rooms. They speak and become "brethren" right away, based on the fact that they both died for essentially the same purpose ("the two are one"). The two figures are personified versions of the things for which they gave their lives, and death is the sacrifice for a greater good. That the two figures died for beauty and truth demonstrates the lengths to which they would go in service of something they regarded as greater than themselves.

Initially, the transcendence of beauty and truth is represented in the fact that the two figures are still aware and speaking, even though they are dead. The reader sees this as a comment, through a picture presented by Dickinson, that these things are immortal. However, the allegory continues by showing the figures eventually succumbing to physical decay, as their names are covered by moss. Because the language and visual presentation is allegorical, the reader is led to wonder what Dickinson is trying to say about the ultimate fate of beauty and truth. But with her speakers rendered silent, the reader is left to draw his or her own conclusions.

Regular Stanzas

Dickinson's poetry is characteristically formal in style and regular in structure and rhythm. "I Died for Beauty" is a perfect example of her regularity of style. The poem is written in three four-line stanzas, all with a rhyme scheme of *abcb*, with the *b* rhymes being near rhymes; in this poem, they are more specifically consonance rhymes because the near-rhyming words are on the same stress and end with the same consonants. The lines for every stanza follow a regular pattern of iambic tetrameter, iambic trimeter, iambic tetrameter, and iambic trimeter. This adherence to style and structure reflects Dickinson's education at Amherst Academy and her ability to tell the story and make her comments within these limitations. Writing in this way requires a particular ability to form lines and use economy of words. From a reader's perspective, the poem has a natural and comfortable feel that makes the poem more accessible. The regular rhythm also frees the reader to focus on the narrative and the subtleties of the imagery rather than be tripped up in unusual or jolting patterns.

HISTORICAL CONTEXT

Realistic Period in American Literature

Although the year of Dickinson's birth, 1830, was also the year that the Romantic Period in American literature began, Dickinson is associated with

COMPARE & CONTRAST

- **1862:** Dickinson has only had about four of her poems published, one in an Amherst College publication and the other three (including "I Taste a Liquor Never Brewed" and "Safe in Their Alabaster Chambers") in the *Springfield Republican* newspaper. Tucked away in her room, however, are volumes of the poetry that she has written over the years.

  Today: Dickinson is one of the most anthologized American poets, studied at virtually every educational level. Dickinson's writing is an ongoing subject of research and analytical papers by literary scholars. Numerous volumes of her poems exist, along with collections of letters, biographies, and scholarly books. Dickinson has taken her place alongside the giants of American poetry, including Robert Frost and Walt Whitman. To many, she is the predominant female voice in the canon of American poetry.

- **1862:** Susan B. Anthony and other suffragettes (women activists who fought for voting rights) participate in political activism with the goal of gaining more equal rights for women. Voting, property ownership, and legal standing are among the top issues of the day. Although Dickinson was not a political activist, she is considered by some historians as having feminist leanings because of her individualism and unwillingness to assume a domestic role that did not interest or suit her.

  Today: Women enjoy the same rights as men and continue to organize themselves for causes specific to women and their position in society. Prestigious women abound. Ruth Bader Ginsberg is a Supreme Court justice; Nancy Pelosi is the Speaker of the House, and Condoleeza Rice is the National Security Advisor; Oprah Winfrey is one of the most influential media figures; J. K. Rowling is one of the most wealthy and successful authors in the world; and Margaret Whitman is President of eBay. Equal pay, maternity leave, and abortion rights are among the top issues of the day.

- **1862:** People communicate with each other through letters, just as Dickinson did. Much history from this time period is preserved in letters and journals, as such forms of writing were very common.

  Today: Very few people write letters anymore. Email, cell phones, and text messaging are the primary means of communication. Because these forms of communication are fleeting, little of day-to-day communication is preserved.

---

the Realistic Period in American literature, which lasted from 1865 to 1900. Where the Romantic Period yielded writing that was optimistic, exalted, hopeful, and at times self-consciously literary, the Realistic Period emerged from a nation struggling after the Civil War and facing economic, industrial, and intellectual change. Because she kept to herself and did not interact with many writers of her day, Dickinson did not set out to become a Realistic writer. She was the product of her time, place, and personality. The Realistic writers were less idealistic than their Romantic predecessors, and they were willing to both look at, and write about, struggle on a collective or individual level. The work of writers like Charles Darwin, Karl Marx, and Auguste Comte were coming more into mainstream thought. Science challenged religion more directly, something that Dickinson understood.

Literary writers were transitioning to the new way of thinking, and new voices rose from the Realistic Period. Authors, poets, and playwrights approached subjects with the intent to present them with more fidelity so that their works would be relevant to their audiences. They left the job of interpretation to the audience or reader. In *A Handbook to Literature*, editors William Harmon and

Hugh Holman note that amidst a number of imitators of Romantic poetry during the Realistic Period were "three new and authentic poetic voices ... [Walt] Whitman's, [Sidney] Lanier's, and [Emily] Dickinson's." Novelists wrote in style and content about growing disillusionment and cynicism. While some of the novelists were harsh and serious, others, such as Mark Twain, adopted the same perspective in a humorous way.

Women in 1860s America

In 1860s Amherst, where Dickinson lived with her family, women had clearly defined roles and expectations within the home and the community. They were encouraged to attend school and learn about literature, philosophy, mathematics, history, and even science, but they were not expected to build careers on their educations. During the late teens, men's and women's educational paths diverged as men launched their careers or went to seminary, law school, or other professional schools. This was the case with the Dickinson children. While Austin advanced to law school, his sisters finished at Amherst Academy and then attended Mount Holyoke Female Seminary. Women's education was taken seriously at this time in history, as evidenced by the establishment of schools like Mount Holyoke, which opened as a seminary for women in 1837. In the next three decades, more colleges for women were founded—Vassar Female College was chartered in 1861 and opened after the end of the Civil War, Smith College was chartered in 1871, and Wellesley College opened in 1875.

Once young women completed their schooling or got married, they assumed their duties at home. As wives and mothers, their duties included all housework, child rearing, and entertaining. The social network was vibrant and important, and hosting visitors and gatherings was part of the woman's responsibilities to her family. Women who did not marry (such as Dickinson and her sister, Vinnie) returned to their parents' homes, where they took on many of the same domestic duties as married women. They were expected to set aside their personal interests in favor of contributing to the smooth running of the household.

CRITICAL OVERVIEW

Many biographers have commented that Dickinson's fascination with death was revealed in her letters. In them, she asks correspondents to describe what it was like to witness a person dying; she wanted to know about their final hours, their presence of mind, and whether or not they felt peaceful. All of this interest, imagination, and detail is poured into her poetry, as noted by Paula Hendrickson in *Dickinson Studies*. "I Died for Beauty" portrays two people who have died, and what transpires after their burial. While it does not speak to the experience of death itself, it does portray a peaceful resignation to death, and it comments on the fleeting nature of human purpose.

During Dickinson's life, only seven of her poems were published. After her death in 1886, her sister, Lavinia ("Vinnie"), set about gathering all of the poems Dickinson had written and pursuing publication for them. The first volume of Dickinson's poetry was published in 1890 to great acclaim, and "I Died for Beauty" was among them. In a review from 1890, a writer for *Critic* praises the volume as "striking and original," adding that its "main quality ... is an extraordinary grasp and insight." Modern readers must remember how unusual Dickinson's poems were to her contemporaries, yet many critics embraced them at once. The reviewer for *Critic* concludes: "Miss Dickinson's poems, though rough and rugged, are surprisingly individual and genuinely inspired." Another 1890 review, this one from the *Nation*, describes Dickinson's poems as "simply extraordinary, and strike notes, very often, like those of some deep-toned organ." Similar praise comes from James Reeves in his much more recent (1994) contribution to *Reference Guide to American Literature*, who claims that "nothing that she wrote is without interest." Singling out "I Died for Beauty," the reviewer for the *Nation* characterizes the poem as having a "Blake-like quality." The critic adds: "The extraordinary terseness and vigor of that weird conclusion runs through all the poems." Reeves regards Dickinson's offbeat style as distinctive, purposeful, and consistent; he explains that "the idiosyncratic vision of which we are speaking is not evident only intermittently, in this image or that turn of phrase, but informs every line, so that despite their differences Dickinson's poems are always unmistakably hers."

One of the great literary critics of the 1950s was John Crowe Ransom, whose poetry and criticism is still studied today. He notes that, like "I Died for Beauty," most of Dickinson's poems are written in the first person, but he explains why this does not always mean that they are about Dickinson herself. He writes:

The former home of writer Emily Dickinson (© James Marshall / Corbis)

If the poems are not autobiographical in the usual sense of following actual experience—and it is not likely that they do ... then they are autobiographical in the special sense of being true to an imagined experience, and that will be according to the dominant or total image which the artist proposes to make up for herself.

In determining Dickinson's place in the American literary tradition, he not only agrees that she holds a position of importance, but he goes so far as to declare: "Whitman and Emily Dickinson were surely the greatest forces of American poetry in the nineteenth century, and both had found their proper masks." Reeves wholeheartedly believes that Dickinson is among the great writers in the English language. He boldly states: "Not all poets have recognized the exceptional resources of this [English] vocabulary, but the greatest, of whom Chaucer and Shakespeare are the preeminent examples, have undoubtedly done so. Dickinson, as a close reading of her poems will confirm, is to be counted among their number."

CRITICISM

Jennifer A. Bussey

Bussey is an independent writer specializing in literature. In the following essay, she looks at a number of Dickinson's poems to place the poet's treatment of beauty and truth in "I Died for Beauty" in a larger context.

Emily Dickinson visited and revisited some of the same themes over the course of her prolific life. In all, Dickinson wrote more than 1,700 poems. She often writes about nature, life, and death; in fact, her poetry so strongly falls into thematic categories that the original 1890 collection of her poetry organizes her poems in the following chapters: Life, Nature, Love, and Time and Eternity. Dickinson is known for her preoccupation with death and her tendency at times to slip into the macabre in her treatments of this theme. Dickinson seems to be so comfortable with her own mortality that she thinks about death in unusual ways, and often in great detail. She writes about the moment of death, the presence of death, and tombs. In "I Died for Beauty," Dickinson adopts a

I Died for Beauty

WHAT DO I READ NEXT?

- *Emily Dickinson: Selected Letters* (2006) was edited by Dickinson scholar Thomas H. Johnson. Dickinson maintained correspondence with a wide variety of people from family members to literary experts. Her letters demonstrate her acute writing ability, and her tendency to slip into poetry, even when writing prose in a letter.

- Daniel Lombardo's *Amherst and Hadley: Through the Seasons* (1998) is a collection of photographs, stories, and history regarding the two towns of Amherst and Hadley, Massachusetts. Lombardo pays special attention to the importance of the season's cycles as they related to the towns and the lives of their citizens in the past. Places that figured into Dickinson's life, including Amherst College, are featured.

- Edited by Wendy Martin, *The Cambridge Companion to Emily Dickinson* (2002) is indispensable to the high school or undergraduate student of American literature. Fourteen essays from respected scholars around the world are collected in this volume.

- Richard B. Sewall's *The Life of Emily Dickinson* (1998) is a National Book Award–winning biography. Sewall's book is very detailed and gets to the heart of the woman, her poetry, and how she achieved her unique and enduring voice.

---

first-person approach to her narrative set in a tomb. It tells of a conversation between two newly-entombed figures.

In "I Died for Beauty" the speaker declares that she died for beauty, and as she was placed in her tomb, another person is placed in a nearby room. She talks to him, and when they discover that she died for beauty and he died for truth, they feel an immediate kinship. Dickinson creates strong parallels in the poem between beauty and

> DICKINSON SEEMS TO HAVE HAD A VERY COMPLICATED UNDERSTANDING OF BEAUTY, AND THESE POEMS SUGGEST A WOMAN STRUGGLING WITH THE ISSUE OF TRUE BEAUTY AND ITS MEANING."

truth. The two seem delighted to have met each other, and they talk until death ultimately renders them silent. No longer can they communicate with each other or have an effect on the world, although Dickinson gives no indication of their moving on to the afterlife. In the last lines of the poem, the same moss that covers their lips (a very physical image of death) also covers their names on the tombstone. In the end, they are mute and apparently forgotten. This allegorical poem makes strong statements about beauty, truth, death, and impermanence. There are two ways to interpret "for"—the speaker may have died in the service of or as a sacrifice for beauty, or she may have died in order to attain beauty.

Dickinson writes about beauty in a handful of other poems, and these may give insight into how the poet understood and valued beauty. In one poem, she states: "To tell the beauty would decrease, / To state the Spell demean" This simply means that explaining why something is beautiful takes away from its beauty. The idea is akin to the literary concept of the heresy of the paraphrase, which contends that literature and art lose something when paraphrased or presented in any other way than the way the artist intended. This is precisely the idea Dickinson puts forth with regard to beauty; it is obvious to those who can see it and it suffers from being analyzed or broken down into elements.

In another four-line poem, Dickinson writes: "So gay a flower bereaved the mind / As if it were a woe, / Is Beauty an affliction, then? / Tradition ought to know." In these short lines, Dickinson tells of a flower so beautiful that it is painful to look at it. Beauty, therefore, can be full of grief "as if it were a woe." Dickinson juxtaposes the beauty and the onlooker's reaction, which leads naturally to the question: "Is Beauty an affliction, then?" She wonders if beauty is less the joy people believe it to be, and is instead burdensome.

1 8 0

Poetry for Students, Volume 28

Her answer is inconclusive and likely unsatisfying to many readers: "Tradition ought to know." In other words, only life experience and the past can answer that question. Perhaps the answer is different for different people.

The last example of a poem dealing with beauty is the most relevant to "I Died for Beauty." It is another four-line poem, but it addresses both beauty and death. Dickinson writes: "Beauty crowds me till I die, / Beauty, mercy have on me! / But if I expire today, / Let it be in sight of thee." The first two lines characterize beauty as invasive, unwelcome, and unkind. It is unrelenting, crowding the speaker right up until the moment of her death, despite her begging for mercy. This image offers a clear answer to the prior poem's question: "Is Beauty an affliction, then?" For this speaker, the answer is a resounding yes, although the manifestation of beauty is unclear. In the last half of the poem, however, she admits to having a need for beauty. She asks beauty not to leave her if she dies today. The speaker wants to die "in sight of" beauty. The speaker clearly has intense feelings about beauty, and those feelings figure prominently in her anticipation of death.

Taken collectively, these three poems characterize beauty as simultaneously indefinable, burdensome, intrusive, and comforting. Dickinson seems to have had a very complicated understanding of beauty, and these poems suggest a woman struggling with the issue of true beauty and its meaning. She does not, however, indicate that it is a great good that is worth taking up as a cause and sacrificing one's life for.

What about truth, the other figure in "I Died for Beauty"? What do Dickinson's other poems say about it? There are only a few other poems that address the subject, but they provide a consistent perspective. In one, Dickinson describes a man who is essentially a loudmouth. Dickinson writes: "He preached upon 'breadth' till it argued him narrow,— / The broad are too broad to define: / And of 'truth' until it proclaimed him a liar,— / The truth never flaunted a sign."

In these lines, Dickinson illustrates the enduring nature of breadth and truth. Both are able to overcome the efforts by one man to discuss them, and the antithetical outcome is that breadth makes the man narrow, and truth makes him a liar. What Dickinson tells the reader about truth is that it transcends human manipulation,

logic, or understanding. It remains steadfast and consistent, regardless of what anyone says about it. It ultimately holds power over those who try to take power from it. In another poem describing truth, Dickinson writes: "There's triumph of the finer mind / When truth, affronted long, / Advances calm to her supreme, / Her God her only throng." Again, Dickinson argues here that truth, no matter how long it is "affronted," or insulted, rises above the efforts of men to reside with God. Dickinson personifies truth as a woman to whom the crowds of men are irrelevant because she is with God. Both of these poems characterize truth as unchanging, powerful, and besieged. What Dickinson does not make clear is how much she values truth. It seems more like an overarching force than something she connects with on a personal level. While it seems like something that is great and enduring, it is difficult to make an argument that her poetry reflects a belief that it is worthwhile to die for truth.

Given this overview, it is likely that Dickinson rejected the view that beauty or truth were worth dying for, and even "I Died for Beauty" indicates this through its treatment of the dead as ultimately silent and nameless. In the end, as Dickinson sees it, people can die under the honorable banners of beauty and truth, but their deaths go the way of all others. Their expressions go mute, their bodies decay, and their names are forgotten.

Source: Jennifer A. Bussey, Critical Essay on "I Died for Beauty," in *Poetry for Students*, Gale, Cengage Learning, 2008.

Evan Carton

In the following excerpt, Carton provides a critical overview of Dickinson's poetry, focusing especially on the spiritual and philosophical themes of her work.

... Dickinson, in the words of several of her critics, writes "poems of epistemological quest," poems that enact "radical inquiry," poems that test "the strength of the imagination against the stubbornness of life, the repression of an antithetical nature, and that 'hidden mystery'—the final territory of death." This is to say, she seeks always to make contact—if not sustained, then repeated contact—with a supreme reality which at once pervades her most intimate surroundings and remains beyond her reach; to this end, she effects the odd fusions of homeliness and extravagance which characterize her language and her

" WHENEVER WE TAKE UP OUR IDEAL, DICKINSON SUGGESTS, WHENEVER WE CLEARLY VIEW THE OBJECT OF OUR QUEST, WE PERCEIVE IT TO BE FLAWED. ITS FLAW, HOWEVER, REFLECTS OUR OWN LIMITATION OR FAILURE."

conceptions. Because the supreme or divine reality that Dickinson pursues is most hidden when it seems immediate and most mysterious when it seems plain, the pursuit must be waged by means of paradox, renunciation, and surprise. What is easily seen or possessed must be resisted if one is to preserve the potential to "taste a liquor never brewed" or to glimpse "The Color too remote / That I could show it in Bazaar—"; failure to suspect the apparent, Dickinson confesses, has led her many times to embrace the deadly illusion of "Wrecked Men" who

> deem they sight the Land—
> At Centre of the Sea—
> And struggle slacker—but to prove
> As hopelessly as I—
> How many the fictitious Shores—
> Before the Harbor be—

The "struggle" must be perpetuated, even at the cost of eliminating altogether one's ability to "sight the Land" and relying on some other, undiscovered kind of vision.

> Renunciation—is a piercing Virtue—
> The letting go
> A Presence—for an Expectation—
> Not now—
> The putting out of Eyes—
> Just Sunrise—
> Lest Day—
> Day's Great Progenitor—
> Outvie

Images of blindness or thwarted vision abound in Dickinson's poems and usually signify achievement, or its potential, rather than frustration. "I see thee better—in the Dark—" ("611"), one poem begins, and another echoes, "What I see not, I better see—/ Through Faith—" ("939"). "'Twas lighter—to be Blind—" ("761"), concludes a third, and Dickinson boasts that her

house of possibility is "Impregnable of Eye—" ("657"). Although eager to cast blindness in its classical role as a trope for inspiration or insight, Dickinson, as "Renunciation—is a piercing Virtue—" suggests, wholly is not reverent toward it. "The putting out of eyes," in its chilling deliberateness, assumes the character of a desperate defense against the temptation to sell out the divine expectation in favor of the dazzling presence, or against the greater fear that nothing superior to what is commonly perceived will present itself ("Lest Day—/ Day's Great Progenitor—/ Outvie"). Dickinson's uneasiness in the face of the rival claims of vision and blindness, presence and expectation, manifests itself in elusive and even deceptive poetry.

> Before I got my eye put out
> I liked as well to see—
> As other Creatures, that have Eyes
> And know no other way—
> But were it told to me—Today—
> That I might have the sky
> For mine—I tell you that my Heart
> Would split, for size of me—
> The Meadows—mine—
> The Mountains—mine—
> All Forests—Stintless Stars—
> As much of Noon as I could take
> Between my finite eyes—
> The Motions of the Dipping Birds—
> The Morning's Amber Road—
> For mine—to look at when I liked—
> The News would strike me dead—
> So safer—guess—with just my soul
> Upon the Window pane—
> Where other Creatures put their eyes—
> Incautious—of the Sun—

Ruth Miller's explicative paraphrase of this poem seems reasonable until one begins to examine her basic assumptions and discovers that they render the poem quite illogical.

Her eyes were put out by the Sun, by her degreeless Noon, by her sudden intuition of a truth so overpowering it shattered her physical sense and replaced that dull way of seeing Nature, that ordinary way ignorant creatures must content themselves with, replaced conventional sight with spiritual vision. When she became aware that all this world of transient nature was not merely to observe but might be possessed, was actually a boon for her taking, that news was too much for her; she was too humble, felt too small and perhaps even fearful of such vision.

Miller first infers from the apparent suggestion of the last two lines that the speaker's eyes were put out not by an act of willful renunciation, as in "Renunciation—is a piercing Virtue—," but by "the Sun." She assumes too that this shatterer of conventional sight is rather the shock of spiritual perception ("her degreeless Noon," "her sudden intuition") than the celestial body itself. These assumptions enable her to interpret the poem as a simultaneous declaration of access and confession of resistance to the overwhelming potential of supersensory vision; but, if they are correct, what danger could exist for the "other Creatures" who have only physical sight? And what explanation could be given for the speaker's stipulation that the news she could not survive would be news of the unlimited appropriative power of her "*finite* eyes"—her physical, and also her *finished* sense of sight? Miller does not address these issues; in fact, she diminishes their gravity for the speaker by misreporting the tense of the verbs in stanzas two through four. "When she became aware ... that news was too much for her," Miller writes. In the poem, the verbs are conditional and the speaker's awareness ("That I might have the sky," and so forth), though imagined, *must* remain hypothetical ("But were it told to me—Today—... The News would strike me dead—").

"Before I got my eye put out" exemplifies perhaps the crucial Dickinsonian situation: that of the quester in mid-quest, indulging the awful possibility that she has sacrificed a presence for an expectation which may prove unfounded, recognizing that the commitment to sacrifice itself is enough to counter (although not enough to dispel) this possibility, and thus sustaining herself between the terrors of complete detachment from and integration with her object. The speaker, here, has forsaken physical sight in preparation for an "other way" to see—a way she expects, as the first stanza implies, to be superior. But now her doubt leads her to imagine being told that she might possess the essential elements of the universe—more than enough to satiate her appetite for splendor—through "finite eyes," through the mode of perception whose ultimacy she has gambled against. It is not the shock of total spiritual perception which would strike her dead; it is the news that such perception would be both illusory and supererogatory. And a report of the absolute *sufficiency* of "finite eyes" to one who has committed herself to the "other way" would constitute precisely such news. Since

her eye has been put out, however, she can only imagine herself succumbing to the temptation of physical sight and runs little actual risk of having its sufficiency proved to her. To hold up to the world one's soul instead of one's eyes is, ironically, a defensive move. It is "safer" because the light of presence can neither divert one from the pursuit of a superior expectation nor subvert the expectation itself. And, because the soul limits itself to an expectative vision, to guessing, its "other way" to see remains an inextinguishable prospect. The danger of the sun, here as in "Renunciation—is a piercing Virtue—," is that its light will satisfy the quester and thus disengage her from the pursuit of a light beyond, detach her from God. Such premature satisfaction, what the "other Creatures" risk—and what they gain—would be deadly for Dickinson.

If death is the reward for submission to the reality of "finite eyes" at the expense of the possibility of the sublime, it is equally the reward for strict allegiance to that possibility. In a poem that is closely related to "Before I got my eye put out," the speaker rejoices in the perpetual failure of her senses (particularly of her vision) to satisfy her ("627"). Everything she perceives hints at "Some Secret" just beyond her grasp, and, in the exultant logic of the poem, she takes these hints to ratify her faith in the superior reality which will unfold before "Another way—to see—." Thus, she confidently may proclaim that "The Tint I cannot take—is best—" and may cast the visible world as the playful secret-keeper that allows her occasional glimpses of the withheld splendor: nature's array of color "swaggers on the eye," landscapes put on an "eager look," summer is a "pleading" which gives way to "That other Prank—of Snow—/ That Cushions Mystery with Tulle." The tone darkens, however, as the final stanza confronts the prospective circumstance of any full revelation.

> Their Graspless manners—mock us—
> Until the Cheated Eye
> Shuts arrogantly—in the Grave—
> Another way—to see—

All that is certain, finally, is that the eye has been cheated and mocked. Its arrogance, in shutting, signals both the stubbornness and the insecurity of the speaker's faith in "Another way—to see—." The quest for "The Tint I cannot take—" offers no greater guarantee against self-delusion than does the rejection of possibility in favor of "As much of Noon as I could take / Between my finite eyes—." Moreover, its uncertain chance of success is contingent upon the death of the quester.

Death imagery informs Dickinson's most triumphant visions of her quest's fulfillment. "The Soul's Superior instants" are instants of "Mortal Abolition" and of the "infinite withdraw[al]" of "friend—and Earth's occasion" ("306"). Her sense of the identity between the death of the self and its achieved contact with supreme reality is keenly paradoxical, and she refuses to mitigate the paradox by invoking the Christian division of the self into mortal body and immortal soul. Instead, she often presents a "me" whose ontological integrity is lost (or on the brink of loss), swallowed up in an aqueous eternity, in the moment of fulfillment.

> Behind Me—dips Eternity—
> Before Me—Immortality—
> Myself—the Term between—
> Death but the Drift of Eastern Gray,
> Dissolving into Dawn away,
> Before the West begin—

Here, the speaker imagines her imminent dissolution in the convergence of earthly and heavenly light. This more beatific than threatening image preludes her vision of an apocalyptic kingdom in which a monarchical figure, triumphing over time and space, makes up both the history and the constituency of his realm through his inexhaustible power of self-apportionment.

> 'Tis kingdoms—afterward—they say—
> In perfect—pauseless Monarchy—
> Whose Prince—is Son of None—
> Himself—His Dateless Dynasty—
> Himself—Himself diversify—
> In Duplicate divine—

But this kingdom remains a rumor ("—they say—"); and, in the structure of Dickinson's poem, the state of ultimate selfhood that it represents is "the Term between" two depictions of a present self's inundation. The third stanza is an ominous mirror image of the first. In it, the "me" is the only small locus of illumination. She is explicitly at sea, and her light is threatened, too, by blackness to the North and South and by a sky that has taken on an oceanic turbulence.

> 'Tis Miracle before Me—then—
> 'Tis Miracle behind—between—
> A Crescent in the Sea—
> With Midnight to the North of Her—
> And Midnight to the South of Her—
> And Maelstrom—in the Sky—

The sea is Dickinson's most frequent symbol of eternity, of the realm in which alone possibility may be realized, and the initial prospect of its invasion is thrilling.

> Exultation is the going
> Of an inland soul to sea,
> Past the houses—past the headlands—
> Into deep Eternity—

The "divine intoxication" of this venture, however, can only culminate in complete submission.

> It tossed—and tossed—
> A little Brig I knew—o'ertook by Blast—
> It spun—and spun—
> And groped delirious, for Morn—
> It slipped—and slipped—
> As One that drunken—stept—
> Its white foot tripped—
> Then dropped from sight—

Whatever she may gain, "The Drop, that wrestles in the Sea—/ Forgets her own locality—" ("284"), loses her integral being. The drowning of a lone individual or a small craft—the simultaneous fulfillment and dissolution that the quester must experience in her integration with the divine—is the subject of perhaps two dozen poems in Dickinson's canon.

Such integration both allures and terrifies, inspiring warring attitudes of dauntless commitment and desperate resistance.

> Escaping backward to perceive
> The Sea upon our place—
> Escaping forward, to confront
> His glittering Embrace—
> Retreating up, a Billow's height
> Retreating blinded down
> Our undermining feet to meet
> Instructs to the Divine.

The final line of this poem affirms the speaker's sustained faith in "the Divine" and her acceptance of instruction to it, but the sense of helpless terror methodically produced by the preceding seven lines is not dispelled. On the contrary, there may lurk a blasphemous suggestion in the equation of repeatedly futile attempts to escape or retreat from a threatening sea with an understanding of the divine. Dickinson's mingled desire and fear to be consumed is consistent with the overtones of sexual seduction in this poem and others like it. Two earlier poems, in particular, trace the progress of a rising tide up the speaker's body; once she flees and once, to prove her love and faith, she submits. In "I started early—Took my Dog—" the speaker's visit to the sea begins innocently enough but quickly turns ominous when she ventures out beyond "the Sands."

> But no Man moved Me—till the Tide
> Went past my simple Shoe—
> And past my Apron—and my Belt
> And past my Bodice—too—
> And made as He would eat me up—
> As wholly as a Dew
> Upon a Dandelion's Sleeve—
> And then—I started—too—
> And He—He followed—close behind—
> I felt his Silver Heel
> Upon my Ankle—Then my Shoes
> Would overflow with Pearl—

When she manages to reach "the Solid Town," the sea withdraws "with a Mighty look." In her successful flight, however, she not only has escaped violation but also has retreated from the sea's imperial realm and from its offer of precious metals and gems, symbols of eternity's splendor. The speaker in "Me prove it now—Whoever doubt," hoping to achieve in death a consummation denied her in life, contains her terror and invites her sacrifice, questioning and "searching" throughout for a sign that her hope is justified.

> Me prove it now—Whoever doubt
> Me stop to prove it—now—
> Make haste—the Scruple! Death be scant
> For Opportunity—
> The River reaches to my feet—
> As yet—My Heart be dry—
> Oh Lover—Life could not convince—
> Might Death—enable Thee—
> The River reaches to My Breast—
> Still—still—My Hands above
> Proclaim with their remaining Might—
> Dost recognize the Love?
> The River reaches to my Mouth—
> Remember—when the Sea
> Swept by my searching eyes—the last—
> Themselves were quick—with Thee!

Although the speaker never shrinks from the tide and desperately reiterates her faith to the last, the tension between doubt and belief is not relieved by death. It is only ossified; her eyes, at the moment of their extinction, are both "searching" and, grimly, alive or "quick—with Thee!" Drowning no more assures the speaker's achievement of the supreme communion she has envisioned than "Shut[ting] arrogantly—in the Grave—" assures "the Cheated Eye" of "Another

way—to see—." The self's completed quest for contact, its integration with God, not only is a self-annihilation but may be a self-deception as well.

Dickinson's terror of the fact of such integration, then, is matched by her terror of its illusoriness. The receptive quester, in her faithful submission to some consecrated deluge, risks the loss of her self; the active and creative quester, in assuming the power to shape and to realize her divine expectation, risks the loss of everything but herself. Dickinson cannot quell her suspicion that the integration over which the self presides is only a wishful fabrication dreamed up to disguise her absolute detachment from her true object, an assertion of tyrannical mastery whose achievement is forgery, devaluation, and failure. That any relation between the self and the divine presupposes the vanquishment of one by the other is the bitter implication of "I make His Crescent fill or lack—."

> I make his Crescent fill or lack—
> His Nature is at Full
> Or Quarter—as I signify—
> His Tides—do I control—
> He holds superior in the Sky
> Or gropes, at my Command
> Behind inferior Clouds—or round
> A Mist's slow Colonnade—
> But since We hold a Mutual Disc—
> And front a Mutual Day—
> Which is the Despot, neither knows—
> Nor whose—the Tyranny—

The third stanza betrays the epistemological groundlessness of the speaker's claim to cosmic power in the first two; perhaps she has been so thoroughly consumed into "His Nature" that she has lost the ability even to distinguish her own impotence from His power. Neither alternative, however, is satisfactory. The possession of the divine that may be achieved by casting God as a puppet, or as a grovelling and insignificant lover, is either an illusory or a grotesquely empty one. Merely to entertain the possibility of such possession, as this poem does, is to cast doubt upon the existence of the divine as anything more than a construct of the creative will ("Which is the Despot, *neither knows—*").

The union of the self and the divine, imperiling the one with annihilation and the other with devaluation, occurs less often in Dickinson's poetry than does the failed attempt at it. Such failure is often maddeningly slight—so slight that sometimes it is almost taken for success. "The Brain—is wider than the Sky—" and "deeper than the sea—," the first two stanzas of poem "632" announce, because it can "contain" and "absorb" them. Upon these preliminary assertions Dickson sets her ultimate claim.

> The Brain is just the weight of God—
> For—Heft them—Pound for Pound—
> And they will differ—if they do—
> As Syllable from Sound—

There is, as Robert Weisbuch notes, a rather weighty irony in the qualifying phrase, "if they do." The difference between "Sound" and "Syllable" is, in his words, "the difference between the thing itself and its imperfect, itemized explanation." Syllables "absorb" and "contain" sound, just as the brain absorbs the sea and contains the sky; but such mastery, as the poem's last two lines subversively intimate, may constitute loss.

When Dickinson sees her poetic quest for contact with a supreme reality as a series of inevitable failures on the verge of success, poetry itself becomes a sadomasochistic exercise in temptation and denial, a counterfeit of possibility—or, to borrow an early poem's striking phrase, "A Diagram—of Rapture!" ("184"). This vision generates the mingled viciousness and anguish of such poems as the following:

> To One denied to drink
> To tell what Water is
> Would be acuter, would it not
> Than letting Him surmise?
> To lead Him to the Well
> And let Him hear it drip
> Remind Him, would it not, somewhat
> Of His condemned lip?

Poetry's evocative power is tremendous, but what it evokes, finally, is a tremendous illusion. The word never substantiates itself; the idea only mimics the thing or summons it as an absence. "Talk with prudence to a Beggar / Of 'Potosi,' and the mines!" one self-incriminating poem warns; for the convergence of powerful illusion with consciousness of illusion may be maddening, or even fatal.

> Cautious, hint to any Captive
> You have passed enfranchised feet!
> Anecdotes of air in Dungeons
> Have sometimes proved deadly sweet!

The liberating possibilities of language neither eradicate nor are eradicated by human limitations. Both captive and enfranchised quester, the poet must breathe a toxic mixture of "Anecdotes of air" and "air in Dungeons."

The poet's language, then, both renders imminent her quest's object and betrays her detachment from it. "'Heaven'—is what I cannot reach!" begins one poem whose eleven subsequent lines nonetheless generate images with which the speaker reaches toward it, images which "decoy" "The credulous" and keep them "Enamored—of the Conjuror—/ That spurned us—Yesterday!" ("239") Dickinson stands uneasily between "The credulous" and "the Conjuror" as the representative of both. The maker of images and arguments to answer her own need to believe, she cannot but suspect at times that she is the only conjuror and that her entire enterprise amounts to a magnificent decoy.

> I know that He exists.
> Somewhere—in Silence—
> He has hid his rare life
> From our gross eyes.
> 'Tis an instant's play.
> 'Tis a fond Ambush—
> Just to make Bliss
> Earn her own surprise!
> But—should the play
> Prove piercing earnest—
> Should the glee—glaze—
> In Death's—stiff—stare—
> Would not the fun
> Look too expensive!
> Would not the jest—
> Have crawled too far!

Here, the game of hide-and-seek is introduced to reconcile the poet's faith in God (the rare period after line 1 provides necessary reinforcement) with her utter lack of evidence. The perfect and benevolent reason of His choice to hide "his rare life" until she has somewhat rarefied her perception is comforting at first. But, once she has had to account for God as the player of a part in a game of her own earnest invention, the possibility soon presents itself that that part is His sole reality. The painfully alliterative third stanza enacts the hardening of metaphor into fact, of temporary attitude into permanent lifelessness. The absence of pronouns in stanzas three and four effects a debased merger of poet and God; both participate in a cruel jest and both fall victim to it. Lively belief, discovering its involvement with artifice, can give way almost instantly in Dickinson's poems to staring emptiness, like the cheap and ephemeral splendor of a travelling circus.

> I've known a Heaven, like a Tent—
> To wrap its shining Yards—
> Pluck up its stakes, and disappear—
> Without the sound of Boards
> Or rip of Nail—Or Carpenter—
> But just the miles of Stare—
> That signalize a Show's Retreat—
> In North America—

Contact on any terms becomes desirable when the poetic quest for reality repeatedly ends in frustration. Even a false faith may be contemplated—"Better an ignis fatuus / Than no illume at all—" ("1551")—and Dickinson may knowingly attempt to generate sustaining fictions, "to think a lonelier Thing / Than any I had seen—," for instance, in order to provide herself the "Haggard Comfort" of an imagined companion ("532"). But such fictions merely enable their maker to feel more keenly the lack that gives rise to them: "Conjecturing a Climate / Of unsuspended Suns—/ Adds poignancy to Winter—" ("562"). In these moods, truth seems to inhere only in pain and death.

> I like a look of Agony,
> Because I know it's true—
> Men do not sham Convulsion,
> Nor simulate, a Throe—
> The Eyes glaze once—and that is Death—
> Impossible to feign
> The Beads upon the Forehead
> By homely Anguish strung.

Not even the image of death, however, bespeaks certain truth. Life does imitate death and death feigns life in a number of Dickinson's poems—"It was not Death, for I stood up" ("510"), "I breathed enough to take the Trick—" ("272"), "A Wounded Deer—leaps highest—" ("165"), and "She lay as if at play" ("369"), to name several—nor can a typological view of such interplay put things securely in order. Typology, Dickinson understands even as she employs it, no matter how faultless or sublime, remains a kind of metaphor, a literary device. The highest reality still must be imagined; and, once imagined, its basis solely in imagination, in fiction, becomes all too clear. This is the paradox that perhaps most centrally preoccupies American literature. The attempt to locate an essential reality and the true foundation of selfhood by means of imagination and language fails by claiming to succeed; the very sources of its power guarantee against its consummation.

That Dickinson's quest continues under these recognized circumstances seems to betray a self-deception on her part, a strategic blindness adopted to sustain her visionary enterprise. This self-deception, however, if it can be labelled as such at all, is of a peculiarly conscious and self-exposing variety. "In insecurity to lie / Is Joy's insuring quality" ("1434"), Dickinson wryly and relentlessly insists. For her, perseverance toward a supreme and unexampled truth requires not that one delude oneself as to language's adequacy or imagination's innate legitimacy, but that one proceed as if they were, or could prove, adequate and legitimate, even while questioning or mocking such procedure. (Ironically, the element of self-doubt or self-mockery tends to preserve the questing self of Dickinson's poetry from the devastation of complete integration with or detachment from its object.) Dickinson's consciousness of her imaginative vision's susceptibility to delusion, then, no more cancels her commitment to the vision than the commitment cancels her consciousness.

The willingness ultimately to be deceived is a requisite for true faith, and faith alone is a more powerful argument when the consciousness that it may foster a delusion presses sensibly against its surface. Understanding this, Dickinson may reaffirm her enterprise as she confesses its insubstantiality.

> Could Hope inspect her Basis
> Her Craft were done—
> Has a fictitious Charter
> Or it has none—

The double vision, projection and reflection, that hope cannot endure is maintained in Dickinson's poetry. Dickinson *does* inspect hope's basis without relinquishing all hope or repudiating her craft. Her art deliberately exposes its artificiality; it admits its fictitious charter and proceeds to found itself squarely upon it.

> Taking up the fair Ideal,
> Just to cast her down
> When a fracture—we discover—
> Or a splintered Crown—
> Makes the Heavens portable—
> And the Gods—a lie—
> Doubtless—"Adam"—scowled at Eden—
> For *his* perjury!
> Cherishing—our poor Ideal—
> Till in purer dress—

We behold her—glorified—
Comforts ~~search~~—like this—
Till the broken creatures—
We adored—for whole—
Stains—all washed—
Transfigured—mended—
Meet us—with a smile—

Whenever we take up our ideal, Dickinson suggests, whenever we clearly view the object of our quest, we perceive it to be flawed. Its flaw, however, reflects our own limitation or failure.

"Doubtless—'Adam'—scowled at Eden—/ For *his* perjury!" Only by the enactment of a conscious fiction, therefore, may our proper ideality and the ideality of our ideal be restored: the adoration of "broken creatures—/ ... for whole—" leads to their transfiguration. Encountering our ideal in faith, we soon find it to have assumed new splendor; "washed," "mended" and "in purer dress," it bestows upon us an ambiguous smile which seems at once beatific and conspiratorial.

Source: Evan Carton, "Dickinson and the Divine: The Terror of Integration, the Terror of Detachment," in *ESQ: A Journal of the American Renaissance*, Vol. 24, No. 4, 1978, pp. 242–52.

Gilbert P. Voigt

In the following essay, Voigt explores the religious and spiritual beliefs that Dickinson held. Many of these beliefs are apparent in "I Died for Beauty."

Thomas Carlyle once remarked that "the chief thing about a man is his religion; and until we know what a man thinks and believes about religion and God, we do not know that man." Hence, any attempt to understand the fascinating but baffling Thrush of Amherst must take account of her religious attitude and creed. It is difficult to determine these, chiefly because of her strange contradictions and startling inconsistencies; her cries of doubt and her confessions of faith; her petulant indictments of God and her confiding appeals to him. One moment she is not sure there is another life; another time she is certain of it. On one occasion she accuses God of duplicity; on another, she expresses "perfect confidence in ... his promises." Sometimes he seems a cruel enemy; again, an infinitely tender friend. In one mood she considers our universe impossible and cruel; in another, she finds human life ecstatically beautiful.

Any Lowell once suggested that these contradictions in Emily Dickinson were due to her

> **SHE WAS A MYSTIC ALSO IN THE RELIGIOUS SENSE OF THE TERM—A CHRISTIAN MYSTIC."**

dual nature, which made her at once a pagan and a "sincerely religious woman." Inherently she was a pagan; by training she had been made religious.

But was Emily Dickinson by nature a pagan? That is, was she irreligious? Some of her utterances seem to show that she was jestingly irreverent. She addresses the Almighty as "Papa above," "our hospitable old neighbor," "the Jehovah who never takes a nap." She even accuses God of unkindness in refusing her prayer for the relief of another's pain and of injustice in excluding Moses from the Promised Land. But we must remember that she was by nature mischievous with a "vein of pert and bubbling rascality" and a penchant for playful and good-natured banter. Hence her picture of the Puritan heaven:

Because it's Sunday all the time
And recess never comes;
And Eden'll be so lonesome
Bright Wednesday afternoons.

At times she was petulant and pouting—in short, childish. She liked to regard herself somewhat kittenishly as God's "old-fashioned, naughty" little girl. She is a striking illustration of the "superficial tendency toward irreverence," which, as Joseph Wood Krutch has pointed out, overlies "the fundamental earnestness of the American character."

But Emily Dickinson was not always childish. Usually she was childlike. Her faith was as simple and as strong as that of a child:

Savior! I've no one else to tell
    And so I trouble Thee,
I am the one forgot Thee so.
    Dost Thou remember me?

When her good friend J. G. Holland died, she consolingly reminded Mrs. Holland that her husband had been on "childlike terms with the Father in Heaven," and that he had "passed from confiding to comprehending." Her own faith was equally confiding; it was a bridge without piers, which bore her bold soul over its "unshakeable span of steel to the mysterious, yet certain Isles of the Blest." In the midst of sorrow and hardships she could feel the hand of her Heavenly Father:

> Far from love the Heavenly Father
>   Leads the chosen child;
> Oftener through realm of briar
>   Than the meadow mild,
>
> Oftener by the claw of dragon
>   Than the hand of friend,
> Guides the little one predestined
>   To the native land.

She could be sure that

> Not one by Heaven defrauded stay.
>   Although He seem to steal,
> He restitutes in some sweet way
>   Secreted in His will.

These are not the utterances of a pagan in either sense of the word.

Carl Sandburg has given Emily Dickinson the felicitous title, "the impish and mystic singer of Amherst." And indeed she was a mystic. First, in the philosophical sense of the term.

> By intuition mightiest things
> Assert themselves, and not by terms.

This was her belief. She was not a logician or a systematic philosopher. Her flashes of intuition were as disconnected as Emerson's.

She was a mystic also in the religious sense of the term—a Christian mystic. Her knowledge of the Triune God was intuitive; she felt his presence constantly. Sometimes he seemed to be a next-door neighbor; at other times, a guest:

> The Soul that has a Guest,
> Doth seldom go abroad,
> Diviner Crowd at home
> Obliterate the need . . .

Occasionally she was caught up into the seventh heaven, like Paul, and permitted a vision of "the colossal substance of immortality." Now and then she felt herself united to God in immortal wedlock:

> Bride of the Father and the Son,
> Bride of the Holy Ghost.

Like other mystics, she emphasized the beauty of God. Human life she found "all aglow with God and immortality." So her sister-in-law has told us. "Her garden was full of His brightness and glory; the birds sang and the sky glowed because of Him." Thus Mrs. Mabel Loomis Todd has written.

But, like other mystics again, Emily Dickinson rejected accepted beliefs and practices: her heaven was not the one "the creeds bestow." The doctrine of original sin she held to be false. Of conversion she felt no need, and her pastor assured her parents that the usual process of conversion was not necessary for her. As for the Bible, she accepted only those parts her experience confirmed.

There is a fairly close parallel between Emily Dickinson and St. Teresa. Both had frail bodies. Both had literary genius. Both were aristocrats. Both were "romantic and ardent." Both were torn between two worlds. Both disliked pretension and spiritual conceit. Both were witty and full of fun. Both were angels of mercy. Both had a direct experience of God.

But mystical as she was, Emily Dickinson did not ignore the needs and claims of the intellect. Indeed, she thanked God for "these strange minds" of ours, even if they do at times turn us against him, even though at the sight of human suffering they look to him with "confiding revulsion." She believed that "faith is doubt"; that our dull human eyes cannot see clearly the spiritual and the supernatural:

> Not "Revelation" 'tis that waits,
> But our unfurnished eyes.

Emily Dickinson's theology may be reduced to three dogmas, her creed to three articles. The first is her belief in the essential beauty and goodness of human life and of the earth. To this extent she was something of a pagan. Her religion was one of joy and beauty and happiness. Her church was a sunny orchard; her chorister a blithe bobolink; her preacher the bright and glorious God himself. Except for death, which snatched her loved ones away, it was "heaven below"; even with suffering and sorrow, there was a predominance of bliss.

The second article of Emily Dickinson's creed is the beneficent power of suffering. Although the sight of pain she could not relieve made of her "a demon," yet she attempted to see the reason and the good in human suffering. She decided that it was God's means of making happiness all the brighter by contrast, of refining and enlightening mankind.

> Must be a woe,
> A loss or so,
> To bend the eye
> Best beauty's way.
>
> . . .

A common bliss
Were had for less;
The price—is
Even as the Grace.

The mysterious path of pain she considered
but the way

With many a turn and thorn
That stops at Heaven.

And if the problem of suffering is beyond
our present power of solution, some day "Christ
will explain each separate anguish" and will provide in Heaven an abundant compensation for
all the sufferings of earth: "What a recompense!
The enthusiasm of God at the reception of His
sons! How ecstatic! How infinite!"

For the third article of Emily Dickinson's
creed is her deep and abiding faith in the immortality of the soul. Toward the close of her shel-
tered life, as the company of her departed loved
ones grew larger and larger, she seemed to live
more with them than with her relatives and
friends on earth. And in her last illness her
thoughts turned constantly to Heaven. "I live
in the sea always now," she remarked to her
beloved Sister Sue, "and know the road."

Not satisfied with her intuitive awareness of
eternity, she was fond of speculating on its
nature. She likened it to an infinite series of seas:

As if the sea should part
And show a further sea
And that a further, and the three
But a presumption be
Of periods of seas
Unvisited of shores—
Themselves the verge of seas to be—
Eternity is these.

Though she had rebelled against the Calvinistic faith of her parents, Emily Dickinson did
not turn to Unitarianism, as did Oliver Wendell
Holmes, or to Episcopalianism, as did Harriet
Beecher Stowe. Nor did she become an agnostic
like Francis Parkman, or an unbeliever like William Dean Howells. She retained her religious
faith, mystical and individualistic as it was. She
suggests the Transcendentalists, but the parallel
must not be pressed. As in other respects, so in
her inner life, she was *sui generis*.

Source: Gilbert P. Voigt, "The Inner Life of Emily Dickinson," in *College English*, Vol. 3, No. 2, November 1941,
pp. 192–96.

Francis H. Stoddard

*In the following letter, Stoddard offers a rebuttal
to an earlier* Critic *review of Dickinson's poetry.
Focusing specifically on "I Died for Beauty" in his
argument, Stoddard attempts to prove that the
poem is not formless despite the fact that it does
not adhere to traditional poetic forms.*

To the Editors of *The Critic*:—

In your issue of Dec. 19 an evidently compe-
tent reviewer refers to the first volume of Miss
Dickinson's poems [*Poems by Emily Dickinson*],
issued a year ago, as a 'volume of curiously formless poems,' and suggests that the fact of the
issuance of several editions proves 'that a great
many persons care little for the form of expression in poetry so long as the thoughts expressed
are startling, eccentric and new.' In the same
review the critic says of the two volumes taken
together that 'their absolute formlessness keeps
them almost outside the pale of poetry.' The
thought here seems to be that real poetry must
have perfection of technique, must have metrical
and grammatical finish: the poems of Emily
Dickinson do not have such finish; hence these
verses are almost out of the pale of poetry. The
major premise here set down has not been
attacked of late. The minor one is not so easily
disposed of. For Miss Dickinson's poems may be
formless, or they may be worded to so fine and
subtle a device that they seem formless, just as
the spectrum of a far-off star may seem blankness
until examined with a lens of especial power. I
wish to examine one poem of Miss Dickinson's,
taken almost at random, and search for the fine
lines of the spectrum. For such example I take
this poem ["*I died for beauty, but was scarce*"]:—

I died for beauty, but was scarce
  Adjusted in the tomb,
When one who died for truth was lain
  In an adjoining room.
He questioned, softly, why I failed?
  For beauty; I replied.
And I for truth,—the two are one;
  We brethren are; he said.
And so as kinsman met a night,
  We talked between the rooms,
    Until the moss had reached our lips,
And covered up our names.

Now the notion here is the notion of the
unity of truth and beauty. If harmony with the
thought is to prevail in the verse we should
expect a closely parallel structure with a figure
in dual accent—*i.e.*, based upon two factors.
Such a figure we get:—

I died' for beauty, but was scarce
  Adjusted' in the tomb',
When one who died' for truth' was lain
  In an adjoin'ing room'.

Two pairs of lines, each with two accents, the similar words being matched in pairs—'*justed*': *joining*', *died*': *died*', *tomb*': *room*'. *Beauty*' and *truth*' do not perfectly match, of course, because not yet proved to be one in nature. These exact correspondences would produce mechanical regularity and overprove the proposition by overemphasizing the innate notion of harmony, if care were not taken. So care is taken to contrast the positions of the members of the separate pars. That is, in the first line, the slurred words *but was scarce* are at the end, while in the corresponding line the slurred words *when one who* are at the beginning. Similarly, the slurred words *in the* in the second line are contrasted in position with the slurred words *in an* in the fourth line.

In the second stanza we have a more perfectly parallel figure, in accord with the development of the notion of harmony between truth and beauty.

He questioned', softly', why' I failed'?
  For beauty'; I replied'.
And I'—for truth'—the two' are one',
  We brethren' are; he said'.

Almost a formal balancing, but with a suggestion of relief; as, for example, in the harmonic echo of *he questioned*', in the opening line, with *We brethren*', in the closing line, suggesting a recurrence of the first verse motive.

In the last verse comes the deeper verity that though truth and beauty are one spiritually, they can never be at one in this world. So at the close the pattern changes and together with the hint of the attainment of perfect harmony we have a reversion both in form and tone. It is a suggestion of the death reversion which springs the thought to a harmony more subtle and remote.

And so as kinsmen' met a night',
  We talked' between the rooms',
Until the moss' had reached our lips'
And covered' up our names'.

The rhyme changes to alliteration which is beginning-rhyme instead of end-rhyme—*night*: *names*. That is, our earthly names are lost in the endless night of death; ourselves, at one with each other, at one with truth and beauty, entered into the endless day of beauty and of truth.

I submit that such art as this may be subtle and mediaval, but it is not formlessness.

Source: Francis H. Stoddard, "Technique in Emily Dickinson's Poems," in *Critic*, Vol. 17, No. 516, January 9, 1892, pp. 24–25.

SOURCES

Allison, Alexander W., et al, eds., "Emily Dickinson," in *The Norton Anthology of Poetry*, Norton, 1983, pp. 804–16.

Dickinson, Emily, *The Complete Poems*, www.bartleby.com/113/ (accessed October 17, 2007).

———, "I Died for Beauty," in *The Complete Poems of Emily Dickinson*, edited by Thomas H. Johnson, Back Bay, 1976.

Harmon, William, and Hugh Holman, eds., "Realistic Period in American Literature, 1865–1900," in *A Handbook to Literature*, Prentice Hall, 2003, pp. 422–23.

Hendrickson, Paula, "Dickinson and the Process of Death," in *Dickinson Studies*, Vol. 77, 1991, pp. 33–43.

"Poems by Emily Dickinson," in the *Nation*, No. 1326, November 27, 1890, p. 423.

"The Poems of Emily Dickinson," in *Critic*, Vol. 14, No. 363, December 13, 1890, pp. 305–306.

Ransom, John Crowe, "Emily Dickinson: A Poet Restored," in *Emily Dickinson: A Collection of Critical Essays*, edited by Richard Sewall, Prentice Hall, 1963, pp. 88–100.

Reeves, James, "Emily Dickinson: Overview," in *Reference Guide to American Literature*, edited by Jim Kamp, St. James Press, 1994.

FURTHER READING

Angelo, Raymond, Leslie A. Morris, Richard B. Sewall, and Judith Farr, *Emily Dickinson's Herbarium: A Facsimile Edition*, Belknap Press, 2006.

> Dickinson began gardening and preserving samples as a teenager. This is a copy of the book where she pressed flowers and herbs, complete with labels and comments.

Bradbury, Malcolm, and Richard Ruland, *From Puritanism to Postmodernism: A History of American Literature*, Penguin, 1992.

> Considered a readable overview of American history, this volume follows the styles of, and reactions to, literature from the earliest days of America up to 1990. Dickinson is given consideration in the author's analysis.

Lundin, Roger, *Emily Dickinson and the Art of Belief*, William B. Eerdmans, 2004.

> Lundin brings together biographical information and Dickinson's poems to explore the poet's Christianity and personal religious beliefs.

Sea Rose

H.D.

1916

"Sea Rose," written by Hilda Doolittle, more commonly referred to by her pen name, H.D., was first published in 1916 and was included in H.D.'s *Sea Garden*, her first collection of poetry. This poem is one of the most popular poems in this first collection and has been frequently anthologized. In "Sea Rose," H.D. rejects the traditional image of the rose as a symbol of feminine beauty and love, and instead provides an image of a flawed and stunted rose enveloped in the sea. This reversal of expected images also suggests why H.D. is regarded as important in any discussion of modern feminist poetry. Her poem suggests that neither the rose, nor a woman, must be perfect to be appreciated. H.D. is perhaps the best known of the Imagist poets, who were followers of Ezra Pound's ideas about a new style of poetry that was direct, concise, and relied mostly on imagery to communicate its message. Indeed, H.D.'s "Sea Rose" is representative of how concise language can be used to create images from words. "Sea Rose" is also included in a collection of her poetry, *H.D. Selected Poems*, published in 1957. The third edition of *The Norton Anthology of Modern and Contemporary Poetry*, published in 2003, contains a selection of H.D.'s poetry, including "Sea Rose."

AUTHOR BIOGRAPHY

H.D. was born Hilda Doolittle on September 10, 1886 in Bethlehem, Pennsylvania. She was one of

H.D. (Hilda Doolittle) *(AP Images)*

six children and the only daughter to survive infancy. Her father, Charles Doolittle, was a professor of mathematics and astronomy, and her mother, Helen, taught art and music at a local seminary. H.D. studied classical and modern language in high school and attended Bryn Mawr only briefly before leaving college in 1906. While at Bryn Mawr, she became friends with poets Marianne Moore and William Carlos Williams. As a teenager, H.D. had been romantically involved with the poet Ezra Pound, to whom she was briefly engaged. Although the two did not marry, H.D. later followed Pound to London, where he introduced her to a literary circle of friends, including D. H. Lawrence, May Sinclair, W. B. Yeats, and Richard Aldington, whom H.D. married in 1913. Several of her poems were published in *Poetry* magazine in 1913, in large part thanks to Pound's efforts. These poems were published under the name H.D. Imagiste, a word coined by Pound to describe H.D.'s Imagism poetry, in which a concise and precise selection of words is used to create images. H.D.'s earliest published poems were very popular and she became the best known representative of the Imagism movement.

Her success as a writer did not, however, ensure happiness in her private life. H.D.'s first pregnancy ended in a stillbirth in 1915, a year before the publication of her first collection of poetry, *Sea Garden*, in which the poem "Sea Rose" appears. H.D. and Aldington separated in 1918, just before the birth of a daughter in 1919. After her marriage ended, H.D. began to live with the novelist Annie Winifred Ellerman, who used the pseudonym, Bryher, for her novels. The two women moved to Lake Geneva in 1920, which continued to be their home throughout the remainder of H.D.'s life. Several collections of poetry published in the 1920s enhanced H.D.'s reputation as an Imagist poet. In addition, *Hymen* (1921), *Heliodora, and Other Poems* (1924), and *Collected Poems of H.D.* (1925) also firmly established H.D. as an important figure in modern feminist poetry. In the 1930s, H.D. began an extended period of psychoanalysis with Sigmund Freud, during which she lived in seclusion in Switzerland.

Although she published infrequently in the 1930s, in the mid 1940s H.D. began a period of more intense work, with the publication of a war trilogy: *The Walls Do Not Fall* (1944), *Tribute to the Angels* (1945) and *The Flowering of the Rod* (1946). H.D.'s last major poetic work was *Helen in Egypt*, published a month after her death in Switzerland on September 27, 1961. During her career, she published poetry, novels, and drama. H.D. won the Guarantors Prize from *Poetry* magazine in 1915, the Brandeis University Creative Arts Medal in 1959 for lifetime achievement, and the Award of Merit Medal for poetry from the National Institute and American Academy of Arts and Letters in 1960.

POEM SUMMARY

Stanza 1

"Sea Rose" begins with a contradiction of both literary and romantic custom. Traditionally, roses are emblematic of romance and beauty. Countless poets have compared a woman's beauty to that of a rose. H.D. reverses the expected and begins her poem with the line, "Rose, harsh rose." Rather than softness and velvety delicacy as would be expected of the rose, this sea rose is hardened, rough, more austere than its cousin, the long-established English rose. This rose is "marred," imperfect and spoiled by its "stint of petals." Rather than a glorious flower with abundant petals, this rose has been blighted and is lacking in its allotment of petals; instead, a "meagre flower" results. H.D. uses only a few words to paint a picture of the sea rose, with its "thin" flower and "sparse" leaves. Rather than the perfect rose of literary tradition, the sea rose is described by words that create an image of blooms too paltry and scanty to fulfill the expected icon of the rose as a symbol love, feminine beauty, and fragile loveliness. This first stanza also suggests that the poet's idea of beauty is not the traditional English garden, of which the rose is the centerpiece, renowned for its beauty. Instead, this poet's rose is wild, stunted, and totally resistant to the severity of life that batters it.

Stanza 2

To the poet, however, this sea rose, though flawed and seemingly incomplete, is "more precious" for its imperfections. The contrast in the next two lines is the customary long-stemmed beauty, which so many lovers embrace as a tool to woo young women. This is the "rose" encased in water and a vase, the "single on a stem" beauty so vividly associated with romantic love. In contrast, the sea rose is "caught in the drift" of the sea, floating in the water and churned by the sea. Its survival in the harsh sea reveals its strength. This is no delicate rose, unable to survive when buffeted about. This sea rose, defined by its lack of beauty and its ability to survive being tossed by the sea is a metaphor for the poet, who is able to withstand life's painful challenges. The year before the publication of "Sea Rose," H.D. was pregnant with her first child, but the pregnancy ended in a stillbirth. Rather than the image of fragility and delicate beauty that is expected in a poem about a rose, H.D. embraces strength and an ability to survive painful events, no matter how difficult the process.

Stanza 3

The third stanza begins the second complete sentence of the poem with the observance that the sea rose is "stunted," having been flung from the sea upon the sand. With its "small leaf," it is easy prey for the coastal winds that lift the sea rose and "crisp" grains of sand, with ease. The rose, now wet from being carried in the sea, is contrasted with the sand, whose crispness describes both the cold of the sand and its crusty, often brittle nature. The rose is able to endure even when buffeted by strong winds. The use of the word "drives" suggests the fierceness of the wind that tosses the rose, which was "flung" from the sea in which it floated onto the sand, with its abrasive ability to wear down

whatever touches it. Sandpaper derives its name from the feel of sand on a beach, and yet sandpaper is capable of wearing away even hard wood. The poet juxtapositions the rose, as victim of the rushing sea and the harsh sands, and still it survives, with its meager petals and small leaves intact.

Stanza 4

In the final three lines, the poet does not waste a single word. With the same brevity of language that offered only sharp words of description, such as "harsh," "marred," and "meagre," the poet returns to the comparison between the sea rose and the romantic rose of poetry. The smell of the perfect lover's rose is one of the most cherished aspects of this flower. The rose smell is so essential that the rose given by a cherished lover is often pressed between sheets of tissue paper, preserved as a memory forever, its "spice" scent intensifying as it dries. The rose smell is so valued that its scent is often duplicated in perfumes. In contrast, the sea rose with its "acrid fragrance" is even more valued. Its scent did not come easily, a gift from a generous nature that imbues the lover's rose with its sometimes cloying scent. Instead, the scent of the sea rose emerges from its "hardened" existence, a byproduct of its survival. This same rose was "lifted" by the sea, whose strength carried it ashore. Its scent is "acrid," pungent, perhaps bitter. All its strength goes to surviving. The sea rose lacks the safety of the lover's cherished handling, the perfect vase to protect and nurture its "spice-rose" beauty. Instead, the sea rose has no extra vigor to give to values of beauty and scent. The sea rose, like H.D., is a survivor. Although buffeted by waves and wind, the rose survives the challenges it faces. In the last line, it becomes clear that the sea rose is a "hardened" victor, that has survived.

THEMES

Disillusionment

The beginning of the twentieth century and World War I brought about the end of Romantic sentimentality in literature, which had lingered even through the Victorian Age. World War I changed the face of literature. H.D. lived in England during this period, where the impact of war was keenly felt. The events of World War I brought about a period of disillusionment and pessimism. The glory of fighting for the Empire

TOPICS FOR FURTHER STUDY

- One of the best ways to learn about poetic form is to write poetry. Place yourself in H.D.'s poetic tradition, and using her poem as a guide, write at least one or two poems that imitate both her style, language use, and content. When you have completed your poems, write a brief evaluation of your work, comparing it to H.D.'s poems. In your written critique of your poems, consider what you learned about the difficulty of writing Imagist poetry.

- Visual artists are often inspired by poetry. Spend some time looking through art books in the library and try to select a picture or illustration that you feel best illustrates H.D.'s poem. Then, in a carefully worded essay, compare the art that you have selected to "Sea Rose."

- Women's lives were undergoing a period of transition in the second decade of the twentieth century. Indeed, women were striving for more freedom and in some cases rejecting traditional patriarchal expectations. Research the suffrage movement (in which women sought the right to vote) that defined this historical period and prepare an oral presentation that focuses on the women who were essential to this movement.

- Many scholars compare H.D.'s poetry to that of the Greek poet, Sappho. In an essay, compare H.D.'s poem to one of Sappho's poems. Include quotations from each poet's work and be prepared to discuss how each poet uses language to create images.

---

was replaced by the reality of dying in trenches. The brutality of war was made significantly worse by the use of airplanes, which made aerial bombing more commonplace. The use of mustard gas and the torpedoing of the Lusitania led to huge numbers of casualties. H.D.'s husband, Aldington, volunteered for the army, and her beloved brother, Gilbert, died during World

War I. World War I made clear that the heroism of war was only an ideal that did not exist in modern warfare. H.D. captures this rejection of sentimentalism in "Sea Rose." The sea rose is not the lover's gift of sweet scent, nor is it an offering of seduction to woo a woman. Instead the sea rose is a flawed beauty that, though harsh and acrid, marred and meagre, still survives being buffeted by the sea and wind. This rose is no fragile sentimental beauty to be pressed between tissue paper and saved for lingering daydreams. In this poem, H.D. rejects the sentimental view of a world so obviously flawed by pain and hatred. Although lacking the sentimental beauty of the garden rose, the sea rose proves able to withstand the reality of life, which is often cruel and filled with pain, just as war proved to be even more cruel than could be imagined.

Rejection of Feminine Perfection

In "Sea Rose," the poet rejects the notion that a flower must attain perfection to be valued. Rather than an exacting number of petals and leaves, with glorious fullness and a scent that adds to its beauty, H.D.'s sea rose is described with a series of adjectives that rebuff the established ideas about floral beauty. H.D.'s rose is "harsh," "marred," "meagre," "sparse," and "stunted." The rose is also a time-honored representative of feminine beauty. The literary tradition in poetry has a history of describing women as willowy as a long-stemmed rose, with cheeks that blush like the pinkest rose, of lips that are full with the crimson color of roses, and even bosoms that are pale like the whitest rose. H.D.'s rejection of this idealism suggests that images of feminine perfection can be similarly rejected in favor of the realistic depiction of beauty. The freedom of the sea rose to go where ever the sea or winds take it is a freedom lacking for women. With this poem, H.D. rejects the conventional ideas that govern women's lives. There is no need to be perfect and no limitations to rule women's lives. Though wild, women are "more precious" than their domestic counterparts. Real women can be imperfect and they can have value, even when they lack the "spice-rose" of the protected and carefully cultivated garden rose.

Survival

"Sea Rose" is a poem whose brevity of language still manages to create an image of survival and strength in sixteen very short lines. Although the sea rose lacks the beauty of the conventional garden rose, the poem still suggests that the sea

---

rose has value separate from the more conventional domestic rose. The sea rose is "lifted" by the blowing sand, rather than lying battered on the shore. This symbol of survival parallels H.D.'s own survival of the stillbirth of her first child in 1915. H.D. rejects the fragility of a world where the rose is perceived as a delicate symbol of love and beauty. In its place, she embraces a world where a "stunted" flower can be pounded by waves and wind and still survive. The sea rose is strong enough to be "lifted" by the blowing sand and still retain a sense of self, clearly defined by the label: rose. Like H.D., herself, the sea rose will survive no matter how battered. The sea rose is "hardened" by all that it has experienced and its scent, though acrid, is still preferred over the scent of the domestic rose, whose endurance has not been tested.

STYLE

Avant Garde

Avant Garde refers to writing that reveals new and innovative ideas and style. The term can be used to refer to either form or subject. The term derives from a French military metaphor that designates a frontal attack. In literature, then, the term suggests that the writer is attacking literary traditions and creating something inventive and original. H.D.'s poem is *Avant Garde* because of the poet's reliance on Imagist techniques and because the subject rejects traditional ideas about roses as iconic symbols of femininity and romantic love.

Free Verse

Free verse is verse with no discernable structure, rhyme scheme, or meter. Free verse allows the poet to fit the poetic line to the content of the poem. The poet is not restricted by the need to shape the poem to a particular meter but can instead create complex rhythm and syntax. Free verse is not the same as blank verse, which also does not use a rhyme scheme. Blank verse almost always adheres to iambic pentameter, while free verse relies on line breaks to create a rhythm. Free verse is most often associated with modern poetry, as it is with H.D.'s poem. There is no pattern of rhyme or meter to "Sea Rose." Instead, the irregular line breaks give the poem more of a sing-song rhythm that is best appreciated by reading it aloud. In this poem, H.D. does not adhere to any standardized meter; nor are the stanzas exactly the same. H.D. creates her own meaning using concise, clear language that does not waste words.

Imagism

Imagism is a style of poetry that was created by a group of poets during the second decade of the twentieth century. H.D. was one of the originating poets who created this style. The Imagist style uses common ordinary language and exact, concise word choice to create an image. Imagist poets reject formulaic language and conventional topics, as well as fixed rhymes and meter. Imagists also embraced the notion of exact imagery that was harsh and unexpected. "Sea Rose," is an example of Imagist poetry. The sparse use of language, with exacting descriptive word choice that create images that are unexpected, such as the "harsh," "meager" rose, captures the Imagist principles. H.D.'s poem also rejects established ideas about rhyme and meter that had long governed poetry. "Sea Rose," contains no rhyme scheme or fixed meter to define it.

Modern Poetry

The label, modern poetry, like modern novels and other forms of modern literature, refers to the poet's strong and conscious effort to break away from tradition. Modern poetry attempts to create a new world by changing perceptions of the old world. Modern literary works identify the individual as more important than either society or social conventions and privileges the mind and the poet's inward thoughts. The imagination of the poet often prefers the unconscious actions of the individual. H.D.'s poetry suggests that poets can be free of conventional ideas about romance and beauty. Her poem moves beyond typical definitions of what is pretty to privilege strength over fragility, just as modern poetry values the freedom to challenge traditions.

HISTORICAL CONTEXT

Early Twentieth-Century Feminism

In "Sea Rose," H.D. rejects traditional ideas about feminism and embraces a definition of feminism that is untamed and imperfect. The sea rose is free to go where ever the sea or winds take it. This is a freedom lacking for women, who in the early twentieth century are constrained by a society

COMPARE
&
CONTRAST

- **1910s:** The British Parliament gives women over thirty the right to vote in national elections in 1918.

  Today: The hard fought effort for suffrage has been forgotten in England and the United States, where the right of women to vote is now taken for granted.

- **1910s:** Women in Great Britain are used to recruit men to join the army and fight in the Great War. Women tell men that joining is a matter of honor.

  Today: Women are no longer used to recruit their fathers, husbands, and sons to go to war. Instead of recruiting their loved ones, women now serve as soldiers and sailors in the military.

- **1910s:** *Poetry: A Magazine of Verse* debuts in Chicago in 1912. It is one of the first magazines devoted to poetry. H.D. publishes some of her very earliest poems in *Poetry*, and other poets published in the magazine around this time include Marianne Moore, William Carlos Williams, Carl Sandburg, and Hart Crane, all of whom are now very well known and were brought to public notice through publication in *Poetry*.

  Today: Though there are now many magazines, journals, and websites that publish new poets, *Poetry* is still known for introducing new poets that go on to achieve lasting fame.

---

that places great value on women as delicate creatures in need of restraint. H.D. had moved to England in 1911 and continued to live there throughout World War I. The world in which she was living was still caught up in traditional values that limited women's lives. Prior to the beginning of World War I, women in England still lacked equality in many areas. Women still had limited opportunities to work. Domestic service continued to be a common avenue of employment open to women. Women were still not permitted to vote in national elections. Emmeline Pankhurst and her daughters had formed the Women's Franchise League in 1889 and quickly won the right for women to vote in elections for local office. By 1906, Pankhurst had established a London office, where her efforts in the suffrage movement became increasingly militant. She was repeatedly jailed and used hunger strikes to bring attention to the suffrage movement. During World War I, Pankhurst and her followers agreed to stop their protests, and the suffragettes who had been jailed were released. During this period there was little progress in the suffrage movement; however, by 1917, the British government needed to have an election. The history professor Joanna Bourke

points out in her article "Women on the Home Front in World War One" that only men who had been residents for twelve months were permitted to vote. But with so many men in Europe fighting the war, there were not enough men to vote. In order to provide enough voters for a national election, women over the age of thirty who owned land were given the right to vote in a general election. Bourke estimates that about 8.5 million women received the vote in 1918. This was the first step in granting women any rights at all. The suffrage movement that was put on hold during World War I never really regained its prewar momentum after the war ended. It would be 1928 before all women in England had the right to vote.

Women and War

World War I did offer some opportunities that freed women from the domestic sphere. Women took the jobs vacated by men, who had gone to fight the war. They worked in factories, manufacturing goods needed for the war effort. They worked farms and harvested crops, and of course, they worked as nurses to care for the wounded, both in England and near the front lines in Europe. In her article, "Women and the Military during

World War One," Bourke explains that the Women's Defence Relief Corps helped to place women in men's jobs, so that men could join the war effort. Women were also trained in a semi-military fashion to defend the home front, and they were used to recruit men to volunteer for the war, as a matter of honor. As was the case during past wars, women had more freedoms during time of war. By assuming men's work, they also assumed the freedoms that accompanied the male sphere. These working women were not paid men's salaries, though. Bourke claims that many employers divided men's jobs among several women or changed job descriptions to circumvent union rules that governed wages. Women who were active in women's rights in England thought that the Great War would change women's lives. In a sense that did happen. After the war, it was difficult to convince women to return to the lives they led before the war. Bourke claims that half of the first group of recruits for the London General Omnibus Company were former female domestic servants. Women also took clerical jobs or began working for the Civil Service. Women earned better wages than they had as domestic servants and they had more independence. However, for most women, the great hopes that World War I would lead to greater equality dissipated after the War. Women who were able to work found that they were paid less than men. The jobs that men held prior to the war were returned to men when the war ended, and most women returned to their traditional roles as wives and mothers.

CRITICAL OVERVIEW

When H.D. died in September 1961, her obituary in the *New York Times* celebrated her accomplishments by recalling the many books of poetry that she had written throughout her life. It was, according to this obituary, the publication of *Sea Garden*, H.D.'s first collection of poems, that established her reputation. The obituary writer refers to H.D.'s work as "exquisite in its deftness," and notes that she was "rated by some recent critics as the most accomplished of the Imagists." The critical comments about her work that are voiced in H.D.'s obituary were not always so flattering during her lifetime. In fact, a *New York Times* review of *Sea Garden* upon its publication in 1916 was certainly less appreciative of H.D.'s talent as a poet. Indeed, the critic writing in this review comments: "There is genuine beauty in *Sea Garden*, but it lacks

Water lily sea rose (© fl online | Alamy)

laughter." The reviewer suggests that H.D. should relax "her taut soul." According to the critic, H.D. is too much the Puritan, too strict in her depiction of nature as hostile. She would benefit more, according to the reviewer, if she were a hedonist, since the self-indulgent pursuit of happiness takes "more strength and more courage" than being a Puritan, which is too difficult to do on a consistent basis. Nevertheless, the negative opinions expressed in this 1917 review are generally uncommon. Usually, reviews of H.D.'s poetry are more mixed, with comments that both flatter and criticize.

Reviewing H.D.'s 1932 collection, *Red Roses for Bronze*, Percy Hutchison, also writing in the *New York Times*, calls H.D.'s poems "rejuvenating and magical." Hutchison refers to H.D. as a "rare lyric genius" whose "work is sculptured with all the care of a worker in marble." However, he quickly shifts to a more critical stance in comparing H.D.'s work to that of one of her contemporaries, Edna St. Vincent Millay. Hutchison claims that H.D. neglects melody in her poetry, and thus, while both Millay and H.D. will enjoy longevity as poets, Millay's poems will be read, while H.D.'s will remain on library shelves. H.D. is a poet, he says, whose technique is too "carefully studied." Regardless, Hutchison feels that H.D.'s poems can rise above their limitations and become "exquisite."

In 1957, with the publication of H.D.'s *Selected Poems*, the critical reception of the poet's work had changed dramatically. Reviewer Babette Deutsch, writing in the *New York Times*, points out that tastes in poetry changed from when H.D. first began writing. H.D.'s earliest works, once so criticized by reviewers, had since become a staple of poetry anthologies. Where earlier critics had complained that her work lacked melody, Deusch celebrates this very feature of H.D.'s poems, referring to "her lyricism" as her most "salient gift." According to Deutsch: "the reader hears a melody not only in the lines themselves but suggested by them."

Deutsch is not the only critic to celebrate H.D.'s poems. After her death, Horace Gregory's tribute, published in the *New York Times* in 1961, sought to remind readers of her talents as a writer. Gregory admires the Imagist quality of H.D.'s work, referring to her poems as "clean and direct." He also states that her "mature achievements" fulfill the "early promise" of her first poems. It is clear from both her obituary and Gregory's tribute, that after her death the critical ambiguity that had once plagued H.D.'s earlier work was replaced by admiration. Further proof of H.D.'s well-deserved place in the canon of modern poets was evident when a 1969 edition of the journal, *Contemporary Literature* was devoted to essays examining her work. Although not every essay in this issue celebrates H.D.'s poetry, the authors do have a common belief that her poetry remains relevant and worth additional study.

CRITICISM

Sheri Metzger Karmiol

Karmiol has a doctorate in English Renaissance literature. She teaches literature and drama at the University of New Mexico, where she is a lecturer in the University Honors Program. Karmiol is also a professional writer and the author of several reference texts on poetry and drama. In this essay on "Sea Rose," Karmiol examines H.D.'s poem as a celebration of unique poetic interpretations.

WHAT DO I READ NEXT?

- H.D.'s *Notes and Thought and Vision & the Wise Sappho* (1969) is a meditation on the sources of imagination and the creative process.

- *Penelope's Web: Gender, Modernity, H.D.'s Fiction* (1991), by Susan Stanford Friedman, is the study of H.D.'s prose work.

- *Winter Love: Ezra Pound and H.D.* (2003), by Jacob Korg, is a comparative study of their lives and influence upon one another's work.

- *Imagist Poetry: An Anthology*, reissued in 1999 and edited by Bob Blaisdell, was originally edited by Ezra Pound. This anthology is a collection of the poetry written by members of the Imagist movement.

- *Sleeping on the Wing: An Anthology of Modern Poetry with Essays on Reading and Writing* (1982), by Kate Farrell and Kenneth Koch, is a collection of poetry selected from the works of twenty-three modern poets. In addition to a collection of wonderful poems, the authors also provide guides to help the fledgling writer create his or her own poems.

- *Sound and Form in Modern Poetry* (2nd edition, 1996), by Harvey Gross and Robert McDowell, is a good basic text to help the student understand form and function in modern poetry. One strength of this book is its emphasis on metrical structure and stanza forms.

- *Forgotten Voices of the Great War: A History of World War I in the Words of the Men and Women Who Were There* (2004), by Max Arthur, provides firsthand accounts of World War I. H.D. lived in London during the war, and her poetry and prose writings were influenced by the suffering that the war caused.

"Sea Rose" might well serve as a metaphor for H.D., whose own life rejected conformity and tradition. Just as the sea rose is an unconventional

> THE SEA ROSE IS A SYMBOLIC REJECTION OF THE ROMANTIC IDEAL OF FEMININITY AND ROMANCE THAT THE TYPICAL DOMESTIC ROSE REPRESENTS."

adaptation of the domestic garden rose, H.D. was not representative of young women at the turn of the nineteenth century. She just did not fit well into the traditional role created for women in early twentieth-century America. She left Bryn Mawr College at age twenty without completing a degree, and she did so because she did poorly in math and English, but she did not leave to marry as so many other young women did during that period. Nor did she choose to marry in the five years after her return home. It is in her poetry that H.D. finds her identity as a poet and as a woman. As a woman poet, she transcends ordinary definitions of a woman as daughter, wife, and mother. Her poetry, like her personal life, reflects an effort to reject conventionality. "Sea Rose" rejects the expected and embraces the uncommon opportunities that present themselves, just as H.D. did in her own life.

When H.D. dropped out of college in 1906, she joined a swelling population of unmarried women, who had no real means of support beyond that provided by their families. Unmarried middle class women like H.D. were rare, though that was quickly changing. By the early twentieth century, women like H.D. were, in fact, becoming far more common in the United States. There were so many unmarried women—as many as one in four by some estimates—that society began to take notice. Indeed, women were beginning to challenge their traditional roles, and this is represented in "Sea Rose." Instead of the domestic rose with its abundance of flowers and lush smell, the sea rose is "harsh," "marred," "meagre," even "stunted." The sea rose is a symbolic rejection of the romantic ideal of femininity and romance that the typical domestic rose represents. The sea rose mirrors H.D.'s rejection of the conformity that surrounded her. In 1911 and during a visit to Europe with Josepha Frances Gregg, H.D. decided to remain in England and not return to the United States. By remaining in London, H.D. effectively rejected the conventional life that awaited her at home. With the exception of several short visits, she never lived in the United States again.

In London, H.D. became a part of the new wave of literary and poetic rebellion, where Ezra Pound introduced her to a circle of poets that included Richard Aldington, T. S. Eliot, and William Butler Yeats, all of whom saw poetry as a way to bring attention to social inequities. In her essay in *The Cambridge History of American Literature*, Irene Ramalho Santos claims that H.D. "conceived of poetry as a way of achieving social change." According to Santos, H.D. did this in a "personal and intimate way, as a subtle and troubled questioner of the culture and the tradition, and the hegemonic (male) intellect, imagination, and sensibility that sustained them." Her poem, "Sea Rose," presents this questioning of culture, as the poem probes conventional ideas about femininity and survival. The sea rose, though battered by the sea and sand, claims its beauty in its survival. It presents the feminine as strong and capable of surviving, even when battered and beaten by forces that would attempt to confine women to the domestic garden of conventionality.

The beginning of the twentieth century was a time of change in both cultural and societal life. This was a period of time in which women's identities were as shifting as the blowing sands in H.D.'s poem. The world in which she was living was still caught up in traditional values that limited women's lives, but it was a world in which women were demanding more equality. This is a time in which modern poets use their texts to interrogate "the crisis of modernity," according to Santos. These poets use poetry to "speak the language of rupture" that is occurring in the modern world, a world in which women are challenging traditions. Santos argues that "assumptions about the individual and collective identities of men and women, long taken for granted in the hierarchical order of the patriarchal tradition, were being challenged by science and technology, the intensification of commerce, and the unprecedented acceleration of travel and communication." World War I highlighted the shifting boundaries between the domestic and private world of women and the salaried and public world of men. Santos notes that "at the beginning of the twentieth century, it had become more difficult than ever before to be a woman in a man's world, precisely because all three—woman, man, and world—were being transformed in many subtle and complex ways." As the world underwent so much change, the ways in which men and women interacted reflected a new tension of change as their lives together became less clearly bound by institutional norms, such as marriage. Her relationship with Gregg is only one example of H.D.'s rejection of conventionality. Even before marrying Aldington, H.D. had been involved in a three-way romantic relationship with Ezra Pound and Gregg. Santos suggests that H.D.'s "intense emotional and erotic attachment" to Gregg, as well as "Pound's betrayal" in becoming involved with Gregg might have contributed to H.D.'s "understanding of herself as a poet." It was as a poet that H.D. understood her role in the world and where she found the strength to reject the traditional values that defined what was expected of women.

Throughout most of the nineteenth century, literature was characterized by the sentimentalism of the Romantic poets and nobility of the Victorian Age. Even before the start of World War I, the late Victorian Age began to give way to the Realist Period in English literature, as literature responded to the scientific revolution of the late nineteenth century. H.D.'s poetry appears right at the cusp of this change. As noted above, one change was in women's demands for more equality. Although the boundaries between women's and men's lives were less clearly defined than in previous centuries, the majority of women still continued to spend their adult lives as wives and mothers. H.D. did become a mother, but she rejected the conventionality of marriage after her union with Aldington ended. Instead, she began a lifelong relationship with the novelist, Annie Winifred Ellerman.

In his essay in *Contemporary Literature*, Joseph N. Riddel claims that H.D.'s "purity and hardness and coldness, her alleged classicism, are qualities of loneliness, a metaphysical estrangement that confronts her at every moment with the perilous condition of her own identity." The hardness and coldness of which Riddel speaks are features of "Sea Rose." With its emergence from the cold sea onto the "crisp sand," the sea rose might be considered to exemplify the isolation of the speaker, but it also signifies survival. Even the perfume of the sea rose is "hardened" into an "acrid fragrance," but once again, the speaker suggests that the sea rose is valued for its difference. While some readers find strength and survival in H.D.'s rejection of conformity, Riddel argues that rejection leads to unwelcome solitude. "And it is precisely this loneliness that calls forth her poems, those words through which

she anxiously seeks connection at once with the solid ground of some remote past." Riddel adds: "only words are not lonely." H.D.'s vulnerability and loneliness may be present in her poetry, but her strength is that of the sea rose; it survives the challenges of change.

In a 1969 interview in *Contemporary Literature*, Norman Holmes Pearson, a long-time friend of H.D.'s, suggests that "only Emily Dickinson will be felt to be her [H.D.'s] superior as a woman poet." Pearson is not alone in his admiration of H.D. In discussing the need for a female poet who might inspire a new generation of women poets, Alicia Ostriker, writing in *Contemporary Literature*, also looks to H.D. to provide a paradigm for women poets who seek to create a new women's literary canon. Ostriker argues that women poets need a model of strength and resistance. Indeed, Ostriker claims that "if a woman is ambitious and means perhaps to be a major poet, she will have read major critics—men of course—writing about the poets she might consider identifying with." These female poets will find that the traits that were valued in women poets of the past were not what might be expected. Instead of strength and resistance, women poets will find that their poetic ancestors were valued, according to Ostriker, for being "*modest.*" Words such as *powerful, forceful, violent,* or *large* were not used to describe women poets. Ostriker says that women poets want models "who are subversive; whose work constitutes a critique of culture." She argues that modern women poets have an obligation to retrieve the subversive nature that was so artfully disguised by earlier female poets, who sometimes had to pretend to be compliant to the values promoted in a patriarchal world that valued women more for their modesty than their talent. H.D. is the perfect poet to fill this role. In "Sea Rose," she is at her best, celebrating the difference and the uniqueness of the individual, even while rejecting the supposed perfection of conventionality.

Source: Sheri Metzger Karmiol, Critical Essay on "Sea Rose," in *Poetry for Students*, Gale, Cengage Learning, 2008.

Eileen Gregory

In the following excerpt, Gregory explores H.D.'s representation of a lyrical spiritual world through flower imagery in the poems collected in Sea Garden, *with specific discussion of "Sea Rose" as well.*

... I suggest that *Sea Garden* is a consciously crafted whole, with similar consistency in landscape, voice, and theme. The landscape is a sufficiently constant feature among the poems that we get the sense of a finite place: desolate sandy beach strewn with broken shells, large promontories and rocky headlands; inland, a barren stretch of sparse but hardy vegetation beyond the beach, and low wooded hills nearby; deeper inland, the marshes and places of luxuriant or cultivated growth. The voice in these poems also possesses consistency. All the speakers have a similar tone and intensity, even in poems dealing with specific dramatic situations and appearing to have sometimes male and sometimes female speakers. This voice is similar to that in H.D.'s translations of Euripidean choruses. Though few of the poems speak of "we," the collective voice is suggested; the "I" dissolves within the pervasive sense of generalized suffering and exaltation, like the single voice in the chorus of tragedy. The poems are often addressed to another person or to a god, and, in a few instances, they are simple meditations. But the most representative address, occurring in more than a third of the poems, is the apostrophe, the vocative voice. It seems in part to function as prayer or supplication, summoning presences, as do some of the poems in the *Greek Anthology*. More than this, the apostrophe, as Jonathan Culler points out, serves to create "a detemporalized immediacy, an immediacy of fiction." The "apostrophic" force is central to lyric power, creating "a fictional time in which nothing happens but which is the essence of happening" (152).

... The poems of *Sea Garden* appear to have been selected and arranged quite deliberately. The separate lyrics are not presented in chronological order, though their order is clearly not random. Furthermore, the volume does not represent merely a gathering of H.D.'s already published poems, for many of the best of these—for instance "Oread," "Sitalkas," and "The Pool"—do not appear until her third collection, *Heliodora and Other Poems*. The unity of *Sea Garden* is not immediately apparent; nevertheless the work gives singleness of affect. It is this affective coherence that first led me to contemplate the possibility of hidden authorial motives.

I find evidence of self-conscious crafting not only in the consistency of landscape and mood but in several details of structuring as well. Similar poems, such as the encounters with gods, the intense dramatic monologues, and especially the five sea-flower poems, are spaced evenly throughout the work, giving the impression of rhythmic or cyclic recurrence of moods and images. Furthermore, there is slight but deliberate progression in the poems depicting times of day (midday, evening, and night), and another, more subtle, progression in the placement of the precincts of the chief gods (the "shrine" at the beginning, the "temple" in the center, the "herm" as a boundary marker at the end). But to perceive the most significant instances of artistic choice in arrangement requires that one grasp the ritual intent of the whole volume: that one enter the sea garden, a world ritually set apart, as an initiate in its mysteries. Seen in this light the volume has a group of three initiatory poems that move us immediately and deeply into the mysteries of the sea garden, and three poems of closure that allow reflection upon the marginal nature of that world and the cultivation of the soul's beauty it allows. Considering first the governing images and themes of the book as a whole, I wish to treat the initiatory poems, others that suggest the character of the sea garden experience, and finally the poems of closure.

The title of the collection points to the governing experience in all its poems. The *garden* is traditionally the place of consummation of love. In H.D.'s poems the garden is still the place of love, but love washed with salt. It is a *sea* garden, inimical to all but the most enduring. The sea represents here the harsh power of elemental life, to which the soul must open itself, and by which it must be transformed or die. H.D. need not have known, but probably did, that sea/salt is the arcane alchemical substance linked to the mysterious bitterness and wisdom essential to spiritual life.

... In the opening three poems we move from an intense, static focus upon a mysterious icon ("Sea Rose"), to a choice for movement and engagement with the sea ("The Helmsman"), and, finally, to a ritual passage of entrance into the sacred mysteries of the sea garden ("The Shrine").

H.D.'s flowers, like Sappho's, represent a moment when a certain poignant beauty takes on "the stature of an eternal condition in the spirit" (McEvilley, "Sapphic Imagery" 269). "Sea Rose" immediately reveals to the reader the necessity to *look through* the image to read that eternal condition. The initiate's work begins with learning *clairvoyance*. This "harsh" rose, "marred and with stint of petals, / meagre … thin, / sparse of leaf," has no conventional worth, but, marked by the inimical elements, is altogether poor. Yet it is "more precious / than a wet rose / single on a stem." Here the typical standards of beauty are reversed, and in the last stanza the "spice-rose" is deficient for not possessing the "acrid fragrance" of this harsh flower. The relentless elements in action are annihilating ("you are caught in the drift … you are flung on the sand"); yet they exalt ("you are lifted / in the crisp sand / that drives in the wind"). The beauty is in the mark of sea-torture.

… "Sea Rose" and these other poems reveal the spiritual potency residing in a surrender to the process of "sea-change." The flowers represent, like those of Sappho, a pure openness to life; however, rather than the fresh, natural virgin threshold of the young girls in Lesbos, these show a virginity, an integrity, *achieved* within desire. Moreover, in these key recurring poems the voice itself reveals its radical openness, its own movement in the wash of feeling. The dominant voice in *Sea Garden* comes from within the sea-washed flower…

Source: Eileen Gregory, "Rose Cut in Rock: Sappho and H.D.'s *Sea Garden*," in *Contemporary Literature*, Vol. 27, No. 4, Winter 1986, pp. 525–52.

Jackson R. Bryer

In the following article, Bryer discusses the popular and critical reputation of H.D. in light of the mid-twentieth century scholars who attempted to reestablish American Imagism and Modernism as critical to the development of American poetry.

From the anonymous reviewer for the *Times Literary Supplement* in 1916 who kept referring to the author of *Sea Garden* as "he" down to William Hogan, longtime book critic of the *San Francisco Chronicle*, who admitted, in a 1960 review of *Bid Me to Live*, that he thought that H.D. had died "years ago," the literary career of Hilda Doolittle was one filled with paradoxes and shrouded in the sort of obscurity and mystery which the poetess herself apparently sought by using initials (and occasionally pseudonyms) instead of her full name. Although, as the first section of the following Checklist makes graphically apparent, H.D.'s verse and prose have been widely published, collected, and anthologized, the second section of the Checklist gives equally convincing evidence that her work has not been the subject of nearly the same amount of serious critical scrutiny afforded such contemporaries as Pound, Williams, Eliot, and Marianne Moore.

> H.D.'S MAJOR CLAIM TO CRITICAL RECOGNITION, THAT SHE WAS THE FIRST AND PUREST OF THE IMAGISTS, HAS NOT ONLY BEEN AN INESCAPABLE AND ALL TOO FACILE MEANS OF SUMMING UP HER ALMOST FIFTY-YEAR WRITING CAREER, BUT IT IS ALSO A KEY TO UNDERSTANDING THE FLUCTUATIONS OF HER CRITICAL REPUTATION DURING THAT CAREER."

H.D.'s major claim to critical recognition, that she was the first and purest of the Imagists, has not only been an inescapable and all too facile means of summing up her almost fifty-year writing career, but it is also a key to understanding the fluctuations of her critical reputation during that career. When her verse began to appear, first in periodicals like *Poetry, The Egoist,* and the *Little Review,* and then in collections such as *Sea Garden* (1916), *Hymen* (1921), and *Heliodora and Other Poems* (1924), its uniqueness and apparently faithful adherence to the Imagist creed as enunciated by Pound elicited virtually unanimous approval from reviewers of the individual volumes and from essayists in the leading literary journals. Amy Lowell proclaimed her "among the most important of recent American poets," while May Sinclair went even further in a review of *Hymen,* declaring, "There is certainly nothing in contemporary literature that surpasses these … poems." Mark Van Doren hailed her as "the most perfect woman poet alive"; Herbert Gorman saw *Heliodora* as "certainly one of the most pleasing books of poetry that have appeared for some time"; and John Donelson, in *The Bookman,* called H.D. "one of the few living poets who speak with absolute accents of genius." Further praise was lavished upon her, in early essays, by F. S. Flint (in *The Egoist*), John Gould Fletcher, and Richard Aldington (both in the *Little Review*). Virtually the only negative reactions were those expressed by English reviewers. Typical of these, the *Times Literary Supplement* found the selections in *Hymen* "deadening and monotonous," and F. L. Lucas, in the *New Statesman,* felt that *Heliodora* was "a sham reproduction of an original that never existed."

During the middle years of H.D.'s career, after the novelty and innovative quality of her verse were no longer noteworthy, critical attention began to dwindle in quantity, while at the same time being more sharply divided in its estimate of quality. There was also a tendency to analyze and characterize the nature of her art rather than simply to be enthusiastic about it. Several commentators, Harriet Monroe, Edward Sapir, and Babette Deutsch among them, viewed H.D.'s verse as decidedly American in spirit, though classical in form. Reviewers of *Collected Poems* (1925) were generally impressed, with Herbert Gorman, Marianne Moore, and William Carlos Williams among those most appreciative; but Robert Hillyer sounded an early and prophetic note of mild dissent when he praised the translations in the book, but called her "metrical and rhymed verse ... unsure, even bungling" in places, and predicted that H.D.'s work would survive not in collection, "but rather, like her admired Sappho, in fragments." A glance at the Checklist will reveal the accuracy of this observation; for, while many of H.D.'s poems have been anthologized three or four times, only a handful—"Orchard," "Oread," "Heat," and "Sea Gods"—have been reprinted continuously since their first appearance.

Adding to the ambiguous critical response during this period were the publications of *Palimpsest* (1926) and *Hedylus* (1928), H.D.'s first two books of "fiction." Reviewers were plainly puzzled but hesitant to dismiss entirely what they did not understand. "It is possible not to like the intricate, subjective manner; but one can hardly fail to gain a sense of something rare, and real, and living," wrote the reviewer of *Palimpsest,* in *The Adelphi.* The same work left Edward Shanks in the *Saturday Review* "with a faint impression that the author has failed to convey something not worth the conveying." Similarly baffled by *Hedylus,* Grace Frank noted cryptically, "For those who can transmute the fragilities and subtleties of H.D.'s seeing and knowing into their own experience, the book will offer rarely suggestive reading." But there were also those unafraid to register more definite opinions. Walter Kohn in the *New Republic* felt that the two books offered definitive evidence that "nowhere in contemporary English prose fiction is there any prose more exquisite than that of H.D., and that nowhere in English prose fiction are human emotions and experiences more immaculately reproduced." On the other side, Gorham Munson called *Hedylus* "not so much caviar as poorly cooked common honest dessert"; and John Gould Fletcher felt that, in *Palimpsest,* "the treatment ... overburdens the theme."

Critical response to *Red Roses for Bronze* (1932), H.D.'s last pre-World War II collection of verse, was also divided. R. P. Blackmur, who had generally approved of her three-act, verse play, *Hippolytus Temporizes* (1927), was now very critical: "Having given her words work to do, she should have made sure that they worked at all times." J. V. Cunningham admitted that H.D.'s verse, which now seemed "thin," might have once been "overvalued because it was pertinent to our lives." But, most important, many reviewers observed that the poems in *Red Roses for Bronze* were very different from the early Imagist verses, and thus began the task, which has actually continued down to the present moment, of distinguishing between H.D. the Imagist and H.D. the poetess and evaluating the two separately. The *Times Literary Supplement* saw the change as not entirely fortunate, noting that "the further removed from everyday, the more significant do her words seem to be." The reviewer for *The Spectator* agreed, feeling that "attempts to handle contemporary experience [have] relaxed the frozen intensity of her verse and thawed it into a rather inconclusive fluidity." But a critic for *The Bookman* claimed that what her new poems lost in beauty, "they gain[ed] for it in dramatic contrast."

The movement in H.D.'s poetry away from Imagist form and classical themes toward a concern with the present world which had been signaled in *Red Roses for Bronze* was intensified in her three-volume series of war poems, *The Walls Do Not Fall* (1944), *Tribute to the Angels* (1945), and *The Flowering of the Rod* (1946). Critics were now confronted directly with the challenge of whether or not they could accept her apart from the movement which had given her work its original impetus. Again, the response was mixed. Elizabeth Atkins called the first volume "the best poem that I have seen arising out of the present war"; Leo Kennedy saw the second as "one of her finest books"; and Martha Bacon felt that the third "will be a delight to all those who care for the poetry which we have inherited and which we long to perpetuate." But the negative voices were clear, if not always reasonable in their standards. Babette Deutsch committed the fatal critical error in faulting H.D. in *The Walls Do Not Fall* for betraying "one of the first principles of imagism by using unwieldy abstractions instead of making each poem a concrete, expanded yet powerful metaphor." Alfred Kreymborg, reviewing *Tribute to the Angels* for the *Saturday Review of Literature*, also seemed oblivious to the changes in its author's themes and method, choosing instead simply to characterize H.D. as "the perfect Imagist, and the one most certain to survive fly-by-night changes in poetry." One is tempted to ask whether or not Kreymborg would have included H.D.'s own change in the fly-by-night category!

But by far the most damaging dismissal of H.D.'s art during the last twenty-five years was Randall Jarrell's in a "Verse Chronicle" in *The Nation*. Jarrell, important not only as a discerning critic of modern poetry but also as a spokesman for an entire generation of post-World War II poets, devoted only one brief paragraph to *Tribute to the Angels*, spending the balance of his review on Alex Comfort's *The Song of Lazarus*. Clearly, Jarrell felt that H.D.'s verse was outdated. For her, he wrote, "imagism was a *reductio ad absurdum* upon which it is hard to base a later style." He dismissed her new poem as "one for those who enjoy any poem by H.D., or for those collectors who enjoy any poem that includes the Virgin, Raphael, Azrael, Uriel, John on Patmos, Hermes Trismegistus, and the Bona Dea."

While it would be foolish to claim that Jarrell's few sentences are responsible for the relative critical neglect which has befallen H.D. in the last two decades, they are nevertheless expressive of the offhand manner in which her poetry has been dealt with during that period. Her five final books (one was published posthumously) were not reviewed widely. Although, as always, she did have her advocates—Horace Gregory and Merrill Moore were perhaps the most vehement—Richard Eberhart, in a *Poetry* review of *Selected Poems* (1957), echoed Jarrell's sentiments, calling her early work "magnificent" but seeing her limitation as an inability directly to tell us "how to live." Her 1960 novel, *Bid Me to Live,* was interesting to reviewers chiefly because of its thinly disguised portraits of D. H. Lawrence and his circle.

Within the last few years, however, there has been evidence, albeit slight, of renewed interest in and appreciation of H.D.'s work. This actually began in 1960 with the awarding to her of the Award of Merit Medal for Poetry of the American Academy of Arts and Letters, a clear indication of the continuing high esteem in which she was held by her peers. It continued with the editorial tribute which appeared in the *New York Times* upon the occasion of her death, in October of 1961. Not only was the very fact of this editorial an important harbinger of the permanence of H.D.'s place in literary history; but also the sentiments expressed established a goal for future students of her work: "Her poetry owes no allegiance to movements and time. The Imagist label was applied to her poems; they did not derive from it. The precision and clarity of her lines, the ability to capture the sharply observed object are qualities that are beyond literary fashions or styles." "Long after the flamboyance of other poets of these years will have begun to wear," predicted the *Times*, "readers will return with pleasure to these cleanly hewn, controlled poems..."

If this prediction has not been fully realized, it is nonetheless true that the years since H.D.'s death have seen the appearance of the first two book-length studies of her life and work. Her poems are continually anthologized in collections ranging from high school texts to scholarly editions. What are needed now are intensive studies and explications of H.D.'s prose and verse, in an attempt to discern and define just what its timeless attributes are. We are now sufficiently removed from both the novelty of Imagism and the emotional impact of World War II to be able to evaluate her work virtually in vacuuo, or at least without undue attention to schools of verse or contemporary events. This special issue of *Contemporary Literature* will, one hopes, begin this new phase of H.D. studies. It is a recognition richly deserved and long overdue.

Source: Jackson R. Bryer, "H.D.: A Note on Her Critical Reputation," in *Contemporary Literature*, Vol. 10, No. 4, Autumn 1969, pp. 627–31.

SOURCES

"The Battle between Rhyme and Imagism," in the *New York Times*, February 4, 1917.

Bourke, Joanna, "Women and the Military during World War One," http://www.bbc.co.uk/history/british/britain_wwone/women_combatants_01.shtml (accessed September 26, 2007).

———, "Women on the Home Front in World War One," http://www.bbc.co.uk/history/british/britain_wwone/women_employment_01.shtml (accessed September 26, 2007).

Dembo, L. S., Introduction, in *Contemporary Literature*, Vol. 10, No. 4, Autumn 1969, p. 4.

Deutsch, Babette, "The Melody Lingers On," in the *New York Times*, September 22, 1957.

Freeman, Ruth, and Patricia Klaus, "Blessed or Not? The New Spinster in England and the United States in the Late Nineteenth and Early Twentieth Centuries," in *Journal of Family History*, Vol. 9, No. 4, Winter 1984, pp. 394–95.

Gregory, Horace, "Speaking of Books," in the *New York Times*, October 22, 1961.

H.D., "Sea Rose," in *H.D. Selected Poems*, Grove Press, 1957, p. 15.

"Hilda Dootlittle, Poet, Dead at 75," in the *New York Times*, September 29, 1961.

Hutchison, Percy, "New Books of Poetry," in the *New York Times*, January 31, 1932.

Ostriker, Alicia, "What Do Women (Poets) Want? H.D. and Marianne Moore as Poetic Ancestresses," in *Contemporary Literature*, Vol. 10, No. 4, Autumn 1969, pp. 485–503.

Pearson, Norman Holmes, and L. S. Dembo, "Norman Holmes Pearson on H.D.: An Interview," in *Contemporary Literature*, Vol. 10, No. 4, Autumn 1969, pp. 435–46.

Riddel, Joseph N., "H.D. and the Poetics of 'Spiritual realism'," in *Contemporary Literature*, Vol. 10, No. 4, Autumn 1969, pp. 447–73.

Santos, Irene Ramalho, "H.D.: A Poet between Worlds," in *The Cambridge History of American Literature*, Vol. 5, edited by Sacvan Bercovitch, Cambridge University Press, 2003, pp. 239–47.

———, Prologue, in *The Cambridge History of American Literature*, Vol. 5, edited by Sacvan Bercovitch, Cambridge University Press, 2003, p. 191.

FURTHER READING

Anonymous, *World War I in Photographs*, Carlton Books, 2002.

This books contains photos taken from the collection of war photos at the Imperial War Museum in London. The photos are augmented by essays that explain the events in more detail.

Clift, Eleanor, *Founding Sisters and the Nineteenth Amendment*, John Wiley & Sons, 2003.

This book chronicles the struggle women underwent as they fought for the right to vote. Clift's book is very readable and is filled with interesting anecdotes that provide a glimpse into this period of history.

Heyman, Neil M., *Daily Life during World War I*, Greenwood Press, 2002.

This book provides details about life during World War I, and includes information about women's lives in England, France, Germany, and the United States.

Ouditt, Sharon, *Fighting Forces, Writing Women: Identity and Ideology in the First World War*, Routledge, 1993.

This book offers a feminist examination of women's experiences during World War I.

Silkin, Jon, ed., *The Penguin Book of First World War Poetry*, Penguin, 1997.

This anthology is a collection of poetry that explores life, death, and patriotism.

Self-Portrait in a Convex Mirror

JOHN ASHBERY

1975

Written in a style often described as verbal expressionism, "Self-Portrait in a Convex Mirror" is the title poem in the collection for which John Ashbery won a Pulitzer Prize, a National Book Award, and a National Book Critics Circle Award, all in 1976. Originally published in 1975 in the collection *Self-Portrait in a Convex Mirror: Poems*, the lengthy title poem was inspired by a painting by the same name, completed in 1524, by the Renaissance painter Francesco Mazzola (1503–1540), who is most commonly known as Parmigianino. The poem is viewed as Ashbery's most accessible in terms of language and style and therefore distinguishes itself from many of Ashbery's other poems, the style of which has often been regarded as unconventional in the extreme. Indeed, many of his other poems have been described as being difficult or impossible to decipher. "Self-Portrait in a Convex Mirror" is counted among the masterpieces of late-twentieth-century American poetry, and it is certainly regarded as Ashbery's personal masterpiece. The work is ostensibly a meditation on Parmigianino's painting, offering lengthy observations on Parmigianino's artistic technique and skill. It also delves into themes such as the nature of art, poetry, and artistic expression, and explores such philosophical issues as the nature of personal identity and the soul. The poem is available in *Self-Portrait in a Convex Mirror: Poems*, published by Penguin Books in 1990.

John Ashbery *(Mikki Ansin / Liaison / Getty Images)*

AUTHOR BIOGRAPHY

Born in Rochester, New York, on July 28, 1927, to a fruit farmer and his wife, John Ashbery spent his youth in Sodus, New York, a small town near Lake Ontario. When Ashbery was thirteen, his nine-year-old brother died of leukemia, an event that scarred his childhood with tragedy and loss. Ashbery attended Deerfield Academy and in 1945 enrolled at Harvard, developing friendships with the poets Frank O'Hara and Kenneth Koch. After earning his bachelor's degree from Harvard in 1949, Ashbery began his graduate studies at Columbia and New York University, where he focused on French literature. His circle of friends at this time included artists and painters, one of which was Jane Freilicher, who illustrated Ashbery's first publication, the limited edition *Turandot and Other Poems* (1953). In 1955, Ashbery was awarded a Fulbright scholarship to study in France; he became an art critic and correspondent in Paris. While in France, Ashbery wrote two poetry collections (*The Tennis Court Oath*,

published in 1962, and *Rivers and Mountains*, published in 1966), both of which were regarded as highly controversial. This was due in part to the experimental form and style of the poems.

Returning to New York in 1965, Ashbery worked as executive editor of *Art News*, holding the position through 1972. Soon after his return to New York, he published the volume *The Double Dream of Spring* in 1970. This was followed by *Three Poems* in 1972. By the mid 1970s, Ashbery was receiving a greater amount of critical recognition for his poetic work and was regarded as one of America's most prominent poets, despite the controversy surrounding his work. He additionally worked as an art critic for both *New York Magazine* and *Newsweek*. In 1975, Ashbery's "Self-Portrait in a Convex Mirror" was published as the title poem in his collection, *Self-Portrait in a Convex Mirror: Poems*. The volume was praised for being more accessible than some of Ashbery's earlier work. The acclaimed volume received the Pulitzer Prize, the National Book Award, and the National Book Critics Circle Award in 1976.

From 1974 through 1990, Ashbery served as Professor of English and a Codirector of the M.F.A. program in Creative Writing at Brooklyn College, and as a Distinguished Professor from 1980 through 1990. During this time, Ashbery continued to write poetry. His works *Houseboat Days* (1977) and *As We Know* (1979) were increasingly described as both difficult to decipher and avant-garde (avant-garde is a term applied to artwork that is viewed as obscure, intellectual, and experimental). Since then, he has worked as the Charles P. Stevenson, Jr., Professor of Languages and Literature at Bard College (in Annandale-on-Hudson, New York). His more recent work includes *And the Stars Were Shining* (1994), *Chinese Whispers* (2002), *Where Shall I Wander* (2005), and *A Worldly Country* (2007). Ashbery's body of work includes poetry, a novel, plays, and essays, and he has received numerous awards and prizes for his achievements, in addition to those bestowed upon *Self-Portrait in a Convex Mirror: Poems*.

POEM SUMMARY

Strophe 1

"Self-Portrait in a Convex Mirror" opens immediately with an explanation of Ashbery's subject. In the first strophe (a distinct division within a poem that is similar to a stanza), Ashbery describes the method by which the Renaissance painter Parmigianino created the painting known as *Self-Portrait in a Convex Mirror*. With short, vivid phrases, Ashbery outlines the way Italian painter and architect Giorgio Vasari (1511–1574) discusses the creation of Parmigianino's convex mirror itself from a sphere of wood. Ashbery catalogs details of the portrait, the way the quality of the light ensures that Parmigianino's face looks life-like, the way the curve of the mirror and its reflection is captured by the artist. Embedded in these technical details are Ashbery's observations on the soul he perceives animated in the eyes Parmigianino has painted. "The soul," Ashbery says, "establishes itself;" yet it "is a captive," longing for freedom, but trapped within the human form; and the human form is trapped within the sphere of our world, "life englobed." Ashbery's extended ruminations on the position of the soul within the body and within the world give way to a return to the technical discussion of the artistry of the portrait. Commenting on the distorting effect of the convex mirror in Parmigianino's painting, Ashbery studies the size of the artist's hand. These observations yield quickly to a meditation on the nature of our perspective of reality: "The whole is stable within / Instability," Ashbery states.

Strophe 2

In the second section of the poem, Ashbery begins a more serious digression from the subject of Parmigianino's painting. His concentration is broken: "The balloon pops." His thoughts wandering, the narrator thinks of his friends, conversations he has had with them, and the ways in which parts of others—their thoughts, their ideas—are absorbed by the self. We are "filtered and influenced" by others in the same way that light is changed by "windblown fog and sand." The self, like art, like nature, is all collaboration. Ashbery meditates on the shifting nature of the world around us, likening Parmigianino's portrait to a person at the center of a sphere. The narrator then describes the vision that passes before one's eyes to reality spinning about a central core like a "carousel starting slowly / And going faster and faster." In trying to capture an instant of this spinning, Parmigianino has been only marginally successful, the narrator notes, observing that it is impossible to record a perfect moment, to "rule out the extraneous / Forever" or to "perpetuate the enchantment of self within self."

Strophe 3

Ashbery, in the third section of the poem, continues to consider what it means to contemplate a painting such as Parmigianino's, particularly when one understands how much more challenging it is to actually capture and express experience. Being able to put *today* into perspective is nearly impossible. The present, the narrator observes, is pregnant with promise and potential: "Even stronger possibilities can remain / Whole without being tested." The pattern of opposition Ashbery explored in the first section is repeated again, as he discusses the flow of potential contained within a room. Such a place, he notes "should be the vacuum of a dream" but instead is continually replenished "as the source of dreams." Once exposed to reality, a dream is forced to try and thrive in a place that "has now become a slum." At this point, the narrator refers once again to Parmigianino's painting, or at least Renaissance art scholar Sydney Freedberg's discussion of it. Ashbery relates Freedberg's analysis of the portrait's use of realism to project disharmony rather than truth. The argument feeds the narrator's discussion of the distortion of dreams and reality. This section of the poem is concluded with the idea that while the nature of dreams shift as they are "absorbed" into our reality, in this process "something like living occurs."

Strophe 4

In the fourth section Ashbery employs Freedberg again to comment on Renaissance art, and the place of Parmigianino's painting within the art of that time period. Ashbery discusses the care with which Parmigianino captured the effects of the mirror's rounded surface upon the artist's reflection. The narrator observes how, in studying the portrait, it is almost easy to forget that the reflection the painting captures is not your own. The effect is one of displacement once the realization that it is not your own reflection is made. Such a startling response is likened by Ashbery to the bizarre experiences of one of (nineteenth-century fantasy and science fiction writer) E. T. A. Hoffmann's characters, or by looking out of a window and being startled by a sudden snowfall.

Strophe 5

Ashbery in the fifth section of the poem begins by briefly relating biographical facts about Parmigianino, how soldiers "burst in on him" during the sacking of Rome (in 1527, by troops of the Holy Roman Emperor Charles V), and spared his life. From Rome, Ashbery moves to Vienna, "where the painting is today" and on to New York, which he views as "a logarithm / Of other cities." Ashbery recounts the history of the creation of the portrait, as well as his own creation of the poem in New York. Ashbery's short cataloging of the details of city life is a reminder of the way he interacts with the portrait, is drawn to it, and is then drawn back again to his own reality, his own creation, forcing the reader into the same flux of attention. This section of the poem transitions the reader away from the artwork of Parmigianino again; the narrator states "Your argument, Francesco, / Had begun to grow stale as no answer / Or answers were forthcoming." Yet Ashbery leaves open the possibility of a continued relationship or exchange with the painting, suggesting that perhaps "another life is stocked there / In recesses no one knew of; that it / Not we, are the change; that we are in fact it / If we could get back to it." This recalls Ashbery's earlier statements about dreams, and the shifting nature between dream and reality: trying to recall the impact a work of art has had on us is similar, Ashbery seems to be suggesting, to the struggle to recollect a fading dream.

Strophe 6

In the final, lengthy movement of the poem, Ashbery turns decidedly to his own creation, having highlighted both the limitations and possibilities of the aesthetic (set of artistic principles) of another artist. Released from the fixed point to which it had been previously anchored, that is, from Parmigianino's portrait, the poem now embarks on a more loosely structured, philosophical exploration of the themes Ashbery has previously touched on, such as the soul's response to art, and the reality of the present moment. "No previous day would have been like this" (l. 382) he states. "I used to think they were all alike, / That the present always looked the same to everybody." As he does earlier in the poem, Ashbery emphasizes a point by pursuing opposing ideas. The reality of one's interpretation of art, and the inspiration it offers is questioned, but accepted as having a place "the present we are always escaping from / And falling back into." Conscious of his own position as an observer, as a person interacting with a piece of art, and that the reader of the poem is in the same position, Ashbery has stressed throughout the poem that a person in such a position is not *exclusively* in this position. That is, the art admirer and the reader of a poem have a place in a reality, in a life in a city, that is separate from, but a part of, their interaction with the art work. "And we must get out of it even as the public / Is pushing through the museum now so as to / Be out by closing time. You can't live there," Ashbery states. He goes on to express the limitations he sees inherent in artistic expression, limitations centered around the impossibility of capturing the truth of a moment in the present. The effect of such an effort is always "the 'it was all a dream' / Syndrome, though the 'all' tells tersely / Enough how it wasn't. Its existence / Was real, though troubled," Ashbery states.

THEMES

Self-Reflexivity

"Self-Portrait in a Convex Mirror" is a work in which the poet examines, through the course of the poem, his own act of creating poetry. This is known as self-reflexivity, and it features prominently as both theme and device in Ashbery's poem. The work is very much *about* its own self-reflexivity. Repeatedly, Ashbery calls attention to the creation not just of art, but of *his* creation of *this* work of art. Additionally, he discusses that this is being done in other works of art as well, particularly in Parmigianino's self-portrait. In the Parmigianino painting, the artist calls attention to the methods by which he accomplished his artistic achievement by having selected such a peculiar format—a painting of a reflection. Furthermore, the mirror is not a simple flat mirror, but a convex mirror. The choice appears to have been made for the sake of artifice alone. Ashbery also notes that Parmigianino's is "the first mirror portrait." Ashbery's own self-reflexivity can be observed in the statements he makes throughout the poem. Repeatedly he refers to his own actions, nestled as they are within his descriptions of Parmigianino's portrait and his reaction to the work. His attention wandering, he notes "I think of the friends / Who came to see me, of what yesterday / Was like" and then uses this as a bridge back to the poem. His memories of yesterday intrude "on the dreaming model / In the silence of the studio as he considers / Lifting the pencil to the self-portrait." He draws attention back and forth, from the painting, to his own life, and back again to the artwork that inspired his meditation.

TOPICS FOR FURTHER STUDY

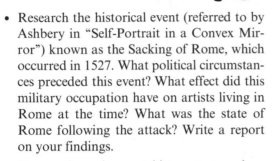

- Research the historical event (referred to by Ashbery in "Self-Portrait in a Convex Mirror") known as the Sacking of Rome, which occurred in 1527. What political circumstances preceded this event? What effect did this military occupation have on artists living in Rome at the time? What was the state of Rome following the attack? Write a report on your findings.

- Browse through an art history text, such as Frederick Hartt's *Art: A History of Painting, Sculpture, Architecture*, and select a painting that you respond to strongly, whether positively or negatively. Compose a poem about the work. Include some physical details about the work itself as well as observations about your emotional response to it.

- Examine the works of Parmigianino (other than *Self-Portrait in a Convex Mirror*) and other Mannerist painters, such as Correggio. Be sure to examine Mannerist sculptors, such as Cellini, as well. Observing their styles, their distortions of perspective or exaggeration of features, sketch or paint a self-portrait emulating the Mannerist style.

- In the sixth section of "Self-Portrait in a Convex Mirror," Ashbery mentions *Mahler's Ninth*, and how it was said that a portion of this piece invoked the sentiment of awakening a moment too late. This is an allusion to the composer Gustav Mahler (1860–1911) and his ninth symphony, the last symphony that he completed before his death. Listen to this symphony (available in the collection *Mahler: The Complete Symphonies*, 2001) and write a brief essay in which you explore why or how such music serves as a source of artistic and philosophical inspiration.

Coming back to his own perspective, Ashbery not only comments on his own response to Parmigianino's painting, but discusses his creation of a poem about it. He speaks of the exact present moment of writing, in "New York / Where I am now." Ashbery emphasizes his continued desire to derive meaning and substance from art: "I go on consulting / This mirror that is no longer mine / For as much brisk vacancy as is to be / My portion this time." Ashbery's self-reflexivity is demonstrated through his fascination with *today*, with his attempts to depict the truth and meaning of the present moment, and his willingness also to portray his process. "All we know / Is that we are a little early, that / Today has that special, lapidary / Todayness." "I used to think they were all alike," Ashbery goes on: "That the present always looked the same to everybody." He speaks then of being drawn back, as if down a corridor, toward art, toward the painting, wondering what "figment of 'art'" it is trying to express, then suggests "I think it is trying to say it is today." The expression of, and experience of the present moment is conflated with artistic expression when Ashbery observes that "Today has no margins, the event arrives / Flush with its edges, is of the same substance, / Indistinguishable." He also meditates on the failure of art to convey that which the artist intends, and in doing so calls into question his own ability to accomplish the same task. "Often" Ashbery says, "he finds / He has omitted the thing he started out to say / In the first place." In pointing out our "otherness" as a viewer of art, he emphasizes the existence of the reader of his poem, of the reader's perception of his own art.

Isolation and Connection

Ashbery quotes Italian painter and architect Giorgio Vasari's claim that Parmigianino set out to copy all that he saw, which was, Ashbery notes, "Chiefly his reflection, of which the portrait / Is the reflection once removed, / The glass chose to reflect only what he saw / which was enough for his purpose: his image." What Ashbery notices about the painting is that the artist in fact depicted only the distorted largeness of his own person ("the right hand / Bigger than the head, thrust at the viewer"). The background, save for a glimpse of the window, is practically empty. The artist himself is the entire world, or globe of the poem, one that is organized "around the polestar of your eyes which are empty / Know nothing, dream but reveal nothing." The self that Ashbery describes portrayed in the painting has become symbolically isolated, by its own hand, from the rest of the world. The artist's own self-involvement has led to its isolation, Ashbery seems to be saying, whereas his own work of art, the poem, seeks to use art to identify connection, to the world, to reality, to a consciousness of the present moment. While Parmigianino's portrait is encapsulated and isolating, this very nature of the artwork prompts Ashbery's philosophical meditations on his own reaction to art, and his place within his own world, which, conveyed to the reader, is an invitation to do the same. Parmigianino's isolation inspires Ashbery's attempt to connect himself to *today*, to his life in New York, which he describes. Through his interaction with the artwork, and his understanding of the possibilities of the reader's reaction to his poem, Ashbery emphasizes both the isolating and connecting nature of art.

STYLE

Mannerism

The term Mannerism refers to an artistic style beginning to be popular during the later years of the High Renaissance (a period of advanced artistic achievement) in Italy, during the early 1500s. Mannerist works of art were highly individualistic and featured distortions of perspective and qualities that were artificial or exaggerated rather than naturalistic. Parmigianino's *Self-Portrait in a Convex Mirror* is itself an example of a Mannerist piece, and Ashbery's poem has similarly been described as Mannerist for its own distortions of perspective: the reader is in effect viewing Parmigianino's portrait from Ashbery's point of view, which is shaped by his own intentions. Like Mannerist paintings which drew attention to themselves as artificial creations through exaggeration, Ashbery draws attention to his own work of art by examining his own act of creating it. It should be noted as well that some scholars view Ashbery's technique as a critique of Parmigianino's Mannerist work. While both pieces are works of self-representation, Ashbery strives to analyze Parmigianino's as well as his own methods of self-portrayal, thereby distinguishing his approach from Parmigianino's by his attempt to eliminate not the self-reflexivity of the work, but the narcissistic and limiting qualities he finds in the painting.

Expressionism

Ashbery's style in "Self-Portrait in a Convex Mirror" is sometimes referred to as expressionistic rather than Mannerist. Expressionism, or verbal expressionism, is the literary equivalent of the artistic abstract expressionism, in which the artist intentionally uses elements of distortion to create a desired emotional effect. The artists Jackson Pollock and Pablo Picasso were among the best known abstract expressionists. The purpose of verbal expressionism is the conveying of emotional truth, rather than the statement, in linear, traditional ways, of logical arguments or ideas. In "Self-Portrait in a Convex Mirror" Ashbery so accurately discusses Parmigianino's painting, he in effect offers a glimpse into the emotions expressed in the painting, presenting the verbal equivalent of viewing the painting itself (or the experience of viewing it), which transcends the mere description of the painting's details. In doing so, Ashbery delineates the possibilities of both verbal and visual modes of expression.

HISTORICAL CONTEXT

Pop Art in 1970s New York

When "Self-Portrait in a Convex Mirror" was written in 1975, visual art in New York was under the influence of several movements, including that of Pop art; Ashbery was, in fact, friends with one of the best known Pop artists of the time, Andy Warhol (1930–1987). A visual artistic movement that began in Britain in the 1950s, Pop art is characterized by the influence of popular mass culture in terms of theme and the techniques the artists employed. A famous example is Warhol's repetition, in garish colors, of the silk-screened image of Marilyn Monroe, or his detailed paintings of Campbell's soup cans. The Pop art movement has been seen alternately as a rejection of, or an expansion of, the modes of abstract expressionism, which remained a prevalent style of New York artists in the 1970s. At once academic (in that it is often difficult to decipher techniques) and designed by way of its subject matter to appeal to a wide audience, Pop art asserted, in much the same way the abstract expressionism did, a faith in the idea of artistic possibility. In some ways, it was characterized by anti-aestheticism, or by the rejection of the notion of controlling artistic principles. Ashbery's poem exhibits similar tendencies, exploring both the shortcomings and the possibilities of art.

COMPARE
&
CONTRAST

- **1520s:** In 1524, Italian explorer Giovanni da Verrazzano (c. 1485–c. 1528) explores the Atlantic coastline of North America. His journey takes him to New York Harbor (where the Verrazzano-Narrows Bridge is, having been named for the explorer) and north to Maine. Inhabitants of the largely uncultivated area are Native Americans.

  1970s: New York City is a cultural center that promotes the arts in a variety of forms, including theater, painting, photography, literature, and music. At this time, punk rock is emerging as a new and rebellious form of artistic expression. Zoo York, graffiti art in the subway tunnel underneath New York City's Central Park Zoo, is also developing. New York City is Ashbery's adopted hometown, and his descriptions of life in the city play an important part in "Self-Portrait in a Convex Mirror."

  Today: New York City remains an international cultural and artistic capital. The city hosts the "People's Poetry Gathering" in which New Yorkers are encouraged to offer individual lines that form a larger poem. Following the September 11, 2001, terrorist attacks, this effort at communal poetry was employed to create a traveling exhibition featuring poems of 110 lines each, one line for each story of the World Trade Center towers destroyed in the attacks.

- **1520s:** Mannerism, as an artistic movement, is in its early phases. Parmigianino's works, including *Self-Portrait in a Convex Mirror* (1524) and *Madonna with the Long Neck* (1534–1540), along with the works of artists such as Rosso Fiorentino, including his *Descent from the Cross* (1521), exemplify this style. Mannerism is characterized by distortions in perspective, exaggerated physical features, disturbing compositions, and often unusual color choices. Given this definition, Ashbery's "Self-Portrait in a Convex Mirror" could be considered a Mannerist poem.

  1970s: Conceptual art is becoming popular, and it is concerned primarily with the idea, or concept expressed, rather than with conventional modes of style or notions of aesthetics. Ashbery's "Self-Portrait in a Convex Mirror" could also be considered in this light, as it explores the ability of art to represent truth; it is, in many ways, *about* art itself.

  Today: Notions about what constitutes art in the twenty-first century continue to shift. Nevertheless conceptual art remains fashionable: in 2005 Simon Starling exhibits his *Shedboatshed* a wooden shed that was turned into a boat, sailed down the Rhine River, and turned back into a shed.

- **1520s:** English-language poetry at this time is dictated by the conventions of the pastoral and lyric forms. Pastoral poetry exalts an idealized, simple world of shepherds and shepherdesses, and it expresses the joys of country life and laments romantic troubles. Lyric poetry of this period features the praising of love and nature, or often of God and spirituality. These types of poems are characterized by structured forms and rhyme schemes.

  1970s: Poetry is influenced by artistic movements such as Surrealism, a cultural movement typically associated with the visual arts but also related to philosophy and literature. Surrealist works incorporate elements of surprise and of unexpected juxtapositions. Ashbery is writing at a time when many poets, Surrealists and otherwise, seek to resist traditional poetic movements and forms, and "Self-Portrait in a Convex Mirror" is an example of a work that is unique in its form and structure.

  Today: Though modern poetry still shows resistance to form and convention, there has also been a revival of poetry crafted with attention to meter, formal rhyme schemes, and traditional structures, an a movement described as New Formalism. Critics sometimes describe it as a "closed" form that opposes or threatens the open, free verse poetry popular in many critical and academic circles.

Italian High Renaissance Art

The subject of Ashbery's poem is the painting by Parmigianino, *Self-Portrait in a Convex Mirror*. The painting was completed in 1524, during the end of the High Renaissance period (a short period of about twenty-five years, beginning at the end of the fifteenth century, and continuing through the beginning of the sixteenth century) of art in Italy and the beginning of the Mannerist period. During the High Renaissance, the highest achievements in painting were characterized by spatial harmony, exquisite arrangements of subjects, and proportions that were naturalistic and graceful. Examples of this period include such famous works as Leonardo da Vinci's (1452–1519) *Last Supper* (completed in 1498), Michelangelo's (1475–1564) *David* (completed in 1504), and Raphael's (1483–1520) *Transfiguration of Christ* (completed in 1520). At the time, however, a new movement, that which became known as Mannerism, was becoming prominent. In Mannerist works, artists such as Parmigianino, Benvenuto Cellini (1500–1571), and Georgio Vasari (1511–1574) distort perspective and depict figures with extremely exaggerated or unnatural features. Political and religious factors are cited as contributors to these dramatic shifts in the visual arts. Florence, the center of artistic creation in the region at the time, lost its political independence in 1512 and was now under the rule of the Medici family. Conditions of the population became miserable, and the city resented its loss of freedom. Concurrently, the Roman Catholic Church began to lose followers to Protestantism. When a member of the powerful Medici family became pope in 1523, political unrest and religious conflict fused. Armies that were supposedly loyal to the Roman Emperor Charles V but were actually not under control at all attacked Rome, under the auspices of addressing the pope's political maneuverings and manipulations. The distortions of Mannerism, then, are said to reflect the social, political, and religious chaos of the time. The disturbing effects of Mannerism stand in sharp contrast to the ordered, graceful, and beautiful imagery of the recent High Renaissance.

CRITICAL OVERVIEW

"Self-Portrait in a Convex Mirror" is perhaps Ashbery's most studied poem; many critics certainly refer to it as his most accessible. Reviewers often comment that the language in it is more straightforward than in his other poems, and that the subject of the poem remains consistent throughout. In 1979, poet, literary critic, and art historian David Shapiro explains in *John Ashbery: An Introduction to the Poetry*: "From the beginning of the poem to the end the poet reenacts both a meditation upon the painting ... and a meditation on the unfolding of his own vital poem." "Self-Portrait in a Convex Mirror" is often described as unique in its ability to verbally convey the visceral, visual impact of the painting, rather than simply describing the physical details of the image, or discussing the manner by which it was created.

In a *Journal of Modern Literature* essay published in 1976, shortly after the publication of Ashbery's poem, Fred Moramarco comments that Ashbery is able "to explore the verbal implications of painterly space, to capture the verbal nuances of Parmigianino's fixed and distorted image. The poem virtually resonates or extends the painting's meaning. It transforms visual impact to verbal precision." Moramarco goes on to explore the way Ashbery attempts to "record verbally the emotional truth contained in Parmigianino's painting." Later critics have reassessed the poem's achievements in this area. Travis Looper, in a 1992 essay in *Papers on Language and Literature* suggests that Ashbery's poem is a study of the failure of language, of the inability of verbal expression to accurately capture meaning. Looper asserts that Ashbery is aware "even as he writes the words of the poem, that the signs are themselves paltry substitutes of the object-realities he would describe." Nevertheless, Looper goes on, the poet continues to use words as signifiers even though he is aware of their inadequacy, otherwise Ashbery would be "undermining the poem even as he writes it. Rather, in human fashion, he persists in that which is ultimately hopeless."

Other critics agree that the poem is *about* representation. Richard Stamelman, in his 1984 essay for *New Literary History*, maintains that Ashbery emphasizes the differences between Parmigianino's act of self-portrayal and the way Ashbery represents himself in the poem. Commenting that Ashbery approaches art from a postmodern standpoint, Stamelman identifies Ashbery's position as one in which "painting and poetry can represent nothing other than their own difficult, often thwarted efforts at representation." A more positive description of Ashbery's views on the possibilities and limitations of artistic representation is offered by David Herd in his 2000 book, *John Ashbery and American Poetry*. Herd observes that in "Self-Portrait in a Convex

Self-portrait of Parmigianino (Girolamo Francesco Maria Mazzola) in a convex mirror (Erich Lessing / Art Resource, NY)

Mirror," "Ashbery's poetic, like Emerson's 'American Scholar,' but unlike Parmigianino's painting, leads the reader beyond the confines and conventions of artistic practice and into an encounter with their own experience."

CRITICISM

Catherine Dominic

Dominic is an author and freelance editor. In this essay, Dominic explores the way the relationship between order and chaos, as portrayed in Ashbery's

"Self-Portrait in a Convex Mirror," functions as a parallel to the relationship between representation and experience.

The self-reflexive nature of Ashbery's "Self-Portrait in a Convex Mirror" (its tendency to refer to itself and its own act of having been created) is a much analyzed feature of the poem. Often the focus of such studies is on the way Ashbery discusses both the limitations and possibilities of artistic representation of any kind. Alternatively, many critics emphasize the ways in which Ashbery compares and contrasts Parmigianino's visual act of self-representation with the

WHAT DO I READ NEXT?

- "Song of Myself," by Walt Whitman, is available in *Leaves of Grass: The Original 1855 Edition* (reprinted 2007). Like Ashbery, American poet Walt Whitman was known for his unconventional poetic structures, his cataloging of human experiences, an often rambling style, and his explorations of the soul and the relationship between the body and the soul.

- "The Over-Soul" (1841), by Ralph Waldo Emerson, is available in *Emerson's Essays* (1981). The prominent scholar and critic Harold Bloom has observed that Ashbery's poetry is highly influenced by the philosophy of American Transcendentalism, which is explored and explained in Emerson's essay.

- *A Worldly Country: New Poems* (2007), by John Ashbery, features Ashbery's most recent poetic compositions. The poems are playful in tone but cover serious themes such as old age and death.

- *Parmigianino* (2006), by David Ekserdjian, contains previously unpublished drawings by Parmigianino as well as a new painting. Ekserdjian analyzes the significance of Parmigianino's works, and he also discusses the painter's artistic development while praising his artistic achievements.

- *Tales of E. T. A. Hoffmann* (1972) is a collection of short stories by E. T. A. Hoffmann. Ashbery makes reference in "Self-Portrait in a Convex Mirror" to the short-story characters created by the science fiction/fantasy writer Hoffmann (1776–1822).

poet's own written act of self-representation. Yet the notion of representation functions in another way in "Self-Portrait in a Convex Mirror." Ashbery uses the debate regarding the merits and limitations of Parmigianino's visual representation (and his own verbal act of representation) as a means of

> IN THE END, ASHBERY'S STANCE, WHICH SEEMED CONTENTIOUS AT THE ONSET OF THE POEM, POSITING CHAOS AGAINST ORDER, NOW APPEARS TO BE AMBIGUOUS."

exploring, in a philosophical manner, the themes of order and chaos.

In "Self-Portrait in a Convex Mirror" the terms "order" and "chaos" are loosened from their traditional connotations, with "order," rather than "chaos" possessing the more pejorative implication. This inversion is revealed in the first section of the poem, when Ashbery, after describing Parmigianino's technical methodology, reflects that the effect the artist has achieved has been to capture the soul: "the soul is a captive, treated humanely, kept / In suspension, unable to advance much farther / Than your look as it intercepts the picture." Through his painting, Parmigianino has attempted to impose order on something that is in reality uncontainable. For as Ashbery goes on to observe, what Parmigianino has accomplished is to capture something in the look on his face in the portrait that reminds the viewer of the idea of the soul. But "the secret is too plain ... / ... the soul is not a soul, / Has no secret, is small, and it fits / Its hollow perfectly: its room, our moment of attention." Here and throughout the poem, the act of representing is shown to be an attempt to impose *order*. The objects of this intent in the poem include the soul, dreams, ideal forms, truth—all elements that by their very nature resist quantification, codification, or other methods of ordering; in this, resistance may be described as chaotic. Interestingly, Ashbery uses the term "chaos" when he refers to Parmigianino's attempt to organize the world depicted in painting around the center point of his eyes, which fail to reflect the artist's soul: "I see in this only the chaos / Of your round mirror which organizes everything / Around the polestar of your eyes which are empty." The paradox of chaos that organizes is repeated in other expressions as well, such as "pure / Affirmation that doesn't affirm anything," and "the whole is stable within / Instability." Such paradoxes emphasizes the very chaotic nature of the unrepresentable ideas Ashbery explores within the poem.

Reflecting on the way one's attention wanders when viewing a work of art, Ashbery catalogs various recent experiences: "I think of the friends / Who came to see me, of what yesterday / Was like." He recalls the way the thoughts of others become a part of us through their words, stressing here the significance of the experiences of everyday living. Turning his attention back to the painting, he questions the artist's ability to capture such things as time, and ideas. Ashbery asks: "Whose curved hand controls, / Francesco, the turning seasons and the thoughts / That peel off and fly away." Through his painting, through the reflection in the mirror, Parmigianino has attempted to order, to organize. Ashbery however describes the world of living, rather than the represented world, in visceral terms "I feel the carousel starting slowly / And going faster and faster," and here the implication is that the world of experience, the chaos of the spinning carousel, and the multitude of images and facts of daily living that "boil down to one / Uniform substance" are preferred over the limiting representations of art.

Ashbery subsequently links this chaotic, vital "magma" to the world of dreams, suggesting that dreams remind us of the elusive truths we frequently forget. In this, dreams are like visual acts of representation, like Parmigianino's painting, and verbal acts of representation, like Ashbery's poem, reminding us that artistic forms "retain a strong measure of ideal beauty / As they forage in secret on our idea of distortion." Such artistic representations, Ashbery is saying, because they are "fed by our dreams," retain some elements of the chaos from which they emerged. Dreams filter a truth that is just beyond our reach, and artists and poets further distill these ideas into artistic representations. And yet, so far removed from the source, the capturing of such ideas with any accuracy is impossible. We forget things "which were ours once." That we retain the notion at least that such connections exist, that we know at least that we have indeed forgotten something, justifies the human need to impose order on chaos, to attempt to represent artistically the true ideas that experience and living often seem to be more attuned to. Artistic representation, Ashbery concedes "is a metaphor / Made to include us, we are a part of it and / Can live in it as in fact we have done." Our need

to question "will not take place at random / But in an orderly way that means to menace / Nobody— the normal way things are done, / Like the concentric growing up of days / Around a life: correctly, if you think about it."

In the end, Ashbery's stance, which seemed contentious at the onset of the poem, positing chaos against order, now appears to be ambiguous. The desire to order, to codify and quantify, is very human and understandable, since what we reach for in the chaos is a sense of the true order and nature of things, a sense of unity. And yet, in this striving, the true forms are always distorted by the very nature of their being represented. "It seems like a very hostile universe," Ashbery states, the one in which such a distorted relationship must exist. Throughout the poem, Ashbery has emphasized the importance of *today*, talking about his current thoughts about his friends, and the conversations they shared, the details of everyday life, such as the "desk, papers, books, / Photographs of friends, the window and the trees." Near the end of the poem, he returns to this idea, that the present moment and our experiences are of the utmost significance. "*This* thing, the mute undivided present, / Has the justification of logic, which / In this instance isn't a bad thing / Or wouldn't be, if the way of telling / Didn't somehow intrude, twisting the end result / Into a caricature of itself." Artistic representation, or "the way of telling", in whatever form it takes, inevitably distorts. But "the mute undivided present" is *happening* rather than being portrayed. It is closer to the chaos, or truth, or to the ideal form that we sometimes touch but ceaselessly forget, and that we consistently try to remember, in the same way we try to remember our dreams once we are awake. Ashbery compares this effort at remembering to "the game where / A whispered phrase passed around the room / Ends up as something completely different." At the poem's end, Ashbery laments that "each part of the whole falls off / And cannot know it knew, except / Here and there, in cold pockets / Of remembrance, whispers out of time." The act of representation is one of disfiguring, of distorting. Parmigianino distorted the proportions and perspective in his painting through the use of the convex mirror, metaphorically isolating the soul through his attempt to portray the true reflection of himself. Ashbery, in contrast, is forthright in his admission that a true reflection cannot in fact be conveyed, and that as humans, we are by our very nature cut off from ideal forms, from whole-ness and unity, our souls imprisoned in our bodies, in our current existence, the way Parmigianino's is symbolically captured within the portrait.

Ashbery's explorations transcend a literary analysis of self-reflexivity and extend into philosophical territory. The notion of ideal forms is a Platonic one, as is the idea that our soul possesses knowledge, or truth, that we have forgotten. Our lives, Plato (c. 428 B.C.E.–c. 347 B.C.E.) explains in works such as the *Meno* are a process of recollecting that which we once knew. Similarly, the idea that our souls are part of a greater whole parallels Ralph Waldo Emerson's conception of an Over-Soul, which he describes in the essay "The Over-Soul" (first published in 1841 and now available in *Emerson's Essays*). Emerson (1803–1882), an American philosopher, poet, and essayist, explores not only the existence of our transcendent, or spiritual natures, but the possibilities of accessing the truth revealed in that nature through acts of quiet contemplation. He argues that while we may experience the world "piece by piece" it is all part of the same whole. Ashbery similarly portrays the apparently fragmented nature of human experience, but also depicts the possibilities of connection, the very yearning for wholeness suggesting that a "Uniform substance / a magma of interiors" does in fact exist.

Source: Catherine Dominic, Critical Essay on "Self-Portrait in a Convex Mirror," in *Poetry for Students*, Gale, Cengage Learning, 2008.

Richard Stamelman

In the following excerpt, Stamelman defines "Self-Portrait in a Convex Mirror" as a postmodern critique of art's ability to capture the complexities of self-expression. Stamelman further argues that the poem explores the contemporary world as a world that is slipping towards meaninglessness.

"Self-Portrait in a Convex Mirror" is a title that has a double identity; it is a name shared by two different works of art: on the one hand, the small Mannerist self-representation (it is only 9 5/8 inches in diameter) painted on a convex piece of poplar wood by Francesco Parmigianino in Parma between 1523 and 1524; on the other, the postmodernist poem of 552 lines composed by John Ashbery in New York, probably between 1973 and 1974. The painted self-portrait is as self-enclosed, condensed, and smoothly englobed as

> FOR ASHBERY PERCEPTION AND REFLECTION ARE A MATTER OF SEEING IN A GLASS DARKLY, IF AT ALL."

the poetic meditation is open-ended, rambling, and fragmented. Where Parmigianino's face floats angelically in a state of perfect, timeless immobility, Ashbery's mind rushes to and fro in a dance of associations, thoughts, and self-conscious reflections. His consciousness moves in a recurring, although decentered, pattern from a meditation of the Parmigianino painting to a contemplation of his own life, to a consideration of the nature of poetic and pictorial representation, and back to the painting once again, where the meditation starts anew. While the painter presents an image of himself at once complete and unchanging, the poet represents the comings and goings of sensations, desires, thoughts, and impressions—"a mimesis," he says, "of how experience comes to me."

Although both works share the same title, they are radically different forms of self-representation. By entitling his poem "Self-Portrait in a Convex Mirror," Ashbery appears to have wanted to reveal the extreme difference between Mannerist and postmodernist aesthetics and the great disparity between the idea of self and the attitude toward reality that those two aesthetics embody. He wanted, in other words, to make his poem serve as a *critical reflection* of the painting: an ekphrastic re-presentation of Parmigianino's self-portrait and at the same time a radical criticism of the illusions and deceptions inherent in forms of traditional representation that insist on the ideal, essential, and totalized nature of the copied images they portray. Whereas portraiture has consistently been regarded as a "meditation on likeness," in Ashbery's hands it becomes a meditation on difference.

The critical difference in Ashbery's poem is literally the difference criticism makes by being inserted into his poetic discourse; poetic expression and critical analysis function together in "Self-Portrait." Wherever he can, he inserts a difference, a sense of critical otherness, that illuminates the disparity between his act of self-portrayal and Parmigianino's, which the poem paradoxically mirrors. Ashbery's criticism of the painting enables him to reveal and thus "dispel / The quaint illusions that have been deluding us" ("Litany," *AWK*, p. 35), not only in the representations of the world, which painting, poetry, and narrative give, but in the fictions one uses to order one's life and past.

Ashbery is a poet of demystifications, differences, and, as will become clear, deconstructions. In the very act of presenting the Parmigianino painting—describing its formal elements, its stylistic mannerisms, the history of its composition—he critically dismantles the portrait, pointing to the sealed, life-denying, motionless image of self it portrays; the poem offers a critical deconstruction of representation itself, or more precisely, of the aesthetic of perfection which gives representations an aura of eternal sameness, enshrining them in the paradise of art so that they constitute what Harold Bloom calls a "supermimesis." The Parmigianino painting as it is taken into and described by Ashbery's poem—so that it is transformed into a text, an *ekphrasis*, an inscribed version of the work of art—dazzles the reader with its triple reflection; it has its source in the mirror image that Parmigianino copies onto a convex surface and which Ashbery four hundred and fifty years later contemplates and represents:

> Vasari says, "Francesco one day set himself
> To take his own portrait, looking at himself
>   for that purpose
> In a convex mirror, such as is used by bar-
>   bers ...
> He accordingly caused a ball of wood to be
>   made
> By a turner, and having divided it in half and
> Brought it to the size of the mirror, he set
>   himself
> With great art to copy all that he saw in the
>   glass,"
> Chiefly his reflection, of which the portrait
> Is the reflection once removed.

Mirroring and meditation constitute the critical reflections which Ashbery's poem projects as it presents and deconstructs Parmigianino's self-portrait. Criticism, the poet suggests, is reflection: a specular interpretation that mirrors and meditates simultaneously. The critic *reflects* the work he studies—quotation, paraphrase, photographic reproduction are mirror images of a special type—by *reflecting upon* it; the

specular thus leads to the speculative, as Ashbery suggests:

> The words are only speculation
> (From the Latin *speculum*, mirror):
> They seek and cannot find the meaning of
>   the music.

... For Ashbery perception and reflection are a matter of seeing in a glass darkly, if at all. While Parmigianino's sixteenth-century *Self-Portrait in a Convex Mirror* presents an image of artistic unity that expresses faith in the representability of world and self through art, Ashbery's critical re-vision of the painting reveals what is a stilled and detemporalized scene of reflection. In Ashbery's postmodernist (and self-reflexive) view, painting and poetry can represent nothing other than their own difficult, often thwarted efforts at representation. By means of this critical meditation Ashbery so completely demystifies the traditional notions of self and representation that by the end of the poem Parmigianino's convex painting is flattened and pushed back into the dead past; self-portraiture is stripped of authority and authenticity; and knowledge appears as no more than the random coalescence of fragments.

... "Self-Portrait in a Convex Mirror" belongs to that group of ekphrastic poems that self-reflexively make a statement about the nature of poetry or art. Ashbery's poem initiates its mirroring of the Parmigianino painting in the following way:

> As Parmigianino did it, the right hand
> Bigger than the head, thrust at the viewer
> And swerving easily away, as though to
>   protect
> What it advertises. A few leaded panes, old
>   beams,
> Fur, pleated muslin, a coral ring run
>   together
> In a movement supporting the face, which
>   swims
> Toward and away like the hand
> Except that it is in repose. It is what is
> Sequestered.

In these fragmentary perceptions, none of which make a complete sentence except for the last, Ashbery quickly sums up the painting's features. Quoting Vasari, he explains how Parmigianino had a wooden convex surface made equal in size to his convex mirror and "'set himself / With great art to copy all that he saw in the glass'." Ashbery will repeatedly question this idea of representing *all* that one sees, thus uncovering the illusions of totality and detemporalized wholeness which such representations contain. Paintings like the Parmigianino self-portrait hide the fact that they have come into existence through arbitrary selections made by the painter from among his perceptions, thoughts, and feelings. Ashbery is aware of the important events and impressions that had to be left out in the process of creating the representation—"this leaving-out business," he calls it in an early poem ("The Skaters," *RM*, p. 39)—exclusions that point to the unreality and the solipsism of totalized representations.

The reductiveness of the Parmigianino self-portrait is not the only flaw Ashbery has discovered; there is also the painting's lifelessness, its static unreality. Repeatedly, Ashbery refers to the protected, embalmed, sequestered, imprisoned face of the painter, surrounded at the painting's base by the large, curved right hand, which is elongated and slightly distorted by the convex surface. This hand both welcomes and defends, seeming simultaneously to move out to greet the viewer and to retreat, "Roving back to the body of which it seems / So unlikely a part, to fence in and shore up the face." The painting represents an autonomous and complete life within its convex globe. But the price paid to bring forth this unified and coherent image is high: it entails the deadening of the painter's spirit and the sacrifice of his freedom. In representing himself, Parmigianino has had to exclude much about his life and world that must have defined him as a person. He has had to reduce his being to a miniature image which conforms to the limits of an artful and timeless prison. Parmigianino's is a cautious self-portrait, and in his striving for a perfect, idealized expression of himself, he distorts the meaning of human existence:

> The soul has to stay where it is,
> Even though restless, hearing raindrops at
> the pane,
> The sighing of autumn leaves thrashed by
> the wind,
> Longing to be free, outside, but it must stay
> Posing in this place. It must move
> As little as possible. This is what the portrait
> says.

The representation freezes one moment in the painter's life and presents it (falsely, Ashbery implies) as representative of that life, its perfect and essential embodiment. Everything is purified,

filtered, self-contained; this is a curtailment of human possibility that moves Ashbery to tears of sympathy:

> The pity of it smarts,
> Makes hot tears spurt: that the soul is not a
> soul,
> Has no secret, is small, and it fits
> Its hollow perfectly: its room, our moment
> of attention.

It is the immobility of the Parmigianino painting, its changeless and unmoving reality, that Ashbery questions. He will have nothing to do with "monuments of unageing intellect." The chaos of life can submit to no artistic control:

> Whose curved hand controls,
> Francesco, the turning seasons and the
> thoughts
> That peel off and fly away at breathless
> speeds
> Like the last stubborn leaves ripped
> From wet branches? I see in this only the
> chaos
> Of your round mirror which organizes
> everything
> Around the polestar of your eyes which are
> empty,
> Knowing nothing, dream but reveal nothing.

Art, Ashbery suggests, is a convention in which artist and viewer agree to suspend disbelief and to pretend that the representation is a coherent, complete re-presentation or reorganization of reality. An art like Parmigianino's gives the illusion of plenitude, but beneath the surface—and surface is all there is—lies nothing:

> And the vase is always full
> Because there is only just so much room
> And it accommodates everything. The
> sample
> One sees is not to be taken as
> Merely that, but as everything as it
> May be imagined outside time—not as a
> gesture
> But as all, in the refined, assimilable state.

To Ashbery the painting's fullness is fundamentally empty: "I go on consulting / This mirror that is no longer mine / For as much brisk vacancy as is to be / My portion this time." ...

Source: Richard Stamelman, "Critical Reflections: Poetry and Art Criticism in Ashbery's 'Self-Portrait in a Convex Mirror,'" in *New Literary History*, Vol. 15, No. 3, Spring 1984, pp. 607–30.

John Koethe and John Ashbery

In the following excerpt, taken from an interview between Koethe and Ashbery, the poet comments on his ideas and feelings about the long poem form in general, and specifically about "Self-Portrait in a Convex Mirror." Ashbery also talks about teaching poetry in universities, and about the movement towards poetry that stresses sound rather than image.

. . . Koethe: More than most poets, you've written long poems periodically. In a way, you've revived the long poem. Are there any kinds of long poems that you would like to write in the future? You've written long prose and sequence poems, and you've written a continuous meditation, Self Portrait in a Convex Mirror.

Ashbery: I would like to do more but I haven't figured out what form they're going to take yet—in fact I prefer to do that after I've already begun. But I like the idea of writing something that takes a great deal of time because your mind changes while you are doing it and the reader isn't aware at what point you left off and put it aside for two months and then came back; there aren't any seams. The long poem seems to gain a kind of richness from being written by not different poets, but a poet who is different each time.

Koethe: Self Portrait in a Convex Mirror, *which expanded your readership, appears philosophically more continuous than some of your poems, in the sense of carrying an argument through to the end. Do you want to do that again, or is that something you wanted to do just one time?*

Ashbery: I guess it's something that I wanted to do just that one time and I think its continuity is actually very specious. It seems to have fooled a lot of people. I think if it were examined closely, it would be found to be just as "incoherent" as my more notorious long poems. It's not a poem that I particularly like—it seems too serious.

Koethe: Creative writing as a subject open to everyone is a recent development in American education. Since the mid-seventies, you've been teaching poetry. What is your experience of teaching poetry and what sorts of techniques do you find work? Do you think it's a good idea on the whole since it's not something that you ever learned when you were young? Do you think there is any danger that creative writing classes "professionalize" poetry in a way that discourages experimentation?

Ashbery: Teaching creative writing is a very good idea for me because I couldn't make a living otherwise. I don't really know how it works although it does seem to work. I've noticed that the work of certain poets gets better during the course of the year, but I don't know how that works. I actually did take a poetry writing course when I was an undergraduate, before such things really existed, and I was so pleased to be noticed once in a while by Theodore Spencer, the poet who was teaching the class. It did a lot for me though the assignments he gave weren't really very interesting or provocative. I think it's very valuable for me to act just the way I am and not pretend to be any smarter or nicer than I actually am and to really be quite silly every now and then. This destroys the artificial barrier between me and the students. They realize that not only am I not any smarter, I'm really not a better person than they are. But I think a lot of poets use creative writing classes for ego trips and invent all sorts of artificial disciplines and act professional. That's not something I do. My classes are really on a sort of low conversational level. Yet I think that the more demotic the discussion becomes, the better it is for all of us.

Koethe: One final area: the difference between written and spoken poetry, and the idea of poetry as something you read on the page as opposed to something you read aloud. Many people think it makes a great deal of difference how you conceive of poetry—as something to be heard or something to be read. Do you think it makes much difference, and do you tend to conceive of your own work as primarily something to be read on the page rather than heard?

Ashbery: I, myself, enjoy reading it rather than hearing it read. On the other hand, the input for my poetry seems to come from colloquial talk and the inaccurate ways we present our ideas to other people and yet succeed in doing so despite our sloppiness. On the other hand, I don't really like to hear it, I would rather see it. I can hear it better when I see it. I seldom go to poetry readings, and I don't like performance poetry. The word "performance" reminds me of a line in *Hebdomeros* by De Chirico. I forget exactly what it is that sets off the hero at that particular point. I think it is the idea of eating oysters, or strawberries and cream. The line is: "It made him flee like Orestes pursued by the Furies." The word "performance" has a similar effect on me.

Source: John Koethe and John Ashbery, "An Interview with John Ashbery," in *SubStance*, Vol. 11, No. 4, Issue 37–38, 1983, pp. 178–86.

Fred Moramarco

In the following excerpt, Moramarco emphasizes the influence of abstract expressionist paintings on the poetic styles of Ashbery and his friend and contemporary Frank O'Hara. More specifically, Moramarco argues that in "Self-Portrait in a Convex Mirror" Ashbery attains a new level of intersection between the poetic and the painterly.

The title poem in John Ashbery's new collection, *Self Portrait in a Convex Mirror*, begins with a precise description of the remarkable painting by Parmigianino which inspired it. Looking at the poem and painting together, one is struck by Ashbery's unique ability to explore the verbal implications of painterly space, to capture the verbal nuances of Parmigianino's fixed and distorted image. The poem virtually resonates or extends the painting's meaning. It transforms visual impact to verbal precision. I am reminded of an antithetical statement by the Abstract Expressionist painter Adolph Gottlieb, whose haunting canvases juxtaposing luminous spheres and explosive brush strokes have all sorts of suggestive connections with Ashbery's poetry. Gottlieb writes about his own painting:

> I frequently hear the question "What do these images mean?" This is simply the wrong question. Visual images do not have to conform to either verbal thinking or optical facts. A better question would be "Do these images convey any emotional truth?"

It seems to me Ashbery's intention in "Self Portrait" is to record verbally the emotional truth contained in Parmigianino's painting. Visual images do not have to conform to verbal *thinking*, as Gottlieb points out, but they can generate a parallel verbal universe, and it is this sort of a universe that Ashbery's poetry has consistently evoked.

... Returning to the collection with which I began this discussion, *Self Portrait in a Convex Mirror*, we find the painterly sensibility evident throughout Ashbery's work linked to the meditative mode that emerged as early as *Rivers and Mountains* but flourished fully in *Three Poems*. The title poem opens with a comment on the distortive quality of art even in its lucidity. In the Parmigianino portrait it describes,

> the right hand
> Bigger than the head, thrust at the viewer
> And swerving easily away, as though to protect
> What it advertises.

What it advertises, of course, is the artist's vision of himself, a vision limited by the confines of the mirror which contains it and misshapen by the contours of that mirror. Ashbery quotes from Vasari concerning the circumstances under which the portrait was made—Parmigianino's determination to copy exactly everything he saw looking into a convex barber's mirror on a similarly shaped piece of wood. The portrait, as we look at it, "Is the reflection once removed," and Ashbery's poem about the portrait removes us yet further from the actual physical reality of Francesco Parmigianino toward a metaphysical reality—a disembodied consciousness evoked by the presence of the portrait. Art captures life, but what is the nature of that life it captures, how much of his life can the artist give to his art and still remain alive? "... the soul establishes itself, / But how far can it swim out through the eyes / And still return safely to its nest?"

The soul of the artist was *in* his being as he painted the portrait. In another sense it is *in* the portrait itself; and in still another sense it is *in* our consciousness as we look at the portrait. Or put another way, it is *in* none of the above places, but rather exists apart from time and place in an uncharted region that is ultimately ineffable. The soul—human consciousness—will not stay contained. It is always

> Longing to be free, outside, but it must stay
> Posing in this place. It must move
> As little as possible. *This is what the portrait says.*
> [emphasis mine]

To convert the feelings evoked by, or contained within, the portrait, or within the poet's own self, into poetry means finding words for the ineffable, a paradoxical and doomed endeavor, but one which the poet, as Ashbery views the role, is destined to undertake continually:

> That is the tune but there are no words.
> The words are only speculation
> (From the Latin *speculum*, mirror):
> They seek and cannot find the meaning of the music.

Self-portraiture, then, emerges fully as a major theme in Ashbery's latest book, but it was, as I think we have seen, his theme all along.

It is, as Barbara Rose has noted, a "theme with a thousand faces," including in the broadest sense, the non-mimetic, painterly face of abstract forms, shapes, and colors. It is a theme he shares with Frank O'Hara, who wrote about "what is happening to me, allowing for lies and exaggerations" and with the abstract canvases of William Baziotes, whose paintings tell him what he is "like at the moment." Looking at life through the mirror of words, the work of O'Hara and Ashbery leads us to shatter the esthetic boundaries between painterly and poetic art. They are our painterly poets, and we need to look at a great many paintings to read them well.

Source: Fred Moramarco, "John Ashbery and Frank O'Hara: The Painterly Poets," in *Journal of Modern Literature*, Vol. 5, No. 3, September 1976, pp. 436–62.

SOURCES

Ashbery, John, "Self-Portrait in a Convex Mirror," in *Selected Poems*, Penguin, 1986, pp. 188–204.

Ashbery, John, and Mark Ford, *John Ashbery in Conversation with Mark Ford*, Between the Lines, 2003.

Emerson, Ralph Waldo, "The Over-Soul," in *Emerson's Essays*, Harper Perennial, 1981, pp. 188–211

Hartt, Frederick, "Part Four: The Renaissance," in *Art: A History of Painting, Sculpture, Architecture*, Vol. 2, 3rd edition, Prentice-Hall, 1989, pp. 627–44.

Herd, David, "John Ashbery in Conversation: The Communicative Value of *Self-Portrait in a Convex Mirror*," in *John Ashbery and American Poetry*, Manchester University Press, 2000, pp. 144–78.

Kalstone, David, "*Self-Portrait in a Convex Mirror*," in *Bloom's Modern Critical Views: John Ashbery*, edited by Harold Bloom, Chelsea House Publishers, 1985, pp. 91–114.

Leckie, Ross, "Art, Mimesis, and John Ashbery's 'Self-Portrait in a Convex Mirror'," in *Essays in Literature*, Vol. XIX, No. 1, Spring 1992, pp. 114–31.

Looper, Travis, "Ashbery's 'Self-Portrait,'" in *Papers on Language and Literature*, Vol. 28, No. 4, Fall 1992, pp. 451–56.

Moramarco, Fred, "John Ashbery and Frank O'Hara: The Painterly Poets," in *Journal of Modern Literature*, Vol. 5, No. 3, September 1976, pp. 436–62.

Plato, *Meno*, translated by. R. W. Sharples, Aris & Phillips, 1986.

Shapiro, David, "Prolegomenon: The Mirror Staged" in *John Ashbery: An Introduction to the Poetry*, Columbia University Press, 1979, pp. 177–78.

Stamelman, Richard, "Critical Reflections: Poetry and Art Criticism in Ashbery's 'Self-Portrait in a Convex Mirror,'" in *New Literary History*, Vol. 15, No. 3, Spring 1984, pp. 607–30.

FURTHER READING

Bloom, Harold, ed., *Modern Critical Views: John Ashbery*, Chelsea House Publishers, 1985.
    Bloom's collection of essays explores Ashbery's poetic aims, as well as his thematic, stylistic, and structural approaches to poetry.

Criswell, David, *The Rise and Fall of the Holy Roman Empire: From Charlemagne to Napolean*, PublishAmerica, 2005.
    This book details the power struggles between emperors and popes throughout the duration of the Holy Roman Empire, providing both a church history as well as a secular history of the time period. This study provides the historical context for understanding the political climate in Italy during the 1500s. The politics of this time greatly impacted the endeavors of artists, such as Parmigianino, whose work inspired Ashbery's poem.

Franklin, David, *The Art of Parmigianino*, Yale University Press, 2004.
    Franklin discusses Parmigianino's inspirations as well as his artistic struggles, and explores the artist's desire to convey, through his art, complex ideas. The book additionally contains numerous photographs of the artist's works.

Friedlaender, W., *Mannerism and Anti-Mannerism in Italian Painting*, Columbia University Press, 1990.
    Friedlaender, one of the world's most prominent art historians, details the elements of the Mannerist movement, discussing it as a reaction against High Renaissance ideals. Friedlaender additionally studies the artistic reaction against Mannerism, that is, the Anti-Mannerist movement.

Heffernan, James A. W., *The Poetics of Ekphrasis: From Homer to Ashbery*, University of Chicago Press, 2004.
    Heffernan studies ekphrasis (the practice of describing works of visual art) as a struggle between two modes of representation and discusses Ashbery's work within this larger framework.

Kraut, Richard, ed., *The Cambridge Companion to Plato*, Cambridge University Press, 1992.
    This collection of essays examines Plato's views on such subjects as knowledge, reality, and poetry, and places Plato's writings within the context of the intellectual and social background of his time.

The Tragedy of the Leaves

CHARLES BUKOWSKI

1963

"The Tragedy of the Leaves" is a narrative poem by Charles Bukowski, a German-American author who is noted for his heavily autobiographical stories of survival and his life as a heavy drinker existing on the fringes of society. His writing deals with raw emotion and harsh experiences, conveyed in simple, direct language and violent and sexual imagery. It is often set in the *Skid Row* areas of Los Angeles, the city that Bukowski called home for much of his life. "The Tragedy of the Leaves" first appeared in the collection *It Catches My Heart in Its Hands: New and Selected Poems, 1955–1963* (1963). It is also available in *Run With the Hunted: A Charles Bukowski Reader* (1993), and is the first poem in the collection *Burning in Water, Drowning in Flame* (1983).

"The Tragedy of the Leaves" is reminiscent of Blues songs in that it describes a tragic and critical point in the life of the speaker, a probable alcoholic who is down on his luck. He wakes in a room surrounded by empty bottles: the potted plants are dead, his woman has left him, and his landlady is screaming for the rent, which is overdue. The poem is typical of Bukowski's work in that it explores the theme of "lowlife" existence through the persona of a downtrodden and marginalized individual.

AUTHOR BIOGRAPHY

The American poet, novelist, and short story writer Charles Bukowski was born Henry Charles Bukowski, Jr., in Andernach, Germany, on August

Charles Bukowski *(Eckarth Palutke | Huntington Library | AP Images)*

16, 1920. He was the only child of an American soldier (Henry Charles Bukowski, Sr.) and a German mother, Katherine Fett Bukowski. In 1922, the family immigrated to the United States, settling in the Los Angeles area around 1925, where Bukowski spent most of his life. The city was later to become an integral part of his writing. He grew up in working-class neighborhoods where other children ridiculed him for his German origins, leading him to feel that he did not belong. Bukowski's father, who worked as a milkman, was sporadically unemployed in the Depression years (the Great Depression began with the stock market crash in 1929 and the economy only fully recovered after the end of World War II in 1945). Financial hardship did not improve his temper, and he regularly beat his son with a razor strop.

Bukowski hated his father and what he represented: the belief that economic and emotional success was won by hard work and patriotism—the American dream. Bukowski later depicted his childhood in his novel *Ham on Rye* (1982).

In an effort to shield himself from his father's brutality, the young Bukowski began his lifelong preoccupation with alcohol. He also suffered from severe acne, which left scars on his face. He underwent painful and ineffectual hospital treatments that cemented his mistrust of authority figures (doctors, fathers, and gods), a theme that recurs in his writing. During his school years Bukowski read widely. He was particularly impressed by Sinclair Lewis's *Main Street*, as well as the work of D. H. Lawrence, and Ernest Hemingway.

After graduating from Los Angeles High School, Bukowski attended Los Angeles City College from 1939 to 1941, studying journalism and literature. He left home in 1941 after an incident in which his father read his stories and then threw his belongings onto the lawn. He drifted across America, working in low-paying jobs such as gas station attendant, lift operator, truck driver, and post office clerk. By this time, his drinking had become habitual.

Bukowski began to write for publication in the mid 1940s, submitting short stories to the *New Yorker* and *Atlantic Monthly*. They were rejected. In 1944, the magazine *Story* published Bukowski's short story "Aftermath of a Lengthy Rejection Slip," which features an alcoholic writer.

In 1944, Bukowski returned to Los Angeles. The city plays a large part in many of his writings. In the same year he met Janet Cooney Baker, with whom he lived for the next decade. She also drank heavily. In the mid 1950s, Bukowski was hospitalized with an alcohol induced bleeding ulcer and nearly died. In 1955, he married the wealthy publisher of a poetry magazine, Barbara Frye, but the marriage ended in divorce two years later. He returned to the post office in Los Angeles in 1958, where he continued to work as a clerk for over a decade. He lived for some years with Frances Smith, and in 1964 they had a daughter, Marina Louise.

Bukowski started to write poems in 1955, but his rise to literary recognition was arduous. Gradually he established a following for his depictions of down-and-out people. His first collection, *Flower, Fist and Bestial Wail*, was published in 1960, when he was forty. He was to follow this collection of poems with over forty others. *It Catches My Heart in Its Hands*, published in 1963, marked the first publication of "The Tragedy of the Leaves." The collection dealt with topics typical of Bukowski's work, such as cigarettes, betting on racehorses, a call girl, and drifters. The book won a 1963 Loujon Press Award.

Between 1966 and 1973 Bukowski wrote a weekly column for the alternative newspaper *Open City* called "Notes of a Dirty Old Man." The pieces were a mixture of realistic fiction, reportage, and anti-authoritarian opinion, and were collected in a book, *Notes of a Dirty Old Man* (1969).

Bukowski gained a wide readership in Germany and France, but it took longer to establish his reputation in his home country of the United States, where he remained virtually unknown beyond a small cult following. This impasse was broken in 1970, when his friend and publisher John Martin of Black Sparrow Press rescued him from wage slavery at the post office. Martin offered to pay the poet a monthly stipend of a hundred dollars if he would do nothing but write. In return, Martin would retain the right to publish his work. The arrangement proved a success for both publisher and author. By the time Bukowski died, his monthly payment had risen to seven thousand dollars, he had nineteen books in print, and he was a bestselling poet.

Bukowski's first collection of short stories, *Erections, Ejaculations, Exhibitions, and General Tales of Ordinary Madness* (1972), covered similar subject matter to his poems: sex, violence, and the absurdities of life. Another collection of stories, the semi-autobiographical *Hot Water Music*, was published in 1983 to considerable acclaim. The protagonists of the stories are often underground writers, similar to Bukowski himself, living in hardship and violence. Bukowski's main alter ego, or autobiographical figure, is Henry Chinaski, a down-and-out writer and a modern version of the Underground Man of the Russian nineteenth-century author Fyodor Dostoevsky. Dostoevsky wrote his novel *Notes From the Underground* (1864) from the point of view of the character of the Underground Man, an anti-hero who is hyperconscious, analyzes his own feelings and actions, feels himself a failure, and finds it impossible to engage fully in a life of action.

Chinaski also appears in many of Bukowski's novels, including *Post Office* (1971), where Chinaski emerges as a figure of rebellion against mean-minded bureaucrats, and *Ham on Rye*. The film *Barfly* (released 1987), for which Bukowski wrote the screenplay, stars Mickey Rourke as Chinaski. Bukowski used his experience of making *Barfly* as the basis of his novel *Hollywood* (1989), which portrays Chinaski as a successful old man leading a respectable life.

In 1973, the film director Taylor Hackford presented Bukowski to a wider audience in a documentary, *Bukowski*, for Los Angeles public television station KCET. The film won the San Francisco Film Festival's Silver Reel Award after being voted the best cultural film on public TV. Bukowski received a National Endowment for the Arts grant in 1974.

Bukowski's hell-raising personality did little to secure his reputation among the literary establishment. He was caught drunk on film praising the dictators Idi Amin and Adolf Hitler in a series of interviews shot by the French director Barbet Schroeder that ran on French TV in the mid-1970s.

In 1976, Bukowski met Linda Lee Beighle, a health-food restaurateur, and they became a couple, marrying in 1985. This marked a more stable and prosperous phase of Bukowski's life. He earned steady royalties in the low six-figure range, bought a home in San Pedro, California, had a swimming pool, and drove a black BMW.

Pulp, a parody of the pulp detective novel, is the novel Bukowski worked on just prior to his death from leukemia in San Pedro, California, on March 9, 1994. It was published posthumously in 1994.

POEM SUMMARY

Lines 1–12

The poem opens with the speaker awakening in his room. There is an atmosphere of dryness and the potted ferns have turned "yellow as corn" and are dead. The speaker's woman has left him, and he is surrounded by empty bottles of the alcohol he has drunk. In a simile (a comparison using *like* or *as*), the empty bottles are compared with corpses drained of their lifeblood. They have become symbols of "uselessness," a word that comments on the speaker's own life.

Into this scene of bleakness, the speaker introduces one hopeful note: the sun, which is "still good." His attention is drawn to a note he has received from his landlady, which has either been written on yellow paper or on paper that is yellowing with age, since its "yellowness" is mentioned. The note is an eviction notice, as the speaker has not paid his rent. The note being "cracked" has a double and possibly a triple meaning: the paper is cracked through age and being dried out; the paper makes a cracking sound as the speaker handles it; and musically, a cracked note is a break in tone, as might be heard in the voice of a singer of a jazz or blues song. In the case of this last meaning, there is an implicit identification of the landlady with a jazz or blues singer. These lines may encompass one, two, or all three of these meanings.

At line 8 the speaker distances himself from the scene he has described to make the wry comment that what is needed now is a comedian or jester to make jokes about the absurdity of pain. The comedian or jester is described as "ancient style" because he was a standard character in traditional stories and dramas dating at least as far back as the ancient Greek period (this period of history is variously defined, but some historians place it between 1000 B.C.E. and 323 B.C.E.). The jester was also found in literature, drama, and folk traditions of medieval Europe, and passed into the drama of William Shakespeare, where he is usually termed a fool. The figure of the jester can connote a variety of qualities: innocence; ignorance; heterodoxy; freedom from observation of cultural, social, or religious convention; joy;

freedom from earthly desires; perversity; audacity; truth; confidence; or cultural power. Traditionally, a jester or fool was given unrivalled license by his powerful or wealthy patron to speak in a disrespectful or honest way to his superiors under the protective guise of comedy. Thus Shakespeare often used a jester or fool (as in *King Lear*) to utter truths to the King that nobody else would dare to broach. The jester is also used to comment on the characters or action in an ironic, detached, or mocking manner.

In this poem, the jester is invoked but then immediately dismissed by the speaker. The jester would be expected to comment on the absurdity of the speaker's pain, but the speaker overrules the jester, saying that the only absurd aspect of pain is its very existence. There is no more to be said on the subject of the absurdity of pain, the speaker says.

The speaker makes a shift back to the action narrated in the poem. He shaves carefully with an old razor.

Lines 13–25

As he shaves, the speaker describes himself as "the man who had once been young and / said to have genius." The speaker juxtaposes the promise and hope that characterized his youth with the failure and disappointment he experiences now. He identifies the tragedy of his life with "the tragedy of the leaves," the plants that were once alive but that now are dead. His use of the third person to talk about himself ("the man who") emphasizes the yawning gap he feels between the promise of his youth and the reality of his life as a mature man who has not fulfilled that promise.

At line 17 the narrative of the poem shifts again as the speaker makes his first decisive move. He walks out of his room into the dark hall of the building where he lives. The landlady stands there waiting for him, cursing ("execrating") him. The word "final" suggests that she is not going to give him a second chance: this is the end of his tenure here. The words "sending me to hell" have both a figurative and a literal sense. In the figurative sense, the words mean that she is cursing or swearing at him, or damning him. Literally, the words mean that she is sending him to hell, just as a vengeful God would send a sinner to hell. This particular hell would be homelessness, life on the streets, and all the dangers and hardships attendant on that state.

The landlady is described in dehumanizing terms: she is reduced to a figure "waving her fat, sweaty arms" and screaming for the rent. This is an ugly picture that does not convey any sympathy for the landlady. The tone, however, shifts markedly in the last two lines. The speaker gives the reason why the landlady is screaming and waving her arms: "because the world had failed us / both." Here, the landlady is brought into the orbit of the speaker, and he identifies with her: both, he says, have been let down by the world. Both are unlucky, both are suffering.

THEMES

Disappointment, Disillusionment, and Failure

The main theme of "The Tragedy of the Leaves" is the disappointment and disillusionment attendant on failure and misfortune in life. The poem captures a moment in the speaker's life when he is down on his luck. He has been drinking; his woman has left him; and he is about to be evicted from his rented room because he has not been able to pay the rent. He contrasts his present situation with the promise of his youth, when he was "said to have genius." That promise has come to nothing, and his life is as hopeless as the dead potted plants in his room. "The tragedy of the leaves" represents the tragedy of his life. Growth, lushness, and vitality have been replaced by decay, dryness, and death.

Alienation

The speaker of the poem is portrayed as being very much alone in his life. He no longer has the companionship of his woman, his supply of alcohol has run out, and his only companions are dead plants. He lives in a rented room from which he is about to be evicted by a hostile landlady. When he uses the phrase "the man who," about himself, the speaker shows that he is even alienated from his younger and more promising self. Mainstream society, prosperity, and employment appear to have passed him by. The descriptors "fine" and "undemanding" applied to the landlady's note may have a sarcastic ring to them: there is nothing fine about the landlady and nothing undemanding about her note, as transpires later in the poem. But these words also emphasize the speaker's cynical, or perhaps even philosophical, detachment from his situation.

The only touch of human warmth in the poem lies in the last lines, "because the world had failed us / both." On this level, the poet is joined to, and not alienated from, his screaming landlady. In their similar suffering and privation

TOPICS FOR FURTHER STUDY

- Interview someone who has experienced extreme poverty and/or homelessness. Find out the circumstances and events that led to their situation. To what extent, in their view, were these events beyond (or in) their control? If they were able to improve their situation at any point, how were they able to do so? Convey your findings in a class presentation.

- Read George Orwell's novel *Down and Out in Paris and London* (1933). Write an essay in which you compare Orwell's treatment of poverty and dispossession with Bukowski's in "The Tragedy of the Leaves."

- Research the causes, nature, and effects of homelessness in a particular region. Identify the main demographic groups that are affected, and why they may be especially vulnerable. Compile a report on your findings, including graphs, photographs, or other visual aids.

- Bukowski has been called a Beat writer (The Beats were a group of writers that reached prominence from the mid 1950s to the early 1960s). Research the Beat poets and the characteristics considered typical of their work. Write an essay discussing which aspects of the Beat movement "The Tragedy of the Leaves" reflects.

lies the only hint of belonging and commonality that can be discerned in the poem.

Life and Death

The speaker's journey into disillusionment and failure is described in terms of the life that he once embodied versus the death that seems about to engulf him. Death is not seen as a fulfillment but as a negation: of hope, achievement, youth, talent, companionship, and vitality. Death is only mentioned explicitly with regard to the dead potted plants, but the speaker is surrounded by imagery of death and emptiness. The landlady herself becomes a figure connoting death: she stands in a dark hallway, "execrating" or cursing the speaker and sending him to hell, just as an angry God might do. She is momentarily transformed into a dark angel of death, a judging and vengeful figure who has come to tell the speaker that his tenancy—perhaps not just of her room, but of life itself—is at an end.

Tragedy and Comedy
The poem's title alerts the reader to the tone of the poem. The tragedy of the leaves is that they were once alive but now they are dying. The leaves are equated with the speaker's life, which once showed promise but which has since turned into a tragedy.

A tragedy can be defined as a work of literature, often a drama, dealing with a serious or sorrowful theme. It typically involves a great person doomed to destruction through a flaw of character or conflict with some external force, such as fate or society. A comedy is a work of literature, often a drama, of light and humorous character with a happy ending. The narrative of a comedy involves the protagonist's triumph over adverse circumstances, resulting in a successful conclusion, often a life-affirming romance or marriage. The genres of tragedy and comedy are often mixed for dramatic effect. Comic characters or jesters may appear in tragedies in order to offer a novel perspective on the tragic story that is unfolding, or to show that even in the midst of suffering, joy has its place.

Bukowski exploits this tradition of introducing a jester to comment on the tragic story of his poem, to make jokes about absurd pain. But he then goes on to subvert the tradition, when the speaker immediately dismisses the jester as having nothing to contribute to this story. The speaker goes on to explain that his life is a tragedy as final as that of the dead potted plants. The tragedy encompasses not only himself, but also his seeming adversary, the landlady: life has "failed" them both equally. However, whereas most tragedy is grandiose in scale, telling the story of the fall of great people, the tragedy of the speaker's life is small, domestic, even mundane: his life has been no more significant than the withering leaves on a dead house plant.

STYLE

Informal Style
"The Tragedy of the Leaves" is written in an informal, conversational style, relatively free from poetic ornament. The sense is that the poet is speaking directly to the reader in the cadences of everyday speech, a technique perfected by the poet William Carlos Williams. Bukowski was also influenced by the novelist Ernest Hemingway's abrupt, spare style. This style is maintained in spite of the poem's tragic theme: there is a complete absence of melodrama. The speaker describes his predicament in a detached, unemotional tone that is all the more moving because it is so matter-of-fact. The poem is written in free verse, with irregular meter and line length, which adds to its informality.

Off Rhymes, Repetition, and Alliteration
While the poem does not rhyme in the traditional way, with words at the ends of lines sharing the same final sounds, it is full of off rhymes, or half rhymes, as they are sometimes called. The off rhymes may fall in the middle of lines, as with "uselessness" and "yellowness", or at the ends of lines, as with "hall" and "hell." There are also repeated words, such as "dead" and "screaming," which produce a chiming effect that creates a sense of foreboding and helplessness against inevitability. Alliteration, where the same initial sound of a word is repeated, is used in "a jester / with jokes," where the *j* sound is repeated. All these effects set up an internal musicality and rhythm that adds to the vibrancy and emotional effect of the poem when read aloud.

Squalid Setting
The poem's setting is typical of Bukowski and the Beat Generation of poets with whom he is sometimes associated. It is a seedy, down-at-heel, rented room in a building populated by poor and desperate people: himself and a landlady who is as deplorable as he. The speaker is surrounded by the detritus of a decayed, barren, and futile life: emptied bottles of alcohol, dead plants, an old razor. The hallway is dark, and the only other person in the poem besides the speaker is not a friend or relative (his woman has left him), but the landlady who wants his rent and is about to evict him. It is a dehumanized and isolating environment that reflects the sense of alienation in the poem.

HISTORICAL CONTEXT

The Beat Generation and Subculture
The American author Jack Kerouac is generally thought to be responsible for introducing the

COMPARE
&
CONTRAST

- **1960s:** The rise of public questioning of the political establishment in the United States is galvanized by the public's disenchantment with the government's involvement in the Vietnam War. "The Tragedy of the Leaves" is told from the point of view of a disenchanted and dispossessed speaker, who stands outside the social and political system and criticizes it because it has "failed us / both."

  Today: Public questioning of the political establishment is widespread in certain circles, fueled by the free exchange of information on the Internet. Examples include opposition to the war in Iraq and the continuing discussion of the events that have unfolded following the terrorist attacks of September 11, 2001.

- **1960s:** Many towns and cities in the United States contain an area mostly populated by the poor, as well as transients, the mentally ill, and alcoholics. The slang term for any such area is *Skid Row*.

  Today: According to a 2004 press release from the National Law Center on Homelessness and Poverty, over any one year "2.5–3.5 million people are homeless; of this number, 1.35 million are children." The Center identifies "increasing rents, destruction of existing low-income housing, and cuts in federal housing programs" as contributing factors. According to the National Coalition for the Homeless, in 2005, the proportion of homeless people who are addicts is 30 percent.

- **1960s:** The Community Mental Health Act of 1963 exacerbates homelessness in the United States. Long-term psychiatric patients are released from state hospitals into the community. Support systems are absent or inadequate, and a large sector of this population is subsequently found living on the streets with no support system.

  Today: According to 2005 figures cited by the National Coalition for the Homeless, "approximately 16 percent of the single adult homeless population suffers from some form of severe mental illness."

- **1960s:** Between 1966 and 1968 in San Francisco, a group calling itself the Diggers opens free stores, where everything in the store is given away, and serve free food to homeless people and others. The Diggers also provide free medical care, transport, and temporary housing. The movement recognizes the rise of a subgroup of people who are homeless or poor out of political choice rather than misfortune.

  Today: The gift economy, in which goods and money are given away without any agreement of repayment, continues in the form of philanthropic acts by individuals, groups, foundations, and corporations. The Freecycle Network is a nonprofit organization registered in Arizona that oversees a worldwide network of gifting groups, aiming to divert reusable goods from landfills.

---

phrase *Beat Generation* around 1948. The term described a group of writers who reached prominence from the mid 1950s to the early 1960s, and who shared many of the same themes and ideas. Kerouac introduced the term to the novelist John Clellon Holmes, who published a novel about the Beat Generation, *GO!*, in 1952, and a type of manifesto in the *New York Times Magazine* titled "This is the Beat Generation" (published November 16, 1952). The novel was a thinly disguised account of the lives of key Beat figures, including Kerouac, Neal Cassady, and Allen Ginsberg. In the novel, as in life, they present themselves as moral pioneers who reject materialism and the values that support it, in favor of adventurous lives involving a search for deeper meaning.

The adjective *Beat* is thought to have been introduced to the group by the American subculture icon Herbert Huncke, who used the word to describe someone living roughly with little money and prospects. Though it seemed that Kerouac initially used the term *Beat* to suggest that he and his circle were beaten down by conformist society, he later added positive connotations, insisting that the word meant upbeat, beatific, and musically on the beat, in correct rhythm. All these connotations of the word passed into the term *Beatnik*, which originally meant a follower of the Beat Generation but came to describe anyone who rejects conventional behavior.

The original group of Beat writers was based in New York, but later, writers based in San Francisco were also identified as part of the Beat movement. The movement was a twentieth-century version of Romanticism, a literary protest movement that emphasized a spontaneous expression of the individual's vital energies and subjective experience. Beats were disaffected people who rebelled against what they saw as the rigid, outdated, and discredited views and conventions that characterized post-World War II American society. They coined a word, *square*, that summed up everything they opposed: conventional morality, received wisdom, authority, racism, imperialism, being out of date or out of touch. Their stance frequently involved alienation, an opposition to war, drug-taking and addiction, inter-racial relationships, an interest in Eastern thought and religion, an ecological sensibility, and decadent, alternative, and self-destructive lifestyles. All these elements permeated their literature.

Other Beat characteristics that passed into the work of poets such as Bukowski include a direct, conversational, and informal style, employed in an attempt to communicate directly to the reader; gritty depictions of unconventional and visceral experience; and the use of antiheroes and low characters. Beat writers tried to show the underbelly of life, the flip side of the American dream.

Jack Kerouac's novel *On the Road* (1957), Allen Ginsberg's epic poem "Howl" (1956), and William S. Burroughs's novel *Naked Lunch* (1959) are considered some of the most important works of the Beat Generation. The role of the Beat writers as subversives was confirmed in 1957, when Ginsberg's collection *Howl and Other Poems* was the subject of a landmark obscenity trial. Its publisher, Lawrence Ferlinghetti, was charged with disseminating indecent writings. The charges centered around supposedly obscene words and images in the poem "Howl." The judge ruled that Ginsberg's poem was not obscene, and stated that freedom of speech and of the press depended upon an author's right to express his thoughts in his own words.

Bukowski was never closely associated with Kerouac, Ginsberg, or other major Beat writers, and has tried to distance himself from them. However, his conversational style, nonconformist stance, and subcultural subject matter have led some readers and critics to identify him with the Beat movement. His poem "The Tragedy of the Leaves" is characteristic both of his own work and of the Beat tradition. It is written in free verse and in an informal style; it features a poverty-stricken and probably alcoholic speaker who lives on the margins of society in a state of alienation from the mainstream; and it points an accusing finger at a society that allows such privation to exist ("the world had failed us / both"). The speaker also shares the Romantic Beat tendency of viewing himself as superior to, and more acutely conscious of truth than, mainstream society. He was once "said to have genius," and he sends away the jester who is ready to dispense conventional wisdom because he himself knows better: "pain is absurd / because it exists, nothing more."

Confessional Poetry

Confessional poetry became popular during the 1950s and 1960s. It is characterized by the poet's revelations of raw, intimate, and often unflattering information about himself or herself, particularly to do with sex, illness, addiction, and despair. Poets who have been classed as confessional include Allen Ginsberg, Robert Lowell, Sylvia Plath, and Anne Sexton. "The Tragedy of the Leaves," can be said to fit into the confessional genre, as it entails the speaker laying bare the disappointments of his life: alcohol addiction, an unfulfilling sexual liaison, poverty, and alienation.

CRITICAL OVERVIEW

The collection in which "The Tragedy of the Leaves" first appeared, *It Catches My Heart in Its Hands*, was published in 1963 to an enthusiastic response from Bukowski's loyal cult following. The poet Kenneth Rexroth, in his 1964 review for the *New York Times Book Review*,

Scene from the 1987 version of Barfly, *with Mickey Rourke, Faye Dunaway, Barbet Schroeder, and Charles Bukowski* (Cannon / The Kobal Collection / The Picture Desk, Inc.)

however, is more guarded in his response. He warily distances himself from the "small but loudly enthusiastic claque" that views Bukowski as "the greatest thing since Homer." Nevertheless, he is generous in his praise of the collection. Rexroth judges the collection to be "simple, casual, honest, uncooked." He adds that Bukowski writes about what he knows: "rerolling cigarette butts . . . the horse that came in and the hundred-dollar call girl that came in with it, the ragged hitchhiker on the road to nowhere." Noting Bukowski's outsider status, Rexroth writes that Bukowski "belongs in the small company of poets of real, not literary, alienation."

Several decades later, Bukowski has become a bestselling poet and his literary reputation has solidified, though some critics remain ambivalent. A 1993 *Publishers Weekly* review of the collection *Run with the Hunted*, which also contains "The Tragedy of the Leaves," notes that the "stunning directness and infamous 'bad attitude'" of Bukowski's autobiographical poetry and fiction are "as captivating as they are repugnant." In a comment that could be applied to

"The Tragedy of the Leaves," the reviewer praises the immediacy and candor of Bukowski's work, along with his "singular blend of cynicism, misanthropy and unexpected sentimentality."

In her review of *Run with the Hunted* for the *New Statesman & Society*, Elizabeth Young calls the collection "poignant and moving," with an acerbic edge and a sense of the frailty of human endeavor. An obituary by William Grimes in the *New York Times*, written after Bukowski's death in 1994, sums up the poet's literary reputation in words that reflect the flavor of "The Tragedy of the Leaves": "Mr. Bukowski was a bard of the barroom and the brothel, a direct descendant of the Romantic visionaries who worshiped at the altar of personal excess, violence and madness."

CRITICISM

Claire Robinson

Robinson has an M.A. in English. She is a former teacher of English literature and creative writing,

WHAT DO I READ NEXT?

- *Hot Water Music* (1983) is a highly acclaimed collection of short stories by Bukowski. The stories examine all manner of dysfunctional relationships. One such story, "The Death of the Father," is a funny yet tragic and moving analysis of the days following the death of Bukowski's father.

- Readers who enjoy Bukowski's tales of womanizing and drifting may like the work of Henry Miller, to whom Bukowski is often compared. *Tropic of Cancer* (published in Paris in 1934) recounts the adventures of a vagabond American who lives on Paris's West Bank, welcoming poverty and ostracism in pursuit of erotic pleasure and his soul's freedom.

- Allen Ginsberg's epic poem "Howl," first published in *Howl and Other Poems* in 1956, is a masterpiece of innovation and dissent. It exercised a major influence on the Beat writers and other antiestablishment figures, including Bukowski. The poem is both a cry of rebellion against conventional society and an expression of sympathy for human suffering.

- *Bukowski and the Beats: A Commentary on the Beat Generation* (2002), by Jean-Francois Duval, is an examination of Bukowski's life and work in relation to other Beat writers. In spite of Bukowski's attempts to disassociate himself from the Beats, Duval finds many historical and thematic links between them, as well as some philosophical and aesthetic differences. He includes anecdotes about Bukowski's meetings with Beat writers, including Lawrence Ferlinghetti, Neal Cassady, Allen Ginsberg, and William Burroughs.

- *Down and Out in America: The Origins of Homelessness* (1991), by Peter H. Rossi, offers a comprehensive picture of homelessness. It explains causes, proposes solutions, and draws contrasts between the homeless of the 1950s and 1960s and the homeless population of today, which is younger and contains more women, children, and African Americans.

---

and is currently a freelance writer and editor. In the following essay, Robinson explores how Bukowski uses symbolism and imagery in "The Tragedy of the Leaves."

John William Corrington, in his 1963 critique of *It Catches My Heart in Its Hands* in the *Northwest Review*, challenges those academic critics who decry Bukowski's "poetry of surfaces." Corrington acknowledges Bukowski's concern with the concrete, observed in minute detail, but interprets it as an aspect of the work's "savage vitality." He notes that the middle stage between act and art, of intellectual analysis and synthesis, simply does not exist in Bukowski's poetry: "Act moves into image directly; feeling is articulated as figure and intellection is minimal." Corrington adds that if there is symbolic value in the work, "the reader is spared a kind of

burdensome awareness of that symbolism on the part of the writer."

Singling out "The Tragedy of the Leaves" for illustration, Corrington writes that it would be folly to read the poem as simple description, but an equal folly to suggest that the poem's surface is simply an excuse for its symbolic significance: "Symbol rises from event ... Bukowski's poem is symbolic as all great work is symbolic: the verity of its surface is so nearly absolute that the situation it specifies produces the overtones of a world much vaster than that of the landlady's dark hall."

Corrington draws attention to an unusual strength of Bukowski that is perfectly exemplified in "The Tragedy of the Leaves": his ability to suggest meaning through symbols and imagery in a way that is so subtle as to be almost invisible.

"

THE POEM CAN BE READ PURELY IN TERMS OF ITS SURFACE MEANING. IT MAKES PERFECT SENSE AS AN OBSERVED SCENE FROM THE LIFE OF A DOWN AND OUT MAN, BUT IT ALSO RICHLY REPAYS A DEEPER READING."

The poem can be read purely in terms of its surface meaning. It makes perfect sense as an observed scene from the life of a down and out man, but it also richly repays a deeper reading.

The images are used to convey the stark opposites in the poem: life and death, hope and despair, comedy and tragedy. It is significant that these opposites are not given equal weight: the balance always comes down on the side of death, despair, emptiness, and tragedy. The jester, a symbol of life-affirming comedy, is introduced but summarily dismissed by a speaker. The speaker, it is suggested, knows more of the reality of life than the jester, a traditional purveyor of wisdom, and he knows it to be unqualified tragedy. Another example of the imagery of opposites is that of the potted plants. These were living once (symbolic of the speaker's life, which was once characterized by growth and promise), but are only presented in the poem as yellow, withered, and dead, like the speaker himself. The concept of death is forced home by the frequent repetition of the word "dead," chiming like a bell ringing the death toll.

Life and death are symbolized in the poem by the opposites of wetness and dryness. The speaker has "awakened to dryness," and the plants have dried up and died. The speaker is surrounded by bottles of alcohol, which he has drained dry. The resonance of this image is reinforced by the simile in which the bottles are compared with "bled corpses," bodies that are not only dead but drained of their life fluid. Thus everything that was once lush and wet with living sap is now dried up and dying or already dead. This idea is echoed by the fact that the speaker's woman has left him. Relationship, which defines so much of a living human being's identity, is no more. The overall feeling conveyed is that the speaker's own life has dried up and is heading fast towards death: he is "the man who had once been young and / said to have genius."

The images of dryness may also symbolize the drying up of the poet's inspiration or flow of creativity. While the speaker is not explicitly described as a poet, the strong autobiographical nature of Bukowski's work, along with the fact that this poem was written at a point in his life when he was struggling in low-paying jobs and finding it difficult to publish his poetry, suggest that he is writing about the death of creativity as well as death in its literal sense. This interpretation ties in with the beginning of the poem, which describes the poet's awakening, a word that connotes the arrival of vision or realization as well as the literal meaning of the end of sleep. In a typically Bukowskian irony, this poet's awakening is to a realization of the death of his creativity. But an awakening it is, and there is the sense that the significance of this point in the speaker's life stretches far beyond the question of whether he can pay his rent.

Certainly, Bukowski believed that drinking alcohol to excess produced a series of deaths and rebirths, as he describes in an interview with Robert Wennersten in *London* magazine:

> Drinking ... joggles you out of the standardism of everyday life ... It yanks you out of your body and your mind and throws you up against the wall. I have the feeling that drinking is a form of suicide where you're allowed to return to life and begin all over the next day. It's like killing yourself, and then you're reborn.

Bukowski is describing a transcendent experience, reminiscent of the descent of a mythical hero into the underworld (the home of the dead), to emerge reborn, transformed in some way. Such a reading is supported by the "dark hall," symbolic of the underworld, and the suggestion of the symbolic role of the landlady as a type of guardian of the gate to the afterlife who judges the speaker's life.

The razor, too, is a discomforting image that emphasizes the proximity of death. The speaker shaves "carefully," raising an implicit question as to what would happen if he were not being careful. The line between his careful shaving and the desperate act of slitting his throat is a fine one. The fact that he is taking care not to slit his throat is almost redundant because the man he used to be, who had "genius," is long gone. In effect, that man is dead, and the man who is left may as well be.

Is there no glimmer of light in this poem? Robert Peters, in *Where the Bee Sucks: Workers,*

Drones, and Queens in Contemporary American Poetry, believes that the speaker mentions the sunlight as a sign that he is "sensing the positive." This is thrown into doubt, however, by what follows. Sunlight is golden, but everywhere else in the poem, yellowness is not a life-affirming quality; usually, it connotes death. The landlady's note may be characterized by "fine and / undemanding yellowness," but it later transpires that it is anything but undemanding. It is an eviction note, which marks not only the end of his tenancy in the building, but also symbolically, the end of his tenancy of life. This notion is reinforced by the all-pervading symbolism of death in the poem. The ferns are "yellow as corn," which would normally be a cheerful image of harvest, but here, it merely means that they are dead. In Bukowski's world, therefore, sunlight and the color yellow are not to be taken at face value.

In addition, it should be remembered that the final image of the poem is of the speaker walking out of the room from which he can see the sun, into the "dark hall." Where is the golden sun now? For the speaker, it has vanished, as darkness envelops him. It is not a peaceful, blessed darkness, either: the landlady is "execrating" or cursing him, "screaming" at him, "waving her fat, sweaty arms," and sending him "to hell." The idea is one of damnation. The landlady becomes symbolic both of an angel (herald) of death and of a judging, godlike figure. She is able to decide the fate of the speaker's soul, and has determined that it does not deserve redemption. Her decision is "final." The dark hallway is reminiscent of the dark tunnel of near-death experiences, except that most of these describe a light at the end. Here, there is no light.

As a comment on modern society, dominated as it is by the capitalist economic model, the poem is bitter in the extreme. The condition of having no money is deemed worthy of damnation. The speaker is, in essence, being thrown into the eternal dustbin because he cannot pay the rent.

The poem's vision would be unremittingly bleak were it not for a single redeeming element. It comes in the final line and a half, and as such is reminiscent of the final couplet of a sonnet, which marks a shift in perspective. Until this point, the landlady has been the villain of the piece: hostile, ugly, loud, and screaming for rent. But in the final lines, the speaker explains why she is as she is: "because the world had failed us /

both." This is a recognition of the common humanity that the speaker and the landlady share. Finally, even this angel of death is caught in the same trap as the speaker, and is as much a victim as he. On this level of sympathy and love, the landlady is no godlike figure damning him to hell, but only another human being who shares his predicament: the desperation of the powerless, the suffering, and the dispossessed.

As Corrington points out, this vast story, in all its depth and resonance, is told without intellectualizing, and without analysis. Rather, it is communicated directly in images that allow the overlying surface description to maintain a perfect integrity and to be understood purely on its own level. So exact is the match between the surface and the deeper symbolic meanings that the deeper level may barely be visible on a first or quick reading. The symbolic meaning does not impose itself on the reader; on the contrary, it whispers, only emerging fully when the reader's mind is quiet enough to let the images speak.

Source: Claire Robinson, Critical Essay on "The Tragedy of the Leaves," in *Poetry for Students*, Gale, Cengage Learning, 2008.

Jean-Francois Duval

In the following excerpt, Duval attempts to disconnect Bukowski somewhat from his association with the Beat writers, and to reconnect him with a more politically active and socially conscious form of countercultural art.

In 1994, the year that saw the renewal of interest in the Beat generation, Charles Bukowski died in San Pedro, California. He was a notable figure of the counterculture. Many newspapers—in Europe particularly—were a bit too quick to present him as Kerouac and Ginsberg's successor. Charles Bukowski would probably better rank in the third section of Leary's classification (as discussed above)—the post-Beat punk era. There is no doubt that Bukowski's "destroy" mythology—dirty and perpetually drunk, surrounded by a pile of beer bottles and boxes—matched the punk aesthetic more closely, and it is probably no accident that Buk's international recognition in the '70s coincided with the advent of *No Future* philosophy.

When he was interviewed in 1978 in Paris by the chief editor of *Paris Métro,* Bukowski made this clear: he declared "that he felt closer to the punks than to the beatniks," and he added: "I'm not interested in this bohemian, Greenwich Village, Parisian

> FOR BUKOWSKI, AMERICA WAS MUCH MORE UNSENTIMENTAL THAN A LYRICAL POEM IN KEROUAC'S STYLE."

bullshit. Algiers, Tangiers that's all romantic clap-trap." Back in 1967 when an American magazine associated him with the beatniks' heroes—"Timothy Leary, Norman Mailer, William Burroughs, Jean Genet, Henry Miller, LeRoi Jones, Lawrence Ferlinghetti, Bob Dylan, Bertolt Brecht, John Cage, Eugène Ionesco, W. H. Auden, Anaïs Nin, Allen Ginsberg and Charles Bukowski"—Buk felt an affinity with only a few of these big names. He clarified this in a letter to his German translator, Carl Weissner: "Genet in portions when he doesn't creampuff out in love with his writing, Brecht in portions, and the very early Auden."

Let's take for instance the way he reports his "encounter" with one of the most famous Beats. In his novel *Women* he tells of a reading that Chinaski, his alter ego, agreed to give in the North. "It was the afternoon before the reading and I was sitting in an apartment at the Holiday Inn drinking beer with Joe Washington."

Suddenly Joe, the event organizer, glances through the window and calls out: "Hey, look, here comes William Burroughs across the way. He's got the apartment right next to yours. He's reading tomorrow night."

Chinaski gets up, goes over to the window and says: "It was Burroughs all right . . . We were on the second floor. Burroughs walked up the stairway, passed my window, opened his door and went in."

Joe suggests a meeting with Burroughs. Chinaski declines. All the same Joe goes to Burroughs and thinks he is doing the right thing in telling him that Chinaski is in the next room; he doesn't have much success. Burroughs barely gives a terse "Oh, is that so?"

A little later, when Chinaski leaves his room to look for an ice machine, he cannot fail to catch a glimpse of the great Bill: "As I walked by Burroughs' place, he was sitting in a chair by the window. He looked at me indifferently."

Fact or fiction (but more fact than fiction, according to his last wife Linda Lee Bukowski) the whole scene is very accurate and the two men are perfect in their respective roles. Burroughs and Bukowski have just one thing in common: a completely mutual indifference. Buk hits home in his description: Burroughs in an armchair in his motel room, stripped of expression, as silent and still as a figure in an Edward Hopper painting.

Burroughs appears here as if in a photographic negative (no meeting, nothing, zero communication). To a certain extent the "Burroughs motif" in this piece has no other function but to give Bukowski the opportunity to explain his link with the Beat writers, via the link's very absence. Burrough's personality, at that moment, reinforces this void: Victor Gioscia described Burroughs at that time as entirely cerebral, becoming more and more like "a vast computer running all the time, making arcane comparisons silently." This is the Burroughs that Buk/Chinaski probably saw through the motel room window.

Bukowski certainly didn't think too much of the Beat writers.

For this reason it seems incongruous to come across him years later, in 1992, on a film and a CD-ROM entitled *Poetry in Motion* principally devoted to the Beats. It is a collection of readings given (sometimes in front of 3000 people) by poets like Ginsberg, Burroughs, John Cage, Robert Creeley, Diane DiPrima, Michael McClure, Gary Snyder, Anne Waldman, and most unexpectedly, Charles Bukowski. The CD-ROM is even introduced by Bukowski who "after drawing a passionately eloquent sketch of Beat poetry, regained his self-control to say that everything is just beer shit. Then he knocked back a glassful of port & got pixelated Quick Time." According to the poet Anne Waldman, Bukowski's role in the film was to represent the opposite standpoint: "He is kind of the voice of dissension, in that film documentary, he is used in this way, as a kind of gallery commentaire, and that commentary is amazing, it's funny his role in there, that kind of growl, it is the slightly bitter but very funny commentator on the scene."

Indeed, the whole of Buk's correspondence between 1960 and 1970 reveals his ambiguous attitude towards the Beat writers (the first volume, *Screams from the Balcony*, was published in 1994, and the second, *Living on Luck*, in 1995). But there was a dilemma—how could he stand apart and remain aloof from a movement that was the basis of a counterculture to which he subscribed? How could he claim a similar aesthetic and state of mind, when there was no way he would fit into a group that had been seminal to the whole underground movement? On one side there was the constellation of Beat writers—Kerouac, Ginsberg, Burroughs, Gary Snyder, Philip Whalen, Gregory Corso, Michael McClure, Philip Lamantia, etc.—a literary movement that linked the West coast to the East coast. On the other side there was a loner, a rebel for all causes, a total dissident even within the counterculture. Bukowski alone embodies the most deprived, most hard-working, most popular fringe of the system's rejects, of the poor in spirit, in literature and in poetry.

Russell Harrison, the author of *Against the American Dream: Essays on Charles Bukowski*, a study that mostly refers to *Post Office* and *Factotum*, notes that Buk was probably the only American poet who addressed the nonintellectual classes and whose poetry related to the concrete and everyday realities of the world of work (although, it was pointed out, he was not really interested in the working class as a group, only as individuals). Those realities he experienced through the hundreds of dead-end jobs, reluctantly toiled at for forty years around the country. It is no surprise his first novel told of his life at the post office (writing *Post Office* inspired Buk in 1969 to leave his job of the past 11 years): the sorting office, the horrors of routine work with no creative outlet, hell for the soul of an artist...

The Beats were more up-market; bums, but heavenly bums. They, too, put their hand to a range of jobs, led a bohemian lifestyle and spent time in prison. Kerouac went to sea with the Merchant Marines, worked in a ball bearings factory and was a brakeman for Southern Pacific Railway as was Cassady. Ginsberg was involved in journalism and advertising. Like Buk, they were no angels. Herbert Huncke was a junkie and notorious thief. Neal Cassady boasted of stealing more than five hundred cars before he was twenty; not for the money but for the pleasure of going for a spin in the Rockies near Denver. Burroughs inadvertently gunned down his wife Joan while acting out William Tell in Mexico, and spent two weeks in prison before being released on bail. Lucien Carr was imprisoned for two years for the murder of a professor who was sexually harassing him. And Kerouac, who

helped Carr conceal the knife, only narrowly avoided prison by marrying Edie Parker with two policemen as witnesses.

But the perspective was different. Bad boys, shady environments and the world of crime attracted the Beats, particularly under the influence of Burroughs. The constraints of work took second place, even if they often had only a few dollars in their pockets. These constraints were also relegated to the back seat in their writing. The essential reality, in which they lived and evolved, was primarily literary, poetical, and musical. Influenced by his reading of Thomas Wolfe, Kerouac considered America principally as a poem. When Ginsberg, aged 17, first met Kerouac he confided that he wanted to study law to help the working classes, Kerouac gently pointed out: "You have never worked a day in your life in a factory, you have no idea about labor."

Kerouac himself was rather removed from the hardships of the world of work, to which he looked at primarily as a poet. In a long article about the Beat revival which appeared in 1996 in the French newspaper *Le Monde*, Samuel Blumenfeld wrote: "During a reading of 'October in the Railroad Earth' in a piano bar in 1959, Kerouac openly scorned the commuters with their tight collars obliged to catch the 5:48 train at Millbrae or San Carlos to go to work in San Francisco, while he—a son of the road—could watch the freight trains pass, take in the immensity of the sky and feel the weight of ancestral America." Carolyn Cassady in *Off the Road* tells of "the extent Kerouac was really keen on the comfort of her home, perfectly ordered, with a bourgeois interior, whose view," Blumenfeld reports sarcastically, "looked over the same Bayshore Freeway that took these commuters with tight collars from their homes to San Francisco." In fact, Kerouac romanticized the people at the bottom, as James Campbell put it rather severely: "The difference between the Beats and the bums they imitated is that the latter would have got off skid row if only they could: their failure had made them beaten, and they wouldn't have cared anything for 'beat,' which it would have been their rights to consider a white middle-class invention."

Bukowski lived in a totally different world to the Beats, alternating long periods as a bum with temporary work. At the beginning of the '70s he said: "At one time I had this idea that one could live on a bus forever: travelling, eating, getting off, shitting, getting back on the bus . . . I had the strange idea that one could stay in motion forever." But he worried about work all the time and he was unable to apply the Beats' carefree attitude to his obligations. He wrote about it (starting his sentence as usual in the lower case, a question of aesthetics): "the years I have worked in slaughterhouses and factories and gas stations and so forth, these years do not allow me to accept the well-turned word for the sake of the well-turned word." He would often tell journalists ironically: "It beats the eight hour job, doing what you are doing. It's better than the eight hour job. Don't you think?" In many respects writing was a way out of this fate. While the Beats danced along the road composing a hymn to their freedom from social proprieties, Buk put in forty years to free himself from the shackles which alcohol and poetry alone helped him to forget at times. As an echo to Kerouac's lyrical motto "the only people for me are the mad ones, the ones who are mad to live, mad to talk," Bukowski, in a letter reproduced in *Reach for the Sun*, in 1992, two years before his death, states: "Thank the gods that the first 50 years of my life were spent with the Blue Collars and the truly mad, the truly beaten." There is no lyricism in his vision of the road. The same year, he writes to an unknown correspondent: "I didn't want the road, I wanted to write so I needed some walls for that."

For Bukowski, America was much more unsentimental than a lyrical poem in Kerouac's style. When he got off the bus in New York, he thought the city seemed more brutal than anywhere else in America. "When you have only $7 in your pocket and look up at those huge buildings . . . I went to every town broke in order to learn that town from the bottom. You come into a town from the top—you know, fancy hotels, fancy dinners, fancy drinks, money in your pocket—and you're not seeing that town at all." . . .

Source: Jean-Francois Duval, "Bukowski: The Counterculture's Dissident," in *Bukowski and the Beats*, edited by Alison Ardron, Sun Dog Press, 2002, pp. 21–36.

Andrew J. Madigan

In the following article, although Madigan focuses on another of Bukowski's poems ("I Met a Genius"), the critic's brief explication does a wonderful job of discussing the theme of autonomy generally found in Bukowski's poetry. Many of the points
made in this essay can be applied to "The Tragedy of the Leaves."

One of the central ideas in the works of Charles Bukowski, particularly in his poetry, is that of the individual's need to have total control over his or her ideas, actions, and sensations. The artist, of course, must be especially sensitive to, and maintain dominion over, the self. In a mass society that attempts to systematically strip the self of autonomy, individuality, dignity, and expression, one must be continually wary. For if the Other—either overtly or through the covert mimesis of social behavior—instructs the self in the small details of existence, it might begin to tell that self how to experience the world and, ultimately, how to *be*.

Quite often, Bukowski portrays this "hegemony of normality" to betray his aesthetic stance. (Although he frequently assumes a native, ignorant, or anti-intellectual posture, Bukowski's odes to the autodidactic ecstasy of the Los Angeles Public Library argue strongly against this.) He seeks autonomy not only with regard to life, but also concerning art. The short poem "i met a genius" explores this theme eloquently:

> I met a genius on the train
> today
> about 6 years old,
> as he sat beside me
> and as the train
> ran down along the coast
> we came to the ocean
> and then he looked at me
> and said,
> it's not pretty
>
> it was the first time I'd
> realized
> that.

With the brevity and poignancy of Li Po, Bukowski deftly implies what would be ineffective if directly asserted. The narrator is almost certainly a writer, the Bukowski-Chinaski who preoccupied the author. One would imagine that Bukowski could have decided for himself whether the vista was beautiful or not, but even the archindividualist is conditioned to accept unconditionally that which society posits as true. Anesthetized by the literary convention of embracing the physical charms (if not always the power and danger) of nature as absolutely good, the narrator has never pondered the opposing view. Why is a "beautiful" pastoral scene beautiful, true, or good? If we do not question this assumption, we are enslaved by it. The writer, Bukowski would adamantly agree, needs to become free of these prejudices to create an authentic, individual, and formidable art.

These concerns are not original to Bukowski, but they are often overlooked or misunderstood in his works. Bukowski is frequently aligned, incorrectly, with the postmodern movement. Whether this is due to the author's wholesale rejection of conventional behavior, morality, and human values, or because critics too often seek to interpret and divide writers by chronology alone, one cannot be certain. One can be quite certain, however, that Bukowski continually and significantly fails to deconstruct the traditional concept of "self." In this respect Bukowski represents a "new defiant individualism" His body of work seeks not to submerge, deny, or obfuscate the self—as with the postmodern critique of the individualist hero and his struggle—but rather to elevate the self, its personal ethos, and its predilections above all else. In fact, Bukowski makes of this search for self a raison d'être, a direction, a religious quest. Thus, it is clear that Bukowski—despite his ethical ambivalence and rejection of form—has more in common with the heroes of premodern American literature (Ahab, Hester Prynne, Huck Finn) than with the antiheros of postmodern fiction.

Source: Andrew J. Madigan, "Bukowski's 'I Met A Genius,'" in *Explicator*, Vol. 55, No. 4, Summer 1997, pp. 232–33.

SOURCES

Basinski, Michael, "Charles Bukowski," in *Dictionary of Literary Biography, Volume 169: American Poets Since World War II, Fifth Series*, edited by Joseph Conte, Gale Research, 1996, pp. 63–77.

Bukowski, Charles, "The Tragedy of the Leaves," in *Run with the Hunted: A Charles Bukowski Reader*, edited by John Martin, HarperCollins, 1993, pp. 172–73.

Corrington, John William, "Charles Bukowski and the Savage Surfaces," in *Northwest Review*, Vol. 6, No. 4, Fall 1963, pp. 123–29.

Grimes, William, "Charles Bukowski Is Dead at 73; Poet whose Subject was Excess," in the *New York Times Book Review*, March 11, 1994.

Holmes, John Clellon, "This Is the Beat Generation," in the *New York Times*, November 16, 1952, p. SM10.

"Homelessness and Poverty in America," National Law Center on Homelessness and Poverty, 2007, http://www.nlchp.org/hapia_causes.cfm (accessed September 10, 2007).

"Increasing Homelessness in the United States Violates International Law," National Law Center on Homelessness and Poverty, January 2004, http://www.nlchp.org/view_release.cfm?PRID=26 (accessed September 10, 2007).

Peters, Robert, "Gab Poetry, or Duck vs. Nightingale Music: Charles Bukowski," in *Where the Bee Sucks: Workers, Drones, and Queens in Contemporary American Poetry*, Asylum Art, 1994, pp. 56–66.

Review of *Run with the Hunted*, in *Publishers Weekly*, Vol. 240, No. 13, March 29, 1993, pp. 34–36.

Rexroth, Kenneth, "There's Poetry in a Ragged Hitch-Hiker," in the *New York Times Book Review*, July 5, 1964.

Wennersten, Robert, "Paying for Horses," in *London* magazine, Vol. 1, No. 15, December 1974–January 1975, pp. 35–54.

"Who Is Homeless?," National Coalition for the Homeless, August 2007, http://www.nationalhomeless.org/publications/facts/Whois.pdf (accessed September 10, 2007).

Young, Elizabeth, Review of *Run with the Hunted*, in *New Statesman & Society*, June 17, 1994, Vol. 7, No. 307, pp. 37–39.

FURTHER READING

Bukowski, Charles, *Ham on Rye*, Ecco, 2007.
This acclaimed novel by Bukowski is the first installment of the life story of his alter ego, Henry Chinaski.

Cherkovski, Neeli, *Hank: The Life of Charles Bukowski*, Random House, 1991.
This biography, by a friend and colleague of Bukowski's, gives fascinating insights into the wild man of contemporary American poetry. Cherkovski analyzes fragments of Bukowski's poetry and prose, relating them to the writer's life.

Conley, Dalton, ed., *Wealth and Poverty in America: A Reader*, Blackwell, 2002.
This is a readable collection of essays by contemporary and historical authors on the complex relationship between the rich and the poor in the United States. It presents theories of where wealth comes from and why it tends to concentrate in the hands of the few.

Farber, David, and Beth Bailey, *The Columbia Guide to America in the 1960s*, Columbia University Press, 2003.
This book provides an accessible overview of the 1960s, the turbulent decade in which Bukowski wrote "The Tragedy of the Leaves." Essays are included on the civil rights movement, the Vietnam War, the women's movement, the sexual revolution, the environmental movement, landmark legal cases, and religion.

Hoffman, John, and Susan Froemke, eds., *Addiction: Why Can't They Just Stop?*, Rodale Books, 2007.
In this overview of the epidemic of addiction in the United States, Cheever examines the impacts of chemical dependency on addicts and their families, and explores scientific discoveries about why addicts find it so hard to quit.

The Wings

MARK DOTY
1993

The American poet and memoirist Mark Doty's lyric poem "The Wings" was published in *My Alexandria* (1993), his third volume of poetry. As of 2007 it was still in print.

"The Wings" and the other poems in *My Alexandria* are informed by Doty's experiences as a homosexual man at a time when AIDS was devastating the homosexual community in general and his own personal life in particular. In 1989 Wally Roberts, Doty's partner of many years, was diagnosed with AIDS. Roberts died of a brain infection in 1994. "The Wings" is an elegiac poem (a poem expressing grief, usually over the death of a loved one) that reflects the themes of mortality, sorrow, loss, and memory that were to become especially pronounced in Doty's work during Roberts's illness and after his death. The poem is partly set at a Vermont auction, as Doty explains in an interview with Christopher Hennessy for the *Lambda Book Report*. "The Wings," as its title suggests, features recurring images of angels, which in the last decade of the twentieth century became iconic figures in art, film, and literature relating to AIDS. The poem is typical of Doty's work in that its images and epiphanies are prompted by everyday experiences, its free verse form, and its conversational style widen its appeal beyond the homosexual community to a general readership. The collection in which the poem appears has won many awards and, with Doty's subsequent volume *Atlantis* (1995), is widely considered to

Mark Doty *(Photograph by Margaretta K. Mitchell. Reproduced by permission)*

be one of the most accomplished and important works to emerge from the AIDS epidemic.

AUTHOR BIOGRAPHY

Mark Alan Doty was born on August 10, 1953 in Maryville, Tennessee, and grew up in a succession of suburbs in Tennessee, Florida, southern California, and Arizona. His father was a civilian employee of the Army Corps of Engineers. In his memoir *Firebird*, Doty describes his troubled relationship with his father, and his mother's alcoholism.

While in Tucson, Arizona, a teacher at Doty's high school introduced him to the poet Richard Shelton, a mentor who encouraged his interest in literature. By the age of eighteen, Doty was confused and frightened about his sexual orientation. Soon after graduating from high school he married the poet Ruth Dawson. He earned a B.A. from Drake University in Des Moines, Iowa, and by 1980, he and his wife divorced. After accepting his homosexuality, Doty moved to New York City and worked as

a secretary. He then earned a master of fine arts degree in creative writing from Goddard College in Vermont. During this period Doty met his long-term partner, Wally Roberts, who worked as a window-dresser in a department store.

For several years, Doty and Roberts lived in Montpelier, Vermont, where they renovated a nineteenth-century house. In his memoir *Still Life with Oysters and Lemon* (cited by Peter Marcus in a review for the *Gay & Lesbian Review*), Doty describes his and Roberts's adventures during their time in Vermont in "the realm of auctions, a time-honored system for the redistribution of the possessions of the dead." This reflects the setting of the poem "The Wings," in which a dead woman's belongings are being auctioned off.

Doty's first collection of poems, *Turtle, Swan*, was published in 1987. In 1989, Roberts tested positive for HIV, an event that was to transform and shape Doty's life and writing. Doty himself tested negative. In the same year, Doty and Roberts visited Provincetown, Massachusetts. The beautiful coastal setting and the large gay community convinced them to settle there. Doty's second volume of poems, *Bethlehem in Broad Daylight*, appeared shortly thereafter in 1991.

Doty's next volume of poetry, *My Alexandria* (1993), in which "The Wings" was included, marked his critical breakthrough. The book was chosen to receive sponsorship as a National Poetry Series publication that same year. It won the Los Angeles Times Book Award for Poetry (1993) and the National Book Critics Circle Award for Poetry (1994). The book also won the T.S. Eliot Prize for best book of poetry published in the United Kingdom in 1995, the first time that the prize had been won by an American author. This volume and its successor, *Atlantis* (1995), took as their main theme the ordeal of Roberts's deteriorating health and death from an AIDS-related brain infection in 1994. *Atlantis* won the Lambda Literary Award for Gay Men's Poetry (1995), the Ambassador Book Award (1996), and the Boston Review's Bingham Poetry Prize (1996).

Doty found writing poetry difficult after Roberts's death, so he turned to prose, writing a memoir about his life with Roberts called *Heaven's Coast* (1996). The book won the PEN/Martha Albrand Award for First Nonfiction (1997). Doty then returned to poetry and published *Sweet Machine* in 1998, and a memoir about his childhood, *Firebird*, in 1999. Doty published an extended essay mixing memoir and art history, *Still Life with Oysters and Lemon,* in 2001. Another volume of poetry, *Source,* appeared in 2001, and explores gay eroticism and post-AIDS mourning. *Seeing Venice: Bellotto's Grand Canal* (2002), is an essay illustrated with photographs of Venice.

Throughout his career, Doty has taught creative writing and poetry at institutions including Columbia University, the University of Utah, the University of Houston, and Goddard College. As of 2007, Doty was John and Rebecca Moores Professor in the graduate creative writing program at the University of Houston.

POEM TEXT

The bored child at the auction
lies in his black rainboots reading,
on the grass, while beneath the tent

his parents grow rich with witness:
things that were owned once, in place,   5
now must be cared for, carried

to the block. A coast of cloud
becomes enormous, above the wet field,
while the auctioneer holds up

now the glass lily severed   10
from its epergne, now the mother of pearl
lorgnette. These things require

the boy's parents so much they don't know
where he is, which is gone: the book
he's brought, swords on its slick cover,   15

promises more than objects or storm.
He's lost in the story a while
but then the sun comes out,

he's been reading a long time,
and he lies on his side with his cheek   20
against the grass. This seems

the original moment of restless dreaming:
shiny rubber boots, a book forgotten
in one hand, a tired reader's face pressed

against damp green. He's the newest thing here.   25
I've bought a dark-varnished painting
of irises, a dead painter's bouquet

penciled, precisely, *Laura M.*
1890. The woman in front of us has bid
for a dead woman's plates, iridescent flocks   30

of blue birds under glaze. When it's all over
his parents awaken the sleeping reader:
his father's bought a pair of snowshoes
nearly as tall as the boy, who slings them both
over his back and thus is suddenly winged.   35
His face fills with purpose;

the legendary heroes put away in his satchel,
he's become useful again, he's moved
back into the world of things

to be accomplished: an angel   40
to carry home the narrative of our storied,
scattering things.

Didn't you want apples on the branch,
not just the cold-scented globes
but winesap or some sharp red   45
ballooning from the bearing wood?

And didn't we find, on Saturday morning,
at the edge of town,
beside a barn twisting
on its foundations, trying to collapse,   50

an abandoned orchard
offering branch after branch,
the ones a little higher
than the deer could reach?

Everywhere under the trees   55
long flattened grasses
where they'd lain, gorged with the low
or windfall fruit. We cut an armload,

trying to jostle nothing loose,
swearing at the sweet ringing   60
when any one fell—
strange how a solid thing

chimes. In a barn down the road
—among the oily lawnmowers,
the cracked motors, sapbuckets   65
and gaskets—a rabbit cage,

two rough-cut painted pine hares
bracing a pen of chicken wire,
their red eyes eager and intent:
a beautiful thing, made for the loved companion   70

of a loved child, ours for two dollars
and irreplaceable. We brought it home,
with the few intact apple branches
and a sheaf of maple burning

the unmatchable color things come to   75
when the green goes out of them
and the rippling just under
blooms through. Some days things yield

such grace and complexity that what we see
seems offered. I can't stop thinking   80
about the German film in which the angels
—who exist outside of time and thus long

for things that take place—
love most of all human stories,
the way we tell ourselves   85
what we dread or wish.

Of all our locations
their favorite is the library;
the director pictures them perched
on the balustrades, clustering   90

on the stairs, bent over
the solitary readers as if,
to urge us on, to say *Here,*
have you looked here yet?

If endlessness offered itself to me today   95
I don't think I'd have done anything

differently. I was looking from the car window
at the unlikely needlepoint wild asters made

of an October slope, blue starry heads
heaped upon each other, too wet and heavy   100

with their own completion to stand.
I didn't even stop, but that brief

yellow-eyed punctuation in a field
gone violet and golden at once,

sudden and gone, is more than I can say.   105
There's simply no way to get it right,

and it was just one thing. Holsteins,
a little down the road, paraded

toward the evening's expected comforts;
two cats in the long grass   110

observed. By a rowboat-sized pond,
one slanting ram floated on the thinnest legs.

There were geese. *There were*:
the day's narration is simple assertion;

it's enough to name the instances.   115
Don't let anybody tell you

death's the price exacted
for the ability to love;

couldn't we live forever
without running out of occasions?   120

In the Exhibition Hall each unfurled
three-by-five field bears
in awkward or accomplished embroidery

a name, every banner stitched to another
and another. They're reading   125
the unthinkable catalog of the names,

so many they blur, become
a single music pronounced with difficulty
over the microphone, become a pronoun,

become You. It's the clothing I can't get past,   130
the way a favorite pair of jeans,
a striped shirt's sewn onto the cloth;

the fading, the pulls in the fabric
demonstrate how these relics formed around
one essential, missing body.   135

An empty pair of pants
is mortality's severest evidence.
Embroidered mottoes blend

into something elegiac but removed;
a shirt can't be remote.   140
One can't look past

the sleeves where two arms
were, where a shoulder pushed
against a seam, and someone knew exactly

how the stitches pressed against skin   145
that can't be generalized but was,
irretrievably, you, or yours.

In September the garden
—this ordered enactment of desire—
is exhilarating again;   150

the new season says
Look what can be done, says
any mistake can be rectified:

the too-shaded lavender
transplanted to a brighter bed,   155
a lilac standard bought

and planted in a spot
requiring height, strong form.
Setting them in place,

attending to the settling of roots   160
between yellowed iris
and flourishing asters,

I'm making an angel,
like those Arcimboldos where the human
     profile
is all berry and leaf,   165

the specific character of bloom
assembled into an overriding form.
And then the bulbs: the slim-necked tulips

such saints of patience, exploding
so long after you plant them   170
they're nearly forgotten. Ignore

or attend, the same thing happens:
buried wishes become blooms,
supple and sheened as skin. I'm thinking

of the lily-flowered kind   175
on slim spines, the ones
that might as well be flames,

just two slight wings that will
blaze into the future;
I have to think they have a will,   180

a design so inherent in the cells
nothing could subtract from them
the least quotient of grace,

or wish to. I dreamed,
the night after the fall planting,   185
that a bird who loved me

had been long neglected, and when
I took it from the closet and gave it water
its tongue began to move again,

and it began to beat the lush green music   190
of its wings, and wrapped the brilliant risk
of leaves all around my face.

We've been out again on the backroads,
buying things. Here's a permanent harvest:
an apple and four cherries   195
stenciled on a chair-back,

the arm-wood glowing, so human,
from within, where the red paint's

been worn away by how many arms
at rest. Polished and played   200

by the blue table and the windows
that frame the back garden,
it's a true consolation,
necessary, become *this*

through its own wearing away   205
by use, festive with its once-bright
fruit. Anything lived into long enough
becomes an orchard.

And I've bought a book printed
in Edinburgh, in 1798—where's it been,   210
clearly never much referred to,
two hundred years? Bound in whorled leather,

it's the second volume of a concordance
of biblical nouns, *A Literal,*
Critical and Systematic Description of Objects   215
in fine and oddly comforting raised type:

SADNESS, by means of which the heart
is made better, weaned
from worldly things. And *THE LIMIT*
of God's house, round about, being most holy   220

imports that even the most circumstantial things
are holy in themselves: contradictory,
and heretical, for this eighteenth-century John
   Brown,
whom the foxed title page identifies only as

"Minister of the Gospels at Haddington."   225
In my afternoon class the students
sit in a circle of chairs on the terrace,
and behind their faces, which seem then

so dizzyingly new, all the rich
commingling of leaves hurry downward   230
into latent shades too subtle
to ever name, colors

we perhaps can't register even once,
and they wonder why the poet we're reading's
so insistent on mortality. I want to tell them   235
how I make the angel, that form

between us and the unthinkable,
that face we give the empty ringing,
and how that form for me appears in a boy
with snowshoe wings slung across his shoulders,   240

or in the child sprawled on the marble floor
of the post office yesterday,
who filled the echoing lobby with random notes
blown on her recorder, music made out of
   waiting.

I let the light-glazed angel   245
in the children's bodies, the angel
with his face flushed in the heat
of recognizing any birth,

I let him bend over my desk and speak
in a voice so assured you wouldn't know   250
that anyone was dying. *Any music's*
made of waiting, he says.

I make him again. *Look,*
it doesn't matter so much
See into what you can.   255
I make the angel lean over our bed

in the next room, where you're sleeping
the sturdy, uncompromised sleep
of someone going to work early tomorrow.
I am willing around you, hard,   260

the encompassing wings of the one called
unharmed. His name is nowhere
in the concordance, but I don't care;
he's the rationale for any naming.

A steady fine-pointed rain's   265
etching the new plantings,
and I'm making the rain
part of the angel. *Try to be certain,*

he says, *where you're looking.*
If you're offered endlessness,   270
don't do anything differently. The rule
of earth is attachment:

here what can't be held
is. You die by dying
into what matters, which will kill you,   275
but first it'll be enough. Or more than that:

your story, which you have worn away
as you shaped it,
which has become itself
as it has disappeared.   280

POEM SUMMARY

The stanzas in "The Wings" are not end-stopped, which means a sentence begun in one stanza does not end until the next, and the occurrences in each section tend to overlap as a result. Because of this, the sections described in the Plot Summary may also overlap.

Stanzas 1–4

"The Wings" is not a linear poem—the events described have no clear beginning, middle, or end. It opens at an unspecified time in the speaker's life, at an auction that is being held in a tent. The speaker of the poem describes a bored child lying on the grass reading while his parents are inside the tent witnessing the sale of the belongings of an unidentified person. The items that were once owned by someone and that had a place in that person's home now need a new home, so they are carried one by one to the auctioneer's block (the platform from which the auctioneer sells the goods).

The speaker's attention momentarily shifts to a growing bank of clouds in the sky before returning to the auctioneer, who is holding various items in turn.

Stanzas 4–9

The boy's parents are so engrossed in the objects being auctioned that they do not know where he is. He is "gone," engrossed in the story in his book. The sun comes out, and the boy forgets his book and lies on his side with his cheek against the grass. The speaker notes that the boy is "the newest thing here," as the objects being sold are all old.

Stanzas 9–14

The speaker turns his attention to a painting of irises that he has bought, dated 1890, composed by a long-dead painter. It is revealed that the auctioned items belonged to a woman who has recently died. When the auction is over, the sleeping boy's parents awaken him. His father has bought a pair of snowshoes almost as tall as the boy. The boy slings them over his shoulder, giving him the appearance of having wings. For the speaker, the boy appears suddenly to be transformed into one of the recurring iconic images of the poem, a winged angel. The speaker sees him as an angel who has the task of carrying home the story of the scattered objects at the auction.

Stanzas 15–20

The action of the poem shifts away from the auction to a time when the speaker's lover is apparently already dead. This is not made explicit, but it is implied by the elegiac tone in which the speaker remembers the times he spent with his lover. He addresses the dead lover, recalling an occasion when his lover wanted to pick apples. The speaker and his lover find the apples growing abundantly in an abandoned orchard. Underneath the trees are flattened patches of grass, where deer have lain after gorging themselves on the fruit. The speaker and his lover cut an armload, trying not to let any fall to the ground (apples that have been in contact with the ground bruise and quickly lose their freshness).

Stanzas 20–24

The action shifts to a barn a short distance from the orchard. The barn is full of old machinery. The speaker and his lover find an old rabbit cage flanked by two carved and painted hares, made for "the loved companion / of a loved child."

They take it home with the apple branches and a bunch of maple branches, as the leaves are showing their fall colors. The speaker reflects that some things are so graceful and complex that they seem "offered." The implication is that they are the gift of a benevolent creator.

Stanzas 24–27

The speaker remembers a German film (*Wings of Desire*, directed by Wim Wenders) about angels who exist outside of time and who long to experience events within time, just as humans experience events. These angels "love most of all human stories" about fear or desire. Their favorite location is the library, where they sit looking over the shoulders of readers but unseen by them, willing them to look at a certain line in a book that could prove significant.

Stanzas 28–40

The action shifts once again to an unspecified time. The elegiac tone and the speaker's musings on death continue to imply that his lover is dead. The speaker is reflecting on remembered times. He thinks that even if "endlessness" (lack of death, and thus immortality) offered itself to him, he would not have acted differently throughout his life. He recalls seeing from his car window a bank of wild blue flowers with yellow centers. Though he does not stop driving, he is speechless with joy at the sight of the flowers as they briefly flash past his gaze. He recounts some other things noticed on his journey, and reflects that to tell the story of his day, it is enough to name the things and events that he has seen. The speaker bitterly rejects the conventional truism that death is the price that a person pays for the ability to love. He feels that it would be possible to live forever and yet never run out of ways and means to feel and express love.

Stanzas 41–49

The action shifts to an art exhibition. Again, the time is unspecified, but the speaker's lover in this section is clearly deceased, and the lover is memorialized by the quilt described throughout these stanzas. The speaker describes one of the exhibits. This is almost certainly the AIDS Memorial Quilt, which was created as a memorial to people who have died of AIDS-related illnesses. The quilt was begun in San Francisco in 1987 by volunteers and, as of 2007, is maintained and displayed by the NAMES Project Foundation. Each patch on the quilt contains the name of a loved one who has died from AIDS, embroidered by their surviving friends or family. According to the speaker, there are so many names that they blur into "a single music" that, when spoken over the microphone, forms itself into the word "You." The "You" refers to the speaker's lover, who, it is implied, is now among the dead. Sewn onto the patch are pieces of clothing owned by the dead during their lifetime. The speaker notes the signs of wear in each piece of clothing that once formed itself around a unique, living human body. That living human body is now, however, missing. Whereas the speaker feels that the embroidered names are "elegiac but removed," a piece of worn clothing is so intensely individual and personal that it cannot be remote. It is, the speaker says, "irretrievably, you, or yours." This statement again refers to his dead lover.

Stanzas 50–62

It is September, and the speaker's attention moves to his garden. It is not made clear whether the speaker's lover is still alive here, but he is not present in this section and does not appear again until stanza 65. The position of this section, immediately following the speaker's visit to the AIDS Memorial Quilt, and the absence of the lover, may suggest that the lover is already dead.

The speaker calls the garden "this ordered enactment of desire" because, he explains, every mistake can be rectified; plants in the wrong place can be moved. In the garden, he is making an angel out of various plants and flowers, like the figures in paintings by the sixteenth-century Italian painter, Giuseppe Arcimboldo, who specialized in realistic but grotesque symbolic portraits of people constructed from plants, fruits, and animals. The speaker calls the tulips in his garden "saints of patience" because they bloom a long time after they are planted. Whether or not the gardener pays attention to them, the same thing happens: "buried wishes become blooms." Taking up the angel imagery of the poem, the speaker says that the tulips are the lily-flowered kind with "wings that will / blaze into the future," an image suggesting hope and purpose. Indeed, a will or design is so firmly built into the cells of the flowers that nothing could diminish their "grace." The word *grace*, as well as connoting beauty, is a theological term meaning a favor or gift from God to man.

Stanzas 62–64

The night after he plants the garden, the speaker dreams of a bird who loved him, but whom he had neglected. He takes it out of the closet where it has apparently been living. He gives the bird water. Its tongue begins to move again, it beats its wings, and it wraps itself around his face in an image suggestive of sensual love. At the same time, in the image of the bird wrapping "the brilliant risk / of leaves all around my face," the word "risk" suggests danger, perhaps of contracting HIV/AIDS.

Stanzas 65–73

The speaker recalls an unspecified time when his lover was alive. He describes an outing when he and his lover go looking for antiques. They find a chair with fruit stenciled on the back, which represents a "permanent harvest." The wood of the chair glows from having been worn smooth by all who have sat in it. The speaker reflects that the chair has become fully itself by being worn away with use, just as land that is farmed for long enough can become an orchard.

The speaker has bought an old book written by the real-life minister John Brown (1722–1787). The speaker reads Brown's entry on "SADNESS," which is defined as a process that makes the heart better and less attached to worldly things. Another entry on the "LIMIT" (boundary) of God's house explains that even things on the outer edge of God's realm are holy. The speaker remarks that this notion was seen as heretical in Brown's time.

Stanzas 73–77

The action shifts to a point in time when the speaker's lover is still alive, but when the speaker is acutely aware of the lover's impending death. The scene is an afternoon class that the speaker is teaching on a terrace during the fall. In spite of the fact that the leaves are falling off the trees at an extremely fast rate, the young students cannot understand why the poet they are reading is so insistent about mortality. The speaker wants to tell them how he creates an angel as a form "between us and the unthinkable" ("the unthinkable" refers to death and eternity, which cannot be thought about both because it is so vast and terrifying, and because it is a concept that cannot be truly grasped). He wants to explain that for him, the angel appears in the form of the boy with the snowshoe wings at the auction, or in the form of a child he saw sprawled on the floor of the post office, playing music on her recorder while she waits for her parents. Because the poem only states that the speaker wants to tell his students about the angel, it is reasonable to assume that he does not actually tell them, perhaps because he fears ridicule or disbelief, or because the story is too personal.

Stanzas 78–82

Again, this section indicates that while the lover is still alive, he is clearly dying, but in the next section this is more ambiguous. The speaker creates an angel in his mind. The angel bends over his desk and speaks in an assured voice that seems at odds with the speaker's knowledge that his lover is about to die. The angel explains that all music is made out of waiting. The speaker makes the angel lean over the bed where his lover is sleeping, and wills the angel to enfold him in his protective wings. The speaker gives the angel a name: "*unharmed*," wishing that he will confer this quality on the sleeping man. He knows that there is, officially, no angel with this name, but he does not care.

Stanzas 83–86

A soft rain is falling on the garden that the speaker has just planted. He makes the rain into part of the angel. The angel tells the speaker that if he is offered "*endlessness*," he should not do anything differently. This confirms the speaker's own thoughts at Stanza 28. The angel explains that the earth is ruled by attachment, whereas where the angel exists (outside of time and space), only the intangible ("*what can't be held*") exists. He says that when you die, you die "*into what matters*"; in other words, intangible things are the only things that matter. This level of reality will kill you, the angel indicates, "*but first it'll be enough.*" This may mean that the experience of this reality fulfills and satisfies in a way that life on earth cannot. The angel adds that each life is a story in progress that wears away simultaneously as it is shaped, and becomes fully itself as it disappears into death. Thus death, the angel implies, is also a kind of birth; it is the birth of a story.

THEMES

Death and Loss

The main theme of "The Wings," in common with the other poems in the collection, is death and loss. Specifically, the poem expresses the

MEDIA ADAPTATIONS

- *My Alexandria*, adapted as an audio cassette narrated by Doty, was published by University of Illinois Press (1995).

---

speaker's attempts to come to terms with the death of his lover. The poem moves in carefully graduated stages from generalized images of death and loss to painfully personal and immediate images. An example of the generalized image is that of the dead woman's objects being sold at the auction. Though this is a poignant scene, the woman is unknown to the speaker. An example of the painfully personal image is that of the items of clothing sewn onto the patch of the quilt. The impermanence of objects is emphasized, such as the glass lily broken from the table centerpiece in the opening lines of the poem, the maple branches adorned with autumn colors that are collected on a road trip, and the falling leaves that are mentioned as the speaker teaches a class.

The poem provides no resolution to the ordeal of death and loss, which is shown as an inevitable part of life. Instead of presenting answers, the poem recounts the process of living through loss and shows how beauty and grace can be distilled from pain.

The Made Object

In his review of Doty's poetry volume *Source*, David Bergman writes, "If there is a transcendent force in Doty's world, it is the transcendence of art." Doty, adds Bergman, repeatedly returns to "that very queer turn-of-the-century belief that art and literature are different from other objects and can bring a kind of salvation, or at least a balm to the spirit." For the speaker in the poem, an important part of the process of coming to terms with the death of his lover is memorializing him through the works of art or crafts that were associated with him. Take, for example, the antiques the two men find and take home with them on their trips along the backroads; and the quilt at the exhibition. It is no accident that the antiques that the men find frequently feature portrayals of living objects such as fruit or animals; they exist as records and memorials of life itself.

Nature, too, is an artist, and her works exercise a similar power: there are the apple branches "ballooning" with vibrant apples; and the maple leaves whose color becomes more intense even as they are dying in autumn. Indeed, all of these made and found objects tell the story of a human life, just as the made object of the poem tells the story of the speaker and his lover. In creating a story, it is enough, says the speaker, "to name the instances."

It is not suggested that made objects resolve the grief that the speaker feels, though perhaps they provide the closest thing to "consolation" that is available to him. They do, however, fulfill the apparently universal "will" or "design" to manifest beauty from death and emptiness. This creative process is perhaps shown as inevitable, just as the tulip in the speaker's garden explodes with beauty and life after a long period of latency within the bulb.

Waiting

As is symbolically suggested by the image in the opening lines of a rain-cloud looming above the boy at the auction, this is a poem about waiting for death. The speaker knows that his lover is dying, and reflects on how he is going to be able to live with this knowledge. Various figures in the poem are shown dealing with the waiting process in their own way. The boy at the auction is reading a story of heroes while waiting for his parents; the speaker, in tending his garden, makes an angel out of plants while he waits for bulbs to sprout; the child in the post office makes music on her recorder as she waits for her parents. Indeed, it is interesting to note the recurring image of a child occupying itself with art (reading, playing music) while waiting for its parents. The angel in the final lines of the poem tells the speaker, "*Any music's made of waiting.*" In other words, art emerges from the time that occurs between "what we dread or wish" and the fulfillment of the thing we dread or desire.

Epiphanies Derived from Everyday Experience

An epiphany is a sudden, intuitive insight into the reality or essential meaning of something, often prompted by an everyday experience. There are many epiphanies in "The Wings."

For example, the poem describes a ram that "floated on the thinnest legs," as if not grounded on earth. The image mirrors the angels of the poem in its ethereal nature. Similarly, the apple and maple branches that the two men find and take home seem "offered," the gift of a benevolent creator. Each propitious discovery of a beautiful antique on the back-roads is an epiphany, telling the story of the person who made or owned it. The beauty of the wild flowers strikes the speaker with such force that the experience is "more than I can say," and he is prompted to drop into a momentary awed silence. Such incidents are presented as not mere chance, but as a manifestation of the inherent will and purpose of all creation to express itself. They speak of the inherent "grace and complexity" in nature, as well as the transitory nature of things.

The Homosexual Experience

"The Wings" contains a background theme exploring how it feels to live as a homosexual man in a predominantly heterosexual world. This theme is symbolically expressed in the speaker's dream of a bird that loves him and that he has for too long neglected. The speaker takes the bird out of the closet where it has been kept, and to come out of the closet, of course, is a colloquial expression indicating the open expression of one's sexuality. To be in the closet, then, is to hide one's sexuality. Thus, the story of the bird symbolically describes the speaker's experience of embracing his homosexuality after a period of denial. Furthermore, after the speaker takes the bird out of the closet, he gives it water. The speaker gives the bird an essential thing needed to sustain life, which is to say that the speaker's acknowledgement of his homosexuality is essential for sustaining his own life.

STYLE

Stream-of-Consciousness

"The Wings" is written in stream-of-consciousness style, a literary technique that relays the speaker's thought processes as they are happening. The style is an aspect of the literary movement known as Modernism, which peaked in the first half of the twentieth century alongside the discipline of psychology, on which it draws, or by which it was largely influenced. Stream-of-consciousness is characterized by associative images or thought patterns, in which one image, thought, or event

TOPICS FOR FURTHER STUDY

- Research the HIV/AIDS epidemic using the early 1980s, when the disease was first identified, as a starting off point. What are the supposed origins of the disease, what causes it, and what are its major symptoms? How has the treatment and progression of the disease changed over the years? Describe how public perception of the disease has changed from the early 1980s to today, and say how and why. Create either a written report or a class presentation on your findings.

- Write a poem about death, grief, or loss, and write a brief prose piece on the same topic. Afterwards, write an essay about what you discovered while writing the poem, and what you discovered from writing the prose piece. How was the poem different from, or similar to, the prose piece?

- "The Wings" often refers to angels both literally and symbolically, and angels appear in many poems, novels, and paintings throughout history. Beginning with the thirteenth century, research the artistic representation of angels up to the present day. During what historical periods was this representation popular, and why? How have symbolic meanings pertaining to angels changed over time? How have they remained unchanged? Citing specific examples, present your findings to the class.

- Write an essay in which you compare and contrast "The Wings" with Thom Gunn's poem "Lament" or his "In Time of Plague," both from Gunn's collection *The Man With Night Sweats* (1992). How does each poem deal with the topic of HIV/AIDS?

---

can set off discussion of another with no consideration to chronological time or physical space. The speaker of the poem does not narrate a chronological progression of events, but looks back from a point in time when his lover is dead to a number of times when his lover was still alive, and also to times when he was dying. The sequence of events and scenarios in linear time is not made clear and is not essential to an understanding of this poem. It would not be correct to say, however, that there is no progression in the poem. Progression occurs on the emotional and psychological level of the speaker as he comes to terms with his lover's death: it is a maturation, or an evolution of understanding, not a cataloguing of any concrete event.

Symbolism

As the poem's title suggests, the major symbolic figures in "The Wings" are angels, but there are many symbolic images and figures throughout the poem. Angels are traditionally held to be messengers between God and people. Another way of describing this role is to say that they carry stories. The first section of the poem concludes with the image of a boy-angel, carrying home the story of the objects once owned by the newly deceased, now scattered at the auction. As the bearer of a story, the angel becomes linked with the artists or craftsmen who make the works of art and the antiques that are an important aspect of the poem. These beautiful objects are shaped by the people who make and own them, and therefore they symbolize and memorialize the human lives of which they were once a part. These objects represent the story of a human being.

The role of angels in the poem is made more explicit in the passage that recalls the angels from the German film *Wings of Desire*. The speaker says that these angels live outside of time and therefore long for the things that take place within time, as human lives occur within time. Most of all, he says, they love "human stories," and so their favored location is the library. The library is full of human stories in the form of books, and full of humans reading those stories and forming new stories with the unseen encouragement of the angels. Here again, the angel is linked to the figure of the story-teller, and, by implication, to the poet, who is also telling a story. The angel thus takes on something of the quality of a muse, a spiritual being who, according to Greek mythology, assisted and guided artists in their creative work.

The angel that the speaker makes in his mind in the final lines of the poem temporarily becomes an extension of the speaker's will or intention. Just as the speaker has created the story of his life with his lover simply by narrating events and naming objects seen during their time together, he hopes to create a different ending to their story by naming the angel "*unharmed*" and having him enfold his lover in his protective wings, in the hopes of preventing the lover's inevitable death. Here, the angel is assigned the traditional role of guardian angel.

Multiple Lines of Narrative

Unusually for a lyric poem (a poem that is an outpouring of the speaker's intimate thoughts and feelings), "The Wings" employs multiple lines of narrative that at first glance seem disconnected from one another. On a closer reading, it becomes clear that the different lines of the narrative interconnect and build on one another, by sharing or expanding on the same theme, image, or symbol. For example, the image of the angel recurs in slightly different forms in several sections of the poem, and the theme of the made object also recurs in different contexts. The effect of these interconnections is to weave together the different threads of the narrative into a unified whole.

Elegy

An elegy is a poem or other work written as a lament for the dead. "The Wings" is an elegy to the speaker's dead lover, though it is also a cautious affirmation of the regenerative powers of life and art.

Religious Poetry

As Roger Gilbert points out in his essay "Awash with Angels: The Religious Turn in Nineties Poetry," "The Wings" is one of a number of works (poems, books, and films) from the 1990s that features angels. The trend, says Gilbert, marked a return to traditional religious iconography after the ironic, postmodern 1980s. In particular, the famous play *Angels in America* (which was subsequently adapted as a film) explicitly linked the subject of AIDS with angels.

Angels are just one way in which Doty lends a religious undertone to his poem. He also uses religious metaphors to express a sense of reverence toward his subject. The clothes worn by now-dead loved ones in the quilt exhibition are "relics," recalling the belief of some Catholic Christians that the remains of saints and other religiously significant items (relics) were sacred. The tulips in the speaker's garden are "saints of patience" because they bloom long after they are planted and forgotten. Patience, it is implied, is a

quality needed to withstand the illness and death of a loved one. There is nothing one can do but wait, as the tulip does, for the inevitable blooming of life and beauty, for the sprouting of the petal-wings that "blaze into the future."

Underlining the religious imagery in the poem is the concept of grace, which has two levels of meaning: the more superficial level of gracefulness, or physical beauty, and the deeper level of divine grace. The speaker sees both types of grace manifesting in the beautiful works of nature such as those in the garden, in the gathered maple branches, and in the wildflowers glimpsed while driving. The fact that physical beauty is experienced as spiritual beauty seems to indicate that the two aspects of grace, which initially seem so different from one another, are actually quite closely intertwined.

HISTORICAL CONTEXT

HIV/AIDS

"The Wings" and the collection in which it appears was inspired by the AIDS-related death of Doty's lover. Acquired Immune Deficiency Syndrome (AIDS, or Aids) is a collection of symptoms and infections resulting from damage to the immune system widely believed to be caused by the human immunodeficiency virus (HIV). Although treatments for AIDS and HIV exist to slow the virus's progression, there is no known cure. The late stages of the illness leave a person susceptible to opportunistic infections and other diseases, which are usually the actual cause of death. HIV is transmitted through contact of a mucous membrane or blood with a bodily fluid containing HIV, often blood, semen, or vaginal fluid. Though the disease may be transmitted through blood transfusions or contaminated needles, as well as from mother to child during childbirth or nursing, it is most often contracted through some form of sexual contact.

While HIV/AIDS can be contracted by anyone, in developed countries homosexual males are particularly at risk. In the United States, homosexual sex is the leading method of transmission. A variety of possible reasons for this have been suggested, including the high risk of rupture of mucous membranes and bleeding during anal sex (raising the possibility of transmission); supposed promiscuity in some homosexual communities; and the use of such recreational drugs as amyl nitrate, favored predominantly in the homosexual community, which may suppress the immune system and raise the likelihood of infection.

The picture of HIV/AIDS infection in the homosexual community in the United States is complicated by a double social stigma. First, homosexuality has long been stigmatized in its own right. Second, HIV/AIDS infection carries its own stigma, which tends to proliferate alongside certain notions and misunderstandings about the disease. These include theories held by some religious groups that HIV/AIDS is God's judgment on homosexuality or promiscuous behavior, which they hold to be sinful. Fear of people with HIV/AIDS is exacerbated by mistaken beliefs about how easily the disease is transmitted.

In the United States, during the 1980s and 1990s, the rate of HIV/AIDS infection in the homosexual community was extraordinary. The disease was not even identified or understood until the early 1980s. As a result, awareness and prevention did not catch up with the rate of infection until the late 1990s. Throughout this period, being diagnosed as HIV-positive was seen as a death sentence, and it often was.

Alexandria

The Egyptian city of Alexandria, after which Doty's collection of poems is named, was founded by the Greek conqueror Alexander the Great around 334 BCE. It quickly became one of the great cities of the Hellenistic (ancient Greek) culture. It was the home of the Library of Alexandria (the largest library in the ancient world). The library was destroyed by fire several times, leading to the loss of irreplaceable manuscripts from all over the world. From the story of Alexandria, Doty borrows the theme of irreparable loss. In addition, the ancient Greek civilization is known to have been not only tolerant of homosexuality, but to have idealized it as a more refined, noble, and spiritual form of love than that of heterosexual relationships.

In an article for the *Independent*, Ruth Padel comments on the significance to Doty of Alexandria and Atlantis. As described by the ancient Greek philosopher Plato, Atlantis was a lost civilization, whose name Doty adopted for his fourth volume of poetry. Padel writes that for Doty, Alexandria and Atlantis present a vision of a "threatened gay utopia, a dream of partnership glowing at the centre of civilised being, refracted through the great myths of unrecoverability:

Cavafy's Alexandria, Plato's Atlantis." "Doty has said of *My Alexandria*, Alexandria . . . is that city of art—that made place, which is both the given and the way that we transform the given" (cited by Deborah Landau in *American Literature*). "The Wings" is full of images of made objects: works of art, craft objects, and antiques, all of which are portrayed as embodying the stories of the people (now dead) who made and owned them. Thus through art, the dead are memorialized and transformed into things of beauty.

Furthermore, one of the major influences on Doty's poetry is the Greek poet Constantine P. Cavafy (1863–1933). Like Doty, Cavafy was homosexual. Doty's *My Alexandria* is named in homage to the poet. Cavafy was born in the city of Alexandria, and he lived there for much of his life. Cavafy's work also touched upon the history of Alexandria, particularly the Hellenistic era when it was under the influence of ancient Greek culture.

John Brown

In "The Wings," the speaker buys an old book published in 1798, a concordance (guide) of biblical nouns written by the real-life John Brown (1722–1787), who was a self-educated author and church minister at Haddington, East Lothian, Scotland.

The speaker remarks that Brown's assertion that even things on the outer edge of God's realm are holy was seen as heretical in Brown's time. This statement is also based in fact. Brown's extraordinary learning led some members of the Secession Church, to which he belonged, to claim that he received his knowledge from the devil. Brown only cleared his name with difficulty.

There is an implied connection between the speaker and Brown, because Brown's thoughts on sadness and the holiness of the things that seem marginalized from God, echo the speaker's own feelings as expressed in the poem. The fact that Brown was condemned as a heretic and had to fight to restore his good name mirrors the experiences of the homosexual community at large, which for centuries was marginalized and condemned by much of mainstream society.

CRITICAL OVERVIEW

On its publication, *My Alexandria* met with immediate critical acclaim. The book contributed to Doty's reputation as "the finest American poet

COMPARE
&
CONTRAST

- **1990s:** Senator Jesse Helms, the North Carolina Republican who has vigorously fought homosexual rights, wants to reduce the amount of federal money spent on AIDS sufferers, because, he says, their "deliberate, disgusting, revolting conduct" (cited by Deborah Landau in "'How to Live. What to Do.' The Poetics and Politics of AIDS") is responsible for their disease.

  Today: In 2007, President George W. Bush announces that the President's Emergency Plan For AIDS Relief (PEPFAR) is meeting its commitment of fifteen billion dollars over five years to support AIDS prevention, treatment, and care.

- **1990s:** In the United States, a majority of states have policies prohibiting discrimination against people with AIDS. However, according to the study "Public Reactions to AIDS in the United States, 1990–1991" by Gregory M. Herek, Ph.D., & John P. Capitanio, Ph.D., roughly forty percent of Americans treat AIDS as a stigma.

  Today: In 2003, the American Civil Liberties Union release the survey "A Report from the Frontline of the HIV/AIDS Epidemic," which details widespread civil rights violations throughout the United States against people with HIV/AIDS.

- **1990s:** The rate of HIV/AIDS infection in the homosexual community is high. There is little knowledge of how to prevent and manage the disease. Treatments are minimal and HIV/AIDS largely results in fatal complications.

  Today: The introduction of anti-retroviral and other drugs in the mid-1990s is reported to have slowed the progression of the disease in infected people and to have dramatically increased their life expectancies. In addition, preventive measures such as the use of condoms during sexual intercourse have reduced the number of reported new HIV/AIDS cases.

- **1990s:** AIDS organizations welcome the 1996 visit by President Bill and Hillary Clinton to the AIDS Memorial Quilt in Washington, D.C., the first public acknowledgement of the quilt by any president.

  Today: Over fourteen million people have visited the AIDS Memorial Quilt at displays worldwide. Through such displays, the NAMES Project Foundation, which maintains the quilt, has raised over three million dollars for AIDS service organizations throughout North America.

of the last 20 years," according to Michael Glover in a review of the book's successor, *Atlantis*, for the *New Statesman*. Glover also called Doty the most forceful and inventive American poet since Robert Lowell.

In an article for *Ploughshares* titled "About Mark Doty," Mark Wunderlich calls *My Alexandria* a "tour de force." Wunderlich praises the book as "perhaps the finest in-depth literary investigation of the AIDS crisis," noting that, "at its center is the anticipation of tremendous loss, an ache that pervades each of the poems." *Los Angeles Times* critic Marjorie Lewellyn Marks also comments on the themes of impermanence and doom, stating that though AIDS is a "pervasive metaphor," "the crystalline sensibility and breathtaking beauty of these poems is redemptive . . . rather than depressive."

Comparing *My Alexandria* with Doty's previous two volumes of poetry, Bruce Smith, in his article for the *Boston Review*, writes that Doty's preoccupations remain the same: "the lush world, its architecture and artifice, and the forms of remembering and inventing—what Doty earlier calls 'something storied.'" Smith calls the poems "enchanting" and likens the patterned texture of the collection to a woven fabric.

In the *Los Angeles Times Book Review*, Ray Gonzalez praises the elegiac poetry of *My Alexandria*, pointing out that Doty manages to find positive truths and beauty amid pain and death. In a comment about other poems in the collection that could easily apply to "The Wings," Gonzalez writes, "Doty encounters death in life and the terrifying surprise that, as the acute poet, he has the courage to extract beauty out of the living monuments created by death." Gonzalez finds a difference between these poems and other anthologies of poems about AIDS because Doty's poetry "does not wish to insist on the concrete moment of mourning or the wish to change the realities of the late century." Instead, Doty finds a new way of responding to the crisis. He writes about the suffering, yet goes on to create in an atmosphere where "the pain, the memories and the surviving beauty strengthen and nourish him."

My Alexandria was also successful in Great Britain, where it won the T.S. Eliot prize. Ruth Padel reviews the collection with largely positive comments in the London-based newspaper, the *Independent*. In her review, Padel summarizes the arguments of Doty's critical supporters and detractors. The detractors say that Doty's poetry displays a fault common to much other American poetry, in that it has slid towards "sentiment that tells rather than shows. It goes for surface prettiness plus the ironed-on appearance of philosophy." Meanwhile, Doty's supporters, Padel notes, applaud Doty's lyricism, with which, these commentators say, "you get on to another plane. The subject is only the take-off point; what matters lies beyond." Weighing the arguments with regard to *My Alexandria*, Padel concludes that there are enough poems in the volume that prove the supporters' case.

CRITICISM

Claire Robinson

Claire Robinson has an M.A. in English. She is a former teacher of English literature and creative writing, and is currently a freelance writer and editor. In the following essay, Robinson examines how the poet explores death and loss in his poem "The Wings."

WHAT DO I READ NEXT?

- Doty's critically acclaimed prose memoir *Heaven's Coast* (1996) tells the story of the years he spent with his lover, Wally Roberts, whose life, and death from an AIDS-related illness, inspired Doty to write *My Alexandria*.

- Thom Gunn's award-winning collection of poetry, *The Man With Night Sweats* (1992), provides a haunting chronicle of the poet's grief over the loss of many of his friends to AIDS.

- The Greek homosexual poet C. P. Cavafy (1863–1933) is one of Doty's major poetic influences and one of the most important poets of European literature. *The Collected Poems of C. P. Cavafy: A New Translation* (2007), translated into English by Aliki Barnstone, contains many of his greatest poems.

- *The Complete Sonnets and Poems* of William Shakespeare (1564–1616) (2002), edited by Colin Burrow, contains some of the most extraordinary love poems ever written by one man to another. Critics are divided as to the exact nature of the relationship described, and some feel that the poems describe sexual love, while others feel the poem describes spiritual love. Read them and decide for yourself. Additionally, this edition has helpful notes and commentaries.

- *AIDS in the Twenty-First Century: Disease and Globalization* (2006), by Tony Barnett and Alan Whiteside, examines the social and economic effects of the HIV/AIDS epidemic, paying particular attention to Africa, where much of the populace is infected (more so than in any other part of the world). Many scientists also believe that the disease originated there. The authors explain how the disease is changing family structures, economic development, and even the security of countries in the developing world.

> " THE LEAVES SHOW THAT LIFE IS GIVING WAY TO DEATH, BUT THERE IS BEAUTY TO BE EXTRACTED FROM THE PROCESS. THE POET MAKES THE POEM, A WORK OF ART (OR A THING OF BEAUTY), OUT OF THE DEATH OF HIS LOVER."

Doty has called AIDS (as cited by Michael Glover in the *New Statesman*) "the great intensifier." Certainly, it intensifies the acute sense of death and loss that pervades "The Wings." This theme is subtly introduced in the first lines of the poem, which opens at an auction where a dead woman's belongings are being sold off. The speaker also sees an old painting he has bought in light of the long-dead person who painted it. Indeed, the word "dead" chimes throughout the lines like the toll of a funeral bell. This is an example of Doty's ability to imbue ordinary phrases with more than ordinary weight through an accumulation of interconnected images, and this can also be seen in the phrase "When it's all over." Superficially, the phrase refers to the end of the auction, but in the light of its position, after the appearance of the dead woman's things and the dead painter's work, it also connotes death.

Emerging from this world of death and loss is a semblance of life. All of the items initially discussed are man-made portrayals of nature, memorials of things that were once alive. The painting bought by the speaker, though it is by a dead artist, portrays a bunch of once-living irises, coated with a preserving varnish. The plates bought by a woman at the auction are decorated with flocks of birds. All the objects sold at the auction tell a story about real, living people, and though their most recent caretaker is dead, they will travel home with the new owners who, the poem says, will care for them. The stories told by the objects will be continued in a new place.

The many angels that appear in the poem take part in this creation and continuation of stories. The first angel appears when the boy slings a pair of old snowshoes across his back; for the speaker, the boy is suddenly transformed into an image of a winged angel. This boy-angel is indeed a kind of messenger, since he will "carry home the narrative of our storied, / scattering things." He will unify the things that are scattered in the aftermath of death into a coherent story. Implicitly, the boy becomes linked in purpose with the poet, as this poem is the story of the poet and his now-dead lover. Story-telling is presented as a way of making some sense of death and loss.

As if cued by the boy-angel to tell the story of the dead, in the second section of the poem, the poet begins to recall his road trips with his now deceased lover. This time, the images of life are not portraits or semblances, but actual living things. The two men find an abandoned orchard containing "apples on the branch." This discovery fulfills a desire expressed by the speaker's lover, rendering it a cherished event. Further reflecting this shift from a world where death dominates (*the auction of the dead woman's belongings) to a world where life is the prevailing theme (*the abandoned orchard), the poet addresses his lover directly, as if he were still alive: "Didn't you want" "And didn't we find," he asks. In the orchard, deer are gorging themselves on windfall apples, an image of unalloyed gratification. Death remains in the background, but not as a forceful presence. It appears in the old barn "trying to collapse" (and not succeeding); in the fact that the orchard is abandoned, the past owners having died or left; and in the two men's attempts to prevent any apples from falling to the ground in case they should be spoiled.

On this trip, as at the auction, the poet and his lover succeed in distilling beauty from death. They find an old rabbit cage flanked by a pair of beautifully fashioned hares, which was once owned by "the loved companion/of a loved child," both of whom are now likely dead. The same theme appears through the image of the maple branches they bring home. The leaves' living green color has been replaced by the "burning" color that appears in autumn. The leaves show that life is giving way to death, but there is beauty to be extracted from the process. The poet makes the poem, a work of art (or a thing of beauty), out of the death of his lover. The speaker wonders at the "grace and complexity" expressed in the apple and maple branches, which make them seem as if they are gifts offered by a divine creator. Thus, the speaker portrays the things of this world, even in the process of losing their life, as hinting at a celestial benevolence.

In the face of such meditations, Doty portrays the enjoyment of sensual and sexual pleasure without guilt or self-recrimination. If the apple-gorged deer in the second section of the poem showed the naturalness of sensual gratification, the wildflowers in the third section represent an intensification of that mood. The flowers, their heads "heaped upon one another," "too wet and heavy / with their own completion to stand," form a startlingly direct symbol of sexual satiety and post-coital exhaustion. Certainly, much poetry pits the claims of sensual and sexual pleasure against those of mortality and the knowledge of death. It is implied that the latter invalidates the former. Doty's poetry takes the opposite stance, consistently affirming the validity of sensuality in the face of death.

The speaker's bitter piece of advice, "Don't let anybody tell you / death's the price exacted / for the ability to love," enforces this theme. These lines have an additional meaning in the context of homosexual love, as some who disapprove of homosexual sex claim that homosexuals who contract HIV/AIDS have brought the disease upon themselves. The speaker of the poem rejects the notion that death is the price paid for love: "couldn't we live forever / without running out of occasions?" He believes that even in a world of "endlessness" where death does not exist, love would persist.

As the moments of joy in the poem grow more vivid, so does the sense of loss. The fourth section of the poem uses the image of an art object, a quilt embroidered with the names of those who have died from AIDS, created by those who have been left behind. This art object is a progression from the precious objects and antiques featured earlier in the poem. Sewn into the quilt are pieces of clothing that belonged to the dead, and which once formed and shaped themselves around "one essential, missing body." These pieces of clothing are unique, intensely personal, and they speak of the dead person more directly than do the embroidered names. In this scene of immense emotion, the poem's theme of death and loss rises to a climax. This is underlined by the speaker's stated failure to find the words to encompass his feelings. He is too overwhelmed by emotion: "It's the clothing I can't get past" and "One can't look past / the sleeves where two arms / were." Where the antiques were poignant but ultimately merely reminiscent of an unknown owner, a piece of clothing

that the dead beloved once wore "can't be generalized but was, / irretrievably, you, or yours."

Falling away from this climax, the speaker shifts the narrative to the topic of planting his garden. The garden, unlike death, is responsive to the speaker's will; it is an "ordered enactment of desire," something that "*can be done.*" The speaker's planting of the garden is full of angelic imagery. In the first instance ("I'm making an angel"), the angel itself is another made object, art created by the speaker out of living plants. The second and third instances of angelic imagery in the garden scene are not conscious creations, but rather they are "offered" gifts, like the maple branches from earlier in the poem. In the second instance, a lily-flowered tulip blooms only because of its inherent will to do so, and the petals of the tulip are described as being like "wings that will / blaze into the future." Here, the angelic imagery connotes hope.

The third instance of angel-related imagery (or at least wing-related imagery) is the most memorable and climactic. The speaker recounts his dream of a bird, and his decision to take care of the bird seems to symbolize allowing homosexual relationships into his life after a period in which he denied his sexuality. The bird's tongue beginning to move is suggestive of kissing or foreplay. The whole experience is one of intense, shimmering vitality, expressed in the phrase, "lush green music." The bird's wrapping of "the brilliant risk / of leaves all around my face" is an ecstatically sensual image which, in the unusual and striking use of the word "risk," acknowledges the ever-present specter of HIV/AIDS. The threat of death and loss is imminent, but it does not diminish the speaker's joy in the experience he describes.

The bird has characteristics both of an animal and a plant. This links it in terms of imagery with the description of the garden that the speaker plants, and with the angel that he forms out of plants in the manner of a painting by Arcimboldo. The bird is further tied to the iconography of angels by the fact that both creatures have wings, and the speaker focuses predominantly on the wings of the angels when they are described. The title of the poem also reinforces this link. The effect of the story of the bird within the poem is to affirm homosexual sexuality and love as a life-enhancing, creative, and joyful experience. The bird, when viewed in context with the angels, further symbolizes that sexual love is a derivative of the compassion and divinity of angels.

The final section of the poem works like an epilogue, or a summing up of what has gone on before. No easy resolutions are offered, but the speaker derives some degree of "consolation" from an antique chair, the wood glowing from having been worn smooth by so "many arms / at rest." The phrase "at rest" has connotations of death as well as of the simple relaxation to be had by sitting in the chair. Once again, the made object memorializes the person that has owned it. Paradoxically, the more the object is worn away, the more it becomes shaped and formed by its owner. The angel that the speaker invokes in the final lines of the poem applies this very principle to human life. It says: "your story, which you have worn away / as you shaped it, / … has become itself / as it has disappeared." Thus, while life itself is the process of dying, as an individual life wears out, more of the inner beauty and essence of that life (*or person) is expressed, like the burning colors of dying maple leaves, or the glow of wood polished smooth by numerous arms. This is the way of nature: "Anything lived into long enough/becomes an orchard." (It is also the way of the craftsman who makes beautiful objects (the painting, the chair) that memorialize the dead, and the way of the artist who tells the story of a loved one. Death and loss, as the things that evoke beauty from all things, are therefore refined and translated into a transcendent beauty in their own right.

Source: Claire Robinson, Critical Essay on "The Wings," in *Poetry for Students*, Gale, Cengage Learning, 2008.

Gale

In the following essay, the critic gives a critical analysis of Doty's work.

Since the publication of his first volume of verse, *Turtle, Swan*, in 1987, Mark Doty has become recognized as one of the most accomplished poets in America. Like the work of James Merrill, Doty's utterings transcend the category of "gay poetry" to appeal to a diverse cross-section of readers; fittingly, Doty has won a number of prestigious literary awards, including the Whiting Writer's Award, the T. S. Eliot Prize (of which he was the first U.S. winner), the National Poetry Series, the *Los Angeles Times* Book Award, the National Book Critics' Circle Award, and the PEN/Martha Albrand Award for first nonfiction. Doty, the son of an army

> THE COUPLE LIVED TOGETHER FOR TWELVE YEARS IN MANHATTAN AND IN PROVINCETOWN, MASSACHUSETTS; WALLY'S ILLNESS AND DEATH FROM AIDS, WITH WHICH HE WAS DIAGNOSED IN 1989 AND TO WHICH HE FINALLY SUCCUMBED IN JANUARY, 1994, WAS TO BE THE CENTRAL EVENT OF DOTY'S MATURATION AS PERSON AND POET."

engineer, grew up in a succession of suburbs in Tennessee, Florida, southern California, and Arizona. An ancestor, Edward Dotey, was, as Doty recounted in a 1996 *Publishers Weekly* interview, "the 'archetypal American scoundrel,'" who arrived on the Mayflower in 1620, fought the first duel on American soil, and filed the first lawsuit in this country.

Doty described himself, in *Publishers Weekly*, as having been "a sissy" in childhood; frightened by his emerging sexual identity, he married hastily at age eighteen. After completing his undergraduate studies at Drake University in Iowa, he got a divorce and moved to Manhattan, where he paid his dues as a temporary office worker. He earned a master's degree in creative writing from Goddard College during part-time semesters; during the same period, he met his lasting love, Wally Roberts, a window-dresser at a department store. The couple lived together for twelve years in Manhattan and in Provincetown, Massachusetts; Wally's illness and death from AIDS, with which he was diagnosed in 1989 and to which he finally succumbed in January, 1994, was to be the central event of Doty's maturation as person and poet. (Doty himself tested negative for HIV.) In the interim, however, Doty was publishing his early work.

A first volume of poems, *Turtle, Swan*, was rejected by the publisher David Godine, only to be accepted by Godine after urgings from author Roger Weingarten whose works had also been published by Godine. On its publication in 1987, *Booklist* praised the "quiet, intimate" *Turtle, Swan* for turning the gay experience into "an example of how we live, how we suffer and transcend suffering," while Marianne Boruch, in

American Poetry Review, called the volume "a stunning arrival." Doty's second collection, the 1991 *Bethlehem in Broad Daylight*, also won praise from critics. Miriam Levine, in *American Book Review*, appreciated Doty's gift for "simple speech," and specified that "Doty's poems work best when he finds his way back and forth between the vernacular and the elegant music of desire and loss." *Booklist* critic Pat Monaghan made a similar comment, delighting in the "combination of extreme formality and extreme accessibility" which made *Bethlehem in Broad Daylight* "one of the most satisfying of recent collections."

Poetry reviewer David Baker commended Doty for "well-ordered poetry whose primary method is anecdotal, whose speaker is singular and personal, and whose vision is skeptical." If there was a problem in Doty's work, Baker hypothesized, it was the poet's "detachment from his own story"—Doty, he claimed, approached his subjects as a "privileged observer and commentator."

If this was indeed a problem, Doty went a long way toward dealing with it in his 1993 *My Alexandria*, which won the National Poetry Series contest and was therefore published by the University of Illinois Press. Here, Doty wrote about the pain of life as seen through the prism of AIDS. Yet, as Ray Gonzalez noted in the *Los Angeles Times Book Review*, "Doty goes beyond the triumph of the plague to write about life beyond this dark century. . . . He has the courage to extract beauty out of the living moments created by death. . . . The pain, the memories and the surviving beauty strengthen and nourish him." Assessing the volume for the *Yale Review*, Vernon Shetley wrote, "Doty's writing displays tremendous craft in ways that have become fairly unusual in our poetry. . . . And one senses in the poetry as well an admirable assurance in the choices he makes."

On the negative side, Shetley felt that Doty relied too much on a rich "gift for phrasemaking"; all in all, however, he hailed *My Alexandria* as evidence of "a big talent at work." Jonathan Bing, the *Publishers Weekly* interviewer, looked back on *My Alexandria* in retrospect as "a watershed" in Doty's career," full of "luminous studies of urban and natural flux." Doty himself told Bing that he thought of *My Alexandria* as "a real change. . . . I was casting about for what would come next. And what came next for me was looking around at the present and adult life," in contrast to the poems of remembered youth in his earlier books.

In February, 1996, James Fenton wrote about *My Alexandria* in the *New York Review of Books* on the occasion of the awarding of the T. S. Eliot Prize to that volume. Fenton pointed out the explicit homage to Robert Lowell in Doty's work, especially in the poem "Demolition," whose subject was strikingly similar to that of Lowell's great "For the Union Dead." "It's a gutsy act," stated Fenton, who also praised the poem "Fog," a response to Doty's and Wally's HIV tests as "the best poem in the book." The volume as a whole, Fenton felt, was "a conscious evocation of a personal bohemia . . . tenderly evoked," and it "hangs together so beautifully that it seems like a single orchestrated work."

My Alexandria also led to the National Book Critics' Circle Prize for 1994, and to the publication of Doty's next volume, *Atlantis*, by a commercial house, HarperCollins, in 1995. *Atlantis* was a response to, and in many respects a description of, Wally's illness and death, and a *Commonweal* reviewer, the poet and memoirist Patricia Hampl, called it simply "miraculous." Hampl loved Doty's casual voice and his ability to make something universal—"an emblem that springs open for us all"—out of an individual tragedy. She compared Doty to Keats in being "poised on exact perception. When he sees the ocean—the salt spray hits you." *Library Journal* contributor Frank Allen praised the poems' painterly descriptions, while *Yale Review* critic Willard Spiegelman applauded both the works' visual quality and their "smooth, graceful" music. Savoring, as other critics had done before, Doty's ability to create beauty out of grief, Allen discerned the influences of Elizabeth Bishop, Amy Clampitt, and above all, Walt Whitman, and concluded, "No recent book so strongly warrants both tears and laughter."

After Wally's death, Doty found himself unable to write or even read. However, the solicitation of a poem by a friend who was editing an anthology led him to the writing, not of a poem, but of a book-length memoir, *Heaven's Coast*, in which he came to grips, in prose, with Wally's life and death. "It was a real gift to be able to write it" at that troubled moment, Doty told Bing, and readers evidently felt the same way, for the book achieved high acclaim and was widely read. Doty deliberately refrained from organizing the book carefully; it was a patchwork quilt of memories, including quotations from friends letters. Bernard Cooper in the *Los Angeles Times Book Review* expressed keen appreciation for this literary strategy: "How else, except with tentative, borrowed strength, can one grapple with the indifference of death?" Cooper called *Heaven's Coast* a "powerful memoir."

Jim Marks in the *Washington Post Book World* found the book "unique among AIDS memoirs" for its author's "refusal to become dominated by his anger" and for his questioning of the appropriateness of beauty as a response to death. Marks found a great deal of appropriate beauty, however, in Doty's prose: "Even his considerable reputation could not have prepared readers for the astonishing beauty of these opening pages." Responding to the scene of Wally's death, Marks wrote, "[Doty] takes us into the moment of death ... in language that, purged of anger and grief, comes close to being transcendent."

Following *Heaven's Coast* was the 1998 poetry collection *Sweet Machine*, a work in which "the poems ... contemplate nature and art as the closest thing we have to an extravagant, if not transcendent, presence," according to a reviewer for *Publishers Weekly*. Though the collection "is the book of a freer, altogether less burdened spirit," maintained a reviewer for *Economist*, *Sweet Machine* nevertheless appears to contain less intense subject treatment and "slacker" writing, according to the reviewer. However, in a review for *Progressive*, Joel Brouwer stated: "In *Sweet Machine*, we see an already masterful poet refusing to lapse into nostalgia or to unthinkingly reuse the poetic strategies that have served him so well in the past. Instead, we find Mark Doty exploring new territories and questioning himself at every turn."

In 1999, Doty published a second memoir, *Firebird*, which a reviewer for *Newsweek* described as "The poet's beautifully written, hallucinatorily evocative memoir of growing up gay in baby-boom America." A reviewer for *Publishers Weekly* said that the memoir is "beautifully and sensitively written," but has less of an emotional impact and more of a mental one. In *Firebird*, Doty recalls his experiences as a young boy growing up, including those of an often difficult family life and an increasing awareness of his homosexuality. The *Publishers Weekly* reviewer commented as well that in the book the author "is at his best when describing his relationship to the idea of beauty and how it influenced his growth as an artist."

In *Still Life with Oysters and Lemon*, Doty presents an extended meditation on a Dutch still-life painting by Jan Davidsz de Heem, painted in Antwerp 350 years ago. The slim volume "takes [the] reader deep into the painting," according to Peter Marcus in the *Gay and Lesbian Review Worldwide*. Marcus noted, "Doty's prose sentences read much like lines of his poetry: they beg the reader to pause, to reread, to consider all their complexities. ... *Still Life* is a meditation on how a painting can capture the ephemeral." In *Lambda Book Report*, Jim Gladstone wrote that the book was "slim yet infinitely rereadable," and in *Library Journal*, Carol J. Binkowski commented that the volume "should be lingered over and reread to uncover the full depth of its beauty and insight."

Source: Gale, "Mark A. Doty," in *Contemporary Authors Online*, Gale, Cengage Learning, 2007.

Roger Gilbert

In the following excerpt, Gilbert analyzes the angel imagery in Doty's poem "The Wings." The critic discusses how Doty "is careful not to let his angels take on a fully supernatural presence," instead endowing them with a real-world, active role in the poem. Gilbert also compares the language of the angel's lines with that from other artistic endeavors from the 1990s that feature angels.

Literary historians looking back on the poetry of the 1990s will surely be struck by what can only be called a plague of angels. Heavenly beings swarmed the decade's books and magazines like locusts. Consider just the titles of poetry volumes published in the last twelve years: by my count at least twenty-seven of them contain the word "angel" or some variant thereof. Many more individual poems published during the period featured angels prominently in their titles or texts. These angels were surprisingly ecumenical, favoring no particular school or mode of poetry but showing up in a wide variety of poetic settings and styles, from buttoned-down formalism to coffee-house surrealism and everything in between. I'd like to consider this obsession with angels as one symptom of a larger shift in tone and style visible even in nonangelic poetry of the nineties. My claim is that the evocation of angels and related figures by poets of many different stripes reflects a more general impulse to revive modes of representation that had come to seem

> "WHAT LENDS THE POEM ITS SPECIAL PATHOS IS THE FIGURE OF THE SLEEPING LOVER, VULNERABLE BUT NOT YET ILL, FOR WHOM THE ANGEL'S PROTECTION IS MOST URGENTLY BEING INVOKED."

increasingly illicit or unavailable in the ironic, postmodern eighties. Angels in particular seemed to offer nineties poets a way to mediate between sharply opposed realms: religion and history, heaven and earth, spirit and matter, the sublime and the profane. As instruments of divine revelation, angels gave poets access to visionary possibilities that had lain largely dormant in the seventies and eighties. Yet as peculiarly passive beings, possessed of little real agency or power, angels allowed poets to measure and describe the corrosive effects of history and materiality on the workings of pure spirit.

It would of course be easy to view the poetic fascination with angels in the nineties as a side effect of that widespread resurgence of eclectic spirituality known as the New Age, and certainly it can't be entirely dissociated from such broader cultural currents. Not surprisingly, apocalyptic imaginings ran wild in the decade leading up to the millennium. At the same time, a countervailing hunger for reassuring images of divine authority seems to have been widely felt. Angels turned up everywhere in the nineties: in movies (*Wings of Desire, City of Angels, Angels in the Outfield, Michael*), on television (*Touched by an Angel*), on CDs (*Voice of an Angel*), *and* on the bestseller list (*A Book of Angels, Angelspeake*). Tony Kushner's brilliant play cycle *Angels in America* was perhaps the decade's most serious and ambitious effort to bring angelic figures into contact with contemporary reality. By comparison, most popular representations of angels were thoroughly banal. As Harold Bloom noted in 1996: "Angels, these days, have been divested of their sublimity by popular culture... In our New Age, the upper spheres, where the angels live, are overpopulated, so that even the least deserving of us can be assigned a guardian messenger" (43). At their most insipid, nineties angels became glorified operators on a heavenly Psychic Hotline, dispensing advice and inspiration on demand. Needless

to say, the angels that haunted the decade's poetry bore scant resemblance to these sentimental cartoons. Often blank, wounded, or ominous, the poets' angels offered little in the way of reassurance or guidance, instead embodying the terrors evoked by the encroaching millennium. Still, we should not dismiss the conjunction of popular and poetic tropes as mere historical coincidence. Despite their marginal position in contemporary culture, poets are never wholly immune to the obsessions of their zeitgeist, though they often produce more compelling and complex renderings of them...

Like Wallace Stevens, for whom angels were necessary fictions to be both celebrated and exposed, many nineties poets treated their angels as explicit constructs inviting a delicate mixture of reverence and detachment. In a 1978 essay entitled "What Was Modern Poetry?" Howard Nemerov offers some remarks that illuminate the characteristic stance of these poets toward their supernatural personae:

> Devils and angels together, goblins and nymphs alike, appear to be progressively forbidden the poets just as they have progressively been exiled from the world, in the interest, it is supposed, of evidence, reason, clear thinking, common sense; but I rather doubt the poets are in a better position for that; and the last state of them is like enough to be worse than the first. For poetry was once the place where these entities did their proper work, where the exact degree of their fictitiousness could be measured against the exact degree of their quite real powers, and both could be experienced ideally, not fatally in the world of action. As Rudolf Steiner said so shrewdly, Think these thoughts without believing them.

(191)

Nemerov is writing at a moment when angels and other supernatural beings had largely disappeared from contemporary poetry; hence the rueful, nostalgic tone of his comments. Since then, of course, angels have made a spectacular comeback, very much in the spirit of Steiner's "Think these thoughts without believing them." Nineties poets often present their angels *sous rature*, as it were, as in these lines by Michael Palmer:

> Thus released, the dark angels converse with
> the angels of light.
> They are not angels.
> Something else.

(*The Lion Bridge* 250)

This gesture, invoking the category of angels while simultaneously questioning or denying it, recurred in many nineties poems, though not always so explicitly. The "something else" that the word "angels" can only approximate remains undefined in this poem; Palmer's emphasis is on both the inescapability and the inadequacy of the traditional icon.

As Nemerov insists, fictitiousness and power need not be mutually exclusive. Many poets who call attention to the imagined or constructed character of their angels ascribe a performative agency to them that produces real effects. Mark Doty's beautiful long poem "The Wings," from his 1993 volume *My Alexandria*, weaves together various images of angels—a boy carrying snowshoes on his back, characters in the German film *Wings of Desire*, a garden planting—with the poet's anxiety over his HIV-positive lover. Doty is careful not to let his angels take on a fully supernatural presence, yet even as fictions they prove surprisingly active. The poem's closing movement begins with the speaker in the role of teacher, expounding the power of artifice:

> In my afternoon class the students
> sit in a circle of chairs on the terrace,
> and behind their faces, which seem then
>
> so dizzyingly new, all the rich
> commingling of leaves hurry downward
> into latent shades too subtle
> to ever name, colors
>
> we perhaps can't register even once,
> and they wonder why the poet we're reading's
> so insistent on mortality. I want to tell them
> how I make the angel, that form
>
> between us and the unthinkable,
> that face we give the empty ringing,
> and how that form for me appears in a boy
> with snowshoe wings slung across his
> shoulders,
>
> or in the child sprawled on the marble floor
> of the post office yesterday,
> who filled the echoing lobby with random
> notes
> blown on her recorder, music made out of
> waiting.

The slight hesitation in the phrase "I want to tell them" suggests that for Doty the making of angels remains problematic, a fragile venture all too susceptible to mockery. Yet if the angel is "that form / between us and the unthinkable, /

that face we give the empty ringing," then without its mediation we would have no way to apprehend or confront those facts that exceed rational understanding: death, birth, infinity, eternity. Doty's emphasis on the private, idiosyncratic quality of his angelic imaginings ("for me") allows him to bridge empirical and visionary registers while recognizing that such acts of bridging are fundamentally poetic or constructive.

Doty's interest in his angel is not merely poetic, however, but deeply personal, as the next stanzas reveal:

> I let the light-glazed angel
> in the children's bodies, the angel
> with his face flushed in the heat
> of recognizing any birth,
>
> I let him bend over my desk and speak
> in a voice so assured you wouldn't know
> that anyone was dying. *Any music's
> made of waiting*, he says.
>
> I make him again. *Look,
> it doesn't matter so much.
> See into what you can.*
> I make the angel lean over our bed
>
> in the next room, where you're sleeping
> the sturdy, uncompromised sleep
> of someone going to work early tomorrow.
> I am willing around you, hard,
>
> the encompassing wings of the one called
> *unharmed*. His name is nowhere
> in the concordance, but I don't care;
> he's the rationale for any naming.

What lends the poem its special pathos is the figure of the sleeping lover, vulnerable but not yet ill, for whom the angel's protection is most urgently being invoked. (Not surprisingly, AIDS was a significant presence in much nineties poetry and undoubtedly played a role in the widespread turn to religious themes and tropes.) In an explicit revisionary gesture, Doty calls his angel "*unharmed*," a name he admits is "nowhere / in the concordance" yet insists is "the rationale for any naming." Making and naming the angel become an apotropaic ritual, a way of imaginatively warding off disaster while acknowledging its inevitability. What the speaker desperately wants from his angel—invulnerability for his sick lover—is not what the angel has to give, however. All this angel can offer is eloquence, an expression of mortal tenderness without the traditional comforts of religion:

> A steady fine-pointed rain's
> etching the new plantings,

and I'm making the rain
part of the angel. *Try to be certain,*

he says, *where you're looking.*
If you're offered endlessness,
don't do anything differently. The rule
of earth is attachment:

here what can't be held
is. You die by dying
into what matters, which will kill you,
but first it'll be enough. Or more than that:

your story, which you have zoom away
as you shaped it,
which has become itself
as it has disappeared.

Although Doty's angel is transparently fictive, as the repeated phrase "I make" concedes, he takes on a kind of oracular authority in these concluding stanzas, offering homiletic reassurances to his mortal creator. The thought expressed is a familiar one, a variant on Stevens's "Death is the mother of beauty," itself a modulation of the ancient carpe diem motif. It's hard to imagine a poet in the ironic eighties writing in this unabashedly lofty vein; for Doty as for other nineties poets, the angelic persona sanctions a kind of utterance that might seem stilted or didactic in the voice of a human speaker. The words spoken here are of course Doty's own, yet by ventriloquistically projecting them into the angel's mouth, he estranges them, giving a face, a name, and a voice to what he had earlier called "the empty ringing."

Where Doty places his angel under the sign of making or artifice, a number of nineties poets place theirs under the sign of unmaking or erasure. For them the angel is not a form between us and the unthinkable but a means of destroying all mediating forms, a way to imagine negation in its purest state.

Source: Roger Gilbert, "Awash with Angels: The Religious Turn in Nineties Poetry," in *Contemporary Literature*, Vol. 42, No. 2, Summer 2001, pp. 238–69.

Deborah Landau

In the following essay, Landau here focuses on the political nature of My Alexandria, *particularly as it addresses issues related to AIDS and homosexuality. The critic notes that although Doty does not adopt a "polemical" tone in these poems, he nevertheless does not merely create a personal, private poetry. Rather, his poems resonate on both a public and a political level, in so doing illuminating*

> AS IN TONY KUSHNER'S *ANGELS IN AMERICA,* UNCONVENTIONAL SPIRITUALITY EMERGES IN *MY ALEXANDRIA* AS A SALVE FOR THE SUFFERING ASSOCIATED WITH THE AIDS EPIDEMIC; DOTY'S ANGELS, LIKE KUSHNER'S, ARE HEALING, REDEMPTIVE, LIBIDINOUS, AND VISIONARY."

"Doty's visionary rewriting of oppressive myths about AIDS."

. . . Doty has said of *My Alexandria,* "Alexandria . . . is that city of art—that made place, which is both the given and the way that we transform the given." I will argue that Doty performs a crucial function in this desolate era not only by providing a record of massive destruction but also by reimagining the terms used to describe such destruction and envisioning possibilities for political, sensual, and spiritual redemption . . .

The poems of *My Alexandria* transform homophobic narratives about the disease, offer comfort to those living with HIV, and encourage empathy from those whose lives have not yet been affected by the virus. In "Dante on Fire Island: Reinventing Heaven in the AIDS Elegy," James Miller praises poems that offer a "blessed moment of recovery when the dead rise from the mass graves dug for them by the fatalistic discourse of public health and join forces with the living against the World, the Flesh, and the Virus." Mark Doty is a poet who envisions sustaining moments despite great suffering and offers his readers a "way to continue." Although Doty's poems are not polemical, they counter reductive representations of people with AIDS, are accessible to a wider audience, and have the potential to improve public response to the epidemic.

Doty's *My Alexandria,* a collection of poems about mortality in the age of AIDS, fulfills Wallace Stevens's dictum that the poet's role is to "help people to live their lives." If Auden was wrong and poetry can on occasion "make something happen," Doty's visionary rewriting of oppressive myths about AIDS may help people live their lives in a more literal way than Stevens intended. Through discursive and ideological revisions, Doty's poems produce humane and comforting narratives that stand in sharp contrast to the hostile sociopolitical climate of the contemporary United States. His poems expose the codes that map meaning onto the HIV-positive body, destabilize the complex cultural networks that construct gay male identity in the context of the AIDS epidemic, and forge a transformed and transforming language in which to articulate love and loss.

My Alexandria enacts a semiological reframing of the AIDS epidemic. The book begins with "Demolition"—a fitting introduction to a volume of poems about mortality in a time of plague. A group of people gather on a city street "joined by a thirst for watching something fall," as a bakery and florist shop topple leaving only "the ghost of their signs faint above the windows / lined, last week, with loaves and blooms." In an image that uncovers the signs that stand in place of substance, "Demolition" exposes the gap between discourse and the material world and (although the poem contains no specific references to AIDS) initiates the thematic concerns of *My Alexandria*—a book largely about the rift between the ideology that surrounds the AIDS epidemic and the specific experiences of people living with HIV.

As the "brutish metal" eradicates the building and its signs, the speaker muses on how "in a week, the kids will skateboard / in their lovely loops and spray / their indecipherable ideograms" (2–3). Nothing can remain blank, but the progression from an ordered, stable structure to this improvisational scribbling suggests hope for a new, fluid language that will shape this space less rigidly. Indeed, by the end of the poem all that remains of the once-solid structure are "gaps / where the windows opened once." Reveling in the freedom of unbounded space, Doty writes: "It's strange how much more beautiful / the sky is to us when it's framed by these columned openings someone meant us / to take for stone" (3).

By challenging the stability of structures that are meant to be taken for stone, "Demolition" sets the stage for later poems in the collection that discursively demolish constraining structures. The "articulate shovel" of "Demolition" functions as a metaphor for the poetry of *My Alexandria*, which "nudges the highest row of moldings" of an oppressive social order so that—at least in the world of the poems—

"the whole thing wavers as though we'd dreamed it, / . . . and   topples all at once."

In "Fog," a poem about the three-week period during which Doty and his companion of twelve years, Wally Roberts, waited for HIV-test results, the speaker stands in his garden filled with "blood color" flowers and laments: "three weeks after the test, / the vial filled from the crook / of my elbow, I'm seeing blood everywhere" (33). While "Demolition" evokes the redemptive power of poetic language, "Fog" enacts such redemption by transforming the cultural coding of AIDS and situating the lovers' dreadful discovery in a world animated by compassionate spirits:

> The thin green porcelain
> teacup, our homemade Ouija's planchette,
>
> rocks and wobbles every night, spins
> and spells. It seems a cloud of spirits
>
> numerous as lilac panicles vie for occupancy—
> children grabbing for the telephone,
>
> happy to talk to someone who isn't dead
>   yet?
> Everyone wants to speak at once, or at least
>
> these random words appear, incongruous
> and exactly spelled: *energy, immunity, kiss*.
>
> Then: M. *has immunity*. W. *has*.
> And that was all. (33–34)

The poem exemplifies Doty's ability to perceive animation in the midst of a dying world and to contextualize grief within a spirit-filled garden. The speaker tells how "one character, Frank, . . . who lived in our house in the thirties, . . . asks us to stand before the screen / and kiss. *God in garden*, he says" (34). Doty's spirituality is unconventional and iconoclastic; his spirits request homoerotic union, and in place of a patriarchal "God" it is an invisible presence that moves in the garden:

> Sitting out on the back porch at twilight,
> I'm almost convinced. In this geometry
>
> of paths and raised beds, the green shadows
> of delphinium, there's an unseen rustling:
>
> some secret amplitude
> seems to open in this orderly space.
>
> Maybe because it contains so much dying,
> all these tulip petals thinning
>
> at the base until any wind takes them.
> I doubt anyone else would see that, looking in,
>
> and then I realize my garden has no outside,
>   only *is*

subjectively. As blood is utterly without

an outside, can't be seen except out of
    context,
the wrong color in alien air, no longer itself.
    (34–35)

Although Doty does not write explicitly about the political world, his transformations are ideological as well as spiritual. Much as the speaker's garden is an "orderly space" in which design is imposed on wilderness, so his blood is coded by the medical establishment when tested for HIV. In the context of the discourses that define the AIDS epidemic, the speaker's blood—or his body—cannot be simply "itself." As Douglas Crimp writes, "AIDS does not exist apart from the practices that conceptualize it, represent it, and respond to it."

In the midst of this "alien air," Doty's speaker describes the process of HIV testing in which their blood

submits to test, two
to be exact, each done three times,

though not for me, since at their first entry
into my disembodied blood

there was nothing at home there.
For you they entered the blood garden over

and over, like knocking at a door
because you know someone's home. Three
    times

the Elisa Test, three the Western Blot,
and then the incoherent message. We're

the public health care worker's
nine o'clock appointment,

she is a phantom hand who forms
the letters of your name, and the word

that begins with P. (35)

Because the terminology of an anonymous bureaucrat is painful and alienating, Doty seeks another language to assimilate this information that will elude—or at least loosen—the grip of the "phantom hand" of systemic discourse. Knowing that the cultural significance of his lover's HIV status is fixed by the word "that begins with P," the speaker resists that language, and will not say the word *positive*:

Planchette,
peony, I would think of anything

not to say the word …

…

Every new bloom is falling apart.

I would say anything else
in the world, any other word. (36)

The speaker's wish to "say any other word" reflects a fierce need to deny his lover's HIV status, as well as a desire for a language that would enable him to narrate this experience in his own terms: a "secret amplitude" to enable breathing room amidst—and despite—the discourses that script the cultural meaning of AIDS. Like James Merrill, who often used the ouija board as a tool for composing poems, Doty takes the ouija board in "Fog" (like Merrill's, "homemade") as a figure for the process of generating alternative narratives and exploring uncharted territory. And, indeed, he does succeed in saying "other words": the word "positive" does not appear anywhere in the poem.

Although Joseph Cady might read the speaker's refusal to say HIV positive as a problematically "counterimmersive" moment that echoes public denial of AIDS, from another perspective Doty can be said to resist oppressive cultural responses in "Fog" by forging alternative narratives to those of public health discourse. The test results are devastating, yet Doty contextualizes Wally's HIV status within a spirit-infused garden and narrates the situation in tender, compassionate language to affirm love and spirituality.

"The Wings"—a poem of anticipatory grief for an HIV-positive lover—is another text in which Doty forges alternative ways to speak about love and loss in the context of the AIDS epidemic. Reflecting on a fall landscape, he writes:

There were geese. *There were*:
the day's narration is simple assertion;

it's enough to name the instances.
Don't let anybody tell you

death's the price exacted
for the ability to love;

couldn't we live forever
without running out of occasions?

In contrast to Liu's portrayal of same-sex couplings as lethal, Doty rejects the link between love and death and challenges narratives that portray homoerotic love as self-destructive. While Paul Monette's poems forcefully refute homophobic myths, Doty goes beyond refusal to transform oppressive ideology ("death's the price exacted / for the ability to love") into a celebration of love between men ("couldn't we live forever / without running out of occasions?").

James Miller describes a similar moment in an earlier poem, "Tiara," in which Doty's speaker tells of overhearing a damning stereotype at a friend's funeral: "And someone said he asked for it. / *Asked* for it." In an interview, Doty summarized the events that occasioned the poem: "'Tiara' is an elegy for a friend of mine who was a drag queen, always out in clubs ... After he died someone said at his wake, 'Well, he asked for it.' I was filled with rage at that ridiculous notion that we invite our own oppression as a consequence of pleasure." In "Tiara," as in "The Wings," Doty does not merely refute this myth but transmutes it into what Miller describes as "a collective defense of our stampeding life in the body":

> given
> the world's perfectly turned shoulders,
>
> the deep hollows blued by longing,
> given the irreplaceable silk
> of horses rippling
>
> in orchards, fruits thundering
> and chiming down, given salt
> and a tongue to long for it
>
> and gravity, what could he do,
> what could any of us ever do
> but ask for it.

These lines exemplify Doty's ability to take a derogatory phrase as an occasion to affirm homoerotic love and desire—what he describes as a "redemptive re-evaluation or revisioning. To say, well, there is a way in which we ask for it! We love the world! We want to have sex! We desire beauty! We love whatever it is that we love."

"The Wings" moves from the myth that HIV is a by-product of gay love to another cultural text, the AIDS Memorial Quilt:

> In the Exhibition Hall each unfurled
> three-by-five field bears
> in awkward or accomplished embroidery
>
> a name, every banner stitched to another
> and another. They're reading
> the unthinkable catalog of the names,
>
> so many they blur, become
> a single music pronounced with difficulty
> over the microphone, become a pronoun,
>
> become You. It's the clothing I can't get past,
> the way a favorite pair of jeans,
> a striped shirt's sewn onto the cloth;

the fading, the pulls in the fabric
demonstrate how these relics formed around
one essential, missing body.

> An empty pair of pants
> is mortality's severest evidence.
> Embroidered mottoes blend
>
> into something elegiac but removed;
> a shirt can't be remote.
> One can't look past
>
> the sleeves where two arms
> were, where a shoulder pushed
> against a seam, and someone knew exactly
>
> how the stitches pressed against skin
> that can't be generalized but was,
> irretrievably, you, or yours.

In contrast to the homophobic ideology that represents AIDS as deserved retribution for sex between men, the quilt offers a compassionate, elegiac narrative for those lost to the epidemic. While the passage foregrounds the specificity of those memorialized, the two moments at which the poem pauses on the pronoun "you" blur the distinction between the dead and the reader to emphasize that those lost to AIDS could be anybody—not only the speaker's beloved but the reader, or someone he or she has loved. Through this blurring, Doty brings his readers into the poem in a way that dissolves the boundaries between one body and another and counters the prevalent tendency to see people with AIDS as Other.

Meditations on the loss brought on by this plague—and an awareness that his lover's name might soon also be embroidered into the fabric of the quilt—inspire the speaker to "make an angel" by planting a garden that enables "buried wishes" to

> become blooms,
> supple and sheened as skin. I'm thinking
>
> of the lily-flowered kind
> on slim spines, the ones
> that might as well be flames,
>
> just two slight wings that will
> blaze into the future;
> I have to think they have a will,
>
> a design so inherent in the cells
> nothing could subtract from them
> the least quotient of grace ...

This garden is the birthplace of Doty's angel and suggests the reincarnation of the speaker's lover into a "human profile / ... all berry and leaf." The image of winged, flame-like flowers evokes a fluid and elusive sphere of physical experience, as if the beloved has been resurrected in a medium that defies all physical and cultural constraints. By claiming irreducible grace for these metaphoric blooms, the poet envisions a redeemed world untouched by the rhetoric that makes "death the price exacted / for the ability to love."

The image of winged blooms leads into a passage celebrating homoerotic desire:

> I dreamed
> the night after the fall planting,
> that a bird who loved me
>
> had been long neglected, and when
> I took it from the closet and gave it water
> its tongue began to move again,
>
> and it began to beat the lush green music
> of its wings, and wrapped the brilliant risk
> of leaves all around my face.

Doty's attachment to the regenerating power of the erotic contrasts sharply with the mutilated genitals of Liu's "Eros Apteros" and Gunn's relegation of sexuality to the irretrievable past. By affirming sensuality despite—and in the midst of—risk, "The Wings" defies what Douglas Crimp identifies as "the comfortable fantasy that AIDS would spell the end of gay promiscuity, or perhaps gay sex altogether."

Although Doty's speaker finds himself holding a book entitled *A Literal, Critical and Systematic Description of Objects*, he turns away from that text to articulate experiences that elude rigid coding:

> all the rich
> commingling of leaves hurry downward
> into latent shades too subtle
> to ever name, colors
>
> we perhaps can't register even once,
> and they wonder why the poet we're reading's
> so insistent on mortality. I want to tell them
> how I make the angel, that form
>
> between us and the unthinkable.

If no one can articulate the "unthinkable," Doty gestures towards unbounded experience by locating himself in an epistemological space between the boundaries of the social order and the unimaginable. The angel enables the poet to speak of experiences that cannot be neatly categorized and certainly would not appear in *A*

Literal, Critical and Systematic Description of Objects.

As in Tony Kushner's *Angels in America*, unconventional spirituality emerges in *My Alexandria* as a salve for the suffering associated with the AIDS epidemic; Doty's angels, like Kushner's, are healing, redemptive, libidinous, and visionary. While for Timothy Liu AIDS brings the extinction of angels ("We often made angels on your lawn, watching the bodies fade a little more / each day, until the wings were gone" ["Last Christmas," *Vox Angelica*, 55]), for Doty, the AIDS epidemic necessitates the creation of angels:

> I make the angel lean over our bed
>
> in the next room, where you're sleeping
> . . .
> I am willing around you, hard,
>
> the encompassing wings of the one called
> *unharmed*. His name is nowhere
> in the concordance, but I don't care;
> he's the rationale for any naming.

Angel-making is Doty's metaphor for the poetry-making process that enables him to speak, at least for a moment, "in a voice so assured you wouldn't know / that anyone was dying." If mainstream discourses script people with AIDS as alone and despondent, Doty's angel-laden poetry forges a language that deems his beloved friend "unharmed." Certainly Stevens's necessary angel is behind Doty's angel, but in contrast to Stevens's central man who singularly "sums us up," Doty's angel stands on the margins of American culture, searching for words that elude systematic terminology and cannot be found in any concordance.

The angel's narrative about mortality gives closure to the poem:

> *You die by dying*
> *into what matters, which will kill you,*
> *but first it'll be enough. Or more than that:*
>
> *your story, which you have worn away*
> *as you shaped it,*
> *which has become itself*
> *as it has disappeared.*

Doty's angel endows the dying man with the power to narrate his own life and death and enables him to retain his autonomy and integrity despite the "alien air" of public rhetoric.

"Brilliance" also revises stereotypes about people with AIDS. "Maggie's taking care of a man / who's dying," Doty writes in the opening lines of the poem, which tells of a man with AIDS who has given up, "paid off his credit card," and "found a home for" his pets since "he can't be around dogs or cats / too much risk":

> He says,
>
> *I can't have anything.*
> She says, *A bowl of goldfish?*
> He says he doesn't want to start
>
> with anything and then describes
> the kind he'd maybe like,
> how their tails would fan
>
> to a gold flaring. They talk
> about hot jewel tones,
> gold lacquer, say maybe
>
> they'll go pick some out
> though he can't go much of anywhere and
>   then
> abruptly he says *I can't love*
>
> *anything I can't finish.*
> He says it like he's had enough
> of the whole scintillant world. (65–66)

The passage above fits Douglas Crimp's description of the cultural stereotypes of people with AIDS—"that they are ... debilitated by the syndrome ... generally alone, desperate, but resigned to their 'inevitable' deaths"—stereotypes that Crimp argues fail to empower people with AIDS to fight to improve the quality of their lives. But "Brilliance" goes on to counter such reductive representations:

> *Later he leaves a message:*
>
> *Yes to the bowl of goldfish.*
> Meaning: let me go, if I have to,
> in brilliance.
>
> . . .
>
> So, Maggie's friend—
> is he going out
>
> into the last loved object
> of his attention?
> Fanning the veined translucence
>
> of an opulent tail,
> undulant in some uncapturable curve,
> is he bronze chrysanthemums,
>
> copper leaf, hurried darting,
> doubloons, icon-colored fins
> troubling the water? (66–67)

The last lines of the poem present the fusion between the sick man and the scintillant fish as a subversive and defiant response to an oppressive

world. Doty's story of a man who retains pleasurable attachment to the sensual world despite his rapidly approaching death contrasts dramatically with Gunn's depiction of dying as a "difficult, tedious, painful enterprise" because the two poems serve contrasting purposes. Gunn's is a cathartic lament in which both speaker and reader are immersed in the details of AIDS-related illness, while Doty's poem is a soothing reverie that counters mainstream representations of people with AIDS and gestures towards a world beyond brutality and suffering.

"Bill's Story" is another exploration of alternatives to conventional narratives about death and dying. The poem is about the speaker's sister Anne, who returns from Africa with dementia— "the first sign of something / we didn't even have a name for, / in 1978." When Anne is hospitalized years later, Doty's speaker recalls:

> my mother needed something
> to hold onto, some way to be helpful.
> so she read a book called *Deathing*
> (a cheap, ugly verb if ever I heard one)
> and took its advice to heart;
>
> she'd sit by the bed and say, *Annie*
> *look for the light, look for the light.*
> It was plain that Anne did not wish
> to be distracted by these instructions;
> she came to, though she was nearly gone
>   then,
> and looked at our mother with what was
>   almost certainly
>
> annoyance. *It's a white light,*
> Mom said, and this struck me
> as incredibly presumptuous, as if the light
> we'd all go into would be just the same.
> Maybe she wanted to give herself up
> to indigo, or red. If we can barely even speak
>
> to each other, living so separately,
> how can we all die the same? (68–69)

Much as the man in "Brilliance" chooses "jewel tones" and "gold lacquer" over muted tones of desperation, here the speaker rejects the mythical white light and muses instead on the transportative power of other colors. "Maybe her light was all that gabardine / and flannel, khaki and navy / and silks and stripes," he says, referring to Anne's preference for eccentric costumes in her work as a performance artist. By writing poems about individual people with AIDS and their own particular acts of expression and triumph, Dory responds to

Crimp's call for "counter-images, images of PWA [people with AIDS] self-empowerment"

Doty's narratives are consoling as well as revisionary. In "Becoming a Meadow" the speaker takes refuge in a bookstore during a snow storm and muses on the words "becoming a meadow," a phrase that he finds particularly beautiful because

> a meadow accepts itself as various, allows
> some parts of itself to always be going away,
> because whatever happens in that blown,
>
> ragged field of grass and sway
> *is* the meadow, and threading the frost
> of its unlikely brilliance yesterday
>
> we also were the meadow. In the bookstore
> while you are reading and I am allowing
>   myself
> simply to be comforted by the presence of
>   stories,
>
> the bound, steady presences on the shelves,
> fixed as nothing else is, I am thinking of my
>   terror
> of decay, the little hell opening in every vio-
>   lated cell,
>
> the virus tearing
> away—is it?—and we are still a part of the
>   meadow
> because I am thinking of it, hearing
>
> the bell-phrase of it: Head of the Meadow
> in my head. The titles of books,
> the letters of the writers' names blow
>
> like grasses, become individual stalks,
> seedheads, burrs, rimed swell
> of dune on which the beach grass is writing
>   its book
>
> in characters unreadable or read:
> the meadow-book
> you are writing, and which you read. (75–76)

The speaker's anxiety about his own HIV status is at the center of this passage, but Doty recontextualizes that pressing question in a calm and fluid world. The meadow is a place in which conventional narratives about mortality dissolve so that—at least in the realm of the poem—the world itself is utterly transformed:

> And if one wave breaking says
> *You're dying*, then the rhythm and shift of
>   the whole
> says nothing about endings, and half the
>   shawling head
> of each wave's spume pours into the trough

of the one before,
and half blows away in spray, backward,
    toward the open sea. (76)

This is another of Doty's revisionary moments. The shift from a single, fixed narrative ("you're dying") towards unbounded space is comforting and decentralizes the question ("the virus tearing / away—is it?") that threatens to define a person's entire identity on the basis of his HIV status.

For Doty, poetry is a medium for imagining temporary exemption from history, from the physical and cultural constraints that circumscribe sensation and experience. By revealing the myths and politics that construct the AIDS epidemic and by depicting individual acts that defy the pressure of those constructions, *My Alexandria* transforms the terms that limit the lives and deaths of people with AIDS. Doty tells of letters from readers that confirm the consoling and redemptive power of these poems: "Some who found their own experience of a lover's illness mirrored or defined; ... straight readers who ... wrote to tell ... about arriving at a new understanding of homosexual relationships." Doty cites these letters as tangible evidence of the transformative potential of poetry: "Wouldn't it be wonderful if poetry could have ... broader impact ... I no longer agree with Auden's famous formulation, since I have seen such potent connections between people formed because of poems. I know that these do not in themselves constitute social change, but I have been lucky enough to be on the receiving end of some remarkable communications from readers."

Many readers have written to Doty to acknowledge the extent to which his poems have helped them cope with the illness or loss of a lover:

> I want to thank you for your collection of poems, *My Alexandria*. A beautiful, beautiful book.

> Lately I have been mourning the death of my lover. I have been trying to understand what I have lost, what exactly I have gained, (ache), how to forgive and how to ask for forgiveness. Your poems opened me and stilled me. Thank you.

Another reader, describing his growing apprehension about the future in light of his partner's worsening health, writes:

> Reading your book of poems heightened and focused my feelings to a degree little else has

done in a long time; what had seemed like a whirlpool of emotions and ideas, as I look both back and ahead, has calmed—I might say has been *refined* by the clarity of your vision and your ability to convey that vision in beautiful form and language.

Others write to express gratitude for Doty's ability to articulate what has not been adequately voiced elsewhere in American culture: "As a young gay writer, I find myself casually marginalized everywhere I turn ... so what a relief it is for me to turn to your words." Another reader writes, "I find a new world in your work ... I walk down a street and hear your words. You have made something that exists outside itself. Something that lives and is there because you have made it possible." Still another shares his reaction to encountering Doty's words: "I had to stop every few minutes to scribble madly in my journal and I kept saying to myself 'Yes! Yes!'"

Although the impact of poetry on the social order may be indirect and obscure, these letters suggest that if Doty's reimaginings of this epidemic were to permeate social conceptions of AIDS, they might make the world a less brutal place. As William Carlos Williams writes:

> It is difficult
> to get the news from poems
> yet men die miserably every day
> for lack
>
> of what is found there.

Commenting on this passage, Doty affirms the relevance of Williams's words: "I believe that 'what is found there' might alleviate misery, if not postpone death ... If 'what is found there' might help us all to re-imagine the disease, and rewrite the repetitive texts of homophobia and fear of otherness, then in fact poetry *might* keep people from dying. Let's hope that whatever contribution we can make is one more shoulder put to the wheel."

Source: Deborah Landau, "'How to Live. What to Do.': The Poetics and Politics of AIDS," in *American Literature*, Vol. 68, No. 1, March 1996, pp. 193–225.

Calvin Bedient

In the following essay, Bedient assesses the language and imagery of My Alexandria. *He comments on the "sunny side" of the poems in the collection, noting that Doty highlights the positive aspects of life while also dealing with themes of illness and death. Bedient criticizes Doty's "ever-*

> ... DESPITE DOTY'S OWN DESCRIPTION OF A VIRAL 'TEARING,' THE WORLD IS A RHYTHMIC WHOLE OF APPARENTLY HARMONIOUS COMINGS AND GOINGS—THE SWEETEST PAGANISM."

present pulled-taffy tone and syntax" but also commends the poet for the vision and imagination he displays in the volume.

Between Pater and Pantheism. Mark Doty walks on the sunny side of Pater's still impressive, pathos-and-beauty-ridden sense of reality. Where Pater emphasized the elemental forces ceaselessly "parting on their ways," undoing us, Doty accentuates the ensemble [in *My Alexandria*]. Life is not a thing of darkness; there are riches for the tasting, the taking, the telling. Consider "the unlikely needlepoint" that wild asters make of an October slope. Life is an obvious good. "It's enough to name the instances." "Couldn't we live forever / without running out of occasions?" Nothing is a poverty: "Anything lived into long enough / becomes an orchard." "*Even the most circumstantial things / are holy in themselves.*" We can make earthly angels of ourselves—make "the rain / part of the angel." Yes, we will die, but first "what matters" will have proved to "be enough. Or more than that." (All quotations are from "The Wings.")

At the end of the century that confirmed psychological abysses and bombed up a global atmosphere of disaster, even such modest affirmations have become wagers. Doty's seem a sort of class embroidery, remote from the Third World. Yet the best hope remains the testimony of some of the survivors of atrocity: the reaffirmation of the simple blessing of sunshine, work, and community that Terrence des Pres summarized in his book *The Survivor*, and Doty is not far from this testimony. Not far at all.

Certainly "The Wings" has authority compared to the romantic apologies of "Tiara" an earlier poem of Doty's reprinted in *Poets for Life*. "Tiara," recounts that tension breaks at a funeral when someone says of the dead man, referring to the closed casket, he's "in there in a big wig / and heels," but returns when someone else says "he asked for it":

> *Asked* for it—when all he did
> was go down into the salt tide
> of wanting as much as he wanted,
> giving himself over so drunk
> or stoned it almost didn't matter who,
> though they were beautiful,
> stampeding into him in the simple,
> ravishing music of their hurry.

"What could he do, / what could any of us ever do / but ask for it," the poet punningly asks at the end, braving the fact that the past tense of the second "could" betrays caution and that the question isn't really rhetorical even if it seals itself off by omitting the question mark. The poem is egregious in its go-for-broke erotic romanticism. Such lines as "the simple [!] / ravishing music [!] of their hurry" and "dreaming and waking men lie / on the grass while wet blue horses [!] / roam among them, huge fragments [!] / of the music we die into [!] / in the body's paradise" are more wide-eyed than sensual, more purple than blue.

In a later poem on a transvestite, "Esta Noche," placed in the first part of *My Alexandria*, Doty applauds the stage-lit black-silk-draped "*la fabulosa Lola*" ("a man / you wouldn't look twice at in street clothes, / two hundred pounds of hard living, the gap in her smile / sadly narrative"):

> Tonight, she says,
> put it on. The costume is license
> and calling. She says you could wear the whole damn
> black sky and all its spangles. It's the only night
> we have to stand on. Put it on,
> it's the only thing we have to wear.

Apart from confusing what you stand on with what you can put on, the lines reduce nature to so much black stuff best used to adorn the "sad" human form. They support a sentimental vanity, at best. (Merrill celebrates a "fabulous" getup in these AIDS days with more Paterian finesse in *The Inner Room*.) But as a seer, Doty has proven commendably ad hoc, experimental, if within a narrow, noncontradictory range. "The Wings" is evidence of this; and two strong poems near the end of *My Alexandria*, "Night Ferry" and "Becoming a Meadow," also provide wiser perspectives than do "Esta Noche" and "Tiara."

In "Night Ferry," the self-admitted fiction of the world as a story (another pedal point in the book) first appears in a gorgeous image for reflected dock lights: "their colors / on the roughened surface combed / like the patterns of Italian bookpaper, / lustrous and promising. The narrative / of the ferry begins and ends brilliantly." The end of the poem both takes up the figure again and pokes an air hole through its paper walls:

> There's no beautiful binding
> for this story, only the temporary,
> liquid endpapers of the hurried water,
> shot with random color. But in the gliding
>   forward's
> a scent so quick and startling
> it might as well be blowing
> off the stars. Now, just before we arrive,
> the wind carries a signal and a comfort,
> lovely, though not really meant for us:
> woodsmoke risen from the chilly shore.

We find here Doty's ever-present pulled-taffy tone and syntax (his voice's prison and its gift). But in this rhythmically beguiling poem we find, too, a caution before the temptations of narcissistic illusion, a lucid bargaining at the table of the little that life offers as comfort, which distinguishes it from "Esta Noche."

If the virus is only implicit in "Night Ferry" (in an interview in the 1994 annual issue of *Provincetown Art*, Doty notes that being under so low-hanging a sword as AIDS intensifies the need to "love what is passing" and "to think about what it means to be temporary"), "Becoming a Meadow" pulls it out of the shadows: "I am thinking of my terror / of decay, the little hell opening in every violated cell, / the virus tearing / away—is it?" Really less a tearing away, as I understand it from Warner C. Greene's article "AIDS and the Immune System" in the September 1993 issue of *Scientific American*, than the virus' con-mannish entry into the cell, its subsequent confusion of the cell's identity by insinuating itself into the cell's chromosomal structure through a semiemulative, quick-change artistry in regard to its own constitution and consequent reduction of the cell to serving as the ground of its replication—a dizzying cycle of extraordinary complexity. (The virus itself has over 9,000 "bases" and more genes at its beck and call than other viruses have ever dreamed of.) The insidious complexity of the virus, not to mention what Greene calls its "rapid Darwinian evolution" (the result of the "error" it makes approximately once in every 2,000 incorporated nucleotides, leading to a constant generation of new variants of viral proteins), flies at a ripping angle from the large view of things that Doty creates in "Becoming a Meadow." Here, and despite Doty's own description of a viral "tearing," the world is a rhythmic whole of apparently harmonious comings and goings—the sweetest paganism. But Doty gives the idea considerable dignity, even so. Standing in a bookstore, "comforted" as usual "by the presence of stories," he remembers a recent walk with his companion in Head of the Meadow by the "waves / endless rows of bold cursive," and even as he thinks of his "terror of decays" he feels that "we are still a part of the meadow." Indeed, the books around him are "like grasses," the "whole place ... / is one undulant, salt-swollen meadow of water" where waves swell again and again "like the baskets of bread / and fish in the story, the miracle baskets." Not uncharacteristically, the elaboration of this conceit is, however elegantly, forced; and the miracle of a Creation renewed in each instant should probably be introduced as more than a simile (as it is, also via "baskets," in a famous passage in Whitman's "Song of Myself"), or not at all—as it is, it feels slipped in and put over. In any case, the following vision, which brings Dante's *terza rima* down to all there is of an earthly paradise, or of any paradise, is perhaps as imaginative, surprising, unfeverish, freeing, and, withal, plausible an affirmation of things as they are as anyone has yet devised in these AIDS days:

> a meadow accepts itself as various, allows
> some parts of itself to always be going away,
> because whatever happens in that blown,
> ragged field of grass and sway
> *is* the meadow, and threading the frost
> of its unlikely brilliance yesterday
> we also were the meadow

Source: Calvin Bedient, "These AIDS Days," in *Parnassus*, Vol. 20, Nos. 1–2, 1995, pp. 197–231.

SOURCES

"2006 Report on the Global AIDS Epidemic," Joint United Nations Programme on HIV/AIDS, 2006, p. 53.

Bergman, David, "The Ineffable Being of Light," in the *Gay & Lesbian Review*, Vol. 9, No. 3, May 2002, p. 38.

Doty, Mark, "The Wings," in *My Alexandria*, National Poetry Series, 1993, pp. 39–51.

Gilbert, Roger, "Awash with Angels: The Religious Turn in Nineties Poetry," in *Contemporary Literature*, Vol. 42, No. 2, Summer 2001, pp. 238–69.

Glover, Michael, Review of *Atlantis*, in the *New Statesman*, Vol. 125, No. 4294, July 26, 1996, p. 47.

Gonzalez, Ray, "Something from Nothing," in the *Los Angeles Times Book Review*, October 31, 1993, p. 12.

Hennessy, Christopher, "Going to the Source: An Interview with Mark Doty," in the *Lambda Book Report*, Vol. 10, No. 11, June-July 2002, p. 13.

———, "Ten Ways of Looking at Gay Poetry," in the *Gay & Lesbian Review*, Vol. 12, No. 5, September-October 2005, p. 11.

Herek, Gregory M., and John P. Capitanio, "A Second Decade of Stigma: Public Reactions to AIDS in the United States, 1990–91," in the *American Journal of Public Health*, 1993, Vol. 83, No. 4, pp. 574–77.

Landau, Deborah, "'How to Live. What to Do.': The Poetics and Politics of AIDS," in *American Literature*, Vol. 68, No. 1, March 1996, pp. 193–94.

Marcus, Peter, "Reflections on Intimacy," in the *Gay & Lesbian Review*, Vol. 8, No. 5, September 2001, p. 42.

Marks, Marjorie Lewellyn, Review of *My Alexandria*, in the *Los Angeles Times*, September 5, 1993, p. 6.

Padel, Ruth, "Books: Every Sequin is an Act of Praise; America's Star Poet Dazzles his Fans. But is their New Emperor Naked?", in the *Independent*, July 11, 1998, p. 12.

"A Report from the Frontline of the HIV/AIDS Epidemic," American Civil Liberties Union AIDS Project, 2003, http://www.aclu.org/hiv/gen/11548pub20030101.html (accessed April 13, 2007).

Smith, Bruce, Review of *My Alexandria*, in the *Boston Review*, Vol. 18, No. 5, October-November 1993, p. 33.

Wunderlich, Mark, "About Mark Doty," in *Ploughshares*, Vol. 25, No. 1, Spring 1999, p. 183.

FURTHER READING

Andriote, John-Manuel, *Victory Deferred: How AIDS Changed Gay Life in America*, University of Chicago Press, 1999.

> This book provides a survey of the ways in which AIDS has changed gay social and political life in the United States. With a mix of journalism, cultural analysis, and personal reminiscences, Andriote's study focuses on the period from the early 1980s, when AIDS first appeared in gay urban neighborhoods, to the 1996 visit of President Clinton to the AIDS Memorial Quilt in Washington, D.C.

Campbell, Catherine, *Letting Them Die: Why HIV/ AIDS Prevention Programmes Fail*, Indiana University Press, 2003.

> This thoroughly researched book analyzes the complex social reasons why people in the AIDS-ravaged countries of Africa continue to die of the disease and why the rate of infection is so high. Campbell argues that people at risk must be involved in protecting the health of their own communities in ways that are culturally acceptable to each individual community.

Creswell, Julia, *The Watkins Dictionary of Angels*, Sterling, 2006.

> This dictionary contains over 2,000 entries describing and defining the various types of angels that appear in the religious texts of the world. The dictionary also includes entries about angels that appear in literature, art, film, myth, and folklore. This book is a useful tool for discovering the many purposes that angels have served in different religions, cultures, art forms, and historical periods.

Pastore, Judith Laurence, ed., *Confronting AIDS through Literature: The Responsibilities of Representation*, University of Illinois Press, 1993.

> This anthology of essays by several authors considers how literature is being used to discuss AIDS as a medical, social, and literary phenomenon. The book includes essays by authors of fiction for young readers and for adults; a sample of creative writing about AIDS, and a section on how AIDS literature can be used by teachers.

The Women Who Loved Elvis All Their Lives

FLEDA BROWN

2004

In the title poem of her 2004 collection, *The Women Who Loved Elvis All Their Lives*, Fleda Brown explores contemporary culture's obsession with the idolized celebrity figures of music and film. Moving smoothly from one point of view to another, and pushing the limits of the imagination to allow the voice of a dead Elvis Presley to be heard, Brown reveals how one of the twentieth century's most indelible cultural icons can become a mirror in which a culture can review and reimagine its priorities, anxieties, and most troubling fissures. Balancing biographical, musical, and cultural focal points, Brown's "The Women Who Loved Elvis All Their Lives" transcends the prosaic details about "the King's" life or the legend of Graceland. The poem reaches instead toward a wider intellectual exploration of Elvis as icon and the face (and voice) of an entire generation. More specifically, this is a poem in which a generation collides with itself, as the man who became a symbol of a generation's passion and energy is portrayed shaking hands with Richard Nixon, a president most likely to be seen as the antithesis of that youthful vibrancy.

AUTHOR BIOGRAPHY

Brown was born in 1944 in Columbia, Missouri, but was raised in Fayetteville, Arkansas, where she graduated from high school. She earned a

B.A. in English in 1969 from the University of Arkansas in Fayetteville, and spent the next six years teaching high school in the nearby town of Springdale. Brown returned to her alma mater in 1976 to earn an M.A. in English in 1976, followed by a Ph.D. in English in 1983. Her doctoral dissertation, "The Split Vision: Four Novels of William Dean Howells," was completed while Brown was working as an instructor at the University of Delaware. She joined the faculty of Delaware as an assistant professor in 1986 and achieved full professor standing in 1995.

An accomplished creative and critical writer, Brown is widely published in such prominent literary magazines as the *Southern Review*, the *Cortland Review*, *Ariel*, and *Kenyon Review*. Her poems have been selected for inclusion in numerous anthologies, including *Anhinga Anthology* (2004) and *All Shook Up: Collected Poems about Elvis*. An active scholar as well as prolific poet, Brown has written about the works of Mark Twain, D. H. Lawrence, W. D. Howells, and British novelists Juanita Casey and Jennifer Johnston. She has also served as editor-in-chief for *The Newsletter of the D. H. Lawrence Society of North America* (1981–1985) and as the associate managing editor of *The Irish Renaissance Annual* (1981–1983).

Brown has been recognized with a number of prominent literary awards, including the Felix Pollak Prize for her collection of poems *Reunion* (2007), the William Allen Creative Nonfiction Award in 2004 for her essay "Anatomy of a Seizure," the First Annual Philip Levine Poetry Prize (University of California) in 2002, and Arkansas's major award, the Porter Fund Literary Prize, in 2001, given for a career that has produced an impressive and substantial body of work. She was also a finalist in the National Poetry Series Contest for her poetry sequence *The Devil's Child* (1999), winner of the Verna Emery Poetry Prize for *Do Not Peel the Birches* (1993), and recipient of the Great Lakes Colleges Association New Writers Award for *Fishing With Blood* (1988). The title poem of this latter collection was used by Kevin Putz as the text for his *"Fishing With Blood": Concerto for Soprano and Orchestra* (1994), which was awarded the American Society of Composers and Publishers (ASCAP) national award and the Broadcast Music Incorporated (BMI) national award for the best composition by a composer under the age of thirty.

Recognized for her wide-ranging intelligence and skill in balancing the popular with the literary, Brown was named the Poet Laureate of the State of Delaware in 2001, the first such state appointment in almost two decades. Three years later, her collection, *The Women Who Loved Elvis All Their Lives* was released to critical acclaim. As of 2007, Brown, who retired from the University of Delaware, was a member of the faculty of the Rainier Writing Workshop at Pacific Lutheran University.

POEM TEXT

She reads, of course, what he's doing, shaking
    Nixon's hand,
dating this starlet or that, while he is faithful to
    her
like a stone in her belly, like the actual love
    child,
its bills and diapers. Once he had kissed her
and time had stood still, at least some point
    seems to   5
remain back there as a place to return to, to
    wait for.
What is she waiting for? He will not marry her,
    nor will he
stop very often. Desireé will grow up to say her
    father is dead.
Desireé will imagine him standing on a timeless
    street,
hungry for his child. She will wait for him, not
    in the original,   10
but in a gesture copied to whatever lover she
    takes.
He will fracture and change to landscape, to the
    Pope, maybe,
or President Kennedy, or to a pain that darkens
    her eyes.

"Once," she will say, as if she remembers,
and the memory will stick like a fishbone. She
    knows   15
how easily she will comply when a man puts his
    hand
on the back of her neck and gently steers her.
She knows how long she will wait for rescue,
    how the world
will go on expanding outside. She will see her
    mother's photo
of Elvis shaking hands with Nixon, the terrify-
    ing conjunction.   20
A whole war with Asia will begin slowly,
in her lifetime, out of such irreconcilable urges.
The Pill will become available to the general
    public,
starting up a new waiting in that other depth.
The egg will have to keep believing in its time-
    less moment   25
of completion without any proof except in the
    longing

of its own body. Maris will break Babe Ruth's record while Orbison will have his first major hit with "Only the Lonely," trying his best to sound like Elvis.

POEM SUMMARY

Stanza 1

"The Women Who Loved Elvis All Their Lives" is a prose poem divided into two clearly marked stanzas. The first stanza introduces an apparently unnamed woman who follows Elvis's career through the media and newspaper reports that follow his every move. The "she" of the opening line of the poem serves a double role, used as both a representative of *all* the women who are fanatic fans of the King as well as standing in for one *particular* woman: Lucy de Barbin, who claimed that her daughter, Desireé, was fathered by Elvis. Though de Barbin is not actually named in the poem, Desireé is. Furthermore, the speaker in the poem seems to indicate that Desireé is her daughter, so it is reasonable to identify the poem's narrator as the fictional voice of de Barbin. Thus, as de Barbin's memories in this opening stanza oscillate between the intensely romantic ("Once he had kissed her / and time had stood still") and the almost painfully prosaic ("bills and diapers").

This opening stanza hinges on a question that "she" asks herself: "What is she waiting for?" Although never answered directly, the question lingers over the remaining lines of the stanza, which introduce Desireé as another of the women waiting for Elvis. Having never known her father, and with her own connection to him remaining a source of much controversy among Elvis fans, Desireé is as split in her reaction to Elvis as her mother. Imagining, on the one hand, that he carries with him a hunger for his child, she is, on the other hand, searching for him in the various men that inhabit the public sphere (President Kennedy and the Pope), and in her various lovers. As the stanza closes, readers are left with an impression of a woman (representative of all women) who lives in a fractured world shaped by "a pain that darkens her eyes."

Stanza 2

The second stanza of "The Women Who Loved Elvis All Their Lives" opens with a particularly resonant word in the poem: "once." This adverb marks the two directions that the second stanza takes. Most obviously, this is a stanza about the remembering of Elvis that comes to define the lives of the generic women from the poem's title. Remembering is a powerful narcotic for these women, allowing them to live a seemingly "time-less" life full of "longing" for Elvis.

But at the same time, "memory will stick like a fishbone" in the lives and imaginations of the women. Living in the past, these women are increasingly aware of "the terrifying conjunction" that the icon of Elvis presents in the poem's opening line. The world in which Elvis rose to prominence has long passed, despite the attempts of the women to arrest it. Elvis has shaken hands with Nixon, the "whole war with Asia" has changed American politics forever, and even the legendary baseball player Babe Ruth has been eclipsed in the record books by Roger Maris. The poem ends with a deep sense of forward motion, into a world of international conflict, sexual freedoms ("The Pill will become available to the general public"), and scandalizing politics that render Elvis's status as a cultural icon less and less relevant to all but the women who continue to cling to his image.

THEMES

The American Dream

For the generation that watched Elvis rise to prominence, the singer was a symbol of the post-war promise of the American Dream. Coined in the early 1930s, the term marked a significant break with the imaginative, political, and economic models of the Old World (Europe). Fueled by the emergence of American big business, the completion of a transcontinental railway, and the promise that came with an energized natural resource industry, the celebration of the "rags to riches" archetypal story became a persistent part of the culture. The belief that any American with a modicum of talent and a strong work ethic would be inevitably successful regardless of their origins was embodied by figures such as Elvis. The American Dream captured the collective imagination of an entire country, and writers have always been drawn to the anguish embodied by the clash between this belief and reality. This theme is most notably explored in F. Scott Fitzgerald's *The Great Gatsby* (1925), John Steinbeck's *Of Mice and Men* (1937), and Arthur Miller's *Death of a Salesman* (1949).

In the early decades of the twentieth century, the American Dream faced some of its stiffest obstacles. The Great Depression, the growing pressures of racial discrimination, and the after-effects of two World Wars left many Americans feeling disenfranchised, cut off from the promise of the Dream. But with the economic prosperity of the postwar period, and with it the rise of suburban America and the emergence of Elvis, the Dream regained its energy. Improvements to home comfort and employment stability combined with a dramatic rise in personal income levels and an expansion of educational options became the hallmark of the modern version of the Dream.

Although the countercultural politics of the 1960s and subsequent decades led to the waning prominence of the American Dream as a wholly positive ideal, it has remained embedded in American culture as both a touchstone of hope and a source of deeply felt frustration.

The Cult of Celebrity

The cult of celebrity is a widespread popular interest in celebrities, like Elvis, who capture the collective fascination of a large portion of a community. This cult is driven, as in the case of Elvis, by publicity and exposure via the public media of the day (television, film, newspapers). The fascination with an individual celebrity moves beyond mere adoration toward a kind of secular worship and even to a full-blown fantasy in which the average person perceives an imagined intimacy with the celebrity. This false intimacy stems from the media deluge of images of celebrities and from reportage that divulges personal details about them.

The rise of the cult of celebrity in the twentieth century is often seen as evidence of the apathy, spiritual weakness, and general dumbing down of contemporary culture. Indeed, there is an almost religious intensity to such a cult as the one that has formed around Elvis. There are the sacred places that cult members make pilgrimages to (Elvis's home, Graceland, and the site of Elvis's grave), sacred times for ritualized remembrance (thousands gather annually at Graceland during the week of August 16, the date of Elvis's

death), and the sharing of relics (Elvis collectibles). All of these rituals closely resemble those of popular world religions. The story of Elvis's life is retold as a legend, which often takes great liberties with well-documented historical truth. For instance, Elvis did not take illegal drugs, though it is popularly believed that he did.

As Brown's poem underscores neatly, the modern world is one in which celebrities are as necessary as the ancient gods and saints.

Nostalgia

Nostalgia is described as an intense longing for an idealized past. Originally appearing in the seventeenth-century, the word is a compound of two Greek words, *nostos* (returning home) and *algos* (pain or longing). Records of the experience of nostalgia are ancient and widespread, providing a major theme in myth and poetry from the Bible and Homer's *Odyssey* onwards.

Although it has come to take on relatively benign connotations in modern society, and has also become a powerful marketing tool, nostalgia was originally seen as a serious medical disorder that could cloud an individual's ability to function in the world. It is this lost meaning that imbues Brown's poem, as the women who love Elvis do so with such devotion and intensity as to get in the way of healthy interactions with the world and with other people. The women Brown describes are in a perpetual state of waiting. They are waiting for the moment when Elvis (or his ideals) will transport them back to a time or a sense of place in which they felt more important, more secure, more in control of their lives, more youthful, and more hopeful.

STYLE

Allusion

Allusion is a brief, and sometimes indirect, reference in a poem to a person, place, work of literature or art, or historical event or era, any of which might be real or fictitious (though allusions most often refer to the real). An allusion might appear in a poem as a direct quotation, as the passing mention of a character or setting, or as a phrase, word, or image borrowed from another work or writer. Brown's "The Women Who Loved Elvis All Their Lives," for instance, becomes a catalogue of allusive references to people and events that mark the setting for this poem and establish

TOPICS FOR FURTHER STUDY

- Research the history of rock and roll music in the United States. Make a timeline that traces the major shifts in the genre, the key songs or artists of each era, the role of teen idols, and the social issues that came to shape rock and roll.

- Do some research into the music or life of your favorite recording artist. With this information in hand, write a series of poems that attempt to describe the art and artist you have selected.

- Write a report about the subtleties and complexities of some of the political or social issues that are drawing attention in your community or country. What aspects of pop culture affect or address these issues?

- Given that "The Women Who Loved Elvis All Their Lives" is interested in the intersection of high art (poetry) and popular culture (Elvis), consider the following interpretative exercise: Design and draw a comic-book style interpretation of this poem or any other poems from Brown's collection of the same name. Feel free to arrange and rearrange the fragments of the poem as you deem necessary or to represent them as they appear in the original text.

---

its cultural density. In this sense, Brown's poem is about a culture in transition, as an allusion to one iconic figure (Elvis) must confront allusions to other, equally iconic men or events: the Pope, President John F. Kennedy, Babe Ruth, and the musician Roy Orbison. Set against the culturally meaningful figure of Elvis, is the accumulation of a network of equally powerful cultural icons that crisscross through the poem. The legend of Kennedy brushes against the legend of Babe Ruth; the legends (and tragic realities) of the Vietnam war collide with the escapist productions of Elvis and Orbison.

Allusions such as those that accumulate in Brown's poem can work to both the benefit and detriment of the work. Allusions imply a common knowledge between reader and writer, operating as a kind of complex delivery system of ideas or meaning. Accordingly, poets tend to make allusions simple and clear so that they might be easily understood. Most readers will at least have heard of the names Babe Ruth, Kennedy, and Nixon, for instance, which gives the poem a density of possible meanings (known as the *allusion field*). Entering into the allusive field of Brown's poem, for instance, a reader might begin to contemplate the similarities between Elvis and Babe Ruth, both of whom were men of voracious appetites, massive egos, and incredible popularity.

At the same time, allusions can lead to an interpretative difficulty. If an allusion is too dense and complex, if it is not readily identified by a reader, or if it does not fit naturally or elegantly into the framework of the poem, its potential meanings are lost and its power diminished. For instance, the allusions in "The Women Who Loved Elvis All Their Lives" are highly meaningful to those who were alive during the 1950s, 1960s, and 1970s;—when the people and events that are mentioned in the poem were very much a part of day-to-day life in America. For those born after the 1980's, however, the allusions in the poem are likely less effective.

Prose Poem

"The Women Who Loved Elvis All Their Lives" is an example of a prose poem (sometimes called a proem), which means that it is written and printed in the more familiar rhythms and structures of prose rather than as more conventional poetic verse. What this means, most obviously, is that Brown's poem has a standardized right margin, familiar sentence form, and identifiable patterns of punctuation and syntax. It is a hybrid of forms (poetry combined with prose) that often leaves readers unsure as to what expectations to bring to the reading experience.

Dating as far back as the Old Testament Psalms and renovated most influentially through the writing of the expatriate American writer Gertrude Stein (1874–1946), prose poems offer an opportunity to create an artistic hybrid that marries elegantly the power of clarity commonly associated with prose and the complexity of language and emotion usually reserved for lyric poetry. In the case of Brown's poem, which explores the collision between image and reality, a hybrid form is a natural choice for bringing together the power of the poetic (High Art) with the attraction to, and accessibility of, popular culture (Low Art).

Prose poems also present readers with a series of potentially meaningful incongruities or tensions. In this case, the tensions address the role of Elvis in contemporary culture. There is, for instance, the disorienting juxtaposition of Elvis and the Vietnam War, with its connotations of violence and chaos. Similarly, private responses to Elvis (from all the women who have loved him) are juxtaposed with the public and political responses to Elvis. Prose poems, in other words, are a natural choice for expressing what Brown calls "the terrifying conjunction" of images and ideas.

HISTORICAL CONTEXT

The Nixon-Presley Meeting

The photo of Elvis shaking the hand of then president Richard Nixon alluded to in the poem actually took place on December 21, 1970. The meeting was initiated by Presley, who wrote the President a six-page letter requesting an opportunity to meet and share ideas about various issues that the singer believed still threatened to split the country along lines of Establishment and anti-Establishment politics. In his letter, Elvis took particular pride in noting that his position as an entertainer of near iconic status allowed him to move more or less freely across this ideological divide, a flexibility that allowed him to speak to people of all ages and all political backgrounds. Elvis's goal was also clearly stated in the letter: he wanted Nixon to secure for him credentials of Federal Agent at Large, a title that would allow the singer to contribute in meaningful ways to the well-being of the country as it fought, Elvis mentioned specifically, the increasingly problematic pressures associated with the rising drug culture.

When the two men did meet, Elvis arrived in full regalia, including a velvet cape, gold medallions, and thick silver-plated sunglasses. He also brought Nixon a gift in the form of a World War II Colt 45 pistol in a finely crafted wooden case, as well as a representative sampling of his personal collection of badges and police paraphernalia. The twenty-eight photographs taken at this encounter capture for posterity a symbolic meeting that to many people on both sides of the political spectrum remains almost incomprehensible. The image of the iconic King of rock and roll (a mere seven years away from an early death brought about from prescription drug abuse) shaking hands with the President (whose own legacy was about to be marred by the Watergate scandal) remains a particularly poignant symbol of both the promise and the disappointment of the American culture of the day.

Elvis and the 1970s

Given that "The Women Who Loved Elvis All Their Lives" emphasizes the cultural context of Elvis's rise to iconic status and subsequent fall from grace, it is important to understand the social and cultural environment of the 1970s. In North America, the arrival of the seventies signaled a number of important shifts in attitudes and politics that coalesced to mark a shift away from the social activism and cultural imperatives that defined the 1960s. Replacing social activism as the 1970s unfolded was an emphasis on pleasure and personal gain.

This shift also coincided loosely with Elvis's reemergence within American consciousness. Far removed from the pinnacle of the mania that accompanied his initial rise to fame in the mid-1950s, the 1970s Elvis was distanced both physically and politically from the radical talent who made television history with three appearances on *The Ed Sullivan Show* and whose crossover appeal was solidified with such early film successes as *Love Me Tender* (1956), *Jailhouse Rock* (1957), and *King Creole* (1958). The Elvis imagined in Brown's poem has, by 1970, found himself eclipsed musically by the 1960s rise to prominence of the bands of the British invasion (most notably The Beatles and the Rolling Stones) and by the psychedelic-rock music scene that included The Grateful Dead, Janis Joplin, and The Doors.

More broadly, the seventies was a decade that was defined by Norman Lear's groundbreaking episodic television show *All in the Family*, which brought socially relevant issues to a diverse, mainstream audience every week. When the series premiered in 1971, American audiences heard words that had never been heard on television before, especially words relating to sexuality, race, class, and political attitudes. One of those issues was the oppressive economic recession that took hold of North America. The decade was plagued by a potent combination of low output, rising unemployment, and dramatic increases in the cost of consumer products that came to be known as *stagflation*, a compound word that joined the terms *stagnation* and *inflation*.

Presley attempted to reestablish himself in this radically changing cultural environment, beginning with his 1968 televised comeback special. This hugely successful show served as a springboard to a series of sold-out live performances in Las Vegas

Elvis Presley is surrounded by female audience members while performing on stage in his television program "Elvis Presley's Comeback Special" (Frank Driggs Collection / Getty Images)

and other major American cities. Thus began what has come to be known as the jumpsuit era of Elvis's career—a period of immense commercial success balanced negatively by deep, and ultimately tragic, artistic and personal problems. By the mid-1970s, Elvis was grossly overweight, losing his personal battle with prescription drugs (though he publicly denounced hard drug use), and plagued by reviews that regularly labeled his performances as mediocre, disappointing, and lackluster.

As the decadence and decay of the seventies came to a close, so too did the life and legend of the King. He died on August 16, 1977, while on sabbatical at his Memphis mansion, Graceland. Only forty-two years old and weighing well over

three hundred pounds, he reportedly fell victim to a cardiac arrhythmia brought on by a volatile cocktail of more than a dozen drugs. As Brown points out in "The Women Who Loved Elvis All Their Lives," the death of the King marked the "irreconcilable urges" to see in the piteous passing of the jump-suited icon a "timeless moment," the end of cultural innocence, youthful dreams, and political idealism.

CRITICAL OVERVIEW

Writing in the journal *World Literature Today*, Fred Dings begins his review of Brown's *The Women Who Loved Elvis All Their Lives* collection with a simple assertion. This is, he begins, "a wonderful book" that evokes "the particular pathos of an era and the lives lived within it. The emotional truth of this writing," he continues, "is never humid in its intimacy, but it is affecting in its delicacy and restraint, nevertheless." Mary Kaiser, reviewing Brown's *Do Not Peel the Birches* in *World Literature in Review: English*, also gives a favorable appraisal in the same vein. In contrast to most contemporary poets who are heavy-handed in their engagement with popular culture, Kaiser argues, Brown has developed a poetic voice that operates most elegantly "in the interface between private reflection and public discourse."

Grace Cavalieri, reviewing *The Women Who Loved Elvis All Their Lives* for the *Montserrat Review*, is quick to emphasize that "you don't have to be an Elvis enthusiast to love this book and place it on the shelf with your favorites." Written in a language that says "exactly what it means, and means what it says," Cavalieri continues, the poems of Brown's collection stay "in our minds like a song we sing under our breath that always tells the truth."

CRITICISM

Klay Dyer

Dyer holds a Ph.D. in English literature and has published extensively on fiction, poetry, film, and television. He is also a freelance university teacher, writer, and educational consultant. In this essay, he discusses "The Women Who Loved Elvis All Their Lives" as a commentary on the death of the American Dream, or the belief in sustainable prosperity and cultural revitalization. Dyer also notes that "the women" of Brown's poem refuse to accept or acknowledge this figurative death through their fixation on Elvis.

As Arthur Miller made tragically clear in his seminal play *Death of a Salesman* (1949), the American Dream did not seem to be coming true very often as the United States entered into the second half of the twentieth century. The Dream to which Miller's Willie Loman so often alludes is built on the unquestioned assumption that, with the maturation of post-World War II economy and culture, America would emerge into a new environment of sustainable prosperity and social advancement. Paradoxically, and despite the achievement of a higher standard of living in the

WHAT DO I READ NEXT?

- Other works by Brown will prove rewarding to readers of contemporary poetry, especially her collection *Fishing with Blood* (1988). Also adapted into a concerto, this is a provocative series of portraits that explores family dynamics.

- Will Clemens's collection *All Shook Up: Collected Poems About Elvis* (2001) includes forty-nine Elvis poems, most of which were written after his death in 1977. Brown's "Elvis Reads 'The Wild Swans at Coole'" can be read alongside contributions from such notable writers as Charles Bukowski, Lucille Clifton, and Joyce Carol Oates. Ranging from sonnets and blank verse poems to free verse, these poems are at once a celebration of an immense and tragically wasted talent as well as a lament for a lost innocence that speaks to individuals and a generation alike.

- For a novel-length exploration of the spiritual and emotional malaise of post-war suburban America, Jeffrey Eugenides's 1993 novel, *The Virgin Suicides*, is a provocative read. Set in the 1970s, the novel recounts the stories surrounding the suicides of the five Lisbon sisters and the impact their decisions have on a seemingly happy community forced to make sense of the deaths. Director Sofia Coppola adapted this novel into a critically acclaimed movie of the same title in 1999.

- For readers interested more generally in books that explore music as a theme and metaphor, Nick Hornby's *High Fidelity* (1995) is an entertaining novel about the romantic and philosophic struggles of a vintage record store owner in London.

post-war era, the much-anticipated *better* life remained an ever-elusive goal for a generation driven forward increasingly by the pressures of what Brown describes as "bills and diapers."

" TRAPPED IN A POST-WAR WORLD THAT IS, ACCORDING TO THE DREAM, SUPPOSED TO NURTURE AND PROTECT THEM, BROWN'S WOMEN FIND THEM-SELVES IMPRISONED WITHIN THE HESITATIONS OF THEIR OWN FAITH."

Defining itself increasingly by the ebb and flow of the Dream itself, post-war American culture became a kind of social and cultural desert defined by conformity. The 1950s was a decade characterized by the development of suburban communities that utterly lack the potential for the cultural and spiritual awakening implied in the American Dream. Tellingly, the residents of these post-war suburban communities rarely, if ever, see their lifestyle as spiritually vacant or overtly homogenous and manufactured. As Brown's enquiry into the imaginations of "the women who loved Elvis" underscores, suburbia has become defined primarily by the mass-marketed ideas of middle-class family values and carefully packaged nostalgia. Emerging as the iconic symbol of this spiritually and creatively vacant culture is Elvis, the one-time King of rock and roll, shaking the hand of a scandal-ridden president who is himself about to become the symbol of political decay.

Ironically, it is the presence of an "expanding" world that energizes Brown's poem. Despite their determined efforts to live perpetually in a "timeless moment" on "a timeless street," the women of the poem gently steer themselves away from "the terrifying conjunction" that was caught forever in the photo of Elvis and Nixon. For Brown's women, Elvis remains forever a dashing young sex symbol "dating this starlet or that" and a creative force that every artist of the day would do "his best to sound like." These women, as Brown suggests, live their lives under the constant control of the past-tense adverb "once." The word is used to indicate that the women live in a kind of Dream that captures an ideal—one that was the case at some point in the past but that is no longer relevant in a changing world. Indeed, staring at the now-iconic photograph of the King and the President, the women cannot deny that however deeply locked

in past images they might allow themselves to be, they cannot stop the "irreconcilable urges" of a culture in transition. In the collective memory of Brown's women, the promises of "once" stick "like a fishbone," sit "like a stone in [the] belly," and linger like "a pain that darkens [their] eyes."

Having risen to prominence as an entertainer, Elvis has been reimagined by Brown's women as a kind of cultural visionary and as an iconic symbol of the youthful hopefulness of a by-gone era. He is a symbol of a time before the Dream was forced to confront the images returning from the "whole war with Asia" that began "slowly" but left a bloody stain across an entire generation. The image of his youthful gyrations and powerful voice become for these women a defining moment of their lives, a symbol of a feeling that they allow to "fracture and change" in order that it might be adapted to suit the landscape in which they now find themselves. The transformations are profound and sadly misguided as Elvis the singer morphs into "the Pope" and then again into "President Kennedy," both of whom are figures that represent salvation.

Trapped in a post-war world that is, according to the Dream, supposed to nurture and protect them, Brown's women find themselves imprisoned within the hesitations of their own faith. Unable and unwilling to move forward into a world that acknowledges the decay of Elvis's significance as a cultural icon, they live as if "time had stood still" and are perpetually hopeful that there exists "some point" that remains "back there," and is "a place to return to." In this sense, "The Women Who Loved Elvis All Their Lives" can be read alongside T. S. Eliot's "The Love Song of J. Alfred Prufrock" (1917), the seminal modernist poem that speaks profoundly to the pressures brought to bear on a life that is lived in terror and in hesitation.

Elvis the singer, frozen in photographic time, is silent in the poem. Nevertheless, having turned away from the "urges" of the world around them, the women attempt to isolate his supposedly visionary promise in their own almost obsessive "love" for the "once" youthful Elvis. But by the 1970s, when the photo of Elvis and Nixon was taken, Elvis had reentered mainstream culture as an exceptionally fat man who represented the materialistic repurposing of a comparatively innocent era. Leaving their longing and waiting forever unanswered, the women are drawn almost hypnotically to their own reimagining of Elvis and his 'golden age' as a rock-and-roll icon. Tellingly, this determined revisioning pulls them toward a confrontation with "the terrifying conjunction" that Elvis has become. Put another way, by trying to live in the glow of the "once" great Elvis, the women unwittingly bring the promise of the past into stark relief against the realities of the present. Just as Elvis, the revitalized megastar of the postwar era, ends his life in a nightmare of gluttony and decadence, the Dream of an almost Edenic postwar prosperity slides towards "whole war" (Vietnam), "the other depth" of a post-Pill sexual revolution, and the rise of new rock-and-roll icons such as Roy Orbison.

As the opening stanza of the poem unfolds, Brown's women are forced to ask themselves a very difficult and intensely reflexive question: "What [are they] waiting for?" Despite the profundity of this question, the women remain static. The most evocative of Brown's women, Desireé, Elvis's illegitimate daughter with Lucy de Barbin, spends her life wondering if her father loves her, wondering if he is "hungry" to spend time with the child he might never have known exists, and waiting "for him, not in the original, but in the gesture copied to whatever lover she takes." Whereas the other women implied in Brown's poem might imagine an intimate connection with Elvis, Desireé's imagined intimacy is far more visceral and poignant.

Not surprisingly, Brown's women turn away from the underlying truths about Elvis, including his obesity, drug abuse, and failing talent. In the end, even the death of the King will fail to illuminate the shadowy appeal of the Dreams that shape this poem: of Elvis as perpetual King, of the 1950s as the perpetual golden age of prosperity, and of the power of an icon to mediate the real pressures of a real life. The culture of Brown's women is evolving in a way they deem unhealthy, fracturing from the political and economic realities of that moment and slipping into what they perceive as a much darker ethos of alienation, anomie, and angst. Sequestering themselves in the private spaces of their homes and encountering their world only through their visions and revisions of Elvis, these women withdraw themselves from the intricacies and questions of their own time, a withdrawal that leads ultimately to disappointment and decay. Their lives, like the word "once," define their refusal to understand the world around them, a denial that essentially stems from an inability to accept the death of the American Dream.

Source: Klay Dyer, Critical Essay on "The Women Who Loved Elvis All Their Lives," in *Poetry for Students*, Gale, Cengage Learning, 2008.

Grace Cavalieri

In the following review, Cavalieri discusses the cultural elements that serve as the foundation of Brown's collection The Women Who Loved Elvis All Their Lives. *These include not only the music of Elvis Presley and of rock and roll in general, but also the presidency of Richard M. Nixon, the cold war with the Soviet Union, and the space race. Cavalieri praises the poems in this collection for their specificity of time and place.*

You don't have to be an Elvis enthusiast to love this book and place it on the shelf with your favorites, for the poetry doesn't sound like anything else you've read. The concept of anecdote sets it in motion but the way story becomes poem, for one thing, is through its philosophical underpinnings. In the case of *The Women Who Loved Elvis* . . . it is imagined memory that comes from the depth of experience—growing up in the 50's and 60's with Sputnik, Kruschev, Nixon as antithesis to another world where the beat of rock and roll is the real centrality, and where life gets its first true meanings.

Elvis may have been considered A WRONG ONE by parents who presumed knowledge of what their children should love. These poems are about the idols for which we developed a deep passion—obsession because someone was setting lyrics to what was happening inside us. This was the time for each of us where we tried and failed to understand our feelings and suddenly heard the first sounds we had not heard before. The power given Elvis was in a way like giving your own thoughts power when there was no one to tell about this tumult, if indeed we knew what to call it.

The History of Rock and Roll started right where you were at the time. Fleda Brown writes poems peppered with irony. As wistful as the flowering of youth may be, here is the steady adult eye watching all that is long-gone-and-remembered with empathy and authority. Technical proficiency is the way fractious worlds move back and forth across time to create structure. If you want to know what a poet can be, take a look at this book, which is set in scenes and rooms with characters and never loses its viewpoint. We are shown clearly what to see.

"I Escape With My Mother In The Desoto" (pg. 36) is a narration I like very much. Here's stanza one:

> Listen, it will be all right. I'll drive. Goodby
> Maxwell Street, we'll say as if we had a
>   secret
> emergency, goodby Bendix spindryer, goodby
> petticoats on the line dripping liquid starch...

The marvel of poetry! In a quatrain, we have character, event, plot, and situation. Should I say cultural history? And do we need to be told the time line?

The last stanza of the six, harks back to the recent past:

> . . .
> knees pulled up on the brand clean chenille
>   bedspread.
> We are going through *Ladies Home Journals*
>   and you
> are a beauty queen, safe in your vault of
>   clichés,
> safe from having to explain anything you
>   mean.

Nowhere in these poems will you get language that does not say exactly what it means, and means what it says. This is why we trust Fleda Brown, and will go where she takes us.

The best of poets are dramatists. This means they start with character. "Priscilla Presley, 1962" (pg. 27)

> She is grateful for how
> the little world of Graceland
> holds her in, teaches her to give up
> the small self to the universal good.
> She is watching him for clues,
> what moves he responds to.
> She learned at fifteen to keep her mind
> ahead of his. She dyed her hair black,
> like his. She is aware of a feeling
> of constant swooning, as if she were
> on her knees, and after she complains
> about Anita, or Ann-Margret, the sheets
> still warm from one of them, she is
> literally on her knees, begging him
> to stop raging, stop throwing lamps
> and chairs and not to send her back
> to Germany...

The long narrative ends with this:

> . . .

After that, the whole gang,
she and the Memphis boys, go out
on the lawn, to watch the King
light his cigar, fly his toy plane.

If the person offstage is often the most important, we know all we need to know about Elvis; and in 36 lines the entirety of their relationship.

The last poem in the book is "The Meditation Garden" (pg. 65) from section IV GRACELAND.

> . . .
> Didn't I believe Whitman when he said
>
> "look for me beneath the soles of your feet?
> Didn't I believe my former husband
> who said "I'll haunt you forever"? But one
> positive note: I've kept singing the old
>
> songs in my lousy voice until they don't
> even recognize themselves. And who's
> to say who's right, with all the cover
> versions since? Whose song
>
> would you say "Blue Suede Shoes" is,
> for instance, Carl Perkins's or Elvis's?

What a marvelous ending. When a writer has such personality as this, she can drag all the hard stuff of human consciousness through—in the name of another—a star perhaps—a celebrity—a sex god, and come out singing. Not by mere chronology nor memory do we make such patterns—poetry that stays in our minds like a song we sing under our breath that always tells the truth.

Source: Grace Cavalieri, Review of *The Women Who Loved Elvis All Their Lives*, in *Montserrat Review*, 2005-2006, 2 pp.

Fred Dings

In the following essay, Dings comments on the relationship between high art and popular art that Brown investigates in The Women Who Loved Elvis All Their Lives. *Among the poems that reflect on this issue is "Elvis Reads the Wild Swans at Coole," which features Elvis reading aloud a poem by Yeats. Dings also discusses the "delicacy and restraint" present in the poems in this collection.*

Fleda Brown's verse collection. *The Women Who Loved Elvis All Their Lives* is a wonderful book. These poems, written from various points of view (including Elvis's), evoke in their aggregate the particular pathos of an era and the lives lived within it. The emotional truth of this writing is never humid in its intimacy, but it is affecting in its delicacy and restraint, nevertheless. So many contemporary poems seem to invoke pop-culture iconography in order to borrow an ethos or pedigree not otherwise present in the poem or to demonstrate the facility and widely ranging arcane and hip knowledge of its author (as in much of the poetry of Albert Goldbarth); these poems, in striking contrast, quietly and powerfully explore the inner sensibility of the private lives from which they speak without opportunism, condescension, cloying sentimentality, or sham nobility.

Readers will also discover within these poems an unasserting, quiet consideration of the relationship of high art and popular, the Apollonian and Dionysian, the metaphysical and the physical. The second poem, a sestina, seems to ask by its form alone if there are points of confluence. Nowhere, however, is this better treated than in the poem "Elvis Reads the Wild Swans at Coole," an intricate proposition announced by the title itself. Here, Elvis is asked to read the famous Yeats poem aloud "to see what a Hunk-a Hunk-a Burnin' Love could do to expose the other, more subtle, longings." By the end of the uncomfortable and awkward reading of the poem, Elvis is "flying off the end of it, trying to swagger, / one hand in his pocket, bravely cocking an eyebrow, // off into the wilds where the girls are screaming, wanting / his babies, no questions asked, ah yes, the subtle grass / of the wilds, and the drum-beat of the human heart." See what I mean?

Source: Fred Dings, Review of *The Women Who Loved Elvis All Their Lives*, in *World Literature Today*, Vol. 79, No. 2, May–August 2005, p. 88.

Janis Flint-Ferguson

In the following review, Flint-Ferguson offers a general assessment of the collection. The critic notes that the pieces "are not poems about those rooms in Graceland or about Elvis's life as much as they are poems about the icon of Elvis Presley."

Obviously, this collection of poems is organized around the impact and influence of Elvis Presley. Each poem recounts biographical, musical, and cultural images of the phenomenon that was Elvis and sets them within snippets of the time period in which he lived. So along with the familiar details of Elvis and Priscilla, Elvis and his mother, Elvis and the Army, are references to Teflon, transistor radios, Ed Sullivan, Sputnik, the pill, Nixon, and the death of Princess Di. None of this follows a strict chronological ordering, but it begins with Elvis in the Sun Records studio and loosely follows through the details of

his life from observers' perspectives. Featured prominently as the last section of the book is a tour of Graceland through the thoughts of fans as they tour the "Living Room," "Elvis's Bedroom," "Lisa Marie's Favorite Chair," "The Jungle Room," and "The Meditation Garden."

These are not poems about those rooms in Graceland or about Elvis's life as much as they are poems about the icon of Elvis Presley: voices recounting how Elvis was a part of their own lives whether through his music, his TV image or his physical presence. "Ho hum, I thought the songs / were for me" says one persona looking over the famed Trophy Room. The poems raise the issue of what popular culture says about what we value while they recount the images of a man rather than the man himself.

Source: Janis Flint-Ferguson, Review of *The Women Who Loved Elvis All Their Lives*, in *Kliatt*, Vol. 38, No. 5, September 2004, pp. 38–39.

SOURCES

Brode, Douglas, *Elvis Cinema and Popular Culture*, McFarland, 2006.

Brown, Fleda, "The Women Who Loved Elvis All Their Lives," in *The Women Who Loved Elvis All Their Lives*, Carnegie Mellon University Press, 2004, p. 26.

Cavalieri, Grace, Review of *The Women Who Loved Elvis All Their Lives*, 2005-2006, in the *Montserrat Review*, http://www.themontserratreview.com/bookreviews/elvis.html (accessed March 30, 2007).

Dings, Fred, Review of *The Women Who Loved Elvis All Their Lives*, in *World Literature Today*, Vol. 79 , No. 2, May-August 2005, p. 88.

Kaiser, Mary, Review of *Do Not Peel the Birches*, in *World Literature in Review: English*, Vol. 68, No. 2, Spring 1994.

Lytle, Mark Hamilton, *America's Uncivil Wars: The Sixties Era From Elvis to the Fall of Richard Nixon*, Oxford University Press, 2006.

Marcus, Greil, *Double Trouble: Bill Clinton and Elvis Presley in a Land of No Alternatives*, Henry Holt & Co., 2000.

FURTHER READING

Adelman, Kim, *The Girl's Guide to Elvis: The Clothes, The Hair, The Women, and More*, Broadway, 2002.
    A playful, gossipy but densely detailed book about the life, the likes, and the loves that came to define the King, with particular attention to

his attitudes towards his weight and his performance style.

Guralnick, Peter, *Careless Love: The Unmaking of Elvis
Presley*, Back Bay Books, 2000.
 A chronological companion book to Guralnick's
exploration of Elvis pre-1960 (*Last Train to
Memphis*, 1994) this book begins with Elvis's
hesitant return to public life following his military
service. Treating all aspects of the King's decline
with a balance of critical distance and respect, this
book is in many ways a classic American tragedy
that reveals Elvis as an intensely troubled man
struggling against pressures that were both out of
his control and very much of his own making.

Haberstam, David, *The Fifties*, Ballantine Books, 1994.
 An excellent exploration of the social and cultural changes that defined the mid-point decade
of the twentieth century, this book discusses
traditional historical subjects (politics and war)
as well as the rise of national television, fast
food, the suburbs, and, of course, Elvis.

Krogh, Egil, *The Day Elvis Met Nixon*, Pejama Press,
1994.
 Krogh was the deputy counsel to President
Nixon in 1970, and his book recounts the
events that led to the famous picture of the
King and the President.

Glossary of Literary Terms

A

Abstract: Used as a noun, the term refers to a short summary or outline of a longer work. As an adjective applied to writing or literary works, abstract refers to words or phrases that name things not knowable through the five senses.

Accent: The emphasis or stress placed on a syllable in poetry. Traditional poetry commonly uses patterns of accented and unaccented syllables (known as feet) that create distinct rhythms. Much modern poetry uses less formal arrangements that create a sense of freedom and spontaneity.

Aestheticism: A literary and artistic movement of the nineteenth century. Followers of the movement believed that art should not be mixed with social, political, or moral teaching. The statement "art for art's sake" is a good summary of aestheticism. The movement had its roots in France, but it gained widespread importance in England in the last half of the nineteenth century, where it helped change the Victorian practice of including moral lessons in literature.

Affective Fallacy: An error in judging the merits or faults of a work of literature. The "error" results from stressing the importance of the work's effect upon the reader—that is, how it makes a reader "feel" emotionally, what it does as a literary work—instead of stressing

its inner qualities as a created object, or what it "is."

Age of Johnson: The period in English literature between 1750 and 1798, named after the most prominent literary figure of the age, Samuel Johnson. Works written during this time are noted for their emphasis on "sensibility," or emotional quality. These works formed a transition between the rational works of the Age of Reason, or Neoclassical period, and the emphasis on individual feelings and responses of the Romantic period.

Age of Reason: See *Neoclassicism*

Age of Sensibility: See *Age of Johnson*

Agrarians: A group of Southern American writers of the 1930s and 1940s who fostered an economic and cultural program for the South based on agriculture, in opposition to the industrial society of the North. The term can refer to any group that promotes the value of farm life and agricultural society.

Alexandrine Meter: See *Meter*

Allegory: A narrative technique in which characters representing things or abstract ideas are used to convey a message or teach a lesson. Allegory is typically used to teach moral, ethical, or religious lessons but is sometimes used for satiric or political purposes.

Alliteration: A poetic device where the first consonant sounds or any vowel sounds in words or syllables are repeated.

Allusion: A reference to a familiar literary or historical person or event, used to make an idea more easily understood.

Amerind Literature: The writing and oral traditions of Native Americans. Native American literature was originally passed on by word of mouth, so it consisted largely of stories and events that were easily memorized. Amerind prose is often rhythmic like poetry because it was recited to the beat of a ceremonial drum.

Analogy: A comparison of two things made to explain something unfamiliar through its similarities to something familiar, or to prove one point based on the acceptedness of another. Similes and metaphors are types of analogies.

Anapest: See *Foot*

Angry Young Men: A group of British writers of the 1950s whose work expressed bitterness and disillusionment with society. Common to their work is an anti-hero who rebels against a corrupt social order and strives for personal integrity.

Anthropomorphism: The presentation of animals or objects in human shape or with human characteristics. The term is derived from the Greek word for "human form."

Antimasque: See *Masque*

Antithesis: The antithesis of something is its direct opposite. In literature, the use of antithesis as a figure of speech results in two statements that show a contrast through the balancing of two opposite ideas. Technically, it is the second portion of the statement that is defined as the "antithesis"; the first portion is the "thesis."

Apocrypha: Writings tentatively attributed to an author but not proven or universally accepted to be their works. The term was originally applied to certain books of the Bible that were not considered inspired and so were not included in the "sacred canon."

Apollonian and Dionysian: The two impulses believed to guide authors of dramatic tragedy. The Apollonian impulse is named after Apollo, the Greek god of light and beauty and the symbol of intellectual order. The Dionysian impulse is named after Dionysus, the Greek god of wine and the symbol of the unrestrained forces of nature. The Apollonian impulse is to create a rational, harmonious world, while the Dionysian is to express the irrational forces of personality.

Apostrophe: A statement, question, or request addressed to an inanimate object or concept or to a nonexistent or absent person.

Archetype: The word archetype is commonly used to describe an original pattern or model from which all other things of the same kind are made. This term was introduced to literary criticism from the psychology of Carl Jung. It expresses Jung's theory that behind every person's "unconscious," or repressed memories of the past, lies the "collective unconscious" of the human race: memories of the countless typical experiences of our ancestors. These memories are said to prompt illogical associations that trigger powerful emotions in the reader. Often, the emotional process is primitive, even primordial. Archetypes are the literary images that grow out of the "collective unconscious." They appear in literature as incidents and plots that repeat basic patterns of life. They may also appear as stereotyped characters.

Argument: The argument of a work is the author's subject matter or principal idea.

Art for Art's Sake: See *Aestheticism*

Assonance: The repetition of similar vowel sounds in poetry.

Audience: The people for whom a piece of literature is written. Authors usually write with a certain audience in mind, for example, children, members of a religious or ethnic group, or colleagues in a professional field. The term "audience" also applies to the people who gather to see or hear any performance, including plays, poetry readings, speeches, and concerts.

Automatic Writing: Writing carried out without a preconceived plan in an effort to capture every random thought. Authors who engage in automatic writing typically do not revise their work, preferring instead to preserve the revealed truth and beauty of spontaneous expression.

Avant-garde: A French term meaning "vanguard." It is used in literary criticism to describe new writing that rejects traditional approaches to literature in favor of innovations in style or content.

B

Ballad: A short poem that tells a simple story and has a repeated refrain. Ballads were originally intended to be sung. Early ballads, known as folk ballads, were passed down through generations, so their authors are often unknown. Later ballads composed by known authors are called literary ballads.

Baroque: A term used in literary criticism to describe literature that is complex or ornate in style or diction. Baroque works typically express tension, anxiety, and violent emotion. The term "Baroque Age" designates a period in Western European literature beginning in the late sixteenth century and ending about one hundred years later. Works of this period often mirror the qualities of works more generally associated with the label "baroque" and sometimes feature elaborate conceits.

Baroque Age: See *Baroque*

Baroque Period: See *Baroque*

Beat Generation: See *Beat Movement*

Beat Movement: A period featuring a group of American poets and novelists of the 1950s and 1960s—including Jack Kerouac, Allen Ginsberg, Gregory Corso, William S. Burroughs, and Lawrence Ferlinghetti—who rejected established social and literary values. Using such techniques as stream of consciousness writing and jazz-influenced free verse and focusing on unusual or abnormal states of mind—generated by religious ecstasy or the use of drugs—the Beat writers aimed to create works that were unconventional in both form and subject matter.

Beat Poets: See *Beat Movement*

Beats, The: See *Beat Movement*

Belles- lettres: A French term meaning "fine letters" or "beautiful writing." It is often used as a synonym for literature, typically referring to imaginative and artistic rather than scientific or expository writing. Current usage sometimes restricts the meaning to light or humorous writing and appreciative essays about literature.

Black Aesthetic Movement: A period of artistic and literary development among African Americans in the 1960s and early 1970s This was the first major African-American artistic movement since the Harlem Renaissance and was closely paralleled by the civil rights and black power movements. The black aesthetic writers attempted to produce works of art that would be meaningful to the black masses. Key figures in black aesthetics included one of its founders, poet and playwright Amiri Baraka, formerly known as LeRoi Jones; poet and essayist Haki R. Madhubuti, formerly Don L. Lee; poet and playwright Sonia Sanchez; and dramatist Ed Bullins.

Black Arts Movement: See *Black Aesthetic Movement*

Black Comedy: See *Black Humor*

Black Humor: Writing that places grotesque elements side by side with humorous ones in an attempt to shock the reader, forcing him or her to laugh at the horrifying reality of a disordered world.

Black Mountain School: Black Mountain College and three of its instructors—Robert Creeley, Robert Duncan, and Charles Olson—were all influential in projective verse, so poets working in projective verse are now referred as members of the Black Mountain school.

Blank Verse: Loosely, any unrhymed poetry, but more generally, unrhymed iambic pentameter verse (composed of lines of five two-syllable feet with the first syllable accented, the second unaccented). Blank verse has been used by poets since the Renaissance for its flexibility and its graceful, dignified tone.

Bloomsbury Group: A group of English writers, artists, and intellectuals who held informal artistic and philosophical discussions in Bloomsbury, a district of London, from around 1907 to the early 1930s. The Bloomsbury Group held no uniform philosophical beliefs but did commonly express an aversion to moral prudery and a desire for greater social tolerance.

Bon Mot: A French term meaning "good word." A *bon mot* is a witty remark or clever observation.

Breath Verse: See *Projective Verse*

Burlesque: Any literary work that uses exaggeration to make its subject appear ridiculous, either by treating a trivial subject with profound seriousness or by treating a dignified subject frivolously. The word "burlesque" may also be used as an adjective, as in "burlesque show," to mean "striptease act."

C

Cadence: The natural rhythm of language caused by the alternation of accented and unaccented syllables. Much modern poetry—notably free verse—deliberately manipulates cadence to create complex rhythmic effects.

Caesura: A pause in a line of poetry, usually occurring near the middle. It typically corresponds to a break in the natural rhythm or sense of the line but is sometimes shifted to create special meanings or rhythmic effects.

Canzone: A short Italian or Provencal lyric poem, commonly about love and often set to music. The *canzone* has no set form but typically contains five or six stanzas made up of seven to twenty lines of eleven syllables each. A shorter, five- to ten-line "envoy," or concluding stanza, completes the poem.

Carpe Diem: A Latin term meaning "seize the day." This is a traditional theme of poetry, especially lyrics. A *carpe diem* poem advises the reader or the person it addresses to live for today and enjoy the pleasures of the moment.

Catharsis: The release or purging of unwanted emotions—specifically fear and pity—brought about by exposure to art. The term was first used by the Greek philosopher Aristotle in his *Poetics* to refer to the desired effect of tragedy on spectators.

Celtic Renaissance: A period of Irish literary and cultural history at the end of the nineteenth century. Followers of the movement aimed to create a romantic vision of Celtic myth and legend. The most significant works of the Celtic Renaissance typically present a dreamy, unreal world, usually in reaction against the reality of contemporary problems.

Celtic Twilight: See *Celtic Renaissance*

Character: Broadly speaking, a person in a literary work. The actions of characters are what constitute the plot of a story, novel, or poem. There are numerous types of characters, ranging from simple, stereotypical figures to intricate, multifaceted ones. In the techniques of anthropomorphism and personification, animals—and even places or things—can assume aspects of character. "Characterization" is the process by which an author creates vivid, believable characters in a work of art. This may be done in a variety of ways, including (1) direct description of the character by the narrator; (2) the direct presentation of the speech, thoughts, or actions of the character; and (3) the responses of other characters to the character. The term "character" also refers to a form originated by the ancient Greek writer Theophrastus that later became popular in the seventeenth and eighteenth centuries. It is a short essay or sketch of a person who prominently displays a specific attribute or quality, such as miserliness or ambition.

Characterization: See *Character*

Classical: In its strictest definition in literary criticism, classicism refers to works of ancient Greek or Roman literature. The term may also be used to describe a literary work of recognized importance (a "classic") from any time period or literature that exhibits the traits of classicism.

Classicism: A term used in literary criticism to describe critical doctrines that have their roots in ancient Greek and Roman literature, philosophy, and art. Works associated with classicism typically exhibit restraint on the part of the author, unity of design and purpose, clarity, simplicity, logical organization, and respect for tradition.

Colloquialism: A word, phrase, or form of pronunciation that is acceptable in casual conversation but not in formal, written communication. It is considered more acceptable than slang.

Complaint: A lyric poem, popular in the Renaissance, in which the speaker expresses sorrow about his or her condition. Typically, the speaker's sadness is caused by an unresponsive lover, but some complaints cite other sources of unhappiness, such as poverty or fate.

Conceit: A clever and fanciful metaphor, usually expressed through elaborate and extended comparison, that presents a striking parallel between two seemingly dissimilar things—for example, elaborately comparing a beautiful woman to an object like a garden or the sun. The conceit was a popular device throughout the Elizabethan Age and Baroque Age and was the principal technique of the seventeenth-century English metaphysical poets. This usage of the word conceit is unrelated to the best-known definition of conceit as an arrogant attitude or behavior.

Concrete: Concrete is the opposite of abstract, and refers to a thing that actually exists or a description that allows the reader to experience an object or concept with the senses.

Concrete Poetry: Poetry in which visual elements play a large part in the poetic effect. Punctuation marks, letters, or words are arranged on a page to form a visual design: a cross, for example, or a bumblebee.

Confessional Poetry: A form of poetry in which the poet reveals very personal, intimate, sometimes shocking information about himself or herself.

Connotation: The impression that a word gives beyond its defined meaning. Connotations may be universally understood or may be significant only to a certain group.

Consonance: Consonance occurs in poetry when words appearing at the ends of two or more verses have similar final consonant sounds but have final vowel sounds that differ, as with "stuff" and "off."

Convention: Any widely accepted literary device, style, or form.

Corrido: A Mexican ballad.

Couplet: Two lines of poetry with the same rhyme and meter, often expressing a complete and self-contained thought.

Criticism: The systematic study and evaluation of literary works, usually based on a specific method or set of principles. An important part of literary studies since ancient times, the practice of criticism has given rise to numerous theories, methods, and "schools," sometimes producing conflicting, even contradictory, interpretations of literature in general as well as of individual works. Even such basic issues as what constitutes a poem or a novel have been the subject of much criticism over the centuries.

D

Dactyl: See *Foot*

Dadaism: A protest movement in art and literature founded by Tristan Tzara in 1916. Followers of the movement expressed their outrage at the destruction brought about by World War I by revolting against numerous forms of social convention. The Dadaists presented works marked by calculated madness and flamboyant nonsense. They stressed total freedom of expression, commonly through primitive displays of emotion and illogical, often senseless, poetry. The movement ended shortly after the war, when it was replaced by surrealism.

Decadent: See *Decadents*

Decadents: The followers of a nineteenth-century literary movement that had its beginnings in French aestheticism. Decadent literature displays a fascination with perverse and morbid states; a search for novelty and sensation—the "new thrill"; a preoccupation with mysticism; and a belief in the senselessness of human existence. The movement is closely associated with the doctrine Art for Art's Sake. The term "decadence" is sometimes used to denote a decline in the quality of art or literature following a period of greatness.

Deconstruction: A method of literary criticism developed by Jacques Derrida and characterized by multiple conflicting interpretations of a given work. Deconstructionists consider the impact of the language of a work and suggest that the true meaning of the work is not necessarily the meaning that the author intended.

Deduction: The process of reaching a conclusion through reasoning from general premises to a specific premise.

Denotation: The definition of a word, apart from the impressions or feelings it creates in the reader.

Diction: The selection and arrangement of words in a literary work. Either or both may vary depending on the desired effect. There are four general types of diction: "formal," used in scholarly or lofty writing; "informal," used in relaxed but educated conversation; "colloquial," used in everyday speech; and "slang," containing newly coined words and other terms not accepted in formal usage.

Didactic: A term used to describe works of literature that aim to teach some moral, religious, political, or practical lesson. Although didactic elements are often found in artistically pleasing works, the term "didactic" usually refers to literature in which the message is more important than the form. The term may also be used to criticize a work that the critic finds "overly didactic," that is, heavy handed in its delivery of a lesson.

Dimeter: See *Meter*

Dionysian: See *Apollonian and Dionysian*

Discordia concours: A Latin phrase meaning "discord in harmony." The term was coined by the eighteenth-century English writer Samuel Johnson to describe "a combination of dissimilar images or discovery of occult resemblances in things apparently unlike." Johnson created the expression by reversing a phrase by the Latin poet Horace.

Dissonance: A combination of harsh or jarring sounds, especially in poetry. Although such combinations may be accidental, poets sometimes intentionally make them to achieve particular effects. Dissonance is also sometimes used to refer to close but not identical rhymes. When this is the case, the word functions as a synonym for consonance.

Double Entendre: A corruption of a French phrase meaning "double meaning." The term is used to indicate a word or phrase that is deliberately ambiguous, especially when one of the meanings is risque or improper.

Draft: Any preliminary version of a written work. An author may write dozens of drafts which are revised to form the final work, or he or she may write only one, with few or no revisions.

Dramatic Monologue: See *Monologue*

Dramatic Poetry: Any lyric work that employs elements of drama such as dialogue, conflict, or characterization, but excluding works that are intended for stage presentation.

Dream Allegory: See *Dream Vision*

Dream Vision: A literary convention, chiefly of the Middle Ages. In a dream vision a story is presented as a literal dream of the narrator. This device was commonly used to teach moral and religious lessons.

E

Eclogue: In classical literature, a poem featuring rural themes and structured as a dialogue among shepherds. Eclogues often took specific poetic forms, such as elegies or love poems. Some were written as the soliloquy of a shepherd. In later centuries, "eclogue" came to refer to any poem that was in the pastoral tradition or that had a dialogue or monologue structure.

Edwardian: Describes cultural conventions identified with the period of the reign of Edward VII of England (1901-1910). Writers of the Edwardian Age typically displayed a strong reaction against the propriety and conservatism of the Victorian Age. Their work often exhibits distrust of authority in religion, politics, and art and expresses strong doubts about the soundness of conventional values.

Edwardian Age: See *Edwardian*

Electra Complex: A daughter's amorous obsession with her father.

Elegy: A lyric poem that laments the death of a person or the eventual death of all people. In a conventional elegy, set in a classical world, the poet and subject are spoken of as shepherds. In modern criticism, the word elegy is often used to refer to a poem that is melancholy or mournfully contemplative.

Elizabethan Age: A period of great economic growth, religious controversy, and nationalism closely associated with the reign of Elizabeth I of England (1558-1603). The Elizabethan Age is considered a part of the general renaissance—that is, the flowering of arts and literature—that took place in Europe during the fourteenth through sixteenth centuries. The era is considered the golden age of English literature. The most important dramas in English and a great deal of lyric poetry were produced during this period, and modern English criticism began around this time.

Empathy: A sense of shared experience, including emotional and physical feelings, with someone or something other than oneself. Empathy is often used to describe the response of a reader to a literary character.

English Sonnet: See *Sonnet*

Enjambment: The running over of the sense and structure of a line of verse or a couplet into the following verse or couplet.

Enlightenment, The: An eighteenth-century philosophical movement. It began in France but had a wide impact throughout Europe and America. Thinkers of the Enlightenment valued reason and believed that both the individual and society could achieve a state of perfection. Corresponding to this essentially humanist vision was a resistance to religious authority.

Epic: A long narrative poem about the adventures of a hero of great historic or legendary importance. The setting is vast and the action is often given cosmic significance through the intervention of supernatural forces such as gods, angels, or demons. Epics are typically written in a classical style of grand simplicity with elaborate metaphors and allusions that enhance the symbolic importance of a hero's adventures.

Epic Simile: See *Homeric Simile*

Epigram: A saying that makes the speaker's point quickly and concisely.

Epilogue: A concluding statement or section of a literary work. In dramas, particularly those of the seventeenth and eighteenth centuries, the epilogue is a closing speech, often in verse, delivered by an actor at the end of a play and spoken directly to the audience.

Epiphany: A sudden revelation of truth inspired by a seemingly trivial incident.

Epitaph: An inscription on a tomb or tombstone, or a verse written on the occasion of a person's death. Epitaphs may be serious or humorous.

Epithalamion: A song or poem written to honor and commemorate a marriage ceremony.

Epithalamium: See *Epithalamion*

Epithet: A word or phrase, often disparaging or abusive, that expresses a character trait of someone or something.

Erziehungsroman: See *Bildungsroman*

Essay: A prose composition with a focused subject of discussion. The term was coined by Michel de Montaigne to describe his 1580 collection of brief, informal reflections on himself and on various topics relating to human nature. An essay can also be a long, systematic discourse.

Existentialism: A predominantly twentieth-century philosophy concerned with the nature and perception of human existence. There are two major strains of existentialist thought: atheistic and Christian. Followers of atheistic existentialism believe that the individual is alone in a godless universe and that the basic human condition is one of suffering and loneliness. Nevertheless, because there are no fixed values, individuals can create their own characters—indeed, they can shape themselves—through the exercise of free will. The atheistic strain culminates in and is popularly associated with the works of Jean Paul Sartre. The Christian existentialists, on the other hand, believe that only in God may people find freedom from life's anguish. The two strains hold certain beliefs in common: that existence cannot be fully understood or described through empirical effort; that anguish is a universal element of life; that individuals must bear responsibility for their actions; and that there is no common standard of behavior or perception for religious and ethical matters.

Expatriates: See *Expatriatism*

Expatriatism: The practice of leaving one's country to live for an extended period in another country.

Exposition: Writing intended to explain the nature of an idea, thing, or theme. Expository writing is often combined with description, narration, or argument. In dramatic writing, the exposition is the introductory material which presents the characters, setting, and tone of the play.

Expressionism: An indistinct literary term, originally used to describe an early twentieth-century school of German painting. The term applies to almost any mode of unconventional, highly subjective writing that distorts reality in some way.

Extended Monologue: See *Monologue*

F

Feet: See *Foot*

Feminine Rhyme: See *Rhyme*

Fiction: Any story that is the product of imagination rather than a documentation of fact. Characters and events in such narratives may be based in real life but their ultimate form and configuration is a creation of the author.

Figurative Language: A technique in writing in which the author temporarily interrupts the order, construction, or meaning of the writing for a particular effect. This interruption takes the form of one or more figures of speech such as hyperbole, irony, or simile. Figurative language is the opposite of literal language, in which every word is truthful, accurate, and free of exaggeration or embellishment.

Figures of Speech: Writing that differs from customary conventions for construction, meaning, order, or significance for the purpose of a special meaning or effect. There are two major types of figures of speech: rhetorical figures, which do not make changes in the meaning of the words, and tropes, which do.

Fin de siecle: A French term meaning "end of the century." The term is used to denote the last decade of the nineteenth century, a transition period when writers and other artists abandoned old conventions and looked for new techniques and objectives.

First Person: See *Point of View*

Folk Ballad: See *Ballad*

Folklore: Traditions and myths preserved in a culture or group of people. Typically, these are passed on by word of mouth in various forms—such as legends, songs, and proverbs—or preserved in customs and ceremonies. This term was first used by W. J. Thoms in 1846.

Folktale: A story originating in oral tradition. Folktales fall into a variety of categories, including legends, ghost stories, fairy tales, fables, and anecdotes based on historical figures and events.

Foot: The smallest unit of rhythm in a line of poetry. In English-language poetry, a foot is typically one accented syllable combined with one or two unaccented syllables.

Form: The pattern or construction of a work which identifies its genre and distinguishes it from other genres.

Formalism: In literary criticism, the belief that literature should follow prescribed rules of construction, such as those that govern the sonnet form.

Fourteener Meter: See *Meter*

Free Verse: Poetry that lacks regular metrical and rhyme patterns but that tries to capture the cadences of everyday speech. The form allows a poet to exploit a variety of rhythmical effects within a single poem.

Futurism: A flamboyant literary and artistic movement that developed in France, Italy, and Russia from 1908 through the 1920s. Futurist theater and poetry abandoned traditional literary forms. In their place, followers of the movement attempted to achieve total freedom of expression through bizarre imagery and deformed or newly invented words. The Futurists were self-consciously modern artists who attempted to incorporate the appearances and sounds of modern life into their work.

G

Genre: A category of literary work. In critical theory, genre may refer to both the content of a given work—tragedy, comedy, pastoral— and to its form, such as poetry, novel, or drama.

Genteel Tradition: A term coined by critic George Santayana to describe the literary practice of certain late nineteenth- century American writers, especially New Englanders. Followers of the Genteel Tradition emphasized conventionality in social, religious, moral, and literary standards.

Georgian Age: See *Georgian Poets*

Georgian Period: See *Georgian Poets*

Georgian Poets: A loose grouping of English poets during the years 1912-1922. The Georgians reacted against certain literary schools and practices, especially Victorian wordiness, turn-of-the-century aestheticism, and contemporary urban realism. In their place, the Georgians embraced the nineteenth-century poetic practices of William Wordsworth and the other Lake Poets.

Georgic: A poem about farming and the farmer's way of life, named from Virgil's *Georgics*.

Gilded Age: A period in American history during the 1870s characterized by political corruption and materialism. A number of important novels of social and political criticism were written during this time.

Gothic: See *Gothicism*

Gothicism: In literary criticism, works characterized by a taste for the medieval or morbidly attractive. A gothic novel prominently features elements of horror, the supernatural, gloom, and violence: clanking chains, terror, charnel houses, ghosts, medieval castles, and mysteriously slamming doors. The term "gothic novel" is also applied to novels that lack elements of the traditional Gothic setting but that create a similar atmosphere of terror or dread.

Graveyard School: A group of eighteenth-century English poets who wrote long, picturesque meditations on death. Their works were designed to cause the reader to ponder immortality.

Great Chain of Being: The belief that all things and creatures in nature are organized in a hierarchy from inanimate objects at the bottom to God at the top. This system of belief was popular in the seventeenth and eighteenth centuries.

Grotesque: In literary criticism, the subject matter of a work or a style of expression characterized by exaggeration, deformity, freakishness, and disorder. The grotesque often includes an element of comic absurdity.

H

Haiku: The shortest form of Japanese poetry, constructed in three lines of five, seven, and five syllables respectively. The message of a *haiku* poem usually centers on some aspect of spirituality and provokes an emotional response in the reader.

Half Rhyme: See *Consonance*

Harlem Renaissance: The Harlem Renaissance of the 1920s is generally considered the first significant movement of black writers and artists in the United States. During this period, new and established black writers published more fiction and poetry than ever before, the first influential black literary journals were established, and black authors and artists received their first widespread recognition and serious critical appraisal. Among the major writers associated with this period are Claude McKay, Jean Toomer, Countee Cullen, Langston Hughes, Arna Bontemps, Nella Larsen, and Zora Neale Hurston.

Hellenism: Imitation of ancient Greek thought or styles. Also, an approach to life that focuses on the growth and development of the intellect. "Hellenism" is sometimes used to refer to the belief that reason can be applied to examine all human experience.

Heptameter: See *Meter*

Hero/Heroine: The principal sympathetic character (male or female) in a literary work. Heroes and heroines typically exhibit admirable traits: idealism, courage, and integrity, for example.

Heroic Couplet: A rhyming couplet written in iambic pentameter (a verse with five iambic feet).

Heroic Line: The meter and length of a line of verse in epic or heroic poetry. This varies by language and time period.

Heroine: See *Hero/Heroine*

Hexameter: See *Meter*

Historical Criticism: The study of a work based on its impact on the world of the time period in which it was written.

Hokku: See *Haiku*

Holocaust: See *Holocaust Literature*

Holocaust Literature: Literature influenced by or written about the Holocaust of World War II. Such literature includes true stories of survival in concentration camps, escape, and life after the war, as well as fictional works and poetry.

Homeric Simile: An elaborate, detailed comparison written as a simile many lines in length.

Horatian Satire: See *Satire*

Humanism: A philosophy that places faith in the dignity of humankind and rejects the medieval perception of the individual as a weak, fallen creature. "Humanists" typically believe in the perfectibility of human nature and view reason and education as the means to that end.

Humors: Mentions of the humors refer to the ancient Greek theory that a person's health and personality were determined by the balance of four basic fluids in the body: blood, phlegm, yellow bile, and black bile. A dominance of any fluid would cause extremes in behavior. An excess of blood created a sanguine person who was joyful, aggressive, and passionate; a phlegmatic person was shy, fearful, and sluggish; too much yellow bile led to a choleric temperament characterized by impatience, anger, bitterness, and stubbornness; and excessive black bile created melancholy, a state of laziness, gluttony, and lack of motivation.

Humours: See *Humors*

Hyperbole: In literary criticism, deliberate exaggeration used to achieve an effect.

I

Iamb: See *Foot*

Idiom: A word construction or verbal expression closely associated with a given language.

Image: A concrete representation of an object or sensory experience. Typically, such a representation helps evoke the feelings associated with the object or experience itself. Images are either "literal" or "figurative." Literal images are especially concrete and involve little or no extension of the obvious meaning of the words used to express them. Figurative images do not follow the literal meaning of the words exactly. Images in literature are usually visual, but the term "image" can also refer to the representation of any sensory experience.

Imagery: The array of images in a literary work. Also, figurative language.

Imagism: An English and American poetry movement that flourished between 1908 and 1917. The Imagists used precise, clearly presented images in their works. They also used common, everyday speech and aimed for conciseness, concrete imagery, and the creation of new rhythms.

In medias res: A Latin term meaning "in the middle of things." It refers to the technique of beginning a story at its midpoint and then using various flashback devices to reveal previous action.

Induction: The process of reaching a conclusion by reasoning from specific premises to form a general premise. Also, an introductory portion of a work of literature, especially a play.

Intentional Fallacy: The belief that judgments of a literary work based solely on an author's stated or implied intentions are false and misleading. Critics who believe in the concept of the intentional fallacy typically argue that the work itself is sufficient matter for interpretation, even though they may concede that an author's statement of purpose can be useful.

Interior Monologue: A narrative technique in which characters' thoughts are revealed in a way that appears to be uncontrolled by the author. The interior monologue typically aims to reveal the inner self of a character. It portrays emotional experiences as they occur at both a conscious and unconscious level. Images are often used to represent sensations or emotions.

Internal Rhyme: Rhyme that occurs within a single line of verse.

Irish Literary Renaissance: A late nineteenth- and early twentieth-century movement in Irish literature. Members of the movement aimed to reduce the influence of British culture in Ireland and create an Irish national literature.

Irony: In literary criticism, the effect of language in which the intended meaning is the opposite of what is stated.

Italian Sonnet: See *Sonnet*

J

Jacobean Age: The period of the reign of James I of England (1603-1625). The early literature of this period reflected the worldview of the Elizabethan Age, but a darker, more cynical attitude steadily grew in the art and literature of the Jacobean Age. This was an important time for English drama and poetry.

Jargon: Language that is used or understood only by a select group of people. Jargon may refer to terminology used in a certain profession, such as computer jargon, or it may refer to any nonsensical language that is not understood by most people.

Journalism: Writing intended for publication in a newspaper or magazine, or for broadcast on a radio or television program featuring news, sports, entertainment, or other timely material.

K

Knickerbocker Group: A somewhat indistinct group of New York writers of the first half of the nineteenth century. Members of the group were linked only by location and a common theme: New York life.

Kunstlerroman: See *Bildungsroman*

L

Lais: See *Lay*

Lake Poets: See *Lake School*

Lake School: These poets all lived in the Lake District of England at the turn of the nineteenth century. As a group, they followed no single "school" of thought or literary practice, although their works were uniformly disparaged by the *Edinburgh Review*.

Lay: A song or simple narrative poem. The form originated in medieval France. Early French *lais* were often based on the Celtic legends and other tales sung by Breton minstrels—thus the name of the "Breton lay." In fourteenth-century England, the term "lay" was used to describe short narratives written in imitation of the Breton lays.

Leitmotiv: See *Motif*

Literal Language: An author uses literal language when he or she writes without exaggerating or embellishing the subject matter and without any tools of figurative language.

Literary Ballad: See *Ballad*

Literature: Literature is broadly defined as any written or spoken material, but the term most often refers to creative works.

Lost Generation: A term first used by Gertrude Stein to describe the post-World War I generation of American writers: men and women haunted by a sense of betrayal and emptiness brought about by the destructiveness of the war.

Lyric Poetry: A poem expressing the subjective feelings and personal emotions of the poet. Such poetry is melodic, since it was originally accompanied by a lyre in recitals. Most Western poetry in the twentieth century may be classified as lyrical.

M

Mannerism: Exaggerated, artificial adherence to a literary manner or style. Also, a popular style of the visual arts of late sixteenth-century Europe that was marked by elongation of the human form and by intentional spatial distortion. Literary works that are self-consciously high-toned and artistic are often said to be "mannered."

Masculine Rhyme: See *Rhyme*

Measure: The foot, verse, or time sequence used in a literary work, especially a poem. Measure is often used somewhat incorrectly as a synonym for meter.

Metaphor: A figure of speech that expresses an idea through the image of another object. Metaphors suggest the essence of the first object by identifying it with certain qualities of the second object.

Metaphysical Conceit: See *Conceit*

Metaphysical Poetry: The body of poetry produced by a group of seventeenth-century English writers called the "Metaphysical Poets." The group includes John Donne and Andrew Marvell. The Metaphysical Poets made use of everyday speech, intellectual analysis, and unique imagery. They aimed to portray the ordinary conflicts and contradictions of life. Their poems often took the form of an argument, and many of them emphasize physical and religious love as well as the fleeting nature of life. Elaborate conceits are typical in metaphysical poetry.

Metaphysical Poets: See *Metaphysical Poetry*

Meter: In literary criticism, the repetition of sound patterns that creates a rhythm in poetry. The patterns are based on the number of syllables and the presence and absence of accents. The unit of rhythm in a line is called a foot. Types of meter are classified according to the number of feet in a line. These are the standard English lines: Monometer, one foot; Dimeter, two feet; Trimeter, three feet; Tetrameter, four feet; Pentameter, five feet; Hexameter, six feet (also called the Alexandrine); Heptameter, seven feet (also called the "Fourteener" when the feet are iambic).

Modernism: Modern literary practices. Also, the principles of a literary school that lasted from roughly the beginning of the twentieth century until the end of World War II. Modernism is defined by its rejection of the literary conventions of the nineteenth century and by its opposition to conventional morality, taste, traditions, and economic values.

Monologue: A composition, written or oral, by a single individual. More specifically, a speech given by a single individual in a drama or other public entertainment. It has no set length, although it is usually several or more lines long.

Monometer: See *Meter*

Mood: The prevailing emotions of a work or of the author in his or her creation of the work. The mood of a work is not always what might be expected based on its subject matter.

Motif: A theme, character type, image, metaphor, or other verbal element that recurs throughout a single work of literature or occurs in a number of different works over a period of time.

Motiv: See *Motif*

Muckrakers: An early twentieth-century group of American writers. Typically, their works exposed the wrongdoings of big business and government in the United States.

Muses: Nine Greek mythological goddesses, the daughters of Zeus and Mnemosyne (Memory). Each muse patronized a specific area of the liberal arts and sciences. Calliope presided over epic poetry, Clio over history, Erato over love poetry, Euterpe over music or lyric poetry, Melpomene over tragedy, Polyhymnia over hymns to the gods, Terpsichore over dance, Thalia over comedy, and Urania over astronomy. Poets and writers traditionally made appeals to the Muses for inspiration in their work.

Myth: An anonymous tale emerging from the traditional beliefs of a culture or social unit. Myths use supernatural explanations for natural phenomena. They may also explain cosmic issues like creation and death. Collections of myths, known as mythologies, are common to all cultures and nations, but the best-known myths belong to the Norse, Roman, and Greek mythologies.

N

Narration: The telling of a series of events, real or invented. A narration may be either a simple narrative, in which the events are recounted chronologically, or a narrative with a plot, in which the account is given in a style reflecting the author's artistic concept of the story. Narration is sometimes used as a synonym for "storyline."

Narrative: A verse or prose accounting of an event or sequence of events, real or invented. The term is also used as an adjective in the sense "method of narration." For example, in literary criticism, the expression "narrative technique" usually refers to the way the author structures and presents his or her story.

Narrative Poetry: A nondramatic poem in which the author tells a story. Such poems may be of any length or level of complexity.

Narrator: The teller of a story. The narrator may be the author or a character in the story through whom the author speaks.

Naturalism: A literary movement of the late nineteenth and early twentieth centuries. The movement's major theorist, French novelist Emile Zola, envisioned a type of fiction that would examine human life with the objectivity of scientific inquiry. The Naturalists typically viewed human beings as either the products of "biological determinism," ruled by hereditary instincts and engaged in an endless struggle for survival, or as the products of "socioeconomic determinism," ruled by social and economic forces beyond their control. In their works, the Naturalists generally ignored the highest levels of society and focused on degradation: poverty, alcoholism, prostitution, insanity, and disease.

Negritude: A literary movement based on the concept of a shared cultural bond on the part of black Africans, wherever they may be in the world. It traces its origins to the former French colonies of Africa and the Caribbean. Negritude poets, novelists, and essayists generally stress four points in their writings: One, black alienation from traditional African culture can lead to feelings of inferiority. Two, European colonialism and Western education should be resisted. Three, black Africans should seek to affirm and define their own identity. Four, African culture can and should be reclaimed. Many Negritude writers also claim that blacks can make unique contributions to the world, based on a heightened appreciation of nature, rhythm, and human emotions— aspects of life they say are not so highly valued in the materialistic and rationalistic West.

Negro Renaissance: See *Harlem Renaissance*

Neoclassical Period: See *Neoclassicism*

Neoclassicism: In literary criticism, this term refers to the revival of the attitudes and styles of expression of classical literature. It is generally used to describe a period in European history beginning in the late seventeenth century and lasting until about 1800. In its purest form, Neoclassicism marked a return to order, proportion, restraint, logic, accuracy, and decorum. In England, where Neoclassicism perhaps was most popular, it reflected the influence of seventeenth- century French writers, especially dramatists. Neoclassical writers typically reacted against the intensity and enthusiasm of the Renaissance period. They wrote works that appealed to the intellect, using elevated language and classical literary forms such as satire and the ode. Neoclassical works were often governed by the classical goal of instruction.

Neoclassicists: See *Neoclassicism*

New Criticism: A movement in literary criticism, dating from the late 1920s, that stressed close textual analysis in the interpretation of works of literature. The New Critics saw little merit in historical and biographical analysis. Rather, they aimed to examine the text alone, free from the question of how external events—biographical or otherwise—may have helped shape it.

New Journalism: A type of writing in which the journalist presents factual information in a form usually used in fiction. New journalism emphasizes description, narration, and character development to bring readers closer to the human element of the story, and is often used in personality profiles and in-depth feature articles. It is not compatible with "straight" or "hard" newswriting, which is generally composed in a brief, fact-based style.

New Journalists: See *New Journalism*

New Negro Movement: See *Harlem Renaissance*

Noble Savage: The idea that primitive man is noble and good but becomes evil and corrupted as he becomes civilized. The concept of the noble savage originated in the Renaissance period but is more closely identified with such later writers as Jean-Jacques Rousseau and Aphra Behn.

O

Objective Correlative: An outward set of objects, a situation, or a chain of events corresponding to an inward experience and evoking this experience in the reader. The term frequently appears in modern criticism in discussions of authors' intended effects on the emotional responses of readers.

Objectivity: A quality in writing characterized by the absence of the author's opinion or feeling about the subject matter. Objectivity is an important factor in criticism.

Occasional Verse: poetry written on the occasion of a significant historical or personal event. *Vers de societe* is sometimes called occasional verse although it is of a less serious nature.

Octave: A poem or stanza composed of eight lines. The term octave most often represents the first eight lines of a Petrarchan sonnet.

Ode: Name given to an extended lyric poem characterized by exalted emotion and dignified style. An ode usually concerns a single, serious theme. Most odes, but not all, are addressed to an object or individual. Odes are distinguished from other lyric poetic forms by their complex rhythmic and stanzaic patterns.

Oedipus Complex: A son's amorous obsession with his mother. The phrase is derived from the story of the ancient Theban hero Oedipus, who unknowingly killed his father and married his mother.

Omniscience: See *Point of View*

Onomatopoeia: The use of words whose sounds express or suggest their meaning. In its simplest sense, onomatopoeia may be represented by words that mimic the sounds they denote such as "hiss" or "meow." At a more subtle level, the pattern and rhythm of sounds and rhymes of a line or poem may be onomatopoeic.

Oral Tradition: See *Oral Transmission*

Oral Transmission: A process by which songs, ballads, folklore, and other material are transmitted by word of mouth. The tradition of oral transmission predates the written record systems of literate society. Oral transmission preserves material sometimes over generations, although often with variations. Memory plays a large part in the recitation and preservation of orally transmitted material.

Ottava Rima: An eight-line stanza of poetry composed in iambic pentameter (a five-foot line in which each foot consists of an unaccented syllable followed by an accented syllable), following the abababcc rhyme scheme.

Oxymoron: A phrase combining two contradictory terms. Oxymorons may be intentional or unintentional.

P

Pantheism: The idea that all things are both a manifestation or revelation of God and a part of God at the same time. Pantheism was a common attitude in the early societies of Egypt, India, and Greece—the term derives from the Greek *pan* meaning "all" and *theos* meaning "deity." It later became a significant part of the Christian faith.

Parable: A story intended to teach a moral lesson or answer an ethical question.

Paradox: A statement that appears illogical or contradictory at first, but may actually point to an underlying truth.

Parallelism: A method of comparison of two ideas in which each is developed in the same grammatical structure.

Parnassianism: A mid nineteenth-century movement in French literature. Followers of the movement stressed adherence to well-defined artistic forms as a reaction against the often chaotic expression of the artist's ego that dominated the work of the Romantics. The Parnassians also rejected the moral, ethical, and social themes exhibited in the works of French Romantics such as Victor Hugo. The aesthetic doctrines of the Parnassians strongly influenced the later symbolist and decadent movements.

Parody: In literary criticism, this term refers to an imitation of a serious literary work or the signature style of a particular author in a ridiculous manner. A typical parody adopts the style of the original and applies it to an inappropriate subject for humorous effect. Parody is a form of satire and could be considered the literary equivalent of a caricature or cartoon.

Pastoral: A term derived from the Latin word "pastor," meaning shepherd. A pastoral is a literary composition on a rural theme. The conventions of the pastoral were originated by the third-century Greek poet Theocritus, who wrote about the experiences, love affairs, and pastimes of Sicilian shepherds. In a pastoral, characters and language of a courtly nature are often placed in a simple setting. The term pastoral is also used to classify dramas, elegies, and lyrics that exhibit the use of country settings and shepherd characters.

Pathetic Fallacy: A term coined by English critic John Ruskin to identify writing that falsely endows nonhuman things with human intentions and feelings, such as "angry clouds" and "sad trees."

Pen Name: See *Pseudonym*

Pentameter: See *Meter*

Persona: A Latin term meaning "mask." *Personae* are the characters in a fictional work of literature. The *persona* generally functions as a mask through which the author tells a story in a voice other than his or her own. A *persona* is usually either a character in a story who acts as a narrator or an "implied author," a voice created by the author to act as the narrator for himself or herself.

Personae: See *Persona*

Personal Point of View: See *Point of View*

Personification: A figure of speech that gives human qualities to abstract ideas, animals, and inanimate objects.

Petrarchan Sonnet: See *Sonnet*

Phenomenology: A method of literary criticism based on the belief that things have no existence outside of human consciousness or awareness. Proponents of this theory believe that art is a process that takes place in the mind of the observer as he or she contemplates an object rather than a quality of the object itself.

Plagiarism: Claiming another person's written material as one's own. Plagiarism can take the form of direct, word-for- word copying or the theft of the substance or idea of the work.

Platonic Criticism: A form of criticism that stresses an artistic work's usefulness as an agent of social engineering rather than any quality or value of the work itself.

Platonism: The embracing of the doctrines of the philosopher Plato, popular among the poets of the Renaissance and the Romantic period. Platonism is more flexible than Aristotelian Criticism and places more emphasis on the supernatural and unknown aspects of life.

Plot: In literary criticism, this term refers to the pattern of events in a narrative or drama. In its simplest sense, the plot guides the author in composing the work and helps the reader follow the work. Typically, plots exhibit causality and unity and have a beginning, a middle, and an end. Sometimes, however, a plot may consist of a series of disconnected events, in which case it is known as an "episodic plot."

Poem: In its broadest sense, a composition utilizing rhyme, meter, concrete detail, and expressive language to create a literary experience with emotional and aesthetic appeal.

Poet: An author who writes poetry or verse. The term is also used to refer to an artist or writer who has an exceptional gift for expression, imagination, and energy in the making of art in any form.

Poete maudit: A term derived from Paul Verlaine's *Les poetes maudits* (*The Accursed Poets*), a collection of essays on the French symbolist writers Stephane Mallarme, Arthur Rimbaud, and Tristan Corbiere. In the sense intended by Verlaine, the poet is "accursed" for choosing to explore extremes of human experience outside of middle-class society.

Poetic Fallacy: See *Pathetic Fallacy*

Poetic Justice: An outcome in a literary work, not necessarily a poem, in which the good are rewarded and the evil are punished, especially in ways that particularly fit their virtues or crimes.

Poetic License: Distortions of fact and literary convention made by a writer—not always a poet—for the sake of the effect gained. Poetic license is closely related to the concept of "artistic freedom."

Poetics: This term has two closely related meanings. It denotes (1) an aesthetic theory in literary criticism about the essence of poetry or (2) rules prescribing the proper methods, content, style, or diction of poetry. The term poetics may also refer to theories about literature in general, not just poetry.

Poetry: In its broadest sense, writing that aims to present ideas and evoke an emotional experience in the reader through the use of meter, imagery, connotative and concrete words, and a carefully constructed structure based on rhythmic patterns. Poetry typically relies on words and expressions that have several layers of meaning. It also makes use of the effects of regular rhythm on the ear and may make a strong appeal to the senses through the use of imagery.

Point of View: The narrative perspective from which a literary work is presented to the reader. There are four traditional points of view. The "third person omniscient" gives the reader a "godlike" perspective, unrestricted by time or place, from which to see actions and look into the minds of characters. This allows the author to comment openly on characters and events in the work. The "third person" point of view presents the events of the story from outside of any single character's perception, much like the omniscient point of view, but the reader must understand the action as it takes place and without any special insight into characters' minds or motivations. The "first person" or "personal" point of view relates events as they are perceived by a single character. The main character "tells" the story and may offer opinions about the action and characters which differ from those of the author. Much less common than omniscient, third person, and first person is the "second person" point of view, wherein the author tells the story as if it is happening to the reader.

Polemic: A work in which the author takes a stand on a controversial subject, such as abortion or religion. Such works are often extremely argumentative or provocative.

Pornography: Writing intended to provoke feelings of lust in the reader. Such works are often condemned by critics and teachers, but those which can be shown to have literary value are viewed less harshly.

Post-Aesthetic Movement: An artistic response made by African Americans to the black aesthetic movement of the 1960s and early '70s. Writers since that time have adopted a somewhat different tone in their work, with less emphasis placed on the disparity between black and white in the United States. In the words of post-aesthetic authors such as Toni Morrison, John Edgar Wideman, and Kristin Hunter, African Americans are portrayed as looking inward for answers to their own questions, rather than always looking to the outside world.

Postmodernism: Writing from the 1960s forward characterized by experimentation and continuing to apply some of the fundamentals of modernism, which included existentialism and alienation. Postmodernists have gone a step further in the rejection of tradition begun with the modernists by also rejecting traditional forms, preferring the anti-novel over the novel and the anti-hero over the hero.

Pre-Raphaelites: A circle of writers and artists in mid nineteenth-century England. Valuing the pre-Renaissance artistic qualities of religious symbolism, lavish pictorialism, and natural sensuousness, the Pre-Raphaelites cultivated a sense of mystery and melancholy that influenced later writers associated with the Symbolist and Decadent movements.

Primitivism: The belief that primitive peoples were nobler and less flawed than civilized peoples because they had not been subjected to the tainting influence of society.

Projective Verse: A form of free verse in which the poet's breathing pattern determines the lines of the poem. Poets who advocate projective verse are against all formal structures in writing, including meter and form.

Prologue: An introductory section of a literary work. It often contains information establishing the situation of the characters or presents information about the setting, time period, or action. In drama, the prologue is spoken by a chorus or by one of the principal characters.

Prose: A literary medium that attempts to mirror the language of everyday speech. It is distinguished from poetry by its use of unmetered, unrhymed language consisting of logically related sentences. Prose is usually grouped into paragraphs that form a cohesive whole such as an essay or a novel.

Prosopopoeia: See *Personification*

Protagonist: The central character of a story who serves as a focus for its themes and incidents and as the principal rationale for its development. The protagonist is sometimes referred to in discussions of modern literature as the hero or anti-hero.

Proverb: A brief, sage saying that expresses a truth about life in a striking manner.

Pseudonym: A name assumed by a writer, most often intended to prevent his or her identification as the author of a work. Two or more authors may work together under one pseudonym, or an author may use a different name for each genre he or she publishes in. Some publishing companies maintain "house pseudonyms," under which any number of authors may write installations in a series. Some authors also choose a pseudonym over their real names the way an actor may use a stage name.

Pun: A play on words that have similar sounds but different meanings.

Pure Poetry: poetry written without instructional intent or moral purpose that aims only to please a reader by its imagery or musical flow. The term pure poetry is used as the antonym of the term "didacticism."

Q

Quatrain: A four-line stanza of a poem or an entire poem consisting of four lines.

R

Realism: A nineteenth-century European literary movement that sought to portray familiar characters, situations, and settings in a realistic manner. This was done primarily by using an objective narrative point of view and through the buildup of accurate detail. The standard for success of any realistic work depends on how faithfully it transfers common experience into fictional forms. The realistic method may be altered or extended, as in stream of consciousness writing, to record highly subjective experience.

Refrain: A phrase repeated at intervals throughout a poem. A refrain may appear at the end of each stanza or at less regular intervals. It may be altered slightly at each appearance.

Renaissance: The period in European history that marked the end of the Middle Ages. It began in Italy in the late fourteenth century. In broad terms, it is usually seen as spanning the fourteenth, fifteenth, and sixteenth centuries, although it did not reach Great Britain, for example, until the 1480s or so. The Renaissance saw an awakening in almost every sphere of human activity, especially science, philosophy, and the arts. The period is best defined by the emergence of a general philosophy that emphasized the importance of the intellect, the individual, and world affairs. It contrasts strongly with the medieval worldview, characterized by the dominant concerns of faith, the social collective, and spiritual salvation.

Repartee: Conversation featuring snappy retorts and witticisms.

Restoration: See *Restoration Age*

Restoration Age: A period in English literature beginning with the crowning of Charles II in 1660 and running to about 1700. The era, which was characterized by a reaction against Puritanism, was the first great age of the comedy of manners. The finest literature of the era is typically witty and urbane, and often lewd.

Rhetoric: In literary criticism, this term denotes the art of ethical persuasion. In its strictest sense, rhetoric adheres to various principles developed since classical times for arranging facts and ideas in a clear, persuasive, appealing manner. The term is also used to refer to effective prose in general and theories of or methods for composing effective prose.

Rhetorical Question: A question intended to provoke thought, but not an expressed answer, in the reader. It is most commonly used in oratory and other persuasive genres.

Rhyme: When used as a noun in literary criticism, this term generally refers to a poem in which words sound identical or very similar and appear in parallel positions in two or more lines. Rhymes are classified into different types according to where they fall in a line or stanza or according to the degree of similarity they exhibit in their spellings and sounds. Some major types of rhyme are "masculine" rhyme, "feminine" rhyme, and "triple" rhyme. In a masculine rhyme, the rhyming sound falls in a single accented syllable, as with "heat" and "cat." Feminine rhyme is a rhyme of two syllables, one stressed and one unstressed, as with "merry" and "tarry." Triple rhyme matches the sound of the accented syllable and the two unaccented syllables that follow: "narrative" and "declarative."

Rhyme Royal: A stanza of seven lines composed in iambic pentameter and rhymed *ababbcc*. The name is said to be a tribute to King James I of Scotland, who made much use of the form in his poetry.

Rhyme Scheme: See *Rhyme*

Rhythm: A regular pattern of sound, time intervals, or events occurring in writing, most often and most discernably in poetry. Regular, reliable rhythm is known to be soothing to humans, while interrupted, unpredictable, or rapidly changing rhythm is disturbing. These effects are known to authors, who use them to produce a desired reaction in the reader.

Rococo: A style of European architecture that flourished in the eighteenth century, especially in France. The most notable features of *rococo* are its extensive use of ornamentation and its themes of lightness, gaiety, and intimacy. In literary criticism, the term is often used disparagingly to refer to a decadent or over-ornamental style.

Romance: A broad term, usually denoting a narrative with exotic, exaggerated, often idealized characters, scenes, and themes.

Romantic Age: See *Romanticism*

Romanticism: This term has two widely accepted meanings. In historical criticism, it refers to a European intellectual and artistic movement of the late eighteenth and early nineteenth centuries that sought greater freedom of personal expression than that allowed by the strict rules of literary form and logic of the eighteenth-century neoclassicists. The Romantics preferred emotional and imaginative expression to rational analysis. They considered the individual to be at the center of all experience and so placed him or her at the center of their art. The Romantics believed that the creative imagination reveals nobler truths—unique feelings and attitudes—than those that could be discovered by logic or by scientific examination. Both the natural world and the state of childhood were important sources for revelations of "eternal truths." "Romanticism" is also used as a general term to refer to a type of sensibility found in all periods of literary history and usually considered to be in opposition to the principles of classicism. In this sense, Romanticism signifies any work or philosophy in which the exotic or dreamlike figure strongly, or that is devoted to individualistic expression, self-analysis, or a pursuit of a higher realm of knowledge than can be discovered by human reason.

Romantics: See *Romanticism*

Russian Symbolism: A Russian poetic movement, derived from French symbolism, that flourished between 1894 and 1910. While some Russian Symbolists continued in the French tradition, stressing aestheticism and the importance of suggestion above didactic intent, others saw their craft as a form of mystical worship, and themselves as mediators between the supernatural and the mundane.

S

Satire: A work that uses ridicule, humor, and wit to criticize and provoke change in human nature and institutions. There are two major types of satire: "formal" or "direct" satire speaks directly to the reader or to a character in the work; "indirect" satire relies upon the ridiculous behavior of its characters to make its point. Formal satire is further divided into two manners: the "Horatian," which ridicules gently, and the "Juvenalian," which derides its subjects harshly and bitterly.

Scansion: The analysis or "scanning" of a poem to determine its meter and often its rhyme scheme. The most common system of scansion uses accents (slanted lines drawn above syllables) to show stressed syllables, breves (curved lines drawn above syllables) to show unstressed syllables, and vertical lines to separate each foot.

Second Person: See *Point of View*

Semiotics: The study of how literary forms and conventions affect the meaning of language.

Sestet: Any six-line poem or stanza.

Setting: The time, place, and culture in which the action of a narrative takes place. The elements of setting may include geographic location, characters' physical and mental environments, prevailing cultural attitudes, or the historical time in which the action takes place.

Shakespearean Sonnet: See *Sonnet*

Signifying Monkey: A popular trickster figure in black folklore, with hundreds of tales about this character documented since the 19th century.

Simile: A comparison, usually using "like" or "as", of two essentially dissimilar things, as in "coffee as cold as ice" or "He sounded like a broken record."

Slang: A type of informal verbal communication that is generally unacceptable for formal writing. Slang words and phrases are often colorful exaggerations used to emphasize the speaker's point; they may also be shortened versions of an often-used word or phrase.

Slant Rhyme: See *Consonance*

Slave Narrative: Autobiographical accounts of American slave life as told by escaped slaves. These works first appeared during the abolition movement of the 1830s through the 1850s.

Social Realism: See *Socialist Realism*

Socialist Realism: The Socialist Realism school of literary theory was proposed by Maxim Gorky and established as a dogma by the first Soviet Congress of Writers. It demanded adherence to a communist worldview in works of literature. Its doctrines required an objective viewpoint comprehensible to the working classes and themes of social struggle featuring strong proletarian heroes.

Soliloquy: A monologue in a drama used to give the audience information and to develop the speaker's character. It is typically a projection of the speaker's innermost thoughts. Usually delivered while the speaker is alone on stage, a soliloquy is intended to present an illusion of unspoken reflection.

Sonnet: A fourteen-line poem, usually composed in iambic pentameter, employing one of several rhyme schemes. There are three major types of sonnets, upon which all other variations of the form are based: the "Petrarchan" or "Italian" sonnet, the "Shakespearean" or "English" sonnet, and the "Spenserian" sonnet. A Petrarchan sonnet consists of an octave rhymed *abbaabba* and a "sestet" rhymed either *cdecde, cdccdc,* or *cdedce.* The octave poses a question or problem, relates a narrative, or puts forth a proposition; the sestet presents a solution to the problem, comments upon the narrative, or applies the proposition put forth in the octave. The Shakespearean sonnet is divided into three quatrains and a couplet rhymed *abab cdcd efef gg.* The couplet provides an epigrammatic comment on the narrative or problem put forth in the quatrains. The Spenserian sonnet uses three quatrains and a couplet like the Shakespearean, but links their three rhyme schemes in this way: *abab bcbc cdcd ee.* The Spenserian sonnet develops its theme in two parts like the Petrarchan, its final six lines resolving a problem, analyzing a narrative, or applying a proposition put forth in its first eight lines.

Spenserian Sonnet: See *Sonnet*

Spenserian Stanza: A nine-line stanza having eight verses in iambic pentameter, its ninth verse in iambic hexameter, and the rhyme scheme ababbcbcc.

Spondee: In poetry meter, a foot consisting of two long or stressed syllables occurring together. This form is quite rare in English verse, and is usually composed of two monosyllabic words.

Sprung Rhythm: Versification using a specific number of accented syllables per line but disregarding the number of unaccented syllables that fall in each line, producing an irregular rhythm in the poem.

Stanza: A subdivision of a poem consisting of lines grouped together, often in recurring patterns of rhyme, line length, and meter. Stanzas may also serve as units of thought in a poem much like paragraphs in prose.

Stereotype: A stereotype was originally the name for a duplication made during the printing process; this led to its modern definition as a person or thing that is (or is assumed to be) the same as all others of its type.

Stream of Consciousness: A narrative technique for rendering the inward experience of a character. This technique is designed to give the impression of an ever-changing series of thoughts, emotions, images, and memories in the spontaneous and seemingly illogical order that they occur in life.

Structuralism: A twentieth-century movement in literary criticism that examines how literary texts arrive at their meanings, rather than the meanings themselves. There are two major types of structuralist analysis: one examines the way patterns of linguistic structures unify a specific text and emphasize certain elements of that text, and the other interprets the way literary forms and conventions affect the meaning of language itself.

Structure: The form taken by a piece of literature. The structure may be made obvious for ease of understanding, as in nonfiction works, or may obscured for artistic purposes, as in some poetry or seemingly "unstructured" prose.

Sturm und Drang: A German term meaning "storm and stress." It refers to a German literary movement of the 1770s and 1780s that reacted against the order and rationalism of the enlightenment, focusing instead on the intense experience of extraordinary individuals.

Style: A writer's distinctive manner of arranging words to suit his or her ideas and purpose in writing. The unique imprint of the author's personality upon his or her writing, style is the product of an author's way of arranging ideas and his or her use of diction, different sentence structures, rhythm, figures of speech, rhetorical principles, and other elements of composition.

Subject: The person, event, or theme at the center of a work of literature. A work may have one or more subjects of each type, with shorter works tending to have fewer and longer works tending to have more.

Subjectivity: Writing that expresses the author's personal feelings about his subject, and which may or may not include factual information about the subject.

Surrealism: A term introduced to criticism by Guillaume Apollinaire and later adopted by Andre Breton. It refers to a French literary and artistic movement founded in the 1920s. The Surrealists sought to express unconscious thoughts and feelings in their works. The best-known technique used for achieving this aim was automatic writing—transcriptions of spontaneous outpourings from the unconscious. The Surrealists proposed to unify the contrary levels of conscious and unconscious, dream and reality, objectivity and subjectivity into a new level of "super-realism."

Suspense: A literary device in which the author maintains the audience's attention through the buildup of events, the outcome of which will soon be revealed.

Syllogism: A method of presenting a logical argument. In its most basic form, the syllogism consists of a major premise, a minor premise, and a conclusion.

Symbol: Something that suggests or stands for something else without losing its original identity. In literature, symbols combine their literal meaning with the suggestion of an abstract concept. Literary symbols are of two types: those that carry complex associations of meaning no matter what their contexts, and those that derive their suggestive meaning from their functions in specific literary works.

Symbolism: This term has two widely accepted meanings. In historical criticism, it denotes an early modernist literary movement initiated in France during the nineteenth century that reacted against the prevailing standards of realism. Writers in this movement aimed to evoke, indirectly and symbolically, an order of being beyond the material world of the five senses. Poetic expression of personal emotion figured strongly in the movement, typically by means of a private set of symbols uniquely identifiable with the individual poet. The principal aim of the Symbolists was to express in words the highly complex feelings that grew out of everyday contact with the world. In a broader sense, the term "symbolism" refers to the use of one object to represent another.

Symbolist: See *Symbolism*

Symbolist Movement: See *Symbolism*

Sympathetic Fallacy: See *Affective Fallacy*

T

Tanka: A form of Japanese poetry similar to *haiku*. A *tanka* is five lines long, with the lines containing five, seven, five, seven, and seven syllables respectively.

Terza Rima: A three-line stanza form in poetry in which the rhymes are made on the last word of each line in the following manner: the first and third lines of the first stanza, then the second line of the first stanza and the first and third lines of the second stanza, and so on with the middle line of any stanza rhyming with the first and third lines of the following stanza.

Tetrameter: See *Meter*

Textual Criticism: A branch of literary criticism that seeks to establish the authoritative text of a literary work. Textual critics typically compare all known manuscripts or printings of a single work in order to assess the meanings of differences and revisions. This procedure allows them to arrive at a definitive version that (supposedly) corresponds to the author's original intention.

Theme: The main point of a work of literature. The term is used interchangeably with thesis.

Thesis: A thesis is both an essay and the point argued in the essay. Thesis novels and thesis plays share the quality of containing a thesis which is supported through the action of the story.

Third Person: See *Point of View*

Tone: The author's attitude toward his or her audience may be deduced from the tone of the work. A formal tone may create distance or convey politeness, while an informal tone may encourage a friendly, intimate, or intrusive feeling in the reader. The author's attitude toward his or her subject matter may also be deduced from the tone of the words he or she uses in discussing it.

Tragedy: A drama in prose or poetry about a noble, courageous hero of excellent character who, because of some tragic character flaw or *hamartia*, brings ruin upon him- or herself. Tragedy treats its subjects in a dignified and serious manner, using poetic language to help evoke pity and fear and bring about catharsis, a purging of these emotions. The tragic form was practiced extensively by the ancient Greeks. In the Middle Ages, when classical works were virtually unknown, tragedy came to denote any works about the fall of persons from exalted to low conditions due to any reason: fate, vice, weakness, etc. According to the classical definition of tragedy, such works present the "pathetic"—that which evokes pity—rather than the tragic. The classical form of tragedy was revived in the sixteenth century; it flourished especially on the Elizabethan stage. In modern times, dramatists have attempted to adapt the form to the needs of modern society by drawing their heroes from the ranks of ordinary men and women and defining the nobility of these heroes in terms of spirit rather than exalted social standing.

Tragic Flaw: In a tragedy, the quality within the hero or heroine which leads to his or her downfall.

Transcendentalism: An American philosophical and religious movement, based in New England from around 1835 until the Civil War. Transcendentalism was a form of American romanticism that had its roots abroad in the works of Thomas Carlyle, Samuel Coleridge, and Johann Wolfgang von Goethe. The Transcendentalists stressed the importance of intuition and subjective experience in communication with God. They rejected religious dogma and texts in favor of mysticism and scientific naturalism. They pursued truths that lie beyond the "colorless" realms perceived by reason and the senses and were active social reformers in public education, women's rights, and the abolition of slavery.

Trickster: A character or figure common in Native American and African literature who uses his ingenuity to defeat enemies and escape difficult situations. Tricksters are most often animals, such as the spider, hare, or coyote, although they may take the form of humans as well.

Trimeter: See *Meter*

Triple Rhyme: See *Rhyme*

Trochee: See *Foot*

U

Understatement: See *Irony*

Unities: Strict rules of dramatic structure, formulated by Italian and French critics of the Renaissance and based loosely on the principles of drama discussed by Aristotle in his *Poetics*. Foremost among these rules were the three unities of action, time, and place that compelled a dramatist to: (1) construct a single plot with a beginning, middle, and end that details the causal relationships of action and character; (2) restrict the action to the events of a single day; and (3) limit the scene to a single place or city. The unities were observed faithfully by continental European writers until the Romantic Age, but they were never regularly observed in English drama. Modern dramatists are typically more concerned with a unity of impression or emotional effect than with any of the classical unities.

Urban Realism: A branch of realist writing that attempts to accurately reflect the often harsh facts of modern urban existence.

Utopia: A fictional perfect place, such as "paradise" or "heaven."

Utopian: See *Utopia*

Utopianism: See *Utopia*

V

Verisimilitude: Literally, the appearance of truth. In literary criticism, the term refers to aspects of a work of literature that seem true to the reader.

Vers de societe: See *Occasional Verse*

Vers libre: See *Free Verse*

Verse: A line of metered language, a line of a poem, or any work written in verse.

Versification: The writing of verse. Versification may also refer to the meter, rhyme, and other mechanical components of a poem.

Victorian: Refers broadly to the reign of Queen Victoria of England (1837-1901) and to anything with qualities typical of that era. For example, the qualities of smug narrowmindedness, bourgeois materialism, faith in social progress, and priggish morality are often considered Victorian. This stereotype is contradicted by such dramatic intellectual developments as the theories of Charles Darwin, Karl Marx, and Sigmund Freud (which stirred strong debates in England) and the critical attitudes of serious Victorian writers like Charles Dickens and George Eliot. In literature, the Victorian Period was the great age of the English novel, and the latter part of the era saw the rise of movements such as decadence and symbolism.

Victorian Age: See *Victorian*

Victorian Period: See *Victorian*

W

Weltanschauung: A German term referring to a person's worldview or philosophy.

Weltschmerz: A German term meaning "world pain." It describes a sense of anguish about the nature of existence, usually associated with a melancholy, pessimistic attitude.

Z

Zarzuela: A type of Spanish operetta.

Zeitgeist: A German term meaning "spirit of the time." It refers to the moral and intellectual trends of a given era.

Cumulative Author/Title Index

Three To's and an Oi (McHugh): V24
Tintern Abbey (Wordsworth): V2
To a Child Running With Outstretched Arms in Canyon de Chelly (Momaday): V11
To a Sad Daughter (Ondaatje): V8
To an Athlete Dying Young (Housman): V7
To an Unknown Poet (Kizer): V18
To His Coy Mistress (Marvell): V5
To His Excellency General Washington (Wheatley): V13
To My Dear and Loving Husband (Bradstreet): V6
To the Virgins, to Make Much of Time (Herrick): V13
Toads (Larkin): V4
The Toni Morrison Dreams (Alexander): V22
Tonight I Can Write (Neruda): V11
The Tragedy of the Leaves (Bukowski): V28
Tranströmer, Tomas
    Answers to Letters: V21
Trompe l'Oeil (Salter): V22
The Tropics in New York (McKay): V4
True Night (Snyder): V19
Two Poems for T. (Pavese): V20
The Tyger (Blake): V2

U

Ulysses (Tennyson): V2
Ungaretti, Giuseppe
    Variations on Nothing: V20
The Unknown Citizen (Auden): V3

V

A Valediction: Forbidding Mourning (Donne): V11
Valentine, Jean
    Seeing You: V24
Vallejo, César
    The Black Heralds: V26
Van Duyn, Mona
    Memoir: V20
Vancouver Lights (Birney): V8
Variations on Nothing (Ungaretti): V20
Vazirani, Reetika
    Daughter-Mother-Maya-Seeta: V25
Viereck, Peter
    For An Assyrian Frieze: V9

Kilroy: V14
View (Bell): V25
Virtue (Herbert): V25
Voigt, Ellen Bryant
    Practice: V23

W

Walcott, Derek
    A Far Cry from Africa: V6
Waldner, Liz
    Witness: V26
Walk Your Body Down (Barbarese): V26
The War Against the Trees (Kunitz): V11
The War Correspondent (Carson): V26
War Is Kind (Crane): V9
Warren, Rosanna
    Daylights: V13
    Lake: V23
The Waste Land (Eliot): V20
Waterfalls in a Bank (Ramanujan): V27
Ways to Live (Stafford): V16
We Live by What We See at Night (Espada): V13
We Real Cool (Brooks): V6
The Weight of Sweetness (Lee): V11
What Belongs to Us (Howe): V15
What I Would Ask My Husband's Dead Father (Hashimoto): V22
What My Child Learns of the Sea (Lorde): V16
What the Poets Could Have Been (Baggott): V26
Wheatley, Phillis
    To His Excellency General Washington: V13
When I Have Fears That I May Cease to Be (Keats): V2
When I Heard the Learn'd Astronomer (Whitman): V22
When I Was One-and-Twenty (Housman): V4
While I Was Gone a War Began (Castillo): V21
Whitman, Walt
    Cavalry Crossing a Ford: V13
    I Hear America Singing: V3
    O Captain! My Captain!: V2
    When I Heard the Learn'd Astronomer: V22
Whoso List to Hunt (Wyatt): V25

Why I Am Not a Painter (O'Hara): V8
Why The Classics (Herbert): V22
Wilbur, Richard
    Beowulf: V11
    Merlin Enthralled: V16
    On Freedom's Ground: V12
Wild Geese (Oliver): V15
Wild Swans (Millay): V17
Wilderness Gothic (Purdy): V12
Williams, William Carlos
    Overture to a Dance of Locomotives: V11
    Queen-Ann's-Lace: V6
    The Red Wheelbarrow: V1
The Wings (Doty): V28
Witness (Waldner): V26
The Women Who Loved Elvis All Their Lives (Brown): V28
The Wood-Pile (Frost): V6
Words for Departure (Bogan): V21
Wordsworth, William
    Lines Composed a Few Miles above Tintern Abbey: V2
Wright, Charles
    Black Zodiac: V10
Wright, James
    A Blessing: V7
    Autumn Begins in Martins Ferry, Ohio: V8
Wright, Judith
    Drought Year: V8
Wyatt, Thomas
    Whoso List to Hunt: V25

Y

Yau, John
    Russian Letter: V26
Yeats, William Butler
    Easter 1916: V5
    An Irish Airman Foresees His Death: V1
    The Lake Isle of Innisfree: V15
    Leda and the Swan: V13
    Sailing to Byzantium: V2
    The Second Coming: V7
Yet we insist that life is full of happy chance (Hejinian): V27
Young, Kevin
    Chorale: V25

Z

Zagajewski, Adam
    Self-Portrait: V25

Cumulative Nationality/Ethnicity Index

Cumulative Nationality/Ethnicity Index

Subject/Theme Index

Cumulative
Index of First Lines

While the long grain is softening (Early in the Morning) V17:75

While this America settles in the mould of its vulgarity, heavily thickening to empire (Shine, Perishing Republic) V4:161

While you are preparing for sleep, brushing your teeth, (The Afterlife) V18:39

Who has ever stopped to think of the divinity of Lamont Cranston? (In Memory of Radio) V9:144

Whose woods these are I think I know (Stopping by Woods on a Snowy Evening) V1:272

Whoso list to hunt: I know where is an hind. (Whoso List to Hunt) V25:286

Why should I let the toad *work* (Toads) V4:244

Y

You are small and intense (To a Child Running With Outstretched Arms in Canyon de Chelly) V11:173

You can't hear? Everything here is changing. (The River Mumma Wants Out) V25:191

You do not have to be good. (Wild Geese) V15:207

You should lie down now and remember the forest, (The Forest) V22:36–37

You stood thigh-deep in water and green light glanced (Lake) V23:158

You were never told, Mother, how old Illya was drunk (The Czar's Last Christmas Letter) V12:44

Cumulative
Index of Last Lines

In the rear-view mirrors of the passing cars (The War Against the Trees) V11:216

In these Chicago avenues. (A Thirst Against) V20:205

in this bastion of culture. (To an Unknown Poet) V18:221

in your unsteady, opening hand. (What the Poets Could Have Been) V26:262

iness (l(a) V1:85

Into blossom (A Blessing) V7:24

Is Come, my love is come to me. (A Birthday) V10:34

is love—that's all. (Two Poems for T.) V20:218

is safe is what you said. (Practice) V23:240

is still warm (Lament for the Dorsets) V5:191

It asked a crumb—of Me (Hope Is the Thing with Feathers) V3:123

It had no mirrors. I no longer needed mirrors. (I, I, I) V26:97

It is our god. (Fiddler Crab) V23:111–112

it is the bell to awaken God that we've heard ringing. (The Garden Shukkei-en) V18:107

it over my face and mouth. (An Anthem) V26:34

It rains as I write this. Mad heart, be brave. (The Country Without a Post Office) V18:64

It was your resting place." (Ah, Are You Digging on My Grave?) V4:2

it's always ourselves we find in the sea (maggie & milly & molly & may) V12:150

its bright, unequivocal eye. (Having it Out with Melancholy) V17:99

It's the fall through wind lifting white leaves. (Rapture) V21:181

its youth. The sea grows old in it. (The Fish) V14:172

J

Judge tenderly—of Me (This Is My Letter to the World) V4:233

Just imagine it (Inventors) V7:97

L

Laughing the stormy, husky, brawling laughter of Youth, half-naked, sweating, proud to be Hog Butcher, Tool Maker, Stacker of Wheat, Player with Railroads and Freight Handler to the Nation (Chicago) V3:61

Learn to labor and to wait (A Psalm of Life) V7:165

Leashed in my throat (Midnight) V2:131

Leaving thine outgrown shell by life's un-resting sea (The Chambered Nautilus) V24:52–53

Let my people go (Go Down, Moses) V11:43

life, our life and its forgetting. (For a New Citizen of These United States) V15:55

Life to Victory (Always) V24:15

like a bird in the sky . . . (Ego-Tripping) V28:113

like a shadow or a friend. *Colombia.* (Kindness) V24:84–85

Like Stone— (The Soul Selects Her Own Society) V1:259

Little Lamb, God bless thee. (The Lamb) V12:135

Look'd up in perfect silence at the stars. (When I Heard the Learn'd Astronomer) V22:244

love (The Toni Morrison Dreams) V22:202–203

Luck was rid of its clover. (Yet we insist that life is full of happy chance) V27:292

M

'Make a wish, Tom, make a wish.' (Drifters) V10: 98

make it seem to change (The Moon Glows the Same) V7:152

midnight-oiled in the metric laws? (A Farewell to English) V10:126

Monkey business (Business) V16:2

More dear, both for themselves and for thy sake! (Tintern Abbey) V2:250

My foe outstretchd beneath the tree. (A Poison Tree) V24:195–196

My love shall in my verse ever live young (Sonnet 19) V9:211

My soul has grown deep like the rivers. (The Negro Speaks of Rivers) V10:198

N

never to waken in that world again (Starlight) V8:213

newness comes into the world (Daughter-Mother-Maya-Seeta) V25:83

Nirvana is here, nine times out of ten. (Spring-Watching Pavilion) V18:198

No, she's brushing a boy's hair (Facing It) V5:110

no—tell them *no*— (The Hiding Place) V10:153

Noble six hundred! (The Charge of the Light Brigade) V1:3

nobody,not even the rain,has such small hands (somewhere i have never travelled,gladly beyond) V19:265

Nor swim under the terrible eyes of prison ships. (The Drunken Boat) V28:84

Not a roof but a field of stars. (Rent) V25:164

not be seeing you, for you have no insurance. (The River Mumma Wants Out) V25:191

Not even the blisters. Look. (What Belongs to Us) V15:196

Not of itself, but thee. (Song: To Celia) V23:270–271

Nothing, and is nowhere, and is endless (High Windows) V3:108

Nothing gold can stay (Nothing Gold Can Stay) V3:203

Now! (Alabama Centennial) V10:2

nursing the tough skin of figs (This Life) V1:293

O

O Death in Life, the days that are no more! (Tears, Idle Tears) V4:220

O Lord our Lord, how excellent is thy name in all the earth! (Psalm 8) V9:182

O Roger, Mackerel, Riley, Ned, Nellie, Chester, Lady Ghost (Names of Horses) V8:142

o, walk your body down, don't let it go it alone. (Walk Your Body Down) V26:219

Of all our joys, this must be the deepest. (Drinking Alone Beneath the Moon) V20:59–60

of blood and ignorance. (Art Thou the Thing I Wanted) V25:2–3

of gentleness (To a Sad Daughter) V8:231

of love's austere and lonely offices? (Those Winter Sundays) V1:300

of peaches (The Weight of Sweetness) V11:230

Of the camellia (Falling Upon Earth) V2:64

Of the Creator. And he waits for the world to begin (Leviathan) V5:204

Of what is past, or passing, or to come (Sailing to Byzantium) V2:207

Oh that was the garden of abundance, seeing you. (Seeing You) V24:244–245

Old Ryan, not yours (The Constellation Orion) V8:53

On the dark distant flurry (Angle of Geese) V2:2

on the frosty autumn air. (The Cossacks) V25:70

On the look of Death— (There's a Certain Slant of Light) V6:212

On your head like a crown (Any Human to Another) V3:2

One could do worse that be a swinger of birches. (Birches) V13:15

"Only the Lonely," trying his best to sound like Elvis. (The Women Who Loved Elvis All Their Lives) V28:274

Or does it explode? (Harlem) V1:63

Or help to half-a-crown." (The Man He Killed) V3:167

or last time, we look. (In Particular) V20:125

Or might not have lain dormant forever. (Mastectomy) V26:123

or nothing (Queen-Ann's-Lace) V6:179

or the one red leaf the snow releases in March. (ThreeTimes My Life Has Opened) V16:213

ORANGE forever. (Ballad of Orange and Grape) V10:18

our every corpuscle become an elf. (Moreover, the Moon) V20:153

outside. (it was New York and beautifully, snowing . . . (i was sitting in mcsorley's) V13:152

owing old (old age sticks) V3:246

P

patient in mind remembers the time. (Fading Light) V21:49

Perhaps he will fall. (Wilderness Gothic) V12:242

Petals on a wet, black bough (In a Station of the Metro) V2:116

Plaiting a dark red love-knot into her long black hair (The Highwayman) V4:68

Powerless, I drown. (Maternity) V21:142–143

Práise him. (Pied Beauty) V26:161

Pro patria mori. (Dulce et Decorum Est) V10:110

R

Rage, rage against the dying of the light (Do Not Go Gentle into that Good Night) V1:51

Raise it again, man. We still believe what we hear. (The Singer's House) V17:206

Remember the Giver fading off the lip (A Drink of Water) V8:66

Ride me. (Witness) V26:285

rise & walk away like a panther. (Ode to a Drum) V20:172–173

Rises toward her day after day, like a terrible fish (Mirror) V1:116

S

Shall be lifted—nevermore! (The Raven) V1:202

Shantih shantih shantih (The Waste Land) V20:248–252

share my shivering bed. (Chorale) V25:51

Show an affirming flame. (September 1, 1939) V27:235

Shuddering with rain, coming down around me. (Omen) V22:107

Simply melted into the perfect light. (Perfect Light) V19:187

Singing of him what they could understand (Beowulf) V11:3

Singing with open mouths their strong melodious songs (I Hear America Singing) V3:152

Sister, one of those who never married. (My Grandmother's Plot in the Family Cemetery) V27:155

slides by on grease (For the Union Dead) V7:67

Slouches towards Bethlehem to be born? (The Second Coming) V7:179

So long lives this, and this gives life to thee (Sonnet 18) V2:222

So prick my skin. (Pine) V23:223–224

Somebody loves us all. (Filling Station) V12:57

Speak through my words and my blood. (The Heights of Macchu Picchu) V28:141

spill darker kissmarks on that dark. (Ten Years after Your Deliberate Drowning) V21:240

Stand still, yet we will make him run (To His Coy Mistress) V5:277

startled into eternity (Four Mountain Wolves) V9:132

Still clinging to your shirt (My Papa's Waltz) V3:192

Stood up, coiled above his head, transforming all. (A Tall Man Executes a Jig) V12:229

strangers ask. *Originally?* And I hesitate. (Originally) V25:146–147

Surely goodness and mercy shall follow me all the days of my life: and I will dwell in the house of the Lord for ever (Psalm 23) V4:103

syllables of an old order. (A Grafted Tongue) V12:93

T

Take any streetful of people buying clothes and groceries, cheering a hero or throwing confetti and blowing tin horns . . . tell me if the lovers are losers . . . tell me if any get more than the lovers . . . in the dust . . . in the cool tombs (Cool Tombs) V6:46

Than from everything else life promised that you could do? (Paradiso) V20:190–191

Than that you should remember and be sad. (Remember) V14:255

that does not see you. You must change your life. (Archaic Torso of Apollo) V27:3

That then I scorn to change my state with Kings (Sonnet 29) V8:198

that there is more to know, that one day you will know it. (Knowledge) V25:113

That when we live no more, we may live ever (To My Dear and Loving Husband) V6:228

That's the word. (Black Zodiac) V10:47

the bigger it gets. (Smart and Final Iris) V15:183

The bosom of his Father and his God (Elegy Written in a Country Churchyard) V9:74

the bow toward torrents of *veyz mir*. (Three To's and an Oi) V24:264

The crime was in Granada, his Granada. (The Crime Was in Granada) V23:55–56

The dance is sure (Overture to a Dance of Locomotives) V11:143

The eyes turn topaz. (Hugh Selwyn Mauberley) V16:30

the flames? (Another Night in the Ruins) V26:13

The garland briefer than a girl's (To an Athlete Dying Young) V7:230

The guidon flags flutter gayly in the wind. (Cavalry Crossing a Ford) V13:50

windowpanes. (View) V25:246–247

With gold unfading, WASHINGTON! be thine. (To His Excellency General Washington) V13:213

with my eyes closed. (We Live by What We See at Night) V13:240

With the slow smokeless burning of decay (The Wood-Pile) V6:252

With what they had to go on. (The Conquerors) V13:67

Without cease or doubt sew the sweet sad earth. (The Satyr's Heart) V22:187

Would scarcely know that we were gone. (There Will Come Soft Rains) V14:301

Y

Ye know on earth, and all ye need to know (Ode on a Grecian Urn) V1:180

You live in this, and dwell in lovers' eyes (Sonnet 55) V5:246

You may for ever tarry. (To the Virgins, to Make Much of Time) V13:226

you who raised me? (The Gold Lily) V5:127

you'll have understood by then what these Ithakas mean. (Ithaka) V19:114